TO THE RESCUE

The Biography of

THOMAS S. MONSON

TO THE RESCUE

The Biography of

THOMAS S. MONSON

Thomas S. Monson

BY HEIDI S. SWINTON

DESERET
BOOK

To Jeffrey

And to our sons: Christian, Cameron,
Daniel, Jonathan, and Ian

Unless otherwise noted, all photographs appear courtesy of the Thomas S. Monson Collection.

Visit us at DeseretBook.com

Library of Congress Cataloging-in-Publication Data
Swinton, Heidi S.
  To the rescue : the biography of Thomas S. Monson / Heidi Swinton.
     p. cm.
  Includes bibliographical references and index.
  ISBN 978-1-60641-898-7 (hardbound : alk. paper)
  1. Monson, Thomas S., 1927– 2. The Church of Jesus Christ of Latter-day Saints—
Presidents—Biography. 3. Mormons—United States—Biography. I. Title.
  BX8695.M56S95 2010
  289.3'32092—dc22
  [B]   2010027460

Printed in the United States of America

10   9   8   7   6   5   4   3   2   1

CONTENTS

CONTENTS

PREFACE

THE PHONE RANG ON THE EVENING of June 18, 2008, at the mission home in Cobham, England. My husband answered, looked at me, and with a smile of surprise said, "President Monson is on the phone; he wants to talk to you."

What had I done to get in such trouble, I wondered, that the President of the Church would call me in England? In his ever-familiar voice, President Monson began, "How are you, Heidi?" He chatted, asking about the mission and the missionaries, "jolly old England" and our family. And then he said, "I have been getting a lot of pressure to have my biography written. I have prayed about it; I've talked with Frances; and I have decided that I want you to write my biography."

"President, I would be honored," I said. Then, gathering my wits, I said, "But I'm in England." I imagine he was nodding, *I know; I called you.* "But you aren't that busy, are you?" he said. "You can get a good start on the book before you get home." I have since learned one of his favorite teachings is, "Remember that faith and doubt cannot exist in the same mind at the same time."

For the next year—still on foreign soil—I pored over biographies of Presidents of the Church and notable figures in history, from John Adams to Winston Churchill to Sir Christopher Wren. I studied, outlined, and catalogued all the talks President Monson has given for the last forty-seven years. We did videoconferences from the mission office with him every month, technology connecting us across the ocean and seven time zones. When I called to schedule the first "interview," Lynne Cannegieter, his personal secretary, asked me how long I wanted to talk to him. Not wanting to impose on his time, I suggested forty-five minutes. There was a long pause. I thought, "Oh, no, I've asked for too much." Then Lynne said diplomatically, "Oh, you'll need more than that. He'll want to talk to you for at least two hours."

In that first session, I remember recognizing quickly that his interest and discussions had little to do with date, time, and place. He sees life and teaches the gospel through the eyes of experience. I learned he is most comfortable answering questions with true life accounts—he doesn't call them "stories" because they are true; they have happened to real people. And most often he was there.

I have read his daily journals from 1963 on. They are a reflection of more than his days. The accounts applaud those with whom he works and has occasion to meet. They are filled with his willingness to follow the promptings of the Lord and with his gratitude for the opportunity.

It became apparent very quickly that this is no ordinary man. He has been schooled by the Lord since his childhood. He has had the association of the Spirit coupled with remarkable faith in Jesus Christ and Father in Heaven. As a result, his biography reflects that premise. His life is not about where he went and what he did when he was there. It is about what he learned in the process. There seemed to me to be no other way to capture the man whose experiences read like the books of Matthew, Mark, Luke, and John. When I sat down to write, I could hear him teaching one experience after another, and I realized that if his biography were to be true to his life, it had to reflect just such a pattern. Hence this book is shaped around his personal accounts and the principles they teach.

I found in the research that volumes could be written describing the hands he has lifted, the hearts he has touched. In any setting where his name is mentioned, accounts of what, when, where, and how he has touched a life are volunteered quickly—not just by one but by many. It was so even when I was halfway around the world.

The other thing I realized, quickly, is that he is as good as he appears. He is the kind of person that people think he is. There is no pretense or show, bravado or self-congratulation. He gives all he has to the moment at hand. I have let those who are close to him share their observations of this uncommonly good man.

And shouldn't he be? He is the Lord's chosen prophet on the earth today. He is not perfect. But to look for his failings is to suggest that mortals can measure and assess the life of such a singular servant of God. We learn from him what we learned from Abinadi, Nephi, Enos, Peter, and Joseph Smith: The Lord calls disciples to his work at the time He needs them. It has always been so.

In this era of the last dispensation, when cultures have squandered their rights to God's inspiration, when men's hearts have failed them and their designs are not in keeping with the teachings of the Lord Jesus Christ, our Father in Heaven has placed a prophet in our midst so that we can carry on.

I have sat in his office, which I have come to call the pool of Bethesda, and experienced what so many others have as well. He looked at me with the kindest of eyes when the weight of this assignment had worn me down, and he asked, "What can I do to help?" What he did was talk to me, engaging the Spirit to speak peace to my soul. I had read of that happening to others; I have had that blessing given to me as a witness that Thomas S. Monson speaks as a prophet of God. The title of his biography, *To the Rescue,* is fitting for a man whose life has been in such service.

There are many who have come to the rescue as this project has unfolded.

I have been fortunate to work closely with Lynne Cannegieter, secretary to the President, who has been in his office for forty-five years. I have benefited from her knowledge, loyalty, honesty, insight, and wisdom.

While in England I asked historical researcher and writer Tricia H. Stoker to join this project as a research assistant. Together we have forged a love for the East German portion of President Monson's service and for the many members in that land whose stories are simply extraordinary. I couldn't have done this work without her.

Both of President Monson's counselors, President Henry B. Eyring and President Dieter F. Uchtdorf, have consented to interviews and given encouragement these many months, as has each member of the Quorum of the Twelve and various members of the Seventy and Presiding Bishopric and general auxiliary officers of the Church. Their perspectives have been invaluable in shaping this biography. In particular, Elder Robert D. Hales has been a guiding hand and voice.

President Monson's children—Tom, Ann, and Clark—participated in interviews and gave a view of their home life and parents so important to the biography, as did his brothers and sisters. I am indebted to President Monson's close friends in Germany and Canada who hosted us as we visited and relived sacred experiences of his past.

I am sincerely grateful to Christine Marin, in the LDS Church History Department, who has provided tremendous help in accessing materials; to Cristy Valentine, Pat Fought, and Renee Wood in President Monson's office and Brook Hales in the office of the First Presidency; all have been cooperative, patient, and supportive—daily. I am grateful for the love of our missionaries and for the faithful Saints we came to know so well in the England London South Mission.

Thank you to all who shared their stories. Many appear in this book, but it would have taken several volumes to include everything.

Deseret Book has a history of publishing the biographies of all the prophets of this dispensation. To Sheri Dew, who has written two biographies of latter-day prophets and has been a mentor and treasured friend, I will always be indebted. To Emily Watts, whose skill at editing is genius; to Richard Erickson, whose design direction is unmatched; and to Cory Maxwell, who is ever the gentleman and always giving encouragement—thank you for the long days and, at the end, long nights. Thanks also to Tonya Facemyer for the typography and to Scott Eggers for the beautiful cover design.

Most important, I am indebted to my husband, Jeffrey, who for these past two years—and our whole married life—has been my inspiration, adviser, dearest friend, and refuge; I love him. Our sons, Cameron, Daniel, Jonathan, and Ian; their spectacular wives, Kristen, Julia, Annie, and Janelle; and our six grandchildren have been my ever-present cheering section. My mother is an example of courage and determination. Barbara Lockhart and many others have been true friends in the Monson tradition; Wayne and Lesley Webster have made it possible to concentrate on fulfilling this work for the Lord.

President Monson has so often counseled members to "eliminate the weakness of one standing alone and substitute instead the strength of many working together." This biography is a witness of such efforts. Still, though many have been at my side, I alone am responsible for the creation and conclusions of this volume. What a privilege it has been. I have come to know that indeed the Lord is on our right hand and on our left, and there are angels round about to bear us up (see Doctrine and Covenants 84:88).

—HEIDI S. SWINTON

INTRODUCTION

TO THE RESCUE

He is more Christlike than the rest of us. He's known for emphasizing and elevating things that are most important, the ordinary things. He is the one for whom the widow and the orphan are not just statements in a book.

PRESIDENT BOYD K. PACKER
President of the Quorum of the Twelve Apostles

IT WAS A RAINY, LACKLUSTER SUNDAY, December 2, 1979, when a gregarious Apostle of God with his long and purposeful stride entered the dreary Dresden hospital in the German Democratic Republic. The moment was quintessential Thomas S. Monson. Following a prompting, he had flown more than 5,200 miles and crossed behind the Iron Curtain at Checkpoint Charlie for one purpose—to give Inge Burkhardt a blessing.

Inge had been in the hospital nine weeks with complications from gall-bladder surgery that developed into pneumonia and a string of other ailments. The doctors recommended a second surgery—of questionable efficacy—in an operating room that had no heat and archaic equipment. When Elder Monson heard of her plight, he got on a plane. Without any prior planning, yet bidden by the Spirit and by his love for the Burkhardts, he traveled across the globe to minister to a single soul.

"We joined our faith and our prayers in providing her a blessing," Elder Monson recorded in his journal. The scene as he

1

departed the hospital grounds will always stay with him. "When looking upward we saw Sister Burkhardt from her bedroom window waving farewell to us."[1]

Looking upward is what Thomas S. Monson does best. He often quotes the verse:

> But chief of all Thy wondrous works,
> Supreme of all Thy plan,
> Thou hast put an upward reach
> Into the heart of man.[2]

The Burkhardts were trapped, as were thousands of other Latter-day Saints, in a country overrun with guards and guns. The government officials allowed religious worship, but anyone participating was suspect. Henry Burkhardt, president of the Dresden Mission for ten years, was singled out by the Communist government as the Church's representative in the land. It was hardly an honor. He did not advance at work; his children were denied educational opportunities; he and Inge were watched all the time.

Ask Henry to recall the single most significant experience he had with Elder Monson during the two decades when the bold young Apostle supervised and visited East Germany, and the tears come quickly. Henry will bypass the meeting he attended with the nation's supreme leader, Erich Honecker, when President Monson asked for and received approval for missionaries to serve in East Germany, then known as the German Democratic Republic—though that day was deserving of front-page news. He will not point to the serene morning on the hill overlooking the Elbe River when Elder Monson blessed the land "for the advancement of the work" of the Lord Jesus Christ and His gospel and made seemingly impossible promises to the Saints held hostage by a totalitarian government. Nor will he describe the many meetings held in rattletrap cars parked on gloomy streets to avoid the ever-present listening devices as a small huddle of men learned from an Apostle how to move the Church forward in a godless land.

No. What stands out in Henry's mind is that day at the

hospital when Elder Monson came just to bless Inge. It was a rescue mission.

While in the country, Elder Monson agreed to an impromptu meeting with the active priesthood leaders in the area; on short notice, thirty-seven of the thirty-nine attended. They met in the Leipzig "chapel," the men bundled in tattered clothing because the furnace had long since quit working. But there was "no lack of warmth in the hearts of the members," Elder Monson noted. "They had their scriptures with them, sang with gusto, and reflected a spirit of devotion to the gospel."[3]

And then he flew home.

Such is the ministry of the man—Thomas S. Monson, sixteenth President of The Church of Jesus Christ of Latter-day Saints, prophet, seer, and revelator.

Jesus Christ, in His ministry at the meridian of time, "went about doing good, . . . for God was with him."[4] He blessed the sick, restored sight to the blind, made the deaf to hear, and caused the halt and maimed to walk. He taught forgiveness by forgiving, compassion by being compassionate, devotion by giving of Himself, and love of His Father in Heaven by loving others—one at a time.

In like manner, Thomas S. Monson has spent his life going about doing good. He has lifted, encouraged, listened, counseled, and shared personal experiences, always for one single purpose—to encourage faith in the Lord Jesus Christ.

Jesus Christ called His disciples to follow Him and become "fishers of men." His disciples today have the same charge. President Monson's most productive "fishing hole" can be likened to the pool of Bethesda, where "a great multitude of impotent folk, of blind, halt, withered"in New Testament times went for healing—to be "made whole."[5] He understands from whence such healing comes: "Let us remember that it was not the waters of Bethesda's pool which healed the impotent man. Rather, his blessing came through the touch of the Master's hand."[6]

For a long time—a lifetime—Thomas S. Monson has gone to those waiting by the "pool," those draped in despair, disappointment, infirmities, pain, and even sin, and joined his faith with theirs that they might be made whole.

The man healed by Jesus Christ at the pool of Bethesda was seemingly obscure. No one reverenced his presence or found greater stature being by his side. But the Savior went right to him.[7] So it is with President Monson. He too goes to the weary and often forsaken, lays hands on their heads, and, in his singularly recognizable voice, provides inspired counsel. "I firmly believe," he has said many times, "that the sweetest experience in mortality is to know that our Heavenly Father has worked through us to accomplish an objective in the life of another person"—to help make someone whole.[8]

"Reach out to rescue . . . the aged, the widowed, the sick, the handicapped, the less active," he has said, and then he has led the charge. "Extend to them the hand that helps and the heart that knows compassion."[9]

When he went to East Germany, he was connecting Inge Burkhardt to the "whole" church and the faith and prayers of its people.

When he chaired the Scriptures Publication Committee, he spent ten years helping put in place greater access to the Lord's words with new study aids that would make members more "whole" in their understanding of the Lord Jesus Christ.

When he sat by his wife's bed in the hospital for seventeen days as she lay in a coma, he beseeched the Lord to intervene. The doctors tried to prepare him for the possibility that she would never wake up. He simply waited on the Lord, knowing his prayer of faith would be answered. She awoke; she had been healed.

When he appears at the funeral of one of his scores of friends and associates—such as Robert H. Hodgen, the carpenter who built his chicken coop and remodeled the family cabin at Vivian Park—he is showing gratitude for service that is known to only a few but is nonetheless a valued contribution.

When he is asked how he finds time to do such things, given the burdens of his ministry, he responds, "I am a very simple man. I just do what the Lord tells me to do."[10]

Following his sustaining at the solemn assembly during the 178th Annual General Conference of The Church of Jesus Christ of Latter-day Saints, President Monson stood before the membership of the Church, thirteen million strong, and encouraged the "less active, the offended, the critical, the transgressor" to come back. He pleaded, "To those who are wounded in spirit or who are struggling and fearful, we say, Let us lift you and cheer you and calm your fears."[11] Come, and be made whole.

For President Monson, being made "whole" does not mean being fixed, repaired, or made good as new. *Wholeness* is much more than that; it is a description of a life on earth filled with the Spirit of God and one in the eternities in the presence of the Father. He wants nothing less for all of God's children: "I plead with you to turn to our Heavenly Father in faith. He will lift you and guide you. He will not always take your afflictions from you, but He will comfort and lead you with love through whatever storm you face."[12]

His self-proclaimed optimism is clearly evident to everyone who knows him or even makes his acquaintance. He starts his first meeting of the day with "Top of the morning," he whistles in the middle of the afternoon, and he advocates with true sincerity finding "joy in the journey" at every turn. Earlier in his ministry he could attend personally to those in need; the pressures and demands of his prophetic office now require that he enlist the help of many others.

For President Dieter F. Uchtdorf, Second Counselor in the First Presidency of the Church, "It is a marvelous thing to be close to the prophet on a daily basis, to sit with him every day and feel of his closeness to the Lord. Always there is something going on and always a need for the First Presidency to act upon things, both spiritual and temporal, as the prophet leads the way."[13]

"Bethesda" in the Bible Dictionary is described as "house of mercy or house of grace." There could be no better description of President Monson's presence—wherever he is. Some of those to whom he ministers look put together on the outside but cry out for help from within their very souls. He hears them. He has continually offered the promise of peace, hope, and comfort in spite of challenges and grief, some seemingly insurmountable. He quotes often the promise of Jesus Christ: "I will go before your face. I will be on your right hand and on your left, and my Spirit shall be in your hearts, and mine angels round about you, to bear you up."[14] He loves that verse, for it speaks of how, through the power of the Atonement, we are made whole.

Like the Israelites' tabernacle of old, his "pool" of healing and love is portable. President Monson takes it with him wherever he goes: to Inge in East Germany, to a troop of scrappy Scouts camping out in a muddy field, to a small village in Tonga or Peru, to the bedside of the sick or dying, and to the marriage of loved ones in the holy temples of God. Indeed, his ministry is best expressed by his attention to the healing of souls.

To him, needs are both programmatic (that's where the welfare plan steps in) and personal (that's where he steps in). Many have described him as "the bishop" of the Church. He has been and always will be a champion of the Church's remarkable welfare program, which has addressed people's needs for more than half a century. But beyond relying upon programs, he steps in personally to assist those who struggle with testimony, suffer illness, grieve the loss of someone close, or make up "the long line of the lonely."[15] The list is endless but ever present on his mind and in his heart. When he is prompted, he goes—to the rescue.

His life is a witness of the importance of following personal inspiration: "When you honor a prompting and then stand back a pace, you realize that the Lord gave you the prompting. It makes me feel good that the Lord even knows who I am and knows me well enough to know that if He has an errand to be run and prompts me to run the errand, the errand will get done."[16] Put simply, he does not gauge where or what or how. "I'll go where you want me to go, dear Lord" is what President Monson is always about.[17] He always has been.

And his wife, Frances, has always been right at his side. Her commitment to his calling has equaled his. She is reserved in her manner, knowing that what she says, does, and puts her hand to will reflect on the calling that her husband bears. Her way of honoring the responsibility to them both is to be his support, any way she can, and to bear testimony of the divinity of Jesus Christ to Saints in many nations.

In tribute to her, he has said, "I could not have asked for a more loyal, loving, and understanding companion."[18]

When President Monson has spoken of "the miraculous strength" and "mighty power"[19] of wives and mothers in the home, he has had his sweet companion as his model. She has traveled with him when she could while caring for their young family, been ever ready to go at a moment's notice when he had people to visit across town, waited good-naturedly while he gave one blessing after another until the quick stop at the hospital turned to hours, and she has never complained. They have seldom sat together during a Church service; she has packed his bag for every trip he's taken; she has fixed his breakfast every day, even if it meant being up at 4:30 A.M. so he could be off for a "fishing" trip.

Called as an Apostle in 1963 by President David O. McKay when the Church was emerging as a worldwide denomination, Elder Monson traveled to every continent while balancing a load of significant committee assignments; he chaired them all. There were weekly stake conferences while he was a member of the Quorum of the Twelve and, later, when he joined the First Presidency, regional conferences. He has attended innumerable groundbreakings and temple dedications, and conducted countless mission tours.

The sheer logistics have not been easy. He has weathered lightning storms encircling his aircraft, delays on the ground and in the air, flight cancellations, lost baggage, eight-hour bus rides in the jungle to make it to meetings, and yet he has arrived—with the Spirit—ready to teach and preach to the members.

A fellow Apostle, Elder Joseph B. Wirthlin, described his long-time friend as "a mighty man of Israel who was foreordained to preside over this Church." In tribute he continued, "While it is a compliment to him that many of the great and mighty of this world know and honor him, perhaps it is an even greater tribute that many of the lowly call him friend."[20]

One of his good friends was Everett Bird. They had chickens in common: Rhode Island Reds, to be exact. Everett kept Elder Monson's chickens in his coop and was proud to show them off because of their owner. Elder Monson said of his chicken keeper: "I am daily impressed that the majority of the good people in the world do not receive any accolades or any publicity but live good lives within a small circle and one day will merit eternal reward."[21]

President Monson truly loves people. He is profoundly loyal to friends and associates. He relates to everyone—everywhere—and many through the years have been surprised and pleased to find that he still remembered them. One particular Sunday, when giving a blessing to his friend Don Balmforth from the old Sixth-Seventh Ward, he encouraged him, "Remember, Don, your influence has been felt on me. Wherever I go, you go. Wherever I speak, you speak. Wherever I serve, you serve." That same Sunday Elder Monson traveled across town to give a blessing to Louis McDonald in a nursing home, and he went later to his own brother Bob's home to give another. His summation: "All in all, a busy day."[22]

That's why his challenge—"to the rescue"—has such resonance and integrity. He has been there.

"His personality is this buoyant, outgoing, hail-fellow-well-met," explains Elder Jeffrey R. Holland. "He's larger than life. He fills that entire six-foot-three frame with enthusiasm. Nevertheless, when recalling an incident in his life or referring to the illness of a General Authority or remembering the passing of a grandchild of one of his schoolmates, he will weep on the spot—instantly. His eyes betray him. He will get red rims around his eyes the minute he talks about something spiritual and something personal."[23]

As an administrator, "he's not fast to judgment, not quick to fire out of the starting blocks," explains Elder Robert D. Hales. "He wants dialogue. He wants it from his counselors and from members of the Quorum. It's quite remarkable. He takes it all in and then he'll pray about it. Don't expect him to give an opinion and have it immediately adopted. He likes to say that he measures twice before he cuts once, but he measures five or six times before he cuts."[24]

Elder Ronald Rasband, Senior President of the Seventy, recalls the friendly hour-long exchange he had with President Monson on the plane returning from the temple dedication in Sacramento. "He is so conversant in regular affairs of life from basketball to Scouting to baseball to fishing to what's happening in town and the barbershop. He has knowledge of the life of the regular person. He loves to talk about it and he makes you feel totally comfortable in any of those settings."[25]

President Monson was not born to worldly wealth, but in his

home the spirit of love abounded. There is no question that he was prepared in his youth for service that may have belied his age but never his ability. He has always been a leader, from his first assignment as secretary in the deacons quorum to the prophetic mantle he carries today. Those who were in his teachers quorum when he was the president can attest that he has never given up on them and did finally get them to the temple. Experience has taught him: "The mantle of leadership is not the cloak of comfort but rather the robe of responsibility."[26]

This is a man who has never left his moorings. His childhood memories reveal much more than simply his growing up. They speak of the security of grandparents, aunts, uncles, and cousins; of the examples of righteous, hardworking parents; and of a Church environment that fostered faith and testimony. Born and bred in a neighborhood with the train whistles blaring and transients knocking at the door, he learned and exercised love for the Lord, concern for the elderly, compassion for the needy, loyalty, hard work, and a profound commitment to duty.

Though he has kept a daily journal since his call to the Twelve in October 1963, he is not linear; date, time, and place are simply the backdrop for him to see the manifestation of the hand of God. On those voluminous pages are recorded his priorities. He writes little about meetings and much about people. He is as comfortable with those who clean the building as he is with ambassadors of nations. Each has equal importance to him. When he speaks of his experiences, he is prompting the listeners to look at their own lives, to look for the Lord sending rescuers in the little things: the visit of a friend, the note, the much-needed affectionate handshake.

A day in March 1995 is a good example. Elder Russell M. Nelson brought Bruce D. Porter, a BYU professor, and his wife, Susan, to President Monson's office for an informal visit. (Just weeks later Brother Porter was called as a member of the Second Quorum of the Seventy.) However, that story began not in the office at 47 East South Temple but in Germany in 1972, when young Elder Porter, a mission secretary, was assigned to help Elder Monson, who was organizing the Düsseldorf Stake from the Ruhr District in the Germany Central Mission. Elder Porter spent three priceless days in the company of Elder Monson as driver, translator, organizer of schedules, recorder, and general ombudsman. Elder Porter did not expect President Monson to remember him—twenty-three years later. But, before Elder Porter could extend his hand in greeting, President Monson bounded across his office with open arms and said, "Düsseldorf!"[27]

President Monson was called as a bishop at just twenty-two years of age in the ward where he grew up. In fact, he and Frances have been members of that same ward and only one other their whole married life. He presided over the Sixth-Seventh Ward of the Temple View Stake, a ward with more than 1,080 members, 85 of them widows. There is no question that those years significantly shaped his perspective and prowess in Church leadership. He had in his care the needy, aged, ill, fatherless, and forgotten who were waiting at the "pool." He found them everywhere he visited. In his five years as bishop he learned his lessons well: listen to the Spirit, act on promptings, and do what the Lord would have you do.

"You develop an appreciation that Heavenly Father knows who you are and He says, 'Here, go do this for me,'" he has explained. "I always thank Him. My only regret is that I don't have more time to do the many things we are called upon to do. I work hard. I work long. I hope I work effectively, but I never feel I have exhausted what I should be doing."[28]

At age twenty-seven he was called into the stake presidency; at thirty-one, as a mission president in Canada; and at thirty-six, as an Apostle called of God. "The Lord selected him by His hand to be the prophet," states Elder L. Tom Perry, who has worked with him in the Twelve since 1974, "and he was well prepared for it and well trained for the time that he was needed there to build our Father in Heaven's kingdom."[29]

His inimitable speaking style has endeared him to millions as he has opened the doctrines and principles of the gospel through personal experiences. Embedded in each one are lessons of life and measures of virtue and character. He draws in his listeners with accounts from his own life or the experiences of people close to him and then leaves application of the principle to them.

To President Monson, "pure religion and undefiled before

God and the Father is this, To visit the fatherless and widows in their affliction, and to keep himself unspotted from the world."[30] He speaks it; he lives it. He expects others to do the same. "Our happiness is completely and utterly intertwined with other people: family, friends, neighbors, and the woman who you hardly notice who cleans your office."[31]

Like the Savior, he champions the widows. The 85 in the Sixth-Seventh Ward were not a number to him. They were noble souls whose station in life was easily transcended by their place in God's eyes. This is a man who sits down in nursing homes and explains the game of football to the women staring at the screen. In the process, he may have missed a meeting, but he "harvested a memory." When he talks with those who seem unresponsive, he enjoys the one-sided conversation, feeling that indeed he has "communed with God."[32]

"He truly is devoted to the rescue of others," President Henry B. Eyring, First Counselor in the First Presidency, has observed. "I thought I knew how he remembers everybody and how he reaches out to the most obscure person. But, it's more than I ever dreamed. I am a better person every day I work with him. I care about others and think about others more than I ever did before. He has had that amazing effect on me."[33]

"The prayers of people," President Monson has taught, "are almost always answered by the actions of others."[34] That's why his visit to Dresden was much more than a quick flight to see a dear friend. It was a reiteration that the Lord God will visit His people "in their affliction." In this case he took the "pool" behind the Iron Curtain.

For nearly five decades he has offered "living water" to those so desperately in need. Church members from Tahiti to Germany have watched him, followed him, and been taught by him with words that speak spirit-to-spirit:

"All can walk where Jesus walked when, with His words on our lips, His spirit in our hearts, and His teachings in our lives, we journey through mortality. I would hope that we would walk as he walked with confidence in the future, with an abiding faith in His Father, and with a genuine love for others."[35]

THOMAS S. MONSON FAMILY

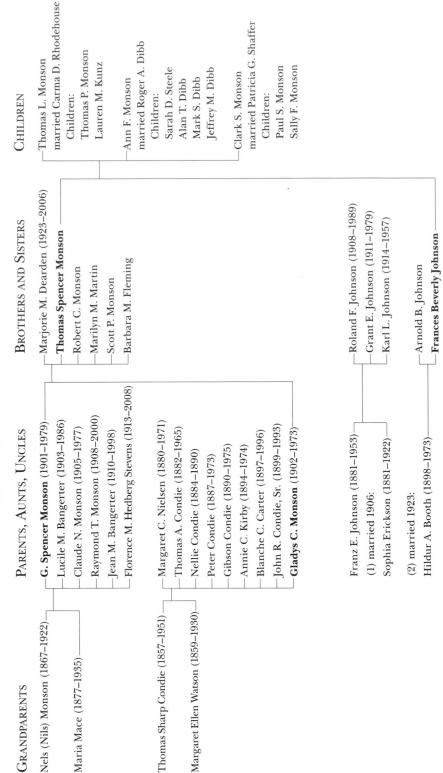

GRANDPARENTS

Nels (Nils) Monson (1867–1922)

Maria Mace (1877–1935)

Thomas Sharp Condie (1857–1951)

Margaret Ellen Watson (1859–1930)

Franz E. Johnson (1881–1953)

(1) married 1906:
Sophia Erickson (1881–1922)

(2) married 1923:
Hildur A. Booth (1898–1973)

PARENTS, AUNTS, UNCLES

G. Spencer Monson (1901–1979)
Lucile M. Bangerter (1903–1986)
Claude N. Monson (1905–1977)
Raymond T. Monson (1908–2000)
Jean M. Bangerter (1910–1998)
Florence M. Hedberg Stevens (1913–2008)

Margaret C. Nielsen (1880–1971)
Thomas A. Condie (1882–1965)
Nellie Condie (1884–1890)
Peter Condie (1887–1973)
Gibson Condie (1890–1975)
Annie C. Kirby (1894–1974)
Blanche C. Carter (1897–1996)
John R. Condie, Sr. (1899–1993)
Gladys C. Monson (1902–1973)

Roland F. Johnson (1908–1989)
Grant E. Johnson (1911–1979)
Karl L. Johnson (1914–1957)

Arnold B. Johnson
Frances Beverly Johnson

BROTHERS AND SISTERS

Marjorie M. Dearden (1923–2006)
Thomas Spencer Monson
Robert C. Monson
Marilyn M. Martin
Scott P. Monson
Barbara M. Fleming

CHILDREN

Thomas L. Monson
married Carma D. Rhodehouse
Children:
Thomas P. Monson
Lauren M. Kunz

Ann F. Monson
married Roger A. Dibb
Children:
Sarah D. Steele
Alan T. Dibb
Mark S. Dibb
Jeffrey M. Dibb

Clark S. Monson
married Patricia G. Shaffer
Children:
Paul S. Monson
Sally F. Monson

1

A HERITAGE OF FAITHFUL SOULS

I can say, as did Nephi of old, that I was born of goodly parents, whose own parents and grandparents were gathered out of the lands of Sweden and Scotland and England by dedicated missionaries. . . . After joining the Church, these noble men, women, and children made their way to the valley of the Great Salt Lake. Many were the trials and heartaches they encountered along the way.

PRESIDENT THOMAS S. MONSON
President of The Church of
Jesus Christ of Latter-day Saints

COME! AND HELP US TO BUILD AND GROW," Brigham Young and his counselors in the First Presidency had declared in a bold missive to Church converts in 1849, only two years after the vanguard company of pioneers arrived in the valley of the Great Salt Lake.[1] Converts scattered across the eastern seaboard of America and the Atlantic responded.

They came "one of a city, and two of a family,"[2] as the Old Testament prophet Jeremiah had prophesied, and they fit the definition of a pioneer that President Monson is so apt to quote: "One who goes before, showing others the way to follow."[3]

Missionaries preached of the restored gospel of Jesus Christ, their message a stark contrast to the hopelessness engendered by the factory smokestacks and crowded industrial ghettos. The missionaries garnered converts by the hundreds, mostly people from the working class, "of clean blood, of noble heritage, of honest frugality and independence, of worthy traditions and unshakable loyalty to truth."[4] The *Birmingham Daily Press* observed that the

13

missionaries "promised to lead [English laborers] out from their Egypt of task-work and subjection" and that converts rallied as if they were following "a new Moses sent from God."[5] It is not surprising that every President of the Church and every President of the Quorum of the Twelve Apostles has roots in the British Isles.

Some of President Monson's ancestors, the Condies, were among the first in Scotland to accept the gospel and be baptized. The Sharps and Watsons followed, caught up in "a rising tide of religious emigration."[6] The Millers came from Rutherglen, Scotland, the Maces from northern England, where the gospel harvest got its start. The Monsons were from Sweden, the land "touched with the finger of beauty."[7]

On a visit to Blekinge, Sweden, President Monson found his grandfather's name in a local record with a note next to it: "Joined the Mormon Church and left for Utah." "We really have few ways today to comprehend the difficulty, the sacrifice, the hunger and deprivation required to build the roads, the culture, the schools, the very basis of today's civilization, in the Salt Lake Valley in the State of Utah," President Monson has said in honoring such believing ancestors. "They came to a new nation, a strange language, and a people whom they did not know; but God they did know, and more important, He knew them and blessed them and prospered them and has been with them."[8]

THE CONDIES

Gibson Condie, born June 14, 1814, and his brother Thomas, born in 1805, mined coal in the little shire of Clackmannan in central Scotland. Gibson and his family were lowlanders. Coal fueled the mills and factories of the burgeoning Industrial Revolution then sweeping across the island. The work was grueling and dangerous. Gibson left the mines and went to work for Thomas, who had quit as a miner some time earlier to manage a local inn.

Thomas allowed LDS missionary William Gibson, one of the first Scottish elders, to hold meetings on the second floor of the Crown Inn. "I am so grateful that one of my ancestors left the coal mines and became a workman in an inn," President Monson has said.[9] In 1847 Gibson and his wife were baptized; later that year Thomas and his family were baptized as well.[10]

Gibson and Cecelia Condie were not adventurers but God-fearing people who had taken the Bible for their guide. Their faith spurred them to seek their new life in a faraway land. In 1848 they left their homes, along with other members of the Clackmannan Branch, bound for the Salt Lake Valley. They and their children, including two daughters from Cecelia's previous marriage, headed out with all their worldly possessions secured in a tiny trunk.

They gathered with other Mormon converts, including Gibson's brother Thomas's family, at the docks in Liverpool and boarded the *Zetland*, then the largest of the chartered Mormon ships and also the newest. On November 10, 1848, the ship, with its 250 Saints aboard, moved down the River Mersey to the ocean and caught the brisk winds for the 3,000-mile journey. "The waves were high, the voyage long, the quarters cramped."[11] Yet with whole-souled devotion they faced this risky seagoing venture, believing that blessings awaited them at the end. For some, the end came sooner than expected.

Far from land, Gibson and Cecelia's young son grew increasingly ill. He had never been strong, and the propensity for disease on ship—"poor food, poor water, no help beyond the length and breadth of that small sailing vessel"[12]—proved too much for the child. He died. The ship's captain directed a brief service, and then the tiny body, wrapped in a canvas and weighed down with iron bars, slipped into its watery grave. And the ship sailed on.

President Monson has reflected on that somber moment: "The father, no doubt with his arm cupped around his wife, choked back tears as he pronounced, 'The Lord gave, and the Lord hath taken away; blessed be the name of the Lord. We will see our son again.'"[13]

The ship docked in New Orleans after forty-four days on the water. It was Christmas Eve.[14]

The Condie brothers, Thomas and Gibson, and their families booked steamboat passage up the Mississippi River to St. Louis, where the two brothers found work in the coal mines in Grove Diggins, a nearby community, to finance the rest of their journey. While in St. Louis, Cecelia gave birth to a little girl, Ellen, on April 27, 1849. In the spring of 1850 Gibson and Cecelia headed west in a company of thirty ox teams. Out on the trail, like so many of the pioneer Saints, "They took an interest to help and assist one another. Sometimes they would have a little amusement, dancing and everything to cheer and comfort them on their journey."[15]

Gibson and his family entered the Salt Lake Valley with a broken wagon, two gaunt oxen, and a determination to serve God. His family knew Gibson as "a man governed in all things by God."[16] They camped at Pioneer Square, where the first pioneers had built a crude stockade for shelter and protection. The area would become home to the Condies for four generations.

There Gibson and Cecelia had five more children. The last was Thomas Sharp Condie, President Monson's grandfather, for whom he was named.

Life in the city revolved around the ward, where the bishop was the religious leader. Wards held preaching meetings every Sunday and fast meetings one Thursday each month. The Condies lived in the Sixth Ward. They were not just pioneer settlers; they were Saints standing firmly with their prophet, Brigham Young. Gibson Condie, a nephew of Gibson and Cecelia born in 1835, was among those who responded to President Brigham Young's impassioned call in 1856 "to bring in" the Martin and Willie handcart companies stranded out on the plains. He was then twenty-one. He and others cut a path through sixteen feet of snow in the nearly impassable canyon leading to the valley so that the rescuers and emigrants could make their way down through the snowdrifts to their final destination. "We were just in time to assist them," Gibson wrote. "We all descended down from Big Mountain to camp. It was dreadfully cold and stormy. We had to have large fires burning all night to keep from freezing to death."[17]

On the wall at Martin's Cove, Wyoming, a list recognizes "Those Who Rescued." On a visit to the landmark, President

Monson said of his relative Gibson Condie, as he gazed at the names recorded on the wall, "Bless his name."[18]

THE MILLERS AND THE WATSONS

Missionaries found the Miller family in the coal-mining town of Rutherglen, Scotland, a royal burgh also known for its weaving, paper manufacturing, and shipbuilding. One of their eleven children, daughter Margaret, would become President Monson's great-grandmother. In the spring of 1848, the Millers too took the route from Liverpool to New Orleans and up the river to St. Louis, arriving at the bustling port in 1849.

Like the Condies, the Miller family went to work hauling coal to the Mississippi River and loading it onto boats at three dollars a ton. The family needed the scanty funds they earned in order to complete their journey. But tragedy struck. That summer cholera raged up and down the Mississippi River, hitting hardest in St. Louis; many of the immigrant families lost loved ones. About 4,500 people died in the epidemic. The Millers were not spared. In the space of two weeks, four of the family members died—including both parents. A family journal records in few words the enormous tragedy:

"Son William, age 18, died here June 22, 1849. Mother, Mary, died here June 27, five days later. Son Archibald, age 15, died two days later, and husband Charles [Stewart Miller] died July 4, a week later."[19]

More than a century later, at the groundbreaking ceremony of the St. Louis Temple in 1993, President Monson would pay tribute to his ancestors: "I feel I am standing on sacred ground in an area where these dear forebears of mine completed their trek to find God and to establish His kingdom here upon the earth."[20]

Due to the enormity of the cholera plague, there were no caskets to be found. The older boys dismantled the family's oxen pens and made caskets for proper burial of their parents and brothers. The nine remaining children, three boys and six girls, ranged in age from twenty-four to three. Now orphaned in a strange city in a foreign land, more than a thousand miles from their longed-for destination, they somehow managed to go west. The oldest daughter was married, and she and her husband became the surrogate parents of the other children. Sparse records indicate that they all left St. Louis in the spring of 1850 with one wagon and the four oxen they used to haul coal. They joined a company of other pioneers and arrived in Salt Lake later that summer, settling in the Sixth Ward near Pioneer Park.

In 1855 Margaret Miller, who had been eleven years old when her parents died, married Alexander Watson, a convert from Calder, Lanark, Scotland, who had immigrated to Utah in 1848 when he was thirteen. He too worked in St. Louis for a time and then came on to Utah, crossing the plains during the summer of 1850. In 1859 a daughter, Margaret Ellen, was born to the Watsons. She married Thomas Sharp Condie on August 2, 1879, and they settled on the corner of Gale Street and 500 South near Pioneer Park.

To this union of Margaret and Thomas Condie came Gladys, President Monson's mother, on October 1, 1902. She was the youngest of nine children—four boys and five girls.

At one time Gladys's father, Thomas Condie, owned one of the largest sheep herds in Utah and was known for delivering most of his flock to market. He hired what he considered the best—Basque shepherds. His hands-on approach to business contributed significantly to his success but pulled him away from home a great deal of the time. His business took him east to the Chicago stockyards to sell his sheep, leaving Margaret to raise the family. When he was home, he regaled his children with tales of wild coyotes and adventures in the dark of night. Successful and resourceful, he retired young, purchasing large pieces of property as an inheritance for his children. When they married, he gave his daughters homes and rental property on Fifth South and Second West; to his sons, he deeded farmland in what was then called Granger, an area south and west of Salt Lake City. He lived all his life on the same block. After his wife, Margaret, died in 1930, he moved in with his daughter Blanche.

THE MACES AND THE MONSONS

John Mace joined the Church in the early 1840s in the company of all his brothers and sisters. Although living in Leeds, Yorkshire, England, the Mace family were actually descendants of French Huguenots, who pronounced the name Macé.[21] (That connection adds another European nation to President Monson's "homelands.") John served as the branch president in Leeds but chose in 1865 to gather to Zion; his wife, Harriet, stayed back until he could provide a home in what she imagined was a true wilderness. He was sent to Cache Valley and set to work preparing a place for his family. Two years later, in 1867, he was called on a mission to England, where he served faithfully in the Leeds area until he was fatally stricken with pneumonia. After his death, most of his family eventually journeyed to Zion.

The Leeds "conference," as it was called, was for decades a stronghold of the Church in England. John's son George, George's wife, Clara, and their children left Leeds, Yorkshire, England in 1883 for Utah. Both George and Clara had worked in what British poet William Blake called "the dark, satanic mills." He was a dyer; she was a weaver. George's first wife, Mary Ann Bowden, had died, leaving him with a one-year-old son, John. George sought a companion who would love the two of them; he found that affection in Clara Judson. They married in 1865 in Leeds. John would always be counted as the oldest of George and Clara's children; he was followed by Harry, James, Caroline, Maria (nicknamed "Rie"), and Mary Ann. Rie would become the great-grandmother of President Thomas S. Monson.

In 1883, George packed up his family, sold their possessions, and bought passage on the steamship *Nevada*. The Mormons on board totaled 352. Steam travel was faster and more predictable than sailing, though icebergs created some peril on the Atlantic crossing. The *Nevada* averaged 250 miles per day.[22] Arriving in Salt Lake by rail from the East, the Mace family settled down, and George took a position with the railroad.

The passengers on the *Nevada* were a mix of Brits and Scandinavians. As with those immigrants before them, they made friends as best they could, given the language barriers. Some even fell in love. Swedish convert Nels Monson was one of them.[23]

Nels Monson was born in Torhamn, in the Swedish province of Blekinge, on April 24, 1867.[24] President Monson has visited the old Svartensgatan chapel where the family would have worshipped. He walked into the empty, aged building, still used as a church facility, and just stood behind the pulpit, reflecting on the fact that his grandfather had borne his testimony from that same spot before leaving his homeland for America.[25]

Their ship, the *Nevada,* sailed from Sweden to Liverpool, where additional passengers from England, Scotland, and Ireland boarded the vessel. For the Atlantic crossing, they were booked on what Brigham Young might have called "the good ship Zion"—one of his favorite phrases. Much good came from the sea journey.

Nels met Rie Mace. He was twenty-four; she was fourteen. He waited seven years and then proposed marriage to Rie. The entry in his journal on the day that they married in the Salt Lake Temple reads, "This is the happiest day of my life. Today I married my sweetheart for time and all eternity. It has been a long seven years waiting for this event."[26]

Just three days after their marriage, Nels boarded a train for the first leg of a journey to Sweden, where he had been called to serve as a missionary. President Monson later said, "That's the kind of man my father's father was."[27] He left behind his bride; he did not return for two years. "Today I walked the pathways of Torhamn [Sweden], where I walked and played as a boy," he wrote in his journal. "I saw the people whom I knew as a boy. I visited many familiar surrounds. My heart was full, but the spirit of the gospel filled my soul. I thought to myself, 'Oh, if only all who could hear my voice could understand the words of truth.'" And then he wrote, "I shall do my best to teach them."[28]

Nels's most frequent journal entry was, "My feet are wet." Another entry of lasting significance read: "Today we went to the Jansson home. We met Sister Jansson. She had a lovely dinner for us. She is a good cook." He continued: "The children all sang or played the harmonica or did a little dance and then she paid her tithing. Five krona for the Lord and one for my companion Elder

Ipson, and one for me." Among the children at the Jansson home was young Franz, who probably sang and joined in the gaiety. Franz, whose name was changed from Jansson to Johnson when he entered the United States of America, later became the father of Frances Johnson, the wife of President Monson.[29]

President Monson has spoken with deep appreciation of "the sacrifice of that grandfather [Nels Monson] and particularly of that grandmother who sustained him while he returned to his homeland to preach the gospel."[30] Of his grandmother he would later explain, she "had been sacrificing for others all her life."[31]

The Monsons have gathered in the temple on occasion to perform sealings for deceased ancestors. President Monson is proud of his heritage. Some of his ancestors left homes and families, buried children and parents, and started over—not just once but repeatedly. With faith in God, they leaned on one another in the harsh, desert clime. President Monson has followed their lead. "Each of us has a heritage—whether from pioneer forebears [or] later converts," he has said. "This heritage provides a foundation built of sacrifice and faith. Ours is the privilege and responsibility to build on such firm and stable footings."[32]

He has further counseled: "Let's develop a tradition of obedience, as our forebears did. As we do, we shall not only be the grandsons and the granddaughters of great men and women, but perhaps we will be the fathers and mothers and the grandfathers and grandmothers of great children and grandchildren."[33]

2

BETWEEN THE RAILROAD TRACKS

What a proud day it was when [Tommy was] born. . . . His mother had great expectations. They have all been fulfilled.

PRESIDENT GORDON B. HINCKLEY
President of The Church of Jesus Christ
of Latter-day Saints, 1995–2008

WHEN THOMAS S. MONSON SPEAKS of his birth and early childhood, he sometimes quotes the words of the Roman poet: "Let ancient times delight other folk; I rejoice that I was not born till now."[1] "Now" for him was Sunday, August 21, 1927, when Gladys Condie and G. Spencer Monson welcomed to their family their second child and first son. He was born early in the day at St. Mark's Hospital on Salt Lake City's west side.

Fitting—it was a Sunday.

After a hospital stay of ten days, typical for the time, his parents took him home to 311 West Fifth South—what many called Condie's Corner—where the Condie families had lived since Gibson Condie first emigrated from Scotland in 1850. Tommy was welcomed by his older sister, Marjorie, almost four, along with a host of aunts, uncles, and young cousins who would be his support, example, and source of entertainment and inspiration in his growing-up years. Gladys's father, Thomas Sharp Condie, owned much of the property on the block. Tom would often kid others that he grew up not east of the tracks or west of the tracks but between them, as two sets of rails ran within a block or two of his home on either side.

Tommy's father, prone to writing verses and letters to his wife and children, penned a poem for his newborn son:

> *Dear Baby Monson with your wee pink toes,*
> *And your wee little mouth*
> *Like the bud of a rose;*
> *May this new world to your wondering mind,*
> *Unfold its treasures good and kind.*
> *Intelligence, wisdom, happiness, too,*
> *Are the riches that I wish for you.*[2]

The Monson family would eventually include four more siblings: Robert (born in 1932), Marilyn (1940), Scott (1943), and Barbara (1948). "Each came with a different personality," Spence was heard to say as he praised his children. "I thank the Lord the wife and I have had the opportunity to tend these spirits."[3] No question, Tommy was "born into a home with loving parents, parents who welcomed us with open arms."[4]

Tommy arrived on the cusp of hard times for the nation. In his birth year, 1927, speculation in stocks hit a fevered pitch. When optimism cooled in 1929 and the market began to wobble, selling prices plunged, and on October 29—"Black Tuesday," as it came to be called—the market collapsed, setting off the Great Depression. Millions lost their savings, their businesses, their farms, and their hopes for the future.

The Depression hit the Intermountain West hard. Between 1929 and 1933, the annual per capita income plummeted from $527 to $300, and unemployment in Utah reached 36 percent, the fourth highest in the country. One-fourth of the banks in the state closed their doors, and 32 percent of the state's population turned to government programs for food, clothing, and other necessities.[5]

LDS Church membership reached 600,000 in 1927, with most of the Saints still living in the West; President Heber J. Grant dedicated the Mesa Arizona Temple, the seventh in operation; and missionary work in Germany was highly successful. Many of the General Authorities walked to work in the fairly new Church Administration Building, carrying sack lunches with them. In 1928 the Church printed the first *Handbook of Instructions* and organized its one-hundredth stake; in 1929 the Mormon Tabernacle Choir officially went on the air with *Music and the Spoken Word,* beginning the longest-running radio broadcast in history. President Heber J. Grant and his counselors exhorted the members to "visit the sick, comfort those who are in sorrow, clothe the naked, feed the hungry, care for the widow and the fatherless."[6] Tom's life would reflect their counsel.

Tommy always took pride that in his birth year Charles Lindbergh made the first nonstop flight from New York to Paris, a daring adventure at the time. His custom-built, single-engine, single-seat monoplane, the *Spirit of St. Louis,* crossed the Atlantic in thirty-three and a half hours. Years later President Monson would pay tribute to Lindbergh, declaring in his recognizable triplet style of speech: "He fulfilled his dream; he reached his goal; he triumphed."[7]

Tommy—Thomas Spencer Monson—was named after his maternal grandfather, Thomas Sharp Condie, and his father, G. Spencer Monson. His great-uncle Peter S. Condie acted as voice to give him a name and blessing on October 2, 1927, in the Sixth-Seventh Ward of the Pioneer Stake. That his mother's uncle pronounced the blessing pointed to the close ties in this deeply rooted pioneer family.

Tommy's father, Spence, had gone to work young. Born May 17, 1901, on a five-acre farm in Murray, Utah, a suburb south of Salt Lake City, he was the oldest child of Swedish emigrant Nels Monson and British convert Maria Mace. He was followed by siblings Grace Lucile, Claude Niels, Raymond Tracy, Maria Jean, and Florence. Spence's father, Nels, with two teams of horses and two wagons, hauled brick for a living, usually four loads a day, earning $1.00 to $1.25 a load.

When Spence was fourteen years old, his father fell seriously ill. Spence quit school and went to work to provide an income for

the family, taking a position at the Arrow Press Printing Company
as a sweep-up boy or "printer's devil." A good student in school,
particularly adept at spelling, Spence was a quick study on the
job. He worked six days a week, steadily advancing from washing
presses to feeding the press to setting up type. At the end of two
years he was making eighteen dollars a week. He had found his
profession. When his family moved to California, hoping the climate would boost his father's health, Spence stayed behind, moving in with his Uncle Elias and Aunt Christine, who was called
Teen.

At eighteen this "dashing, handsome man," along with his
cousin Bill and friend George, began circulating among the local
dances. He met Gladys Condie at the Pioneer Stake's Wednesday
night dance, which had a reputation as "one of the largest and
best in Salt Lake City," with "the best dancing and the prettiest
girls."[8] One of those pretty girls was dark-eyed, dark-haired Gladys
Condie, whose card, he soon learned, was filled with suitors. One
night, he and his friends showed up for the costume ball; many
of the other young men, not wanting to dress up, had purposely
stayed away. Spence asked Gladys, "the girl in striped socks,"
to dance. He walked her home that night, and their courtship
began.[9]

One evening Gladys broke a date because she was ill. The
same thing happened the next night and the next. Concerned,
Spence went to the florist and bought a bouquet of sunflow-
ers, only to learn as he presented it to her that she was suffering dreadfully from hay fever. He was careful thereafter to bring
chocolates.

Spence became a regular visitor to the Condies' summer cot-
tage in Provo Canyon at Vivian Park, sleeping in a tent at the rear
of the cabin with Gladys's sister's beau, John Nielson. Vivian Park
became very much a part of their life in years to come. On her
nineteenth birthday, Spence presented Gladys with a ring.

On a stormy morning, December 14, 1922, Spence and Gladys
took the streetcar to the Salt Lake Temple, where George F.
Richards, temple president, performed their marriage. A winter
blizzard did nothing to dampen the evening celebration held at

the Condie home. Gladys's mother served more than 200 guests a full turkey dinner with all the trimmings.

The newlyweds settled into one of Thomas Condie's properties, a duplex at 311 West 500 South, which he had presented to them as a wedding gift. Spence called it "a love nest," though it took weeks of cleaning, scrubbing floors, and painting woodwork to make it so. Living close to the streetcar came in handy, since two years would pass before they could save enough to purchase their first car, an Oldsmobile.

In 1923, Spence turned down a business offer in California, not wanting to leave home, friends, and relatives. (Twenty-five years later his son Tom would make the same choice.) Instead, he took a position in a new print shop, Western Hotel Register, which opened its doors with a few cases of foundry type and a hand press. He ended up working there for fifty years. He always wore a hat and had ink under his fingernails. He was also known for his patient doggedness about getting the work done. On November 16, 1977, the announcement of his retirement stated, "You are invited to drop in at the Western Hotel Register, 740 South Main, from 4–6 P.M. to greet G. Spencer Monson as he retires after 60 yrs as a printer and the doors of this pioneer printing institution are closed."[10]

Gladys had lived all of her life on the same street; she was educated in Salt Lake City schools and at the University of Utah. She had a ready smile and a confidence that prompted quick conversation with just about anybody. She was the youngest, the tallest, and, the family agrees, the most outgoing of her family members: sisters Margaret, Annie, and Blanche, and brothers Thomas, Peter, Gibson, and John. (Another sister, Nellie, had died as a child.) Gladys loved to talk. On the streetcar she always sat next to perfect strangers, sharing her opinion about everything from what they should name their children to where they should go on vacation to where they should shop. She also spent a good deal of time talking on the phone with friends and was particularly solicitous of those who were homebound. When the children's friends called, they often got Gladys, prompting such comments as, "I had a good talk with your mother today because you weren't home." President Harold B. Lee, her stake president in the Pioneer Stake, described Gladys as one "with a youthful zest for living."[11] She passed on that trait to her oldest son, Tom.

"What an interesting woman she was," President Monson says of his mother. "She had a sense of humor and a ready laugh."[12] Of all the Monson children, Tom is considered to be the most like her. She liked to give people nicknames: young Tommy quickly earned the title of "Nervous Willy" because he was always anxious to get things done—a tendency that has stayed with him.

Spence Monson was as quiet as his wife was loquacious. "He could smile and laugh, but not in the robust way the Scottish did."[13] He was content to let Gladys direct discussions and dominate conversations. He liked to just sit back and watch the family, smiling as they interacted. To his credit, his family "never heard from his lips one word of criticism of another."[14]

Indeed, Tom was greatly influenced by his family in his early years, his parents in particular. "Honor thy father and thy mother" was expected, as was respect for his grandfather, aunts, and uncles, who lived up and down the street in what was almost a family compound. The four Condie sisters and their husbands all lived within three or four doors of each other in homes that their father had given them. Each duplex had a rental to provide extra income for the daughters. Blanche and her husband, Richard LeRoy "Speed" Carter, lived in one with Tom's Grandfather Condie, who had lost his wife in 1930. His oldest daughter, Margaret, and her husband, John "Jack" Nielson, lived just west of them. Other family members—Annie and Andrew Raymond "Rusty" Kirby, Gibson and Hilda Condie, and John and Gertrude Condie—lived for a time in what they called the Terrace, a string of four attached homes behind the duplexes. Eventually the Condie brothers, Thomas W., Peter, Gibson, and John R., moved to the farm property in Granger.

To them, Tommy was more like a son than a nephew. He recalls, "We were in and out of each other's houses. We never knocked or rang the bell." They answered each other's phones— one telephone line handled all four families—and Gladys liked to listen in to the others' conversations. Their number was 3-4724.[15]

It was Tom's uncles Rusty, Speed, and John who taught him to fish the Provo River and the surrounding lakes and reservoirs; they were his frequent fishing companions for years.

The Condie property also included the Blue Front Grocery Store, which had been built years before so that the Condie children would not race across the train tracks to purchase penny candy at the local shop. The second generation—including Tommy and his cousins—frequented the store, as did other neighborhood children.

The families lived in modest two-story, red-brick duplexes. There were no sidewalks or concrete gutters, and the railroad tracks ran close by. In the background was the familiar whistle of the nearby trains. As the trains went by, everyone quit talking because no one could hear. After they had moved on down the track, Gladys would get up and adjust the pictures, and then the conversation would resume.

To Tommy, theirs was a home "made of love, sacrifice, and respect."[16] The kitchen table was surrounded by yellow plastic chairs that were cold in the winter and sticky in the summer. The refrigerator was cooled by blocks of ice. There was a coal-burning stove in the kitchen, and a coal Heatrola in the dining room on the main floor heated the whole house, though it barely kept the chill off. The parents slept in the front bedroom, Marge and later Marilyn and Barbara in the center bedroom, and Tommy and Bob and later Scott in the back bedroom, with a hot-water bottle at the foot of each double bed. Most winter mornings, Tommy curled up on the carpet in front of the Heatrola as his father stoked a new fire. Tommy would retrieve the morning newspaper, reading the headlines, the sports section, and finally the comics. His love for newspapers began early and has continued throughout his life.

"Love thy neighbor as thyself" meant something in the Monson home. And although his mother may not have read to him regularly from the scriptures, she taught him compassion, charity, honesty, duty, and hard work by her every action. He quickly came to understand that "care for the poor, the sick, the needy were everyday dramas never to be forgotten."[17]

Lanky, mustached Grandpa Condie enjoyed sitting on the swing on the front porch. Tom recalls, "He didn't speak much, but he liked company."[18] With his "tough Scottish blood," Tom's grandfather lived until he was nearly ninety-four; he was one of the oldest residents in the valley. In 1947 the *Deseret News* hailed the "Pioneer Son" on his ninetieth birthday and reported that this man who was "born June 20, 1857 in a 'dugout' home on what is now West Fifth South, now lives within two blocks of his birthplace."[19]

One day, ninety-year-old Robert Dicks, a British emigrant the family knew as "Old Bob," sat down on the front porch swing beside Grandpa Condie. Tommy sat near them.

"Mr. Condie," Old Bob began, "I am a sad man today. I have been put out of my home." The house in which he was living was scheduled for demolition as industry began to encroach on what had been a family neighborhood. Tommy glanced across to where widower Old Bob lived. By any standard, it was not much.

In a plaintive voice, the old man continued, "I don't know what to do. I have no family, no place to go, and no money."

Tommy's grandfather just kept swinging and didn't say anything for a few minutes. Finally he reached in his pocket and took out his old coin purse. Many a kid had begged for a nickel for candy from that coin purse. He took out a key and handed it to Bob. "Mr. Dicks," he said, "I was born in that house next to me there. It's vacant, and I don't particularly want to rent it anymore. You take that key, move your things there, and stay as long as you want. Nobody will ever put you out again."

Tears welled up in Old Bob's eyes and coursed down his cheeks, then disappeared in his long white beard. Grandpa Condie's eyes were wet too. Old Bob had a home. That day, Grandpa Condie stood ten feet tall in his grandson's eyes.[20]

Spence Monson, Tom's father, worked six days a week and most evenings. Discretionary time was practically nonexistent. However, he almost always made the family's breakfast, as he had since the morning after his wedding to Gladys, when he had asked her, "What's for breakfast?" and she had replied, "I don't know." The newlyweds had crackers and cheese that morning.

After that, Spence usually prepared bacon and eggs, sometimes with fried potatoes and orange juice, or cereal with bananas and toast, along with bottled peaches or pears. Some days he even put doughnuts or sweet rolls on the table. Tom did not inherit that culinary proclivity from his father, although as a boy he learned to make fudge and hot cocoa.

Sunday dinner was a big event in the Monson home, featuring roast beef with gravy and mashed potatoes. On Monday the family ate leftovers from Sunday dinner. On Tuesday they had stew from the end of the roast. Wednesday they had pork chops, and on Thursday a sirloin steak that fed everyone at the table. Friday was lamb chops or fish, and Saturday link-sausage sandwiches. Variations included lima beans and ham one night, homemade meat pies another. Chopped fruit salad with marshmallows was a favorite, as was rice pudding. Gladys was known for her cakes. She often tinted each layer a different color—green on the bottom, pink in the middle, and yellow on the top—and covered the whole cake with thick chocolate frosting. Even Old Bob got one of Gladys's cakes for his ninetieth birthday, with nine candles, one for each decade.

Every Sunday Gladys would prepare a plate of food for Old Bob; before the family sat down to dinner, she would send Tommy off with the plate. One Sunday he asked, "Why don't I take it down later?"

His mother responded, "You do what I say, and your food will taste better."

He wasn't sure what she meant, but he headed off for Old Bob's, waiting anxiously as aged feet brought his neighbor to the door. Bob reached for a dime to reward the delivery boy. "Oh, Mr. Dicks," said Tommy, "I wouldn't want to take your money. My mother would tan my hide."

"My boy, you have a wonderful mother," Bob said as he patted Tommy's blond hair.

When Tommy got back, his dinner did taste better. "I didn't realize," he recalls, "I was learning a most powerful and important lesson about caring for those less fortunate."[21]

In the evenings, families would gather on the Monsons' porch and listen to their favorite radio programs. While the younger boys liked the Lone Ranger, Jack Armstrong, Little Orphan Annie, and Dick Tracy, the adults insisted on the Hit Parade, each one listening for the list of favorite songs for the week. The heavy-weight fights also drew the men's attention.

Another favorite family activity was a trip to the farm. The four Condie brothers' farms stood side by side, and "a weekend on the farm was to be savored."[22] Tommy enjoyed the freedom of the farm, the animals, walking in the fields, and swimming in the canal. He loved the quiet of the night with the lights of Salt Lake City a long distance away. He watched his uncles milk the cows and tried it himself. The aroma of dairy cattle always hung in the air. The water was brackish; city water had yet to be piped to the "country." The main dish on Friday and Saturday nights was simple bread and milk.

On Sundays at the farm, the family would go to the old Granger First Ward meetinghouse, built at the turn of the century on the southeast corner of 3200 West and 3500 South. The main hall was separated into four classes with curtains. "I learned that if you sat where the curtains joined and had good hearing, you could listen to four lessons simultaneously," President Monson says with a smile.[23]

On Sunday afternoon Tom's father and mother would pick him up from the farm to bring him home, but on the way they would go from one relative's home to another enjoying home-made ice cream.

This was an extended family—aunts, uncles, cousins—that spent time together. They went on vacations, stayed at the summer cabin, and gathered for holidays and Sunday night get-togethers—even after some moved from the "family block." When Tom was older and wanted to say thank you to his aunts—Margaret, Annie, and Blanche—for being "like a second mother," he took them to the Hotel Utah Roof Garden for lunch. They loved it; they loved him.

The family enjoyed some luxuries even during the Depression, including out-of-state vacations. Every other year, in February, they traveled to California for two weeks. As usual, it was an extended-family affair, including aunts and uncles, cousins, and Tommy's Grandpa Condie. Uncle John Nielson took his 1935 Buick, and Spence drove his 1928 Oldsmobile or, some years later, a 1937 Studebaker. On the way they would stop at Dick's Café in St. George. Tommy's father was the printer for the restaurant's menus, and he would talk with its owner, Dick Hammer, as the family had lunch. Tommy always ordered the meat pie. Then they would again be on their way.

When they got to California, the family stayed at the Hotel Edmund in Ocean Park near Santa Monica and ate their meals in the cafeteria. Tommy loved the sunshine—what there was of it, since they usually visited in winter when it rained most of the time. He and his cousins and brothers and sisters spent the days on the beach making sand castles and collecting shells. In the evenings they would stroll out on the piers, listening to the calls of the vendors hawking hot dogs and popcorn and the operators of rides inviting them to step up and enjoy a whirl.

On the drive home to Utah, Tom's Uncle John would entertain the children with stories of his life as a cowboy on the range. As he regaled them with his adventures, "he became tall in the saddle, complete with chaps, spurs, holster and gun, red bandana and 10 gallon Stetson hat." He also knew every shrub and cactus and would point them out as they rode along at 35 miles per hour, calling out: "greasewood . . . sage . . . scrub oak . . ."[24]

In 1941, Uncle "Moose" and Aunt Margaret piled their son Jack and nephew Tom in their five-year-old Buick and set off for Yellowstone National Park. At each stop for dinner, Tom ordered a hamburger steak; it was the only item on the menu he recognized. On Fishing Bridge at Yellowstone, Tom's fishing expertise came in handy when the wind blew Jack's baseball cap into the river. Tom, always quick to come up with a plan, maneuvered his fishing line over the cap as it made its way downstream. Then, to the amazement of his aunt, uncle, and cousin, he hooked the cap and reeled it in.

On the return journey, the Buick gave them some trouble. It seemed the old car was always acting up, but Tom let that memory pass when four years later he decided to buy it. His first car, it was a lemon on the road to Yellowstone and it was a lemon in Tom's hands the entire time he owned it.[25]

President Monson is always proud to say that life at 311 West Fifth South shaped who he is today. "Some of the things you are raised with sink deep when you are young," he has said.[26] Indeed, service, compassion, and family togetherness were all around him. Years later, Harold B. Lee, who had presided over the Pioneer Stake, where the Monsons lived, said of Tom's parents, "Here was a father and mother who gave [their children] what money could not buy."[27]

President Monson sums up his feelings this way: "When we have sampled much and have wandered far and have seen how fleeting and sometimes superficial a lot of the world is, our gratitude grows for the privilege of being part of something we can count on—home and family and the loyalty of loved ones. We come to know what it means to be bound together by duty, by respect, by belonging. We learn that nothing can fully take the place of the blessed relationship of family life."[28]

He has also taught: "The family holds its preeminent place in our way of life because it is the only possible base upon which a society of responsible human beings has ever found it practicable to build for the future and maintain the values they cherish in the present."[29]

"All of us remember the home of our childhood," he has said. "Interestingly, our thoughts do not dwell on whether the house was large or small, the neighborhood fashionable or downtrodden. Rather, we delight in the experiences we shared as a family. . . . What we learn there largely determines what we do when we leave there. . . . The thoughts we think, the deeds we do, the lives we live influence not only the success of our earthly journey; they also mark the way to our eternal goals."[30]

3

"I Want to Be a Cowboy!"

To understand Thomas Monson you have to reach back to his childhood. You have to watch him grow up on the west side of town in a family devoted to one another, a family who worked hard through the Depression. He worked. You have to recognize the help of Church leaders who were there for him—no matter what. He is still that Tom Monson.

ELDER M. RUSSELL BALLARD
Quorum of the Twelve Apostles

WHEN TOMMY MONSON WAS IN third grade, his teacher announced the city's plans to place a monument, a statue of a boy and girl raising a flag, on the grounds of the City and County Building in downtown Salt Lake. A time capsule was to be placed in the base of the statue, and all the students in the city schools had the opportunity to place in that capsule statements of what they wanted to be when they grew up. Tommy went home for lunch and told his mother of the morning's activity.

"What did you tell them you wanted to be?" she asked.

He responded with great excitement, "A cowboy!" That ambition was traceable, perhaps, to the influence of Uncle John and all his tales of life on the range.

"Oh, no, Tommy," his mother responded. "You go back and change that to a lawyer or a banker!"[1]

Dutifully the would-be cowboy returned and told his teacher to change his entry to a banker. Ultimately, the closest he got to being a cowboy was watching western movies. As for being a banker, he did become a director of Commercial Security Bank, which not long afterward merged with Key Bank. He served as a member of its executive committee, and chairman of its compensation committee and audit committee.

When Tom was called as an Apostle in 1963, his mother was asked by many, "Gladys, it's amazing your son grew up to be an Apostle. How did you do this?" Her response was always, "It wasn't easy, but I persevered."[2] She didn't tell them of his childhood dream to be a cowboy.

"Grandma probably didn't have to do very much to keep my dad on the straight and narrow," President Monson's son Clark suggests. "He was sort of wired that way from the beginning. Dad always knew who he was. A lot of people could see he was someone who was going to be successful and go places. My grandmother took credit for that in her own humorous way."[3]

Tommy's childhood seemed to come straight from the cover of *The Saturday Evening Post,* with a Norman Rockwell kind of charm. He was the boy with the tousled blond hair, the broad smile, a fishing pole in one hand, marbles in the other, and a dog yapping at his feet.

He has always believed every boy should grow up with a dog of his own. With his cousin Richard Carter, he would set out in the neighborhood with a wagon that had an orange box precariously positioned on top where they could stow stray dogs. One afternoon they locked the captured dogs in Tom's family coal shed, not sure what to do with them next.

His father came home from work and, as was his habit, took the coal bucket out to the shed to fill it. When he swung open the door, he was nearly knocked to the ground by six dogs wanting their freedom. "As I recall," Tom explained, "Dad flushed a little bit, and then he calmed down and quietly told me, 'Tommy, coal sheds are for coal. Other people's dogs rightfully belong to them.'" Not only did Tommy learn about the inadvisability of borrowing other people's pets, he learned a lesson from his father "in patience and calmness."[4]

Another time Tom "found" a mangy dog while staying at the family cabin at Vivian Park. It belonged to a local sheepherder, but Tommy hoped he wouldn't miss it. He was wrong. The man came to the cabin looking for his dog, and Tommy reluctantly handed it over. "Tommy," said the man, "you wouldn't want this dog. He's part coyote."[5]

But Tommy did want the dog—or any dog, for that matter. Finally his Uncle John found him one. The mongrel was not much to look at. Evidently abandoned on the desert, he was "a sorry mess, with a cast on one leg, a splint on another, and a broken tail."[6] But Tommy accepted him appreciatively and named him Duke. Boy and dog became fast friends.

Tom's love for dogs continued throughout the years. Early in his marriage to Frances he ran an ad in the classified section of the newspaper seeking a brown and white English springer spaniel. He got a phone call from a man who asked what exactly he was looking for in a dog. Tom explained that he wanted a dog he could train for hunting, and the man said, "You really don't want a springer spaniel. What you want is a new breed of dog called a German shorthaired pointer." The man proceeded to extol the virtues of the breed, indicated that he just happened to have a litter, and offered Tom his pick. The caller was a good salesman; Tom ended up buying the pup for what he considered a steep price: twenty-five dollars. He named the dog Freck von Windhausen and called him Freck.

Tom tried unsuccessfully to teach Freck to "heel" in walks around the block. His granddad, sitting on the swing, caught sight of him coming around for the third or fourth time. He hollered, "Tom, what did you give for that little dog?"

Tom was not going to tell him twenty-five dollars. He reduced the price, responding, "Five dollars."

His grandfather's reply was scorching: "Ya darn fool. You paid four dollars and six bits too much!"

That assessment certainly seemed right. The dog was no good at hunting or much else; he was high-strung, and he churned the backyard up in dust. Tom and Frances's young son Tommy could not compete for a place to play. Frances finally announced, "The dog has to go."

First, Tom gave Freck away to a man who within days was back,

36

saying the dog had chased the repairman servicing the kitchen appliances. He gave him to another, who returned him with the report, "He howled all night and the neighbors complained." Finally, one of Tom's business associates offered to take the dog to a farmer in Idaho, who later reported he was "the best hunting dog ever!"[7]

In many ways, Tommy grew up like any other little boy in a humble neighborhood in the depths of the Depression. He never looked back with remorse or sorrow at his modest upbringing. He saw it as what made him.

The children from one of the neighborhood families wore galoshes because they had no shoes. Their mother bought rummage-sale clothing that would fit more than one child in the family. Occasionally, when Tom would stop on his way to school for one of his friends from this particular family, the children would be eating a bowl of cereal covered in warm water. "There was no milk; . . . there was no sugar—only cornflakes and water."[8]

One of Tommy's earliest memories was his first day of kindergarten at the Grant Elementary School, two blocks away from his house. He counted it an adventure to leave "the comfort and security of my own home and a loving mother and to venture forth into the real world and the experiences which were to follow."[9] Each class had about twenty-five students.

On the first day of school, the older boys—age eleven—inducted the kindergartners—age five—into the school by sitting them on the drinking fountain. Tommy learned "to run fast." That's how life was there. Two of the teachers wore wigs; one had peroxided hair. To young Tommy, that was scandalous! As was the tradition in kindergarten, the children would take a nap midway through the class, but Tommy had trouble sleeping because he "wanted so much to be doing things rather than resting," which confirmed his mother's nickname for him: "Nervous Willy."[10]

As the elementary school years passed, Tommy received consistently good marks for his scholarship and citizenship, with an occasional note of a lapse in "work habits" and "self control." He found he was not too keen on mathematics but enjoyed nature classes, geography, and English, even asking for extra work so that he could pursue his studies outside the limited time in class. He was captivated when Miss Birkhaus, his sixth-grade geography teacher, rolled down the maps of the world and with her pointer began covering the globe, identifying the distinctive features of each country, language, and culture. Little did Tommy imagine he would one day travel to those distant lands, becoming friends with people from many different countries.

Music teacher Miss Sharp's love of music was contagious, and, even today, President Monson has been known to break into song at a variety of functions. When he addressed 86,000 people in a stadium celebration of the rededication of the Mexico City Temple, he serenaded the enormous crowd with his high school Spanish rendition of "El Rancho Grande." The crowd erupted with cheers and applause.

Miss Stone, the librarian, often complimented young Tommy for spending his free time with a book in hand by the window in the library. She would look over and nod approvingly. What she didn't know was that he was reading *Chanko, the Homing Pigeon* tucked inside a more scholarly publication. He was also partial to *Toby Tyler, or Ten Weeks with the Circus.* He particularly enjoyed the series of "The Big Little Books" that cost ten cents each and fit in the palm of the reader's hand. The chunky, small, hardcover picture books were all the rage in the 1930s with their thrilling adventure stories; some of Tommy's favorites were *Chester Gump at Silver Creek Ranch* and *Houdini's Big Little Book of Magic.*

His Grandmother Monson loved to read to Tommy and his siblings. One Christmas she gave him a large storybook, which she then read to him.

Tommy was also a familiar face at the Chapman Library on Eighth West. He and his friend Reo Williamson would check out books three times a week. Each had a library card, and each was "keen" on filling up his card.

"Reading is one of the true pleasures of life," President Monson has said. "In our age of mass culture, when so much that we encounter is abridged, adapted, adulterated, shredded, and boiled down, it is mind-easing and mind-inspiring to sit down privately with a congenial book."[11]

Tommy didn't spend all his time with his nose in a book,

though. He had a fun-loving streak and was, at times, a bit of a prankster. He did the things typical of a young lad with an eye for adventure. After exercising the self-appointed prerogative of an older brother to turn out the lights, he set about scaring his little brother until the frightened boy ran to his parents' room in fear. Uncle Jack Bangerter had shot a deer and mounted its head on the boys' bedroom wall, and Tommy would spin tales of the animal coming to life and charging into the room. Little brother Bob would be out the door and down the hall before he finished.

Tommy dreamed of joining the Grant School Drum and Bugle Corps. The boys in the Corps came to class ten minutes late and were dismissed ten minutes early so that the flag on the school grounds would be appropriately raised and lowered. That was their duty. To participate, Tommy needed a bugle. That year, it was first on his list for Santa Claus, and on Christmas morning there it was. He was thrilled. He didn't even think about needing to learn to play the bugle.

Unfortunately, the music teacher who had traditionally pre-pared the boys retired before Tommy got his bugle. Undeterred, every weekday before and after school he would join the Corps in the ceremonies of raising and lowering the flag. He loved marching and hearing the sound coming from those who *could* play. When the Drum and Bugle Corps participated in competi-tion with other schools on the grounds of the City and County Building, the Grant School students came in second. Jefferson School took first. At one point the boy marching in front of Tommy turned and, with a scowl, charged, "You're blowing off key!"

Tommy responded, "That's impossible. I'm not even blowing!" He had perfected puffing out his cheeks to give the illusion of blowing, but not a sound came from the shiny bugle.[12] He still has the instrument—and his skill level has not improved.

The two blocks from home to school and back again seemed quite a journey, but the neighborhood was familiar. Tommy walked to school many days with his friend Luis, whose family was from Mexico. The two were sometimes late for school because

Luis's mother "felt that an Anglo boy should also have a tortilla for breakfast." One day Tommy and Luis had to stay after school and write "I will not talk in class" fifty times in a notebook. About fifteen minutes into the punishment, they heard the sound of an automobile horn. Turning quickly, Luis announced, "That is my father honking; I must go." The teacher gave permission, and Luis raced from the room, handing her his notebook on the way out. As Tommy continued to write, he thought to himself, "Luis's father doesn't have a car!" What Luis did have was a very quick mind.[13]

One teacher, Miss Lawson, piqued Tommy's interest in birds. By the time he was ten and in fifth grade, he was the president of the Junior Audubon Club at Grant School. He learned to identify birds from pictures and later from bird-watching. Upon hearing the announcement of a birdhouse-building contest at school, he enlisted the help of his Uncle Richard LeRoy Carter, a sign painter whose nickname was "Speed" because he was so unhurried and exact in all that he did. The two spent hours painting the birdhouse a striking gray-green, and Speed then adorned the eaves with lilac blossoms. Tommy pronounced it "the most beautiful birdhouse one could imagine."[14]

The birdhouses were displayed on the window ledge in the classroom. Tommy stood by proudly as the students admired his birdhouse; then one of his classmates brushed past, knocking it to the floor and chipping the overhang of one of the eaves. Though it was repaired, Tommy was devastated by the mishap.

In his final year at Grant School, Tommy at age eleven was now among the oldest in the school and had distinguished himself as a good student. He was named a member of the Junior Traffic Patrol, complete with a white belt and a red flag and the responsibility to help fellow students cross the streets. He prized the certificate he was awarded at the end of his term, which noted he had served with "distinction" and was signed by William C. Webb, Chief of Police.

At home, Tommy and his brother Bob raised rabbits. Their Uncle John built them a hutch in the backyard, and the boys would sell the furs to the hide companies across the street for ten cents apiece and the meat to the local grocery stores for twenty-five cents.

Then pigeons caught Tommy's fancy. From the windows of the library at Grant School, he and his friends studied the pigeons strung across the long row of garage roofs directly below. There must be a way, they concluded, to capture the beautiful creatures, which were much better than stray dogs. With a simple box trap, tripped by tugging a string attached to a vertical stick, Tommy and his friends caught common pigeons—"commies," they called them—in the backyard of Bob Middleton's home, just across the fence from Tommy's. "They didn't amount to much," Tom remembers, but his lifelong interest in pigeons took flight.[15]

It was 1938. America had not yet recovered from the devastating Depression. War in Europe was but a year away. Names like Hudson, Packard, LaSalle, and De Soto were the rage in all the automobile showrooms. But Tommy and his eleven-year-old friends were not thinking of cars or wars. Their minds were on pigeons.

When Tommy's friend Bob Middleton's father installed a beautiful window in his son's coop to keep the cold wind from disturbing the birds, Tommy longed for such an addition to his own. One day Bob's father came over unannounced, carrying a window. He went to work installing the glass and frame in Tommy's makeshift coop. "I had never before experienced such a sense of gratitude for something which another person had, on his own, done for me," he recalls.[16] Tommy learned what it felt like to receive from others. The scripture, "When ye are in the service of your fellow beings ye are only in the service of your God," took on real meaning.[17]

Tommy and his pal Bob Middleton were proud of their pigeons until they met John Fife. John lived on Sixth South just west of Gale Street. He and another friend had constructed a loft—an old shed made of used lumber—where Tommy and the other boys in the neighborhood could gaze for hours at his prize Birmingham roller pigeons. John was clearly "the pied piper of pigeondom." Wherever he went, Reo Williamson, Kenny Petersen, Harold Watson, Norman Drecksel, Junior Thompson, Bob

Middleton, and Tommy Monson followed. They loved watching John's rollers perform. Tommy's "trapped" pigeons were a poor match.

Birmingham roller pigeons originated in England and became highly popular for their ability to rapidly roll backward in tight somersaults, the flurry of rotations giving the appearance of a ball of feathers twirling in midair. This ability to roll is not taught but is genetic. When they recover from the spin, they return to their flock, called a "kit" in competition.

Tommy bought his first pair of rollers from John Fife: a black badge hen and a brown beard cock. He named them "Rump" and "Rolly." Actually, to obtain them he traded a pheasant rooster that he had captured as it scurried up Gale Street. As time went on he would most often trade twenty-pound gunnysacks of wheat scavenged from the boxcars at Husler's Flour Mill. He and his friends would painstakingly sweep out the kernels that would lodge between the metal wall of the car and the six-foot tongue-and-groove lining. Only once does he recall actually paying in cash the price of $1.50 for a beautifully matched pair of mealy red-bars with white markings on their heads, wings, and tails.[18] He and John Fife became lifelong friends.

Tommy's father, Spence, considered Tommy's hobby as a pigeon fancier wasteful, impractical, and costly. It may have been. But Tommy loved watching the birds and caring for them. He built his own pigeon coop out of scrap lumber. It lacked the polish of John's, to be sure. John's had specially designed nests, which he had trimmed to size from wooden orange crates, and was whitewashed inside and out. But Tommy was inventive, creating a lean-to style enclosure to take advantage of one side of the backyard garage. Unfortunately, the location at the rear of the lot was easily accessible to pranksters and pigeon thieves, who preyed on his loft a number of times.

Tommy began showing his pigeons at county and state fairs. As he got more adept at raising his Birmingham rollers, he began to win ribbons—blue and purple, mostly. By then he had begun to breed the birds for color and appearance.

He did the same with chickens. He always had a chicken

coop, along with his pigeons. He would get the eggs and incubate them and hatch them out. There was quite a stir once when his half-grown chicks escaped from under the kitchen stove, where he was keeping them warm in a box until their feathers had grown enough for them to be in the yard. The chicks ran wildly through his mother's bridge club. The women ran about the house, trying to get the chicks back into the brooder box.

Today, President Monson's backyard has pigeon lofts prominently situated in the center of the lawn. He also has a chicken coop. Both are far more sophisticated than those he envied in his youth. He still attends the local shows, where he checks out all the pigeons and chats at length with his many pigeon-fancier friends, who for years have shared his avocation.

As a child, Tommy was both resourceful and entrepreneurial. He would sit in Blanche and LeRoy Terry's living room and clip coupons from *Pictorial Magazine, Collier's*, and *The Saturday Evening Post*, which he sent away to receive complimentary products such as Jergens Lotion and Lifebuoy Soap. He tried selling Christmas cards door-to-door, but because of the financially difficult times, his relatives didn't respond. Finally he reached the Griffith home on Gale Street. "They were probably as impoverished as any family in the ward," he remembers, "yet Sister Griffith, out of compassion for a young boy, purchased six Christmas cards."[19] Tom and his sister Marge peddled salve one summer at fifty cents a jar until their father found out. He promptly retrieved the salve, refunded the neighbors' money, and ended his children's sales careers.

Tommy went with Marge every Saturday to her elocution lessons with Mrs. Hoffman and spent hours listening to her practice and present readings. He soaked up her expressive language along with the drama and special techniques she was learning for public speaking—gestures, voice inflections, pauses, and facial expressions.

His mother insisted that he attend Primary every Wednesday, and it became for him, in that era of the pervading gloom of the Depression, "a bright light of hope." Tommy's "marvelous Trekker teacher," newlywed Nancy Taylor, had enthusiasm and interest in the boys. They "looked upon her as an ideal," and she had the

43

knack for motivating the boys to meet their Trail Builder objectives. "It wasn't necessarily that our teacher was well educated and had a lot of degrees after her name; she had none of those. It wasn't because the boys in the class were particularly enlightened or unusually well motivated and well behaved; on the contrary. But that which cemented the relationship between the teacher and her boys was the fact that she loved us, and she taught us the gospel."[20] She introduced each one individually to the Trail Builder program and taught them the song: "We are the boy trail builders, out west where the sunsets glow; where the brooks flow down like silver from the heights of the virgin snow."[21] President Monson can still sing it.

Tommy was ten years old when he began earning the Trail Builder badges. His Uncle John had some lumber, and he helped Tommy build a treasure chest. Tommy's treasure chest, where he kept his badges, became much more than well-finished wood. His uncle's "strong left hand driving the nails" became a memory, a symbol of an uncle's willingness to help the nephew he loved.[22]

The Trail Builders were not an easy bunch to handle. Tommy's energy level and curiosity were difficult to channel. One day he saw Sister Georgell, the Primary president, sitting in the chapel crying. He approached her and asked innocently, "May I help, Sister Georgell?"

She explained that she could not control the Trail Builders in Primary opening exercises. What he didn't realize was that he, Tommy Monson, was at the center of the disruptive boys. He magnanimously committed to help Sister Georgell, and the rowdiness in Primary came to an abrupt end.

Many years later, when performing the marriage for one of Sister Georgell's grandchildren in the Salt Lake Temple, President Monson saw her there and shared the account with those gathered. She said, "Oh, you weren't that bad at all."[23]

When Melissa Georgell was in her nineties, she lived in a nursing facility in the northwest part of Salt Lake. During his Christmas rounds one year, President Monson stopped to visit his beloved Primary president. He found her in the lunchroom staring at her food, shifting it from one corner of the plate to another. As he spoke to her, he saw her eyes look blankly at him and about the room. "I gently took her fork from her and began to feed her, talking all the time I did so about her service to boys and girls as a Primary worker and the joy which was mine to have served later as her bishop." Not even a quick glimmer of recognition crossed her face. Two other residents spoke up: "She doesn't know anyone, not even her own family," one reported. "She hasn't said a word for a long, long time," said the other.

Lunch ended, and Tom, much taller than that little Primary lad, stood to leave. "I held her frail hand in mine, gazed into her wrinkled but beautiful countenance, and said, 'God bless you, Melissa, and Merry Christmas.' Immediately she spoke, 'I know you. You're Tommy Monson, my Primary boy. How I love you.' "[24]

That kind of love and camaraderie and goodness from his circle of family, friends, and Church teachers did much to shield Tommy from the horrors of the Great Depression. Those formative years also helped shape the heart and soul of a prophet. "I am quick to acknowledge the hand of the Lord in my life," he has stated. "I've never doubted it, even as a little boy."[25]

The Monsons opened their doors—literally—to the needy. Because of the Depression, hordes of men hitching rides on the rails came into town looking for work. Living close to the tracks as they did, the Monsons had many transients knock at their door, caps in their hands as they groped for what to say. Finally, out would come, "Pardon me, but is there any work we can do to get something to eat?" No one was ever turned away.

Gladys Monson had no fear. These were not criminals; these were displaced men who had nothing and were trying to make a go of it. She would lead them to the sink and tell them to wash up while she got them some lunch. She would fix exactly what Spence had for lunch—a ham or beef sandwich, potato chips, a piece of cake, and a glass of milk or a soda. Then she would sit down and in her motherly manner ask them, "Where are you from?" They were busy eating, and she was busy asking questions; she was genuinely interested in them. They had to listen to her counsel, and she had plenty. "She would lecture each on how he ought to consider returning to his home and how he ought to be

45

a good person while he was riding the rails and how he should write home to reassure those who were no doubt worried about him."[26]

Tommy never understood how they knew just which house to approach. He *did* know that when he repainted the picket fence, his mother instructed him to leave one slat as it was. He sensed that somehow signaled a welcome to those in need.

Such experiences taught him to be generous and accepting. His father was a man of few words, but when it came to helping others, his actions spoke volumes. Compassion was taught in the Monson home, and the lessons were learned well. "We have no way of knowing when our privilege to extend a helping hand will unfold before us," President Monson has said. "The road to Jericho each of us travels bears no name, and the weary traveler who needs our help may be one unknown."[27]

Christmas was always a memorable time in Tommy's boyhood. For the Monson children, as with most children, it was a long time coming every year. The family would decorate the chandeliers, run streamers from the center of the room to the corners of the living and dining rooms, and adorn the tree with bubble lights and treasured decorations that spoke of seasons past. Spence began a tradition early in their marriage of writing a poem or letter to Gladys for Christmas and her birthdays. One year, he penned:

> How many a mile together we've trod
> Closely together, as peas in a pod
> Although at times I'm quite a bore
> I hope together we'll celebrate more.[28]

As a Primary boy, Tommy participated each year in the annual Christmas pageant in the Sixth-Seventh Ward. One year he was one of the three wise men, with a bandanna wrapped about his head, his mother's precious Chickering piano-bench cover draped over his shoulder, and a black wooden cane in his hand. He was convincing with his assigned lines: "Where is he that is born King of the Jews? For we have seen his star in the east and are come to worship him."[29]

There was more to his message, but although the words have faded from his memory, his feelings of the moment have held fast: "The three of us wise men looked up, saw the star, journeyed across the stage, found Mary with the young child, Jesus, then fell down and worshipped Him and opened our treasures and presented gifts: gold, frankincense, and myrrh. I especially liked the fact that we did not return to the evil Herod to betray the baby Jesus, but we obeyed God and departed another way."[30]

That black wooden cane today occupies a special place in the Monson home, representing the message of that first Christmas and the commitment and love for Jesus Christ for which President Monson clearly is known: "May we ever be guided by the supreme Exemplar, even the son of Mary, the Savior Jesus Christ—whose very life provided a perfect model for us to follow. Born in a stable, cradled in a manger, He came forth from heaven to live on earth as a mortal man and to establish the kingdom of God."[31]

One December Tommy's mother took him to "Toyland" in a Salt Lake department store. To lure shoppers, the store had advertised a drawing for a beautiful Shetland pony. Each child was to write a note telling why the pony would be a welcome Christmas gift, and the signed notes were placed in a large box right next to the pony, then stabled in the toy department. At the appointed day and hour of the announcement, Tommy and his mother were there in the crowd of buoyant children, each expecting to take the pony home. So certain was Tommy that he would win that he already had piled straw and hay out in his sister's playhouse in the backyard—fine quarters for his new pony. But his name was not read, and he was heartbroken.

As they left the store, Tommy noticed a bundled-up man ringing a bell to direct attention to a small kettle suspended from a triangle frame. His mother paused and deposited in the container what looked to be a silver dollar. She turned to Tommy and said, "Do you have any money you would like to give to the poor for Christmas?" Tommy reached in his pocket and produced two nickels, all he had, and dropped them into the kettle, one after the other. "That day," he recalls, "I didn't win the pony, but I received a far greater gift, even 'the smile of God's approval.'"[32]

Tommy's parents tried to keep Christmas from being a fran-tic, overcommercialized activity. Rather, they emphasized cele-brating love and selflessness. President Monson's Christmas mes-sage year after year has reiterated the lessons learned so young, as in his quotation from David O. McKay: "The Christmas spirit is the Christ spirit, that makes our hearts glow in brotherly love and friendship and prompts us to kind deeds of service. It is the spirit of the gospel of Jesus Christ, obedience to which will bring 'peace on earth,' because it means—good will toward all men."[33]

He particularly remembers one Christmas when he learned that "the difference lies in what is in the heart—not what is in the hand."[34] He was ten or eleven years old, and he begged his parents for an electric train. "My desire was not to receive the economical and everywhere-to-be-found wind-up model train," he has related. "Rather, I wanted one that operated through the miracle of elec-tricity." Depression era notwithstanding, his parents—through some sacrifice—placed the longed-for train under the tree. On Christmas morning, he played for hours with the transformer, moving the engine forward and back on the tracks, pushing and pulling the cars. When his mother told him she had purchased a wind-up train for Mrs. Hansen's son, Mark, who lived nearby, Tommy asked to see it. The engine was short and blocky—not long and sleek like the expensive model he had cruising around his track. He did notice an oil tanker car that was part of the inex-pensive set bound for Mark. Tommy's train didn't have such a car, and after great coaxing his mother let him pluck that car out of the box and place it with his. Her words, "If you need it more than Mark," did not dissuade him. He was pleased with the addition to his already remarkable set.

Tommy dismissed his mother's disappointment in him as the two of them took the remaining cars and engine down the road to Mark. He was a year or two older than Tommy but was thrilled with the gift. He wound the key to his engine—not electric like the one up the street on the floor of the Monson home—and watched, beaming, as the engine with its two cars and caboose chugged around the track.

"What do you think of Mark's train?" Tommy's mother asked,

looking at her son, who was nearly out the door before he responded, "Wait just a moment—I'll be right back." Up the street he raced, scooped up the oil tanker from Mark's train and another car from his own set, and ran back to the Hansens'. With a smile he announced, "We forgot to bring two cars that belong to your train." Mark added the two, carefully coupling them to the others. Tommy "watched the engine make its labored way around the track and felt a supreme joy difficult to describe and impossible to forget."[35]

Years later at general conference he told the train story to illustrate what he had learned at his mother's knee about how to live the Golden Rule. A few days later May Hansen, Mark's sister, called to thank him for the sermon, which had meant so much to her ailing mother; she had never forgotten Tommy's kindness that Christmas long ago.

Sister Hansen died within the week after the phone call, and Elder Monson spoke at her funeral. Reconnecting with Mark and his family was for him a blessed moment of reflection on how to share the love of the Lord. "I feel it was providential that I delivered the message concerning the train at the time that I did," he recounted.[36] It was just in time to bless Sister Hansen with that memory.

"Learning the gospel, bearing a testimony, leading a family are rarely if ever simple processes," President Monson has acknowledged. "Life's journey is characterized by bumps in the road, swells in the sea—even the turbulence of our times."[37] That turbulence during the Depression was calmed by the expressions of kindness and goodness in the Monson home. Tommy learned those core values, much like the two thousand stripling warriors of the Book of Mormon who "had been taught by their mothers."[38] In his case, God did "deliver" him from the bitterness and disappointment of the country in crisis.

The Lord kept teaching him what mattered most.

The family always gathered for Thanksgiving dinner. Gladys put the turkey in the "big oven" over at Annie's, and the sisters took turns checking its progress. Spence had charge of setting the table after he got home from four hours at the print shop and before he and the boys went to the annual University of Utah versus Utah State football game, which started at noon. Rusty, Spence, Rich, Jack, Tom, and Bob scrambled to get there for the kickoff. The Monsons were Ute fans, and in 1940 they cheered Marge's new boyfriend, Conway Dearden, on the football team and then watched as she marched on the field with the "Spurs" club at halftime.

One year, the home was buzzing with Thanksgiving preparations when Charlie Renshaw, a friend from over the back fence, stood outside, as was the custom of these young friends, and hollered, "Tom-my!"

When Tommy answered the summons, Charlie said, "It sure smells good in there. What are you eating?"

Tommy told him it was turkey, and Charlie asked what turkey tasted like.

Tom responded, "Oh, about like chicken," to which Charlie asked, "What does chicken taste like?"

Tom ran into the kitchen, snatched a piece of breast meat, and handed it to his friend. "That's good!" the boy said.

When Tom asked what Charlie's family was having for dinner, the answer was, "I dunno. There's nothing in the house."

Tom pondered. He knew his mother always found something to feed those who came to the door. He had no extra turkeys, chickens, or money. But he did have two pet rabbits, a male and female, the pride of his life, beautiful New Zealand whites. He motioned to his friend and headed for the specially constructed rabbit hutch built by one of his uncles. He reached in and grabbed his two pet rabbits, put them in a gunnysack, and handed the bag to Charlie.

"Rabbit meat tastes better than chicken," Tom said. "Their hide makes really good knuckle pads when you are playing marbles. You know, you can sell the hides for a quarter each over at the hide company. These two rabbits will give your family a good dinner."[39]

Charlie was on the fence—the boys used the fences like sidewalks in his neighborhood—and heading for his yard before Tom could close the door to his empty rabbit hutch. He realized he had given all he had. He had met someone else's need and did not regret it. The pattern was in place: "I was an hungred, and ye gave me meat. . . . Inasmuch as ye have done it unto one of the least of these my brethren, ye have done it unto me."[40]

His life has continued to be a tangible expression of the Lord's words.

4

LIKE HUCK FINN ON THE RIVER

Perhaps growing up in very common, unassuming surroundings, he has always been able to see and appreciate the value and the good, the gifts in everybody, particularly those of humble circumstances.

ELDER D. TODD CHRISTOFFERSON
Quorum of the Twelve Apostles

IN 1930 WHEN SINCLAIR LEWIS accepted his Nobel Prize in literature he wisely stated, "I learned, as a boy, that there is something very important and spiritual about catching fish."[1] Tom Monson would agree. He didn't know as a young lad that his adult years would follow the pattern of the ancient Apostles James and John, to whom Jesus said, "From henceforth thou shalt catch men."[2] Tommy just knew he loved to fish.

To learn to fish, Tommy had to be patient, watchful, determined, resilient, and strong. His fishing skills—in the water at least—began at Vivian Park on the Provo River. The setting was idyllic in a Huck Finn kind of way.

He had almost been born at Vivian Park in August 1927. His mother had returned to Salt Lake City just in time to check into the hospital before delivering her first son. From the time Tommy was a babe in arms, the Monsons, along with their Condie aunts, uncles, cousins, and grandfather, packed up and spent most of the summer at their mountain cabin at Vivian Park in Provo

Canyon. Every year they left home on the Fourth of July and did not return until Labor Day.

Tommy's father, Spence, and his uncles John Nielson and Speed Carter stayed in the city to work, commuting every Wednesday night to the cabin with a carload of groceries and again each Saturday evening "for the weekend." For those two months, Tommy fished and swam, fished and hiked, fished and rode horses and "enjoyed every minute of it." Those were days "before radio and television in the canyon; hence, conversation was the only time-passer throughout the day."[3]

The cabin was nothing fancy, with a tongue-and-groove exterior, indoor plumbing, a coal shed, a coal stove for cooking and heat, a screened sleeping porch facing the creek, and one bedroom, with a second added later so that the family could sleep eleven "comfortably." There was a front room with a small couch on one wall. A long table on the other provided a setting not just for meals but for playing spoons and other games, telling stories, and talking late into the night. Talking and telling stories was what the Condies did best.

The Vivian Park property had been in the family for years. Tommy's Grandfather Condie had bought a lot for twenty-five dollars and built a cabin on it. Tommy's grandparents were among the first residents in Vivian Park; a handful of his relatives followed suit. There, in the cool canyon air, Gladys found relief from the asthma that plagued her each summer. There was no electricity in the cabin in the early days. Water boxes, strategically placed in South Fork Creek, which ran right outside the front door, allowed the mountain stream to flow through and cool the perishables. Across the creek and closer to the main road there was a dance hall with a hardwood floor, which offered Saturday night dancing with live bands and was used on Sunday morning for church. There was no telephone except at the nearby store, which was operated for nearly thirty years—well into the 1940s— by Edna and Grover Purvance. The store stocked some grocery items, fishing tackle and bait, and newspapers, and it had a pinball machine. Tommy would wait by the rails for the train to make its way up the winding canyon; as it approached Vivian Park, the engineer would toss the bundle of newspapers off. Tommy would carry them to the store, taking out his family's subscription copy. Back at the cabin, he would check the scores of the baseball games, and his aunts would read what was happening "in town."

The cabin was not built with a great deal of professional skill. By 1986 Tom and his brother Bob were its sole owners. That year, Tom bought Bob's share and had extensive remodeling done, with carpentry, plumbing, and electrical upgrades. He replaced the exterior wood siding with vinyl. "While it is inadequate in size and obviously worn with age, it is still the summer home of my youth," he explains. He checks on the cabin almost every week, as he does the family's second home in Midway, Utah.[4]

Tommy had great fishing instructors in his uncles. His Uncle John bought him his first fishing pole and started him on what became a lifelong love. The two walked up along the railroad tracks at Vivian Park to fish a certain part of the Provo River. "Uncle John taught me how to approach the stream, how to bait a hook, how to lower the line in the most appealing way, and how to retrieve the fish when one would strike the bait," he remembers.[5] His Uncle Speed taught him to thread a minnow and to be patient and wait for the big fish. Uncle Rusty was another familiar fishing partner. Tommy also watched older, successful fly-fishermen who frequented the Provo River and learned what he could, copying their style.

Many mornings about 4:00 or 5:00 A.M. Tommy would slip out of the cabin with his dog Duke, giving his mother a kiss on the cheek before he left. "I don't know how in the world she slept," he has said, "knowing the perils which a young boy could encounter when fishing in an area where the water was deep, the banks steep, and the morning dark."[6]

He fished with night crawlers in the summer and with minnows in the fall. Some evenings he would fish alone, particularly midweek. He was not above showing off his skill, catching a big fish for Wednesday or Saturday night to present to his father and uncles. His brother Bob and his cousins often tagged along. They considered Tom "a great fisherman" because he always caught more fish than they did. When the fish had eluded him, he would stay two or three extra hours until fishing legally closed at nine P.M. rather than come in early. Those last five minutes sometimes brought in the desired catch.

Tommy became quite the fisherman. Secret Island, as he called it, was an excellent stretch of water for fishing. South Fork Creek split near the cabin and created a small island about twelve feet wide and thirty feet long. River birch of all sizes thrived on the island and on both sides of the creek, making the setting ideal not just for catching fish but for being outdoors in general. "Thinking back on those days," President Monson muses, "I regret the absence of a spinning rod, which would enable a fisherman to put the lure or the bait in places otherwise inaccessible."[7] The boys fished with Japanese gut leader, rather than the nylon he uses today.

And, like all good fishermen, he has the story of the one that got away.

It was Labor Day weekend and the end of another glorious summer at Vivian Park. Late one night, Tommy was fishing with a newly purchased line and a number-six grey-hackle, yellow-body fly. He and his friend Blaine Nuttall were casting just below what they called the rapids, downriver from the swimming hole. As he tells it: "Suddenly there was a loud splash in the water and I realized that a monster trout had taken my fly. The fish immediately began his run down the river, stripping out all of my line from my reel and taking me with him. I literally chased that fish for a third of a block, feeling that he would break my tackle if I didn't run after him. He then stopped, giving me a chance to rest and to get my bearings, but immediately commenced a second run, going clear down to the Vivian Park bridge, where he stopped momentarily. Then he swam to a position below the bridge, where he again stopped."

Tommy knew there was no way he was going to get that fish out of the water without help. His friend Blaine jumped in the water, attempting to get the fish. "This frightened the fish, and he began his final run down the river. I chased him as far as I could for another fifty yards, and then the water was up to my waist. His sheer weight caused my pole to come down toward the water and, with all the line extended, the fish broke the six-pound test leader and was gone. I have never felt so bad about losing a fish."[8]

Tommy determined that he would turn to heavier tackle and minnows for bait. He returned to the cabin, retrieved his bait rod and some twenty-pound test leader, and took a pail of minnows down into the slow water. He was rewarded. "That night," he recalls, "I caught the biggest fish I have ever caught on the Provo River." It was twenty-four inches long, about six and one-half pounds in weight, and Tommy landed it with the heavier tackle. It was not "the monster"—but it certainly was large by all other measures.[9]

Even in his youthful hobbies, Tom liked things to be orderly. The boys fished by seniority, stringing along the riverbank by age. Tom would go first and then, in order, his cousins Jack Condie, Rich Carter, Phil Condie, and Jack Carman, and finally Tom's brother Bob, always last. Down the river they would troop, fishing on either side, but the rule was that each had to stay in his position. Most of the fish were caught by those farthest upstream.

Fishing wasn't all about the river and the water. At times Tommy would stake his pole, his line safely in the water, and sit on the bank looking up at the mountains around him. He would imagine he could see the shapes of animals in the scrub oak. Occasionally the spell would be broken by the bleating of a sheep grazing on the hillside or in the rich grass that lined the sides of the railroad track.

For Tom Monson, the Provo River was then and is now his "pool of Bethesda," where he gets away to be renewed, refreshed—to be made whole. There and on fishing trips to Alaska, Idaho, and several lakes in Utah he has thrown his line out to the water, and his catch has had little to do with what was fooled by the fly. Whether on the banks or in the boat, when fishing he has been able to let go of all the pressing issues, the problems that were and are his. The break allows him, like the blind man whose eyes the Savior swathed in mud, to return to his work "seeing."[10]

At the cabin, young Tommy shared a bed on the screened-in front porch with his Grandpa Condie. When large numbers of relatives came, they would sleep three people across on each of the three beds on the porch. At night his grandfather would tuck his small, black leather purse—holding the key to his house and some silver coins—under his pillow. Grandfather would counsel Tom in the ways of life and answer his questions. "As we would lie there on a morning, with the east sun streaming through the screened porch, I would ask him to tell me stories about his early days as a boy and as a sheep rancher in the Great Salt Lake Valley."[11] When Grandpa Condie grew tired of entertaining his namesake, he would recite with drama:

> *I'll tell you a story about Jack and Ory*
> *And now my story's begun.*
> *I'll tell you another about Jack and his brother,*
> *And now my story is done.*[12]

Tommy learned to swim in the Provo River. The "old swimming hole" was a twenty-foot-deep portion of the river with a massive rock in the center that had fallen in, he assumed, when the workmen constructing the railroad from Provo to Heber were blasting through the canyon. The pool was dangerous; its current moved swiftly around the large rock, sucking and spilling into whirlpools. It could prove treacherous for a novice or inexperienced swimmer.

But the swimming hole was a favorite gathering place where the families spread blankets, picnicked on the sandy beach, and then braved the frigid water. When he was young, Tommy played on the bank, making a series of dams and sand castles while his mother and Aunt Blanche would sidestroke down the current, through the whirlpools, and around through the eddy about twenty times. Tommy learned to swim by watching how everyone else swam. When he made his first solo swim down the current, his family surrounded him on all sides. What a sense of exhilaration he felt when he completed this first dangerous passage through the whirlpools and back to the safety of the riverbank. "I'm certain our duty and responsibility are frequently to swim upstream and against the tide of temptation and sin," he has said, applying the lessons of the swimming hole. "As we do so, our spiritual strength will increase, and we shall be equal to our God-given responsibilities."[13]

One warm summer afternoon when he was about twelve or thirteen, Tom took a large, inflated inner tube from a tractor tire, slung it over his shoulder, and walked barefoot up the railroad track that followed the course of the river. He entered the water about a mile above the swimming hole, sat comfortably in the tube, and enjoyed a leisurely float down the river he now knew well. "The river held no fear for me, for I knew its secrets," he says.

That day some Greek families were holding a reunion at Vivian Park, with food, games, and dancing. A few left the party to wade in the river. Afternoon shadows were already creeping across the swimming hole and its whirlpools.

Tom later described: "As my inflated tube bobbed up and down, I was about to enter the swiftest portion of the river just at the head of the swimming hole when I heard frantic cries, 'Save her! Save her!'" A young lady swimmer, accustomed to the still waters of a gymnasium swimming pool, had waded into the river on the railroad track side below the big rock. She had gone so far out that she had come to an unseen dropoff and was swept into the treacherous whirlpools. None of the party could swim to save her.

"I saw the top of her head disappearing under the water for the third time, there to descend to a watery grave. I stretched forth my hand, grasped her hair, and lifted her over the side of the tube and into my arms." At the whirlpool's lower end, the water slowed and Tommy paddled his way to the frantic relatives and friends. First they threw their arms around the water-soaked girl and kissed her, crying, "Thank God! Thank God you are safe!" Then they pulled Tom to shore and began hugging and kissing him. Embarrassed, he quickly returned to the tube and continued his float down to the bridge.

He would later recount the aftermath of the rescue: "The water was frigid, but I was not cold, for I was filled with a warm feeling. I realized that I had participated in the saving of a life. Heavenly Father had heard the cries, 'Save her! Save her,' and permitted me, a deacon, to float by at precisely the time I was needed."[14]

Tommy was a curious, enthusiastic, fearless youngster—somewhat prone to getting into trouble. He sometimes played with Danny Larsen, whose family lived in Provo and summered at Vivian Park as well. They were the Huck Finn and Tom Sawyer duo.

One day they decided to clear an area in the June grass where the family could all have a big bonfire that evening. Often the family gathered around a campfire at night, roasting marshmallows and hot dogs. For some reason, Tommy thought that setting fire to the June grass would burn a circle sufficient to allow for the bonfire that night and then the grass would just extinguish itself. To the horror of Tommy and Danny, the June grass blazed like a gasoline fire and the flames began to follow the wild grass up the mountainside, endangering the pine trees. Within minutes every available man at Vivian Park was dragging wet burlap bags to smother the blaze. Tommy learned a truth he has drawn upon all his life: Look beyond the immediate to the possible conclusion of an activity.

Like most little brothers, Tommy enjoyed playing pranks on his older sister. One day when his sister Marge, one of her girlfriends, and two boys were sunning themselves on the sand at the side of the river, he and his coconspirator Danny devised a clever plan. They determined to slip below the swimming hole, shape two large mud balls with a live frog embedded in each, and then drop a mud ball on the stomach of each of the sleeping girls. They quietly moved to the sunbathers and let go of their globs of mud, which landed on target. Splattered, the two girls sat up "straight as a string," and the frogs jumped into their faces. Tommy and Danny were doubled over with glee when the two husky boys picked them up and threw them into the river, hollering, "Sink or swim!" They swam.

Marge, Tommy, and Bob all liked to ride horses at the rental facility just up from their cabin. On Saturdays when their father arrived, they would coax and plead until he gave them each a quarter to rent a horse for half an hour. They made the most of the time, taking the horses on a good run and then walking them back to cool off. The stable hands usually gave Tommy a mount that was spirited; they knew he could handle such a horse. One day when he was about fourteen, he was on a fast horse when another rider, a girl, cried out in alarm as her horse galloped off. Tommy, remembering how cowboys in the movies would lash their horses, reach over, and catch the reins of a horse that had bolted, did just that—and rescued the girl! That was about as close as he would come to being a cowboy.

One year a mudslide caused by a heavy rainfall swept into the Provo River, blocking it solidly and backing the water up into Vivian Park. Tommy worried that he and his family "might perish" as they watched the water edge closer and closer to the cabin. While his parents tried to allay his fears, the sheer volume of mud and its potential to destroy their cabin community haunted him. He and a friend, John Swertfager, finally felt confident enough to go out on a raft to survey the damage. Treetops that had once been high above their heads were now at eye level. Fish—the largest Tommy had ever seen—swam by just out of his grasp. "It was rather eerie to float past the store at Vivian Park—only the roof was showing," he recalls.[15] When his uncles and father came up from the valley for the weekend, they took the circuitous route through Midway in Heber Valley and then had to be ferried from the highway to the cabin, which was untouched by the water. Eventually the mudslide was cleared, but Tommy had new respect for the forces of nature and the hand of God that protected his family.

Through the years, President Monson has often shared illustrations drawn from his experiences at Vivian Park, where he learned so many lessons about reaching out, holding fast, keeping focused, never giving up, watching for the moment to help others, and carrying a prayer in your heart. There are no coincidences, he says, recognizing that his experiences in life have taught him to look for the Lord's hand. One example:

"My boyfriends and I would take pocketknives in hand and, from the soft wood of a willow tree, fashion small toy boats. With a triangular-shaped cotton sail in place, each would launch his crude craft in the race down the relatively turbulent waters of the Provo River. We would run along the river's bank and watch the tiny vessels sometimes bobbing violently in the swift current and at other times sailing serenely as the water deepened.

"During such a race, we noted that one boat led all the rest toward the appointed finish line. Suddenly, the current carried it too close to a large whirlpool, and the boat heaved to its side and capsized. Around and around it was carried, unable to make its way back into the main current. At last it came to an uneasy rest at the end of the pool, amid the flotsam and jetsam that surrounded it.

"The toy boats of childhood had no keel for stability, no rudder to provide direction, and no source of power. Inevitably their destination was downstream—the path of least resistance.

"Unlike toy boats, we have been provided divine attributes to guide our journey. We enter mortality not to float with the moving currents of life, but with the power to think, to reason, and to achieve.

"Our Heavenly Father did not launch us on our eternal voyage without providing the means whereby we could receive from Him guidance to ensure our safe return. Yes, I speak of prayer. I speak, too, of the whisperings from that still, small voice within each of us; and I do not overlook the holy scriptures, written by mariners who successfully sailed the seas we too must cross."[16]

The lessons of Vivian Park etched themselves deeply in young Tommy Monson's heart, where he could draw upon them for many years to come.

At the end of each summer, on Labor Day, the family would pile into two or three cars and drive to Midway to swim in the acclaimed hot pots there. Aunts, uncles, and cousins from the farm came as well. Schneitter's and Luke's, the two well-known hot-pot resorts, allowed only their overnight guests in their pools, so the family always went to Beuhler's Hot Pots and practically had the whole place to themselves.

For three or four hours they swam in the hot mineral springs, quite different from the bone-chilling river. The cousins would have a contest to see who could stay in the hottest pool the longest. Tom can still remember being "cooked in the hot water."

Then "we'd go back to Vivian Park, pack the car, go home, and start school the next day."[17]

And thus would end another successful summer.

A postscript: In later years, when President Monson was visiting the Vivian Park cabin one evening, he noticed several BYU students, some sitting close to one another watching television in the recreation area of the park. They had rigged a generator to provide energy for the TV; others had a volleyball game going on as well. And the words he often quotes to students came to his mind: "Backward, turn backward, O time, in thy flight; make me a boy again, just for tonight."[18]

5

BECOMING A GENTLEMAN

Why would the prophet of God, in his first appearance before the priesthood holders in a general priesthood meeting, wiggle his ears? I think the answer is that he wanted the young men in the Church to know that he could understand them. He was a boy once. He does a pretty good job of conveying his humanity to the Church.

ELDER MARLIN K. JENSEN
First Quorum of the Seventy

I ALWAYS LOOKED UP TO MY brother Tom and his friends," brother Bob, five years Tom's junior, recalls. "They were the type of people I wanted to be when I grew up."[1]

For the most part they were worthy of emulation.

But Tom and his friends were a handful for any Sunday School teacher. One Sunday morning Sister Lucy Gertsch came into the classroom. She saw immediately her task: to tame the unruly youth. Years later, in a letter to "Elder Monson—dear Tom," she described that first day:

"When the Superintendent took me into that basement room, Bill Mayne was astraddle the bench, some were on the high window sill and others were playing leap frog. I don't know where you were, but I don't recall that you were ever a problem child. You just happened to be in that group because of your age. You were a lively, good boy. Many people would find it hard to believe that an LDS Sunday School could be so undisciplined. Bill Mayne said, 'We'll run her out like we have all the rest.' What he didn't know was that I had Swiss blood in me and a conquering spirit, too. . . . As it was all I could do was stand there and give a silent prayer. Luckily I had been to the show the night before entitled 'Boys Town' and I recognized that the class [members were] good boys with a problem. Love is the only solution I had."[2]

Tom and Lucy made an immediate connection because she had grown up in Midway, Utah, and she included in her lessons descriptions of the beautiful valley with its expansive green fields and curious hot pots, all favorites of the Monson family.

Lucy brought to the classroom as honored guests Moses, Joshua, Peter, Jacob, Nephi, and, most of all, the Lord Jesus Christ. "Though we did not see them, we learned to love, honor, and emulate them."[3] Gospel scholarship grew—and so did deportment. It didn't take long for the boys to love Lucy.

"From the Bible she would read to us of Jesus, the Redeemer and the Savior of the world. One day she taught us how the little children were brought to Him, that He should put His hands on them and pray. His disciples rebuked those that brought the children. 'But when Jesus saw it, he was much displeased, and said unto them, Suffer the little children to come unto me, and forbid them not: for of such is the kingdom of God.'"[4]

Many Sundays the class left feeling as did the disciples on the way to Emmaus: "Did not our heart burn within us?"[5] She did indeed open the scriptures to them. From that class and others with similar spiritual energy came the foundation of Tom Monson's testimony of Jesus Christ.

One Sunday Lucy suggested a party and the class was enthusiastic. During the following weeks she kept careful records as they brought in their scarce nickels and dimes to fund the cakes, cookies, pies, and ice creams they imagined. They had reached their goal when one Sunday in January Lucy announced that the mother of their classmate Billy Devenport had passed away. Many thought of their own mothers and imagined Billy's pain.

The lesson that day drew from the scriptures in the book of Acts: "Remember the words of the Lord Jesus, how he said, It is more blessed to give than to receive."[6] In the middle of the lesson,

Lucy mentioned the dire economic condition of Billy's family and then asked, "How much money do we have in our class party fund?" Depression days prompted a proud answer: "Four dollars and seventy-five cents." Then she suggested, "How would you like to follow this teaching of the Lord and take your party fund to the Devenports as an expression of your love for them?" The vote was unanimous. Lucy provided a large envelope and inside went the precious party fund.

The little group walked the three city blocks, knocked on the door, and greeted Billy and his father, brothers, and sisters. The absence of Mrs. Devenport was felt by all. Lucy handed the grieving father the envelope. "Our hearts were lighter than they had ever been, our joy more full, our understanding more profound," President Monson recalls. "This simple act of kindness welded us together as one. We learned through our own experience that it is indeed more blessed to give than to receive."[7]

Years later the class held a reunion for the "Lucy Gertsch Thomson Class of 1940." Those "rowdy" boys had gone on to become gentlemen indeed: Don Balmforth, carpet contractor; Richard Barton, physician; Don Brems, millwright; John Giles, fireman and railroad engineer; Bryant Giles, language professor; Jack Hepworth, chemist; Alfred Hemingway, film company executive; Robert Marsh, teacher; Bill Mayne, industrial plumber; Leland Weeks, photographer; Leon Robertson, university budgeting and finance officer; Tom Monson, member of the Quorum of the Twelve Apostles.

When President Monson hears the words of the familiar hymn, "Thanks for the Sabbath School. Hail to the day," he thinks of Lucy Gertsch, and also of other treasured leaders such as Thelma Jensen, Larry Green, Pearl Snarr, and Francis Brems. Their examples of Christlike service profoundly influenced him "not so much for what they said, but what they were and how they loved the Lord."[8] They shared life's lessons of kindness, generosity, courage, and honor. Lucy said of those days of teaching, "If one loves, prays and studies, God blesses those efforts."[9] That lesson was not lost on Tom. Love, the theme of his life, was shaped profoundly in classrooms in the basement of a pioneer ward.

Years later, a woman called and asked him, "Do you remember Francis Brems, your Sunday School teacher?" President Monson said that he did. Actually, Brother Brems wasn't really a teacher; he was a "bouncer" assigned to sit at the rear of the class and, if anyone raised a ruckus, to sit down next to the troublemaker. He was in class every Sunday.

The caller went on to explain that Brother Brems had reached the unheard-of age of 105; he was deaf and blind but he could speak. "He lives in a small care center but meets with the family each Sunday," she continued. "Last Sunday, Grandpa announced to us, 'My dears, I am going to die this week. Will you please call Tommy Monson and tell him this. He'll know what to do.'"

The next evening President Monson was at Brother Brems's side. "I could not speak to him, for he was deaf. I could not write a message for him to read, for he was blind. What was I to do? I was told that his family communicated with him by taking the finger of his right hand and then tracing on the palm of his left hand the name of the person visiting and then any message. I followed the procedure [and spelled] T-O-M-M-Y M-O-N-S-O-N. Brother Brems became excited and, taking my hands, placed them on his head. I knew his desire was to receive a priesthood blessing. The driver who had taken me to the care center joined me as we placed our hands on the head of Brother Brems and provided the desired blessing. Afterward, tears streamed from his sightless eyes. He grasped our hands, and we read the movement of his lips. The message: 'Thank you so much.'"[10] Within the week, just as Brother Brems had predicted, he passed away. President Monson spoke at his funeral.

"Who touches a boy by the Master's plan is shaping the course of a future man," President Monson will often quote to youth leaders. Of his own life he has said, looking back, "Every class in Primary, Sunday School, seminary, each priesthood assignment had a larger application. Silently, almost imperceptibly, a life was molded, a career commenced, a man made."[11] That man became a prophet. His teachers were not surprised.

Perhaps one of the reasons he uses hymns so often in his talks is that as a young boy he learned them in Sunday School, and the messages stayed with him. He sees hymns as tools to teach principles. "Come, All Ye Sons of God," "How Firm a Foundation," "Israel, Israel, God Is Calling," and "Ye Elders of Israel" were sung again and again. When the ward chorister put the congregation through the paces of learning a new song, they *learned* it. Stella Waters would wave her baton within inches of the deacons' noses and beat time with a heavy foot that made the floor creak. "As we sang the hymns of Zion," President Monson recalls, "we not only learned the music; we also learned the words."[12] If they responded well, she let them choose the next song. A favorite was:

> *Master, the tempest is raging!*
> *The billows are tossing high!*
> *The sky is o'ershadowed with blackness.*
> *No shelter or help is nigh.*[13]

Tommy loved the words, the intensity of the tune, the drama in the imagery. As a boy, he could fathom somewhat the dangers of a storm-tossed sea but perhaps not the dangers he would see and counsel young deacons to stay away from in years to come: "The demon of greed; the demon of dishonesty; the demon of debt; the demon of doubt; the demon of drugs; and those twin demons of immodesty and immorality."[14]

Tommy was ordained a deacon November 5, 1939, by the stake patriarch, Frank B. Woodbury. After his ordination, the priesthood hymns held even greater significance for him. The words of the opening song his first Sunday as a deacon, "Come, all ye sons of God who have received the priesthood," sank deep.[15] Even today, he looks back on what he felt that day, a young deacon amid men who were—not by age but by priesthood responsibility—his peers. He always viewed holding the priesthood as a trust from God. He has counseled, "Let us consider our callings, let us reflect on our responsibilities, let us determine our duty, and let us follow Jesus Christ our Lord."[16] That commitment began when a twelve-year-old boy met with his fellow brethren.

The members of the bishopric took a personal interest in Tommy, reinforcing the lessons of the Master that he saw displayed at home. Never did he waver from honoring his parents— they were his guideposts, but others also showed him the way. His priesthood advisers stressed the sacred responsibility to pass the sacrament; they emphasized proper dress, a dignified bearing, and the importance of being clean inside and out. It was in those Aaronic Priesthood years that he learned the lessons of service in the Church that would shape the rest of his life. He has taught young men: "All who hold the priesthood have opportunities for service to our Heavenly Father and to His children here on earth. It is contrary to the spirit of service to live selfishly within ourselves and disregard the needs of others."[17]

The ward had two deacons quorums. In 1940 Tommy served as second counselor in the first quorum and in 1941 as secretary to the second quorum of deacons in the Sixth-Seventh Ward in the Pioneer Stake. He enjoyed the precision of record keeping and other secretarial tasks and was proud to serve in a Church calling. At one ward conference officers' meeting, a member of the stake presidency asked him to stand and bear testimony of his feelings about his Church assignment. He doesn't remember what he said, but by that time he had begun to develop a sense of obligation for proper performance and adherence to his priesthood duties, and his thoughts may have reflected that resolve.

Another of those duties was to collect fast offerings. "I would cover a portion of the ward on fast Sunday morning, giving the small envelope to each family, waiting while a contribution was placed in the envelope and then returning it to the bishop. On one such occasion, an elderly member, Brother Wright, who lived alone, welcomed me at the door and, with aged hands, fumbled at the tie of the envelope and placed within it a small sum. His eyes fairly glistened as he made his contribution."[18]

Thomas Monson has never forgotten Ed Wright. And he uses those Aaronic Priesthood experiences today when he teaches youth about this sacred duty: "I recall that the boys in the congregation over which I presided had assembled one morning sleepy-eyed, a bit disheveled, and mildly complaining about arising so early to fulfill their assignment. Not a word of reproof was spoken, but during the following week, we escorted the boys to Welfare Square for a guided tour. They saw firsthand a lame person operating the telephone switchboard, an older man stocking shelves, women arranging clothing to be distributed—even a blind person placing labels on cans. Here were individuals earning their sustenance through their contributed labors. A penetrating silence came over the boys as they witnessed how their efforts each month helped to collect the sacred fast offering funds which aided the needy and provided employment for those who otherwise would be idle."[19]

His counsel is clear: "We could well expect more today from our Aaronic Priesthood quorum presidencies, for I know we would achieve better performance if we expected such."[20]

Tommy was still a fun-loving youth, and he and his friends were mischievous, though never mean-spirited. They were known to hitch rides on switch engines in the rail yard and to play pranks on cars in the street. One day after school, walking down Second West, he and his schoolmates came upon the dog catcher's truck parked outside a sausage shop. Since "all boys hate dog catchers," they surveyed the truck, noticing that the dog catcher had left the lock hanging by its hasp. That was all they needed. Concerned for the dogs "on their way to the death chamber," Tommy reached out and lifted the lock, giving seven dogs a reprieve; the dogs dutifully chased the boys for blocks.[21]

One Halloween Tommy and his friends "came into possession" of a life-size dummy, stuffed with straw and dressed in shabby men's clothing. The story was that it had been made at the state prison for a Halloween dance of the family of one of the inmates and discarded at the end of the event. The boys were elated when they stumbled on "him."

The boys' minds began to race: How could they make use of this dummy they dubbed "Charlie"? It didn't take long before they were huddled in the honeysuckle bushes at the side of the chapel, and when a car would approach, they would throw the dummy out in front of the vehicle, giving the impression that the driver had hit someone. They would hear the brakes screech and the driver scream, and they thought this was great fun.

The boys would then retrieve "Charlie" and wait for the next car. And the next. It was when they threw him in front of a City Lines bus that things got out of hand. The driver slammed on the brakes, passengers screamed, and one lady fainted. For Tommy and his chums, "that was the highlight of the evening." Word got out quickly to a counselor in the bishopric, John Burt, who confiscated Charlie and marched down to the furnace room of the ward building. As he opened the door to the furnace, the deacons threatened, "If you burn our dummy we will not pass the sacrament."

"How you act on Sunday is up to you," said Brother Burt, looking at the foolhardy deacons. "How I act is up to me." Charlie went into the flames, and the deacons were sent home. They were angry.

On Sunday morning the young men did not take their usual seats. But as the meeting began, they also began to think about Brother Burt's words. One by one they stood and made the "embarrassing walk" to their appointed places and passed the sacrament with repentant hearts.[22]

President Monson would draw upon that lesson in teaching deacons all around the world: "Are you living your life in accordance with that which the Lord requires? Are you worthy to bear the priesthood of God? If you are not, make the decision here and now, muster the courage it will take and institute whatever changes are necessary so that your life is what it should be."

He has said many times to young men: "Yours is the privilege to be not spectators but participants on the stage of priesthood service."[23]

Tommy usually made his way to priesthood meeting alone. But when his father's favorite General Authority, LeGrand Richards, was scheduled to address the Pioneer Stake priesthood meeting in the Fourth Ward chapel, Spence and Tommy went together. For Tommy, those moments with his dad were precious.

On one occasion, still a young deacon, Tom was assigned to speak about the Word of Wisdom at a stake meeting. His father wrote the message. His stake president, Paul C. Child, leaned over to Tommy after he sat down and congratulated him on his message, but added, "In the future you will not need to read your talks. You have the ability to deliver one without reading it." Tommy took his advice to heart.

The young men were rambunctious but teachable. "It seems like yesterday that I was secretary of the deacons quorum of my ward. We were tutored by wise and patient men who taught us from the holy scriptures, even men who knew us well. These men who took time to listen and to laugh, to build and to inspire, emphasized that we, like the Lord, could increase in wisdom and stature, and in favor with God and man. They were examples to us. Their lives were a reflection of their testimonies. Youth is a time for growth."[24]

As a deacon he watched the priests as they officiated at the sacrament table. One priest, Barry, had a particularly fine voice, and his reading of the sacrament prayers was inspiring. The others often complimented him on his "golden" voice, as if he had been participating in a speech contest. He became a bit proud. On the other hand, Jack, one of the other priests, was hearing impaired, and his diction was unnatural and at times garbled.

One Sunday, Jack with "the awkward delivery" and Barry with "the beautiful voice" sat at the sacrament table together. The congregation sang the hymn; the priests broke the bread; then Barry knelt to pray. Nothing happened. Soon, the deacons and other members of the congregation were checking to see what had caused the delay. The picture still lingers in Tom's mind of Barry "frantically searching the table for the little white card on which were printed the sacrament prayers." It was not there. Embarrassed, Barry flushed crimson.

Then Jack, with his bearlike hand, pulled Barry back to the bench. He knelt on the footstool and began to speak the words he had memorized: "O God, the Eternal Father, we ask thee . . ." The deacons—and Barry—gained great respect that day for Jack, who, though handicapped in speech, had done his duty by committing to heart the sacred sacrament prayers.[25]

Youth of the ward looked forward every year to the season of road shows. They "knew what a production was." To this day

President Monson is an advocate for road shows, dance festivals, and other such events. He considers them both uplifting and edifying—even, as was the case for him, life changing. In recent years, grand events have accompanied temple dedications. He recognizes, "They enable our youth to participate in something they truly find unforgettable. The friendships they form and the memories they make will be theirs forever."[26]

Myriel Cluff and later Betty Rushton Barton directed the productions in the Sixth-Seventh Ward. In November 1940 the Sixth-Seventh Ward entry, "Through the Rays of the Sun," won first place in the stake and went on to take first place in competition at Kingsbury Hall on the University of Utah campus for the best road show in the valley. "It portrayed the spirit of Pioneer Stake, for it showed how individuals all over the world come together through the gospel."[27]

In the production, Tom and the other twelve-year-olds were Eskimos. Dressed in white, they performed a dance portraying hunting seals on the ice. Other age-groups in the ward represented the Deep South and the Orient. Tom's sister Marge had the featured role, reciting the poem by Emma Lazarus that appears on the Statue of Liberty to advance the idea, "Through the rays of the sun all lands and people are seen."

The day of the regional competition, Marge came down with laryngitis. She sucked lemon peels and took hot honey remedies and other concoctions from ward members, but to no avail. No voice. The words, "Give me your tired, your poor," were not going to be heard from her. Tom told her he would pray for her and he would get all the Eskimos to do so as well. He gathered the deacons, and they got down on their knees and offered a prayer. Her voice came back and the Sixth-Seventh Ward was "judged as having the finest road show in the Church." Through prayer and faith, they represented well their "great stake of Zion."[28]

"President Monson has always been a person of great faith and a person of prayer," Bishop H. David Burton observes. "He uses those great gifts to bless the lives of many today."[29]

A long-standing tradition for the youth of the Sixth-Seventh Ward was to commemorate the restoration of the Aaronic

Priesthood by traveling to Clarkston, Utah, a small community about a hundred miles north of Salt Lake City. There the boys would visit the grave of Martin Harris. "Most of our time was devoted to learning about Martin Harris, one of the Three Witnesses of the Book of Mormon, whose body rests in this peaceful cemetery," President Monson recalled. "No doubt he is the cemetery's most illustrious occupant. However, I strolled beyond the granite shaft bearing Martin Harris's name and read tombstone inscriptions of others less prominent but equally as faithful. Some of the ancient tombstones contained interesting reminders, such as 'We will meet again,' or 'Gone to a better place.' One that I still remember read: 'A light from our household is gone; a voice we loved is stilled. A spot is vacant in our hearts that never can be filled.'"[30]

He remembers still the "reverence and awe" he felt when they stopped at the Logan Temple grounds. "As boys are inclined to do on a spring day, we would lie on the lawn and gaze at the temple spires, which vaulted to the blue sky, and note the silky, wispy white clouds as they hurried by. I thought of the pioneers buried in that small cemetery. As a result of the sacred ordinances performed in the holy house of God, no light need be permanently extinguished, no voice permanently stilled, no place in our heart permanently left vacant. Oh, how those early pioneers loved the temple!"[31]

In 1942 the bishop called Tom Monson as president of the teachers quorum. Glen Bosen was first counselor and Fritz E. Hoerold second, with John Hepworth, secretary. Though the young men in his quorum grew up, married, and moved away, Tom never let go of his sense of responsibility for them. His love for a favorite verse, quoted time and again, may have had its birth in this setting: "Do your duty, that is best; leave unto the Lord the rest."[32]

The teachers quorum presidency occasionally held their meetings at the home of one of their leaders, Brother Miller, concluding the evening by playing a game of Monopoly and eating homemade meat pies. Tommy received his patriarchal blessing there as well from patriarch Frank B. Woodbury, Sister Miller's father; she had acted as his scribe.

Harold Watson, Tom's teachers quorum adviser, shared his love of pigeons; he raised the sophisticated Birmingham roller pigeons. One day Brother Watson asked Tom if he would accept a gift of a pair of purebred Birmingham roller pigeons. Tom was elated. The very next day, Tom was there when Brother Watson got home from work; he'd been waiting an hour. "He took me to his pigeon loft, which was in the upper area of a small barn located at the rear of his yard. As I looked at the most beautiful pigeons I had yet seen, he said, 'Select any male, and I will give you a female which is different from any other pigeon in the world.'"

Tom chose, and then Brother Watson placed in his hand a tiny hen. Tom asked what made her so different.

"Look carefully, and you'll notice that she has but one eye."

Sure enough, one eye was missing; she had met up with a cat.

"Take them home to your loft," Brother Watson counseled. "Keep them in for about ten days and then turn them out to see if they will remain at your place."

Tom followed the instructions. After the recommended time, he released them. The male strutted about the roof of the loft and then ducked back inside to eat. But the one-eyed female flew off immediately. Tom called Brother Watson and asked, "Did that one-eyed pigeon return to your loft?"

"Come over and we'll have a look."

As the two walked out to the loft, his adviser commented, "Tom, you're the president of the teachers quorum. What are you going to do to activate Bob, who is a member of your quorum?"

As Tom answered, "I'll have him at quorum meeting this week," Brother Watson reached up to a nest and handed him the one-eyed pigeon. "Keep her in a few more days," he said, "and try again."

The same thing happened. Tom called Brother Watson and again they walked out to his loft. The conversation went something like this: "Congratulations on getting Bob to priesthood meeting. Now what are you and Bob going to do to activate Bill?" Bill and his family had been the recipients of the party fund from Lucy Gertsch's class.

Each week the pigeon flew back to the Watson loft. Each

week Tom and his adviser talked about the activity of his quorum members. "I was a grown man before I fully realized that, indeed, Harold Watson, my adviser, had given me a special pigeon: the only pigeon in his loft he knew would return every time she was released. It was his inspired way of having an ideal personal priesthood interview with the president of the teachers quorum."[33]

From Harold Watson and many others Tom learned patience, persistence, duty, and spiritual reliance on the Lord. "What a privilege to learn the discipline of duty. A boy will automatically turn from concern for self when he is assigned to 'watch over' others," he says.[34] He likes to talk about Brother Watson and the pigeons, but the story has little to do with a one-eyed pigeon. With Brother Watson he was learning how to help others to be made whole.

Another ward member, James Farrell, father of a large family of all girls, operated the Spring Canyon Coal Company. It was a one-man operation: one old truck, a pile of coal, one shovel, and his weathered hands. He worked long hours, early morning to late evening, and still his family struggled to survive. But they were at every meeting and every ward activity. In fast meetings, this giant of a man always stood and expressed his thanks to the Lord for his family, his work, and his testimony. "The fingers of those rough, red, chapped hands which turned white as he gripped the back of the bench" made an impression on young Tom. When Brother Farrell bore witness of "a boy who, in a grove of trees near Palmyra, New York, knelt in prayer and beheld the heavenly vision of God the Father and Jesus Christ the Son," Tom knew what he said was true; he could feel it.[35]

The humble people of the Sixth-Seventh Ward influenced Tommy dramatically. These were good-hearted, hardworking folk; people with testimonies of their Lord and Savior; people grateful for their blessings, though such blessings may have appeared meager in the eyes of the world. With their help, the pattern was set for Thomas S. Monson's lifetime of service, compassion, hard work, and testimony.

6

SCHOOL DAYS

When you talk about President Monson, you talk about the man who cares about the boy without the coat in winter or the worker who came home last night having lost his job or the widow who has no husband and is lonely. Those have been President Monson's gifts and messages throughout his life, and it just so happens that this is the climate or environment we find ourselves in today. For me, President Monson is truly the prophet of this day.

ELDER RONALD A. RASBAND
Presidency of the Seventy

At GRANT ELEMENTARY SCHOOL, Tommy had played softball on a gravel playground, invariably dropping the fly ball or striking out at the plate. He was destined for the outfield rather than second base or shortstop.

But at Horace Mann Junior High, Tom became an athlete, surprising everyone, including himself. He had faced the disappointment and youthful humiliation of being chosen last for many a team. Maybe it was that his father never had time to go out and play catch with him. Maybe he just needed to grow into his arms and legs. He knew what it meant when the team captain sent him to the outfield, where he was standing one day when a "miracle" happened. He had a fielder's glove inscribed with the name of Mel Ott, the premiere player of the day, but it hadn't improved Tom's game. On this particular day, however, local slugger Red Sperry hit a long fly ball to center field. As Tom ran back to catch it, he heard the runner say, "I'm safe. He'll miss it." That taunting was all it took. Though Tom ran like the wind, he realized that the ball was beyond the reach of his glove. So he reached with his bare hand, said a little prayer—and caught the ball. With that catch came a new sense of confidence, a new Tom.

Once he knew he could catch a fly ball, he built on that success—hitting well, then pitching. In time he was selected first for the team, then captain of the team. He became highly successful as a fast-pitch pitcher in softball, proving that there comes a change when you keep working at things: "The Lord blesses you and you will succeed."[1]

He and his friends and brother played softball in the dirt alley behind their homes. The makeshift field was cramped but satisfactory as long as you hit the ball to "center field." But if you hit the ball right, disaster loomed. Mrs. Shinas lived in a little house tucked between the Monson duplex and Uncle John and Aunt Margaret's—right off first base—and she watched the boys play from her kitchen window. She was cross and difficult to get along with, never missing a chance to scold the boys as they played in the alley or the street. She and her husband had no children and rarely came out of their home, nor did they socialize with their neighbors. Every time a softball landed near her porch, Mrs. Shinas would hurry out, grab it, and take it inside, limping because of a stiff leg. Sometimes her dog helped retrieve the errant balls. Needless to say, the stash of softballs inside her door made her a prime target for pranks.

One day, Tommy decided to call a halt to the standoff. The boys had long since given up playing ball in the alley—they had run out of balls. As he watered the front lawn, he decided to water Mrs. Shinas's lawn as well. When he watered the Monson rosebushes he watered the Shinas bushes, too. He continued his expanded watering throughout the summer and into the fall. He hosed the Shinases' lawn free of leaves when they started to fall and stacked them in piles at the street's edge to be burned or gathered.

Not once that summer or fall had he seen Mrs. Shinas. Then one evening she opened the front door and beckoned to him as he did his outside chores. Tommy hopped the short fence, and she invited him into her living room, where she presented him with milk and cookies. Then she went into the kitchen and returned with a large box filled with balls, several seasons' worth. "Tommy, I want you to have these baseballs, and I want to thank you for being kind to me," she said. They became friends. But more than that, Tommy learned one of those life lessons: "Do unto others as you would have them do unto you."[2]

The success of the local baseball club, the Salt Lake Bees, in the Pioneer League became almost an obsession with Tom. He went to every game, knew the name of each player, followed the batting averages, and after a game would run the bases, pretending he was a big leaguer. At the time, what a great distance it seemed to run from first base to second to third and then to home plate!

Tom's friends at West High School remember him as loyal and industrious, fun-loving and friendly. He and his friend Earl Holding, who would eventually become a wealthy entrepreneur, believe they were the only two who never saw a West High football game. They weren't apathetic; they were working.

Tommy was twelve when he began working after school and on Saturdays at the print shop where his father worked. He would sweep the floors, tidy the washroom, run errands, and fill in as a pair of extra hands, earning five dollars a week. One afternoon he absentmindedly tucked his wages in the pocket of his Levi's and forgot about it. "Horror of horrors," on Monday, the Levi's went off to the laundry. When he realized it, he knelt down "then and there" and prayed that somehow or other that five-dollar bill would make its way back to him. He waited anxiously for Thursday when the laundry would be returned, clean and fresh. He opened the bag and placed each item on the kitchen table. When he got to his Levi's he thrust his hand in the money pocket and there was his five-dollar bill—wet, but safe. He has often quipped, "That was the first laundered money I had ever seen." That night, he thanked his Heavenly Father for that answer to prayer.[3]

Tom gradually moved up to become an apprentice at the print shop, Western Hotel Register, at 740 South Main. Every afternoon he made the rounds of all the restaurants in town, collecting changes for their next-day menus. Only once did anyone offer him anything to eat, though he was in the kitchens of them all. From that beginning he went on to become general manager of Deseret Press, chairman of the board of Deseret News Publishing Company, board member of Deseret Book, and president of the Utah Printers' Association.

His classmate Earl Holding, like Tom, started out at the bottom, cutting the grass at the Covey Apartments, which his parents managed. He later bought the apartments and then Covey's Little America hotel facility in Wyoming, which he expanded to a four- and five-star chain of hotels. He eventually purchased Sinclair Oil, Sun Valley resort in Idaho, and Snowbasin resort in Utah's Ogden Canyon. "Working didn't hurt us any," Tom observed when being named in 2006 to West High's Hall of Fame.[4]

Three high schools served the city population when Tom attended: West, South, and East. West was the oldest; East was its primary rival; South was in between them geographically. Students attended for two years, as juniors and seniors; some could opt for a third. Tom's West High class included 384 students. Tom was president of the Spanish club, a member of the student council and of the eligibility and awards committee, and a sergeant in ROTC.

He excelled in English, geography, and history. He once commented that if he were to go back and reshape his profession, he would consider becoming a history professor. His office has one book cabinet full of World War II books that detail aspects of the war. There is no question that his interest was spurred by his growing up in the midst of war and his later responsibility for the European area, home to many World War II battlefields. He "did not do so well in zoology," and Spanish was a disappointment. That first year he learned to ask for a glass of water and memorized some other "packaged" conversation. His second year, his Spanish teacher, the "most outstanding in the valley," married and left teaching. West High administrators replaced her with an older teacher who confessed on the first day, "I haven't studied Spanish since I was nineteen years old." Still, Tom had several Hispanic friends and acquired basic Spanish language skills that have helped him in many of the Latin countries on his Church assignments.

His mother encouraged him to take a shorthand class in high school. She anticipated that one day he might be involved in the war, and having skills for an office job might keep him off the front line, where her brother Pete had served in World War I. Surprisingly, Tom quite liked shorthand and was good at it. It didn't hurt that the "prettiest girls" at West High were in that class, including LaRee Teuscher, Jean Moon, Jackie Devereaux, and Joy Timpson.

The students danced at the Rainbow Rendezvous on Main Street, bought fudge brownies at Mrs. Backer's Bakery just south of the school next to the seminary building, and ate at Burt's Hamburger Stand right across the street from the school, which today looks just like it did when Tom attended.[5]

Tom's height and strength would have made him a natural for basketball. But his work after school limited his opportunities to practice, and he had access to only the small-size court in his ward. In one Church ball game, the coach sent Tommy onto the floor right after the second half began. He took an inbounds pass, dribbled the ball toward the key, and let the shot fly. Just as the ball left his fingertips, he realized why the opposing guards had not attempted to stop his drive: he was shooting for the wrong basket! He immediately offered a silent prayer: "Please, Father, don't let that ball go in." The ball rimmed the hoop and fell out. But the crowd showed no mercy. They began a chant: "We want Monson, we want Monson, we want Monson—*out!*"

Many years later, as a member of the Quorum of the Twelve, he joined a small group of General Authorities in a visit to a newly completed chapel in northern Utah where, as an experiment, the Church Physical Facilities Department was trying out a tightly woven carpet for a gymnasium floor.

"While several of us were examining the floor, Bishop J. Richard Clarke, who was then in the Presiding Bishopric, suddenly threw the basketball to me with a challenge: 'I don't believe you can hit the basket, standing where you are!'"

He was some distance behind what is now the professional

three-point line. He had never made such a basket in his entire life. Elder Mark E. Petersen of the Twelve called out to the others, "I think he can!"

Elder Monson's thoughts returned to the "embarrassment of years before, shooting toward the wrong basket. Nevertheless, I aimed and let that ball fly. Through the net it went!"

Throwing the ball in his direction again, Bishop Clarke once more issued the challenge: "I know you can't do that again!"

Elder Petersen spoke up, "Of course, he can!"

He describes the words of the poet coming to his mind and echoing in his heart:

> *Lead us, O lead us,*
> *Great Molder of men,*
> *Out of the shadow*
> *To strive once again.*

He shot the ball. It soared toward the basket and went right through.[6]

Another sport Tommy enjoyed was duck hunting. He didn't own a gun himself—his mother wouldn't have one in the house—but he talked his Uncle Speed into buying an old double-barreled Stevens shotgun for thirty-five dollars.

Tom and his cousin Richard Carter went out to the Copper Club Marsh one afternoon late in the season to shoot. They were not club members; they were trespassers. Not only that, but Tom had not bought a hunting license. He had borrowed one from his friend Reo Williamson. Walking across a dike in the late afternoon haze, almost dark, the two caught sight of a flock of ducks. They could not resist, although hunting was legally over for the day. They stood up and fired at the birds, missing all of them. When they got to their car, they found a federal game warden waiting to greet them. He issued Tom a ticket, bypassing Richard, who was too young. The boys had to appear before a justice of the peace, who lectured them on being good sportsmen and never shooting after hours. He then levied a ten-dollar fine.

A few days later a list appeared in the daily newspaper of all those who had been arrested for violating the hunting and fishing laws of Utah: "Shooting after hours, Reo L. Williamson; fine $10." Tom never mentioned to Reo "his" brush with the law.[7]

War broke out in Europe in 1939. For Tom, life went on as usual except for the cloud of uncertainty and conflict hanging over his home and neighborhood. The German military invaded Poland in September 1939 and then marched across border after border of European neighbors. Japan bombed Pearl Harbor on December 7, 1941, a Sunday. Tom and his father were driving home from visiting relatives when they heard the news; his father pulled over to the side of the road as they listened to the sober announcement. The two just sat in stunned silence. The raid pushed the United States into the conflict. Tom went from being a child of the Depression to becoming a youth of the war. At school, the administration announced a contest for the best patriotic oration by a student. Tom's presentation, "Our Flag: The Symbol of America," won first place.

Recognizing that the Church had congregations across the globe, the First Presidency in April 1942 issued an official statement on war: "Hate can have no place in the souls of the righteous. . . . Live clean, keep the commandments of the Lord, pray to Him constantly to preserve you in truth and righteousness, live as you pray, and then whatever betides you the Lord will be with you and nothing will happen to you that will not be to the honor and glory of God and to your salvation and exaltation. . . . Then, when the conflict is over and you return to your homes, having lived the righteous life, how great will be your happiness—whether you be of the victors or of the vanquished—that you have lived as the Lord commanded."[8] Those words would be reflected in Elder Monson's service to the German Saints years after the war ended.

The war economy gave employment to many of Tommy's neighbors who desperately needed work, but rationing made gasoline, sugar, shoes, meat, butter, eggs, and candy bars especially hard to get. And he learned much in those years about shock, sorrow, loneliness, and heartache as he watched the conflict shatter lives of people he knew and loved.

His friend Arthur Patton had enlisted. "He had blond, curly hair and a smile as big as all outdoors," Tom recalls. "He stood taller than any boy in the class. I suppose this is how, in 1940, as the great conflict which became World War II was overtaking much of Europe, Arthur was able to fool the recruiting officers and enlist in the navy at the tender age of 15. To Arthur and most of the boys, the war was a great adventure. I remember how striking he appeared in his navy uniform. How we wished we were older so we too could enlist."

When Tom passed the Patton house, Mrs. Patton often opened the door and waved him in to hear the latest news from Arthur. Following the order of the day, she hung a blue star in the living-room window in his honor. She was so proud. That star represented to every passerby that her son wore the uniform of his country.

In March 1944, Arthur's ship was attacked in the Pacific. He was one of those lost at sea, one month from his nineteenth birthday. A gold star replaced the blue one hanging in his mother's window, announcing the fall of her soldier son. Mrs. Patton was devastated.

President Monson has never forgotten the day that he went, a youth with no experience of such pain, to the door of the Patton home, hoping words of comfort would come to him. Mrs. Patton opened the door, and her arms reached out as she embraced him like she would have hugged Arthur if he had come home. Tommy suggested that they pray, and Mrs. Patton acknowledged that she belonged to no church, had no belief. "Tell me, Tommy," she said, "will Arthur live again?"

Years later, Tommy, by then Elder Monson, began his 1969 general conference message by addressing Arthur's mother: "Mrs. Patton, wherever you are, from the backdrop of my personal experience I should like once more to answer your question, 'Will Arthur live again?'" He then outlined the basic elements of the plan of salvation.

"I had little or no hope that Mrs. Patton would actually hear the talk," he said. She was not a member of the Church. But he later learned that a miracle had taken place. Latter-day Saint neighbors of Mrs. Patton, who was now living in California, invited her to their home to listen to a session of conference. They could not have known what Elder Monson was going to say. "She accepted their invitation," he notes, "and thus was listening to the very session where I directed my remarks to her personally."

Just weeks later, he was astonished to receive a letter postmarked Pomona, California, from Mrs. Terese Patton. She wrote:

> Dear Tommy,
>
> I hope you don't mind my calling you Tommy, as I always think of you that way. I don't know how to thank you for the comforting talk you gave.
>
> Arthur was 15 years old when he enlisted in the navy. He was killed one month before his 19th birthday on July 5, 1944.
>
> It was wonderful of you to think of us. I don't know how to thank you for your comforting words, both when Arthur died and again in your talk. I have had many questions over the years, and you have answered them. I am now at peace concerning Arthur. . . . God bless and keep you always.
>
> Love,
> Terese Patton[9]

Little did he know, the day he knocked on Mrs. Patton's door, how much comfort he would offer to her in years to come.

And so the years went by, until finally it was time to move on from high school. When Tom graduated, his family was so proud of his accomplishment. His Aunt Blanche wrote him a note that he has kept: "My—but I am proud of you tonight. Just think—you are graduating from High School—not only that but an 'A' student. . . . Love Aunt Blanche."[10]

He never misses his high school reunion; the classes of 1942, '43, and '44 join together. He is quick to say, "New friends are silver, but old friends are gold." The reunion is one of the few places where the President of The Church of Jesus Christ of Latter-day

Saints puts on a name badge that reads "Tom Monson" and where people still call him "Tommy." Clearly, he enjoys just getting together with old friends. He has not forgotten them, nor does he reserve his attention only for those who share his religious beliefs. Jane Beppu Sakashita, a friend from "way back," was amazed when she received a letter from him after her brother passed away. "I'm Buddhist," she explained. "How grateful I was to hear from him; I mean, a person of his stature to remember me and take time to send a letter of condolence." She sent a letter back and congratulated him on his new position as President of the Church. "He replied to my letter and then I wrote to him again. I said, 'I know you only by Tommy. Is it appropriate for me to call you Tommy?'"

President Monson wrote back, signing the letter, "Tommy."[11] Who he was then is still a big part of who he is now.

7

THE GREATEST LESSONS

He was always being prepared for something, from the time he was the deacons secretary, teachers president, ward clerk, or young men's superintendent. Whatever his calling has been, he has devoted 100 percent of his energy to it. And he really cares about people. He has always forfeited his personal time to help those in need, providing blessings, compassion, and companionship.

LYNNE CANNEGIETER
Personal Secretary to
President Thomas S. Monson

WHEN PRESIDENT MONSON LOOKS back at pivotal experiences in his life, his years at the University of Utah come quickly to mind: "Here I studied. Here I learned. Here I taught. Here I met the beautiful girl who became my wife. Here I entered as a boy and emerged as a man."[1]

Most West High students didn't consider any institution besides the University of Utah for their higher education. The streetcar made regular runs up the hill to the U, which had been founded in 1850 by Brigham Young.

During the Depression, W.P.A. laborers had constructed several grand buildings, which comprised most of the campus. A number of them clustered around a circle, creating an intimate yet imposing university campus with the striking, pillared John R. Park Administration Building built in 1914 as the centerpiece.

It was an era of campus queens, football victories, afternoon dances, and big bands. Almost every student had a part-time job, and looming heavily over the campus was the inevitable call for the male students to serve their country. Paper shortages delayed textbooks; many were not available until halfway through the courses.

Tom enrolled at the U as a freshman in 1944; he had just turned seventeen. His father paid his tuition—$104 for fall, winter, and spring quarters combined. Tom attended classes in the mornings and worked for his father in the afternoons and on Saturdays until 1:00 to pay for books, other collegiate expenses, and dating.

Tom had a system for his study that he later shared with many college students: "Have discipline in your preparations. Have checkpoints where you can determine if you're on course. Study something you like and which will make it possible for you to support a family. . . . You can't get the jobs of tomorrow until you have the skills of today. . . . Make certain as you prepare that you do not procrastinate." He even had specific techniques that worked for him in the classroom. "In academic preparation, I found it a good practice to read a text with the idea that I will be asked to explain that which the author wrote and its application to the subject it covered. Also, I tried to be attentive in any lecture in the classroom and to pretend that I would be called upon to present the same lecture to others. While this practice is very hard work, it certainly helps during test week." He was quick to add, "It is not the number of hours you put in, but what you put in the hours that counts."[2]

Tom's favorite subject at the university was United States history. Right at the top of his list of favorite professors was G. Homer Durham, who brought history to life. "The love in his classroom opened the windows" of Tom's mind. He took to heart Dr. Durham's teaching: "The past is behind; learn from it."[3] History was much more than date, time, and place to him. He came to know some of the great figures of history, men he respected, wished to emulate, and would later use as examples for college students on the cusp of life's decisions. The signers of the Declaration of Independence were among them. These were men of principle. "There were about three million people who lived in the American Colonies at the time of the Revolution," he told a gathering. "They could only get fifty-six people to sign the Declaration of Independence. It took a lot of courage, because they knew if this failed, they were going to hang by the neck until dead. When you stop to think of it, it is pretty wonderful that they got even fifty-six to meet in Philadelphia and pledge their lives, their fortunes, and their sacred honor."[4]

Courage to act on principle describes Tom Monson.

During one quarter, he had a speech class at 8:00 in the morning from Dr. Royal Garff, a renowned professor. One partic-ular day, he and his fellow students waited—and waited—for the instructor to arrive. Finally, someone from the office came into the room and announced that Dr. Garff's wife had just died. He would not be attending that day. Students were looking around wondering what to do when Tom said, "You can leave, but I am staying here to pay honor to our professor, who needs our sup-port." No one left, and they spent the remainder of the class time in silent contemplation.[5]

Physical education courses were required, and Tom enrolled in advanced swimming and basketball. His coach, Charlie Welch, proved to be both a competent instructor and a "wonderful per-son." One morning during roll call a young man walked purpose-fully into class dressed in a navy uniform. The sailor went up to Charlie and said, "I want to thank you for saving my life."

The story quickly unfolded. "You once told me that I swam like a lead ball, yet you patiently taught me to swim. Two months ago, far off in the Pacific, an enemy torpedo sank my destroyer. As I swam my way through the murky waters and foul-tasting, dan-gerous film of oil, I found myself promising, 'If I ever get out of this mess alive, I'm going to thank Charlie Welch for teaching me how to swim.' Today I came here to say 'thank you.'"

Tears came readily to Charlie's eyes that day as he quietly re-ceived his reward.[6]

Tom passed his swimming class, though the tests were rigor-ous. He had good, strong strokes perfected in the currents of the Provo River. In the pool he had to demonstrate his mastery of the crawl, the back, the side, and the breast stroke, swimming five lengths of each. More grueling was a thirty-minute stretch of treading water. Then came the diving, followed by the "most trying assignment": swimming the length of the pool using feet only for both the crawl and the breast strokes. He was "grateful he passed" and could see how that training had saved the life of Charlie's student.

Tom also took institute classes, enjoying the midweek inspiration that had typically come mostly on Sundays. The institute employed two teachers, Dr. Lowell Bennion and Dr. T. Edgar Lyon; their gospel scholarship and service interests lifted Tom's sights. Classes were held in the University Ward Chapel, which had housed the institute for more than a decade. Not until 1949 did it move one block south to a purpose-built facility, and years later to a complex on the south side of campus. The massive color tile mosaic of Jesus Christ reaching out His arms was a fitting entrance to religious study with its inscription: "And he went up to the mountain to teach them."

Academic pursuits were not the only things occupying Tom Monson's attention in those days. At the University of Utah Hello Day Dance in 1944, he had a friend from West High on his arm when he first caught sight of fellow freshman Frances Johnson dancing with another student to the popular tune "Kentucky." He resolved to meet her but didn't catch her eye again that evening.

It was a month before he happened to see her a second time. One afternoon, while waiting for the streetcar near campus, he saw her chatting with a few friends at the bus stop. Tom recognized one of them from Grant Elementary but could not remember his name. Not sure how to approach the situation, he hesitated—just briefly—when into his mind came a phrase he had committed to memory, "When the time for decision arrives, the time for preparation is past." He squared his shoulders and stepped forward to greet his former grade-school acquaintance.

"Hello, old friend," Tom said. "How are you?"

The young man politely introduced Tom to the two young ladies with him, and they all rode the streetcar to town. As Tom bid the three good-bye, he quickly took out his student directory and underlined the name *Frances Beverly Johnson*. Ever the consummate proofreader, he noted a typographical error in her middle name—"Berverly."

Tom wasted no time. That night he called to ask Frances to the dance at the Pioneer Stake gym that weekend. He has said that he will always remember his first visit to her home to pick her up for that date.

Tom's home environment was noisy, his siblings gregarious; everyone was "part of the action." Whenever his older and "very beautiful" sister, Marjorie, brought to the house a beau—and there were many—Tommy and his younger brother took turns standing on a chair in the kitchen peering through the window in the door to the front room to check him out.

There were no such antics at the home of Franz and Hildur Johnson on Yale Avenue on the east side of town. Frances, named after her father, Franz, was the only daughter. Her home environment was proper and dignified. On Tom's first visit, her father and mother both welcomed him; they were dressed up as if they were going out, but that formality was just to meet him. His nervousness increased.

Franz Johnson asked, "Your name is Monson?"

Tom replied, "Yes, sir."

He said, "I think that is a Swedish name."

Tom said, "Yes, sir."

Then Franz walked over to a cabinet drawer and brought out an old picture of two missionaries with top hats and canes. He turned to the young suitor and asked if he were related to one of the missionaries in the photo, an elder by the name of Elias Monson.

"Yes, sir," Tom said, then added, "that is my father's uncle. Elias Monson was a missionary in Sweden."

Immediately, Frances's father began to weep as he described the visits his family had enjoyed with Elias and his companions in their home in Sweden. He threw his arms around Tom's neck and embraced him. Then Frances's mother embraced him. Frances looked at Tom and said, "I'll go get my coat."[7]

In subsequent visits they talked further of Frances's Swedish parentage. Her father, Franz, along with his parents and his eleven brothers and sisters, had lived in a two-room farmhouse in the little country village of Smedjabacken. Besides President Monson's Great-Uncle Elias, the family had known Nels Monson, Tom's grandfather. When Nels had returned to Sweden on his mission he had stayed at their home, and later he had received the tithing of Sister Monson's grandmother.[8]

Franz was a widower when he married Frances's mother, Hildur. His first wife, Sophia, had died in 1922, leaving him with three sons, Roland, Grant, and Karl. He and Hildur were married in 1923, and they had two children, Arnold and Frances.

Hildur Booth Johnson had been raised in the village of Eskilstuna in a home built by her grandfather. One of the marks of the Swedish people is their meticulous care for their homes and farms. Not only is that home still standing but, after visiting it many years later in Sweden, Sister Monson pronounced that it "still looks so nice."[9] In Eskilstuna, Hildur's family had a lovely home and the opportunity to make a good living. But they left their homeland when Hildur was eighteen, arriving in Salt Lake City with only what they could carry. They had chosen to gather with the Saints for the blessings that would come to their family. One of those blessings was Frances Johnson meeting Tom Monson.

By the time Tom left the Johnson home for his first date with Frances, he knew he had "halfway won the hand of the Johnsons' daughter." Next he had to convince Frances. He has said, "I am so grateful for my mother-in-law, a Swedish girl who became one of the first members of her family to join the Church. She indeed did seek the truth; and she indeed did trust in the Lord. And she brought into the world a lovely daughter who is my wife and companion, who I can assure you is her husband's keeper, and the keeper of her children as well—a noble daughter of our Heavenly Father."[10]

Frances was what her mother called "a quiet child, easy to get along with." She spoke Swedish, often used at home, before she spoke English, though she is quick to admit that she doesn't remember the language now.

She attended Emerson Elementary, Roosevelt Junior High, and then West High's archrival, East High. She and Tom were born the same year and liked many of the same things—being outdoors, enjoying nature, hiking in the mountains, and spending time with family. Tom found in Frances a young woman with a sense of humor. "She laughed readily," she had a host of friends, she was "charitable and kind," and she exhibited "a great deal of empathy."[11] Both were enrolled in institute classes. They were well suited for one another.

Frances's mother had taught her the same principles of charity and kindness that Tom's mother had taught him. "I remember my mother taking me into a department store when I was a little girl to buy me a dress and a coat," she has said. "It was during the Depression. Everyone was having a hard time, but the family next door was having an especially difficult time. My mother bought a dress for me and one for my little girl friend because she knew her parents wouldn't be able to buy one."[12]

Tom and Frances shared a love for the big bands that were so popular at the time, and they went to dances most Saturdays. They even had a chance to dance to the music of such legendary band leaders as Tommy Dorsey, Jimmy Dorsey, Stan Kenton, and Glenn Miller when they played in the area. President Monson still remembers the words to their favorite songs and has no qualms about quoting them and singing them.

Frances was light on her feet. One of her older brothers was quite shy and unsure of himself on the dance floor. He often took Frances to dances at the university so he could improve his steps and gain the confidence to ask a girl for a date. Those dance practices helped Frances hone her skills as well. She and her friends also performed Swedish dances at Lagoon, an amusement park north of Salt Lake, on Midsummer's Eve, a Swedish national holiday.

Tom and Frances often doubled-dated with friends from the Sixth-Seventh Ward, ending the evening at Don Carlos's drive-in having a barbecued beef sandwich and a pineapple malt. They dated often but did not "go steady"—at least, not at first.

New Year's Eve of 1944 found Tom and Frances and friends

at the home of Dick Barton for midnight refreshments. Dick's mother, Betty, had prepared more than a casual nibble—she had spread a feast, and they sat back eating and listening to records. But the evening was cut "short" when Frances announced she had to be home by 2:00 A.M. because she had to work the next day. "What kind of a company would expect you to work on New Year's Day?" Tom asked. "The Deseret News," she replied. She worked there in the copy room. Interestingly, Tom would come to know the Deseret News Publishing Company firsthand years later when he started a career there.

Though they enjoyed each other's company, Tom and Frances were not prepared to get serious. World War II still blazed in Europe and the Pacific, and every young man faced interruption of his life and schooling. "The daily newspapers carried the news of battles raging, men dying, cities being obliterated; hospitals filled with grievously burned and maimed servicemen."[13]

During the summer of 1944, Tom had taken a job at the naval supply depot in Clearfield, Utah, where he worked in the receiving division as a typist. After a month he was moved up to become an inspector, charged with examining boxcars containing valuable equipment that had been damaged. Tom was a quick study. When the chief complimented him, saying he was "his best inspector," Tom was more than flattered, he was stunned.[14] Even though his heart was not in the job, his work ethic was impeccable.

Tom entered military service in 1945, just as the British, French, Americans, and Soviets were carving Berlin into four sections. The war in the Pacific continued, and Tom had no choice but to enlist or be drafted. By enlisting, he could choose between the different branches of the service—navy, army, marines, or the one that paid the best, the merchant marines. Frances thought he would look best in a navy uniform because he was so tall and thin. His mother had read in the paper that the army had the most casualties. So the navy it was.

Ten days before his eighteenth birthday, Tom and his father entered the recruiting office in the Federal Building and signed him up. Two chief petty officers, "with many stripes on their sleeves indicating years of service," gave a rousing talk to the forty-four young men assembled; forty-two of them, including Tom, passed the physical exam. The recruiters extolled the merits of the regular navy over the naval reserve. They emphasized the benefit of the best training and schools in the four-year commitment and the navy's tendency to give those in the actual navy preferential treatment. There were no such assurances for those in the naval reserve, since their commitment was not for four years but only for the duration of the war plus six months.

Most of the group chose the regular navy. Tom was one of the holdouts. He turned for help to his father, but Spence was weeping and saying he didn't know anything about the armed service. Tom sent a prayer heavenward, earnestly hoping that the Lord would answer it, and He did. "The thought came to me just as clearly as though I had seen a vision, 'Ask those chief petty officers how they chose.'" Tom turned to the recruiter and asked, "When the choice was before you, which did you choose?" The man looked uneasy as he admitted that he had joined the naval reserve. Tom put the question to the other recruiting officer, whose answer was the same. "If the reserve was good enough for you," Tom said, "I want to follow your example."[15]

That proved to be an inspired decision. The war ended just months after he enlisted—Tom did not fight in the trenches of Europe or the sea battles of the Pacific—and his service to his country was completed at the end of one year. Had he been in the regular navy, his commitment would have been four years and his "entire life would have been altered." His understanding that "the door of history turns on small hinges, and so do people's lives," may have begun in that recruiting station in 1945.[16]

Before Tom left for basic training, his bishop recommended that he receive the Melchizedek Priesthood. Tom phoned his stake president, Paul C. Child, to set up an interview. President Child was known for his love and deep understanding of the scriptures. He was also known for his searching, detailed probing of the scriptures with those he interviewed. So when Tom called for an appointment, he was reasonably nervous.

"Hello, President Child. This is Tom Monson," he said. "I

have been asked by the bishop to visit with you relative to being ordained an elder."

"Fine, Brother Monson. When can you see me?" President Child replied.

Knowing that President Child's sacrament meeting was at six o'clock, Tom suggested five o'clock, hoping that the interview would be brief.

"Oh, Brother Monson, that would not provide us sufficient time to peruse the scriptures," said President Child. "Could you please come at two o'clock and bring with you your personally marked and referenced set of scriptures."

When Sunday arrived, Tom appeared at President Child's home on Indiana Avenue at the appointed hour. He was "greeted warmly, and then the interview began."

"Brother Monson, you hold the Aaronic Priesthood. Have you ever had angels minister to you?"

"No, President Child."

"Do you know," said the president, "that you are entitled to such?"

Again Tom said, "No."

Then President Child requested, "Brother Monson, repeat from memory Doctrine and Covenants section 13, which tells of the ordination of Joseph Smith and Oliver Cowdery to the Aaronic Priesthood."

Tom began, "Upon you my fellow servants, in the name of Messiah, I confer the Priesthood of Aaron, which holds the keys of the ministering of angels . . ."

"Stop," President Child directed. Then in a calm, kindly tone he counseled, "Brother Monson, never forget that as a holder of the Aaronic Priesthood you are entitled to the ministering of angels." He then asked Tom to recite section 4 of the Doctrine and Covenants: "Now behold, a marvelous work is about to come forth among the children of men. Therefore, O ye that embark in the service of God, see that ye serve him with all your heart, might, mind and strength, that ye may stand blameless before God at the last day . . ."[17]

Tom never forgot the spirit he felt in President Child's home.

It was "almost as if an angel were in the room." And the message of the fourth section he had recited would become more than words revealed in 1830—those words would become a standard for him in his service to the Lord.[18]

With Tom's military commitment looming, he and Frances had a serious talk. "I think I will come back," he told her, but with war no one knew for sure. He had classmates and friends who had not returned from the conflict. "It wouldn't be fair for you to just sit home," he told her as he contemplated his indefinite commitment to the navy. "Date while I am away," he suggested generously, an idea that would later cause him to ask, "What was I thinking?"

Tom's orders for active military duty were slow in coming. Week after week he would bid a fond farewell to Frances and to his family, only to find that his orders were not in the Friday mail. Finally, on October 6, 1945, he shipped out for San Diego. His family and friends came to see him off at the train depot not far from his house. John Burt from the bishopric came as well. Just before the train pulled out, John placed a copy of the Missionary Handbook in Tom's hand. Tom looked quizzically at him and said, "I'm not going on a mission." John answered, "Take it anyway; it may come in handy."

Tom adapted easily to the regimen of military life. He was not one to rebel at authority; he liked structure and had learned from his youthful pranks that the best policy was to stay out of trouble. For the first few weeks, he felt as though the navy were trying to kill him rather than train him on how to stay alive.

The first Sunday of basic training, the drill sergeant lined everyone up and announced, "Today everybody goes to church. All of you Catholics meet in Camp Farragut. Forward, march! Don't see me until three this afternoon. Now, all of you who are Jews go meet in Camp Decatur. Forward, march. Now, the rest of you Protestants meet in the big theater on the base. Forward, march."

Tom wasn't a Protestant, a Jew, or a Catholic. He was a Mormon, so he stayed in place, along with a handful of other men. He has said, "One of the sweetest expressions I have heard came from a petty officer when he said, 'What do you fellows call yourselves?' It was the first time I realized I wasn't standing alone."

The men responded, "We're Mormons."

The petty officer scratched his head and then directed them, "Go find somewhere to meet, and don't bother me until this afternoon." They marched away almost to the cadence of the Primary rhyme: "Dare to be a Mormon; dare to stand alone. Dare to have a purpose firm, and dare to make it known."[19]

That Tom Monson was a member of The Church of Jesus Christ of Latter-day Saints became well known. One of his fellow sailors, Eddie Foreman, who worked in the same office, later wrote in a letter to him: "The eyes of so many of us were watching you as the Devil did his best to lead you astray.

"We were out at La Jolla Shores having an Office-Beach party. Beer was being served. . . . You were kind of a natural leader even then among us. They would not leave you alone. . . . I can see you so clearly right now in my mind—that skinny, tall kid with your smile and sense of humor to laugh your way through saying no, so no one would take offense, pushing it away, repeating, no, no. How would it have hurt you? It would have hurt us, Tom—those of us who were watching you. The Lord could still have made you an apostle if you had taken that beer, but what would it have done to us who remember that moment in time so many years ago? How grateful I am to you, President Monson, for that example, for the stalwart you were as a young man in the military service and for what it means to me as I raise my hand in the square to sustain you without any reservation whatsoever."[20]

When the two reunited many years later, Eddie said to Tom, "You seemed calm under stress and perfectly in control, with complete trust in your religious beliefs." Eddie had wanted that for himself, so he had studied the gospel and had become a member of the Church. Tom had known neither of his friend's conversion nor of the role he himself had played in it.[21]

One day the drill officer announced, "All of you who know how to swim will be permitted to go into San Diego for your first liberty. Those of you who don't know how to swim will remain here at the base and undertake a course in swimming, because such is required before you graduate from boot camp."[22] The navy didn't take anyone's word that he could swim. Before boarding the buses, the sailors had to strip down, jump into the deep end of the pool, and swim to the shallow end. There were some in the crowd anxious to go to town who had lied, thinking they would not actually be expected to prove they could swim. The petty officer let those men flail frantically in the deep end before he reached out, almost reluctantly, with a safety pole to pull the hapless recruits—one after another—to the side. Tom's swimming prowess made it easy for him to pass the test.

San Diego had a sea of white sailor hats dotting nearly every square foot of downtown. When Tom stepped from the bus he was quickly approached by those who promised to escort him and his buddies to the strip-tease theater, the houses of prostitution, and, oddly enough, the evangelical churches. He and his pals chose simply to stroll about the city.

The navy conducted a classification test to determine the aptitude of each recruit. One hundred was a perfect score. Tom scored perfectly on the ability to identify flag semaphore code and Morse code. He quickly grasped "able . . . baker . . . charley . . . dog . . . easy . . . fox." (He can still race through the list, complete with hand motions.) His recognition of the vessels of the different fleets—Japanese, German, Italian, British, French, and U.S.—was flawless. His proficiency in identifying the actual type of vessel was also excellent. In the test, a vessel would show on a screen and the sailor would have to press the button and give identification. "For example, a destroyer escort—DE—you would say DE Japan or DE USA. A Two Stacker would be a Light Cruiser, and you would say Light Cruiser French, Light Cruiser Italian. And BB was Battleship—always easy to identify because they were so large."[23]

Tom's mechanical aptitude was not as stellar. With some self-deprecation he revealed that his score on that test was somewhat below perfect. When he had a chance to look through his own file, he found that the testing data confirmed what he already knew: "Not mechanically minded."[24]

Each day began with the clear sound of the bugle playing

reveille and ended with the mournful sound of taps in the evening, indicating "lights out." Tom couldn't help but reflect on the Grant Elementary School Drum and Bugle Corps playing those familiar tunes, which to him had come to represent "duty, honor, and country." Honor stands right next to duty in President Monson's mind. "It is an expression of our inner selves, a commitment to do that which is right," he has said.[25]

He witnessed graft and corruption among sailors and officers but was particularly touched by the opposite, as exhibited in the faith of an eighteen-year-old seaman, Garth Hallet, who every night knelt by his bed to pray. A sailor whose last name was Jonitz returned to the barracks one night in a drunken and hostile mood. Garth, a Catholic, was kneeling in prayer. The surly Jonitz shoved and then kicked him. Immediately two others jumped down from their bunks, grabbed Jonitz, and took him to the shower room. When they returned, they said Jonitz had "slipped on a bar of soap and was injured." He spent three days in sick bay, and "never again did he speak or act disrespectfully toward another person who was honoring his religion."

Tom "admired Garth Hallet for kneeling in prayer. We Mormon boys would pray while lying on our bunks, but he had the courage and felt the need to get out of the bunk and, in view of all, kneel down and offer his personal prayers."[26]

During basic training the company commander instructed the recruits that the best way to pack clothing in a sea bag was to place a hard, rectangular object at the bottom of the bag. That way clothes would stay firm. Tom had just the right hard, rectangular object—the Missionary Handbook. For twelve weeks it served a useful purpose.

But it didn't just sit in the bag. The night before their Christmas leave, the barracks room was quiet except for the moans of Tom's buddy Leland Merrill, a fellow Mormon, in the adjoining bunk.

"What's the matter, Merrill?" Tom asked.

He replied, "I'm sick, really sick."

Tom suggested he get to the base dispensary, but he and Merrill both knew that would mean they wouldn't let him go home for Christmas. The moans got louder and more frequent. In desperation, Merrill whispered, "Monson, aren't you an elder?" Tom acknowledged that he was. Merrill then said, "Give me a blessing."

Tom had never given a blessing; he had never seen anyone give a blessing to the sick. He prayed for help, and an answer came, "Look in the bottom of your sea bag." There, at two o'clock in the morning in a barracks of 120 sailors, many of them aware something was going on, Tom "emptied on deck the contents of the bag." He then took to the barracks' night-light that hard, rectangular object he had stashed at the bottom, the Missionary Handbook, and read how to bless the sick. "With about 120 curious sailors looking on," Tom blessed Merrill that he would get well. Before he could stow his gear, "Leland Merrill was sleeping like a child." The next morning as they prepared to ship out for home, Merrill, with a broad smile on his face, said, "Monson, I'm glad you hold the priesthood."[27]

At the end of his twelve weeks of basic training in San Diego, Tom was granted a ten-day leave. Wanting to surprise Frances and his family, he came home unannounced. It was Friday, and he called Frances immediately to ask her out for that night. She declined; she already had a date. He asked her to break it, but her sense of propriety and commitment won out. However, they dated almost every night that followed. A few months later, on another ten-day leave, he backtracked on his earlier magnanimous suggestion that she date other men in his absence.

Tom enjoyed the navy. He was assigned to what was known as "Ship's Company" at the San Diego Naval Training Center. His shorthand skills got him assigned as a yeoman—secretary to the commanding officer of the classification division. "This was a rather high honor, since those who made the assignments had their pick of all the recruits flowing through that massive facility." He became a trainee yeoman replacement for Howard Foy from Memphis, Tennessee, a rather dour, rough-speaking, chain-smoking sailor. Foy threatened him with sea duty when he mixed things up, but, as with Mrs. Shinas, the neighbor of his youth, Tom soon won him over and they became good friends.

At the end of the training, Foy handed him a large envelope. "Monson," he said, "in this envelope is a diagram of all the dozens upon dozens of four-drawer filing cabinets that line the entire south wall of the classification division. There are instructions in the envelope that give you all that you need to know about each of these files. Don't open it until I have been away from here forty-eight hours and hence have been discharged from the navy."

Tom waited the prescribed time and then opened the envelope to find that he need only concern himself with every fifth drawer in the filing cabinets. Foy had padded the filing cabinets with drawers and drawers of clippings from magazines and newspapers. The sheer number of files and the seeming complexity of the system insured that he, and only he—not his commanding officers—could navigate the volume of information.[28]

As a side note: Thirty years later the Monsons tracked down Howard Foy, took him a book about the Mormons, and invited him to a stake conference where Elder Monson was speaking. Both Howard and his wife, Lucille, came, bringing two friends with them. In his message during the conference, Elder Monson talked about his navy experiences and paid tribute to Howard. His words struck a chord, and Elder Monson watched his navy buddy wipe a tear from his eye. After the meeting, Howard and Lucille and the other couple came forward and Howard's friend indicated that the message had just about convinced him to join the Church.[29]

The classification office was a fit for Tom Monson, with his organizational skills. Occasionally he "worked the system."

"I remember a young man with whom I worked by the name of Olsen. He came up to me—red-faced and infuriated. He said, 'Monson, read this letter from my girlfriend and you'll cry with me.' I read the letter and it said something like this: 'So happy that you are now assigned in the classification division of the United States Navy. Since you've been in the navy, our mutual friend Robert from Minneapolis has been dating me, and I would feel it a great honor if you would arrange to have Robert assigned to a base near Minneapolis so that we could continue dating while you are serving there in San Diego.' Olsen turned to me and said, 'Do me a favor, will you? How far away from Minneapolis can you send this man?' I said, 'How about San Francisco?' 'Not far enough!' 'Well, how about Hawaii?' 'Not far enough!' 'Well, here's a ship going to Hong Kong, how about that?' 'Just right, just right.' I confess that we cut Robert's orders for Hong Kong."[30]

Tom wrote to his own girlfriend, Frances, every day he was in the navy to make sure she remembered him. "I was a romantic, still am," he says. He would go to the commodore's garden and pick a snapdragon to tuck into a letter he sent to her. He knew it would dry up, but it was the sentiment that counted.

He went to church on the base, "but it wasn't as good as being home at our own ward on Easter Sunday," he wrote his father. His letters were filled with the doings of an eighteen-year-old far from home. "Went over to the marine base and bought a pair of swimming trunks for $2.60" and then went "swimming on the beach of La Jolla," he wrote, where he experienced the "fun of riding in on the breakers."[31]

On New Year's Eve, he went out to Mission Beach to listen to music, but he didn't date the girls. He had watched many of his navy friends get involved with girls. One message given by President Heber J. Grant in a priesthood meeting Tom had attended in the Tabernacle stayed with him. "He said, in essence, that men who commit . . . sins do not do so in the twinkling of an eye. . . . Our actions are preceded by our thoughts, and when we commit sin, it is because we have first thought of committing that particular sin. . . . The way to avoid sin is to keep our thinking pure."[32] So Tom steered clear of relationships, contenting himself during that New Year's show with listening to the music from two bands trading off every half hour. They were big names, including Stan Kenton and Charlie Barnett, he remembers. "It was good music, 1944 music."[33]

Tom's military experience, while offered in the same cause, was nothing like the account that had so impressed him in his youth, that of the "Lost Battalion," the 77th Infantry Division in World War I, trapped behind enemy lines during the Meuse-Argonne offensive. Men volunteered readily, fought gallantly, and many died bravely in what was one of history's great rescue operations. The heroics were not lost on Tom, who saw the hand of God in that service.

Years later he would stand on an old bridge spanning the River Somme where the Lost Battalion had crossed as it made its steady but unhurried way through the heartland of France. He tried to imagine what the River Somme had looked like to the soldiers who had crossed that same bridge. Some came back; some didn't. Acres of neat, white crosses stand as unforgettable reminders of the toll of human life spent on the battlefields of Vimy Ridge, Armentières, and Nueve Chappelle. The words of the poem "In Flanders Fields" came easily to his mind:

> *In Flanders fields the poppies blow*
> *Between the crosses row on row,*
> *That mark our place; and in the sky*
> *The larks, still bravely singing, fly*
> *Scarce heard amid the guns below.*
>
> *We are the Dead. Short days ago*
> *We lived, felt dawn, saw sunset glow,*
> *Loved and were loved, and now we lie*
> *In Flanders fields.*[34]

Naval service left an imprint on Tom Monson that has surfaced many times. "The planners of war rarely face the suffering that the people do. It's when whole families and entire cities face suffering that we see the real horror," he has said. He has stood by soldiers who lost their sight, their limbs, even their will to go on. "We ought to be grateful for peace every day of our lives, but we ought to be vigilant to prevent the types of warfare, the aggressive behavior, the dominance of one military force over another that we have witnessed in the past."[35]

When the war ended, Yeoman Third Class Thomas S. Monson had to serve only six more months to fulfill his active duty commitment. His official honorable discharge—making him eligible for the GI Bill for his college education—was dated July 30, 1946. Senior Chaplain Ralph A. Curtis of the U.S. Naval Personnel

Separation Center wrote to his parents: "The great majority of servicemen are now returning to peace-time pursuits, to their families, churches and home communities. We are thankful that your son is one of them."[36]

President Harry S Truman sent a letter of thanks to the yeoman for his service. "To you who answered the call of your country and served in its Armed Forces to bring about the total defeat of the enemy, I extend the heartfelt thanks of a grateful Nation. . . . We now look to you for leadership and example in further exalting our country in peace."[37]

That fall of 1946, "Johnny did come marching home again, as did the Toms, the Dicks and the Bobs."[38] Under the GI Bill, young men thronged college campuses across the nation. With them came what they had learned on the fronts in Europe and the Pacific. They were more serious than before, more disciplined and hardworking. They were determined to move forward, doing well in class and preparing for their professions. Tom Monson was among them.

8

STARTING A FAMILY

My mother is the other part of my father's success story because she has been supportive of him in everything he's done.

ANN MONSON DIBB

LDER M. RUSSELL BALLARD, who began his studies at the University of Utah in the summer of 1947, remembers that there was "quite a bit of competition among the men on campus. They were older, more mature, and more experienced, and they were better students. So it was tough." Yet he recognized the value of learning from those who had been exposed to the rigors and traumas of war: "You heard things that you wouldn't have heard if the only people in the classes had been your friends just out of high school."[1]

Tom attended a business law class with one of the football team stars. The athlete never prepared for the oral recitations or the class discussions. "In the classroom, he was just a phony. He was clever, all right." Perhaps too clever. The final examination was "closed book." Tom's classmate came to class that winter morning wearing sandals. As the examination began, he placed his open textbook on the floor, removed his bare feet from the sandals, and, with toes saturated with glycerin, opened his textbook. Skillfully, with those "educated" toes, he turned the pages to find the answers to the questions asked. "He received an A grade, as he did in other classes. Nominated for honors, praised for his intellectual acumen, he passed the examinations of school but failed the test of manhood."[2] As he prepared for his comprehensive exams, the dean of his discipline announced for the first time that an oral exam rather than a written test would be given. The athlete failed and remained another year in school to fulfill his graduation requirements.[3]

Years later, standing before university students, President Monson said, "During the last half century, there has been in this country a gradual but continual retreat from standards of excellence in many phases of our life. We observe business without morality; science without conscience; politics without principle; wealth without works." He counseled, "Refuse to compromise with expedience. Maintain the courage to defy the consensus. Choose the harder right instead of the easier wrong. By so doing, you will not detour, but rather will ever remain on the way to perfection."[4]

While in school at the U, Tom began working afternoons and evenings on a wastepaper truck with his sister Marjorie's husband, college football star Conway Dearden. Tom was earning money so that he could purchase an engagement ring for his girlfriend, Frances Johnson. A printing position would have been safer. One afternoon, on the corner of Third South and Main Street, he fell from the top of the truck to the pavement, shattering both wrists. Given the severity of the fractures, he should have been treated by a specialist, but the attending physician set both arms in casts—without anesthetic. He was forced to withdraw from school and complete his term with home study. But he stuck with it, and that diligence paid off. Attending summer school, he graduated from the University of Utah in August 1948, just one quarter behind his entering class, though he had been gone for a year in the navy. He graduated with honors, which thrilled his mother but frustrated him. He recognized that "with a bit more effort and motivation" he could have received "high honors."[5] A lesson learned.

Tom had planned from the start to graduate from the School

of Business. "Marketing, management, corporate finance, and economics held a fascination that has never dimmed," he says.[6] He was not typical—he never changed his major. He completed the 93 hours in lower division classes to be admitted to the School of Business and fulfilled 183 total hours to graduate from the School of Business. His degree was in marketing, with a minor in economics.

Tom appreciated the business faculty. One marketing professor in particular, O. Preston Robinson, Tom considered to be one of the finest teachers he ever had. Dr. Robinson believed in "friendly persuasion," consistently inspiring his students with a spirit of "You can do it."[7] They worked hard in his classes; he opened doors for them. Dr. Robinson invited Tom to work as his assistant in teaching and grading papers. "He not only taught us at the classroom level but he was busy on the streets of Salt Lake City, in the retail establishments, in the wholesale concerns, and in the industrial empires to make room for his own trained graduates."[8]

Dr. Robinson had led Tom, lifting and inspiring him. Tom eventually taught a class at the University of Utah in sales management and later one in salesmanship with Dr. Robinson. The professor would be influential in Tom's career choice.

Meanwhile, Tom's relationship with Frances Johnson had continued to blossom. Tom proposed in the spring of 1947. He was from what he calls the "old school," which he describes as: "Serve your country, graduate from the university, and get a job before getting married." He recognizes that times have changed. He has said that he would "probably get married sooner" if he could go back.[9]

Tom took his mother with him to Davis Jewelry to pick out an engagement ring. He brought it home, showed it to his family, and then tucked it in his pocket for later. On the night he planned to ask Frances to marry him, he picked her up and they stopped off at his home. Seeing the two of them together, his four-year-old brother, Scott, announced with great glee, "Tommy has a ring for you, Frances." The story is legend in the family. There is some tongue-in-cheek speculation as to whether or not Tom has ever forgiven Scott.

Tom and Frances had been engaged for about a year when they set their wedding date for September 14, 1948. However, his mother, Gladys, was expecting a baby and was late in delivering, so the two postponed the wedding to October 7. Barbara Monson was born, and three weeks later Gladys was standing in Tom and Frances's reception line. On January 2, 1949, Tom gave his new little sister a name and a blessing in the Sixth-Seventh Ward sacrament service.

Benjamin L. Bowring, who would later serve as temple president in both Los Angeles and Hawaii, performed the marriage in the Salt Lake Temple in what was known as the mirror room. Large numbers of guests did not attend wedding ceremonies in those days; the only people there were Tom's mother, Gladys; Peter and Flora Hepworth, who were temple workers and members of the ward; and Frances's mother and father. Standing in for Elder Mark E. Petersen, who was out of town on assignment, Brother Bowring counseled the couple: "Every night, kneel by the side of your bed. One night, Brother Monson, you offer the prayer, aloud, on bended knee. The next night, you, Sister Monson, offer the prayer, aloud, on bended knee. I can then assure you that any misunderstanding that develops during the day will vanish as you pray. You simply can't pray together and retain any but the best of feelings toward one another." He then promised, "Pure love will fill the room and fill your hearts."[10]

They have followed that counsel.

Years later, when President David O. McKay, ninth president of the Church, extended the call to Thomas S. Monson to serve in the Quorum of the Twelve Apostles, he inquired about Tom's family. Tom related the formula for prayer that had guided them. President McKay listened, then sat back in his large leather chair and, with a smile, responded, "The same formula that has worked for you has worked for Emma and me all the years of our marriage."[11]

Tom and Frances greeted friends and family at the Johnson home the evening of their wedding. Vivid in Tom's memory are

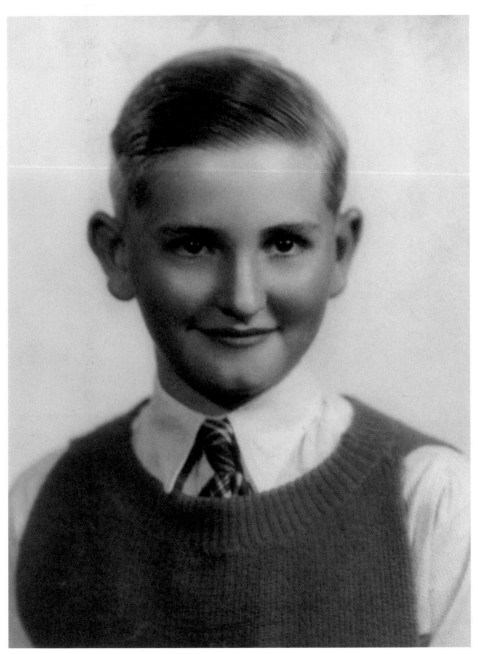
A young Thomas S. Monson.

Paternal family: Thomas S. Monson's great-grandfather Mons Akesson; grandfather Nels Monson; and father, G. Spencer Monson.

Nels Monson family about 1906. Left to right: G. Spencer (1901–1979), Nels (1867–1922), Grace Lucile (1903–1986), Maria Mace (1877–1935), Claude Niels (1905–1977).

Young G. Spencer Monson had to quit school
at age fourteen to help support the family.

Tommy, his father, G. Spencer, and his grandfather
Thomas Sharp Condie on vacation in California.

Tom's mother, Gladys Condie Monson, in her childhood.

Part of the Condie family. Clockwise from left: Blanche, Annie, Gibson, Margaret Ellen Watson Condie (Tom's grandmother), Gladys (Tom's mother), and John Robert.

The Condie sisters. Left to right: Gladys, Blanche, Annie, and Margaret.

Thomas Sharp Condie, Tom's
maternal grandfather.

Margaret Ellen Watson Condie,
Tom's maternal grandmother.

The Monson family home at 311 West Fifth South, with Tom's sister
Marilyn Monson Martin and her infant son, 1967.

Tommy Monson, 1928.

Sister Marge and Tommy in a cart pulled by a goat.

Tommy and sister Marge on a family
vacation at Ocean Park, California.

Tommy at the beach in California.

Tommy on his tricycle at the Fifth South home.

Vivian Park in Provo Canyon, where Tommy and his family spent every summer. He still visits the cabin regularly.

The Condie clan at Vivian Park. Left to right: Vera Stewart Swertfager (neighbor at Vivian Park), Uncle John Nielson, Aunt Margaret Condie Nielson, Mother Gladys, Father Spence, Grandmother Margaret Ellen Watson Condie holding Tommy Monson, Grandfather Thomas Sharp Condie (behind), sister Marjorie Monson (in front), cousin Helen "Penny" Nielson, one of the Phillips girls, Uncle Jack Condie, cousin Thelma Condie.

At home on Fifth South on his wooden pony.

Living out his dream of being a cowboy.

Cousins posing at a photo gallery in Ocean Park, California.
Left to right: Jack Carman, Richard Carter, and Tommy.

The Sixth-Seventh Ward Sunday School class of 1941. Tom, front row, second from right; teacher, Lucy Gertsch, back row, fourth from left.

Tom, at age thirteen, with his catch of the day at Vivian Park.

Fishing in Star Valley, Wyoming, with son Clark, July 19, 1971.

Frances at the University of Utah.

Tom at graduation from West High School.

Public Schools

SALT LAKE CITY, UTAH

Report of School Progress
in the
Articulating Unit

19 40 -19 40
2nd Semester

Pupil Mensen Tommy

School HORACE MANN HIGH

Home Room Teacher Sarah Ann Pardell

Principal Gertrude Arbuckle

TO PARENTS

This report shows the estimates of the results being achieved by this pupil in the classroom work in the school and indicates probable rate of progress through the regular school program.

Parents are requested to sign this report and to confer with teachers when the pupil's progress does not appear to be satisfactory. If more detailed information is desired it will be given by the principal upon request. Parents are invited to visit the school as often as possible. The signature of the parent merely indicates that the report has been examined. It does not necessarily mean indorsement of the report.

L. JOHN NUTTALL, JR.
Superintendent of Schools

Form 263 B —10-6-38—8000

SCHOLARSHIP, CITIZEN

ITEM	*INDEX OF ACCOMPLISHMENT				DET
	REPORT PERIOD				FIRST
	1st	2nd	3rd	4th	
English	S	S	S	S	Sarah Ann Pardell
Math	S	S	S	S	C. McLeod
Eng. Cook	S	S	S	S	B. Aysart
Art	S	S	S	S	Hoyer
Gen. Shop	S	S	S	S	C. S. Fairbank
Music Reading	S	S	S	S	B. Kendall
Phys. Ed. 3	S	S	S	S	A. C. Cawkes
Natural Science	S	S	S	S	M. Sanford

Adaptability					
Cooperation					
Creativeness					
Dependability					
Effort					
Self-Control					
Work Habits					

	1st	2nd	3rd	4th
School Days	24	20	20	28
Days Present	24	20	20	28
Times Tardy			0	

*INDEX OF ACCOMPLISHMENT—S means that achievement is SATISFACTORY
NS means that achievement is NOT SATIS

Rate of

STATUS	REPORT PERIOD			
	1st	2nd	3rd	4th
Pupil is making normal grade progress				
Pupil will probably require more than the normal amount of time				
Pupil may need special program adjustment				

Tom's report card from Horace Mann Junior High in 1940.

SALT LAKE CITY HIGH SCHOOLS

WEST HIGH SCHOOL

This Certifies that **THOMAS S. MONSON** HAVING COMPLETED THE STUDIES PRESCRIBED BY THE BOARD OF EDUCATION FOR GRADUATION FROM THE HIGH SCHOOL AND HAVING CONDUCTED HIMSELF IN A SATISFACTORY MANNER THROUGHOUT THE COURSE IS HEREBY AWARDED THIS

DIPLOMA

GIVEN AT SALT LAKE CITY, UTAH
THIS EIGHTH DAY OF JUNE 1944

Ivan L. Baker
PRINCIPAL

James T. Worlton
SUPERINTENDENT OF SCHOOLS

D. D. Stockman
PRESIDENT OF BOARD OF EDUCATION

SEAL OF THE SALT LAKE HIGH SCHOOLS
NOBIS NON CONSTANTIA NATIOS

Tom attended West High School and graduated, as he describes it, "into the war."

Tom joined the navy in 1945 and was stationed in San Diego, California.

At brother Scott's wedding, October 7, 1966. Standing, left to right: Barbara,
Scott, Marilyn, Bob, Tom, Marjorie; seated: Gladys and Spence.

G. Spencer and Gladys Condie Monson in 1971.

the words of one of his Swedish aunties, then eighty years old. Short in stature, she reached up and pulled her nephew down so she could congratulate him. "Oh, Tom," she said, "I am glad you have married a Swede." The Scandinavians are fiercely nationalistic, and when Tom married Frances, he married all the traditions of Sweden as well. He has embraced most of them, although he never managed to develop a taste for lutefisk, pickled fish.[12]

Due to the rush of young families getting settled following the war, housing was scarce when the Monsons were married. The young couple moved into the Condie family's terrace of apartments at 508 South 200 West, in a unit where his Aunt Annie and Uncle Rusty had lived. Rent was twenty-five dollars a month, which left some cash for the newlyweds to use in redecorating. The apartment had a coal stove in the kitchen, a coal Heatrola in the living room, and an icebox on the back porch. There was no water heater except the water jacket connected to the coal stove. That first year, Tom arranged for a natural gas line into the house; a gas stove would replace the coal-burning range, and a gas-operated Heatrola would heat the living room. Tom and Frances felt like royalty: "Gone were the cold days and nights." Even today, they "appreciate a warm house."[13]

Tom was employed at the time as manager of the classified advertising department at the Deseret News, and Frances worked in the payroll section of J. C. Penney, a large national department store. Both worked downtown and often went home the five blocks for lunch, where they opened a can of Franco-American Spaghetti and listened to western songs on the radio. One of their favorites was Eddie Arnold's "Anytime."[14]

Tom was serving as the ward clerk when they married. In 1949, in a bishopric meeting, he listened to the bishop lament about the low attendance in the YMMIA and the fact that they needed a new superintendent. Tom spoke up and said that he didn't know whom they were going to get, but he felt sorry for the man; only ten people had been at the MIA adult class that Tuesday.[15] He left the meeting to take roll in elders quorum but was summoned back to the bishop's office, where he was asked to be the new superintendent of the Mutual. He responded, "Who will serve as ward clerk?" The bishop said, "We'll work that out." Clerks were more plentiful than men who could inspire attendance.

Tom missed his duties as ward clerk but was successful bringing many out to MIA who had been lost.

By that time, Tom had rejoined the naval reserve, with the intent to acquire a commission as an officer so that if a further conflict should break out he would be an officer rather than an enlisted man. He attended drill every Monday night at Fort Douglas and studied hard to qualify for a commission in the navy. He passed every examination: mental, physical, and emotional. Finally, the letter came from Denver, Colorado: "You have been accepted to receive the commission of an Ensign in the United States Naval Reserve." He was thrilled, as was Frances.

But before accepting the commission, he was called as a counselor in the ward bishopric. Unfortunately, the bishop's council meeting was on the same night as his navy drill. He had to make a decision. At the time he did not realize it was one of the most important he would ever make.

What he did know was that he had in his hands the chance to be an officer. He prayed about it. He felt prompted to visit with his boyhood stake president, Elder Harold B. Lee. He explained how hard he had worked for the commission and how much it meant to him. Then he showed Elder Lee the letter of appointment.

Elder Lee paused and then said, "Here's what you should do, Brother Monson. You write a letter to the Bureau of Naval Affairs and tell them that because of your call as a member of the bishopric, you can't accept that commission in the United States Naval Reserve."

Tom's heart stopped. That wasn't what he had hoped to hear.

Elder Lee continued, "Then write to the commandant of the Twelfth Naval District in San Francisco and tell him that you would like to be discharged from the reserve."

Tom said, "Brother Lee, you don't understand the military. Of course they will decline to give me that commission if I refuse to accept it, but the Twelfth Naval District isn't going to let me off. A noncommissioned officer will surely be called up, with a war brewing in Korea. If they are called back, I would rather go

110

back as a commissioned officer, but I won't if I don't accept this commission. Are you sure this is the counsel you want me to receive?"

Elder Lee put his hand on Tom's shoulder and reassured him, "Brother Monson, have more faith. The military is not for you."[16]

Tom went home. He declined the commission and returned the forms to the office in Denver. Then he composed a letter to the Twelfth Naval District requesting a discharge from the naval reserve. Miraculously, it was granted. His discharge was in the last group processed before the outbreak of the Korean War. His headquarters outfit was soon activated and dispatched to Korea. Six weeks after his call as a counselor Tom was called to be the bishop of his ward.

That experience illustrated what President Monson has taught for years: "Decisions determine destiny." Decades later, he said, "I would not be standing before you, had I not followed the counsel of a prophet, had I not prayed about a decision, had I not come to an appreciation of the important truth: The wisdom of God oft times appears as foolishness to men. But the greatest single lesson we can learn in mortality is that when God speaks and a man obeys, that man will always be right."[17]

Tom was only twenty-two years old when he became the bishop of the Sixth-Seventh Ward, and from that point on, he and Frances rarely sat together in sacrament meeting. "She has been supportive from the day we married," President Monson has said. "She knew I put a lot of stock in that word 'duty.' I'm very mindful of responsibility. She knew that. She has never complained."[18]

After nearly two years of marriage, with no children in sight, Frances became concerned, wondering if she would ever be a mother. She decided she should obtain her patriarchal blessing, hoping it would relieve her mind on the subject. She and Tom visited Patriarch Charles Hyde, and Frances received her blessing.

"I first realized the truthfulness of the gospel and that our Heavenly Father knows us and loves us and knows everything we do when I had my patriarchal blessing," Frances has said. "As he placed his hands upon my head, he didn't say anything for a while, and I was frightened. I thought, 'I am not going to get a blessing. He doesn't have anything for me.' But as he started to speak and gave me my blessing, I had certain questions in my heart and in my mind, and he answered those questions. He had not known me before and could not have known what questions I had, and yet our Heavenly Father knew, and He answered the questions for me. President Hyde said, 'This blessing is given to you under inspiration of our Heavenly Father, which you yourself can feel.' And I knew that my Heavenly Father loved me, that He knew what I wanted and needed."[19]

Their first child, Thomas Lee Monson, named for his father and for Tom's mentor Elder Harold B. Lee, was born on Monday, May 28, 1951. The night before, Frances and many others in the neighborhood had followed a fire engine to a gigantic fire at the Utah Poultry Company on Fourth South and Third West. The next morning she delivered her first child.

That weekend, since Frances and the baby would be staying in the hospital for more than a week, as was the custom then, Tom went ahead with a fishing trip in Idaho that he had planned. He says he has never heard the end of it. His story is that Frances encouraged him to go, promising she would "just rest" till he was back. Frances has "mentioned" the expedition and its timing "many times."[20] He is a "serious" fisherman. But that fishing trip was a "serious" mistake.

Tom had "always favored the name Ann,"[21] and when the second little Monson, a daughter, was born June 30, 1954, there was no question what she would be called. Frances had a difficult delivery and little Ann had a hard start, but both mother and daughter made a full recovery before too long.

Clark, the third and final child, was not born until 1959, when the family lived in Canada as his father was serving as mission president there.

"I am very proud of you, Frances," Frances's father, a furniture refinisher, told her in 1953 shortly before he died. "I am proud of your husband, Tom. You will both receive many blessings because of your loyalty and devotion to the gospel, your home and family."

With their young family, the Monsons felt that promise. "Life was very good" to them.[22]

President Boyd K. Packer has observed, "You can't talk about President Monson without talking about Frances. She's a wonderful woman. She has supported him through all the patterns of their life."[23] Elder Richard G. Scott adds, "She is so loyal; she would do anything for him and for the work he has been called to do. They certainly have deep love for each other."[24]

Living in a family property on Condie's Corner, Tom and Frances established more than a home—they established a pattern of living. For years President Monson has quoted the Lord's instruction given through the Prophet Joseph Smith in 1832, that His people should "establish . . . a house of prayer, a house of fasting, a house of faith, a house of learning, a house of glory, a house of order, a house of God."[25] He and Frances set out to do that. "Where in all the world could we find a better blueprint to fashion the home, the house, the family—one's self?" he has taught. Such a home "will meet the building code recorded in Matthew—the house built upon the rock. It will withstand the rains of adversity, the floods of opposition, the winds of doubt everywhere present in our challenging world." In his classic style, he identified three "points to ponder" in establishing such a home where the Lord is the general contractor: "Kneel down to pray, step up to serve, and reach out to rescue."[26] This exemplifies the home he and Frances established.

For Frances, home has always been where she is most comfortable. From the very beginning of their marriage, she made their home inviting and serene—like herself. "Our homes are to be more than sanctuaries; they should also be places where God's Spirit can dwell, where the storm stops at the door, where love reigns and peace dwells," President Monson has told the Saints. He knows firsthand what that is like.[27]

9

"DECISIONS DETERMINE DESTINY"

He really has walked with the "kings" of the earth for a long, long time. And he has kept the common touch in a remarkable way.

ELDER ROBERT C. OAKS
Presidency of the Seventy, 2004–2007

THOMAS S. MONSON JOINED THE workforce on the cusp of what some have called "the fabulous fifties." Though the Cold War prompted further divisions between nations, and the conflict in Korea required drafting America's young men into the military again, at home Disneyland opened, the interstate highway system started laying down its grid, the civil rights movement got a boost on a bus in Alabama, Liberace and Lawrence Welk charmed viewers on television, and Perry Mason began his nine-year run of mystery programs. *Perry Mason* was then and still is President Monson's choice of television shows.

That he would work for a publishing company seemed natural, though the one who opened the doors for him at the Deseret News knew nothing of his journeyman training. On July 1, 1948, Dr. O. Preston Robinson, Tom's nationally recognized marketing professor, sent three of his soon-to-be-graduating seniors for interviews with Amos Jenkins, advertising director of the

Deseret News. He hoped at least one would be hired as a classified advertising sales representative.

Tom had options. He had excelled in school and entered a market hungry for his training. He had taught marketing at the University of Utah, and Dean Dilworth Walker invited him to join the faculty and teach full-time. After giving the post "prayerful consideration," he determined that his heart was in the work of advertising and marketing, not in teaching about it.

Big-name companies came to the University of Utah campus to interview those graduating. Tom went into his interviews well prepared. He received outstanding offers from Standard Oil of California and Procter and Gamble. He had also received an offer from the Deseret News Publishing Company. When he later counseled students that "decisions determine destiny," he had certainly seen that in his own life.

Tom considered, "If I accept the Procter and Gamble offer or the one from Standard Oil, I will be doing a lot of traveling, and I don't like to travel. I will not be able to go fishing on my favorite stream. I will not be able to hunt ducks or pheasants out on the marsh in the autumn. I will have to leave my neighborhood and my parents, aunts, uncles, and cousins. I have a young family." He then made his deliberations a matter of prayer.

His decision was a demonstration of faith and principle mixed with duty and responsibility. Salary issues and prospects of vacations on sunny beaches were not even in the equation. "There are factors within you and within me," he has taught, "even basic principles with which we have been imbued from our creation, which seem to call out and demand of us our best. Those particular years and those cravings and those bits of inspiration seem to be telling you and me, 'Seek the best in life. Look for opportunities where you can be of greatest service.'"[1]

He turned down Procter and Gamble and Standard Oil and took the position with the Deseret News Publishing Company, perhaps the least "exciting" of the three. He was appointed assistant classified advertising manager.

As it turned out, in the decades that followed, his Church responsibilities kept him from doing much hunting or fishing, and probably no one in the Procter and Gamble or Standard Oil organizations has traveled more than Thomas S. Monson.

That first year, the Deseret News launched an aggressive postwar expansion to broaden its market, introducing a Saturday morning paper and enlarging its staff in both news and advertising. As the evening paper went head-to-head with its morning competitor, the *Salt Lake Tribune,* circulation more than doubled.

Since Tom had already apprenticed as a printer, instead of coming up through the staff line he was placed in sales. He joined a "talented and individualistic group, including Amos Jenkins, a charismatic advertising director; Susie Miller, who knew every real estate agent and auto dealer in Salt Lake City; Ralph Davison, a hard-pushing manager of national ads; and Kenneth Bourne, retail advertising manager, who always wore a hat, indoors and out, hiding a lack of hair."[2] Within a relatively short time Tom was named classified advertising manager.

As part of his training, Tom spent several weeks in the San Francisco Bay area, working one week at the *San Francisco Chronicle,* another at the *San Francisco Examiner,* another at the *Oakland Tribune,* and one at the *Oakland Post-Inquirer.* He lived at the Hotel California for that long month and quickly tired of being away from home. If anything, that stint reaffirmed that he had been right to choose a position at home. He returned from California with innovative policies and procedures for classified advertising.

For years, the *Salt Lake Tribune,* a morning paper, had exceeded the afternoon *Deseret News* by many comparisons. In particular, the *Deseret News* ran a "poor second" in the classified advertising business. Though the paper had carried a classified section since the 1890s, the listings did not produce the readership or responses advertisers desired. Ever the optimist, Tom was undaunted. He has always contended, "In our chosen fields, the obstacles confronting us may be mountains in their appearance—even impassable in their challenge to our abilities. Press forward we must."[3] And he did.

As manager of classified advertising, with a staff of eleven, he set out to boost readership with a bold circulation campaign. He saw "selling a difficult product in a secondary position" as just the setting "for effective and hard work."[4] The highlight of that position was working with Robert Cutler in the creation and implementation of a promotion program he called the "Benny Beaver Action Ads." The new approach was wildly successful, and regional and national convention representatives from other newspapers, the San Francisco papers in particular, clamored to learn how to institute the same campaign—word for word. Tom spoke at Bob Cutler's funeral on August 14, 2000, and reminisced about those early years in his career when fine men such as Bob had helped show him the way.

He applied in his everyday work what he calls "Wisdom's Seven Watchwords: Vision, Patience, Balance, Effort, Understanding, Courtesy and Love." He applied them in his business career, in the community, in his Church assignments, and in his home. If these principles are followed, he has taught, "we will have happier lives, more fulfilling experiences and that satisfaction within our hearts that we have been the vehicle through which our Heavenly Father's power has been made manifest."[5]

And he sought to lift his associates' sights with a strict work ethic: "Complaining is not thinking. Ridiculing is not reasoning. Accountability is not for the intention but for the deed. No person is proud simply of what he or she intends to do. . . . Only the human mind has the capacity for creativity, imagination, insight, vision and responsibility."[6]

M. Russell Ballard, just returned from a mission to England, met Tom Monson in his father's showroom at Ballard Motor Company, 633 South Main. "From that time, I watched Tom Monson all through his life and was not a bit surprised that he would be called as a mission president and then on into the Quorum of the Twelve," says Elder Ballard. "I don't know of anybody in those days who had better people skills than Thomas S. Monson. Everybody loved him. He was able to laugh with them; he was realistic, down to earth. He knew all the dealers by their first names; they all knew him by his first name."[7]

In 1952, the Deseret News and Tribune organizations called a truce, of sorts, when they signed a joint operating agreement to reverse the financial losses both were experiencing. Elder Mark E. Petersen, general manager and chairman of the board of Deseret News, had helped engineer the pact. For this previously unheard-of move, they had to enlist Congress for antitrust legislation to allow the combination. As part of the agreement, the Deseret News took over the Tribune's *Salt Lake Telegram,* an afternoon publication, and *Deseret News* subscribers received the Sunday morning edition of the *Tribune.* It would not be the last reorganization for the two competitors.

The circulation and advertising wars that the two papers had waged for decades were over, and the prospect of both parties operating in the black looked promising. A joint agency operation—50 percent owned by each newspaper for thirty years— would handle production, circulation, and advertising, operating one set of presses instead of two, one mechanical department instead of two, one circulation department instead of two, and one advertising department instead of two. Both papers would be printed on presses on Regent Street, a couple of blocks from the Deseret News Richards Street offices, and the advertising staff would move to the Tribune building. That meant a merger of the classified staffs.

Tom was asked to terminate employment for half of his people, step down as classified advertising manager, and become assistant classified advertising manager in the new Newspaper Agency Corporation (NAC), with responsibility for real estate and automobile sales. He was named an officer of the new NAC. The move took him by surprise. He voiced his concern to the assistant general manager of the Deseret News Publishing Company, Preston Robinson, his former professor. Certainly he had more to offer than the current classified advertising manager of the Tribune, he suggested. Robinson agreed but indicated that the decision had been made.

Moving to what had been enemy territory was a leap of faith for this enterprising and increasingly visible advertising executive. The joint operating agreement, however, was a blessing to both newspapers, halting the debilitating quarrels that had consumed time, energy, and resources for a very long time. Still, tension and competition between the editorial staffs continued.

With the creation of the NAC, the Deseret News forfeited its right to publish a Sunday paper, which Tom recognized quickly as "one tragic mistake." In the coming years the worth of the Sunday paper tripled in value. Little did Tom realize then that in thirty years he would be the principal representative of the Church in negotiating a renewal of the Newspaper Agency Corporation agreement. He would be in a position to correct the mistake.

Tom's day off was Monday. In the classified advertising world, Saturday was one of the busiest days, so Tom's five-day work week began on Tuesday. He liked to go duck hunting on Mondays with his Uncle Rusty. Much more came from their hunting excursions than simply watching for ducks. Rusty and Tom furthered a camaraderie; Rusty "was a wise teacher and a sound philosopher." Though not a member of the Church, "he was a good man and honorable in every respect." They also took fishing trips on the Provo River, to Pinedale, Wyoming, and to the Strawberry Reservoir. Uncle Rusty ran a gas station, but he was always available to enjoy nature at every opportunity. "He truly appreciated the handiwork of God."[8]

In December 1952, Preston Robinson called Tom to his office with a new job proposal. He wanted Tom to return to what was then called the Deseret News Press and begin a training program to become Dr. Robinson's assistant general manager. He intended to have Tom spend a year or two working in the Deseret News Press division and then an equivalent period of time in the newspaper editorial division so that he would have a background in advertising, editorial, and commercial printing when he advanced.

Working at the Deseret News Press was like going home.

Tom had apprenticed as a printer at his father's business under Sheldon "Shelley" Weight. Tom was a quick study, and he had quick hands. "When you are an apprentice, you do all the dirty work, wash up the presses and do the menial tasks," he says.[9] Tom gained the reputation for never getting his fingers caught in the presses, which says something about his instincts and his laser-sharp eye. Tom and Shelley became lifelong friends, and at Shelley's funeral, Elder Monson praised his mentor "for being the kind of man he was" and setting the example of "such a wonderful work ethic" in a labor-intensive business.[10]

At Deseret News Press, thanks to his prior apprenticeship, Tom completed the outlined in-service in each of the departments in record time. But he felt that the highlight of his in-service training period was the opportunity to become "so close to all of the employees at the Press. These employees are some of the finest men and women in the world."

He understood what Elder Stephen L Richards meant when he said, "Life is a mission and not a career." He saw his work as much more than getting a project out the door on bid and on time. He really got to know the people with whom he worked. His journal reads like a who-was-who at Deseret News Press for decades as he said good-bye to them one by one, speaking at their funerals.

In no time, Tom was named assistant sales manager and then sales manager of the Press division.

In those years he forged strong ties with men he would serve with in the future as he oversaw the publication of Church materials. In particular, he got to know Gordon B. Hinckley, who directed the missionary office with its catalog of mission literature numbering well over one hundred items. One of Brother Hinckley's tasks was to keep an adequate supply on hand of all the items needed around the world. One of Tom's tasks was to help him. The two would plan what to print, how many to print, and when to print or reorder. "The biggest job was placing orders for the Book of Mormon," Tom recalls.[11] During the 1950s the press printed new, revised, or updated translations of the Book of Mormon in Spanish (1950 and 1952), Portuguese (1951, 1952, and 1958), French (1952 and 1959), Finnish (1952), German (1955 and 1959), Japanese (1957), Norwegian (1959), and Swedish (1959). That intense exposure to the printing of the scriptures was just the beginning of Tom's involvement in publication of the Church's holy writ.

He also became well acquainted with those for whom he

published books. In his role as sales manager, he developed a very good working relationship with Deseret Book Company. Alva Parry had been named general manager at Deseret Book, and the two worked closely together. One of the first things Tom did was to become acquainted with the books published by Deseret Book and to analyze each one. He updated the inventory system, since the printed but unbound books were stored at the Deseret News Press. He found that the company was in transition, going from publishing a few titles a year to producing many. He noted that they used a reduced size of type and margins in order to get more on the page. He recommended increasing the type size from 10 point to 12 and increasing the size of the books to six inches by nine inches, making the final published product more inviting to read. He also recommended using different designs and more color on the book jackets. Each of his suggestions was implemented, and Elder Adam S. Bennion's book *The Candle of the Lord* garnered first prize for production in a national book publishers competition.

"Books became friends," he explains. "As I watched them go from manuscript to finished product, I was in on the creation, and I felt a love for a book, even before I read it."[12]

Alva Parry relied on him to keep track of the inventory of Deseret Book Company's books, which helped Deseret News Press monopolize Deseret Book's business. Many of the books were written by General Authorities, and in the process of their printing, Tom developed strong associations with these Church leaders. President David O. McKay, President Stephen L Richards, President J. Reuben Clark, Jr., Elder Mark E. Petersen, and Elder LeGrand Richards all appreciated his trained eye for detail, composition, type, paper, and design. Tom's experiences with "some of the most noble of God's leaders" are highlights in his life, for they gave him direction "from the brilliance of their minds, from the depths of their souls, and from the warmth of their hearts."[13]

President J. Reuben Clark, Jr., was such a man. The two shared humble backgrounds and high ideals, a devotion to welfare principles, and a prodigious work ethic. Both were avid readers and whole-souled disciples of Christ. President Clark grew up in

Grantsville, Utah, where "simple food and simple pleasures were the order of the day; but there existed also high ambitions."[14] He served for over two and a half decades in the First Presidency under Presidents Heber J. Grant, George Albert Smith, and David O. McKay.

Tom Monson and Alva Parry were summoned one day to President Clark's office, where he pushed back the rolltop on a desk in his office to reveal stacks of yellow legal pads, their edges curled and pages fanned from constant use. President Clark outlined a publishing project, and for eight months he and Tom met almost daily at 2:00 P.M. to prepare his book, a harmony of the New Testament Gospels. That book was clearly President Clark's life's work. He had begun the manuscript as a law student, and it showed. Those stacks of yellow legal pads were filled with the handwritten notes and analysis that ultimately became the monumental work *Our Lord of the Gospels*. President Clark was known for his attention to exactness and his passion for detail. Even something seemingly small, such as the letter *s* inverted on the printed page, would distract him and cause him angst. Tom, with his printer-proofreader eye, would share with him that insistence on accuracy. In their daily interchanges they discussed much more than what was included in the books of Matthew, Mark, Luke, and John. They talked at length of the doctrines and ministry of Jesus Christ.

In President Monson's library is a personally inscribed, leather-bound copy of this classic harmony of the four New Testament Gospels. The section entitled "The Miracles of Jesus" brings back to President Monson's mind, as if it were yesterday, a poignant day when President Clark asked him to read aloud several of these accounts while he sat back in his large leather chair and listened. That was a day in Tom's life "never to be forgotten."

"President Clark asked me to read aloud the account found in Luke concerning the man filled with leprosy. I proceeded to read:

"'And it came to pass, when he was in a certain city, behold a man full of leprosy: who seeing Jesus fell on his face, and besought him, saying, Lord, if thou wilt, thou canst make me clean.

"'And he put forth his hand, and touched him, saying, I will:

be thou clean. And immediately the leprosy departed from him.' [Luke 5:12–13.]

"He [President Clark] asked that I continue reading from Luke concerning the man afflicted with palsy and the enterprising manner in which he was presented for the attention of the Lord:

"'And, behold, men brought in a bed a man which was taken with a palsy: and they sought means to bring him in, and to lay him before him.

"'And when they could not find by what way they might bring him in because of the multitude, they went upon the housetop, and let him down through the tiling with his couch into the midst before Jesus.

"'And when he saw their faith, he said unto him, Man, thy sins are forgiven thee.' [Luke 5:18–20.]

"There followed in the scriptural account snide comments from the Pharisees concerning who had the right to forgive sins. Jesus silenced their bickering by saying:

"'What reason ye in your hearts?

"'Whether [it] is easier, to say, Thy sins be forgiven thee; or to say, Rise up and walk?

"'But that ye may know that the Son of man hath power upon earth to forgive sins, (he said unto the sick of the palsy,) I say unto thee, Arise, and take up thy couch, and go into thine house.

"'And immediately he rose up before them, and took up that whereon he lay, and departed to his own house, glorifying God.'" [Luke 5:22–25.]

As Tom read, President Clark removed a handkerchief from his pocket and wiped the tears from his eyes. He commented, "As we grow older, tears come more frequently." Tom said later, "After a few words of good-bye, I departed from his office, leaving him alone with his thoughts and his tears."[15]

Those spirit-filled moments of tutoring, those hours overflowing with gratitude to the Lord for His divine intervention to relieve the suffering, heal the sick, lift the weary, even raise the dead were not lost on Tom, himself a young bishop dealing with an overabundance of such issues.

Putting the final touches on his research, President Clark

indicated that he wasn't certain about one particular section relating to the number of times the Savior appeared following His resurrection. "Let me think about it over the weekend," he said. He was going out to his farm in Grantsville, west of Salt Lake, to clear his mind and resolve the issue. That Sunday morning the phone rang at the Monson home and Frances answered. The caller said, "Is Bishop Monson home?"

She replied, "No, he's at church."

The caller asked, "Do you think a bishop ought to be in church on Sunday?"

Frances no doubt wondered, "Who is this?" With composure, she responded, "Oh, I would think so."

The caller said, "I would agree with you. This is President J. Reuben Clark. Would you have Brother Monson call me when he returns?"

When Bishop Monson called back, President Clark said simply, "Tom, you may remove the question mark from the number I gave you. It is correct."

Tom would later note, "I felt President Clark had received a confirmation by the Spirit as well as through his research regarding the question which he had about the manuscript."[16]

Tom also shepherded two important books through to final printing for Elder LeGrand Richards: *A Marvelous Work and a Wonder* and *Israel, Do You Know?* The unedited manuscript of *A Marvelous Work and a Wonder*, he later explained, read the way Elder Richards spoke: "It was almost all one long sentence!"[17] Elder Richards taught Tom about the value of unselfish service when he refused a royalty for his books. Elder Richards believed, as did Tom, "We are not simply filling a job. We can indeed seek to excel and bring credit to the Church in the process. We can be pillars in the community; we can be the pivot point around which other Latter-day Saints will have opportunities. We can achieve for our families blessings and benefits if we have the vision to see the end from the beginning."[18]

There would come a time when Tom would author many of his own books, including *Pathways to Perfection* in 1973; *Be Your Best Self*, 1979; *Favorite Quotations from the Collection of Thomas S.*

Monson, 1985; *Live the Good Life,* 1988; *Inspiring Experiences That Build Faith: From the Life and Ministry of Thomas S. Monson,* 1994; and *Faith Rewarded: A Personal Account of Prophetic Promises to the East German Saints,* 1996; plus a number of small booklets and even an illustrated book that has become a Christmas classic, *A Christmas Dress for Ellen,* 1998. In 1985 he privately published an autobiography, *On the Lord's Errand,* for family members.

From his mentors, Tom learned more than just how to operate a printing business. The general manager of the Deseret News Press was Louis C. Jacobsen, a Danish immigrant who had attended school only to the third grade. He taught Tom much. Louis had served as bishop of the neighboring Fifth Ward in the same stake and had, like so many, faced poverty and ridicule growing up. "In Sunday School one Sabbath morning," wrote Tom, "the children made light of his patched trousers and his worn shirt. Too proud to cry, young Louis fled from the chapel, stopping at last, out of breath, to sit and rest on the curb that ran along Third West Street in Salt Lake City. Clear water flowed in the gutter next to the curb where Louis sat. From his pocket he took a piece of paper that contained the outlined Sunday school lesson and skillfully shaped a paper boat which he launched on the flowing water. From his hurt, boyish heart came the determined words, 'I'll never go back!'

"Suddenly through his tears, Louis saw reflected in the water the image of a large and well-dressed man. Louis turned his face upward and recognized George Burbidge, the Sunday School superintendent. 'May I sit down with you?' asked the wise leader. Louis nodded.

"There on the gutter's curb sat a good Samaritan ministering to one who was in need. Several paper boats were formed and launched. . . . Many years later Lou himself presided over that same Sunday School. . . . He never failed to acknowledge the traveler who rescued him along a Jericho Road."[19]

Though Tom learned quickly from Louis and others, when he was given responsibility to buy the paper for the press, one paper representative from a large company derided the appointment to Tom's father, Spence. He was certain that Tom would flounder in the assignment because he lacked "experience." Spence, who rarely praised anyone, was quick to retort that his son would "surprise the man and would do just fine."[20]

In March 1957 Tom cochaired the convention of the Printing Industry of Utah at Hotel Utah and another for Utah and Idaho; the next year he became president of the organization. He served as a member of the board of directors of the Printing Industries of America from 1958 to 1964, with a reputation as a "wise, forward-thinking leader who made countless friends from all corners of the industry."[21] In April 2009 he was inducted into the Utah Printers Hall of Fame.

At a printing convention in Dallas, Texas, in the late 1950s, Tom climbed aboard a sightseeing bus to tour what is sometimes called the "City of Churches." As they would pass one stunning church after another the driver would comment, "On the left you see the Methodist Church," or, "There on the right is the Catholic Cathedral." As they passed a particularly striking red brick chapel sitting on a hill, the driver drawled, "That building is where the Mormons meet." A woman spoke up from the rear of the bus, "Driver, can you tell us something about the Mormons?" He pulled the bus over to the side of the road and said, "All I know is that they meet in that building." And then he asked, "Is there anyone on this bus who knows anything about the Mormons?"[22]

No one spoke. Tom searched faces and realized that they knew nothing. So he pulled himself to his feet and for the next fifteen minutes gave what Peter described as "a reason of the hope that is in you."[23] Another oft-remembered scripture, "If ye are prepared ye shall not fear,"[24] gave him courage to speak out.

He joined the Advertising Club, the Utah Association of Sales Executives, and the Salt Lake Exchange Club. He shaped the Exchange Club's "Religion in American Life" program, which won first place in the national competition. When the Exchange Club national chairman came to Salt Lake to bestow the honors, Tom arranged for him to meet President David O. McKay. The three visited together for close to an hour, with President McKay addressing national issues of concern that signaled the country "was slipping from its moorings." The national chairman listened intently. When he and Tom left the President's office, the chairman stopped in the foyer of the Church Administration Building and said, in a solemn voice, "You know, David O. McKay looks like a prophet. He speaks as a prophet would speak. He thinks as a prophet would think." Tom noted the chairman's quizzical expression and said, "My friend, the reason David O. McKay looks like a prophet, speaks like a prophet, and thinks like prophets is simply answered, 'He is a prophet of the living God.'" For the guest, the visit had been "life changing."[25]

Tom quickly gained a national reputation in printing. "I have a printer's eye," he says. "If anything isn't lined up the right way, a letter is just a little off its feet, if the sheet isn't perfect, it just stands out and says 'help.'"[26] But it's not just the printing he notices, it's the people who put the printed materials together, who set the type and watch the press and work in the bindery. Such faithful workers evoke for him the words of the Lord: "Well done, thou good and faithful servant: thou hast been faithful over a few things, I will make thee ruler over many things: enter thou into the joy of thy lord."[27]

In 1948 the Deseret News Press had relocated from downtown near the temple grounds to the wartime Remington Arms Plant in an industrial area of Salt Lake City near 1700 South and Redwood Road. In 1967, nearly twenty years later, it would separate completely from the Deseret News. In 1980 the Deseret Press became the Printing Division of the LDS Church, giving up its name and its years of service to other commercial entities in order to meet the needs of a growing Church operation.

Tom oversaw the Deseret Press transition from letterpress printing to offset printing. Deseret Press was the largest plant of its kind west of the Mississippi, and the work poured in and out. The jobs were mostly massive projects, including telephone directories, full-color magazines, trade journals, catalogues, edition-bound books—many for Deseret Book—and a host of projects for the Church, particularly the Missionary Department.

When honored at a homecoming program in 1986 at Dixie College, Tom was presented with a book written by famed historian Karl Larson. Obviously the school was proud of the subject,

I Was Called to Dixie, and Tom was proud as well. He had printed the book. Such connections happened often.[28]

Years earlier, when Tom had instructed college students in business classes, he always emphasized the importance of being understanding. He would use the example of one of the employees in a bookbindery assembly line who was consistently tardy. His fellow workers lost patience. They had to wait, losing valuable production time, until he arrived, which was particularly irksome because they were all paid by the piece. The foreman, exasperated, announced, "This is the last time. If you are late again, don't even come into my office." The tardy worker nodded—and the very next day was late again.

Tom would ask, "If you were the foreman, what would you do?" "Give him another chance," some would reply. "Fire him," said others. Tom would reveal that both were wrong. He told them that the worker should be asked *why* he was late. "Don't take action until you find out the circumstances of the person," he said, urging the students to be careful to get the facts.[29]

One evening Tom got a call from the Utah Highway Patrol informing him that they had found a huge pile of paper, each sheet printed on one side, on the banks of the Jordan River in Salt Lake City. They assumed that the pile had come from the Deseret News Press because the sheets were printed with the Joseph Smith story. "That would be ours," Tom replied and indicated he would be right down. Sure enough, 20,000 sheets from the plant sat there on the ground. Tom surmised that one of the men on the night shift had gotten a little tired and quit watching, and that a piece of metal had broken off and gouged the pages as they fed automatically through the press. Every sheet of the 36-page pamphlet was unusable.

The morning after the telephone call, Deseret News Press truck drivers picked up the pallet and returned it to the plant, stacking the ruined paper conspicuously in Tom's office, as instructed. When the 3:00 P.M. shift came on, the man who had been responsible entered Tom's office, saw the stacks of paper, and said, "I guess I'm through."

"Yes, you are," Tom said, "because you didn't call me. I had to find out from the police department. If you'd called me, I wouldn't be nearly so harsh."

A year later, the man came back and described his plight. He was out of work, and his wife and children were suffering. "Do you have any idea what I can do now?"

"Yes, I do," Tom replied. "That was a year ago. Go punch your time card for the 3:00 shift; you haven't forgotten how to be a good printer." Tom explained that he had put behind him the visit to the Jordan River and so should the pressman. The pressman worked his shift until he retired.[30]

Tom's actions toward all of the employees were consistent with his philosophy: "You can live with yourself if you treat people the way you would like to be treated."[31] He encourages, "Cherish associations with others. I have learned everyone can teach me something. I love to learn something from each person with whom I associate."[32]

Such traits would serve him well in the many assignments to come in his life.

10

ALWAYS A BISHOP

As a young bishop in a ward which required much attention to needy persons . . . he rose to the occasion; and from his intimate association with the problems of the everyday world, he developed a sensitivity which has characterized his life.

PRESIDENT HAROLD B. LEE
President of The Church of
Jesus Christ of Latter-day Saints, 1972–1973

N OT MANY YEARS AGO, President Monson and his wife, Frances, drove slowly around each of the blocks that had once comprised the Sixth-Seventh Ward in the center of Salt Lake City. The streetscapes had changed. Of the houses and apartment buildings where the more than one thousand ward members had once lived, only three were still standing, and those structures looked nothing like the homes they had once been. One was overgrown with trees and bushes; one housed a small office; the other simply was boarded up. A large hotel complex spread across the block where the Sixth-Seventh Ward chapel had stood; the Growers Market behind it was gone. The area as he knew it had essentially been erased, and major connecting roads to freeways cut right down the middle of what once were the neighborhoods of his ward.

He parked the car, and the two just sat for a while. Precious memories filled his thoughts: memories of people who taught him so much, whose lives were part of his, whose needs were many and resources few, people to whom he would always be Bishop Monson.

Decades earlier, on Sunday, August 21, 1927, the Sixth-Seventh Ward of the Pioneer Stake received a new bishop, Richard D. Andrew. Gladys Monson was in the hospital at the time; she had just given birth to her first son. When her husband, Spence, came up to visit her in the maternity ward, he said, "Mother, we received a new bishop today."

Gladys, holding up their new son, replied, "And I have a new bishop for you."[1]

In fulfillment of those "prophetic" words, twenty-two and one-half years later, on May 7, 1950, Thomas Spencer Monson was sustained by the congregation as bishop of that same Sixth-Seventh Ward. Three days later, May 10, 1950, Elder Alma Sonne, an Assistant to the Quorum of the Twelve Apostles, ordained Tom to the office of bishop. He succeeded thirty-six-year-old John R. Burt, neighbor and lifelong friend, who was called as second counselor to President Adiel F. Stewart in the stake presidency of the Temple View Stake, which had been organized in 1947 from the Pioneer Stake. For just six weeks prior to his call, Tom had served as a counselor to Bishop Burt.

Tom became probably the youngest bishop in the Church at the time. There were 1,541 wards in the Church in 1950, most of them in the Intermountain West, western Canada, and southern California. The membership of the Church had passed 1.1 million but represented less than one-tenth of one percent of the world's population. Stakes in the Church totaled 180, 47 percent of them in Utah. The Church was organized in fewer than 50 nations or territories, with 43 missions and some 5,156 missionaries. The Church operated eight temples and was microfilming records in the United States and Europe for genealogy purposes.[2]

At age twenty-two, Tom was now bishop to his parents, his brothers and sisters, and many of his Condie relatives. He was definitely the youngest ever called to such service in his ward. The area of the Sixth-Seventh Ward had become increasingly transient but was still inhabited by some old-line families who had settled there in pioneer days. He described the ward as 25 percent established families such as his, 25 percent transient families, and the remaining 50 percent somewhere in between.[3] A 1935 local newspaper article suggested, "The people of the ward are of the poorer class. But there is found in the congregations and socials a spirit of humbleness and camaraderie not found in larger growing wards. Seemingly their common lot in life has brought the members of the ward closer together and created to a greater degree the spirit of brotherly kindness and love."[4]

Long years ago, when the Apostle Paul wrote an epistle to his beloved associate Timothy about the work of a bishop, he said nothing about age. "If a man desire the office of a bishop, he desireth a good work," he said, to which Tom often added, "a good *workout!*" Paul continued, "A bishop then must be blameless . . . vigilant, sober, of good behaviour, given to hospitality, apt to teach . . . not greedy of filthy lucre; but patient. . . . Moreover he must have a good report of them which are without."[5] Tom took the counsel to heart: "These words burned into my soul when I read them."[6]

For him, "The magnitude of the calling was overwhelming and the responsibility frightening." He recalls, "My inadequacy humbled me. But my Heavenly Father did not leave me to wander in darkness and in silence, uninstructed or uninspired. In His own way, He revealed the lessons He would have me learn."[7]

And learn he did.

President Harold B. Lee once described Tom's five years of service as bishop in the Sixth-Seventh Ward as equaling that of a bishop serving twenty-five years in any other ward, anywhere in the Church. Of his experience as bishop, President Monson has said, "I have seen hunger and want and I have watched wonderful people grow old and infirm. I developed very young in life a spirit of compassion for others who might be in need, regardless of age or circumstance."[8]

He had learned a powerful lesson before the Lord could use him in such a demanding position. He occasionally chose to go out on the first two days of the duck-hunting season if weather conditions were just right. On the opening Saturday night in the fall of 1949, he and his brother Bob surveyed the sky and reckoned the next morning would be just perfect for hunting: cold, blustery, foggy, and damp. The two woke early and headed north to the area near Corinne where they kept their boat. The drive was more than an hour, but they were heartened that the skies were overcast, the gray stillness just perfect for what they had planned.

They loaded their shotguns and trudged through the marsh to their boat, then stashed their gear in the flat-bottomed craft and dragged it into the water. Tom was in back, Bob in front. As Tom rowed, the craft struck a sandbar and Bob climbed out to push the boat clear. Neither can clearly explain what happened next, but Bob lost his footing, slipped into the mud, and pitched forward just as his 16-gauge shotgun fell from the bench in the boat and discharged, shooting straight at where Bob would have been standing had he not just lost his balance. The shotgun blast barely missed his broad back.

The two brothers looked at each other—ashen. Tom got out of the boat and sat down on the side; Bob joined him. Neither spoke for a long time. Finally, Tom said, "Let's go home."[9]

He never again went hunting, fishing, or anything else of the kind on Sunday. That "near miss" on the Sabbath in a marshland far from where he should have been got his attention. He had been protected but chastened "to measure up to the stature of [his] true potential."[10]

Just months later, Thomas S. Monson was called to the bishopric of the Sixth-Seventh Ward, and then, in weeks, he became the bishop, the "father" of the ward. "Why I was called as a bishop, I can't tell you," he has said. "Only the Lord would know that."[11]

The Sixth-Seventh Ward was a combination of two of the original nineteen congregations created by Church President Brigham Young on February 14, 1849, under the umbrella of the Salt Lake Stake, with John Smith as president. In 1862 members began construction of their chapel—rock by rock. Most other chapels at that time were frame or adobe, but the Seventh Ward chapel was constructed of stone, fifteen years in the building, and the ward was proud of that heritage. Bishop Monson often likened the structure to one of his favorite songs:

Firm as the mountains around us,
Stalwart and brave we stand
On the rock our fathers planted
For us in this goodly land.[12]

But that part of town was wearing out. By the early 1920s, railroads and industry began crowding out the Latter-day Saint population. New wards and stakes began to chip away at the enormous boundary of Pioneer Stake, and both the Sixth and Seventh Wards faced declining membership.

On November 12, 1922, the two wards, which for more than seventy years had sat side by side, were consolidated in a most unusual way. The bishop of the Sixth Ward stood at the pulpit of his ward building for the last time and announced that at 10:15 that morning they would leave that chapel forever. "We will march out the front doors and, to the music of the Poulton Brothers Brass Band, will proceed down Third West, then left on Fifth South, moving forward until we enter the doors of the Seventh Ward Chapel and become members of the newly created Sixth-Seventh Ward." At the same hour, the bishop of the Seventh Ward told his congregation, "In just a few minutes, the doors of this chapel will swing open as we welcome to this building the members of the Sixth Ward. I have just one word of advice to give you regarding these fine people: Be careful what you say about any of them; they are all related."[13]

Thus was born the Sixth-Seventh Ward. President Monson, who would shape and reshape wards and stakes for decades as a visiting General Authority, has remarked, "I don't think any other ward was ever created in quite that fashion."[14]

At the time Tom was called as bishop, another member of the ward who had served for sixteen years in the bishopric had expected to receive that assignment. Chagrined at being "passed over," he and his wife quit attending. No number of personal visits, calls, or prayers brought them back. Their sudden inactivity alarmed their son, who was then serving a mission. One Sunday, when the speaker scheduled for sacrament meeting was a dear friend of their missionary son, Bishop Monson again turned to the Lord and prayed for this couple's hearts to be softened. Little did he know that the missionary son had sent a telegram that same hour reading:

"Be at Church this Sunday. I know you won't let me down.

"Your Missionary Son."

As usual, Bishop Monson was standing at the door to the chapel before sacrament meeting. Just two minutes before the meeting was to start, the two came up the steps. He was thrilled. "Welcome home," he said. "We've missed you. We need you."[15] And they *were* needed. When Bishop Monson was released five years later, the husband was called as the new bishop to replace him.

Positioned on the wall of every office Thomas S. Monson has occupied since being called as bishop has been a familiar print of the Savior, painted by Heinrich Hofmann. "I love the painting, which I have had since I was a twenty-two-year-old bishop and which I have taken with me wherever I have been assigned to labor. I have tried to pattern my life after the Master. Whenever I have had a difficult decision to make, I have always looked at that picture and asked myself, 'What would He do?' Then I try to do it."[16]

He learned that lesson in a poignant way early in his term as bishop. On the evening of a stake leadership meeting, Bishop Monson took his seat with the other bishops in attendance. Earlier in the day, a classmate from the University of Utah had asked him to visit his uncle, a less-active member of the Sixth-Seventh Ward, who was gravely ill and in the hospital. Bishop Monson indicated that he had a stake priesthood meeting that evening but would pay a visit when it concluded.

As the session dragged on, he kept watching the clock, trying to balance a growing sense of urgency with the uneasiness of leaving in the middle of the meeting. During the closing song, he bolted. Arriving at the hospital, he hurriedly checked at the desk for the room number and then raced up the stairs to the fourth floor. As he came down the hallway, he could see a cluster of people and activity at the door of a room—his ward member's room. The nurse looked at him and said, "Are you Bishop Monson?"

"Yes," he replied heavily, concerned that perhaps he was too late.

"The patient was asking for you just before he died," she said.

Remorse consumed him. He had not responded immediately to the prompting of the Spirit, had let his obligation to attend a meeting take precedence over the needs of one of his people. From this experience Thomas Monson learned a lesson and a truth that has defined his life: "Never postpone a prompting."[17]

That first year as a bishop, he continued the chapel's much-needed "face-lift" begun by Bishop Burt, which included painting the building inside and out. The men in the ward installed new benches and a new sacrament table, carpeted the aisles and the stand where the pulpit stood, and hung new lighting fixtures. They also completely repainted the stake recreation center next door. Tom involved some of the older men in maintaining the chapel and caring for the lawn and flower beds for both buildings. All retired, with meager pensions, these men took their assignments seriously and felt they were "much needed."[18]

The Sixth-Seventh Ward building became a sanctuary for the members and for their bishop. President Monson has said that "every bishop needs a sacred grove to which he can retire to meditate and to pray for guidance. Mine was our old ward chapel. I could not count the occasions when on a dark night at a late hour I would make my way to the stand of this building where I was blessed, confirmed, ordained, taught, and eventually called to preside. The chapel was dimly lighted by the streetlamp in front; not a sound would be heard, no intruder to disturb. With my hand on the pulpit I would kneel and share with Him above my thoughts, my concerns, my problems."[19]

The new look of the chapel boosted the spirits of the ward members and attracted the attention of the neighborhood. Bishop Monson invited guest speakers to address the congregation, including Elder Mark E. Petersen, who had become a dear friend at the Deseret News, and President Joseph Fielding Smith, for whom Bishop Monson did extensive printing. Sacrament meeting attendance doubled, then quadrupled, filling the entire chapel each Sunday.

Elder Harold B. Lee, Bishop Monson's former stake president, noted the changes to the chapel and wrote Tom a letter congratulating him on his "accomplishments as bishop" in a "beautifully decorated meeting house," and more particularly "in the faith . . . engendered among the people through keeping the commandments of God."[20]

President J. Reuben Clark, Jr., had counsel for him as a new bishop. His words still ring true today. Reading from Ecclesiastes, he advised: "Fear God, and keep his commandments: for this is the whole duty of man."[21]

Bishop Monson was inspired by the words of the President of the Church, George Albert Smith, who counseled, "It is your duty first of all to learn what the Lord wants and then by the power and strength of your holy priesthood to so magnify your calling in the presence of your fellows that the people will be glad to follow you."[22]

Bishop Monson had served almost one year when President George Albert Smith died, April 4, 1951. David O. McKay was sustained as the ninth President of the Church April 9, 1951, with Stephen L Richards as his first counselor and J. Reuben Clark, Jr., as his second. This shift in position for President Clark from first counselor to second caused something of a stir. Up to that time, President Clark had served as the first counselor to both President Heber J. Grant and President George Albert Smith. President McKay had been the second counselor to both prophets.

President McKay explained why he had chosen his counselors in that order: "I felt that one guiding principle in this choice would be to follow the seniority in the Council [of the Twelve]. These two men were sitting in their places in that presiding body in the Church, and I felt impressed that it would be advisable to continue that same seniority in the new quorum of the First Presidency."[23]

President Clark spoke following President McKay, and his remarks taught a powerful lesson: "In the service of the Lord, it is not where you serve but how. In The Church of Jesus Christ of Latter-day Saints, one takes the place to which one is duly called, which place one neither seeks nor declines."[24]

President Clark's grace and his reverence for the opportunity to serve the Lord were not lost on Bishop Monson. He and the rest of the Church saw in action the testimony of this mighty man whose willingness to serve was an expression of his testimony. As Tom met almost daily in counsel with this veteran Church authority, helping him prepare his book *Our Lord of the Gospels,* he came to know firsthand this principled leader who became a dear friend and mentor.

The new Sixth-Seventh Ward bishopric set as their first objective to provide an assignment for each ward member. "A dignified call would be preceded by earnest prayer." And each call would include "an explanation concerning what was expected." As part of engaging members in the work of the Lord, the bishopric prepared and printed a small pamphlet that detailed "the pioneer history of the ward, the friendly nature of the membership and the need for all to serve."[25]

That pamphlet, *A Guide to Happiness through Gospel Service,* identified five fundamentals for successful teaching in the Sixth-Seventh Ward:

- A personality filled with religious quality: "Whatever ideals we would impress upon others we must first have realized in ourselves."
- A genuine interest in people: "There is no substitute for this human quality of interest and enthusiasm for truth, and of concern about and love for humanity."
- A knowledge of the gospel: "Have an understanding of the Standard Works of the Church, and a working knowledge concerning how gospel principles when applied can bring happiness into the heart of man."
- A wholesome attitude: "The teacher who succeeds accepts the standard program of the Church and is willing to abide by the counsel and instruction given by those placed in authority over him."
- A utilization of good teaching methods: "He finds the time who has a burning desire to do his duty well."[26]

The pamphlet concluded, "Due to the location of our Ward in the commercial and industrial area of the city, you will observe as you labor that a great portion of the Ward membership is in a state of transition, with many families moving to and from the Ward each month. This condition should not be a detriment to your work but rather a stepping stone. You will have a greater opportunity to touch more lives for good."[27]

Tom's ebullient personality and perspective are evident on every page. "To live greatly, we must develop the capacity to face trouble with courage, disappointment with cheerfulness, and triumph with humility," he encouraged. "We are sons and daughters of a living God in whose image we have been created."[28] He has continued to see every member as a teacher: "No person can escape the influence of his own example. . . . A mediocre teacher tells, a good teacher explains, a superior teacher demonstrates; but the great teachers inspire."[29]

President Monson is a man who likes things done just right, with precision and order. As bishop he followed the conventional procedure of ordaining a young man to an office in the Aaronic Priesthood during the opening exercises of priesthood meeting. One Sunday he invited a young man forward and read his name and the office he was to receive. The chair was placed so that the young man would face the audience, as was the tradition. "As we proceeded, a member of the high council, an ardent temple worker said, 'Excuse me, Bishop. Whenever I am participating in an ordination, I always turn the chair so the occupant faces the temple.' He then had the young man stand up, pick up the chair, and face it toward the temple. Then he had the youth sit down.

For the bishop, that was a moment of decision. Realizing that the brother was well-meaning, and at the same time not wanting to diminish the importance of the temple, Bishop Monson mustered his courage to follow the established pattern in a priesthood ordination and said respectfully, "My dear brother, that might be fine in some places, but in this ward the candidate faces the body of the priesthood." He turned the chair back to the original position, and the ordination went forward.[30]

Bishop Monson saw his transient ward as an opportunity to

reach out and bring back those less active. "Since so many of our members are constantly newcomers we must ever be on the alert to carry with us a friendly and helpful attitude."[31] Every month an average of thirty members moved in and thirty moved out. He kept in touch with them after they moved as best he could. Ten years later, on an assignment in Samoa, he tracked down a young islander who had once lived in his ward. He counseled the young man to get his life in order and live the principles of the gospel. As bishop, he extended calls to some ward members who were no longer attending, and many came back and remained active.

He had the help of the Lord in staffing a ward thin on leadership. On one occasion, he and his counselors pondered where they were going to find a new leader for the young men, at the time called the superintendent of the YMMIA. That morning when he was riding the bus down south Main Street, he had noticed a former member of the ward, Jack Reed, walking along the street by the post office. "If only Jack Reed still lived in our ward, what a wonderful superintendent he would make!" he commented in a later bishopric meeting. His first counselor spoke up, "Bishop, did you know that Jack Reed has just moved back into our ward?" "I didn't know it," Bishop Monson replied. "But the Lord did." That reliance on the Lord, that trust and faith, was born and bred in the Sixth-Seventh Ward, where they nearly had to "pray in" a leader.[32]

The Spirit prompted Bishop Monson with other callings of ward members as well. Stake President Adiel F. Stewart asked for each ward to recommend two capable Melchizedek Priesthood holders to serve as stake missionaries. It was hard enough to staff the ward, let alone to send strong members to serve in stake positions. When President Stewart said—in jest—"If those names are not forthcoming, I will have to requisition your counselors," Bishop Monson and his counselors went to the Lord in prayer. Then they turned to their card file, where they kept a three-by-five card on each head of family. "We would be fools to recommend Richard Moon," they agreed. "He is the finest assistant superintendent of the Sunday School we have ever had." As Bishop Monson tried to return the card to the file, it stuck to his fingers as if glued. He finally relented, "The Lord needs Richard Moon as a stake missionary more than we need him as an assistant Sunday School superintendent." He called the stake president and was asked to go see Brother Moon and extend the call. They found him not at his home on Gale Street but at his mother's house just blocks away. "Bishop, our prayers have been answered," Isabel Moon, Richard's mother, said of the call. Her son had been caught in the Korean War limitation on the number of missionaries called and had not been allowed to serve. "This is certainly from the Lord," she said. Brother Moon became an outstanding stake missionary and returned to the ward a seasoned leader.[33]

One earlier bishop of the Seventh Ward had served for more than forty years. That was not to be the case for Bishop Monson, who set a record for his youth but not his longevity, serving a more usual five-year term. And it certainly was not the case for his counselors in such a transitory ward. He had several over the course of his service: Joseph M. Cox, Alfred Eugene Hemingway, Donald Balmforth, Raymond L. Egan, and Elwood A. Blank.

Staffing challenges notwithstanding, he moved the work forward effectively in his part of the vineyard. The key to President Monson's service was and is his "great faith," explains Bishop H. David Burton, Presiding Bishop of the Church, who has worked with him for many years. When things are "very difficult or very complex or have some implications that are very challenging, he always relies on his faith. 'We're in the Lord's hands,' he will say. 'He'll take care of it. Do the best you can and don't worry.'"[34]

President Monson has always "had a love for the older people" —those easily forgotten at the top of the stairs or the back hallway, in the basements of small, dilapidated dwellings on obscure roads like Gale Street and Orchard Place. Those were his widows like those of the Old Testament Zarephath and Nain, though they went by other names: Zella Thomas, Elizabeth Keachie, Nel Ivory, Nettie Woodbury, Ellen Hawthorne, Edla Johnson, Jessie Cox, and so many more. There was the widow with three crippled daughters who was losing her home; those who sat by the window hoping family would come; the widow who called ahead to others on "his route" to say, "He's coming. He just left my home"; the one with a birthday or a heartache.

As the years passed, he stayed close to his widows. "To such homes he sends you and me," he has said.[35] "And while they might feel they benefit by my visit," he later noted, "I know I come away a better man for having spent perhaps a half hour or hour reminiscing with each of these sweet sisters who are in the late years of their lives."[36] He promised to speak at their funerals—all eighty-five—and he made it to every one, though he sometimes had to slip out of a meeting or fit the service in between general conference sessions. It was a remarkable feat, given that he was often on the road five weeks at a time in his assignments as an Apostle. But none of them left this world before he got home. The funeral file in President Monson's office started out as a small metal box with a stack of funeral programs inside. It grew to fill a file drawer with alphabetical listings.

One evening, driving down the street where an elderly couple lived, Bishop Monson felt prompted to stop for a quick visit. The couple had not been attending church, remaining instead in the shelter of their home. The wife, Emily, answered the door and exclaimed, "All day long I have waited for my phone to ring. It has been silent. I hoped that the postman would deliver a letter. He brought only bills. Bishop, how did you know today is my birthday?" Bishop Monson answered as he stepped into the modest home, "God knows, Emily, for He loves you."[37]

When the Sixth-Seventh Ward had its one-hundredth anniversary celebration, Bishop Monson was determined that his Grandfather Condie would attend the sacrament meeting. His grandfather—who held the office of a priest in the Aaronic Priesthood—had not been to Church for as long as Tom could remember. Tom shaved his grandfather, bathed him, and took him to the barber for a haircut and mustache trim to "doll him up for the event." He had his grandfather sit next to him on the stand. Midway through the meeting, his grandfather felt he had stayed long enough and attempted to get up and leave. Bishop Monson's persuasive powers were put to the ultimate test to keep

Grandfather Condie in his seat for the remainder of the service. After all, he was the oldest living member of the ward.

President Monson's life exemplifies counsel he has given to others: "Visits to the homes of quorum members, blessing the sick, helping a member with a project, or comforting grieving hearts when a loved one passes on are all sacred privileges of priesthood service."[38]

Augusta Schneider, a widow from the Alsace-Lorraine region of Europe, was another member of the Sixth-Seventh Ward. She was fluent in French and German but spoke haltingly in English. Tom continued his visits to her long after he left the ward. One year she presented him with a gift "of great value." Pinned to a lovely piece of felt, six by eight inches, were the medals her husband had received in World War I as a member of the French forces. "I would like you to have this personal treasure which is so close to my heart," she said. President Monson's protests were ignored. "The gift is yours," she continued. "You have the soul of a Frenchman." She had offered "the widow's mite." She died shortly after their visit. And he spoke at her funeral.

Like so many of his experiences, this account has a sequel. While attending the dedication of the Frankfurt Germany Temple, which would serve many German, French, and Dutch members, President Monson felt impressed to take along the precious medals. Why, he didn't know.

During a French-speaking session of the dedication, he recognized in his conducting notes that the members were from the Alsace-Lorraine region and that the organist's last name was Schneider. His mind immediately went back to that dear little sister and her medals, and he realized why he had brought them with him. In his remarks, he related the account of his association with Augusta Schneider, then stepped to the organ and presented the organist with the medals. He then suggested that since his name was Schneider, he had responsibility to pursue the family name in his genealogical activities.[39]

President Monson has often shared the verses of a poem that speak clearly of his service as a bishop and over the years since:

"Father, where shall I work today?"
And my love flowed warm and free.
Then He pointed out a tiny spot
And said, "Tend that for me."
I answered quickly, "Oh no, not that!
Why, no one would ever see,
No matter how well my work was done.
Not that little place for me."
And the word He spoke, it was not stern;
He answered me tenderly:
"Ah, little one, search that heart of thine;
Art thou working for them or for me?
Nazareth was a little place,
And so was Galilee."[40]

Each year at Christmas Bishop Monson worked in the "little places," presenting each of his widows with a box of candy, a book, or a roasting chicken. Some of them may even have gotten chickens he raised himself; he has nearly always raised chickens. While serving as the bishop, he created a welfare project for the ward, remodeling a chicken coop at 325 West 500 South at the rear of his Aunt Margaret's property. On a bright February day, the men in the ward poured the concrete, painted the coop, and constructed a run. Bishop Monson then purchased thirty laying hens, which the ward maintained, with the eggs going to the needy members. In a subsequent stake service project he arranged for the youth to give a "spring cleaning" to a different chicken coop, one operated by the Temple View Stake. They uprooted, gathered, and burned large piles of weeds and debris. By the light of a glowing bonfire, the cleaning crew munched on hot dogs as they surveyed the tidy surroundings. The chickens were not impressed. The noise and fire so disturbed the fragile, temperamental population of the laying hens that most of them went into a sudden moult and quit laying eggs for several months.

In the years to come, as an Apostle, a member of the First Presidency, and as President of the Church, President Monson would often hark back to his experiences with the needy in the

Sixth-Seventh Ward. At a Welfare Executive Committee meeting, Julie Beck, Relief Society general president, posed a simple question to the Brethren, "What is Relief Society?" President Monson responded with an experience concerning two Relief Society sisters, Elizabeth Keachie and Helen Ivory, who on their route to solicit subscriptions for the *Relief Society Magazine* had found Charles and William Ringwood, father and son, living in an old garage at the end of a tiny alley. Their visit to that last "house," with a shabby curtain at the one window, had little to do with magazine circulation, he said. They rescued two lost souls. To President Monson, the saving work performed by Relief Society sisters and others is not about programs or assignments. It's about people.

He has described gazing upon those two faithful and dedicated women, sitting on the bench at the funeral of Charles Ringwood. "I have contemplated their personal influence for good," he has said, "and the promise of the Lord has filled my very soul: 'I, the Lord, am merciful and gracious unto those who fear me, and delight to honor those who serve me in righteousness and in truth unto the end. Great shall be their reward and eternal shall be their glory.'"[41]

That is Thomas S. Monson. He understands what the Lord requires: simple willingness to serve people, to look in the forgotten corners, down the dark streets, and into the eyes that seem to have lost hope. "Charles Ringwood was the oldest deacon I had ever met," President Monson says. They got him to the temple. They got him ready to go to his heavenly home. Brother Ringwood died just weeks after going to the temple.[42]

Bishop Monson had attended only two funerals in his life before his call as bishop. After his call, he conducted two funerals his first week, and they were just the beginning. One time he conducted and spoke at three funerals in one day.

He likes funerals because he feels that they provide an ideal setting for teaching the truths of the gospel. He has said, "Because our Savior died at Calvary, death has no hold upon any one of us . . . we laugh, we cry, we work, we play, we love, we live. And then we die. Death is our universal heritage. All must pass its portals. Death claims the aged, the weary and worn. It visits the youth in the bloom of hope and the glory of expectation. Nor are little children kept beyond its grasp."[43]

One of the funerals he conducted as bishop was that of his own grandfather, Thomas Sharp Condie, who died February 3, 1953, at age ninety-three. He had suffered a stroke following surgery for cancer. He was a family man whose influence on his grandson cannot be overstated.

One by one, Bishop Monson's family members passed on. On May 10, just three months after Grandfather Condie's death, Tom's uncle Richard LeRoy Carter died. The family endearingly called him "Uncle Speed" because of his methodical manner. He was the "slowest eater" in the family, the one who "measured every step" and took life at a snail's pace, a fishing partner of nephew Tom. He never joined the Church, but his funeral service was conducted by Bishop Monson.

Speed Carter's only son, Richard, had chosen to serve a mission rather than enter the military. While he and fellow ward member Howard Hagen were in the mission home, the Church and the military announced a restriction that, effective immediately, any missionary candidate who had not been set apart or ordained would be excused from missionary service to join the military. Richard had been set apart for his mission to Canada, but Howard was to be set apart the next day. Instead, he was required to go into the service. In 1950 there were 3,015 Latter-day Saints who were called to serve missions; by 1952 the number had dropped to 872.[44]

While Richard was serving as a missionary, his father, Speed Carter, suffered a heart attack very early one morning. Tom arrived at his home in time to give him a blessing and then stayed for hours with him at the hospital, where Speed died.

Tom sent a telegram to Richard's mission president and then phoned to make sure that Richard heard about his father. Bishop Monson conducted the funeral, and Elder Carter stayed in the field, becoming a "most outstanding and productive" missionary.

Speed's death was hard on his wife, Aunt Blanche, who was almost like a second mother to Tom. She had lost both her father— who had lived with them—and her husband within months, and her only child was far away in Canada. But with her resilient nature, Tom noted, she looked outside herself, as she had all her life, having family members over for dinner and lifting the spirits of others. During the Depression, when Speed had been unemployed, she had gone to work for the Civil Service to help provide for the family.[45]

Months later, on August 20, 1953, Franz Johnson, Frances's father, died. He had retired as a furniture finisher but had taken a temporary job refinishing benches and furniture in a ward in Moscow, Idaho. When he returned, he was diagnosed with leukemia. "He was a wonderful man: patient, quiet, faithful," and his daughter takes after him.[46] Christmas Eve that year at the Johnson home, though it featured the traditional Swedish dinner, was not the same.

The Sixth-Seventh Ward was a close-knit community in spite of the transient nature of its inhabitants. Ward reunions have always drawn a crowd. While Tom was bishop, a member of the reunion committee one year called at each ward member's home selling tickets for the banquet at a dollar apiece. Those who had moved from the area received a newsletter and notice with a reservation card. Another year, at the 106th celebration, the ward offered a history book, *Through the Years,* which sold for $1.50 a copy. Bishop Monson, who was employed at the Deseret News Press at the time, made certain the sixty-four-page book was done right, with "durable leatherette binding and the finest quality paper."[47]

The ward members loved the bishop and demonstrated their affection. At one ward event, a group of them sang a specially written tribute to their young leader, using the well-known tune of Davy Crockett:

> *Thomas, Thomas Monson, tops in this world of men.*
> *Born in the city not long ago*
> *There he learned what he wanted to know*
> *Didn't fight Indians or kill buffalo,*
> *But here at home, he's known where'er you go.*
> *Bishop, Bishop Monson, Bishop of the Sixth-Seventh Ward.*

Now tonight this party's just for you
And your wife, yes, we're glad she's here, too.
We waited long planning what we would do
So you would know that we are proud of you.
Bishop, Bishop Monson, tops in the world of men.[48]

In many of their minds, regardless of what Church positions he would eventually come to hold, Thomas S. Monson would always be their bishop.

11

"HE WENT ABOUT DOING GOOD"

In a message he gave to all of the General and Area Authorities, he said that one of our responsibilities is to help the members feel the Savior's love. That's who he is. His whole ministry is focused on discerning the needs of an individual and offering a smile or a pat on the back—doing some simple, very gracious thing that you never would really expect the President of the Church to do.

ELDER DAVID A. BEDNAR
Quorum of the Twelve Apostles

THOMAS S. MONSON'S INTRODUCTION to the Church's welfare program came ten years before he was called as a bishop. He was twelve years old, a new deacon, when his bishop asked him to take the sacrament to a bedfast brother who longed for that blessing. On that sunny morning, Tommy didn't mind the three-quarter-mile walk down the street and across the railroad tracks to the modest residence. He knocked at the kitchen door and heard a feeble voice say, "Come in." He uncovered the sacrament for Brother Wright, who was so weak that he needed to ask Tommy to place the bread in his trembling hand and press the cup of water to his lips. Recognizing the overwhelming gratitude of Brother Wright, Tommy felt "the spirit of the Lord" in the room, and he recognized that he "stood on sacred ground."

Brother Wright asked him to "stay awhile," and the elderly man proceeded to bear his testimony: "Tommy, this Church is divine. The love which the members have one for another is an inspiration." He then talked of the Relief Society president, Sister

Balmforth. "Do you know what she did one week many years ago?" he asked. "She took her little red wagon, went to members' homes and gathered a jar of peaches here, a can of vegetables there, and brought to my cupboard shelves the food that sustained me." Brother Wright cried as he told of the experience and "described watching the Relief Society president walk away from his home, pulling behind her, over the bumpy railroad tracks, the red wagon of mercy."[1]

Welfare to President Monson has always been about filling the "red wagon" with whatever is needed: food, clothing, friendship, or personal attention. The welfare plan "would never succeed on effort alone," he has attested, "for this program operates through faith after the way of the Lord."[2]

The Monsons' stake president, Harold B. Lee, had launched a welfare program in the Pioneer Stake before being tapped by President Heber J. Grant to organize the effort for the whole Church. In 1932, at the bottom of the Great Depression, President Lee and his counselors, Charles S. Hyde and Paul C. Child, met in the stake building just next door to the Sixth-Seventh Ward chapel and made plans to help the people of their stake. They had cause to be concerned: Fifty percent of the members in their eight wards and one branch were unemployed, including high councilors and bishops. (The Monson family was not among them.) "In those early days," President Lee would later explain, "we set out not knowing where to go; we knew we had to go somewhere because we had reached rock bottom."[3]

Bishop Monson would begin bishopric and ward council meetings with a pertinent scripture to center everyone's thinking on their duties. One of his favorites was: "Wherefore, be not weary in well-doing, for ye are laying the foundation of a great work. And out of small things proceedeth that which is great. Behold, the Lord requireth the heart and a willing mind."[4]

Bishop Monson became known—and loved—for his heart and willing mind, as expressed in the attention he paid to the welfare of the people in his congregation. He has said, "I always considered myself as a bishop who erred on the side of generosity; and if I had it to do again, I would be even more generous."[5]

He believed that "those receiving welfare assistance should work to the extent of their abilities for that which is received. There are many creative ways leaders can provide work opportunities." He had a crew of elderly retired men whose assistance was repaid by their working on maintaining the grounds and the interior of the Sixth-Seventh Ward building and the adjacent stake hall. He has said, "A Church dole would be worse than a government dole, because it would fail in the face of greater light. Church practices portray more honorable aims, more glorious potential."[6]

Bishop Monson served as chairman of the Temple View Stake bishops' council and as counselor in the regional bishops' council, "a great honor for such a young but capable leader."[7] Elder Glen Rudd, who served as bishop in the adjoining Fourth Ward and later became a General Authority, observed, "He probably has had more actual experience in distributing welfare commodities than any other man living in the Church today. The spiritual blessings of a properly administered welfare program far exceed the physical blessings."[8]

Welfare to Tom Monson has always been about building from within and using the needs of others to strengthen those called upon to assist. "Welfare to him is not a program," states President Henry B. Eyring, who worked closely with welfare when he served in the Presiding Bishopric. "Welfare is people having two effects on others: Helping when they are down, lifting them up—and building their faith in Jesus Christ in the process."[9]

Though programs and their applications adjust over the years, President Monson testifies that "the basic principles of welfare do not change. They will not change. They are revealed truths." He has identified guiding principles in welfare as work, self-reliance, sound financial management, a year's supply, care for the extended family, and wise use of Church resources. He has taught: "We have learned to care for the widow, the orphan, the indigent, those impacted by accident, illness or old age. Ours is the added responsibility to cope with the challenge of changing needs, altered circumstances—even new attitudes and different expectations. Where do we turn? Where shall we go for our help? I answer: Back to basics; back to the revelations of the Lord; back to the utterances of God's prophets; back to the fundamental principles which have undergirded the welfare program of the Church."[10]

Bishop Monson's personal approach to welfare is demonstrated by the fact that he was such a well-known figure at the old Salt Lake County Hospital on State Street. One evening he was summoned to bless a patient in one of the units. As he approached her, he saw the woman in the next bed pull the sheet up to cover her face. He gave the blessing and turned to leave but felt prompted to go back and see who was in the adjacent bed. As he lifted the sheet, he saw a woman who lived in his ward. "Why did you pull the sheet over your face?" he asked. She said, "I thought you were coming to see me, and when you stopped at the other bed, I was embarrassed." He responded, "The Lord knew you were here and brought me back. I am here to give you a blessing."[11] The woman was Kathleen McKee.

Several months later, Bishop Monson received word that Kathleen McKee had died. Hospital records indicated no next of kin; she had listed Thomas Monson as the one to be notified at her death. Upon his arrival at the hospital, the attendant presented him with a sealed envelope containing a lone key to Kathleen's modest basement apartment. Her home showed that she had enjoyed few luxuries. She lived alone, had never married, and had joined the Church "in the twilight of her life." On her desk sat a letter beneath two Alka Seltzer bottles containing quarters, representing her fast offering for the month. She had written in her careful hand:

> Dear Bishop Monson,
>
> I think I shall not return from the hospital. In the dresser drawer is a small insurance policy which will cover the funeral expenses. The furniture may be given to the neighbors.
>
> In the kitchen are my three precious canaries. Two of them are a beautiful yellow-gold in color and are perfectly marked. On their cages I have

noted the names of friends to whom they are to be given. In the third cage is Billie. He is my favorite. Billie looks a bit scrubby, and his yellow hue is marred by gray on his wings. Will you and your family make a home for him? He isn't the prettiest, but his song is the best.

Sincerely,
Kathleen McKee

He realized there was much more to Kathleen's life than her bare basement rooms. She "was much like Billie, her prized canary with gray on its wings. She was not blessed with beauty, gifted with poise, nor honored by posterity. Yet her song helped others to bear their burdens more willingly and to shoulder their tasks more ably."[12] She had befriended many neighbors in need, cheering and comforting one who lived down the street and was crippled. She brightened others' lives. Put simply, she had gone about doing good.

Late one night, just as Bishop Monson left the apartment of another widow, the door opened across the hall. The woman standing there asked in a heavy Greek accent, "Are you the bishop?" He nodded. Then she said, "My name is Angela Anastor. No one visits me or my bedfast husband. Do you have time to come in and visit with us, even though we are not members of your church?"

He provided a blessing to her husband that night and stopped by as often as possible in the months to come. Eventually she was baptized and worked tirelessly in helping translate Church materials into Greek. When her husband died, President Monson spoke at his funeral.[13]

Bishop Monson was especially skilled at turning welfare needs into opportunities for other members of his ward to serve. One such example was that of the Guertler family. Karl Guertler, who lived in Ogden, Utah, had rented a very modest apartment in the Sixth-Seventh Ward for his brother Hans, who was coming to the United States from Germany with his wife and children after

World War II. Karl had contacted Bishop Monson to let him know he would soon have new ward members living in the apartment, and then Karl and Bishop Monson went to look at the empty apartment together. It was just a few weeks before Christmas, and Bishop Monson was heartsick as he contemplated the bleak Christmas these German immigrants would have in the dark and dingy apartment.

Over the following days, Bishop Monson asked the priesthood members, the Relief Society, and the youth to help make the apartment more inviting and to fill the shelves with food for the Guertlers, who would arrive a few days before Christmas.

On the evening the Guertler family arrived at the apartment, the aroma of new wallpaper filled the room; thick carpet covered the floors; furniture sat ready to be used; and kitchen cupboards were lined with food, as was the new refrigerator. A Christmas tree decorated by the youth stood in one corner. Skilled members of the ward had done painting and electrical work and had installed new flooring. Many needed items had been donated by local suppliers, including a new Hotpoint range. The ward members opened their arms that night to the beleaguered but very grateful travelers, who had been ill prepared to start over in a new land. They all sang Christmas carols—the Guertlers in German, their new brothers and sisters in English.

Bishop Monson recalled that as the ward members left that night, one girl turned to him and asked, "Why is it that I feel better than I've ever felt before?" Bishop Monson reminded her of the last verse of the Christmas hymn they had just sung, "O Little Town of Bethlehem."

> How silently, how silently, the wondrous gift is giv'n!
> So God imparts to human hearts the blessings of his heav'n.
> No ear may hear his coming;
> But in this world of sin,
> Where meek souls will receive him, still the dear Christ enters in.[14]

Welfare took another form for Bishop Monson when he wrote to and received mail from ward members who were in prison. Not unusual was the conclusion of one letter in June 1955: "Bishop, please answer soon. I like to hear from you."[15]

If people moved away from the area, he wrote in farewell, "Remember always that all of you are welcome at any time here in the old Sixth-Seventh Ward, where to us you will always be lifetime members."[16] He also wrote regularly to ward members serving missions.

In 1950, Church President George Albert Smith sounded "a prophetic warning" that it would not "be long until calamities will overtake the human family unless there is speedy repentance. It will not be long before those who are scattered over the face of the earth by millions will die . . . because of what will come."[17] Two and half months later, on June 25, 1950, war broke out in Korea, a war that would claim some 2.5 million lives.

Twenty-three young men from the Sixth-Seventh Ward served in the military during the Korean War. Church authorities requested that each LDS serviceman receive both the *Church News* and the *Improvement Era,* as well as a personal letter from his bishop each month. The Sixth-Seventh Ward priesthood quorums "with effort" funded the subscriptions, and Bishop Monson wrote the letters. Having served in the navy, he knew what it felt like to get a letter from home.

Every month he wrote twenty-three personal letters, handing the stack to Iola Moon, a woman in the ward, who mailed them. One of his young men wrote back from the front lines of Korea that amidst the shelling on a Sunday morning, he and those in his platoon who were members of the Church partook of the sacrament—which they passed in a helmet.

One month Sister Moon glanced through the pile of letters to be mailed and asked, "Bishop, don't you ever get discouraged? Here is another letter to Brother Bryson. This is the seventeenth letter you have sent to Lawrence Bryson without a reply."

"Maybe this month," was his response. And he was right. The reply came, postmarked APO San Francisco because the young man was serving "on a distant shore, isolated, homesick, alone."

On December 25, 1953, he wrote: "Dear Bishop, I've been owing you this letter for some time now. But even as I write it, I don't know what I'll talk about or say. This is the first time I have ever written or tried writing a bishop. How are you and your family? How is Church? How was Christmas? I sure would have liked to be there. It's quite a change from Christmas at home and Christmas here. Well, I've run out of words already. As you can see I'm still the same backward kid you knew." He then said, "Keep the letters coming," and asked to be remembered to everyone in the ward. He added a postscript: "Thank you for the *Church News* and magazines, they're great, but most of all thank you for the personal letters. I have turned over a new leaf. I have been ordained a priest in the Aaronic Priesthood. My heart is full. I am a happy man."[18]

Years later, at a stake conference, Brother Bryson would seek out Elder Monson after the meetings to report, "I serve in the presidency of my elders quorum. Thank you again for your concern for me and the personal letters which you sent and which I treasure."[19]

At times Bishop Monson had help providing "in the Lord's way." One autumn he received a call from a member he rarely saw at Church. "Bishop," the man said, "I've got two semi trucks and trailers loaded with oranges and bananas, and if you can use them at the storehouse, I would like to send them down as my tithing." Bishop Monson replied, "We can use all of it." He immediately called Bishop Jesse M. Drury at Welfare Square.

Under the direction of Bishop Drury, all of the trucks were emptied with volunteer help and their contents distributed. Bishop Monson had already contacted the bishops in the region with a report of the fruit availability. As Bishop Monson gratefully wrote out the tithing-in-kind receipt, his gratitude extended beyond the trucks of produce. The brother who donated the fruit—and his wife—had been embroiled in a local controversy that easily could have embittered them and turned them against the Church; others had dropped out of activity for less reason. Instead, they "brought forth fruit" from what they knew to be the Lord's vineyard. The man later became a sealer in the Salt Lake Temple, and Elder Monson spoke at his funeral.[20]

Not forgotten in his "bishoping" were the needs of youth—one at a time. As in most wards, some of the youth struggled, some stood firm; some waffled in the middle. Tom knew a great deal about the Church's youth program, having served in the YMMIA superintendency when he was only seventeen years of age. He had brought a fresh perspective to the assignment; the superintendent and his other assistant had been sixty-four and fifty-nine years old, respectively. Now, as bishop, he and his counselors determined that they would "lend every effort to insure that not one boy or girl was lost." Genuine love and a sense of duty were to guide their efforts. Their results, he attests, were "miraculous."[21]

"It is not necessary," he counsels, "to buy the activity of our youth. . . . To measure the goodness of life by its delights and pleasures is to apply a false standard."[22] In the summers he took the young men to Vivian Park, and on a separate occasion the Relief Society and Young Women leaders took the young women. Some of the young people had never visited the mountains, seen a natural water feature like the Provo River, or roasted hot dogs over an open fire.

He worked with one young man, Robert, who lived in Marguerite Court with his mother. Robert stuttered and stammered severely. Self-conscious, shy, fearful of himself and everyone else, he would not take assignments in Church and never spoke up. Then one day, by some miracle, he accepted the assignment to perform a baptism. Bishop Monson sat down next to him in the Tabernacle baptistry and walked him through the process. They had gone over the procedures in priesthood meeting, and Robert knew what was expected.

By appearances, Robert was well prepared in his white baptismal attire. But when the bishop asked how he was doing, Robert stammered almost incoherently that he felt "terrible." Bishop Monson, with his arm around the lad, suggested they each offer a prayer that he "would be made equal to the task." They did so, right there in the baptistry. When the clerk read, "Nancy Ann McArthur will now be baptized by Robert Williams, a priest," Robert stepped forward as he had been taught, took Nancy's hand, and led her into the water. "He then gazed as though toward heaven and, with his right arm to the square and with the power of the Aaronic Priesthood, repeated the sacred words,

'Nancy Ann McArthur, having been commissioned of Jesus Christ, I baptize you in the name of the Father, and of the Son, and of the Holy Ghost.' His presentation was flawless. Not once did he stammer. Not once did he stutter. Not once did he falter."

Bishop Monson congratulated Robert in the dressing room. Robert's eyes fell downward—yet again. In his stammering voice he struggled to say, "Thank you."[23]

Years later, President Monson spoke at Robert's funeral and reported that he had once performed a baptism with perfect precision and had tried his best throughout his life to honor his priesthood.[24] There were thirteen in attendance at Robert's funeral that day. Because they were short on pallbearers, President Monson and his security officer stepped in to help. He concluded, "I went to the Salt Lake Cemetery so that I might complete my responsibility on earth to this choice young man."[25]

Another young man in the Sixth-Seventh Ward, Richard Casto, repeatedly missed quorum meetings. One particular Sunday, Bishop Monson went to Richard's home during priesthood meeting. His mother and stepfather said Richard was at work at the West Temple Garage. Bishop Monson, determined to do all he could to get Richard to church, searched but could not find him. Finally he had the inspiration to check the grease pit at the side of the station. Two "beady eyes" stared up at him. "You found me, Bishop," said Richard. "I'll come up." The two talked, and Bishop Monson left with Richard's commitment to attend priesthood meeting the next week. Richard was true to his word.

Though the family moved from the ward, Richard arranged to have Bishop Monson speak at his missionary farewell. Richard related that the turning point in his determination to fill a mission came one Sunday morning—not in the chapel, but as he gazed up from the depths of a dark grease pit and found his quorum president's outstretched hand.

Forty years later, Richard sent a letter to "his bishop." "The boy in the grease pit is fine and still true to the faith," he wrote. "I would probably never have gone on a mission or met my wife or had the family I have today if you hadn't taken the time to come over and get me back on the straight and narrow. . . . As I ponder the events in my life, I am so grateful for a bishop who looked, found, and showed a great interest in one who was lost. I thank you from the bottom of my heart for all that you did and have done for me personally. I love you."[26]

He signed the letter, "the boy in the grease pit."

Richard Casto has now served twice as a bishop himself.

Another of Bishop Monson's "incorrigibles" wrote: "You probably thought many times that I may not have understood or even heard some of the advice and teachings you gave to me, by example, as well as precept. I want to assure you now that I did hear and I did understand, and I do deeply appreciate your help. As I recall many youthful mistakes which I made, I can also remember a very steady, consistent influence which kept me from allowing those mistakes to get full control of my future.

"One morning in particular comes to mind when you called and asked why I was not at priesthood meeting opening exercises. My lame excuse was no clean white shirt, after which you promptly offered me one of yours. I quickly found one of my own and arrived at meeting late, but I did arrive."[27]

President Monson has never lost sight of the power of such singular experiences in a youth's life to yield "eternal dividends."[28]

When President Monson reaches back in memory to his time as a bishop, he dwells on the words of President John Taylor: "If you do not magnify your callings, God will hold you responsible for those whom you might have saved had you done your duty."[29]

One Sunday the owner of a nearby drugstore called to say that earlier in the day a young boy from the area—and ward—had come into his store and purchased an ice cream sundae from the soda fountain. When he went to pay, he took the purchase money from a fast offering envelope and forgot to take the envelope with him. The man knew that Tom was the bishop and called him. As he described the boy, Bishop Monson immediately recognized who it was.

As he drove to the home, he prayed for divine direction. The boy's mother invited him into a dimly lit room where a few pieces of shabby furniture were situated. His indignation left as he realized the plight of the family. He asked the mother if she had any food in the house, and she tearfully shook her head. Her husband had been out of work for quite a while and they had no money for rent or food. Soon they would be evicted.

He turned from his intent to discuss the fast offering envelope left at the drugstore and began making plans for immediate assistance. Besides arranging for food and other needed items, he put the priesthood leaders to work on helping provide some form of employment.[30]

President Monson has not just left the door open for people to return to activity and fellowship in the Church—he has actively gone out and found them. If there were a theme to his ministry, perhaps it would be, "Reach out to rescue." He has been doing it all his life.

"There are so many out there who plead and pray for help," he maintains. "There are those who are discouraged, those who long to return but who don't know how to begin. . . . Let us have ready hands, clean hands, and willing hearts, that we may participate in providing what our Heavenly Father would have others receive from Him."[31]

One to whom he reached out was Harold Gallacher. His wife and children were active in the Church, but not Harold. His daughter Sharon had asked Bishop Monson if he would "do something" to bring her father back into activity. As a bishop, he felt prompted one day to call on Harold. It was a hot summer's day when he knocked on Harold's screen door. The bishop could see Harold sitting in his chair, smoking a cigarette and reading the newspaper. "Who is it?" Harold asked sullenly, without looking up.

"Your bishop," Tom replied. "I've come to get acquainted and to urge your attendance with your family at our meetings."

"No, I'm too busy," came the disdainful response. He never looked up. Tom thanked him for listening and departed the doorstep. The family moved without Harold ever attending services.

Years later, a Brother Gallacher phoned the office of Elder Thomas S. Monson and asked to make an appointment to see him.

"Ask him if his name is Harold G. Gallacher," Elder Monson told his secretary, "and if he lived at 55 Vissing Place and had a daughter named Sharon." When the secretary did, Harold was startled that Elder Monson remembered such details. When the

160

two met some time later, they embraced. Harold said, "I've come to apologize for not getting out of my chair and letting you in the door that summer day long years ago." Elder Monson asked him if he were active in the Church. With a wry smile, Harold replied: "I'm now second counselor in my ward bishopric. Your invitation to come out to church, and my negative response, so haunted me that I determined to do something about it."

"They will come back," says President Monson, "if we look up for heavenly help as we reach out to rescue."[32]

Few fell through the cracks in the Sixth-Seventh Ward. Everyone was needed and of great value. As the prophet, President Monson continues to sound the call, "Come back," to all who have distanced themselves from the Lord and His gospel. At his first general conference as President of the Church, he spoke from his experience and his heart:

"Throughout the journey along the pathway of life, there are casualties. Some depart from the road markers which point toward life eternal, only to discover the detour chosen ultimately leads to a dead end. Indifference, carelessness, selfishness, and sin all take their costly toll in human lives.

"Change for the better can come to all. Over the years we have issued appeals to the less active, the offended, the critical, the transgressor—to come back. 'Come back and feast at the table of the Lord, and taste again the sweet and satisfying fruits of fellowship with the Saints.'

"In the private sanctuary of one's own conscience lies that spirit, that determination to cast off the old person and to measure up to the stature of true potential. In this spirit, we again issue that heartfelt invitation: Come back. We reach out to you in the pure love of Christ and express our desire to assist you and to welcome you into full fellowship."[33]

That is welfare to Thomas S. Monson: touching individual lives, going about doing good for people in need, and reaching out to include everyone in the circle of love and fellowship that the gospel provides.

12

"HAVE COURAGE, MY BOY"

The Lord had to make Thomas Monson big because of the size of his heart.

ELDER RICHARD G. SCOTT
Quorum of the Twelve Apostles

TOM HAD BEEN SERVING AS bishop for almost five years when he and Frances began looking for a permanent home outside the stake. They found one in Bountiful that suited them, a split-level facing south, newly completed and ready for a young family. But a call at stake conference put their plans on hold.

On Saturday, June 25, 1955, President Joseph Fielding Smith and Elder Alma Sonne interviewed all the bishops, high councilors, and stake presidency members in the Temple View Stake prior to a reorganization of the stake presidency. The next day, at the stake conference in the Assembly Hall on Temple Square, Bishop Monson was sitting with the youth in the choir loft when President Smith announced the names of the new stake president, Percy K. Fetzer, and his first counselor, John R. Burt. Then he read the name of the second counselor: Thomas S. Monson. It was the first Bishop Monson had heard of the calling. President Smith said, "If Brother Monson is willing to respond to this call to be a counselor in the stake presidency, we will be pleased to hear from him now." The scene was reminiscent of the days when missionaries were called to fields of labor from the congregation at general conference in the Tabernacle with no advance notice.

As Bishop Monson, now President Monson, stood at the pulpit and gazed out at his many friends and neighbors, the choir's last song came to mind, and he drew from those words:

> *This world is a stage of excitement.*
> *There's danger whatever you do.*
> *But if you are tempted in weakness,*
> *Have courage, my boy, to say "no."*

Tom deftly shifted the words to say: "Have courage, my boy, to say yes."[1] He understood that "the call for courage comes constantly to each of us—the courage to stand firm for our convictions, the courage to fulfill our responsibilities, the courage to honor our priesthood."[2]

He called the moment a "heart stopper." He would have more such moments as he matured in Church service.

Tom was released as bishop three weeks later, on July 17, 1955. The Presiding Bishopric of the Church—Joseph L. Wirthlin, Thorpe B. Isaacson, and Carl W. Buehner—expressed thanks for his service, saying in a letter: "You retire with the love and respect of the members of the ward, as you do with our confidence and good will. The office of bishop is a great responsibility. It requires much work, the sacrifice of time and association of loved ones, but carries with it spiritual blessings and personal satisfaction that we feel sure are adequate compensation."[3]

Tom brought youth to the stake presidency. He was twenty-seven years old. Closest in age to him was John R. Burt, thirteen years his senior. The three presidency members would kneel each Sunday morning at the stake office and then go about the Lord's work. President Percy Fetzer believed in delegating significant responsibilities to his counselors. He assigned President Monson to supervise the Aaronic Priesthood, Young Women, Primary, Sunday School, athletics, budget, and all special activities—and to preside at one-third of the ward conferences held in the stake each year. President Monson appreciated that delegating style of leadership, "for it builds leaders and illustrates to the stake members that a presidency presides, rather than just one man."[4]

The high council members were likewise charged to take their assignments seriously. Tom had observed that as a bishop. At stake meetings in his bishopric days, the stake presidency would display a board showing the statistics of the different wards. The board was so large that it had to be made in two parts, with hinges in the center connecting the top and bottom halves. Kasper J. Fetzer (father of stake president Percy Fetzer), a member of the stake high council and a cabinetmaker, used this visual aid in meetings, often to the chagrin of the ward leaders. Half the wards would appear above the hinges and half below. Bishop Monson worked hard to keep his ward "above the hinges," though one evening he received a call from Brother Kasper Fetzer, who, in his thick German accent, said, "Bishop, I thank you for having your home teaching report in on time."

Bishop Monson recognized that line as simply an introduction; his report was always on time. Brother Fetzer continued, "Bishop, I don't understand the line on the report where you say you have twelve families that are inaccessible. What does that word mean—*inaccessible*?"

Tom explained that these were members who had "rejected" the home teachers, who wanted nothing to do with the Church.

"What!?" Brother Fetzer countered. "They do not want the priesthood of God to visit them?"

"That is correct."

Brother Fetzer then asked, "Bishop, could I please come to your home and obtain the names of these families and visit them as your helper?" Bishop Monson was "overjoyed" that a high councilor was going to help him.

Kasper Fetzer was on his doorstep within the hour. To vindicate himself, Bishop Monson listed the most difficult family first. Off went Brother Fetzer to the Reinhold Doelle family, who lived in a spacious home, perhaps the finest in the ward, surrounded by a white picket fence and patrolled by a large German shepherd dog. As Brother Fetzer lifted the latch, the dog charged. Instinctively, Brother Fetzer called out in his native German—and the dog came to a halt. He patted the dog, speaking softly in German, and the two became friends. His actions opened the door, and the family received a visit—the first of many—from home teachers.

Brother Fetzer returned to the Monson home late that Sunday, saying, "Bishop, you can cross from your inaccessible list seven of the families, which will now welcome the home teachers."[5] For Bishop Monson, it was a lesson learned: "Wherefore, now let every man learn his duty, and to act in the office in which he is appointed, in all diligence."[6]

There is more to the story. Years later, Tom stood next to Sister Doelle in line at a wedding reception. She reported that her family now lived in California, and then she asked about their wonderful home teacher, Kasper Fetzer. "His visit changed our lives," she said. They had determined to go back to Church, and she was now serving in an auxiliary presidency in her Palm Springs ward.

Similarly meaningful experiences became a part of President Monson's new assignment. For example, one October the three members of the Temple View stake presidency were attending general priesthood meeting in the Tabernacle. They arrived two hours early, hoping to find good seats, and were among the first to sit down. While they waited, President Percy K. Fetzer related an experience from his missionary days in Germany. He told his counselors that one rainy night, when he and his companion were presenting a gospel message to a group assembled in a schoolhouse, a number of protestors showed up, threatening violence. At a critical moment, an elderly widow stepped between the elders and the angry crowd and said, "These young men are my guests and are coming to my home now. Please make way for us to leave."

The challengers stepped back, and the missionaries with their benefactress walked unharmed to her modest home. She prepared a meal, and then the elders taught her the gospel. Her young son refused to join them, skulking behind the kitchen stove where it was warm.

"While I don't know if that woman ever joined the Church," said President Fetzer, "I'll be forever grateful for her kindness that rain-drenched night thirty-three years ago."

The Tabernacle benches had been filling as he had talked. Two brethren sitting directly in front of them were chatting like old friends, though they had just met. "Tell me how you came to be a member of the Church," Tom overheard one ask the other. The brother responded, and the three on the bench behind him heard his story:

"One rainy night in Germany, my mother brought to our house two drenched missionaries whom she had rescued from a mob. Mother fed the elders, and they presented to her a message concerning the work of the Lord. They invited me to join the discussion, but I was shy and fearful, so I remained secure in my seat behind the stove. Later, when I once more heard about the Church, I remembered the courage and faith, as well as the message, of those two humble missionaries, and this led to my conversion. I suppose I'll never meet those two missionaries here in mortality, but I'll be forever grateful to them. I know not where they were from. I think one was named Fetzer."

At this point, the two counselors turned to look at President Fetzer. Tears were streaming down his cheeks. President Monson remembers that President Fetzer tapped the man on the shoulder and said, "I'm Bruder Fetzer. I was one of the two missionaries whom your mother befriended that night. I'm grateful to meet the boy who sat behind the stove—the lad who listened and who learned."[7]

President Monson admits he doesn't remember the messages from that priesthood meeting, but he will "never forget the faith-filled conversation that preceded the commencement of the meeting." At a stake conference some years later, he shared the experience, and Ernest Braun, a retired tailor, once again introduced himself after the meeting as the boy behind the stove. As always, Elder Monson credited "the hand of the Lord" in prompting him to speak on that subject to the congregation, for he "rarely used this particular illustration."[8] Scripture came to his mind: "In nothing doth man offend God, or against none is his wrath kindled, save those who confess not his hand in all things."[9] Elder Monson would see that divine hand many times in his service in Germany years later when he would call Percy Fetzer to his side to work with the German Saints—those who had the courage to befriend missionaries and stay strong in the gospel.

After President Monson had served for two years in the stake presidency, as the neighborhood gave way to further commercial ventures and the family environment deteriorated, he and Frances again wanted to look for a home in a more suitable area. Tom asked Elder Mark E. Petersen of the Quorum of the Twelve, who directed the Deseret News and its Press, if it were "unfair" for him to consider moving. Elder Petersen thoughtfully responded, "Your obligation to that area is concluded."

Frances found property out in rural Holladay, some forty blocks south of the Monsons' residence. Her requirement was a location close to a bus line. The family had only one car, and she could not imagine them ever having another. They bought a one-acre lot at the end of a quiet cul-de-sac southeast of town for $3,500 and built a red brick home with a one-car garage.

President Fetzer released President Monson at the June stake conference in 1957.

The Monsons moved on Pioneer Day, July 24, 1957. The setting was a far cry from downtown, where they had had practically no yard. Now they had an acre of ground—in the country. Cows grazed in nearby fields. As with most new homes, "there wasn't a blade of grass in the front or the back,"[10] no curtains on the windows, no flower beds or trees. And no train tracks. Gradually, the four of them—Tom and Frances and their children, Tommy and Ann—settled in, planting lawn and an orchard and building a fine coop for Tom's pigeons and another for his chickens.

Their new ward, the Valley View Third Ward of the Valley View Stake, was building a new chapel to accommodate the area's growing population. At the time, the Church relied on members to assist in the building with both funding and labor. The bishopric called Tom to the building committee, with the assignment to telephone members of the ward and "invite" them to work on the construction. They presented him with a list of priesthood holders in the ward, indicating that they would tell him which of the men would be inclined to help. Tom responded, "I don't know any of these men; why not just let me find out who will serve?" Very few declined. He worked right alongside them in their service.[11]

The bishopric also called Tom to work with senior members of the Aaronic Priesthood. "While the work was slow, and success did not come easily," he reflected, "the Lord did bless me with a measure of success."[12] He knew what to do, for the Savior had taught, "What man of you, having an hundred sheep, if he lose one of them, doth not leave the ninety and nine in the wilderness, and go after that which is lost, until he find it? And when he hath found it, he layeth it on his shoulders, rejoicing."[13]

Though he worked diligently to fulfill his many responsibilities, Tom also recognized the importance of balance in life. He enjoyed breeding and raising chickens and pigeons in his "free" time. It was not unusual for his Birmingham roller pigeons to receive blue ribbons at county and state fairs. His entries at the Fancy Feather Association winter shows also took first place. He won in most categories—breeding and performance in particular. At the club's show in 1959, with 133 birds competing, his red-bar, bald-head, Birmingham roller pigeon won first place.

Tom also served for a time as secretary of the Utah State Roller Club. The Utah group entered his pigeons and those of another breeder, considered the best in the state, in the national contest in New Jersey, which had thousands of birds from all over the country entered in the competition. Son Tommy picked up the "pigeon passion" from his father.

Frances planned outings to the zoo and up the canyon, and she established traditions for birthdays and holidays. All the Monsons celebrated holidays and birthdays together. And "together," for them, included their extended family of brothers, sisters, aunts, uncles, and cousins. On Sunday evenings, even after Tom and Frances moved into their new home, they regularly returned to visit with Tom's parents and younger brothers and sisters, and on birthdays the whole family met at his Aunt Annie's and Uncle Rusty's. In the summer they all went to Vivian Park—hiking, swimming, sitting around the campfire, and fishing.

At the family gatherings, Tom's mother continued to be the life of the party and his father the contented observer. One Father's Day, with eighteen people packed into the front room of the Monsons' duplex, Spence Monson opined: "Family is life indeed."

Tom and Frances enjoyed spending time with relatives. "As parents," he later taught, "we should remember that our lives may be the book from the family library which the children most treasure."[14]

To stay connected with Tom's older sister, Marjorie, and her husband, Conway, who lived in California, the family occasionally made reel-to-reel tape recordings at parties with everyone saying something, singing a song, or reciting a verse. "The wife and I are proud parents of six children . . . the finest children in all the world," Spencer Monson was recorded as saying in his deliberate, measured cadence. Gladys piped in with an accolade for each one.

The grandchildren picked up the family tradition of memorizing poems and readings. And they liked to sing. "Heart of My Heart" was a favorite that they sang into the microphone over and over with gusto. The older children told stories or gave recitations; the younger ones, with Frances at the piano, sang Primary songs such as "'Give,' Said the Little Stream." Year after year someone offered a rendition of "All I Want for Christmas Is My Two Front Teeth." Little Ann delighted everyone one evening with her new song, "I'm So Glad When Daddy Comes Home." Tom narrated the activities as the children sang the "Hokey Pokey" and "Jumbo the Elephant."

"Whose little girl are you?" Tom would ask young Ann teasingly. "My Daddy's" would be her quick reply. When young Tommy came to the microphone, he said with some authority, "Now, listen." And then he would rattle through what was on his mind.

Tom, Frances, and their children typically celebrated a Swedish Christmas each Christmas Eve with Frances's family, the Johnsons, and they also began what became a Monson Christmas tradition of reading with the family the story of the Savior's birth from the book of Luke. Tom would use such occasions

169

to emphasize: "Giving, not getting, brings to full bloom the Christmas spirit. Enemies are forgiven, friends remembered, and God obeyed. The spirit of Christmas illuminates the picture window of the soul, and we look out upon the world's busy life and become more interested in people than things. To catch the real meaning of the 'spirit of Christmas,' we need only drop the last syllable, and it becomes the 'Spirit of Christ.'"[15]

Other traditions for the Monsons included caroling with their neighborhood friends out on the circle in front of their home and reading *The Mansion*, a story by American clergyman Henry Van Dyke. Tom would also read *A Christmas Carol*, by Charles Dickens. He especially liked the sentiment: "I have always thought of Christmas time, when it has come round—. . . as a good time: a kind, forgiving, charitable, pleasant time; the only time I know of, in the long calendar of the year, when men and women seem by one consent to open their shut-up hearts freely, and to think of people below them as if they really were fellow-passengers . . . and not another race of creatures bound on other journeys."[16]

Tom Monson could have written those stories himself, as they expressed the deep feelings of his heart: "In this marvelous dispensation of the fulness of times, our opportunities to give of ourselves are indeed limitless, but they are also perishable. There are hearts to gladden. There are kind words to say. There are gifts to be given. There are deeds to be done. There are souls to be saved."[17]

13

"O Canada"

There is not any part of missionary work that President Monson hasn't influenced. He served in every role in the Missionary Department during the course of his life. He's toured most of the missions. You'd have to say just a handful of people in any generation would even be in the same category. He's in a league by himself in terms of being a great missionary.

Elder Quentin L. Cook
Quorum of the Twelve Apostles

In the morning session of general conference, April 6, 1959, Joseph Anderson, clerk of the conference, reported the Church's statistical and financial data, which included the names of eight newly called mission presidents. Thomas S. Monson was one of them. It was the first time that the name "President Monson" would be placed before a general conference congregation; it would not be the last.

President Stephen L Richards, First Counselor in the First Presidency, had extended the mission call on February 21, 1959. He had called Tom at the Deseret News Press and asked, "Brother Monson, could you come and visit with me at your convenience?" This was a man Tom knew well. He had printed books for President Richards and saw in him a "great theologian, beautiful linguist, master craftsman of the English language."[1]

Tom asked what time would be best, and President Richards responded, "Could you come now?"

Being summoned to the Church offices was not unusual for

Tom, since he handled most of the Church's printing projects. On the drive to President Richards's office, he reviewed in his mind the progress of the General Handbook of Instructions, close to being printed at the Press. He had worked with President Richards on that publication for months. When he was ushered into the office on the southwest corner of the main floor—room 101, the same office President Monson would one day occupy as a member of the First Presidency for twenty-three years—President Richards, rather than reviewing the printing project, asked about Tom's current Church assignments, praising his past service as a young bishop and as a member of a stake presidency. He looked at Tom and asked, "You haven't been on a mission?"

"No," Tom replied, explaining that he had served in the navy.

President Richards then extended a call to him to serve as mission president of the Canadian Mission, one of fifty missions in the entire Church. He informed Tom that he would be on a leave of absence from the Deseret News Press and that he was to leave within the month. The Monsons were barely settled in their new home; Frances was having difficulty with her third pregnancy; Tom had more jobs on the press than ever before; he was busy in Church assignments in his ward and stake. But he did not pause. "Yes," he said, "I will serve wherever the Lord needs me."[2]

That would be the last time Tom would see President Richards alive. On May 19, 1959, one month into the mission, he received a telegram from Church headquarters: "With profound sorrow we tell you President Richards passed away yesterday. Funeral Friday." It was signed by David O. McKay and J. Reuben Clark.

Tom went home to tell Frances about the call. He explained the change ahead in their life and what it would mean for their young family. Schooled as a bishop's wife in a very difficult ward, she was prepared to accept the assignment. Son Tommy, nearly eight, was excited at the thought of such an adventure—until he learned they wouldn't be back for three years. Ann, just four, was very much a daddy's girl and was happy to go as long as her family was there.

"To be called as a mission president at age thirty-one was unusual then and it is so today," suggests Elder Quentin L. Cook of

172

the Quorum of the Twelve. "We think we are calling somebody young who is in his late fifties. He was a fabulous mission president."[3] Elder Cook points out the legacy of President Monson's service in Canada—his missionaries have been bishops, stake presidents, and mission presidents as well as great fathers and great mothers. As for President Monson, he learned missionary service from the ground up, and when he later toured missions as an Apostle, he tried to interview every single missionary, building their faith in Jesus Christ with his sincere testimony.

Today, most newly called mission presidents have at least six months to prepare for their service, as well as the benefit of several days of intensive training from Apostles and other Church leaders. The Monsons had just weeks. But those Apostles Tom knew well stepped in to help prepare him. Elder Harold B. Lee indicated that missionary work was different from being in a bishopric or a stake presidency, where wives are not included in discussions or deliberations. "Frances will be your best counselor," he said. He gave further "pointed counsel" that has become a central theme in President Monson's personal Church service and that he has shared repeatedly in leadership settings. "Remember, my friends," Elder Lee said, "whom the Lord calls, the Lord qualifies." He shared other wisdom with them: "When you are on the Lord's errand, you are entitled to the Lord's help," and, "Remember, God shapes the back to bear the burden placed upon it."[4]

Farewells for departing mission presidents were a tradition at the time. The Monsons' meeting on April 12, 1959, focused on the scripture, "Be thou humble; and the Lord thy God shall lead thee by the hand, and give thee answer to thy prayers."[5] Prayer was then and continues to be so much a part of President Monson's life and ministry. He has taught, "No . . . sincere, prayerful effort will go unanswered: that is the very constitution of the philosophy of faith. Divine favor will attend those who humbly seek it. . . . He who notes the sparrow's fall will, in His own way, acknowledge us."[6]

President J. Reuben Clark, Jr., spoke at the Monson farewell and concluded the meeting by advising Tom never to be embarrassed to answer a question with the words, "I don't know." The mission field was not the place to address or encourage speculation, President Clark said, emphasizing, "We get in difficulty if we think we know all the answers." He illustrated with an experience of a mission president who brought an investigator to see him, hoping he would answer the man's difficult questions. To each one of the ten questions, President Clark said, "I don't know."

"Brother Monson," he then said, "if a member of the First Presidency can answer 'I don't know' to ten consecutive questions, a mission president should not hesitate to respond the same way."[7] President Monson took the counsel to heart and has shared President Clark's recommendations with Church leaders, particularly mission presidents, for years.

Before departing, Tom and Frances and their two children visited with President Clark, then age ninety-one, to say a final farewell. Tom realized that his dear friend was failing and would probably not be there to greet him at his return. Tenderly, President Clark took their son Tommy up on his knee and kissed his hands, then did the same with Ann. Turning to the parents, he expressed his love for them and told them how much they would be missed. "We're expecting our third child," Tom said. "If the child is a son, we shall name him after you."

President Clark asked, "What name will you call him?"

"His name will be Clark," Tom said.

President Clark, with a twinkle in his eye and a wry smile, said, "Well, don't be afraid of the Joshua Reuben!"[8]

Seven months later, Tom sent President Clark a telegram announcing the birth of Clark Spencer Monson on October 1, 1959, in Toronto, Canada. He weighed 10 pounds 4 ounces. The delivery was difficult; Frances reacted to a drug that caused her blood pressure to skyrocket. Tom was not allowed in the room with her for several hours, and baby Clark wasn't brought to her side until the next day. When she was discharged from the hospital, Frances was grateful to find her mother at the mission home ready to care for her and fix meals for the missionaries. Hildur, used to managing the cafeteria at the Salt Lake Federal Reserve Bank, felt right at home in the kitchen.

Upon receiving word of the baby's birth, President Clark

immediately wrote a letter to his namesake: "To Clark Spencer Monson: I am rather in hopes that this may be the first letter for you to receive in this mortal life, and as such I invoke upon you all of the blessings which the Lord has to bless and to encourage those who come to earth in these last days of the Fullness of times. . . . God bless you, Clark, in every way in which it is well that He should bless you. May He never cease to remember you."[9]

When the Monsons left for Canada, they stored their furniture at Frances's mother's home and moved Tom's parents and three of his younger siblings, Scott, Marilyn, and Barbara, into their house. Tom had to farm out his pigeons and chickens. He has remarked that he will never forget the tender scene as they left their home. Frances, with tears in her eyes, stroked the doorjamb of the front door, her last act at the home that they had built and that she so loved. She, like pioneer women before her, "faced an unknown future, a new life, a greater destiny as [she] well knew," and she too "faced it with faith in God."[10]

The young family took the train to Toronto, Canada, which was rapidly emerging as the financial and business center of that nation. Toronto was also the hub of Church activity east of Alberta. Two days later, April 26, 1959, they arrived in a snowstorm at the same railroad station where for the next three years President Monson would meet or wave farewell to 480 missionaries.

Toronto, capital of the province of Ontario, was both an agricultural center with rich farmlands and a growing industrial area. The name *Toronto* is believed to be of Indian origin, meaning "meeting place," and such would be the case as the gospel and the people "met" through expanded missionary efforts. By the late 1950s, when the Monsons arrived, the city's population had reached one million.

The area, commonly called Upper Canada, would become home to the Monsons. In 2010, at the cultural celebration held in conjunction with the dedication of the Canada Vancouver Temple, the Church's 131st temple, President Monson delighted the thousands gathered by wearing on his lapel a Canadian flag pin with tiny flashing lights. They cheered when he changed the opening song to "O Canada."

When the Monsons got to the mission home, immediately they had a family of 130 missionaries; that number increased to 180 by 1962. President Monson would later reminisce, "The next three-year period was one of the happiest of our lives, as we devoted full time to sharing the gospel of Jesus Christ with others."[11]

President and Sister J. Earl Lewis, who had presided over the mission for three and a half years, took the Monsons on a two-week tour of the mission. They attended a number of member and missionary meetings and were introduced to the area.

The spacious mission home at 133 Lyndhurst Avenue needed repairs and renovation. Periodically, plaster fell in chunks from the ceiling to the living-room floor; the pipes were old, the furnace temperamental. But Frances worked hard to make it feel like home. The four floors housed not only the Monsons but also the missionaries who served in the office, which was on the third floor; the elder who served as a counselor in the mission presidency, along with his companion; incoming and outgoing missionaries; and at times those missionaries who were sick. "I wouldn't trade that old mission home and all those missionaries, the sick ones and homesick ones," President Monson has said. "[Frances] loved those missionaries and they knew it. I think she did more good than she realizes."[12] All who occupied the house ate together as family. Not surprisingly, breakfast, lunch, and dinner talk was mostly about the mission. In their three years in Canada, the Monsons had only three meals alone—at the Royal York Hotel Coffee Shop for Christmas Day dinner in 1959, 1960, and 1961.

Tom, twelfth mission president since the area had been reopened in 1919, grasped quickly the work ahead of him and felt the weight on his shoulders of presiding over the entire provinces of Ontario and Quebec.[13] There were no wards or stakes, just fifty-five branches with more than five thousand members in nine scattered districts. Some lived more than a thousand miles from Toronto. The nearest temple was in Cardston, Alberta, more than two thousand miles to the west.

At first introduction, the missionaries were surprised that their new president was so young. President Monson was not much older than the majority of the missionaries. Then they heard him speak, felt that firm grip of his handshake, and watched him interact with others. "It didn't take long to recognize the marked difference between him and the missionaries. He had a unique ability to blend with the missionaries and lead," recalls Stephen Hadley, the first missionary to serve with him as a counselor. "He spoke with a special spirit."[14]

"To know Tom Monson is to love him," says Everett (Ev) Pallin, who became his first counselor in the mission presidency. "He is so warm. When you meet him, you feel there is a connection. His themes in his talks seem very simple, yet they always come down to loving and caring and serving each other. That's what the gospel is all about. If we do that, then everything else falls in place."[15]

"Be positive yet gracious in your work as a missionary as you meet your brothers and sisters and open the gospel to their view," President Monson encouraged. "You are blessed with authority and with talents. Use that authority and those talents to their fullest as you serve here in the mission field. Yours is a labor of love—and this labor will bring you joy."[16]

President Monson believed that spirituality was essential to missionary success. "Our teaching, our training, and our testifying will quicken our own spirituality and awaken in those to whom we minister a dedication and determination to follow in the footsteps of our Lord."[17]

The Canadian Saints found in their new president great optimism. They enjoyed his humor and reveled in his teachings of the Savior and His ministry. He showed up at everything, everywhere. There was rarely a wedding or a social event where he didn't make an appearance. He called members when they were sick, visited them at the hospital, and spoke at their funerals. And he engaged them in teaching the gospel.

"President Monson created an excitement and momentum that encouraged Latter-day Saints to stay in Ontario and build up the Church there," observed Everett Pallin.[18] Before his era, many members moved to Utah or Alberta, where the Church was already strong. By the time he left, they were staying in Ontario. He had the ability to unite entire congregations in a common cause, whether it was building a chapel, fellowshipping new members, inviting neighbors to listen to the missionaries, or preparing for the first stake in Canada.

The mission had a small chapel on Ossington Avenue in Toronto, which Heber J. Grant had dedicated in 1939. The Hamilton branch had a modest structure built by the Church; the Kitchener branch met in a home that had been converted into a chapel. All other congregations met in "vintage" chapels purchased from other denominations or in rented quarters such as lodge halls, schools, or hotels, where they often had to clean up debris from a civic gathering or even a dog show from the night before.

Feeling the weight of his calling, President Monson went into the backyard behind the mission home shortly after they arrived, getting down on his knees and pouring out his heart to his Father in Heaven. In this makeshift "sacred grove," he promised, "I will give this mission everything I have, but I have just one wish—that I'll not lose a missionary." He recognized that "every missionary is the pride of his father and his mother, and they have entrusted that precious boy or that precious girl to me."[19] The Lord honored that request. President Monson's ability to keep his missionaries in the field is legend.

President Monson's first experience conducting a mission tour was with Elder ElRay L. Christiansen, an Assistant to the Quorum of the Twelve, who arrived four months into the Monsons' service. Seven-year-old Tommy appreciated how kind the leader was, showing interest in a young man who was lonesome for his grandfather. Elder Christiansen "looked upon missionary work as a serious enterprise." He interviewed all the missionaries. He also met with all the priesthood leaders in the district and counseled them on how they might best prepare to become a stake. President Monson watched and learned from this well-schooled General Authority and would in years to come employ the same exacting approach in his mission tours. Upon his return to Salt Lake City, Elder Christiansen reported he was "much impressed" with the mission and was "lavish" in his praise for the young mission president who obviously had his arms around the work.[20] He was surprised that President Monson knew the names of all the missionaries. He didn't know of Tom Monson's gift for committing names to memory. Elder M. Russell Ballard, who presided over that mission a decade later, recalls sitting on the stand in Canada with Elder Monson: "He would tell me, well, that's Brother So-and-so and that's Sister So-and-so, and he would remember their circumstances. His memory was unbelievable when it came to calling up names. You've got to have that gift come with you from the other side of the veil."[21]

Elder Bruce R. McConkie, at that time a member of the First Council of the Seventy, wrote to his friend Tom: "May I say that I have heard most excellent expressions relative to your good work as a mission president, both from Elder Christiansen who just returned and from others who have seen you operate. This is, of course, exactly what I expected would be the case."[22]

Prior to a General Authority visit, President Monson and the mission staff spent a great deal of time preparing. Those who have worked with him over the years have seen that dedication to getting things exactly right, being thoroughly prepared. None of the missionaries wanted to let their president down.

Others who toured the mission included Elder Mark E. Petersen, Elder Spencer W. Kimball, and Elder Franklin D. Richards. Elder Petersen's report reflected the comments of the others on subsequent visits: "President Monson is doing fine work. . . . He is a leader and inspires confidence in the missionaries. His counselors are giving him great assistance in administrative and proselyting work, stepping up mission activity. . . . All branches are under local administration. Elders quorums have been organized and most of the mission districts are well manned by local members. The mission building program is going forward . . . with eight new chapels soon to be built."[23]

Canada has a significant place in early Church history, and President Monson wanted his missionaries to have a witness that they indeed were preaching on sacred ground. Canada was the first foreign mission field of the Church; Joseph Smith preached his first sermon outside the United States in Canada in 1833 and observed that "great excitement prevailed in every place we have visited. The result we leave in the hand of the Lord."[24] President Monson often refers to section 100 of the Doctrine and Covenants as the "Canadian revelation": "Behold, . . . I have much people in this place, in the regions round about; and an effectual door shall be opened . . . in this eastern land."[25]

One assignment President Monson took especially seriously was what he now describes as "the privilege of showing the missionaries how to serve the Lord."[26] He believes, "The power to lead is also the power to mislead, and the power to mislead is the power to destroy,"[27] a principle he would teach repeatedly to new mission presidents, Church leaders, and teachers for years to come. He based his approach on a favorite scripture: "Therefore, strengthen your brethren in all your conversation, in all your prayers, in all your exhortations, and in all your doings."[29] He imagined the scene in every home of his missionaries: the parents of every missionary kneeling each day in prayer and asking Heavenly Father to bless that son or daughter in the mission field. "In that prayer," he has told new mission presidents in their training, "they ask a blessing upon you, for you in effect become a mother and a father to their child."[28]

His great faith inspired the missionaries. "There is a golden thread that runs through every account of faith from the beginning of the world to the present time," he has taught. "Abraham, Noah, the Brother of Jared, the Prophet Joseph, and countless others were obedient to the will of God. They had ears that could hear, eyes that could see, and hearts that could know and feel. They never doubted."[30]

One of President Monson's first travels was to Timmins, as far north in his mission as he could go. When he came back, Frances was teary. "Why are you crying?" he asked.

"I'm homesick," she said. "Aren't you?"

"You do the crying for us," he replied. "I've got 130 missionaries I've got to take care of, and if I cry, I will have them crying!"[31] The work went on, and Frances was more than up to the task. She waded into every assignment diligently, from directing Relief

Societies around the districts to running what amounted to a full bed-and-breakfast operation with great composure, efficiency, and quiet style.

But Frances didn't like to speak or command attention. One of the elders prepared an agenda for a zone conference that had Sister Monson speaking for twenty-five minutes. When President Monson told her of the "assignment," he did so with a chuckle— and then cut back her time to something more comfortable for her.

About eight months after the Monsons arrived in Toronto, Elder S. Dilworth Young of the First Council of the Seventy visited them on his way to another assignment. Elder Young later wrote to President Monson, "You're a mission president for three years. You're a husband and a father for eternity. Keep that in mind. Your dear friend, Dil."[32]

Busy as he was, President Monson consciously carved out time to spend with his children. In the evenings, he and Tommy would sit in the mission office and play checkers. President Monson was a whiz at checkers. As a young man, he had played checkers with his bishop but lost repeatedly. Tired of being defeated, he purchased a book that identified various strategies for checkers, one of which was to label each square with a number and make moves accordingly. He committed all the moves and techniques to memory and seldom lost again in those contests with the bishop—or with anyone else.

Young Tommy came to know the community well when he signed up to deliver the *Toronto Telegram*. He found the school curriculum and traditions very different from those at home; they followed the English system, which allowed for forms of corporal punishment. One day he came home with "eyes as big as saucers," telling of how the boy in front of him had been rapped on the knuckles with a ruler for being "out of order."

On Ann's birthday in 1959, her father and mother took her to see Queen Elizabeth, who was riding in a parade. "Ann, if you wave to the Queen, she will wave back to you," he promised. Ann did as instructed and marveled, "She not only waved to me, she smiled. How did she know it was my birthday?"[33]

Ann started kindergarten in Canada, and she too became a missionary. She spoke to her teacher, Miss Pepper, about how happy she was to be a Mormon, and she shared the Book of Mormon and the *Children's Friend* with her. Years later, when Miss Pepper retired, she visited Salt Lake City to see for herself what her young pupil found so engaging. The Monsons were out of town on an assignment and came home to a letter that read, "Dear Ann, I came to Salt Lake City today to see what you folks had because a little girl of five shared the Book of Mormon and the *Children's Friend.* Your courage one cannot deny. I went to Temple Square. I went to the visitors' center and now I see why you had that courage and testimony. Sorry I missed you." Miss Pepper died shortly after returning to Canada. Still the missionary, Ann performed the temple work for her first teacher in Toronto.[34]

Ann gave her first Church talk in the Ossington chapel. The Saturday before she was to speak, she could not find the paper with the talk she had written. She glanced in the parakeet cage and saw it there, serving as a cage liner. She did not retrieve it. She had prepared her talk on the Prophet Joseph Smith and memorized it—as her father had instructed. She gave it the next day with no notes.[35]

President Monson involved his family in missionary work whenever possible. Missionaries would practice their teaching on Tommy, Ann, and even Clark. The children were willing subjects, much as Tom had been years earlier when he had listened to his sister rehearse her readings.

Two years younger than President Monson, Ev Pallin served the full three years as his first counselor, working specifically with the branches and districts. A convert himself, he understood missionary work. He would go to the mission home first thing in the morning and give his schedule to the mission secretary. President Monson would be having breakfast with his family, and the two would chat. They traveled on weekends to quarterly conferences, staying with members in the various areas. With nine conferences each convening four times a year, the men weren't home much. "President Monson is a great person to work with, so complimentary," Ev explains. "He treated me as an equal. I was tutored under him. The rest of my life in big decisions I would know how he would treat the situation and that's what I would do."[36]

President Monson's second counselor—who would today be called an "assistant to the president"—worked with the missionaries. Stephen Hadley, one of those missionary counselors, had experiences with his president that were lifelong lessons. "I learned from President Monson that being a leader means more than just being there. It means being there *for another*. He has always been there for us—not just for me but for his entire contingent of missionaries."[37]

Transfers were not blocked into six-week rotations, as is typically the schedule in missions around the world today. New missionaries arrived all month long. President Monson remembers thirty coming one month, thirteen at one time. During his tenure, the age of eligibility for missionary service was lowered from twenty to nineteen. He worried that the new missionaries might be less prepared, but "they didn't miss a beat."[38]

Ask his missionaries today what they remember about their president, and they will talk about his teachings, his example, his exuberance, his intellect. "He inspired confidence," one says. "You had the strong feeling that he really cared for you," another adds. "You trusted his ability."[39] One newly arrived missionary, Elder Michael Murdock, was sitting in a sacrament meeting when the bishop announced that the mission president would conclude the meeting. As President Monson walked up the aisle, he patted the new elder on the back, just a slight pat, but it provided reassurance. "I knew that he loved me," Michael Murdock recalls. "I carried that with me all my mission."[40] Ev Pallin says, "You think of John the Beloved when you think of Tom Monson. Everything happens because of love, as far as he is concerned."[41]

Many of the missionaries saw in their president what they imagined the Prophet Joseph had been like as a leader. He had the same youthful vigor, the same strong leadership characteristics, and the same humility. He had a happy way of handling things, always positive, always decisive. But he "wouldn't stand for any monkey business." He had the ability to make the missionaries feel good, Ev recalls, "even when he was chastising them. He had a rare combination of leadership skills."[42]

The missionaries knew where their president turned for counsel. He had brought with him the portrait of the Savior that had hung in his office when he was bishop. (It still hangs in his office today.) Before working on transfers, one of them recalls, he would "get up from his chair and we would kneel and pray to receive the direction of the Lord. He offered a prayer and then had me offer a prayer."[43]

President Monson worked from a board on the wall with pictures of missionaries, as had his predecessor. But he developed his own method for moving them around. His missionary counselors were always astounded by the president's capacity to remember all the considerations. "He relied on the Lord. We watched it, and his choices always seemed to fit into the Lord's larger plan."[44]

Canada was leaning away from religion. In 1960 the electorate approved theaters and halls to show movies, plays, and concerts on Sundays; Sabbath sports events were already allowed. Catholics were the largest denomination; the United Church of Canada, second; and the Anglicans, third. Immigrants from Italy, Germany, Poland, Hungary, and even the Ukraine provided a fertile field for missionaries.

Missionaries in Welland on the Niagara Peninsula began teaching a group of Italian-speaking immigrants. These investigators invited the missionaries in and were willing to listen, but they did not understand the discussions, as none of the elders spoke Italian. Right around that same time, President Monson was contemplating transfers in that area. As he reviewed the missionaries, "trying to place them, by the will of the Lord, with the right companion and in the right place," he stopped at the name of an Elder Smith. He pondered why he was drawn to that elder's name. A transfer seemed premature. Yet the impression to move Elder Smith over to the Niagara Peninsula came so strongly that he made the move.

The next week, tears came to his eyes as he read in the missionary letters: "Dear President Monson, I know you were inspired in sending Elder Smith to us in Welland. We are teaching ten

Italian-speaking families whose English skills are limited. In my heart I had been praying for a companion who could speak Italian. You found the only missionary in the mission who spoke Italian." President Monson had known nothing about the elder's language skills. He recalls, "With a name like Smith, you don't think he is going to speak Italian."[45]

The miracles continued. President Monson placed one new missionary from a rural area with a companion in the city of Oshawa. The two knocked at a door in a thick, blinding blizzard. Elmer Pollard answered the door and, taking pity on the two elders, invited them in. They shared their message and then asked him if he would join them in prayer. He agreed—if he could offer the prayer. His words astonished the elders. "Heavenly Father," he said, "grant that these two unfortunate, misguided missionaries might see the error of their ways and return to their homes. They have come to a land about which they know nothing to teach that about which they know so little. Amen." He walked the missionaries to the door and sent them on their way. His last words to the two were quite caustic: "You can't tell me you actually believe Joseph Smith was a prophet of God!"

He didn't wait for a reply. He shut the door, ending the exchange. The elders were walking away when the new missionary turned to his companion and said: "Elder, we didn't answer Mr. Pollard's question. He said we didn't believe Joseph Smith was a true prophet. Let's return and bear our testimonies to him." His companion hesitated but finally agreed.

They again knocked at the door, and when it was answered the unseasoned elder spoke: "Mr. Pollard, you indicated we didn't believe Joseph Smith was a prophet of God. I testify to you that Joseph was a prophet; he did translate the Book of Mormon; he saw God the Father and Jesus the Son. I know it." The missionaries departed the doorstep.

"I heard this same Mr. Pollard, in a testimony meeting, state the experience of that memorable day," President Monson has said. The once caustic investigator described: "That evening, sleep would not come. I tossed and turned. Over and over in my mind I heard the words, 'Joseph Smith is a prophet of God. I know it. . . .

I know it. . . . I know it.' I could scarcely wait for morning to come. I telephoned the missionaries, using the address which was on the small card they had left behind containing the Articles of Faith. They returned, and this time, with the correct spirit, my wife and family and I joined in the discussion as earnest seekers of truth. As a result we have all embraced the gospel of Jesus Christ. We shall ever be grateful to the testimony of truth brought to us by courageous, humble missionaries."[46]

Sister Monson claims her own converts. Running a busy mission home, she one day took a phone call and spoke with a person whose Dutch accent came through clearly. He asked, "Is this the headquarters of the Mormon Church?"

She assured him it was, at least for the Toronto area, and asked how she could help. The caller said, "We have come from our native Holland where we have had an opportunity to learn something about the Mormons. My wife would like to know more. I would not." Frances, being the good missionary she was, said, "We can help you." She wrote down all the pertinent information.

"This is a golden referral," she told the missionaries on the staff excitedly as she gave them the names of Jacob and Bea de Jager and their family. But, as sometimes happens, they put off contacting the de Jagers. Days turned to weeks, and she continued to remind them, "Are you going to call on that Dutch family tonight, elders?" After a few more days she would prod again. Finally, exasperated, she said, "If you aren't going to call the Dutch family tonight, my husband and I will!"

Elders Newell Smith and James Turpin committed to a visit that night. They returned to the de Jager home the next night and the next as the family received the teachings of the gospel and the spirit filled their hearts. Every one of them joined the Church—even the father who had professed in the beginning to have no interest.

Brother Jacob de Jager became the elders quorum president before his company transferred him to Mexico. He later served as a counselor to several mission presidents in Holland, then as a regional representative, and finally as a member of the First Quorum of the Seventy from 1976 to 1993. The de Jagers claim the special distinction of being "converts of Sister Monson in Canada."[47]

President Monson focused on involving members in finding and fellowshipping investigators and new converts. They would join in the teaching and could speak with authenticity of their own conversions. Brother and Sister Anthony Belfiglio, who once were Catholic, could ask all the right questions, such as, "What parish are you in?"[48] Brother William Stoneman could say how he lost his job as the chief bookbinder of the United Church of Canada when he joined The Church of Jesus Christ of Latter-day Saints. He would testify, "I found a better job—but more than that, I found greater truth, all the truth, and you will too. May we pick you up on Sunday? We'll sit by you during our meetings and then we'll be able to answer your questions."[49]

"That kind of member involvement produces converts who stay and who build and who serve," President Monson emphasized at a reunion in 2002 at the Ossington chapel. He knew of what he spoke. In attendance were converts who had joined the Church when he was a mission president nearly half a century before. He continues to admonish: "No mission in the Church will ever achieve its full potential without member missionary cooperation and involvement."[50] In an area like Canada, thin on membership, the missionaries could not keep busy working strictly from referrals. President Monson held to what worked in his mission and what he felt inspired to do. That included tracting and door-to-door contacting to find and rescue those lost to the ways of God. But he always credited the member program with the most dramatic increase in the number of converts.

President Monson's ecumenical spirit was ideal for the diverse culture of his mission. He understood that there was room for every person's faith and every person's service. In speaking to a crowd gathered to commemorate the beginnings of the Church in Canada, he embraced the diverse nature of the country, saying: "I believe that we have seen in our lifetime a great movement toward an understanding that we're all God's children, whatever our color, whatever our faith, whatever our background."[51]

Standardized lessons had yet to be integrated into missionary work, so President Monson created a seventy-five-page handbook that included general instructions, ideas regarding preparation, and helps for proselyting. His words in the introduction ring as true now as they did then: "Our missionary handbook is dedicated to the purpose of finding honest souls, helping them to gain a firm testimony of the restored gospel, and bringing them into the kingdom of God."[52] At district and mission leadership conferences, he worked from a four-point plan that included (1) appointing and training coordinator couples in every branch to assist in the interaction of investigators and new converts, (2) increasing the emphasis on investigators attending Church services, (3) introducing a district missionary program to supplement the work of full-time missionaries, and (4) accelerating the missionary teaching process by meeting with investigators on a more frequent basis.[53]

In 1959 President Monson initiated an extensive building program throughout the mission to get the Saints out of rented halls, unfinished basements, Elks lodges, and third-floor walk-ups. He told the story of taking an investigator into the basement of the Moose Hall, saying, "Here's where the true Church of Jesus Christ meets," and hearing a woman ask, "What is the purpose in your religion of the animal head on the wall?"

The answer, "Oh, we're just meeting here temporarily."

Then came the question, "Oh, is your church temporary in our city?"[54]

President Monson put in motion the building program to change such perceptions. Success in the missionary effort required having chapels for services.

Building fever swept the mission, and by March 1961 new ward buildings were completed in Timmins and Oshawa. President Monson started planning for meetinghouses in Toronto, St. Catharines, St. Thomas, London, and Sudbury. When he purchased land for the Etobicoke stake center, the $27,000 check was "the largest check" he had ever held in his hand. On December 11, 1966, Elder Monson, then a member of the Quorum of the Twelve, came back to dedicate that stake center. An overflow crowd of more than 1,700 attended. By then the stake had grown to 4,957 members, an increase of 2,654 in six and half years.[55] The members were fine people, schooled in the gospel and committed to the work.

One of President Monson's early visits among the Canadian Saints was to the struggling St. Thomas Branch. The members— just three families—met in a dilapidated "Orange Hall," named for a fraternal order of William of Orange. Irving Wilson served as branch president; he blessed and helped pass the sacrament and conducted the meetings. Brother Wilson envisioned a new chapel just like one recently completed in Sydney, Australia, and pictured in the *Improvement Era*. He wanted an identical chapel in St. Thomas. President Monson suggested that in time such a structure could be built.

"We don't want to wait," said Brother Wilson. He asked for additional missionaries, promising to provide sufficient referrals to keep them busy. President Monson looked at Brother Wilson's sincerity and eagerness and couldn't say no. He sent six missionaries to St. Thomas.

Brother Wilson operated a small jewelry store and met with the missionaries in his back workroom. They knelt in prayer, and then he said, "This is the beginning of a new day in St. Thomas. We are going to build a chapel." They needed members. "You do the teaching, I'll get them here," Brother Wilson told the missionaries. He reached for the phone directory and turned to the Yellow Pages, explaining, "We ought to have a building designed by a Mormon architect, and since we don't have an architect who is a member of the branch, we need to convert one." He went down the list of architects until he found a name he recognized. He did the same for others, including a builder, barrister, mechanic, and brick mason. He invited the individuals to his home, introduced them to the missionaries, and bore his testimony, as did his wife. Within two and a half years, the fledgling branch of three families had expanded to more than two hundred members. And then they built their chapel.

Brother Wilson believed that their building merited a Wurlitzer organ, a step above the regular-issue Hammond organ. The Church would contribute only enough for the standard

Hammond model. But Brother Wilson was not to be deterred. He called the head of the Church Building Department and asked, "If we can get a Wurlitzer organ for the same price as a Hammond, will you agree to pay?" Permission was given, and Brother Wilson found a Wurlitzer.

At the first meeting in the new building, five different organists participated. They invited nonmembers to come and play the new Wurlitzer, and as those "guest organists" sat through the meetings, listening to the talks and the hymns, each one became an investigator and then a member.[56]

When President Monson first arrived in Toronto, missionaries were serving as district presidents over eight or ten branches; others were branch presidents. As quickly as possible, he moved local priesthood leaders into those responsibilities, allowing the missionaries more time to focus on finding investigators and teaching the gospel. This also provided leadership experience for the members, who had a lot of talent but little administrative experience in the Church.

When President Monson attended the North Bay Branch in a remote corner of Ontario, he found a small congregation of sisters, a handful of investigators, and one priesthood holder, Brother Donald Mabey. Recently transferred to the area by a diamond products company, Brother Mabey had executive experience in business, but he was a thirty-five-year-old deacon who had never had any priesthood responsibility in the Church. He rarely even attended church. Still, he held the highest priesthood authority in the North Bay Branch. President Monson called him to be the branch president.

"I am not qualified," Brother Mabey responded, citing his total lack of experience in the Church. "Surely there is someone else who can do it."

"No, Brother Mabey, if there were, I would not be calling you," President Monson said. Brother Mabey finally accepted the calling, and the branch flourished under his care, as did his testimony and commitment.[57]

Because of the great distances in the mission, much of President Monson's communication to and from the missionaries was by post or telegram. On one occasion, he received from a missionary in the north a telegram that said, "President, the temperature is 40 degrees below freezing. Please advise."

President Monson sent a telegram back: "Dress warm, work hard, and don't look at the thermometer."

The district leader in Kitchener, Ontario, a city of some 80,000 people, wrote, "Dear President Monson: We have tracted out the city of Kitchener. Please tell us where to go next."

President Monson responded, "Dear Elder: Happy to hear that you have tracted out the city of Kitchener. Now if you will teach and baptize the people in Kitchener, that will be your next assignment."[58]

When President Monson learned that the Kingston area to the east had seen but one convert baptism in six years, he decided it was time to exert great faith. For years, missionaries assigned to "Stony Kingston" had marked their time there on the calendar like days in jail. One day Sister Monson read aloud to President Monson an entry in a book she was reading: "Brigham Young entered Kingston, Ontario, on a cold, snow-filled day. He labored there thirty days and baptized forty-five souls."

The passage gave President Monson an idea. He moved all missionaries out of Kingston—they were happy to leave—and then he waited. Soon he announced that "a new city" would be opened for missionary work and described it as "the city where Brigham Young proselyted and baptized forty-five persons in thirty days." The speculation began, and in weekly letters several missionaries hinted they would like the chance to open this new bonanza for missionary work. He assigned missionaries to Kingston—again—and it became "the most productive city in the Canadian mission." All involved learned an important lesson. The city had not altered its appearance; the population had remained the same. "The change was one of attitude. Doubt yielded to faith."[59] Indeed, "they just picked up the plow and plowed on."[60]

President Monson's optimism was contagious. To him, "Success is contingent upon our effective use of the time given us. When we cease peering backwards into the mists of our path and craning forward into the fog that shrouds the future and simply concentrate upon doing what lies clearly at hand, then we are making the best and happiest use of our time. Success is the ratio of your accomplishments to your capabilities."[61]

Creation of the Toronto Stake, the 300th stake in the Church, was a major milestone in the mission. President Monson had watched carefully as new stakes were established, most of them in the western United States. The Alberta Canada Stake, organized in 1895, had been the first stake outside the United States. He admits to holding his breath for fear that Toronto would be the 299th stake rather than the landmark 300th. When Puget Sound in Washington State became the 299th stake, he was delighted. Some time later when he visited the Puget Sound Stake on assignment, he began his message by saying, "I am honored to be here in the 299th stake of the Church." The members marveled at his ability to know precisely when that stake was created and what number they were in sequence in the Church. He didn't divulge that he had been watching from Upper Canada and hoping another stake would round out the 200s.

He asked his first counselor, Ev Pallin, who was familiar with the city, to recommend a facility large enough to hold the stake organization meeting. Brother Pallin found just the right place: the Odeon Carlton Theatre in downtown Toronto, which was closed on Sundays. When he told President Monson about it, Brother Pallin said, "You'll like it because of the organ. You will feel like you are in the Tabernacle." President Monson took Frances to a movie, *The Story of Ruth,* at the Odeon, but he didn't see much of the film. He was busy walking up and down the aisles counting seats. The next time he met with Brother Pallin, he said of the Odeon, "That's the place."

It would require 90 percent attendance of the members in the new stake to fill the seats. President Monson and Brother Pallin organized both a 437-voice children's chorus and a 325-voice Relief Society chorus in order to bring out as many people as possible. The creation of the stake was announced throughout the mission, and people came from everywhere. The conference drew 2,250 people, 92 percent of the new stake's membership, "the largest assemblage of Latter-day Saints ever to come together in the history of the Church in Ontario."[62]

Elder Mark E. Petersen and Elder Alma Sonne organized the Toronto Stake, the first stake in Eastern Canada, made up of three districts. William M. Davies, president of the Toronto District, was called as president. Now the Saints in the area would have all the blessings of a fully organized stake, including their own patriarch. Instead of having to travel to the Detroit Stake for their patriarchal blessings, they could receive them in their own area.

Three years had yet to be set as the standard length of service for a mission president. Most served about that—some a little more, some a little less. In January 1962, after almost three years in Toronto, President Monson received word that the management of the Deseret News Publishing Company was being reorganized and that he was slotted for a prominent position. A few months earlier, Preston Robinson, general manager of the Deseret News Publishing Company, had invited him down from the mission field to meet him at a printing company in Detroit to look over a new web-offset press. The Deseret News was making the move to web-offset printing, in which the paper is fed into the press on a continuous roll, printed on both sides in full color, folded, and then prepared for delivery at the end of the press. The Deseret News bought a press like the one President Monson and Brother Robinson saw.

So when President Monson received a letter of honorable release from his mission, he was not surprised. He was prepared to leave the mission but not ready to turn over to another "the wonderful missionary force." He was convinced then and is still today "that it was the finest group of missionaries to be found anywhere in the world."[63] His roots had gone deep, and Canada had become "a treasured and hallowed nation" to him.[64] The Monsons left "a little of their hearts" in Toronto.

Frank Pitcher and his wife, a couple from Calgary, Canada, replaced the Monsons, assuming responsibility for the mission on February 1, 1962.

President Monson left an imprint on his missionaries that was lasting. One of his elders, Wayne Chamberlain, recalls his own "exit interview" in 1961: "I sat in front of my mission president; he was thirty-three years old. He was the most dynamic man I had ever met in mortality. He had given me a vision of what this great gospel of Jesus Christ was all about and who Joseph Smith was and, most important, how to be an effective missionary. But he gave me one bit of advice that I have never forgotten. He said, 'I am giving you a temple recommend. This will now be the most valuable possession in your world and in your life.' Then he said, specifically, 'I want you to use it and I expect you, Elder Chamberlain, to always be worthy to hold that recommend.'"[65]

As each missionary departed, President Monson explained that missions are a training ground for future service in the Lord's kingdom. He did not realize how completely he was speaking of his own life to come.

14

CALLED TO GENERAL CHURCH COMMITTEES

President Monson's heart is like the heart of the Lord. President Monson would treat the janitor cleaning the banister the same way he would treat the ambassador from Russia who comes in to visit him. Because of his sense of the eternal nature of people, he doesn't see the world in terms of economic or social status. He sees as the Lord would see, and he reaches out.

ELDER NEIL L. ANDERSEN
Quorum of the Twelve Apostles

AT THE END OF JANUARY 1962, the Monsons left the Canadian Mission. They had not opted to take their replacements, the Pitchers, on a grueling tour of the mission like the one they had taken when they had first arrived. But they did sponsor two open houses so the new mission president and his wife could meet the missionary leadership and the member leadership.

The Monsons purchased a new, aqua-colored Pontiac Star Chief automobile in Detroit, bade the missionaries, members, and neighbors good-bye, and headed home to Salt Lake City. Even the gruff, complaining next-door neighbors were sorry to see the family leave. President Monson's efforts to make friends with this couple, who had resented the comings and goings at 133 Lyndhurst at all hours of the day and night, had been highly successful. He had sent his missionaries to help in their garden, to shovel their walks, and to do odd jobs. He had won them over.

Frances had made an impact on the neighborhood as well. When she had arrived there had been women living all along the tree-lined street who, because of a slight here or an offhand comment there, hadn't spoken to each other in years. Frances brought them together at events at the mission home, and slowly those tensions eased. When the Monsons returned to Salt Lake, they left behind neighbors who watched out for one another.

The family drove the southern route across the United States, trying to avoid winter weather, but they still encountered ice storms in Missouri. They visited Frances's brother Arnold Johnson and his wife, Janice, and their children in Phoenix and then continued on to Disneyland in California, where the children had their first experience at "the Magic Kingdom." Then they turned the car for home.

When they got caught in a terrible storm about twenty miles south of their destination, Frances suggested they just turn around and spend the night in Provo. But Tom made the decision to continue on. That evening, after they reached home, the phone rang. John R. Burt from the Temple View Stake presidency, a close friend, was on the line with a request. His father, John H. Burt, had passed away, and his last wish had been that "Bishop Monson" would speak at his funeral. Tom was happy to honor the request. The service was the next day, so he had miraculously arrived home just in time—a pattern he would see repeated many times in years to come. With many from the Sixth-Seventh Ward in attendance, he paid tribute to his old friend, calling him "Truly a man of God."[1]

Tom submitted a report to the Church of his "mission labors," dated February 3, 1962, in which he indicated that he and Frances felt "richly blessed" to have served in Eastern Canada. "The Lord has poured out His spirit on the people of that land. Cities that never had baptisms before are now producing converts every month. One of the recent innovations is the work among the French-speaking people. Now six missionaries are assigned to this part of the work. A French-speaking Sunday School is now functioning in Montreal, and the effort is beginning to show results."[2]

The Church in Canada had grown in membership under his direction. In 1958, the year before he arrived, 266 were baptized, which amounted to an average of 2.13 converts per missionary;

in 1959, 309 became members, 2.44 converts per missionary; in 1960, 462 joined the Church, 3.31 converts per missionary; and in 1961, 1,005 new members were added to the rolls, 5.49 converts per missionary.[3]

Elder Franklin D. Richards, who knew the mission from his earlier tour, praised President Monson for his service, writing: "We are going to miss you, but I am sure an important assignment awaits you here. One thousand and five baptisms in 1961 is a great blessing to all." He signed his letter, "Frank."[4]

Tom immediately returned to work at Deseret News Press as assistant general manager. It was by then the largest printing plant west of the Mississippi River. He may have expected to assume a position as staff assistant to longtime associate and mentor Preston Robinson, since at one time that had seemed Tom's niche. But Robinson had other things in mind. He decided that Tom's administrative and leadership skills could best be used in an executive post. Tom had received other offers, including a far more lucrative partnership with a local real estate firm that would clearly have been a better financial proposition. But the Deseret News Press had provided a stipend while he served in Canada. They had held a job for him. Loyal to the core, he honored his association and did not look twice at the other opportunities.

Just a month later, in March 1962, he was promoted to general manager of the Press and Louis C. (Lou) Jacobsen, who had held that post since 1950, was named an adviser and consultant.

Tom made sure Lou had a presence at the plant and did not feel pushed aside. Lou had begun his career as an errand boy and had been with the Deseret News for fifty-eight years. Wilford Wood, a well-known entrepreneur, commended Tom for how he approached Lou's retirement. Tom had said to Wilford Wood, "If you come down to the plant you will see Lou and me sitting side by side, the same as we were before, and happily working together." Said Wood, "No one else would do such a thing for a most worthy worker and companion but you. . . . All of this because of your deep love, wisdom, understanding, and thoughtfulness of someone who likes you and who needs you and whom you appreciated."[5]

Tom was well loved by the employees at the Press. "After you returned from Canada and we became associated at the Deseret News Press, no one encouraged me as much as you did, although you hardly knew me," Max Zimmer wrote twenty years later. "When my dear mother passed away—whom you did not even know—you honored her and all of us by attending her funeral in Ogden; I did not even dare to inform you beforehand, let alone to invite you!"[6]

Printing processes across the country were changing dramatically. Letterpress operations were giving way to offset printing and lithography. The Press had remodeled extensively and upgraded its machinery as the company made the transition. The equipment Tom had evaluated in the East—a high-speed, five-unit, web-offset, state-of-the-art press—was now in place at the plant. The new presses were a far cry from the first printing efforts in the valley in January 1849, when President Brigham Young and his secretary Thomas Bullock had set the type for the first fifty-cent bills to be used as currency.[7]

For nearly two years after his return from Canada, Tom directed the massive shift in the operation at the Press, which required retraining the mechanical personnel. To help reshape the Press, he named LeRoy DeKarver as plant manager and William James Mortimer as sales manager, a position Tom had once held.

Though very much a businessman, Tom had a management style that was similar to that of a bishop "managing" a ward: mingling with the employees, getting to know their families and their ambitions, as well as upgrading the overall performance of the organization.

One evening he drove fellow employee Sharman Hummel home from the plant. In their conversation, he learned that the Hummels were soon to be sealed in the Manti Temple. Tom asked him if there were a story behind his joining the Church. Ever the missionary, Tom loved what he heard and would later share Sharman Hummel's story from the pulpit.

Sharman explained that he had been living in the East. On one occasion he was journeying west by bus to establish himself in a new company, after which he was going to send for his wife and children. All the way from New York to Salt Lake City the bus trip was uneventful. But in Salt Lake City a teenage girl sat down next to him. She was on her way to Reno, Nevada, to visit an aunt. He turned to her and said, "I guess there are a lot of Mormons in Utah, aren't there?"

She replied, "Yes, sir."

"Are you a Mormon?" he asked.

The girl said, "Yes, sir."

"What do Mormons believe?" he asked, not expecting much of an answer.

The teenager recited the first Article of Faith. And then she talked about it. Then she gave him the second one and talked about it, then the third, fourth, fifth, and sixth up to the thirteenth; she knew them all consecutively and talked about each one.

"When we came to Reno," Sharman continued, "and we let that young girl off into the arms of her aunt, I was profoundly impressed. On the way to San Francisco I thought, 'What is it that prompts a teenager to know her doctrine that well?' When I arrived in San Francisco, the very first thing I did was to look through the Yellow Pages for the Mormon Church. I called the mission president, J. Leonard Love, and he sent two missionaries to my home. I became a member of the Church, my wife became a member, all of my children became members, and all with whom I visited as a stake missionary have become members because a young girl had learned her Articles of Faith in Primary and, in her humble way, taught me what she believed."

Sharman confessed to Tom that he had but one regret: He had not asked the girl's name. "I've never been able to thank her," he said. Tom replied, "Maybe it's just as well, Sharman. In this way, every teacher of every Primary girl may, in her own mind, believe perhaps that it was someone she had taught who brought this great blessing to you and to so many people."[8]

Tom stayed in touch with the Hummels. In 2007, when the family came to Salt Lake City for the wedding of a daughter, they stopped by President Monson's office for "a wonderful visit" that included Brother and Sister Hummel, their six daughters, four sons-in-law, and twelve grandchildren. President Monson was delighted that the entire family had remained active in the Church. Each of the married daughters had been to the temple. "Countless are those who have been brought to a knowledge of the gospel by the members of this family—all because a young girl had been taught the Articles of Faith and had the ability and the courage to proclaim the truth to one who was seeking the light of the gospel."[9] When President Monson thinks of the Hummels, he remembers the words of the Apostle Paul: "For I am not ashamed of the gospel of Christ: for it is the power of God unto salvation."[10] He reminds people, "We not only teach with words; we teach also by who we are and how we live our lives."[11]

Though Tom often stayed late at the office, he was a dad when he was home. He mowed the lawn with the help of the boys. He planted a vegetable garden and enlisted the children to pull weeds; he took them bowling and to the movies, swimming at the Deseret Gym, sleigh riding in winter, and to the Pioneer Day parade in summer. For the parade, they set up chairs in front of his father's printing enterprise on Main Street and cheered for Tom's brother Bob when he rode by on his horse, positioned on the front row of the Ute Rangers and carrying the organization's flag. Often Tom took the boys fishing and duck hunting, two of their favorite pastimes.

Family was ever important to Tom. In the summers, the relatives continued to gather at Vivian Park. "I never visit Vivian Park but what I don't become nostalgic with respect to my boyhood experiences at this canyon home," he confided in his journal.[12] His son Clark's fondest memories as a child are of the big breakfasts at Vivian Park with all the family, evening campfires roasting hot dogs and marshmallows, and the family chat. "Often it would be my dad leading the conversations, steering the conversations," Clark recalls. "If my dad and [his sister] Marjorie were together, they really loved to talk, and it was always fun for me to be around them."[13]

President Monson's son Tom remembers one family get-together at the cabin, with everyone enjoying the traditional potato salad, chicken, chili, and roasted hot dogs, when he sat with his father's Uncle Rusty up on the porch. "Every time a kid would open the door and close it softly, Rusty would say, 'That one is not a Condie,' and then a kid would come rushing through the door and bang the door shut, and he would say, 'That one's a Condie.' That's where Dad gets it," Tom suggests. "In many ways Dad is much more a Condie than a Monson. The Monsons were much more sedate. Condies were all action all the time, and they were big on hunting and fishing. Dad grew up learning hunting and fishing from his uncles on the Condie side."[14]

Amidst his professional and family responsibilities, Tom also found continuing opportunities for Church service. On his first evening home from Canada, in fact, he heard from his stake president, Rex C. Reeve, who officially extended to him a call to serve on the stake high council. Elder Delbert L. Stapley set him apart for the position.

Elder Vaughn J. Featherstone, then a member of the Valley View Stake high council and later a General Authority, recalls President Rex Reeve putting forward Thomas S. Monson's name. Though many knew the returning mission president, Brother Featherstone did not. After Tom reported on his mission to the high council, Brother Featherstone was so impressed that he went to President Reeve and said, "You need to put him in my chair (I think I was about seventh chair on the high council at the time) and put me in the bottom chair on the high council." The stake president responded, "Well, it doesn't work that way." Brother Featherstone said, "I know, but he is something else."[15]

The two were "kindred spirits." Tom found in Vaughn Featherstone "a most guileless and able leader, as well as a dear personal friend." They would ultimately serve together in Church leadership for thirty years.

Tom's tenure on the high council was brief but effective. One of his assignments was to increase attendance at stake conference. He knew how to do that; he had filled a theater in Toronto with more than 2,000 members when the first stake in that area was created. He set to work, and the following quarterly conference had the largest turnout ever. He had invited all the children ages eight to eleven to sing in a Primary chorus, and "of course their parents and loved ones came, and it was a wonderful conference."[16]

But Tom's experience in Canada had prepared him for more than filling choir seats. He came home having had a rich personal experience that had given him a broad understanding of the growing missionary program, the needs of fledgling units, and the international reach of the gospel. In addition, because of his association with many General Authorities before his mission as their printer, and on his mission during their tours, it was no surprise that he was quickly tapped to work on a general Church level.

In March 1962, when Tom had been home for less than two months, Elder Spencer W. Kimball invited him to his office and called him to serve as an area supervisor for nine stake missions. The First Presidency announced his appointment to what they termed Area Number 3, and he was released on April 15 from the Valley View Stake high council. As an area supervisor, one of twenty-five, he was charged with providing encouragement and training in stake missionary activities and missionary labors in general. He felt right at home promoting again the program of "Every Member a Missionary," a work that he truly loved and felt bound by duty to perform.[17]

His printing responsibilities made him a frequent visitor to the Church Administration Building at 47 East South Temple. One day he encountered President David O. McKay and his counselor Hugh B. Brown coming down the front steps of the building. After a brief exchange about his experience in Canada, Tom had turned to cross the street to the Deseret Book Company when President McKay called out, "Brother Monson!" Immediately Tom returned to President McKay's side. Looking into the former mission president's eyes, President McKay said, "Remember, Brother Monson, once a missionary, always a missionary." Tom nodded in understanding, and the prophet concluded the dialogue, "That's all, Brother Monson; that's all."[18]

The area supervisor program was "in the growing-up process," and Church leaders were still figuring out how best to utilize the talents of the new leaders.[19] The intent was to increase member missionary activity in the wards and stakes. Elders Spencer W. Kimball, Ezra Taft Benson, Mark E. Petersen, and Delbert L. Stapley comprised the Committee on Area Supervision of Stake Missions. Elder Stapley was Tom's direct contact for his area. "We shall try to keep close to you," Elder Kimball, who chaired the committee, assured the supervisors, with an offer to make available any of the four General Authorities for meetings of groups of stake leaders.

Tom and the others called were counseled to do their work "*through* the stake presidencies and not *over* them." Elder Kimball recommended using the power of suggestion: "Would you like to do this?" "What would you think of this suggestion?" "Have you thought of this?" They were to hold "development meetings," not "workshops," and were trained in the basics of goal setting and planning.[20]

Tom supervised the Winder, Wilford, Monument Park, Monument Park West, Hillside, Highland, Parleys, Sugarhouse, and Wasatch Stakes. He submitted monthly reports directly to Elder Kimball, in which he was encouraged to report unusual changes in activity, both increases and decreases, and to add "a few words" about the work.[21]

The Apostles kept a close eye on the work, and when conversions for the first five months of the year fell below the previous year's number, and reports indicated that the number of stake missionaries had reduced by hundreds, the area supervisors were encouraged to impress on stake leaders the need for a greater emphasis on missionary work.

Preparing to visit the Wasatch Stake in Heber City, Utah, Tom reviewed the reports and "was appalled by the relatively few serving as stake missionaries." He had enthusiasm for stake missionary work, particularly since the member-missionary program had been one of the keys to his success in Canada. He assured committee chairman Elder Kimball that "this stake would soon have more than four stake missionaries." At a meeting in Heber, he randomly called the bishop of the Midway Second Ward to find out how many of the brethren in his ward were serving as stake missionaries.

The bishop answered, "None."

Tom continued, "Bishop, how many nonmembers of the Church do you have living within your ward boundaries?"

"One, Brother Monson," the bishop replied, to Tom's surprise.

Not to lose his point, Tom countered, "And what are you doing to bring that precious nonmember to the waters of baptism?"

"He is the ward custodian, and his wife is active as a teacher in Primary," the bishop explained. "We're making progress."

Tom concluded the interview, "God bless you, Bishop. Keep up the good work."[22]

The encounter taught Tom a lesson. Never again would he walk into an assignment without knowing what to expect. Even today, prior to a regional stake conference broadcast, he will assemble the group of speakers and go over the service in detail, as well as facts regarding the stakes in the area.

That October, three area supervisors—Tom included—received congratulations from the Missionary Committee for "the increase in hours of proselyting" in their areas. Others had dipped.[23] Also noted was the increase in baptisms in several of the areas. One area showed a 7 percent increase, and from there the numbers climbed to 24 percent, 35 percent, 81 percent. The highest increase was 160 percent, in Brother Monson's area. Figures also showed a "definite improvement in the efficiency of the work in some areas." Brother Monson's was one of them.[24]

Tom was just getting acclimated to the Missionary Committee when the First Presidency appointed him to a second general priesthood committee, the Priesthood Genealogy Committee. He was one of the first twenty-one members called to serve in that specific capacity, many of them former mission presidents.[25] He continued as a member of the Missionary Committee as well.

There were four general priesthood committees in operation at that time. They represented initial steps in the Correlation effort that the First Presidency had put in the able hands of Elder Harold B. Lee in 1960. At the time there was no harmonizing of courses of study in the auxiliaries or the priesthood quorums, and many of their materials changed each year.

President David O. McKay would remember studies

Newlyweds Tom and Frances Monson at their wedding reception at the
Johnson family home, 1046 Yale Avenue, October 7, 1948.

Bishops' council of the Temple View Stake. Bishop Thomas S. Monson
is seated on the far right.

Sixth-Seventh Ward Adult MIA Class in 1949 when Tom Monson (seated in front, center)
was YMMIA superintendent.

Tom attended church in the venerable Sixth-Seventh Ward building until 1957. One of the original nineteen chapels in the Salt Lake Valley, it was demolished in 1967.

Thomas S. Monson was a bishop at age 22, a member of a stake presidency at 27, a mission president at 31, and an Apostle at 36.

Bishop Monson (back row, third from right) with Sixth-Seventh Ward
elders quorum, May 21, 1950, after they received highest honors
among elders quorums of Temple View Stake for 1949–50.

At Temple Square, about 1957, with friend and fellow counselor in the
Temple View Stake presidency John R. Burt and his wife, Irene.

Tom and Uncle Rusty Kirby at the Salt Creek Gun Club in 1956.

Uncle Rusty Kirby at his Phillips 66 gas station on Parley's Way in Salt Lake.
Occasionally Tom would help out with pumping gas.

In the backyard of the Monson home in Salt Lake City with two
of his prize Birmingham roller pigeons.

The pigeon loft in the Monson backyard.

Deseret News classified advertising manager Tom Monson and staff, about 1950.

Tom Monson was at home with all aspects of the printing business, from purchasing paper to selling advertising to working with the presses.

The Deseret News Press in the 1950s was one of the West's largest commercial printing firms.

At the Deseret News Press in November 1956. Left to right: Louis C. Jacobsen, President J. Reuben Clark, Jr., Tom Monson, Rowena Miller, Alva H. Parry, Elder Mark E. Petersen.

At the Deseret News Press with
President David O. McKay and
David Lawrence McKay.

With President McKay and O. Preston
Robinson, editor and general manager
of the Deseret News operation.

Checking a printing plate at the Deseret News Press.
Tom was a familiar presence in the back shop.

G. Spencer Monson at Western Hotel Register, where Tom apprenticed as a youth.

At Western Hotel Register in November 1977 when father, G. Spencer (center), retired from the printing profession. Monson sons (left to right): Scott, Bob, and Tom.

President and Sister Monson served their mission
in Toronto, Canada, from 1959 through 1962.

Monson family: Ann (4), Frances, Tom, and young Tommy (8),
just before their move to the Canadian Mission.

President and Sister Monson with mission leadership at a conference in 1959.

The mission home on Ossington Avenue in Toronto, Ontario, Canada.

President J. Reuben Clark, Jr., with his namesake, Clark Spencer Monson.

The Monsons returned home from Canada in 1962. Left to right: Frances, son Tom, Clark, father Tom, Ann.

Young Tom in front of the family home with Peg, the family's English springer spaniel.

The Monsons as son Tom prepares to leave for his mission to Italy.

undertaken in 1912 and again in 1920 that addressed some means of correlating programs. In the 1940s, the First Presidency advanced an idea "that the auxiliaries might consolidate, cooperate, eliminate, simplify, and adjust their work." President J. Reuben Clark, Jr., speaking on behalf of the First Presidency, explained, "The sole ultimate aim and purpose of the auxiliary organization of the Church is to plan and make grow in every member of the Church a testimony of the Christ and of the gospel, of the divinity of the mission of Joseph Smith and of the Church, and to bring the people to order their lives in accordance with the laws and principles of the restored gospel and priesthood."[26]

In the 1950s, three types of organizations were gaining strength in the Church: an ecclesiastical structure directed by priesthood leaders; auxiliaries operating with their own general officers, conferences, publications, and teaching manuals; and Church departments overseeing such areas as education, social needs, buildings, accounting, and public affairs. It became clear that the blurred lines of accountability and responsibility would not facilitate the anticipated growth of the Church as it added international congregations of diverse cultures and languages. The first stakes outside North America and Hawaii were organized in 1958 in the Netherlands and in 1961 in Berlin, Germany.

After more than a year, Elder Lee and his committee had concluded that "more was needed than simply ensuring that all gospel topics were being treated adequately in the Church's curriculum." At the center of the issue was protection of the family unit, once held sacrosanct in Western society but now threatened by "modern" movements. Elder Lee proposed an organization at the general Church level to bring about "more coordination and correlation between the activities and programs of the various priesthood quorums and auxiliary organizations."[27]

In general priesthood meeting on September 30, 1961, Elder Lee explained: "Correlation means merely to place the priesthood of God where the Lord said it was to be—as the center and core of the Church and kingdom of God—and to see that the Latter-day Saint homes also have their place in the divine plan of saving souls."[28] He outlined that the goal was consolidation and simplification of Church curricula, Church publications, Church buildings, Church meetings, and many other important aspects of the Lord's work. President McKay called it "one of the greatest undertakings that has yet been presented to the Priesthood."[29]

The plan included the four priesthood committees and the formation of an All-Church Coordinating Council with three correlation committees: children, under the direction of Elder Gordon B. Hinckley; youth, under the hand of Elder Richard L. Evans; and adults, chaired by Elder Marion G. Romney.

President Hugh B. Brown presided at the first meeting of the Priesthood Genealogy Committee, held in the Montgomery Ward building on First South and Main Street in Salt Lake City, where the Genealogical Society was then housed. He outlined the committee's responsibilities and emphasized "a general new thrust on genealogy and the formation of family societies for the purpose of stimulating genealogical research." He spoke of missionary work going "forward in the spirit world at an accelerated pace, compared to how it is going forward in our earthly existence."[30] He then quoted the words of President Joseph F. Smith, who described the work of Joseph Smith, his brother Hyrum, Brigham Young, and other faithful Apostles "preaching to the spirits in prison." President Smith had taught: "Through our efforts in their behalf, their chains of bondage will fall from them, and the darkness surrounding them will clear away, that light may shine upon them and they shall hear in the spirit world of the work that has been done for them by their children here, and will rejoice with you in your performance of these duties."[31]

President Brown indicated that Elder N. Eldon Tanner, out of town at the time of the meeting, would direct the committee going forward. After ten weeks of training, the members would begin attending all stake conferences throughout the Church over a six-month period. Tom visited fourteen stake conferences from January to June of 1963.

Being with General Authorities was, for Tom, "a highlight of the service." He joined Elder Howard W. Hunter for a conference of the Gridley Stake in northern California. It was a learning experience for him as a newly called member of the Priesthood

Genealogy Committee. "Brother Hunter treated me with love and deference," he said. The two performed many ordinations and settings apart, which took a substantial amount of time, and they missed their plane for San Francisco. The only option was to rent a car and drive to San Francisco to make their next connection. They stopped en route at the home of President Hunter's youngest son, Richard, and his wife, Nan, who were new parents. "A surprised Richard answered the knock at the door with a crying child in one arm. He saw his father and the two embraced and exchanged an affectionate kiss on the cheek." Elder Hunter said to his son, "Welcome to fatherhood, with its attendant responsibilities." The child never quite stopped crying. That touching scene caused Tom to acknowledge, "I'm happy we missed our plane out of Gridley."[32]

Tom's first assignments as a general Church committee member took him to California, Nebraska, New York, Canada, Idaho, and Arizona with Elders Joseph Fielding Smith, Marion G. Romney, Sterling W. Sill, Victor L. Brown, Henry D. Taylor, and others. In particular, he appreciated the opportunity to work with Elder N. Eldon Tanner, whom he had met in 1959, shortly after beginning his mission in Toronto. This prominent Canadian would be called as an Assistant to the Quorum of the Twelve Apostles, then to the Quorum of the Twelve, and then as a counselor to four Presidents of the Church.

"At the time I met him," Tom recalls, "President Tanner was president of the vast Trans-Canada Pipelines, Ltd., and president of the Canada Calgary Stake. He was known as 'Mr. Integrity' in Canada. During that first meeting, we discussed, among other subjects, the cold Canadian winters, where storms rage, temperatures can linger well below freezing for weeks at a time, and icy winds lower those temperatures even further. I asked President Tanner why the roads and highways in western Canada basically remained intact during such winters, showing little or no signs of cracking or breaking, while the road surfaces in many areas where winters are less cold and less severe developed cracks and breaks and potholes.

"Said he, 'The answer is in the depth of the base of the paving materials. In order for them to remain strong and unbroken, it is necessary to go very deep with the foundation layers. When the foundations are not deep enough, the surfaces cannot withstand the extremes of weather.'

"Over the years I have thought of this conversation and of President Tanner's explanation, for I recognize in his words a profound application for our lives. Stated simply, if we do not have a deep foundation of faith and a solid testimony of truth, we may have difficulty withstanding the harsh storms and icy winds of adversity which inevitably come to each of us."[33]

Tom also became acquainted with many of the stake leaders in the Church. He was assigned to speak at stake conferences on the subject of genealogy from January to May. Committee members held a specialized leadership session on Saturday afternoon and addressed the topic of genealogy in a Saturday evening leadership meeting. In the Sunday morning and afternoon sessions of the stake conferences, they again spoke about genealogy. Tom learned quickly that genealogy was perhaps one of the "most misunderstood among all the programs of the Church."

The committee members' primary assignment was to "convince the membership of the Church that they need not be specialists; they need not be in their eighties; they need not be exclusively genealogists in order to understand the responsibility" to seek out their kindred dead and to perform their temple work, what he described as their "sacred duty."[34]

Committee members carried with them a visual aid, about three feet by three feet. "When we would come down the stairs to get off the plane anywhere it was windy, we almost had a sail in our hands, and we could almost fly off that gangplank," Tom recalled.[35]

He taught the principles relating to genealogy work by using an illustration from his mission about the secretary of one of the genealogy committees, Myrtle Barnum, in one of the districts in Canada. For years she had gathered family history data concerning the St. Lawrence River area but had come to an "iron wall in her work she could not penetrate." She poured out her soul to Heavenly Father and literally made a plea that somehow He would intervene, somehow the way would be opened. And then she continued her research.

One day she was traveling down the main street of Belleville, Ontario, and came to an old bookstore. She felt compelled to enter and began to browse. Her eye caught sight of a two-volume set on the top shelf, and she knew she had to see those books. She asked the clerk the names of the two books; at her request he climbed a ladder, pulled down the books, and read, *Pioneer Life on the Bay of Quinte, Volumes 1 and 2.* She thought they might be novels, but as she leafed through the pages, she realized they were nothing but family histories. Quickly perusing them, she realized that "one volume supplied that key which opened the lock to the mystery which had frustrated her work."

Elated, she asked the price. The clerk responded that the books were very rare. "Two hundred dollars," he said. The quorum of elders in the district purchased the set, and the books did indeed resolve her stalemate. She, "with faith, nothing wavering, had performed her duty," Tom said. The books were later sent to Church headquarters, where it was found that they also held the missing keys for the family line of President Henry D. Moyle, whose forebears had come from the Bay of Quinte, near Belleville, Ontario. "Faith is requisite to this work," Tom would conclude.[36]

In June 1962, while serving on the two general priesthood committees—Missionary and Genealogy—the equivalent of auxiliary general boards, Tom received a phone call from Elder Marion G. Romney. "Brother Monson," he said, "I've been instructed by the First Presidency and the Twelve to call you to become a member of the Priesthood Adult Correlation Committee of the Church." Elder Romney indicated that he himself was chairman of that body and then said, "This takes precedence over any assignment you have. You'll be released from the other duties." As he was so close to completing his work on the Priesthood Genealogy Committee, Tom asked for and received permission to finish out the genealogy assignment. He was released from the Missionary Committee.

Tom was among the fifteen Church leaders appointed to

one of the three standing committees of the newly established All-Church Coordinating Council—the Adult, Youth, and Children's Committees.[37] He served on the Adult Committee until his appointment as a member of the Quorum of the Twelve in October 1963.

The Adult Committee was soon doing more than curriculum planning. Tom was appointed to a special committee to study and make recommendations for reshaping the ward teaching program, which had been in place since the turn of the century. With the new thrust of correlating Church programs to support the family, ward teaching was a beginning point in terms of priesthood involvement.

The committee studied the needs and issues in homes and families, shifting the emphasis to address family needs more directly. What emerged was a new name, *home teaching*, and, in the "spirit of correlation," a program that would be overseen by the priesthood quorum leaders rather than the bishop. On the general Church level, the program would fall under the direction of the Quorum of the Twelve, not the Presiding Bishopric, as in the past. "Home teachers" would have stewardship over the general welfare of the families to which they were assigned, rather than just deliver a monthly message. They would continue monthly visits but would no longer present a set lesson. They would be encouraged to rely on the Spirit and their own initiative to lift and spiritually strengthen "their" families.

On the day the committee presented their recommendations to Church leaders, they assembled in the auditorium on the third floor of the Church Administration Building. Tom recalled, "An air of excitement and anticipation filled each heart when President McKay entered the room."[38]

Elder Romney set the tone: "The purpose of the home teaching program is to have every member of every family do his duty." Elder Harold B. Lee shared President McKay's remark about the home teaching program: "This is not just a step forward, but a bound forward." With exuberance President McKay had continued, "My soul rejoices! . . . I think this is growth. It warms my soul."[39]

As the prophet stood at the pulpit to speak, everyone could

feel that "something bold was in the making." Tom observed as he watched President McKay, "My, he reflects the bearing of a prophet." For Tom, such meetings were just beginning.

President McKay again declared what the First Presidency had written in the letter to Elder Lee setting the Correlation effort in motion: "The home is the basis for the righteous life, and no other instrumentality can take its place or fulfill its essential functions." And then he impressed upon the gathering, "Carry the gospel into our homes; this is our greatest responsibility," and concluded, "The home teaching program and principles which Correlation has enunciated to us today come from God the Father and are endorsed by His Son Jesus Christ, and I want you to know I am an advocate of that which you have heard today."[40] President Monson remembers the moment "as if it were yesterday."

He was sitting near the back of the room when the impression came to him that he was going to be called upon to offer the closing prayer. "I had not had that impression before, and I just sat there wondering why I should feel that way." At the conclusion of the meeting, Elder Lee said, "We will now call on Brother Thomas S. Monson, of the Adult Correlation Committee, to come forward and offer the benediction on this meeting."[41] It was not the only prayer he would offer in the presence of the prophet of God.

Plans were made to introduce the new priesthood home teaching program at stake conferences during the last half of 1963. President McKay named Tom to the new Home Teaching Committee; he was the only carryover from the Adult Correlation group that had formulated the program. In his new assignment he attended stake conferences, as he had when serving on other general priesthood committees, to teach the leaders and members how to accomplish "home teaching." He often shared the words of President John Taylor, who warned, "If you do not magnify your calling, God will hold you responsible for those whom you might have saved, had you done your duty. And who of us can afford to be responsible for the delay of eternal life of the human soul? If great joy is the reward of saving one soul, then how terrible must be the remorse of those whose timid efforts have allowed a child of God to go unwarned or unaided."[42]

The priesthood home teachers were to go into the homes and build a truly personal relationship with each family member—characterized by mutual trust, love, equality, and concern. Brother Monson was a natural for the assignment, which stressed, "We are truly our brother's keeper" and "We should love our neighbor as ourselves."[43]

Home teaching would draw together the strengths of Aaronic Priesthood holders, both young and old, with high priests and elders. The new program required each ward to establish a home teaching committee, which later became the Priesthood Executive Committee, including the bishopric and other priesthood leaders. Each ward also was instructed to organize a ward council, which met monthly and included the Priesthood Executive Committee and the heads of auxiliaries. The ward council was a coordinating body for ward functions and a forum for determining how to help individuals in need.

To introduce home teaching to members and leaders, the committee developed a thirty-minute film with an accompanying loose-leaf binder.[44] Tom assisted in the design, preparation, and printing of the materials. The printer in Tom appreciated that it "represented the largest book binding order in the history of the Church or in the state and one of the biggest commercial printing jobs which the Deseret News Press had ever produced."[45]

The committee members carried their specially produced film, "Of Heaven and Home," to stake conferences throughout the Church. Tom sat through the film so many times that he memorized the dialogue and became "a personal friend of each of the characters."

One summer day he and his wife were driving through American Fork, Utah. While stopped at a red light, he looked at the car next to him. "There was a man I recognized," he recalls. "I said, 'Hello, Dave!' He looked at me and waved." Frances asked, "Who was that?" Tom replied, "Oh, that's Dave Bitton."

"And then," he says, "I realized there was no such person—'Dave Bitton' was the character from the home teaching film that I had seen every Saturday night for six months. But he had become almost a personal friend of mine."[46]

Years later, Tom saw the fruits of home teaching as it touched his own family. At the fiftieth wedding anniversary of his sister Marge and her husband, Conway, in California, Tom sat by their home teachers. "We are working on them," the home teacher said. Tom's sister and her husband had not been back to the temple since they were married in 1943. Their son was serving as a bishop, a son-in-law was in a stake presidency, but Marge and Conway had not been very active in the Church. Both had recently faced serious health issues and were miraculously healed, and they had begun attending Church more frequently. A return to the temple came eventually. Tom credited the change to "home teachers who cared."[47]

In September 1963, Tom was assigned to attend a conference in the North Box Elder Stake in northern Utah with Elder Thorpe B. Isaacson, an Assistant to the Twelve. However, President Henry D. Moyle, First Counselor in the First Presidency, died suddenly just four days before the conference. Church authorities planned his funeral for the Saturday of the stake conference. Elder Isaacson, needing to attend the service, asked Tom to go forward with the stake conference, saying he would join him for the Sunday meetings.

That same week, Tom and Elder Harold B. Lee spoke at the funeral services for Alfred C. Thorn, a longtime member of the Sixth-Seventh Ward who had served on the Pioneer Stake high council at the time Elder Lee had been the stake president. During his message, Tom shared a letter he had read while serving as ward clerk prior to being called as bishop. The letter was to Bishop Thorn, Alfred's father, who had presided over the Seventh Ward for forty years. It read: "Dear Bishop Thorn: As you know, Bishop Harrison Sperry of the Fourth Ward has been called on a mission to England. So that he will not lose his bishopric while he's on a mission, we would like you, Bishop Thorn, in addition to looking after the affairs of the Seventh Ward, to attend to the affairs of the Fourth Ward in his absence."[48]

Following the service for Alfred Thorn on September 28, 1963, Tom commented to Elder Lee, "I surely feel sad in the passing of President Moyle. It will be difficult for someone to fill his shoes."

President Lee acknowledged that each man fills his own shoes, rather than attempting to fill the shoes of another, but that the Lord would provide a successor to President Moyle.[49]

15

A Special Witness

If you just add up the hours, simply count the years, you can see how Thomas S. Monson has been thoroughly, totally committed and devoted to his calling. He came to it at such an early age. He's been doing this a very long time.

Elder Jeffrey R. Holland
Quorum of the Twelve Apostles

It was a quiet Thursday afternoon at the Deseret News Press. Tom was meeting with an insurance adjuster when his secretary, Beth Brian, alerted him that he had a phone call. Tom was engrossed in talking with the agent. Having learned that the adjuster was not a member of the Church, he was telling him the Joseph Smith story before presenting him with a copy of Elder Gordon B. Hinckley's book *What of the Mormons?* which had recently come off the press.

His secretary finally opened the door and said, "Did you remember you have a telephone call holding?" He immediately picked up the telephone and found Clare Middlemiss, secretary to President David O. McKay, waiting on the line. She indicated that President McKay wanted to speak with him, whereupon Tom excused the claims adjuster.

"Brother Monson, how did you enjoy your mission in Canada?" President McKay began.

Tom responded that it had been "a delightful experience."

"How did you leave the Canadian Mission?" the President asked.

Taking the question literally, Tom responded, "In a car we bought in Detroit."

President McKay chuckled and rephrased the question, "What condition did you leave it in?"

"Oh," said Tom, "the best condition we knew how, President."

"Fine," President McKay said, and then asked if Tom could come and visit with him "sometime."

"Surely," Tom responded. "When would you like to see me, President?"

"Could you come right now?"

Tom had printed books for President McKay, but no level of familiarity would make him take casually an invitation to the office of the President of the Church. He checked his watch; it was 2:30 P.M. His car was at the shop being repaired, so he borrowed a car, drove to the Hotel Utah, parked in their lot, and bounded up the stairs of the Church Administration Building.[1]

It was two days before general conference, October 3, 1963, and there was a vacancy in the Quorum of the Twelve Apostles. But those two facts did not even cross Tom's mind. He felt honored to meet with President McKay, whose heart was kind and his manner gracious. Tom saw in him the ways of the Savior.

President McKay invited Tom into his office and had him sit on his right, very close to him. "With great emotion and obvious pleasure he got right to the point. 'Brother Monson,' he said, 'with the passing of President Henry D. Moyle I have named Elder Nathan Eldon Tanner to be my Second Counselor in the First Presidency, and the Lord has called you to fill his place in the Quorum of the Twelve Apostles. Could you accept that calling?'"

The moment was sacred. Tom remembers feeling overwhelmed, shocked, and unable to speak. "Tears filled my eyes, and after a pause that seemed like an eternity, I responded by assuring President McKay that any talent with which I might have been blessed would be extended in the service of the Master in putting my very life on the line if necessary."

President McKay then told him of the "great responsibility"

being vested in him, "expressed the confidence of the General Authorities," and welcomed him to their ranks, promising that this would be "a most rewarding experience" and one in which his talents and energies would be used to the maximum. He asked him not to tell anyone except his wife.[2]

Tom went back to his office, retrieved his car from the shop, and went home. Frances wondered what he was doing there in the middle of the afternoon. He was a successful and confident businessman, a proven Church leader, but the call caused him to take stock of his life and what lay before him. He mentally retraced his visit with the prophet of God and the call to the holy apostleship. He thought about how it would affect his family, their future, his career. Then he went outside and cut the lawn.

That evening he ate little at dinner. Afterward he asked Frances to take a drive with him, ostensibly to deliver some proofs. "I couldn't imagine why, all of a sudden, he would want to go out for a drive. We took our youngest son, who was three," she recalls, "and we drove to This Is the Place Monument, on the east bench of Salt Lake City, where he parked the car. We got out and walked around the monument, reading the inscriptions."

The stately monument, placed there in 1947 to commemorate the centennial of the pioneers' arrival in the Salt Lake Valley, was named for Brigham Young's famous declaration, "This is the right place, drive on." Tom felt oddly connected to the scene, with Brigham Young "standing as a sentinel pointing the way . . . his back turned to the privations, hardships, and struggle of the long desert way." His outstretched arm pointed forward.

Frances asked, "What's wrong? You have something on your mind."

He told her of his visit with President McKay and his call to the Quorum of the Twelve Apostles. She remembers being both "surprised and humbled" at this "most significant call" and its "overwhelming responsibility."[3]

With young Clark trailing along, the two of them walked around the monument, speaking of the great sacrifices of the early settlers, their unexpected trials, and their willingness to do all they were asked. At this monument honoring the early pioneers, the Monsons were in good company.

That night neither Frances nor Tom slept well. Tom's feet were so cold that he had to get up and pull on stockings. "I must have been in a state of shock," he suggests, "for I am told that this is one of the symptoms. At five A.M. I heard a rooster crowing, and I realized that I had not closed my eyes."[4]

That morning, before leaving for general conference, Tom called his parents and told them to be sure to watch the first session. He told them that sometimes a returning mission president might be called upon to speak. He and Frances took the children to her mother's home and recommended that she too watch conference on television.

And he took a call from Max Zimmer, one of the employees at Deseret News Press, who recounted twenty years later:

"On that fateful Friday morning, October 4, 1963, I felt especially concerned about my translation assignment because in those early days of conference translations, the translation facilities were quite primitive. I finally felt that I needed your help and called you . . . asking you to utter a silent prayer in my behalf when you would attend the Friday sessions. Little did I realize what a momentous morning this was in your life! You must have felt apprehensive so shortly before that crucial session. Yet, with great calmness and your usual quiet reassurance and loving spirit, you listened to me and gave me your full attention and promised [to pray for me]. You are indeed a champion of the lowly and simple people in the Church, such as me."[5]

Tom found a seat in the Tabernacle with the Priesthood Home Teaching Committee of which he was a member, along with Hugh Smith, Gerald Smith, Jay Eldredge, and others. As he sat down, Hugh, whose sense of humor was well-known, said, "You don't want to sit there! On two previous occasions the men who were sitting next to me were called to be General Authorities."

Tom sat down. He could feel the gaze of the members of the Quorum of the Twelve, who knew of his appointment.

Frances sat with Thelma Fetzer, whose husband, Percy, had served with Tom in the Temple View Stake presidency. It was the section where the Primary general board members sat, as Thelma served on that board.

The conference was broadcast from the Tabernacle to an overflow gathering in the Assembly Hall next door on Temple Square, over a loudspeaker system to the grounds, and by KSL television and radio "to the largest worldwide audience in the history of the Church," more than fifty stations, including some in Hawaii and Canada.[6] President David O. McKay presided and conducted.

In his welcoming remarks, the venerable Church President acknowledged the passing of President Henry D. Moyle on September 19, 1963, and added, "I like to think he will be listening in here with us this morning."[7] His further remarks touched a theme that set a course for Tom's ministry and his ever optimistic approach. "The true end of life is not mere existence," President McKay said. "The true purpose of life is the perfection of humanity through individual effort, under the guidance of God's inspiration. Real life is response to the best within us. To be alive only to appetite, pleasure, pride, money-making, and not to goodness and kindness, purity and love, poetry, music, flowers, stars, God and eternal hopes, is to deprive one's self of the real joy of living."[8]

President McKay, who had been called as an Apostle at age thirty-three, asked President Hugh B. Brown, new First Counselor in the First Presidency, to read the names of those to be sustained, including the changes in leadership. Before presenting the names, President Brown admonished the congregation, "This is not a mere formality, but is a right given by revelation." He then proceeded, including in the lengthy list Nathan Eldon Tanner as Second Counselor in the First Presidency and Thomas S. Monson as the new Apostle.[9] At age thirty-six, Elder Monson was the youngest man called to the apostleship in fifty-three years; he was seventeen years younger than the next youngest, Elder Gordon B. Hinckley, who had been sustained to the Twelve two years earlier.

"I don't remember the opening song ["The Heavens Are Telling," sung by the Singing Mothers of Mesa, Arizona] or much of what took place in the early part of that session," Elder Monson wrote later, "but I do remember distinctly hearing the names of the Council of the Twelve read and then hearing my own name read as a newly appointed member of this sacred Council."[10]

Members of the Quorum of the Twelve included President Joseph Fielding Smith and Elders Harold B. Lee, Spencer W. Kimball, Ezra Taft Benson, Mark E. Petersen, Delbert L. Stapley, Marion G. Romney, LeGrand Richards, Richard L. Evans, Howard W. Hunter, Gordon B. Hinckley, and Thomas S. Monson. For seven years he would be the junior member of the Twelve. He had long respected these men, their spirits and spirituality. They had been his examples, latter-day disciples who had left their nets at the call, "Follow me." Now he was one of them.

Elder Monson rose to take "that long walk to the stand" as an astonished Hugh Smith whispered, "Lightning has struck a third time!" He took his seat next to Elder Hinckley at the end of the second row. The two would sit side by side in the Quorum for eighteen years and would serve together in the First Presidency for another twenty-two. President Tanner, who had been called to the Twelve only a year before, had sat in that same seat before his call to the First Presidency.

President Tanner spoke, and then it was Elder Monson's turn. He recalls that he tried to remember the advice of President J. Reuben Clark, Jr.: "There are two times when a talk should be brief: when we are appointed or when we are released from a position."

This tall, handsome, newly sustained General Authority, raised up in the Depression, schooled with the world at war and yet seasoned by the Spirit, spoke without script or teleprompter. He would deliver thirty-seven years' worth of general conference messages from that pulpit in the grand, noble Tabernacle before the Conference Center would be built.

His remarks that day were titled, "I Stand at the Door and Knock." The Church membership was introduced to his thoughtful style, his bold presence, and his penchant to teach the gospel through examples from his own life, characteristics that would distinguish his messages in the years to come.

"President McKay, President Brown, President Tanner, my brethren, and brothers and sisters," he said, "from the depths of humility, and with an overwhelming sense of inadequacy, I stand before you and pray earnestly for your prayers in my behalf.

"All of us are saddened by the loss of President Henry D. Moyle. I also miss the presence of President J. Reuben Clark, Jr., and President Stephen L Richards who served in the First Presidency.

"Some years ago I stood at a pulpit and noticed a little sign that only the speaker could see, and the words on that sign were these: 'Who stands at this pulpit, let him be humble.' How I pray to my Heavenly Father that I might never forget the lesson I learned that day!

"I feel to thank my Heavenly Father for his many blessings to me. I am grateful to have been born of goodly parents, whose parents were gathered out of the lands of Sweden and Scotland and England by humble missionaries, who through the bearing of their testimonies touched the spirits of these wonderful people.

"I am so grateful for my teachers and leaders in my boyhood and young manhood in a humble, pioneer ward in a humble, pioneer stake. I am grateful for my sweet companion and for the influence for good which she has had upon my life, and to her dear mother who had the courage in far-off Sweden to accept the gospel and to come to this country. I am so happy that the Lord has blessed us with three fine children, our youngest born to us in the mission field in Canada. I am grateful for these blessings. I am grateful for my friends and for O. Preston Robinson and my associates at the Deseret News with whom I have so closely worked these past fifteen years. . . .

"I think of a little sister, a French-Canadian sister, whose life was changed by the missionaries as her spirit was touched as she said good-bye to me and my wife two years ago in Quebec. She said, 'President Monson, I may never see the prophet. I may never hear the prophet. But President, far better, now that I am a member of this Church, I can obey the prophet.'

"My sincere prayer today, President McKay, is that I might always obey you and these, my brethren. I pledge my life, all that I may have. I will strive to the utmost of my ability to be what you would want me to be. I am grateful for the words of Jesus Christ, our Savior, when he said:

"'I stand at the door and knock. If any man hear my voice and open the door, I will come in to him. . . . ' (Rev. 3:20.)

"I earnestly pray, my brothers and sisters, that my life might merit this promise from our Savior. In the name of Jesus Christ. Amen."[11]

Elder Russell M. Nelson remembers his father, a prominent leader in advertising who had utilized Tom Monson's printing expertise on many occasions, commenting, "This man will become the President of the Church." Elder Nelson continues, "My father was an observer of the Church, a member in name. But he knew. I have always had that feeling of awe and also that feeling of how heavy it would be to have people say, 'Here's a future president of the Church.' Tom Monson has lived with that all these years."[12]

Elder Monson's fellow Apostles welcomed him from the pulpit. President Tanner hailed his "fellow Canadian," whom, he warmly said, "I sustain with all my heart." Added to these words of encouragement and support were the "firm handshakes" of his fellow Brethren. Elder Monson has said he will "never forget the warm hug" from Elder Mark E. Petersen.[13]

Later that evening, the Monsons went to their Canadian Mission reunion. Elder Monson's children and parents attended as well. As they walked in, the assembled missionaries stood and sang, "We Thank Thee, O God, for a Prophet." "At that moment," he later said, "the awareness that members of the Council of the Twelve are sustained as prophets, seers, and revelators seemed to penetrate every fiber of my being."[14]

None of his missionaries were surprised at his call. "We all thought he was going to be a General Authority," one of them, Michael Murdock, observed. "You always feel like you can sustain the Church leadership, but with him I couldn't raise my hand up quick enough to sustain him."[15]

That weekend, Elder and Sister Monson began their lifetime of personal attendance at general conference—with Elder Monson seated on the stand. His journal record of that first conference spells out his discomfort in his new position. "I felt so strange and out of place sitting among the members of the Council of the Twelve," he wrote. "As I looked into the congregation I could see so many men who could have so capably filled the assignment which was extended to me."[16] Elder Hinckley, a longtime friend, did his best to make him "feel at home." Elder Monson appreciated his friendship and that of Elders Howard W. Hunter and Richard L. Evans.

In the Sunday afternoon session of the conference, Sister Annette Richardson Dinwoody sang a solo, "I Know that My Redeemer Lives." The words seemed just for him that day:

> *He lives to silence all my fears.*
> *He lives to wipe away my tears.*
> *He lives to calm my troubled heart.*
> *He lives all blessings to impart.*[17]

Elder Monson felt the spirit in the words and later wrote, "It was beautiful."[18]

Elder David Bednar, called as an Apostle in 2004, was just eleven years old at the time President Monson took his place in the Quorum of the Twelve. "My entire adult life President Monson has been a fixture at general conference," states Elder Bednar. "His counsel about showing love, especially to family, had such an influence. I would expect that, unconsciously, there were times when I said 'No' to pressing demands so I could say 'Yes' to our children because of the influence of President Monson. He's always been there; he has always been an influence."[19]

Elder Monson's call came at a time when the Church was on the move around the world. In order to meet the growing needs of the Church, the Brethren were traveling extensively. Earlier that year President McKay had dedicated a chapel in Merthyr Tydfil, South Wales, the birthplace of his mother; President Moyle had made two trips to England and toured the Pacific Northwest; President Brown had toured South American missions; Elder Tanner had traveled to the Philippines, the Orient, Australia, Samoa, Alaska, and Canada. Elder Monson too would soon be living out of a suitcase for up to five weeks at a time.

In 1963 there were thirty-eight General Authorities to serve the 2,117,451 members in the Church's 389 stakes and 77 missions. There were 11,653 full-time missionaries serving.[20] Church membership in the United States had reached 1.5 million and was increasing in the world at the rate of roughly 100,000 members a year.[21] What once had been a fairly homogeneous group in western America was now worldwide. Church programs needed to embrace the rich spiritual, social, cultural, and physical needs of all the Saints. Many of the members had known only one prophet, David O. McKay.

General Authorities had organized the first non–English-speaking stakes in The Hague, Netherlands, and in Mexico City and had established a Language Training Mission. The Polynesian Cultural Center would be dedicated that year, and the Oakland Temple would be dedicated the next year, bringing the number of operating temples to thirteen.

On Monday night, October 7, 1963, the Monsons celebrated their fifteenth wedding anniversary, treating their family and Frances's mother to dinner at the Hotel Utah Coffee Shop. "They have been happy years," he noted in his journal. "We are so grateful for our three children and the love which we have for each other. Frances is an ideal companion for me, for her personality balances mine."[22]

As they sat in their booth at the coffee shop, he could feel "everyone's eyes" on him. The reaction of the three children to his call was "most interesting." Tommy had said, "It's kind of tough having your Dad an Apostle; everyone expects so much of you." Ann "expressed her happiness at all the attention which the call had brought to her and the family." Clark, of course, was "too young to understand the significance of the call." Tom's mother and father, "while they don't comprehend the magnitude of my assignment, feel honored in it, as does Frances's mother, Hildur."[23]

Telephone calls, letters of congratulations, and telegrams poured into Elder Monson's office and home. He was sobered by "the great responsibility to live worthy of the confidence and trust which so many people have placed in me."[24] The Relief Society general presidency called him to an urgent meeting at their office "to discuss problems with the magazine," which was printed at Deseret News Press. When he arrived, they ceremoniously presented him with a fine attaché case as a token of their appreciation for his service at the Press and an acknowledgment of his weighty calling.[25]

William James (Jim) Mortimer, a close business associate, wrote: "You have brought dignity and distinction to the printing industry of Utah. Coming from the ranks of the printers who are not afraid to smear their hands with the ink that prints words of truth, you have shown to us all that this is a business of more than mere ink on paper. . . . Now new duties take you away from active association with the industry, but we gratefully acknowledge that through the years you have shown to all the higher road of honesty, integrity, and hard work. The printing industry is better because of you."[26]

A *Deseret News* editorial extolled how he would bring "enthusiasm, vigor, friendliness, devotion, humility and ability to a choice group already rich in these important qualities." The paper noted his "rich and varied experiences in the Church" and "fine background in business education and management" and concluded, "[He] is endowed with a contagiously engaging personality which will serve well the Council of the Twelve in its great responsibility of spreading the gospel throughout the world."[27]

But he found perhaps the greatest comfort in an idea expressed some time later by Elder Harold B. Lee, longtime mentor and friend, who said of those called to serve in the leading councils of the Church: "I heard the late Orson F. Whitney, a member of the Twelve, deliver a very impressive sermon in the Tabernacle prior to his passing [1931]. He moved his hand down over the pulpit below him where the General Authorities were sitting and said, 'Now Brothers and Sisters, I don't think that these, my Brethren, are necessarily the best living men in the Church. I think there are other men who live just as good lives and maybe better lives than these General Authorities, but I'll tell you what I do know, that when there's a vacancy in the ranks of the General Authorities, the Lord seeks out the man who is needed for a particular work and calls him to that service. I've watched that over the years."[28]

Tom confided in his journal that Thursday, October 10, 1963, was one of the "most dramatic days" of his life. He met for the first time with the First Presidency and the Quorum of the Twelve in a special room on the fourth floor of the Salt Lake Temple. All of the First Presidency and the Quorum of the Twelve were present. This pleased President McKay, who commented that this was the first time the body had been complete and together for some time. The group dressed in their temple robes and assembled for prayer.

A chair was placed in the center of the room and "we all participated in the setting apart of Hugh B. Brown as First Counselor in the First Presidency and N. Eldon Tanner as Second Counselor. President McKay was mouth for these blessings," Tom recorded.

President McKay then called upon President Smith to ordain Elder Monson an Apostle and set him apart as a member of the Quorum of the Twelve, "as one of the special witnesses of our Lord and Savior Jesus Christ in this dispensation," dedicating his "whole life to the work of the ministry as a servant of our Master, the Lord and Savior of this world."[29]

Having President Smith's hands on his head was a special privilege and further testimony to Elder Monson of the divinity of his call. Joseph Fielding Smith had been ordained an Apostle by his father, Church President Joseph F. Smith, who was ordained an Apostle in 1866 by Brigham Young. The Three Witnesses, Oliver Cowdery, David Whitmer, and Martin Harris, ordained Brigham Young in 1835, having been called by revelation to choose the Twelve Apostles.[30]

In giving Elder Monson his apostolic charge, President McKay outlined his responsibility as an Apostle of the Lord Jesus Christ and explained how the Brethren adhere to the principle of unity, "wherein each member of the Council is to express his views without hesitation; but when the decision of the Council is made, its will is to be carried out wholeheartedly."[31] He has always scrupulously adhered to that charge. The President then called on the Brethren to sustain Elder Monson in his calling, and the vote was unanimous. Elder Petersen expressed his confidence and admiration for his friend, now an ordained Apostle, saying, "There stands before us an Israelite in whom there is no guile." The tributes are keepsakes in President Monson's memory.[32]

Elder Harold B. Lee's influence in Elder Monson's apostolic service emerged quickly. In the temple, Elder Lee ushered him into the dressing room of the senior Brethren—President Smith and Elders Lee, Kimball, Petersen, and Stapley, men he had revered for years. Elder Monson would continue—at Elder Lee's invitation—to dress with the senior Brethren until he was called to the First Presidency. Elder Lee asked him to name a favorite hymn. He replied, "How Firm a Foundation," feeling in a particular way the emotion of fleeing to Jesus for refuge.

Elder Lee later explained the process and preparation of those called to the holy apostleship: "The beginning of the call of one to be President of the Church actually begins when he is called, ordained, and set apart to become a member of the Quorum of the Twelve Apostles. Such a call by prophecy, or in other words, by the inspiration of the Lord to the one holding the keys of presidency, and the subsequent ordination and setting apart by the laying on of hands by that same authority, places each apostle in a priesthood quorum of twelve men holding the apostleship. . . . Each apostle so ordained under the hands of the President of the Church, who holds the keys of the kingdom of God in concert with all other ordained apostles, has given to him the priesthood authority necessary to hold every position in the Church, even to a position of presidency over the Church if he were called by the presiding authority and sustained by a vote of a constituent assembly of the membership of the Church."[33]

The official group portrait taken of the Quorum of the Twelve in 1963 showed a conspicuously tall and youthful new addition. Seven of those pictured would become Church Presidents.

Elder Monson joined Elder Hunter and Elder Hinckley in the junior quartile of the Quorum. He felt the support of the Brethren and came to admire the frank exchanges and discussions in council as the Church leaders wrestled with issues and events on the world stage and addressed policies and programs worldwide.

The following weekend, Elder Monson fulfilled the assignment that had been given to him as a member of the Priesthood Home Teaching Committee to travel to Edmonton, Canada, in the company of Elder Harold B. Lee and Priesthood Welfare Committee member Glen L. Rudd. For Elder Monson, it was a good time to be "going home" to Canada. He expressed his pleasure: "It is rather inspirational that on this, my first weekend as a General Authority, I should be with Brother Lee, who has played such an important role in my life, and that three former members of the Pioneer Stake should be assigned as the traveling representatives to that conference."[34]

In addition to addressing members in the stake meetings, the two Apostles set apart missionaries, and the three men visited a Church welfare farm. Just as they arrived, a man rode up on a large horse and asked Brother Rudd if he would like to ride. Born and raised in the city, he was sure he would fall off. "I have got my best suit on, and I don't think it would be good for me to ride," he said. The man offered the horse to Elder Monson, who, not too sure of protocol, declined as well, using his suit as the reason. Then Elder Lee spoke up, "I've got my best suit on, and I want to ride that horse." He rode off for about ten minutes and came back "full blast," according to Brother Rudd. Elder Lee had been raised riding horses in Idaho.[35]

At the conference's leadership meeting, Elder Monson addressed the important principles of successful interviewing. He "certainly prayed for the inspiration of the Lord in this extemporaneous assignment" and "felt the inspiration" during the presentation. "The presence of the newest apostle brought out a near record attendance," wrote Elder Lee of the occasion.[36]

While President McKay had indicated that Elder Monson might "continue for a time" with his daily work at the Deseret News Press, President Lee counseled him to move quickly toward disassociating from his printing responsibilities so that he might give his "full attention to the work of the Twelve." At that time, some of the Brethren still maintained a regular work schedule in addition to their duties as General Authorities. But just as he had acted upon Elder Lee's advice not to accept a commission in the navy, Tom prepared to step down from his post at the Press. "Brother Lee was one of the wisest teachers the Church has ever produced," he has said.[37]

Following his second meeting in the temple, Elder Monson wrote in his journal, "I am slow in becoming adjusted to the fact that I am a member of the Council of the Twelve and have the opportunity of sitting with such spiritual giants as the Brethren in the Council. Following our meeting we have lunch with the First Presidency in the dining room. This is the time where all of us put aside the press of a business agenda and enjoy one another's companionship. I marvel at President McKay's alertness. He freely quotes from Shakespeare and keeps current on all problems of the day. He is indeed a prophet of God and teaches us by example how we should live and love."[38]

During the next fifteen months, by his own count, Elder Monson attended at least fifty-five different stake conferences throughout the United States, Mexico, and Central America. Also filling his schedule were such tasks as conducting missionary interviews, counseling, dedicating meetinghouses, attending ceremonial functions, and preaching the gospel.

On the first Thursday of every month, the members of the First Presidency and the Twelve met in the temple in a "particularly sweet" fast day service where they partook of the sacrament. At Elder Monson's first such session, President McKay announced in the solemnity of the moment, "Before partaking of the sacrament, we would like to be instructed by our newest member, Elder Thomas S. Monson, on the atoning sacrifice of the Lord Jesus Christ."

He has described the moment as "a heart stopper."[39]

Standing before the august group, and with faith and courage born of years of service and study, he bore testimony of the Atonement of Jesus Christ.

Things lightened up considerably at lunchtime. During the course of the casual discussions, President McKay asked Elder

Monson if he had read the story in the *Reader's Digest* titled, "I Quit Smoking."

Elder Monson nodded and said he thought the man who wrote it had been inspired.

President McKay smiled. "The author was a woman," he said, "but she was inspired." He then asked, "Brother Monson, do you know Shakespeare?"

"Yes, President," he said with some hesitancy.

President McKay, a former English teacher, then asked, "Do you think the Bard of Avon really wrote the sonnets attributed to him?"

"Yes, I do," replied Elder Monson.

"Wonderful," he exclaimed. "So do I."

Elder Monson hoped they were now through with Shakespeare. He had majored in business, had worked in business, and felt uncomfortable with where the conversation was going.

President McKay, however, did not let up. "What is your favorite work of Shakespeare?" he asked.

Elder Monson paused—perhaps more with a desperate prayer than a reasoned thought—and replied, "*Henry VIII.*"

"And do you have a favorite passage?" President McKay asked.

Another "heart-stopper" moment. Then he thought of Cardinal Wolsey, that man who had served his king but neglected his God. "The lament of Cardinal Wolsey," Tom said with confidence and then recited, "Had I but served my God with half the zeal with which I served my king, he, in mine age, would not have left me naked to mine enemies."

President McKay beamed. "Oh," he said, "I love that passage too." He then changed the subject, for which Elder Monson was "extremely grateful," since his knowledge of Shakespeare was "running very thin."[40]

Though President McKay was a General Authority before Elder Monson was even born, they were alike in many ways. Both came from hearty pioneer families but were raised outside the loop of Church visibility. Both had been called at a very young age, and thus each became what could be termed the "institutional memory" for the Church in his long years of service. Both engaged the members with their distinctive speaking styles, their love for poetry and verse, and a recognition that the "real test of any religion is the kind of man it makes."[41] One of President McKay's favorite quotations expressed the sentiments of Elder Monson's heart as well:

> *There is a destiny which makes us brothers,*
> *None lives to himself alone;*
> *All that we give into the lives of others,*
> *Comes back into our own.*[42]

These were years of physical decline for President McKay, but Elder Monson recognized him as the Lord's inspired servant: "As I listened to the prophet, I inwardly thanked Heavenly Father for sustaining him and for providing such a noble leader for His Church as is President McKay. I am especially grateful that it was he who called me to my holy office, for one cannot help but be a better man for having been close to President McKay."[43]

In November 1963, the *Improvement Era*, the Church's predecessor to the *Ensign* and *Liahona* magazines, introduced Elder Monson to Church members, describing him as respected by his peers "for his adaptability" and honored "for his tremendous power." His leadership qualities "are apparent to all who know him: modest, humble, kind, helpful, able, cheerful, adaptable, and sincere, he epitomizes the true Latter-day Saint. . . .

"The thousands of those who have known and loved Elder Monson . . . recognize him as a devout but not a dour Latter-day Saint. To those who have heard his voice on the telephone or talked to him in person, the very cheer of his greeting—the responsiveness of his conversation—his knowledgeable ways—the added testimony comes that these qualities which they have enjoyed will be extended throughout the Church to the blessing of the Saints and the glorification of our Father which is in heaven."[44]

Forty-five years later, in October 2008, President Monson stood again before the membership of the Church, which had swelled many times since his call in 1963. He said, "This conference marks 45 years since I was called to the Quorum of the

Twelve Apostles. As the junior member of the Twelve then, I looked up to 14 exceptional men, who were senior to me in the Twelve and the First Presidency. One by one, each of these men has returned home. When President Hinckley passed away eight months ago, I realized that I had become the senior Apostle. The changes over a period of 45 years that were incremental now seem monumental."[45]

As he began his apostolic duties, the years ahead would bring challenges and blessings unforeseen, but for now, Elder Monson was determined just to plunge in and do his best to accomplish whatever was asked of him.

16

SERVING IN THE TWELVE

I am so grateful that our lives have intertwined over the years. I look forward to long association on both sides of the veil. Thanks for being on top of so many things administratively and yet for noticing and caring about people.

ELDER NEAL A. MAXWELL
Quorum of the Twelve Apostles, 1974–2004

THOUGH YOUNG IN AGE, Elder Thomas S. Monson came to the apostleship well seasoned in Church service. He had presided over a mission and had served on general priesthood committees, in a stake presidency, and as a bishop. He had spoken at stake conferences and worked closely with General Authorities in printing their books and other Church materials. He knew what the Lord expected from him: "Not to be ministered unto, but to minister."[1]

"To be a member of the Quorum of the Twelve means, among other things, to be a member of committees that oversee important Church concerns. It means attending weekly conferences 'for the rest of your life,'" he has explained. But what resonated with him beyond the workload was what "one of the Brethren once said, it means absorbing assignments and opportunities for service that require total commitment to the work of the Master to buoy and lift, teach and train, lead and direct the Saints of God. It means accepting the burdens and strengthening the hopes of the Church and its people."[2]

233

The Quorum of the Twelve met with the First Presidency in the temple every Thursday—and still does. Elder Monson quickly appreciated the "spirit of devotion" prevalent at the meetings "where the outside world seems to be shut out and an inner spiritual peace permeates the attitude of every man present."[3] His journal entries for those Thursdays are replete with his witness of the prophet: "I never cease to marvel at the spirituality evidenced in this meeting. President McKay is indeed a prophet."[4]

Weeks after Elder Monson was sustained, President McKay suffered a slight stroke. At the end of October, Elder Monson noted, "Attended the temple meeting at 8:30. The meeting is not nearly so enjoyable when President McKay is not able to be in attendance. We miss our prophet."[5] Though President McKay missed many of the meetings as his health declined, Elder Monson marveled at his "recuperative capacity." After one general conference, he recorded, "The Lord completely sustained President McKay and he conducted the sessions. Three weeks ago, he would not have been able to accomplish this feat."[6]

When the Quorum partook of the sacrament together, Elder Monson described it as "one of the most sacred moments in our lives, patterned after the occasion where the Savior gave the sacrament to the Twelve Apostles. . . . We cannot but recall in sacred memory the administering of the sacrament of the first Twelve Apostles in the meridian of time. We are closer to them at this time than we are at any other time in our association one with another."[7]

Elder Monson became a prodigious journal keeper, noting the events and meetings he attended, his official assignments, his "errands for the Lord," his tender moments with his family.

His early months in the Quorum of the Twelve were filled with "firsts." His first meeting as an Apostle with the representatives of the Priesthood Home Teaching Committee "seemed rather strange." His last previous attendance at such a meeting had been as a committee member. Three of the number were close friends from the old Pioneer Stake: Percy K. Fetzer, Theodore M. Burton, and Glen L. Rudd.[8]

He spoke for the first time at the Institute of Religion at his alma mater, the University of Utah, on October 15, 1963, set apart missionaries for the first time on October 16, and presided at his first stake conference on October 19 and 20 in the Willamette Stake in Eugene, Oregon. He performed his first temple marriage October 25. He had his first official photograph taken October 28 and admitted being "rather pleased . . . normally I have a difficult time in picture taking." He conducted his first stake division November 2 and 3 in the Salem Oregon Stake, in company with Elder Howard W. Hunter, and gave his first address at Brigham Young University on November 5 in the Smith Fieldhouse, which was "filled to capacity" for his message, "The Three R's of Choice."[9] He attended his first board of trustees meeting for Brigham Young University on December 5, his first Council on the Disposition of Tithes meeting on December 12, where he had "a keen awareness of the responsibility" placed upon him, and his first funeral for a General Authority for Levi Edgar Young on December 16. In the midst of those first hectic weeks, he was also summoned to jury duty but was summarily struck from the list by the defendant's attorney. He was excused just in time to attend a priesthood board meeting.

Elder Monson's schedule was soon packed with mission tours, committee meetings, and training sessions. He supervised auxiliary presidencies and spoke at seminary graduations and baccalaureate exercises. On weekends, and for weeks at a time, he was on the road, whether that meant in the air or on a boat, a bus, a car, or a train. He was young, able, willing, energetic, and committed. Little wonder that, during that first year, he slept in his own bed less than half the time. "One doesn't appreciate sleeping in his own bed until he has the experience of sleeping in a strange bed every Saturday of his life," he once observed.[10]

Despite the grueling schedule, he would emphasize, "I come home every Sunday night feeling that I have benefited immeasurably by the conferences and the spirit of the people and grateful for the opportunity to serve the Lord."[11]

Whether his assignments took him to stakes close to home or far away, the goals were always the same: to strengthen the stake leaders and the members, to give direction, and to provide spiritual counsel. He was amazed at "how the gift of discernment is given to those who have the responsibility of visiting stake conferences."[12] As Isaiah wrote of the last days, "Enlarge the place of thy tent, and let them stretch forth the curtains of thine habitations: spare not, lengthen thy cords and strengthen thy stakes."[13] He was prepared to do that and much more.

In addition to attending conferences, he dedicated chapels, which were popping up everywhere as the Church building program boomed. On one weekend, at the Williamson Ward chapel in Vidor, Texas, the bishop confessed that the congregation had "prayed him there," explaining that they had wanted him to come and that the Lord had fulfilled their righteous desire.[14]

In November 1964 he attended the dedication of the Oakland Temple, which he called "a glorious occasion." It was his first time participating in a temple dedication. The temple, set on a hillside overlooking the San Francisco Bay area, was the thirteenth in the Church, the second in California. The words of Peter meeting with the Savior in a different but similarly hallowed setting coursed through Elder Monson's mind, "Lord, it is good for us to be here."[15] He spoke on the last day of the proceedings and "felt the blessings of our Heavenly Father sustaining me on this occasion."[16]

Elder Monson was always one to do his duty, get things done, and leave people feeling uplifted. "He takes into account the personal aspect of everything," observes Elder Marlin K. Jensen. He has heard President Monson recount the experience he had when he was a young member of the Twelve and President McKay sent him to California to a conference. There was a problem in the stake. One of the bishops had had a statue of Christ installed in a recessed area in the chapel. During the sacrament service, a light would come on and illuminate the statue. The stake president had not been successful in getting the bishop to remove the statue, and the Brethren had to worry about that kind of departure from approved practices. President McKay said to Elder Monson, "While you are at this conference, take the stake president, go see the bishop, bring this practice to an end, and make sure the bishop feels well about it." He did just that.

"President Monson has always been an example to me," Elder Jensen explains, "of getting the job done and getting it done in a way that people do feel well about it. He just assumes that people are doing the best they know how and will do better if we can help them."[17]

As a member of the Twelve with a young family, Elder Monson juggled the rigorous duties of his office with spending time with his wife and children. He attended the "Daddy-Daughter Date" party of the Valley View Third Ward with nine-year-old Ann in February 1964. "This was the first time I had been to an activity with my daughter, Ann, and we had a very good time. I don't know when I have seen her happier or more elated over an event. She is a lovely girl and a choice spirit. I am proud to be her father."[18]

The family picked him up from the airport one evening and headed for the Salt Lake County Fairgrounds. "To my surprise," he wrote, "I found that our Birmingham roller pigeons had swept the County Fair, winning the trophy for the outstanding young bird and a rosette for the outstanding old bird. Our white Plymouth Rock chickens also took top honors in their class but were nudged out for the trophy by a beautiful buff Orpington cock."[19]

He had given all but about a dozen of his birds away when the family had moved to Canada. Upon their return, he had re-cruited friends from the Sixth-Seventh Ward to help him remodel his pigeon coops into what he called "a showplace," and he and his son Tommy began again to breed pigeons, mostly for show purposes. Judges focused on "appearance, confirmation, a good head, and a powerful stance—sometimes with an arched neck—feather quality, and appropriate depth of keel between back and breast bone,"[20] explains President's Monson's son Tom, who took over more and more responsibility to care for the pigeons.

At other competitions, young Tommy won purple sweepstakes ribbons and awards for his "Champion" roller. The newspaper carried a picture of Tommy holding two of his birds. He was also on the cover of the annual show catalogue. When Elder Monson attended a stake conference in the Alpine Stake just south of Salt Lake, he took some of Tommy's homing pigeons to the conference and released them just before the 8:30 A.M. session. He was delighted to find when he got home that all had returned safely.

He took Tommy to Los Angeles on the train to meet distinguished pigeon breeders. "We saw some of the finest performing Birmingham roller pigeons I have yet seen. This was especially true of those in Mr. Patrick's loft," he noted.[21] They concluded their little adventure visiting a museum where the stuffed passenger pigeons particularly impressed Tommy.

"Pigeons aren't really pets," his son explains. "They aren't like a dog. If you give a name to a couple of them it is just to remember where you are on your breeding charts. You breed them and try to enhance qualities."[22] Today, Tom cares for all the pigeons— sixty of President Monson's and another hundred of his own— housed in the backyard of the President's home.

President Monson's son Clark, when he was older, gravitated to hawks as a hobby rather than pigeons. He also loved ghost towns, and the Monsons scoured the back roads of Utah to see the tumbledown relics. On October 27, 1967, Clark Spencer Monson was baptized by his father, who said, "It is a pleasure to have Clark in the home, and we feel honored to be his parents."[23]

He took Clark to California on the train to visit Disneyland. "I don't know when I've seen Clark so happy. 'Dad, will you go on one or two rides with me?' he asked. I answered, 'Clark, this time I'm going on all the rides with you'—and I did. At 10:00 P.M., tired but happy, we returned to the motel for a good night's rest."[24]

Elder Monson remembered being a teenager and sitting down in the living room of his stake president, Paul C. Child, where he was grilled on his scripture knowledge. Now he was attending conferences in the Salt Lake Valley and sitting down again with general Church Welfare Committee member Paul C. Child, his former stake president. This time the two were sitting together on the stand. Years later, when both Paul Child and his wife were living in a local nursing facility, President Monson made regular visits and sometimes spoke in Sunday services. As part of one message, he paid tribute to President Child. He later wrote, "I feel that much good was done for this venerable Church leader to hear one of us extol his virtues and acknowledge his influence rather than waiting for a funeral occasion to do so. . . . I told Frances upon returning home that I think I accomplished more good during that particular visit than in many conferences I may attend."[25]

But in those first few months Elder Monson was torn between the pressure of his new calling and his work at the Press. He would leave a temple meeting and return to his office at Deseret News Press, where he would "work late into the night." He was "finding it difficult to discover enough hours in the day to manage the Deseret News Press and take care of [his] church responsibility."[26] Finding a successor for his position at the Press took longer than expected; it was January 10, 1964, when officials named John Brown from Pacific Press in California to the post. Mr. Brown would stay a year and a half.

Elder Monson's last day at the Press, January 31, 1964, was exactly two years to the day after he had returned to work following service as president of the Canadian Mission. "I am happy that remarkable growth has occurred at the Deseret News Press," he expressed at that emotional time, "and am happy to leave the organization following a successful financial year. It will seem strange not to be a part of the Deseret News Publishing Company. This will be the first time that I have not had some connection with the firm since July of 1948."[27]

In 1964 he was named a member of the board of directors of Deseret Book Company, a position that would draw upon his lengthy experience in the printing and publishing fields. In 1965 he became a member of the Deseret News Publishing board of directors and eventually chairman of the board, serving until 1996, when the decision was made that General Authorities would no longer serve on boards of directors. In 1965 the Printing Industries of America awarded Elder Monson a certificate of recognition, hand engraved, "for his outstanding business accomplishments, industry leadership, personal integrity, religious devotion."[28] He would continue to keep apprised of the newest developments in printing, often visiting printing establishments in foreign countries and at international fairs. But the day-to-day buzz in the printing plant was behind him.

Leaving the business was "rather difficult," since he had spent a "lifetime of work participating in and directing a printing institution." All of that was coming to an end. He noted in his journal, "My first association with printing was as a copy boy for the Western Hotel Register back in 1942. I have been associated with it ever since and have loved it. When I walk though the plant, memories flood my very being, and I know I will find it hard to leave the people whom I have loved so dearly."[29] He didn't abandon those people. He has performed marriages in the temple for their children, has spoken in their wards, and, of course, has eulogized them at their funerals.

It was truly the end of an era. On February 3, 1964, Elder Monson attended the funeral of Louis C. Jacobsen, his "dear friend" and predecessor at the Deseret News Press. The service was very well attended, "for Louis was a friend to one and all." He had exerted "a marvelous influence" on Elder Monson's life. "He taught me to appreciate my family as he appreciated his," Elder Monson claimed. "His motto was, 'A man has but three things: His God, his family and his friends.' . . . We will miss him much—there is so much to miss."[30]

Elder Monson moved into office 211 on the second floor of the Church Administration Building on February 4, 1964, four months after being sustained as an Apostle at conference. There was a bit of an office shuffle going on. Bernard P. Brockbank, an Assistant to the Twelve, was moving into the fourth-floor office of Nathan Eldon Tanner, who moved to the first floor, which freed up an office for Elder Monson. He wrote in his journal, "Little did I dream years ago as I came to these offices for the purpose of being ordained a high priest and for other conferences pertaining to Church and personal matters that I would be occupying one as a member of the General Authorities."[31]

His first secretary was Ann Jones Lee. Lynne Fawson took her place in June of 1965—and never left. "Her skills were abundant and her attitude was excellent," he said, and she became invaluable. His many volumes of journals are replete with his appreciation for her work: "I am grateful for an excellent secretary who is a very choice individual."[32] When her children were small she worked from home, and then she job-shared when they were in school and ultimately returned to full-time work. She, like President Monson, often worked beyond quitting time. He considers her "the most competent secretary in the building, or, for that matter, anywhere I have observed competent secretaries at work. Her shorthand skills are superb, and the decorum of the office is maintained at a level most appropriate. She greets people in an intelligent and friendly manner and conducts without flaw the many intricate responsibilities which devolve upon her."[33]

When she began working for Elder Monson, Lynne was waiting for a missionary, Bill Cannegieter, who was serving in the Northern Indian Mission. When he returned, Elder Monson performed their marriage in the Salt Lake Temple. He testified when they received their first of three adopted daughters, "Our Heavenly Father has directed this particular placement—namely, this special child in a very special family." He stood in the circles when their daughters Jennifer and Kristen were given names and blessings, and he sealed the children in the temple to their parents.[34]

Elder and Sister Monson have celebrated birthdays and holidays with the Cannegieter family, and have been with them at difficult times as well. Second daughter Michelle died of sudden infant death syndrome when she was only six weeks old. The Lord guided Elder Monson to find words of comfort and knowledge of life after death for this precious family: "I turned to *Gospel Doctrine* which contains the writings of President Joseph F. Smith, perhaps the most prolific of our Church presidents with respect to the setting forth of principles of doctrine. I noted that page 452 was turned at the upper corner, after the fashion that I mark a particular page to which I later desire to refer. I noted the heading 'Condition of Children in Heaven.' I then read for several pages concerning the truths taught by Joseph Smith the Prophet regarding children who die in infancy. I was particularly touched by the statement as recorded by Joseph F. Smith: 'Joseph Smith declared that the mother who laid down her little child, being deprived of the privilege, the joy and the satisfaction of bringing it up to manhood or womanhood in this world, would, after the resurrection, have all of the joy, satisfaction and pleasure, and even more than it would have been possible to have in mortality in seeing her child grow to the full measure of the stature of its spirit.' I was touched by the simplicity of this statement. Later, when I telephoned Lynne to advise her of the statement, I retrieved my book, that I might read the information to her verbatim. To my astonishment, there was no turned-down page nor any evidence of a crease to indicate that the corner of the page had ever been folded. Whether or not there was a fold originally, I shall never know, but I do know that I recall such. Perhaps in the plan of our Heavenly Father, known only to Him, this was an indication, even a marker, to direct me to a comfort source to help a grieving mother and father."[35]

The Monsons count the Cannegieters as family.

Elder Monson's first committee assignment as an Apostle came from President Tanner, who assigned him as an adviser to the YWMIA and YMMIA organizations. Elder Monson, with his youth and energy, was a natural. Thus began a connection to the youth of the Church and their leaders that has never been broken. He loved the dance festivals in the stadium at the University of Utah that brought youth from all over the Church for the yearly celebratory activities of June Conference. He presented the trophies for All-Church athletic tournaments. He spoke at youth devotionals and participated in Scouting events.

It's no wonder that he has favored renewing such activities across the Church on a local level. He joined others of his Brethren in encouraging the youth festivals held in conjunction with Joseph Smith's 200th birthday celebration in 2005 as well as cultural celebrations prior to temple dedications. At general conference in 2009 he described 900 youth in Panama City, Panama, and 3,200 in Twin Falls, Idaho, dancing and presenting messages of faith in Jesus Christ. "I am an advocate for such events," he said. "They enable our youth to participate in something they truly find unforgettable. The friendships they form and the memories they make will be theirs forever."[36]

During his early years as an adviser to the MIA, Elder Monson helped shape the program as it fit into the Correlation efforts of the Church. He worked to buffer the encroachment of society's increasingly lax values. He noted: "All about us we see a lowering of moral standards. We see accepted on every hand the permissive society and all that goes with it."[37] At a June Conference held for the MIA organizations, he called on the Young Women leaders to fulfill their callings. "Our duty is to guide our girls to the celestial kingdom of God," he said. "Remember that the mantle of leadership is not the cloak of comfort but rather the robe of responsibility."[38] He has taught that truth in every nation he has visited.

In the ensuing years, the adult MIA programs would be split; the Young Men and Young Women organizations would be administered as priesthood programs; and June Conference, which had been the showcase for so many years, would be eliminated. All the changes were made with the intent to bolster the family and increase the focus on Jesus Christ.

Just a year after being sustained to the Twelve, Elder Monson was assigned to make a recommendation regarding the future of his "grand old pioneer ward," which had played such an important part in his life. The area increasingly had become home to commercial development.

The Sixth-Seventh Ward had absorbed the Fourteenth Ward in 1957 when that original unit in the valley had "dwindled to a shadow of its former greatness." Now it too was being collapsed into the neighboring Fourth Ward. In a Thursday temple meeting, Elder Harold B. Lee made a motion to tear down the old Sixth-Seventh Ward building. Although it was difficult for him, Elder Monson conceded the necessity of following Elder Lee's proposal.

The building, which had stood for nearly a hundred years, was razed on June 10, 1967. Built in 1867 for a cost of $12,000, it was the only red sandstone building of its type remaining in the city. Before it was destroyed, Elder Monson rescued the pulpit where he had spoken in his youth and where he had knelt as a bishop in late evening prayers. It was fitting that when, in June

2009, he dedicated the new Church History Library in Salt Lake City, he stood at that beautifully carved, preserved pulpit. For him it represented what one of his favorite poetic statements says so well, "God gave us memories that we might have June roses in the December of our lives."[39]

The Sixth-Seventh Ward area continued to decline and decrease in numbers and leadership. Five years after the building was razed, Elder Monson and Elder Boyd K. Packer received the assignment to examine the status of all the stakes in the central portion of Salt Lake City for possible readjustment of boundaries. They were assisted by two former leaders in the area, Percy K. Fetzer and Glen L. Rudd. They devised a plan to draw strength from stakes in the valley that had an abundance of leadership. They would import leaders from such areas to bolster the city center stakes in positions such as counselors to bishops and other leadership roles. The Liberty Stake's Fourth Ward—home to those remaining in the Sixth-Seventh Ward area—began receiving couples from the Monument Park and Hillside stakes. For three decades, this arrangement successfully shored up the area.

Eventually, building on those pioneering efforts, an inner-city project, under the hands of Utah Area President Alexander Morrison and the stake president of the Salt Lake Central Stake, expanded beyond the Liberty Stake, with missionaries drawn again from surrounding Salt Lake stakes. By now the missionaries' responsibility was not to serve in leadership roles but rather to support those who had been called to positions in their own wards. Today, those missionaries—in true Monson fashion— spend much of their time helping with the welfare needs of the members, drawing upon what has become a vast network of support and expertise. More than 6,000 have served in what began as inspiration to place a couple here and a couple there.

As the work of the kingdom continued to accelerate, Elder Monson's schedule was grueling. On June 1, 1965, he recorded, "The Scout Relationships conference ran overtime, the Adult Correlation Committee was in process, and a meeting with the presidency of the Rose Park Stake commenced earlier than I had anticipated. Since my attendance was required at all three meetings, I shared the time on a proportionate basis. I prefer to schedule my time a little more loosely than occurred today."[40]

But members of the Church did not see him racing from meeting to meeting and country to country. To them, he seemed always to have time for individuals. His accounts of personal experiences became the hallmark of his teaching.

Elder Ronald A. Rasband, of the Presidency of the Seventy, explains: "If you just want to hear a good story about the old Sixth-Seventh Ward, that's what you will hear. But if you have ears to hear about how he ministered to the widows in his ward, how he visited those widows and spoke at their funerals, you'll learn something from that. You just have to be willing to learn—it's a different style from that which many other leaders have, a very instructive style."[41]

President Monson uses illustrations to put a name and a face on programs, to give purpose to committees and meetings. To him, there's no question—people matter most. That's why in the midst of an intense debate, or as an answer to a question in a committee meeting, he may say, "Let me share an experience with you." His recognizable leadership style is to relate the issues to people, grounding decisions not in academic tenets but in human terms. At a reunion of his Sixth-Seventh Ward, he told those in attendance, "Your lives are my sermons."

In the Sunday morning session of October conference in 1967 he spoke on "Meeting Your Goliath," which proved to be an appropriate topic. During his message a man began shouting from the congregation that it was *his* turn to speak, hollering, "That's enough, Elder; turn it off!" Elder Monson glanced quickly at the First Presidency for direction and then, at their nod, continued his message as if nothing had happened. Ushers escorted the heckler from the building, but he did not go quietly. Later in the day the same young man attempted to break into the afternoon session to repeat his performance. The ushers restrained him, and this time he was taken to jail, though no charges were filed.[42]

The incident did not get in the way of Elder Monson's communicating his message. A non-LDS sales executive who "happened on to" his talk on the radio wrote, "Your talk on 'Meeting

Your Goliath' hit me right between the eyes, and since that day I haven't smoked a cigarette (I was at three packs a day). And a couple of other Goliaths, though not completely dead, lie bleeding and mortally wounded." He explained that he had used the message with his agency sales force, reading them the entire talk. "Our 23 agents—Protestant, Catholic and Jewish—all feel that you are obviously a man with a divine gift."[43]

In addition to using personal experiences and scriptures in his messages, President Monson loves to quote from hymns, poems, plays, and musicals that teach truths. He usually leaves a play or musical having scrawled in the program a particularly insightful phrase or a statement that spoke to his heart. For example, he often turns to playwright George Bernard Shaw and his acclaimed *Pygmalion,* which became the musical "My Fair Lady," to illustrate how to treat people: "The great thing, Eliza, is not having bad manners or good manners or any particular set of manners, but having the same manners for all human souls; in short, behaving as if you were in heaven, where there are no third-class carriages and where one soul is as good as another."[44]

As Elder Monson's responsibilities expanded, he continued to reach out to those in need, like the Apostle Peter at the Gate Beautiful in biblical times, who said, "In the name of Jesus Christ of Nazareth rise up and walk. And he took him by the right hand, and lifted him up."[45] That focus on "the one," that willingness to stop, to pay heed to the Spirit's prompting, defined him long before he was called as an Apostle, and that expression of God's love has continued throughout his life.

Put simply, he finds goodness in everyone. He values the many ways people contribute to the building of God's kingdom on earth. He doesn't expect everyone to be equal in skill, talent, or capacity, but he does expect them to do their duty, to be willing and committed, to try. As an administrator, he has always been known as decisive and insightful, never imperious or dictatorial. He is kind and compassionate, with a firm hand but a tender touch.

Elder Monson is an advocate of service "unheralded," which is often life-changing, and not just for the recipient. He observes:

"In each instance [of service to another] you will realize that you have returned with no diminution of ability but with a heart filled with gratitude, for you will find you have been on the Lord's errand and have been the beneficiary of His help and blessings."[46]

To the poor and downtrodden, the forgotten and seemingly common, those who don't have anyone else, President Monson has always been particularly attentive. William Edwin "Ed" Erickson was an example of this. Ed grew up in the Sixth-Seventh Ward and never left, eventually becoming the caregiver for his aged and ailing mother. He suffered from poor eyesight but was intelligent and a hard worker. Tom, eighteen years Ed's junior, became his bishop and, as such, made certain Ed's temporal needs were met. The two developed a friendship that lasted throughout Ed's life. Ed didn't have many friends—but he had Elder Monson.

Ed had a goodness that spilled out into others' lives. He had worked for the Salt Lake City Streets Department most of his life, making little money and spending hardly any. He was "one who would do anything for anybody."[47] He was a proud member of the Mormon Battalion and volunteered weekly at Welfare Square. Ed walked everywhere. His poor eyesight made it impossible for him to obtain a driver's license, and so he had no car.

Ed's mother eventually passed away, and their small home in the Sixth-Seventh Ward fell victim to the ever-encroaching businesses and industry of downtown Salt Lake City. Through all of this, Elder Monson made certain Ed had a clean, affordable apartment in which to live, one close enough to downtown Salt Lake City for Ed to walk to Lamb's Café every morning for his breakfast.

Elder Monson invited Ed to join with the Monson family whenever they attended such events as the rodeo or the circus. He would have Ed do work at the Monson residence so he could provide Ed some spending money without his feeling that it was a handout. He occasionally took Ed to the Little America coffee shop for lunch, always celebrating Ed's birthday there with a small group of friends.

When Ed was nearing the end of his life, he finally unwrapped his last new shirt—bought after the Second World War when Harry Truman was president. When he died on February 21, 2005, at age ninety-five, he left his life savings—a relatively significant amount—to the Primary Children's Medical Center, to assist children with vision problems, and to the LDS Church's missionary fund, to contribute to service he was unable to perform himself. Said President Monson in tribute to his friend: "What makes it good is that he gave all he had."[48]

Ed is only one of many for whom Tom Monson cared over the years, finding them extra work, making time to listen to their worries, giving encouragement when things were hard. He called Ed his "counselor," and Ed, in jest, often asked where he and President Monson would be going on assignment each week. Ed knew Tom Monson cared for him.

To a gathering of the Young Women of the Church in 2009, President Monson spoke of what he had learned from Ed Erickson: "Have the courage to refrain from judging and criticizing those around you, as well as the courage to make certain everyone is included and feels loved and valued."[49]

Making others feel loved has been a hallmark of President Monson's life and ministry.

17

"HE WAS EVERYWHERE"

Tom Monson was so young and energetic when he was called. Not only was he junior in the Quorum but at thirty-six he was junior in age. He was younger than his Brethren by nearly twenty years. From the very beginning of his service, he got a lot of assignments and carried a lot of freight, which was a tribute to how well he was thought of by the Brethren and by the Lord.

ELDER JEFFREY R. HOLLAND
Quorum of the Twelve Apostles

THE TUESDAY FOLLOWING OCTOBER conference in 1966, Frances came to find her husband at the office and tearfully reported that her doctor had discovered a tumor that would require immediate surgery. She was admitted to the hospital the next day. Elder Monson recorded, "Brother [Harold B.] Lee pronounced one of the most inspired blessings I have ever heard. We felt a reassurance following his prophetic utterance which brought peace to the soul."[1]

Early in the morning on Thursday, October 6, Frances was taken to surgery. To Elder Monson, "the minutes seemed like years and the hours an eternity." But he was reassured by the knowledge that his Brethren "were at that moment in session in the upper room of the temple, uniting their faith and prayers in behalf of my dear wife."[2]

No report has been more joyfully received than the word that the tumor was benign. As Dr. Vernon Stevenson related the good news, Elder Monson told him that the next day would be their eighteenth wedding anniversary, to which the doctor replied, "You are a very fortunate man. This could have gone either way. Your wife will be with you for many years." Elder Monson then said, pointing to the Salt Lake Temple, "that the men I loved most had been remembering [the doctor] in their faith and in their prayers that very morning." The doctor replied, "This makes me feel very humble."[3]

Elder Monson remembers the next meeting in the temple, when he partook of the sacrament: "I silently expressed my gratitude to my Heavenly Father for the wonderful fashion in which He has blessed my companion." President Hugh B. Brown called on him to bear his testimony, and Elder Monson acknowledged that he and his wife Frances "suddenly came face-to-face with the thought there could be a malignancy." Frances's mother had been diagnosed with cancer just a few months before, which had added to their anxiety.

"We felt through it all that we were in the hands of the Lord, and we had confidence that whatever His judgment might be, that would be the right thing for us. . . . My sweetheart read her patriarchal blessing wherein the Lord told her she would be by my side for many, many years, and she told me not to worry. She said, 'I am going to be all right.'

"Last evening as we had our family home evening, each one of my children became closer to me than had heretofore been the case. And I want to bear my testimony that in the Monson household, we are proud to serve the Lord. We are humbled by the great responsibility that has come to us, and our desire as a family is to uphold you Brethren and constantly serve the Lord and be amenable to His desires, and do those things that He would like us to do."

He concluded his words to his Brethren, "I am the least among you and pray that I may be worthy of my association with you."[4]

Elder Monson's words from his April conference message the year before took on new meaning for him and his family: "Those who have felt the touch of the Master's hand somehow cannot explain the change which comes into their lives. There is a desire to live better, to serve faithfully, to walk humbly, and to live more like the Savior."[5]

The same week as the cancer scare, Elder Monson was privileged to perform his younger brother Scott's marriage in the Salt Lake Temple. Scott had served his mission in Sweden. After about a year in the mission field, he had written in a letter to his father, Spence, "Every Sunday I start the day off going to priesthood meeting. I know you haven't attended priesthood much for a long time. I keep thinking how nice it would be when I am going to priesthood meeting on Sunday if you could be doing the same."

Spence got up early the next Sunday and started putting on his white shirt and suit. Gladys asked where he was going, and he responded, "To priesthood meeting." She said with surprise, "You haven't gone to priesthood meeting in ages," to which he responded, "Well, the boy wrote me and said that he thought it would be a nice idea if I attended priesthood the same day he does. So I thought I would do it."[6]

Scott's marriage ceremony was the first of his children's temple sealings that Spence Monson attended. He served as one of the witnesses.

Family was then and has always been important to Thomas Monson. He understood well the basis of the correlation movement beginning to make its way through the Church system, the overall thrust of which was to protect the family. He also grasped the importance of each family member gaining a greater understanding of the gospel through correlated programs.

Elder Monson's imprint is visible in those early correlation efforts and in nearly every Church department, program, and auxiliary, as well as every company owned by the Church since the early 1960s. He also was integrally involved in the training and teaching of spiritual and temporal principles and stewardships. As one person said who worked with him closely, "He was everywhere."[7]

It is simply not possible to catalog or chronicle the countless activities of each separate committee, each chairmanship, each leader or missionary Elder Monson counseled, each proposal he reviewed, or each country he visited, dedicated, or blessed. In every area of administration, especially as correlation efforts restructured and redefined the work of the Church, he played a vital role. He served on every major committee and in many cases was asked to be the chair. He attended innumerable meetings; he was always reaching out to rescue someone in need. He was busy.

Elder Monson was the junior member of the Twelve, and his appointments to key committees may have raised some eyebrows—even his. He wisely concluded, "For a junior member to have all the heavy committee assignments means you'd better know what you are doing."[8]

Under direction from the First Presidency, Elder Harold B. Lee provided the overall leadership and vision for the Correlation Committee, but he relied on Elder Monson to bring many of his ideas to fruition. Elder Lee knew he could count on Elder Monson to help shape Church programs that would promote faith, growth, and stronger testimonies of the principles of the gospel according to family and priesthood all working together.

During the next twenty years, the correlation efforts slowly dismantled the autonomous operations of the Church auxiliaries and departments, replacing them with a system focused on the family with priesthood coordination.

Correlation meant more than standardizing the Church's curriculum so that all gospel topics were taught "as completely as possible at least three times during these three age levels of life: children, youth and adults."[9] It was designed to manage the rapid growth and buffer the societal issues the Church faced in many nations, as well as to clarify and establish lines of organization, beginning with the First Presidency and moving through the Twelve Apostles to stake presidents, bishops, and families. At the heart of the plan were auxiliaries and quorums correlated within priesthood lines, with the ultimate aim of supporting and sustaining the family in an era that saw an eroding of the very foundation of family life in society.

The word *correlation* took on new meaning for everyone associated with the far-reaching plan. Rather than "a cold, academic term," it became an entity of "tremendous sacredness and worth."[10]

In 1965 Elder Monson succeeded Elder Marion G. Romney

as the chairman of the Adult Correlation Committee, the major correlation body of the Church. Elder Monson was humbled by the "tremendous responsibility." He told his Brethren, "I know of the great capabilities of Elder Romney, and I hope and pray that the Lord will make me equal to the assignment."[11] He worked very closely with Elder Harold B. Lee. At one point he suggested to Elder Lee that he (Elder Monson) perhaps had too many significant assignments. Elder Lee's response was quick, "If I had wanted someone else to do this work, I would have called him."[12]

Elder Monson soon learned that everything that didn't fit in the children or youth categories, anything they didn't know what to do with, was handed off to the Adult Correlation Committee. He immediately began an exhaustive study of pending manuscripts of all handbooks and courses of study. There were many. One of the major issues was the introduction of new lesson material each year, not necessarily connected to a stated purpose. He reported to Elder Lee, "The Adult Committee is aware that we are now entering a new and very important phase of the correlation program in the Church. We feel that it is important to keep certain basic things in mind. Our ultimate aim is to help every member of the Church to walk uprightly before the Lord, to experience the kind of joy which the Lord has in mind for us, and to be saved and exalted in His celestial kingdom. For this to be accomplished, every member of the Church must understand, love, and live the principles of the gospel. If he has an inner motivation based on such understanding, loving, and living, he will do the right things for the right reasons."[13]

Elder Monson emphasized to the committee that they needed to think in terms of "one Lord, one faith, one boy, one girl, one program."[14] That was what he wanted to have happen with all adult leaders in the Church as they caught the vision of correlation and were trained in the leadership principles that facilitated its implementation. A focus on family home evening, with Monday set aside as the designated day for holding it, was renewed in 1965 and has become an important tradition to buttress the family from encroaching worldly influences. The thrust to strengthen the family through the priesthood correlation of the 1960s has borne fruit more than fifty years later as family life has been attacked in the world but the Church has stood firm.

Elder Lee also called Elder Monson to chair the Leadership Training Committee. This committee developed training for two groups: (1) priesthood leaders at priesthood meetings and conferences, and (2) specialists in teaching, library work, music, recreation, and other areas on a ward, stake, or regional basis, as the Brethren determined necessary. Every plan went forward for approval to the Correlation Committee and then to the Quorum of the Twelve and First Presidency. The Brethren, in turn, would take that training model to stake conferences and regional meetings with priesthood and auxiliary leaders. Elder Monson selected two able leaders to work with him on the Leadership Committee: Wendell J. Ashton, with whom he had worked in Adult Correlation and who had a strong presence in community affairs and was a stickler for detail, and Neal A. Maxwell, whom he knew by reputation for innovative teaching and modern methods of training, and who served as a member of the YMMIA Board and a University of Utah administrator. As the workload increased in subsequent years, Elder Monson asked for two more to join the committee: James E. Faust and Hugh W. Pinnock. David B. Haight and J. Thomas Fyans assisted as staff members.

Elder Monson was not just putting in place theoretical leadership skills, methods, and techniques. He was also training leaders how to teach true principles. "All of you are teachers," he has said. "No person can escape the influence of his own example. . . . A mediocre teacher tells, a good teacher explains, a superior teacher demonstrates; but the great teachers inspire."[15]

The committee members studied highly successful training methods of large corporations, historical efforts in the Church, and scriptures that infused their planning with spiritual insight. They recognized that one of the central responsibilities of General Authorities is to speak by revelation, teaching the basic concepts of the framework of The Church of Jesus Christ of Latter-day Saints. Some of the first topics developed in the Leadership Training Committee were as basic as "How to Call and How to Release," "How to Listen Attentively," "How to Give

Direction," as well as other themes drawn from the General Handbook of Instructions. The committee developed materials to focus attention on listening as an essential element in teaching, learning, and leading.

Elder Monson advanced a leadership outline for the second half of 1969 that had as its focus: "How to Improve Our Ability—Individually and Organizationally—to Reach the Lost Sheep." No one knew that subject better than Thomas Monson.

Some of the committee's most effective training programs were drawn from notes Elder Monson had taken as a bishop: "The Duties of a Bishop" and "The Organization and Duties of a High Council." Elder Harold B. Lee—an Apostle and former stake president in the area—had trained leaders in the Temple View Stake in those two areas with precision and persuasion. That Elder Monson had kept those notes—and still has them today—says much about the training he received. The Leadership Training Committee slated that exact training for the whole Church, and it was readily approved by the Quorum of the Twelve and the First Presidency.

In February 2004, in a worldwide leadership training broadcast—the current iteration of training venues—President Monson would again bring forward those training notes from Elder Lee and teach a new generation of priesthood leaders about "The Bishop and the Spiritual and Temporal Well-Being of the Saints." He drew five circles on the board to represent the areas of influence and responsibility of the bishop and identified them as follows: The bishop is the presiding high priest and father of the ward; the bishop has responsibility for the Aaronic Priesthood; the bishop cares for the needy; the bishop is responsible for finances; the bishop is the common judge. He concluded by saying that the "sacred and God-given responsibilities [of the bishops] . . . were authored in heaven to bless in our day each member of the Church."[16]

By 1967 Elder Lee was discussing with Elder Monson other structures to connect with the leadership of the Church beyond the Priesthood Committee structure. The First Presidency led by President Heber J. Grant had called Assistants to the Quorum of the Twelve in 1941 to add additional strength at the general level. Since then, the Church had grown dramatically in new members and in new districts, wards, stakes, and missions, and the correlation program called for a more synthesized leadership model.

After lengthy discussions among members of the Quorum of the Twelve and the First Presidency, a new level of priesthood leadership emerged: "regional representatives of the Twelve." Their calling was "to carry counsel to and to conduct instructional meetings in groups of stakes or regions."[17] These men would be not General Authorities but high-level advisers who would serve as liaisons between the stakes and the Quorum of the Twelve.

Elder Lee immediately drew upon Elder Monson's well-honed skills in managing and motivating others, his capacity to think broadly, and his tenacity and discipline to train those called as regional representatives. The first day-long session of training for these newly called men, held on September 28, 1967, established a tradition of leadership training that has continued as an integral part of general conference proceedings. Elder Lee noted in his journal, "Thomas S. Monson and his associates, Neal A. Maxwell and Wendell Ashton, have done a tremendous job in expediting and planning for all the details."[18]

The next year, as the committee prepared for another round of training meetings, what he described as "the highlight of the six-month period," Elder Monson went to see Elder Lee in the hospital, where he was recovering from surgery. "He taught me a great lesson," Elder Monson said, "one all leaders should learn."

"Tom," Elder Lee said, "you know better than I what should take place tomorrow, and if you were given the assignment to act in my stead you would carry on and everything would go better than if I were there." He continued, "You know the order of the Church and I know the order of the Church, and therefore, Spencer W. Kimball, as the man next to me, should be the man to whom the correlation torch should be handed for tomorrow's seminar." He then asked, "Would you be to him what you have been to me, a faithful helper in the cause of Christ?"

Elder Monson responded, "That will be fine with me, Brother Lee."

Then Elder Lee asked him for a blessing.

The next day, Elder Kimball, with the binder of conducting and speaking notes, went forward to teach "a magnificent lesson on the government of the Church." Later that afternoon, a weary Elder Kimball wrote the young Apostle a note in his distinctive script: "I can't give my talk. I can hardly stand. Please speak. Say anything you want. Let me go lie down during the intermission and see if I might recoup my strength." Elder Monson stood as instructed, speaking at length until, walking slowly to the pulpit, Elder Kimball carried on. "It was just before he had heart surgery," Elder Monson later explained, "and Elder Kimball literally, physically, could not have given that talk but for the help of the Lord."[19]

For the next several decades, regional representatives provided training to priesthood and auxiliary leaders in their designated geographical areas. At April conference in 1995, the 284 men then serving as regional representatives were honorably released. Since 1967, 1,072 men had served in that capacity.[20] They were replaced with Area Authority Seventies (later called Area Seventies), who would continue the course of regional representatives but would have additional responsibility to meet the growing needs and pressures of the worldwide Church.

Elder Monson's influence extended beyond internal programs and training to outside connections as well. His experiences growing up close to uncles who were not members of the Church, and in a neighborhood of many different religions—or no religion at all—had taught him to get along with everyone. When President David O. McKay turned to him with assignments to represent the Church in the broader community, he was amply prepared to do so.

Tom substituted for "fellow Canadian" President Hugh B. Brown at the Interfaith Service in Lethbridge, Alberta, Canada, in June 1967. He spoke both days in what was the largest religious service ever held in southern Alberta, sharing the speaker's stand with the Archdeacon of the Anglican Church, Cecil Swanson; the Roman Catholic Bishop of Calgary, the Most Reverend Francis J. Klein; and the Right Reverend of the United Church of Canada,

W. C. Lockhart. He felt "a little uncomfortable following the robed dignitaries" but right at home speaking of the Savior Jesus Christ.

"The formula for finding Jesus has always been and ever will be the same—the earnest and sincere prayer of a humble and pure heart," he said to the large gathering.[21]

He attended an ecumenical session honoring the hundredth anniversary of the Episcopal Church in Utah and was the guest of Bishop Richard Watson at a special luncheon for church heads of the various congregations in the city and state. He was comfortable with leaders of other faiths; they were comfortable with him.

He was recognized by the community for his outreach. On March 8, 1966, the University of Utah awarded him the Distinguished Alumni Award, the first of his many civic recognitions. His mother, who had always been a great advocate of education, was "perhaps the proudest person in the audience," which included his parents, aunts and uncles, brothers and sisters, his children, and even childhood friends. Others on the podium with him receiving awards were Utah Governor Calvin L. Rampton; Frank S. Forsberg, who became the United States Ambassador to Sweden; Dean Olson, founder of Olson Brothers Egg Company in Los Angeles; and Joseph Jensen, developer of petroleum and water resources.

In those years the Brethren served on many boards in the community, not just those of Church-owned businesses. Elder Monson was named to a three-year term on the University of Utah's Alumni Board.[22] Mountain Bell, at the time the Intermountain West's largest phone service company, tapped Elder Monson for a seat on their Utah Advisory Board. Several years later, he was moved up to the Mountain Bell Board located in Denver, Colorado, where he served alongside prominent community leaders from several western states. The board meetings were held in Denver, which meant that once a month he was traveling on a plane to attend them.

Commercial Security Bank asked him to sit on their board. He served as the chairman of their audit committee for twenty years. After he had served for about three years, Commercial

Security Bank decided to change their board meetings to a certain Tuesday each month. Elder Monson approached Richard (Dick) Hemingway, president of the bank, and explained that he would need to resign his position because his meetings of the Mountain Bell board in Denver were already held on that same Tuesday. Dick Hemingway responded, "Each month has thirty days. There are twenty-nine other days that we could hold our board meeting, and we'll be happy to do so." The bank changed to a different Tuesday.[23]

When another, larger bank approached Elder Monson to take a seat on its board, which would require his resignation from Commercial Security Bank, he was flattered but remained loyal to his current post.

When Commercial Security was sold to Key Bank, a much larger operation, the new owners asked Elder Monson to stay on the board. He served until March 1996, when the First Presidency determined that General Authorities would no longer sit on outside boards. The new chairman, Maurice P. Shea, wrote, in gratitude for Elder Monson's service: "On behalf of Key Corp. and Key Bank, your efforts and support will be missed. As a friend, I will miss you even more. I enjoy our discussions about [Larry] Bird and the Celtics and Ted Williams and his Red Sox. As we Irish are fond to say: 'May the road rise up to meet you, may the wind be always to your back. May the sun shine warm upon your face, May the rain fall softly upon your fields and until we meet again, May God hold you in the palm of his hand.'"[24]

His years on the bank board were not all about the bottom line. He became great friends with bank executives Richard (Dick) Hemingway and Robert (Bob) Bischoff. In May 2001 Bob lay critically ill in the hospital following surgery for pancreatic cancer. President Monson felt impressed to visit Bob at the hospital. Their exchange was tender. Bob told President Monson that the illness had brought him to a full realization of what was really important in life. "He expressed to me the inner desires of his heart to study the doctrine of the Church and to become a member and to go to the house of the Lord," President Monson later recalled. President Monson gave him a priesthood blessing and then embraced him.[25] Bob died two days later. President Monson spoke at his funeral, paying tribute to his dear friend who had also served as a member of the Deseret News Board, describing him as "a man of integrity, a man of valor, a man of judgment and a man of good will."[26]

Elder Monson had a great affinity for print media. He soon gained an appreciation for broadcast media as well. In September 1964, the First Presidency clustered its broadcasting companies under a new parent company, Bonneville International Corporation. Bonneville provided centralized support in financing, engineering, purchasing, promotion, advertising, and other essential tasks to the Church-owned radio and television stations but did not take over the policies or operations. It was a bold step into what would be a vital communication network for the next forty-plus years. Elder Monson was asked to serve on Bonneville's board and was "very pleased with this appointment."[27] He also was appointed to the board of directors of KSL, the local broadcasting station in Salt Lake City. It was becoming clear that in order to spread the message of the gospel, the Church needed access to the airwaves across the country and around the world. In later years, satellite transmission also became vital.[28]

Elder Monson was one who would speak his mind. While often the popular thing to do was "voice one's approval," he consistently "had to be honest" with himself, and after analyzing the facts he would voice his personal opinion, whether or not it was "popular." He always lined up with the final decision, however.[29]

His leadership style has always been to encourage expression of opinions and counsel, whether those ideas mirrored his thinking or not. As Church President, he has been known to say, "You don't help me," when committee members have withheld opinions on a pressing matter. Those who have worked at his side agree he is very open to counsel. "He wants it absolutely straight," they say, and has little patience for those in the room who wait to see what is the "right way" to come out on a particular issue. He would often hold up President N. Eldon Tanner as an example. "Here is a leader, a man who is integrity through and through, a man who has the capacity to be a true counselor . . .

unyielding, undeviating, seeking first the kingdom of God and His righteousness."[30]

Although President Monson has typed all of his talks on a typewriter placed on the kitchen table, he has been at the forefront of the Church's embracing new technologies, as he chaired the committees that instituted new systems. He still remembers attending a presentation for an innovation that people said would revolutionize office work. It was called "word processing."[31]

From Church committees to ecumenical efforts to community boards to new enterprises, Thomas S. Monson truly was "everywhere" in his ministry as an Apostle of the Lord Jesus Christ.

18

NEAR AND FAR

A man filled with the love of God, is not content with blessing his family alone, but ranges through the whole world, anxious to bless the whole human race.

JOSEPH SMITH, JR.
President of The Church of Jesus Christ
of Latter-day Saints, 1830–1844

MARK MENDENHALL WALKED across the stage at BYU commencement in 1983 to be "hooded" for his doctorate in social psychology. The Marriott Center was packed with family members and friends of the graduates, Elder Monson among them, sitting on the stand as a representative of the Church Board of Trustees. "That made it perfect for me," Mark later recounted; he had known and loved Elder Monson since childhood.

In Mark's youth, his father, Earl, had been a labor missionary operating the Church's sheep and cattle ranch in Temple View, New Zealand. The community, just outside Hamilton, was essentially a "company town" of Church labor missionaries, teachers and administrators at the Church College of New Zealand, and temple workers who served in the New Zealand Temple. It was multicultural, consisting mostly of Maoris, New Zealanders, Australians, Tongans, Samoans, and some Americans.

The Mendenhalls' spare bedroom often accommodated visiting General Authorities, and periodically from 1965 to 1968, Elder

Monson was one of them. Earl took him fishing on Lake Taupo, one of the most beautiful lakes Elder Monson had ever seen. The first time they went, it rained all day, but Elder Monson was not thwarted. He landed four five-pound rainbow trout and lost perhaps that many more. His fishing partners were not so fortunate.

"My memory of him around the house is of him always being cheerful, upbeat, and full of life," Mark recalls. "As a child I saw him 'behind closed doors' if you will, outside of the official nature of his calling, conversing with my dad and other men and telling stories. I never, ever, saw him or heard him say or do anything that was below the dignity of his calling. I always felt that here was a man of God."

Knowing that young Mark was a stamp collector, Elder Monson always brought him stamps from some of the mail he received at his office in Salt Lake. On one visit, he delighted Mark with a first-day issue of stamps for Tonga. "It was the pure love of Christ being shown to a young boy by a servant of God," says Mark, who still wonders, "How could he remember me, given the crush of his workload and responsibilities?"[1]

Now, as Mark prepared to receive his doctorate in front of his "stamp benefactor" from childhood, he wondered if Elder Monson would remember him. Perhaps, because he carried his father's given name, Elder Monson just might. Mark kept his eyes on Elder Monson and then stepped forward at the announcement of his name: "Mark Earl Mendenhall."

"I saw him visibly jerk his head up a bit and immediately look over to me. I looked straight into his eyes, and he looked into mine and nodded his head to me with a smile, indicating to me what I took to be 'job well done' or perhaps 'you have honored your father and mother.' I nodded back in return as an expression of gratitude for all that Elder Monson had done for my parents over the years."[2]

Mark Mendenhall's experience is just one illustration of Elder Monson's capacity to touch individual lives in the course of an incredibly taxing schedule. Throughout the world, for years and years, similar scenes have played out, unheralded, even unknown by the world but recorded in the hearts of grateful participants.

During his first two years as an Apostle, Elder Monson

supervised the North America West Area, making trips for mission tours, conferences, and special meetings. Other assignments those first years also took him to Nebraska, New Mexico, Ohio, Oregon, Texas, and Minnesota—and several times to Toronto, Canada, where he was pleased to find that the Church membership in some areas had more than doubled since his mission there.

President McKay asked that during their visits to missions, the General Authorities interview all the missionaries. Elder Monson always did his duty. He was grateful when the chapel furnace worked so he didn't have to interview in his overcoat. That first year he interviewed 1,700 missionaries—as many as 50 a day—and the next year he did it again. Interviewing missionaries became very much a part of his mission tours. Years later, he was interviewing in a dark little room and without looking up reached out to shake the next missionary's hand. He felt something cold and wet in his palm. A dog had slipped into the room, and he had it by the nose.

Airplane travel was often tricky. Many times Elder Monson was fogged in, rerouted, grounded, forced to board another plane, or stranded in airports, and he never had time to spare to get to his destination. Sometimes he was simply ticketed poorly, as with one lengthy return flight from Seattle that stopped in San Francisco, Los Angeles, and Las Vegas before landing in Salt Lake. The pilot of a flight to Canada announced that they were unable to land because of fog. Elder Monson offered a silent prayer, and immediately the pilot's voice came on again, "We have been advised that there has been a momentary clearing in our approach to the airport and we will take full advantage of this."[3] Such prayers parted the clouds on several occasions, allowing Elder Monson to get on with what he had been assigned to do. When air travel wasn't possible, he would drive hundreds of miles and then interview, hold meetings, and get back on the road for another long drive.

In June of 1965 the First Presidency divided the world into new areas: five in the United States; North America Spanish; South America; British Isles; West Europe; East Europe; the Orient and Hawaii; and the South Pacific. President McKay assigned Elder

Monson to oversee the South Pacific Area, one of the farthest reaches from Church headquarters. Elder Paul H. Dunn of the Seventy would serve with him.

Elder Monson had been to the South Pacific previously. On that visit, he and Frances had departed on February 5, 1965, leaving the children at home in the care of Frances's mother, known by them as "Mormor" (the Swedish term for maternal grandmother). The Monsons' visit to the Sauniatu School on Upolu, Samoa, the area President McKay had visited in 1921 and 1955, was memorable. As Elder Monson spoke to them, he felt prompted to invite the 200 youngsters to come forward and shake his hand one by one. He first dismissed the thought because of his tight schedule, but the prompting came again. He asked the person in charge if he might personally shake the hand of each child. The administrator responded with an outburst of joy, explaining, "Our prayers have been answered. I told the children that if they had faith, and that if they all prayed, that the apostle of the Lord would personally greet each one of them when he visited Sauniatu."[4]

Everywhere Elder and Sister Monson went, they met with missionaries. Frances, comfortable in the setting, "gave good counsel." Her remarks reminded her husband of their "experiences together in the mission field."[5]

When they arrived back in Salt Lake City on March 9, Frances was rushed to the hospital, where she was admitted with concerns that she might have cholera. When the doctors instead reported salmonella, a type of food poisoning, everyone was relieved. She came home a few days later, weak but on the mend. She was soon on her feet. That was important because just a few days later the family—Elder and Sister Monson, Tommy, Ann, and Clark—held one of their long-established ping-pong tournaments in the basement. Frances was the winner.

After reporting that first tour to President McKay, who had himself spent a great deal of time in the South Pacific, Elder Monson left their meeting with tender feelings: "When one is in the presence of President McKay, he always feels uplifted and leaves the interview a better man."[6]

Later that year, after Elder Monson had been officially assigned to supervise the South Pacific Area, he made a second trip there, this time in company with President Hugh B. Brown. They had planned visits to Samoa, Tonga, Fiji, New Zealand, and Australia. They arrived in Auckland, New Zealand, on October 21, 1965, where they "observed President Brown's eighty-second birthday" by speaking at a regional missionary gathering. At a special conference in the Hamilton Stake, they addressed 2,000 members, who became immediate "friends." Later in their travels they had a special audience with the chief of state of Samoa and the prime minister of New Zealand.

For many days prior to the Brethren's visit to the Church school at Mapusaga, American Samoa, the faculty and children had been fasting and praying for moisture. A severe drought had completely depleted the water supply, which was totally dependent upon rainfall. During the early morning conference sessions, the heavens opened and drenched the area with rain. A pilot who arrived shortly after the downpour was heard to say, "This is the most unusual weather pattern I have ever seen. Not a cloud in the sky except over the Mormon school at Mapusaga. I don't understand it!"[7]

In Apia, Western Samoa, the two General Authorities met with 1,300 members of the stake. At each session, Elder Monson and President Brown spoke with the aid of translators so that remarks made in English could be translated for members who spoke only Samoan. Elder Monson observed what he called "a miracle of the interpretation of tongues" as President Brown was speaking:

"A counselor in the mission presidency leaned forward and spoke to the stake president; these men were native Samoans. They had observed that the congregation was receiving the message of President Brown without the aid of the interpreter. He was promptly excused from the assignment and President Brown spoke another forty minutes. Everyone in the congregation, English-speaking and Samoan-speaking members alike, understood his words."[8]

President Brown cut his tour short, flying home from Auckland, New Zealand; Elder Monson continued the visit alone.

Prompting President Brown's hasty return to Church headquarters was President McKay's surprise announcement of two new counselors appointed to the First Presidency—Elder Joseph Fielding Smith, President of the Quorum of the Twelve, and Elder Thorpe B. Isaacson, an Assistant to the Twelve. A few months later, Elder Isaacson had a debilitating stroke and President McKay called Elder Alvin R. Dyer, another Assistant to the Twelve, as a counselor in the First Presidency. Neither Elder Isaacson nor Elder Dyer was ever named to the Quorum of the Twelve.

Elder Monson carried on to Fiji and to Tonga, where he met with Prince Tui Pele Hake, son of Queen Salote and brother of the Crown Prince. He finished his journey in Tahiti. Upon returning home, he shared with his family the challenges the members faced to get to the temple. The discussions piqued daughter Ann's interest. A few years later, while serving as vice president of the seminary council of the Salt Lake Valley, she launched a campaign, unknown to her father, to raise funds to assist families in the South Seas to receive their temple blessings. The students from many high schools contributed modest amounts and worked on various projects until they exceeded their goal of $8,000. One evening the seminary officers gathered at the Monson home and surprised Elder Monson with the money. He arranged to send the proceeds to the president of the Samoan Mission with a letter asking that the funds be used to help families go to the temple. President Monson observed, "A small sacrifice by seminary students had resulted in eternal blessings for others. They loved as Jesus loves."[9]

For the next two and half years, Elder Monson flew over the Pacific eight times, losing a day and getting it back as he crossed the international date line going and coming. When possible, Frances accompanied him for at least half the trip. The flights over thousands of miles of ocean might have been where he developed his dislike for flying at night, which continues to this day. But ever a student of history, he completed reading the six-volume series of the *Comprehensive History of the Church* during the long plane rides to the South Seas.

His itinerary would exhaust even the most intrepid traveler.

He was usually gone for three or four weeks—occasionally even five—and he had little contact with Church headquarters or home when he was away. Communication was mostly by mail. President Joseph Fielding Smith, then his Quorum President, corresponded in letters, which were slow to arrive. A phone call to the States was almost unheard of; many islands had no phone service at all. He traveled mostly by small vessels, and the weather determined whether the boats could actually get through the reefs and to the islands.

During one of Elder Monson's trips to Australia, while traveling with mission president Horace D. Ensign, their plane stopped at the mining town of Mount Isa, Australia. Elder Monson was surprised to find a woman and her two children waiting at the airport to meet him. The woman, Judith Louden, explained that in her four years of membership in the Church, she had never lived in an organized branch; her husband was not a member. They talked, and Elder Monson was preparing to reboard when Sister Louden pleaded, "You can't go yet; I have so missed the Church." Suddenly, over the loudspeaker came the announcement of a thirty-minute mechanical delay of the flight. They continued their exchange, and she asked how she could influence her husband to join the Church. Elder Monson counseled her to include him in their home Primary lesson each week and to be to him a living testimony of the gospel. Then he promised to send her a subscription to the Church magazines and additional helps for teaching her family. "Never give up on your husband," he said. And then he and President Ensign reboarded the plane and were gone.

A few years later, speaking at a priesthood leadership meeting in Brisbane, Elder Monson shared the story of Mount Isa and the significance of teaching and living the gospel in the home. He concluded, "I suppose I will never know if Sister Louden's husband ever joined the Church, but he couldn't have found a better model to follow than his wife."

One of the brethren in the congregation got to his feet. "Brother Monson, I am Richard Louden," he said. "The woman of whom you speak is my wife and the children are our children.

We are a forever family, thanks in part to the persistence and patience of my dear wife."[10]

Wherever he went in the South Pacific, Elder Monson found Saints devoted to the gospel. Many named their children after leaders in the scriptures or, in the case of Pearl of Great Price Harris, after the book itself. Everywhere he traveled, Elder Monson touched the hearts and hands of the people. "Usually our love will be shown in our day-to-day associations with others," he taught. He had those day-to-day experiences in the South Pacific.[11]

On a trip to Papeete, Tahiti, he felt impressed to leave the stand during the singing to shake hands with an elderly man he had noticed who was seated near the front. The man's name was Tahauri Hutihuti, and he came from the Tuamotu Islands. Elder Monson learned that this noble brother was a champion pearl diver and had been a devout member of the Church throughout his entire life. When Tahauri heard President McKay's prophecy that someday a temple would be built in the Pacific, he immediately began to save for that day, hiding a portion of his earnings beneath his bed. When the New Zealand Temple opened in 1958, Tahauri used his $600, saved over the course of more than forty years, to take his family to the temple. It was clear to Elder Monson why he "was so impressed to extend to him a special greeting during the process of the meeting."[12]

He has shown that kind of individual attention to others many times in his ministry. Minutes before the Saturday afternoon session of general conference began in April 2010, when everyone was seated, President Monson walked down from the stand to put an arm around the shoulders of Eldred G. Smith, former Patriarch to the Church, acknowledging the faithfulness of the 103-year-old stalwart servant of God and grandson of Hyrum Smith, the Prophet Joseph's brother.

And that love is returned. Back in Papeete on a later visit, Tahauri Hutihuti stood in line to greet Elder Monson, who was being thanked for his visit in the traditional fashion, one shell lei at a time being hung around his neck until they nearly covered his face. Tahauri said he had "no gift to bestow except the love of a full heart." The two embraced, and Tahauri gave Elder Monson a kiss on the cheek.[13]

Elder Monson felt right at home with the humble people of the Pacific Islands. He taught them principles of the gospel; they taught him as well. Late one evening during one of his visits, a small boat slipped up to the crude pier of a small island. Two Polynesian women helped Meli Mulipola from the boat and guided him up the well-worn path leading to the village where Elder Monson was meeting with a group of priesthood leaders. Meli was blind, having lost his sight while working on a pineapple plantation, and he "sought a blessing under the hands of those who held the sacred priesthood." His wish was granted and he received the requested blessing. Brother Mulipola then fell to his knees and offered his own prayer, "Oh, God, thou knowest I am blind. Thy servants have blessed me that if it be thy will, my sight may return. Whether in thy wisdom I see light or whether I see darkness all the days of my life, I will be eternally grateful for the truth of thy gospel which I now see and which provides me the light of life." Meli rose to his feet, thanked Elder Monson and the others for providing the blessing, and disappeared into the dark of the night. "Silently he came; silently he departed," remembers President Monson, "but his presence I shall never forget. I reflected upon the message of the Master: 'I am the light of the world: he that followeth me shall not walk in darkness, but shall have the light of life.'"[14]

At one of Elder Monson's visits to Brisbane, Australia, the stake recorded the largest stake conference attendance in its history. The newspaper had announced his arrival: "Top Mormon Visits Here." In Melbourne he visited the great War Memorial, an imposing landmark in the southern Australian city. He was drawn to the messages of the monument and later spoke of how he had felt in such "sacred" surroundings:

"In that edifice, as you walk through its silent corridors, there are tablets which note the deeds of valor and acts of courage of those who made the supreme sacrifice. One could almost hear the roar of the cannon, the sound of the caissons, the piercing scream of the rocket, the cry of the wounded. One could feel the exhilaration of victory and, at the same time, the despair of defeat. In the center of the main hall, inscribed for all to see, was the message of the memorial. The skylight overhead permitted easy reading, and once per year, at the eleventh hour of a November day, the sun shines directly upon that message and it fairly stands up and speaks: . . . 'Greater love hath no man than this, that a man lay down his life for his friends.' The challenge of today is not necessarily that we should go forth upon the battlefield and lay down our lives, but rather that we should let our lives reflect our love of God and our fellowman by the obedience we render His commandments and the service we give mankind."[15]

And so it went. He created stakes, reviewed finances, met with legal representatives, restored blessings, addressed and interviewed missionaries, blessed local members who were sick, spoke at stake conferences, looked for buildings that would make suitable mission homes, attended traditional dance presentations, and was once even escorted from the dock by a brass band playing "Onward, Christian Soldiers." Visit after visit, he took boats on choppy seas to meet with people who had not seen a General Authority in decades, if at all. On one occasion he returned home just in time to speak at the funeral of a widow from the Sixth-Seventh Ward, one of his eighty-five.

In Auckland, New Zealand, he had "a fine interview" with Elder Ryan Jones, the only son of a widowed mother from the Lost River Stake in Idaho. The missionary's mother, Belva Jones, had been diagnosed with cancer, but she hadn't told her son; he had been on his mission only two months, and there was real fear in the family of the dread disease. Her husband, Ryan's father, had died of cancer not long before Ryan became a missionary. Belva's brother, Folkman Brown, director of Mormon Relations for the Great Salt Lake Council of the Boy Scouts of America, had come to Elder Monson's office to ask his advice. Should the young missionary be told of his mother's illness? If so, who should tell him?

Elder Monson told Folkman to leave the matter in his hands, for he was going to New Zealand and would determine the best course when he spoke with the elder. At Hamilton, he made "a very difficult decision" and, in company with the mission president, took the young man aside and advised him of his mother's cancer. "I felt it was better talking to the boy while President Hugh B. Brown and I were there to give him help, rather than for him to hear the news at a time when he was more alone." As he broke the news, Elder Monson "felt the power of [Elder Jones's] testimony and faith in God, and the capable young missionary determined to stay on his mission."[16]

Not long afterward, Elder Monson was assigned to the Lost River Stake in Idaho. He considered the assignment a manifestation of the hand of the Lord. The mother of the missionary in New Zealand was sitting in the congregation. Following the service, President Monson gave her a firsthand report concerning her son, how he had reacted to the news, and how much Ryan loved her. Then he and the stake president gave her a blessing. "Of all the General Authorities who could have been assigned to the Lost River Stake conference," he wrote of the tender experience, "I happened to be the one so assigned, being the only one who would have been able to provide a current report after personally visiting the son of the dear woman."[17]

Countless letters have come to President Monson from those whom he has touched in all corners of the world. Typical is the letter from John Telford, a young man from Elder Monson's home stake who had received a mission call to Samoa in 1965 and was assigned to Elder Monson to be set apart.[18] Brother Telford was ecstatic. He considered Elder Monson partly responsible for his decision to serve. A few years before, he had attended a sacrament meeting and heard recently returned mission president Thomas Monson speak. "The Spirit in that meeting was stronger than at any previous time that I could remember in my life," he later wrote to President Monson. "I don't recall all that was said, but I will never forget the feelings that I had and the renewed commitment that I made to someday go on a mission myself."[19]

During one of his visits to Tonga, Elder Monson found that the mission president, John H. Groberg, had an infant son, born on the island, who was experiencing serious health problems. "Elder Monson must have had some spiritual premonitions," related Brother Groberg, "for he confided in my mother [who had come to help when the baby was born] that if the baby had further problems we should not hesitate to take him immediately to the United States." The entire island—even the Queen of Tonga—had celebrated little John Enoch's birth, but he was not thriving. President Groberg received a surprise call, following the mission tour, from Elder Monson, who inquired again about the baby and repeated what he had said before: "If necessary, do not hesitate to send your wife, Jean, and the baby to the United States for help." Jean Groberg followed Elder Monson's counsel and boarded a flight for Utah, where the baby was immediately whisked to Primary Children's Hospital and had surgery. "After much prayer and pondering," the Grobergs decided to leave the baby with his grandparents during the last year of their mission so he would be close to the hospital and doctors for care. Jean flew back to Tonga to be with her husband and their other children.

Some months later, when creating the first stake in Tonga in company with Elder Howard W. Hunter, Elder Monson spoke of visiting with little John Enoch Groberg at his grandparents' home before coming to Tonga. He described "how healthy and happy the little boy was and what a major contribution the faith and fasting and prayers of the Tongans had been in John Enoch's ability to survive and live and grow." Across the congregation, he saw "thousands of reverent nods of understanding," and "tens of thousands of tears freely flowing."[20]

The organizing of a stake in Tonga was so significant that the king of Tonga gave the Apostles and their wives a private audience and then decreed that the entire Church service would be broadcast over national radio the next night, allowing members on faraway islands to hear the momentous event. "What a remarkable thing," President Groberg observed, "to have the witness of two Apostles heard by an entire nation."[21]

When Elder Monson ordained one of the new high councilors a high priest, the man told him, "Today prophecy has been fulfilled." In 1938, Elder George Albert Smith, while visiting the island, had ordained the man an elder and said at that time, "The day will come when one of the Apostles will lay his hands upon your head and ordain you a high priest."[22]

The Hunters and the Monsons were led to the airport,

accompanied by a brass band playing "76 Trombones" from the popular musical *The Music Man*. One brother, Uliti Uata, approached Elder Monson rather shyly and indicated that his wife had given birth to a new son just a few days before. "We would like to name him after you," he said. Elder Monson beamed, "Certainly." The child has carried the legacy of the weekend's events in his name: Thomas Monson Uata.[23]

Elder Monson's sense of humor was manifest during one particular visit to Australia in the midst of a severe drought, where he noted with some amusement the names of the stake presidents—President Percy Rivers and President William Waters. He called this to the attention of his traveling companions, one of whom reminded Elder Monson that his name was Harry Brooks. The missionaries who met them at the airport were Elder Rainey and his companion, and when he registered at the hotel, the clerk could not locate the reservation until, in searching the cards, he found Thomas S. *Monsoon*.[24]

Following the division of the Sydney Stake in May 1967, Frank Lord, whose wife was the stake Primary president, approached Elder Monson with tears in his eyes. He explained that he had not been a member of the Church all during the years his wife had so enjoyed her own association with the Saints. "Brother Monson," he said, "your message the last time you attended the Sydney Stake conference was the turning point in my life. I knew within my heart after hearing your testimony that the gospel was true and made then the decision to enter the waters of baptism." Elder Monson wrote in his journal, "Such a comment brings me to the depths of humility and a true awareness of the responsibility which I have."[25]

What were his teachings and testimony on those many visits? What stirred the hearts of the people to increase in faithfulness? Always he taught the simple truths of the gospel and fit the message to the people—no matter where he was: "May you love and serve God. May you also love your fellowman. May you have peace within your hearts and contentment within your souls."[26]

On October 6, 1967, the First Presidency authorized missionaries to serve in New Caledonia. Seven months later, Elder Monson caught the once-a-week flight from New Zealand to Noumea, New

Caledonia, a French territory 3,000 miles from Tahiti, to dedicate the land for the preaching of the gospel. First thing in the afternoon, he and mission president Karl Richards met with government officials. "We always go in the front door," Elder Monson has reiterated, explaining how the Church honors the government of the land. In New Caledonia, it had taken many years to crack open that door and get the approvals of the government.[27]

Early in the morning on May 2, 1968, Elder Monson and President Richards stood on the top of Mont Coffyn, overlooking the bay and gentle hills of Noumea, with Teahu Manoi, president of the Noumea Branch; his wife and daughter; and his counselor, Mahuru Tauhiro. Before the prayer, the small group sang "The Morning Breaks, the Shadows Flee." Then Elder Monson "invoked the blessings of our Heavenly Father upon the government officials and the people, to the effect that the work may not be hindered but may go forward." President Richards interpreted for the Tahitians present. There was not a dry eye in the small assembly. It was one of Elder Monson's "most faith-promoting experiences," his first opportunity to dedicate a land.[28]

Elder Monson loved the people of the South Pacific. He traveled long hours to minister to them. In Samoa, the land where Robert Louis Stevenson is buried, he visited the writer's home. While standing near the white frame house, situated in a clearing amidst dense vegetation, he imagined being "carried back to the life and times of its occupant, who best summed up an attitude toward our daily occupations when he declared: 'I know what real pleasure is, for I have done good work.'"[29]

In June 1968, in the normal rotation of assignments, the First Presidency transferred Elder Ezra Taft Benson from Europe to oversee the work in the Orient. They assigned Elder Monson to supervise the European missions: Germany, Italy, Austria, and Switzerland. He could never have imagined what was ahead.

With Frances and young Tom accompanying him, he flew first to Paris on July 22, 1968, and then to Stockholm, Sweden. The three attended a reunion in Eskilstuna, Sweden, to meet relatives of Frances's mother. Although none of the Swedish relatives spoke English, and none were members of the Church, "the bond of family love was nonetheless warm and friendly." It was their first visit to "their homeland." The next day they visited the old family farm in Smedjebacken in Dalarna, where Frances's father and his family had lived. "We felt we were on precious soil as we viewed the old house, the old barns, and realized how our families had crossed one another's pathway through the gospel."[30]

The Monsons stayed in Hamburg, Germany, with the mission president, Stan Rees, and his wife. Young Tom was delighted to be with the Rees children and would have been happy to stay there while his parents continued the tour. But they did not leave him behind. Elder Monson addressed a seminar for mission presidents in the German-speaking area and interviewed each of them; he and Frances and Tommy also attended the road show presentations. Austria won.[31]

On July 31, 1968, Elder Monson and the Reeses made a brief afternoon visit behind the Iron Curtain. "What a stark contrast," Elder Monson observed, "as one passes through Checkpoint Charlie and finds freedom snuffed out and Communism dominating all." They visited the Soviet War Memorial, then crossed back over into the West, where he noticed a simple wreath honoring those who had lost their lives trying to escape over the Berlin Wall. Evidences of World War II bombing were still everywhere to be seen in the East. West Berlin, in contrast, looked like a new and prosperous city, "yet deep down one knows it is beleaguered and surrounded by Communism."[32]

They traveled next to Athens, Greece, scaling the hill reputed to have been the place where Paul delivered one of his powerful sermons, and the next day went on to Rome, then Zurich and Bern, where they toured the Swiss Temple, the first in Europe, and then again boarded the rails, this time for Heidelberg. There they met up with Elder Monson's sister Marilyn and her husband, Loren—who was in the military, stationed in Germany—and their son, Robert. The six traveled to Frankfurt together, and from there the Monsons flew back to Paris and on to Glasgow, Edinburgh, and London.

London may have been the highlight of the trip for young Tommy, for he and his dad took a train ride of several hours to the outskirts of London to meet Bernie Stratford, a famous breeder of Birmingham roller pigeons. "After a full day of straining our necks watching pigeons, we returned to London and the next day, August 12, were on our way back to the States."[33]

Elder Monson was back at the office as soon as they returned home, catching up on correspondence and work that needed his attention. That week he also made a trip to BYU to deliver a message to a genealogical convention.

He had a preliminary grasp of the state of the Church in Europe and was prepared to help the mission presidents and members take the next steps in strengthening the base and adding new members. Months later an assignment to South America—a future stronghold for the Church—increased his understanding of the Church worldwide. In Montevideo, Uruguay, he met with the 100 missionaries in the Uruguay Mission before attending the conference of the Montevideo Stake, a newly created unit, the first stake in the country.

He then flew to Buenos Aires, Argentina, to attend a stake conference there. Years later a stake president would describe how President Monson's visit to that stake had affected him personally. Sebastian Felipe Rodriguez was of missionary age at the time but was not sure he wanted to serve a mission, not sure he even knew that God existed. He went to conference hoping that something would inspire him. As he left the meeting, Elder Monson reached across the rope barrier and extended his hand to the young man. "You are going on a mission, aren't you?" he asked. "You will do the Lord a great service." And then he was gone. It was an answer to prayer. A future leader of the Church in that country was set clearly on the path by the personal attention of Elder Monson.[34]

In São Paulo, Brazil, Elder Monson met with the two stakes, recently divided, for a quarterly conference. The city had lost all electrical power in the area, but an enterprising missionary had connected an automobile battery to a portable loudspeaker system, and the meetings went forward. The highlight of the conference for Elder Monson was naming Leonel Abacherli as the patriarch of the three-month-old São Paulo East Stake. Elder Monson mentioned the appointment to the patriarch of the São

Paulo Stake, who beamed. He explained that he, Jose Lombardi, had given Sister Abacherli her patriarchal blessing just months before and felt impressed to tell her that her husband would be a patriarch himself. Little did he expect the prophecy to be fulfilled within sixty days' time.

Elder Monson flew home on a Friday and was off to a conference in Phoenix, Arizona, for the weekend.

On assignment to create a servicemen's stake in Europe, Elder and Sister Monson made their first trip to the Holy Land, touring the city of Jerusalem, marveling "at the rocky hillside and rugged terrain" and wondering "how Jesus the Christ and others made their way through such a desolate region."[35] They viewed the model of the ancient city, the marketplace, and other significant biblical sites. They met in Beirut, Lebanon, with the handful of missionaries serving there, where missionary work struggled, and made adjustments to some of the policies. The pace was grueling, but Elder Monson never seemed to mind, never recording in his journal the slightest hint of weariness.

In Italy he met with missionaries and members; one man had ridden his bicycle and taken the train six and a half hours to get to the meeting. Elder Monson witnessed that same devotion and faith across the continent and in the Scandinavian countries. The numbers were small but growing, and the need to focus on helping one another live the gospel was everywhere apparent. Home teaching languished at 10 percent in some areas, and some sacrament meeting attendance figures were at 10 percent as well. But not in East Germany. The willingness of the Saints there to watch over one another and join together to worship Almighty God was all they had.

On Saturday, November 9, 1968, Elder Thomas S. Monson made his first real journey into that nation cut off from the world. There he would find devotion and commitment, in spite of the severe oppression. His assignment would be one of the longest individual assignments ever given a member of the Twelve. It would become a most significant chapter in his ministry—the rescue of the East German Saints.

19

"Weary Not"

For me, as a German, of course we claim President Monson, as he is claimed by everyone around the globe. He makes everyone feel that they are first in his attention; that is one of his great talents. The actual blessings he brought to our country and to Europe are so real and so significant and so singular in their value that I really believe that the Lord had prepared him to be an instrument in changing the history of Germany.

President Dieter F. Uchtdorf
Second Counselor in the First Presidency

Since the Berlin Wall had gone up in 1961, no General Authority had attempted to visit the Soviet Zone in Germany. It was now 1968, and, "trusting in the Lord," Elder Monson, newly assigned to the European nations, decided he would be the one to make that visit. He immediately contacted the United States government to determine what—exactly—he would find in divided Germany, particularly behind the Iron Curtain. The U.S. State Department official tried to discourage him from making any trips into East Germany, called then the German Democratic Republic (GDR),[1] explaining that the United States had no diplomatic relations with that country. He was blunt: "If anything happens, we can't get you out."[2]

Elder Monson went anyway.

"You simply had to realize," he explained years later, "that the objective was higher than any earthly authority, and with trust in the Lord you went."[3]

This was not just another assignment to another part of the

279

world. Behind the Iron Curtain were members very much in need of help—of rescue. To a great extent, Germany would define Thomas Monson's apostolic ministry. It was in Germany that he saw, even in tragic circumstances, the Lord's love for the down-trodden and forgotten. It was in Germany, on the other side of the world, that this strong and vigorous young Apostle applied his seasoned administrative skills and a heart to match. There he built upon his years of experience with the widows in the Sixth-Seventh Ward, adding to that cadre women who had lost their husbands in war and families bereft of loved ones.

The first time Elder Monson announced to Frances that he planned to visit the German Democratic Republic, he asked if she would like to go with him. She replied, "Tom, we have children to raise. You go, and I will stay here and watch the children. Then if you don't come back, they will have one of us to give them guidance!"

"Pray for me," he said.[4]

Elder Monson would visit a Germany that had been divided by the victors into four military zones, occupied by American, British, French, and Russian armies. Quickly, the United States, England, and France had begun to rebuild the shattered economy of "their" Germany. Russia, on the other hand, isolated its portion and established a police state where censorship and travel restrictions set back recovery efforts for half a century. Bombed-out buildings covered in soot from cheap coal marked the landscape. In a famed address given in 1946, Winston Churchill, former prime minister of Great Britain, stated, "From Stettin to the Baltic to Trieste in the Adriatic, an iron curtain has descended across the continent."[5]

Those who were able, hundreds of thousands of East Germans, fled to other nations during those first years after the war. Fully a fifth of the population got out. Among those escaping the Russian rule were hundreds of Latter-day Saints.

President David O. McKay had traveled to West Berlin in 1952, and 1,300 members had been allowed to cross over from the East Zone to hear him speak, some selling the little they had, even furniture, to make the trip. The day after, the GDR government refused to allow East German citizens to visit Berlin. In August 1955

Elder Spencer W. Kimball spoke of his "glorious vision" of what would happen if the members stayed in Germany and did their part "unselfishly to rebuild the great kingdom."[6] Elder Adam S. Bennion visited West Berlin in July 1956, and President Henry D. Moyle spoke to the Saints in Leipzig in 1958; it was a reunion for him because he had labored there as a missionary years before. As had Elder Kimball, he emphasized that the Church was "entering a new era which will require the people to remain in their own native lands to build up and strengthen the Church there; and by doing so, they will lay the foundation for the establishment of regular Church organizations."[7] The last visit from Church headquarters before Elder Monson arrived was by Elder LeGrand Richards in 1959. The members heard the message, "Stay in the Zone," and many did "because of the words of the prophets."[8]

After World War II, the city of Berlin, located deep in the Soviet Zone, had, like Germany itself, been divided into four sectors under the four military powers. The American, English, and French sectors became known as West Berlin; the Soviet sector became known as East Berlin. On the morning of August 13, 1961, West Berliners awoke to find a barbed-wire wall encircling their side of the city, with armed guards lined up along it to "protect" the citizens of the Soviet Zone, now the German Democratic Republic, from Western influences. Communications, too, had been shut down, the major street crossings blocked, subway and rail stations closed, and travel between the East and the West sealed off. That September, Erich Honecker, a tough Communist who had scrambled to authority after the war, directed the construction of miles of concrete that became known as the Berlin Wall, the most infamous barrier in the world. A barren no-man's-land, patrolled by troops with orders to shoot anyone trying to cross into the West, further separated the countries.[9]

The fewer than 5,000 Church members who had remained in East Germany—many following previous prophetic counsel to help build up the Church in their homeland—faced punitive practices by the government, designed to discourage religious activity. The intent was to supplant Christianity with socialist dogma and practices. The GDR constitution of 1949 granted churches the right to exist—unlike in other Communist countries—but made religious practice very difficult and always suspect.[10] A government office of religious affairs controlled church activities, though it stopped short of preventing its citizens from worshipping. The state required notice of meetings and even monitored Sunday services; it prohibited missionary activity of any kind and did not allow any scriptures, handbooks, manuals, or even hymnals to come into the country. It denied entry to universities and advancement in the workplace to any citizen demonstrating religious inclinations. The little missionary work that was allowed for a time in East Germany after the war was performed by Church members living within the GDR—many of them newly returned soldiers who had barely survived the conflict.

Certainly the Latter-day Saints were few in numbers compared to the larger Christian denominations, such as the Catholics and Protestants, but being less obvious did not shield them from constant surveillance and even persecution. That the LDS Church's headquarters were in the United States, that the majority of the membership was there as well, and that the Church had been founded on American soil only added to the government's suspicions of the Mormons.[11]

Germany, though, had long been a stronghold for the Church. In the first half of the twentieth century, the area around Freiberg, Dresden, and Leipzig was "one of the most productive areas of membership growth" in the Church. The official records of the East German Mission, organized in late 1937, noted that the mission had a population of 7,267 members in 1939 and "was one of the largest missions (by population) in the world at that time."[12] In fact, Germany stood third in the world in total number of Church members; the United States and Canada were first and second, respectively.[13]

Some of the Church's German branches that now fell in the Soviet Zone had first been established before many in the newly settled communities in Utah.[14] The Dresden Branch, for example, was organized October 21, 1855; German convert Karl G. Maeser served as president. He and most of the branch emigrated to Utah in 1856; he returned to Germany as a missionary in 1867, serving three years, and then returned to Utah to take the position of principal of Brigham Young Academy, which later became BYU. A man of firm and unfailing faith, Maeser is famous for his charge that at the Academy not even "the ABCs would be taught without the Spirit."[15] (On July 14, 2001, President Monson dedicated a larger-than-life statue of Dr. Maeser placed at the Dresden stake center in the heart of town.)

In the mid-1930s, Adolf Hitler's regime began to rebuild the German military and reacquire territory lost in the First World War. During this period, LDS Church meetings were interrupted by Nazis, and local Church leaders were interrogated. After the 1938 annexation of several countries into Germany, including Austria and parts of Czechoslovakia, Hitler's intent was clear. The German political aggression created concerns for the leaders of the Church. Hitler's ambitions seemed at odds with the welfare of the German Saints.

In order to judge the perilous situation, President Heber J. Grant and other Church leaders toured Germany and other European nations in 1937. The visit gave Saints in Europe the rare opportunity to be in the presence of the prophet of God. They were not disappointed. President Grant encouraged them "to appreciate and assume their full responsibilities as Church members and bearers of the priesthood" and to no longer "place so much reliance upon the [missionaries]."[16] The following year, local members were called upon to take over the offices, which they did with integrity and earnestness.[17]

As war loomed in June 1938, President J. Reuben Clark, Jr., then First Counselor in the First Presidency and a former U.S. diplomat, toured the European missions and then met with the mission presidents in Berlin. He suggested that with mounting tensions, each mission president needed to devise a method of withdrawing missionaries. He helped determine the safest location to send missionaries. "We didn't really realize that within six weeks of that time, we'd be starting to evacuate the missionaries," President Franklin J. Murdock of the Netherlands Mission reported. "I don't think President Clark realized that it was that soon."[18] The first withdrawal occurred in 1938, though it was more a trial run, as missionaries returned to their fields of labor when tensions in Germany subsided. A year later, on August 24, 1939, while Elder Joseph Fielding Smith was touring the European missions, a telegram from the First Presidency ordered a second and final evacuation of all 697 foreign missionaries serving in European missions, including mission presidents. One week later, on September 1, 1939, Europe went to war.

As the missionary evacuation began, the responsibility for the East German Mission was turned over to local members. On September 25, 1939, Thomas E. McKay, who was the last mission leader to leave the European continent, sent a letter to all members in Germany, encouraging them as they took over the responsibility for running the mission: "We pray sincerely to our Heavenly Father, that He might protect and bless those that have been called to arms and that He might strengthen those who have remained at home for the additional responsibilities that rest upon your shoulders. Pray, live a pure life, keep the word of wisdom, pay your tithing, visit and participate in all the meetings, keep free from finding fault and bearing false witness, sustain those that have been called to preside and it is our promise that the Lord will guide and lead you in all things and that you, even in the midst of afflictions and difficulties, will find joy and satisfaction. Be always mindful that we are engaged in the work of the Lord and that Jesus is the Christ."[19]

When President Thomas McKay reported to authorities at Church headquarters, he assured them that the German Saints understood the gospel and were well qualified to carry on. Some of the leaders were second- and third-generation members. K. Herbert Klopfer, a twenty-seven-year-old German Mission translator who was given responsibility for the East German Mission after President McKay left, soon reported to Salt Lake City, "Meetings are held regularly and are well attended. . . . Everyone is doing his duty."[20]

When the Relief Society all over the Church celebrated its centennial in March 1942, with the war in full force, over 500 attended the event in Hamburg, making it one of the largest Relief Society commemorations in the Church.[21] And "on June 27,

1944, the branches in Germany held a memorial in honor of the one-hundredth anniversary of the martyrdom of Joseph Smith."[22]

But the war took a tremendous toll. Food rationing was severe. Planes attacked day and night. Two and a half million Germans were killed in a six-month period in 1944. Among them was the acting East German Mission president, K. Herbert Klopfer. He had been a genius at organization, juggling the affairs of the mission even with his assignment in the German military. The story is told of his attending a sacrament service in Denmark—in his German uniform. When he stood to sing with the Saints, they recognized him as a fellow member and "brought him into the fold." He died a prisoner of war on the Russian front. His counselors, Paul Langheinrich and Richard Ranglack, continued to provide leadership, strength, and counsel to the beleaguered members.

The Church members carried on faithfully, though as the war progressed, attendance at meetings dropped because of the disruption of everyday life and the members' moving to rural areas seeking safety. "But the spirit has not suffered," one district president reported. "Less-active members of the Church came back and joined us again," Church leader Henry Burkhardt recalled. Nobody became less active or fell away from the Church. "We all looked for something to hold on to."[23]

At the time, the sacrament was passed in both Sunday School and sacrament meeting Churchwide.[24] Because of the cold and lack of fuel during the winter in the GDR, the sacrament water froze in the cups. The members chipped away the ice and partook. The few priesthood leaders who were not away fighting in the war blessed babies and baptized eight-year-old children, plus a few converts. To connect with outlying branches, Church leaders traveled by bicycle until the roads were destroyed and their bicycles stolen. Then they walked. As the war intensified on several fronts, with more men—from ages fifteen to sixty—drafted into service, some of the branches lost all priesthood leadership. Sisters continued to meet. They held Primary and joined in choir practice to draw upon the power of the Spirit. They shared accounts of their miracles and acknowledged the Lord's hand in their lives.

As the war progressed, the horrors did as well. By the end, the people were exhausted, starving, homeless, and waiting for the return of their soldiers—many of whom did not return. But the members were not disheartened. They looked forward, their faith deepening; it was all they had. And it was enough. Duty, honor, covenants, and cooperation were what sustained them and stirred them on. No wonder Elder Monson loved them.

The scripture "Go ye forth as your circumstances shall permit"[25] took on new meaning. "We can roll up our sleeves and get to work, and the Lord will do the rest," one brother commented as they set about rebuilding a horse barn to serve as a makeshift meeting place.[26]

The members lived on potato peelings and had only the ragged clothes on their backs, but they found refuge with one another, sometimes fifty to a room because their homes were gone. In January 1946, just seven months after the war ended, Elder Ezra Taft Benson of the Quorum of the Twelve arrived in Europe by Church assignment. He was one of the first civilians given permission to travel in Germany. The stories of his ministry in the war-torn countries are epic in nature. He was able, because of the welfare plan of the Church, to distribute food, clothing, bedding, and medical supplies. At the sight of boxes piled on boxes filled with life-saving rice and beans, mission leader Richard Ranglack "broke down and cried."[27] Elder Benson had come to "rescue one and all."[28] He traveled over 60,000 miles during this ten-month "mission of mercy," navigating bombed-out bridges and damaged roads. The Saints came by the thousands to hear him speak. They were mostly pale, thin, and dressed in rags, but "the light of faith" shone in their eyes.[29] He taught the people "to be forgiving, [for] there are really no victors and no losers." In war, he said, "everyone loses."[30]

"Only with a faith in the ultimate consummation of the Lord's purposes can people, with all their earthly possessions swept away, continue with spirits sweet and hearts free from bitterness," Elder Benson said as he left the country at the conclusion of his assignment. "I promise you the richest blessings of eternity inasmuch as you continue faithful."[31] That promise would be repeated by

Thomas S. Monson, another young and vigorous Apostle, more than twenty years later.

Elder Monson arrived in West Berlin on July 31, 1968, for his first visit as the supervisor of the Europe area and its missions in Germany, Austria, Switzerland, and Italy. Stanley D. Rees, president of the North German Mission, headquartered in Hamburg, met him. President Rees had responsibility for the northern states of West Germany (the Federal Republic of Germany) and West Berlin as well as East Berlin and all of the East German sector (the German Democratic Republic, Poland, Hungary, and other countries behind the Iron Curtain). Together, the men cautiously crossed through the checkpoint at the border to travel very briefly into East Berlin. And then Elder Monson and President Rees presented themselves at the border to return to West Berlin. Elder Monson found that, even with a U.S. passport, departure from East Germany was a long process.[32] For the next twenty years he would cross into East Germany several times a year, but he was never casual about the experience.

"It was a little bit frightening to go through Checkpoint Charlie and see the machine guns and the shepherd dogs and Doberman pinschers waiting for a false move on your part," he later recalled. "The border guards never smiled. They would attempt to stare you down."[33]

At Elder Monson's first visit, Church records in East Germany showed 4,641 members on the rolls in 47 branches and 7 member districts, with 47 baptisms in 1968, of which 17 were converts.[34] The German and Italian missions had nearly 1,000 missionaries— almost all of them from the United States—serving in European countries, but none behind the Iron Curtain. In East Germany, the percentages for sacrament meeting attendance, home teaching, and other Church activities were far higher than in West Germany or in the other European stakes and districts.

On his second trip to East Germany, on November 9, 1968, Elder Monson joined President and Sister Rees and they again crossed at Checkpoint Charlie into the East Zone. He asked President Rees to pray that the guards would be blinded to "their true purpose" in visiting. This time they were going deep into the country, to Görlitz on the southern border, across from Poland and Czechoslovakia. As they passed through the inspection, they "were among a very few who were not asked to open their suitcases so the guards could make a detailed inspection of all the contents."[35]

As he and the Reeses drove toward Görlitz, they passed through rural areas where farm machinery was horse-drawn, with not a tractor in sight. "The weather was cold and foggy; hence, a very dismal atmosphere pervaded the scene," Elder Monson wrote.[36] The autobahns were void of traffic, indicating the scarcity of automobiles in East Germany. Those who did have cars wrapped themselves in blankets because their vehicles, for the most part, had no heaters.

Elder Monson had long been intrigued with the history of the wars that had been fought on German soil and enjoyed reading about the First and Second World Wars. In college he had seriously considered majoring in history and becoming a teacher. One of the many bookcases in his office is filled with history books of that period. He has read them all.

On this November 1968 visit, Elder Monson and President Rees stopped at Dresden, one of the most heavily bombed cities during the war. On three evenings in February 1945, Allied bombs had taken the lives of 25,000 to 40,000 people in Dresden.[37] Only a few new structures signaled the massive rebuilding necessary but still not much in evidence. Early missionaries had established a Church unit in Dresden in 1855, and members still held to that legacy; no war was going to compromise their place in God's kingdom.

The hotel accommodations in Görlitz were "the most archaic" of any Elder Monson had seen. His room was cold, with a ceiling fifteen feet high, "a bed that resembled a box," an ancient sink, and a Communist flag at the window. "Lavatory facilities existed only on the second floor of the hotel, and these were most inadequate."[38]

Elder Monson and President and Sister Rees arrived at the Görlitz meeting unannounced. Such would always be the case in the decades ahead because of those who "watched and listened" in this Communist country. Attendance that day totaled 235. The members at first mistook Elder Monson for a missionary because he was obviously American and so young. But the members soon heard the mighty timbre in his voice and felt the power in his testimony and the strength of his spirit.

This was the first time since before the beginning of World War II that a General Authority had visited Görlitz. As a member of the Twelve, Elder Monson brought with him the scriptural commission of "power to open the door of [God's] kingdom unto any nation whithersoever [the First Presidency] shall send them."[39]

Thomas Monson's love affair with Germany began with this meeting in Görlitz. The congregation was filled with people who were Saints in the purest sense of the word. Theirs was a strength born of surviving Hitler's regime; almost every family had lost a loved one in the war. Most had lost their homes and their possessions. Elder Monson felt compassion for them. "It is one thing to make great sacrifice and emerge victorious," he observed. "It is another thing to make great sacrifice and find yourself defeated."[40]

Sister Edith Krause served as Elder Monson's interpreter that day in Görlitz. "I found that frequently she was interpreting her version of what I should be saying," he later remarked, "and that was fine with me." When he referred to "President McKay," for instance, she said instead "David O. McKay," recognizing that soldiers who were listening would take exception to the reference to a "president."[41]

When the Russians were invading the city near the end of the war, the branch president, fearful that his home would be searched, took the Church records to Edith and said, "Protect these, and the Lord will protect you." Edith lived on the third floor of her apartment building. Not long after, Russian soldiers ransacked the first two floors of the building and were headed up the stairs to the third floor when "miraculously, their leader called them back and they went on their way to another block." The Church records and the family remained safe.[42]

Like other Latter-day Saints, the Krauses were punished for their attention to the Church. Their nineteen-year-old son,

Helaman, had been offered a full scholarship to the university if he would join the Communist Youth Party. He declined, saying he would prefer to pay his own way. He was allowed entrance only because his grades were superior, the highest in his entire school. Elder Monson wished that such a fine young man could serve a mission but knew it would not be possible "at this particular time."[43]

That first meeting in Görlitz took place on the second floor of a damaged warehouse on a dingy street. The people were poor. They had little to ease their daily burdens. They had no patriarch, no wards or stakes—just branches. They could not receive the blessings of the temple. But they had hope. "The Spirit knows no borders; it needs no approvals to reach the hearts of those who are true to their beliefs," Elder Monson noted.[44] And these people were truly Latter-day Saints.

Despite the conditions in Görlitz, the congregation exuded "a marvelous spirit," new life, hope, and resilience. A hymn they sang at the meeting was particularly appropriate:

> *If the way be full of trial, Weary not!*
> *If it's one of sore denial, Weary not!*
> *If it now be one of weeping*
> *There will come a joyous greeting,*
> *When the harvest we are reaping—Weary not!*[45]

Elder Monson had "never heard such singing." Indeed, "the Saints showed their love for the Lord by the manner in which they sang the hymns," and there was a unity that came from joining their voices. The messages in the meeting were superb; Elder Monson "felt uplifted and inspired," marveling at the speakers' "knowledge of the gospel and the scriptural messages which were provided, which spoke of gospel study and gospel scholarship."[46]

These members had nothing but scriptures for study and teaching. One man explained, "We received a directive from President Burkhardt [then counselor in the mission presidency based in Hamburg] that all unauthorized religious materials, books, manuals, etc., were to be destroyed. I was heartbroken. I had, over the years, scraped together a small but nice library of Church materials, for which I had no official authorization. I sat in front of an open fireplace. 'No,' I said to myself. 'I can't do it.' But in the end, I burned all of the books and manuals." Less than two weeks after that, the secret police knocked on his door. "They searched my house for unauthorized printed material. I had none. From that experience I learned a great lesson about inspired leaders and listening to their counsel."[47]

Elder Monson was touched by the sincerity of these wonderful Saints. He was humbled by their circumstances. "I have met with few congregations which have demonstrated a greater love for the gospel,"[48] he recalls. As he stood at the pulpit, filled with emotion, he "felt the inspiration" and "followed it," departing from his prepared text. The words he spoke were life-changing for him and for the German Saints as he made them a promise:

"If you will remain true and faithful to the commandments of God, every blessing any member of the Church enjoys in any other country will be yours."[49]

That evening, back in his hotel room, the full impact of what he had promised hit him. "They had no patriarchs for patriarchal blessings, a wall prevented them from going to the temple for their endowment, they had no missionaries among them, they had no ability to hold youth conferences, they couldn't print any of our church material."[50] On his knees he prayed, "Father, I am on Thy errand; this is Thy Church. I have spoken words that came not from me, but from Thee and Thy Son. Wilt Thou, therefore, fulfill the promise in the lives of this noble people."[51] There coursed through his mind the words from the Psalmist, "Be still, and know that I am God."[52]

At that landmark meeting in Görlitz, Elder Monson met Henry Johannes Burkhardt, who would become a key figure in the Church in East Germany. Henry, a third-generation member, grew up in Chemnitz, a city of 375,000. In 1939, at the outbreak of the war, Chemnitz—renamed Karl-Marx-Stadt by the government after the war—had three thriving branches. The Chemnitz Center Branch had 469 members; it was officially the largest branch of the Church in all of Germany and had a fully functioning program of auxiliary activities. Some of Henry's friends were captivated by the Hitler Youth movement. Henry was not. He preferred his Church activity, though he would be denied educational opportunities and work advancements because he never joined the movement.

The Chemnitz Center Branch lost at least fifty of its members in the war, more than any other branch in the mission. On March 5, 1945, massive air raids had reduced the city of Chemnitz to rubble. The first attack came just before noon; another followed in early evening. Henry, who had taken refuge in the basement with a wet blanket over his head, "thought he would not survive." But the war taught him lessons that he would use the rest of his life. He learned "to be without fear," a strength he would draw upon to defend the Church in countless experiences standing before government officials.[53] He was known for his religious affiliation; the state police kept a file on him. He had been called as a counselor in the East German Mission (later renamed the Northern German Mission) in 1952, serving as best he could behind the Iron Curtain.

Elder Monson described Henry as "an individual who typifies the faith and devotion of the people." Henry worked day and night. On a later visit to Dresden, Elder Monson wrote, "[We] had to tell [Henry] to go home—that he should sleep in his own bed rather than catching a few hours' rest on a cot—so dedicated was he to the welfare of the Saints. He earned the trust of the Brethren. He was the man on whom we placed so much responsibility and to whom we looked for leadership for our Saints there."[54]

Because it was difficult for the North German Mission president to receive approval from the GDR to visit Church members behind the Iron Curtain, Elder Monson proposed the creation of the Dresden Mission, with headquarters at Dresden and with Brother Henry Burkhardt as the new mission president. It would not be a true mission, as no missionaries could enter or leave the country, but there would be far less problem with the German government if it were called the Dresden Mission, with local leadership, remaining as autonomous as possible. Elder Monson proposed that Percy K. Fetzer, a regional representative, former mission president in Hamburg, and former Temple View Stake president in Salt Lake City (with whom Tom Monson had served), be assigned to work with the Dresden Mission as though it were a full-fledged stake in order to give them all the help and training possible. "Percy knows the people well, speaks German fluently, and, because he does not reside in West Germany, is able to come and go rather freely." Brother Fetzer was unanimously approved in the meeting of the Quorum of the Twelve.[55]

President Burkhardt chose as counselors Erich Walter Krause and Gottfried Richter. These were men filled with the Spirit of God and steeped in the ways of working within the German Democratic Republic. Walter traveled around from branch to branch among the forty branches and kept the buildings in some state of repair. Gottfried operated a stationery store, which gave him access to hard-to-find supplies such as carbon paper. Since no materials or manuals could be brought into the country, and printing and publishing were strictly forbidden, all information and courses of study had to be typed, using carbon paper to make copies.

Elder Monson continued to visit East Germany, meeting with leaders, missionaries, and members. On the evening of June 14, 1969, a testimony meeting filled "with a glorious spirit" concluded a five-day genealogical workshop. The members had provided not just their self-imposed quota of 10,000 names but more than 14,000 names. "I don't know of a day in my life," wrote Elder Monson, "when so much good has been accomplished."[56] The faithfulness of the Saints, "their absolute unity and trust in their Heavenly Father," were simply remarkable.

The next day, at a leadership meeting of the branch presidencies and district presidencies of the Dresden Mission, President Henry Burkhardt introduced materials from the new General Handbook of Instructions. This thrilled the leaders, who, by nature, "delight in following detailed instructions to the very letter."[57]

Elder Monson had just completed overseeing revisions of the Church's General Handbook of Instructions—a project that had taken three years. While in the temple one Thursday morning, he had said to Elder Spencer W. Kimball, "With all my heart I wish we had one copy of the newly completed German language edition of the handbook available in the German Democratic Republic."

"Why can't you simply mail one?" Elder Kimball asked.

Elder Monson replied, "The importation of such literature is forbidden. There is no way."

Elder Kimball said, "I have an idea, Brother Monson. Why don't you, since you have worked with the handbook, memorize it; and then we'll put *you* across the border!"

Elder Monson laughed, and then he looked at Elder Kimball and realized he wasn't joking. Elder Monson was skilled at memorizing, but he soon realized it was an impossible task—and would have been for anyone. He already knew the material, so he worked on learning the different categories so that he could go into East Germany and type for the Saints a workable copy.

When he crossed the border, he said to one of the leaders, "Give me a typewriter and a ream of paper and let me work." He sat down at the table in the branch office and began to type the handbook as if he were sitting at home at the kitchen table preparing a talk. He was about thirty pages into it when he stood up to stretch and walk around the room. He was startled as he noticed on a shelf what appeared to be the General Handbook of Instructions. He picked it up. Not only was it the Handbook, it was in German. Though his work had been unnecessary, he was well versed concerning the Handbook for many years. How a Handbook came to be in East Germany, no one would say.[58]

One of those in attendance at the leadership meeting in June 1969 where President Burkhardt taught from the Handbook was Horst Sommer, who had met Elder Monson at the Görlitz Branch the November before. After that meeting the Sommers had spoken to Elder Monson about their ill son, and he had responded, "Matthias will get another priesthood blessing, and then the Lord will decide whether he will become well or whether the Lord will take him into His presence." Brother Sommer explained that Matthias had died not long after Elder Monson's counsel. There was silence. Brother Sommer, then serving as branch president, saw "the face of the Apostle become light, and he looked to the heaven for a time. Then he said: 'Don't be afraid for your son. He is in the presence of the Lord, and he works there very hard. It is your responsibility to be strong in the gospel so that you can go where he is already.'" Not knowing that Brother Sommer's wife was home ready to deliver their third child, Elder Monson continued, "The Lord will send you another son, and this son won't be your last child." Sister Sommer had another boy, as Elder Monson had prophesied, and eight years later they had a girl.

Years later, on August 26, 1995, when President Monson dedicated a new chapel in Görlitz, Sister Sommer approached him, sure that after twenty-six years he would not remember the family. When she started to speak, he stopped her, stood up, and said to all in the room, "Here is the lady who lost a child and was promised another one." That last child, Tabea, now eighteen years old, was in the room and began to weep. The Sommer family gathered around Elder Monson and embraced him. For them, "it was a very holy hour."[59]

Frances could see why her husband felt so at home with the German people. "I believe you are a German at heart," she told him. "You like everything orderly."[60] Percy Fetzer saw a likeness as well, commenting, "You have a Swedish name, Monson, but you are a German at heart."[61]

A month after returning from the June 1969 visit to Germany, Elder Monson invited Percy Fetzer to his office and told him that the First Presidency and Quorum of the Twelve had approved Percy's being ordained a patriarch, with authority to provide patriarchal blessings to worthy Saints in Eastern Europe. Though Karl Ringger, an ordained patriarch in Switzerland, had been able to provide some blessings to members when he was behind the Iron Curtain, there were far too many for him to accommodate on his infrequent visits. In Dresden alone there was a backlog of 800 worthy persons requesting patriarchal blessings. Thus, Elder Monson had recommended that Percy Fetzer be called. His promise in his first meeting in Görlitz was being fulfilled.

Brother Fetzer, with his special assignment, was able to give patriarchal blessings in East Germany and other Communist countries. When he was in Selbongen, Poland, giving blessings to a family named Konietz, he was inspired to promise "a young son that he would serve a mission in another country." He then promised the daughter "that she would marry in the house of God." To the parents, he promised that "they and the entire family would be together in a holy temple." Inasmuch as Poland's borders were closed, Brother Fetzer worried about the blessings he had given.

When he returned home, he called Elder Monson and asked to meet with him. As he sat down in Elder Monson's office, he wept. "Brother Monson," he said, "I have pronounced blessings which cannot be fulfilled, but I was persuaded by the Holy Spirit to say what I did. What shall I do?"

Elder Monson quietly motioned for Percy to join him in a kneeling prayer. At the conclusion of their prayer, the two "knew that somehow the blessings would be fulfilled."[62] Not long after, a Polish treaty allowed all German nationals trapped at the end of the war in Poland to go west. The Konietz family moved to Dortmund, in West Germany, and Brother Konietz eventually became a bishop. In 1973, Percy Fetzer, who had been called as president of the Swiss Temple, with his wife, Thelma, as matron, performed their family sealing in that temple. To Elder Monson's mind came the familiar truth: "The wisdom of God ofttimes appears as foolishness to men, but the greatest single lesson we can learn in mortality is that when God speaks and a man obeys, that man will always be right."[63]

During Elder Monson's visits to Europe, he was often accompanied by whoever was serving as mission president of the North German Mission. Elder Hans B. Ringger, a stake president in Switzerland who eventually became a General Authority, accompanied him on many of his visits. Elder Ringger's unique background, devotion to the Lord, Swiss citizenship, and multilingual capabilities made him invaluable in working with the Saints in the Eastern bloc countries. Brother Ringger praised the many experiences he had during those years working at Elder Monson's side, saying that "his great spirit and love for the people" was a significant boost to the Saints. "He gave them hope that they had a future. He showed them his love for them and supported them wherever he could."[64] It was a historic and heartfelt work.

While visiting the Germany Central Mission in Düsseldorf in October 1970, Elder Monson met with the missionaries, including Elder Marc Larson. Just two weeks earlier, he had been scheduled to attend a conference in the Grand Junction Colorado Stake. During the conference, the stake president asked him to meet with Hale and Donna Larson, whose son Marc had just announced that he was leaving the mission field before completing his service. He agreed to meet with the distressed parents.

"Where is your son serving?" Elder Monson asked them.

"In Düsseldorf, Germany," they replied.

Elder Monson placed his arms around Brother and Sister Larson and said, "Your prayers have been heard and are already being answered. With more than twenty-eight stake conferences being held this day attended by the General Authorities, I was the one assigned to your stake." He explained that he would be in Düsseldorf the next week and would meet with their son.

He met with Elder Larson, who committed to completing his mission—and did so.[65]

Elder Monson's visits to Europe were frequent. He grew to love the area of Berchtesgaden, one of the most picturesque spots in West Germany's Bavaria. He visited this charming village as often as he could. In the summer, the square is filled with men in embroidered leather shorts or knee-length lederhosen, and the women wear frilly blouses with full skirts and aprons. Dozens of small shops line the square. Just beyond the shops is a dock, where one can board one of the electric-powered boats that travel from Berchtesgaden to points of interest across Königsee, a beautiful clearwater lake surrounded on three sides by steeply rising flanks of alpine mountains. Elder and Sister Monson often enjoyed taking the boat to St. Bartholomä Church, founded by monks in the twelfth century, and then back to Berchtesgaden. The lake's position, surrounded by mountains, creates an echo that is known for its clarity. On the boat tours, the Monsons particularly enjoyed the traditional boat stops where a trumpet was played to highlight the echo.

One of Elder Monson's most tender experiences in Germany was with Dieter Berndt, who would one day serve as a stake president in Berlin. It began with Edwin Q. "Ted" Cannon, who had served in Germany as a missionary before the war. One day Ted carried to Elder Monson's office some slides that he had found among his mission pictures. He told Elder Monson that he had been home forty years and was just getting around to cataloging the slides. Among them were some Ted could not specifically identify. Every time he had planned to discard them, he had been impressed to keep them, although he was at a loss as to why. They were photographs he had taken when he served in Stettin, Germany, and pictured a family—a mother, father, and two small children, a girl and a boy. He remembered that their surname was Berndt and that there was a Berndt serving as a regional representative in Germany. He wondered if this Brother Berndt might be able to identify the Berndts in the photograph.

Elder Monson indicated that he was leaving shortly for Berlin and would be seeing Dieter Berndt. He agreed to show him the slides, to see if he might recognize the family in the photographs.

Wrote President Monson later: "The Lord didn't even let me get to Berlin before His purposes were accomplished. I was in Zurich, Switzerland, boarding the flight to Berlin, when who should also board the plane but Dieter Berndt. He sat next to me, and I told him I had some old slides of people named Berndt from Stettin. I handed them to him and asked if he could identify those shown in the photographs. As he looked at them carefully, he began to weep. He said, 'Our family lived in Stettin during the war. My father was killed when an Allied bomb struck the plant where he worked. Not long afterward, the Russians invaded Poland and the area of Stettin. My mother took my sister and me and fled from the advancing enemy. Everything had to be left behind, including any photographs we had. Brother Monson, I am the little boy pictured in these slides, and my sister is the little girl. The man and woman are our dear parents. Until today, I have had no photographs of our childhood in Stettin or of my father.'"[66]

The two wept together, and Dieter carefully placed the slides in his briefcase. At the next general conference in Salt Lake City, he had occasion to visit Brother Cannon and thank him for following the inspiration to keep the slides for forty years.

On Elder Monson's East German visits he usually met with President Burkhardt, whom he considered "a giant of the Lord who goes forward in directing our affairs behind the Iron Curtain without regard to any consequence." For safety's sake, they held their meetings in an "automobile so that no listening devices could record our conversation."[67] If members had phones in their homes, they often were tapped. It was a common practice for neighbors to report on neighbors. Even some members in the Church branches had been coerced into submitting reports to the government about the activities of their leaders.[68] It wasn't so much Elder Monson who was at risk as it was the Church leaders who were citizens of the country.

At the conclusion of such a "meeting" in Erfurt, East Germany, in October 1970, Elder Monson told Henry of President Harold B. Lee's concern for him. "Tell Brother Burkhardt," President Lee, then serving in the First Presidency, had said, "that he and his associates, while absent from our presence, are never absent from our prayers and our thoughts. We commend them for their spirituality; we sustain them in their important responsibilities."[69] Elder Monson recounted in his journal, "As Henry walked from our car into the rainy night, I could not help but realize that the day of sacrifice is not over and there serve in the Church today men equally as dynamic and spiritually powerful as in any dispensation."[70]

Another evening, in the rain in a rented car, Elder Monson felt impressed to ask Henry, "If your government received a letter from the Presidency of the Church inviting you to attend a worldwide general conference, do you believe they would possibly grant approval?"

Brother Burkhardt responded with his ever-present great faith, "I believe the Lord will open the way."[71] It took two years of regularly submitted invitations, but the government finally relented, allowing Brother Burkhardt—always under scrutiny—to go to general conference in Salt Lake City, there to personally give the First Presidency a full report of the Dresden Mission. President Burkhardt had to leave his wife and children at home as "hostages" in order to ensure his return. During that first visit, he spoke at the final portion of the German-speaking conference in the Assembly Hall held in conjunction with general conference. He enjoyed a great reunion with German members he had not seen in many years.

Next, the first counselor in the Dresden Mission presidency, Walter Krause, and his wife, Edith, were allowed to come to general conference. While in Salt Lake City, they attended the temple. It was a momentous day on April 3, 1973, when Elder Monson stood in the circle as President Kimball ordained Brother Krause to the office of patriarch to provide blessings to those in the Communist countries. The numbers of members desiring their blessings were so great that Patriarch Percy K. Fetzer could not possibly carry the load himself. But the calling of Brother Krause, long respected and tireless in his service, sent an important message to the sequestered Saints, that one of their number could so serve. Elder Monson counseled that when people receive their patriarchal blessings, they receive hope.[72]

In 1974, Gottfried Richter, second counselor in the Dresden Mission presidency, and his wife were permitted to attend general conference, which meant they too could visit the temple. Miraculously, in 1975, the East German officials rescinded a previous denial of Henry and Inge Burkhardt's visa. It had taken many prayers to get the two of them together to general conference. Both the Richters and the Burkhardts were endowed and sealed by Elder Monson in the Salt Lake Temple and "literally bathed with their tears the little cloth which adorned the sacred altar."[73]

In the years ahead, a small trickle of members from East Germany found a way to Salt Lake City to attend the temple or general conference. Elder Monson was always hosting someone and arranging opportunities for his visitors to meet Church officers. On one such occasion, a sister from East Germany was meeting with President Kimball and Elder Monson. She related how she had looked forward to the day President Kimball was coming

Tom Monson in the congregation at general conference awaiting the announcement of his call to the Quorum of the Twelve Apostles, October 4, 1963.

At his first general conference meeting. Right to left, Elders Thomas S. Monson, Gordon B. Hinckley, Howard W. Hunter, Richard L. Evans, and Ezra Taft Benson (at the pulpit).

Greeting President David O. McKay with his counselors (left to right:) Alvin R. Dyer, Hugh B. Brown, Nathan Eldon Tanner, and Joseph Fielding Smith, December 1968.

On the steps of the Church Administration building at 47 East South Temple in 1967.

Photo courtesy Deseret News

Presenting one of his first messages as an Apostle.

With Elders Howard W. Hunter and Gordon B. Hinckley in a conversation
with President Spencer W. Kimball in April 1970.

Photo courtesy Deseret News

With Elder Mark E. Petersen, a friend and mentor.

Sitting with Elder Gordon B. Hinckley at general conference. The two sat next
to one another in the Quorum of the Twelve for eighteen years and served in the
First Presidency together for more than twenty-two.

Being greeted warmly by the Saints in the South Seas on the Monsons' 1965 visit.

Meeting Tahauri Hutihuti, about age eighty-four, in March 1965. Brother Hutihuti had saved his earnings from pearl diving for forty years to attend the New Zealand Temple.

At the Taj Mahal, August 1971, on a stop between a Scouting World Jamboree
in Tokyo and a Church area conference in Manchester, England.

At the London England Stake in front of the Wandsworth Chapel
on Nightingale Lane, where the mission home used to stand.

On assignment to Africa near Victoria Falls, Rhodesia, November 29, 1974.

At Estoril, Portugal, April 22, 1975, where he dedicated the land for the preaching of the gospel. Directly behind Elder Monson stands the mission president, W. Grant Bangerter.

At the dedication of the Freiberg Germany Temple in June 1985. Right to left:
Elder Thomas S. Monson and his wife, Frances; Elder Robert D. Hales and his wife, Mary;
Elder Joseph B. Wirthlin and his wife, Elisa; Emil Fetzer.

In Haiti to dedicate the land for the preaching of the gospel in 1983.

Receiving Honorary Doctorate of Laws from Brigham Young University at the April 1981 commencement. The newly installed university president, Jeffrey R. Holland, reads the citation.

Receiving honorary degrees from Utah Valley University in May 2009. President Monson received an Honorary Doctorate of Communication and Sister Monson received an Honorary Doctorate of Humane Letters.

Signing a new agreement on June 1, 1982, to continue the Newspaper Agency Corporation contract for joint printing and advertising. President Monson represented the Deseret News and John W. (Jack) Gallivan the Salt Lake Tribune.

Touring the Deseret News Press with President Spencer W. Kimball and Elder Gordon B. Hinckley as the afternoon paper is printed.

Following a priesthood meeting of the newly established Dresden Mission in East Germany on June 14, 1969. Elder Monson is on far right, front row.

After organizing the Dresden Mission on June 14, 1969. Left to right, front row: Walter Krause; Henry Burkhardt, Dresden Mission president; Gottfried Richter; back row: Elder Monson; Percy K. Fetzer; Stanley D. Rees, Hamburg Mission president.

Görlitz meetingplace in an abandoned factory building where Elder Monson promised the East German Saints they would receive all the Lord's blessings.

Addressing the Saints through a translator at the organization
of the Düsseldorf Germany Stake on June 4, 1972.

On a hill overlooking the Elbe River, Elder Monson gave a prayer of dedication for the land
of East Germany on April 27, 1975. Left to right: Gary Schwendiman, Elder Monson, Walter
and Edith Krause, Gottfried and Gertraude Richter, and Henry and Inge Burkhardt.

At the dedication of the new chapel in Görlitz with longtime German friends, including Elder Dieter F. Uchtdorf (left), on August 27, 1995.

Presenting "First Steps" statue to Erich Honecker, head of state of the German Democratic Republic, with (left to right) Elder Russell M. Nelson, Henry J. Burkhardt, Manfred Schütze, and Frank Apel.

On August 26, 1996, walking down the path from the sacred spot on a hilltop between Dresden and Meissen where he offered the 1975 prayer of dedication for the German Democratic Republic.

to Dresden. "She had counted the weeks and then the days and then the hours until she would see the prophet of the Lord and hear him—a lifelong, treasured experience." It was not to be. Her mother became ill and she could not leave her for the trip to Dresden where the prophet would speak. "All of my hopes were gone," she related to those seated in the President's office. She would "never see the prophet of the Lord."

As she related her experience, President Kimball walked around from behind his desk and took her hand and kissed her on the forehead. She had fulfilled the commandment to honor her mother, and the Lord had granted a far greater blessing than that which she had ever hoped to receive.[74]

In August 1973, Elder and Sister Monson attended an area conference in Munich, West Germany. The Tabernacle Choir, then on tour in Europe, came to the conference. President Burkhardt and his counselors had been allowed to attend, although their wives and families were kept behind the Wall. "We had pledged to the German government that all those who were permitted to attend would return," said Elder Monson. When an elderly woman passed away during one of the meetings, true to their word, the Church leaders made certain that her body was returned to East Germany.

That kind of attention to the laws of the land and respect for the government leaders and the rules they imposed would benefit the Church in years to come, as did the massive amount of information "collected" by those who watched what was going on. Years later Brother Burkhardt was allowed to see his government file, fat and filled with dates, quotes from talks, comments "overheard," and reports of meetings. But Elder Monson had repeatedly counseled the members to abide by the twelfth Article of Faith: "We believe in being subject to kings, presidents, rulers and magistrates, in obeying, honoring and sustaining the law." The fact that they obeyed the laws of the land, difficult as that may have been, that they sought changes and permissions through the proper channels and did not rebel or challenge authority, worked in their favor. They proved themselves trustworthy and were blessed.

What happened in the German Democratic Republic influenced the Church's being allowed into other countries. Elder Russell M. Nelson later explained that as President Monson and he worked with leaders of other nations behind the Iron Curtain, they invited those leaders to examine the impact of the Church on the citizens of East Germany. Those governments sent teams into the GDR to talk to the leaders and to satisfy themselves that the doctrines of the Church were helpful for their people. Not only were the Saints "good citizens, productive, honest, and law-abiding, but the fact that they don't use alcohol and drugs . . . that are so prevalent in so many societies today has made them want more of that for their own people."[75]

During a visit to Dresden in April 1975, Elder Monson, who had just come from dedicating Portugal for the preaching of the gospel, felt impressed that he should also dedicate the German Democratic Republic, which as a separate country had never received a priesthood dedication from one of the Quorum of the Twelve. Acting on that inspiration, early in the morning of April 27, 1975, he gathered together a few of the leaders and went with them to a little outcropping overlooking the Elbe River. The group included President Burkhardt and his counselors and their wives and President Gary L. Schwendiman (acting as translator) and his wife, of the Germany Hamburg Mission. They walked through the woods for about twenty minutes; the sky was gray, with an intermittent drizzle. Elder Monson spent a few minutes describing the significance of a prayer of dedication.

Standing in a clearing, with the city of Meissen on the right and Dresden on the left, he offered a prayer "which was confirmed in its entirety by the Spirit of the Lord."[76] He later said: "There we bowed our heads and supplicated our Heavenly Father in dedicating this land for the purposes of His work."[77]

Elder Monson delivered a beautiful prayer of dedication in which he expressed gratitude for the presence of the Church in the land, mentioned the great faith of the members, invoked the blessings of Heavenly Father upon the Saints and their posterity, pleaded for a way for the faithful to receive the blessings of the temple, and asked for a return of missionaries to the land. He sought for "the program of the Church in its fulness" to come again to the people, indicating that they had "through their faith . . . merited such blessings." The prayer was history in the making.[78]

He later wrote: "During the prayer, a rooster happened to crow in the distance, signaling the beginning of the day; church bells began to chime down in the valley, signaling it was a Sabbath day. During that time, I felt heat on my hands. I knew we were in a rainstorm, but as we concluded the prayer and looked heavenward, it had cleared. A shaft of sunshine was coming right down to that little outcropping which engulfed us in its warmth. The warmth which we felt on our hands and our faces happened to be from that ray of sunshine from heaven, which confirmed to me that it was the dawning of a new day, acknowledged by our Heavenly Father." Elder Monson was reassured "that the hand of the Lord was with this work."[79]

That beautiful spot on the hill where the prayer was offered is, for President Monson and the people of East Germany, sacred ground. He recorded that up to that time, he had never "enjoyed a more spiritual experience as a member of the Council of the Twelve than the experience of offering the prayer in this Communist-controlled land, invoking the blessings of our Heavenly Father on as faithful a group of Saints as ever existed."[80] On occasion, he has returned to that sacred spot, always feeling the Spirit there.

In the district conference following the dedication of the land, Elder Monson felt impressed, as he looked at the congregation getting settled for the meeting, to ask seventeen-year-old Sabine Baasch to bear her testimony. Earlier, he had asked President Burkhardt to select two young people to share their testimonies. To his surprise, Sabine was on President Burkhardt's list as well. A member of the choir, she not only spoke but then sang an impromptu solo of the hymn, "O My Father." Her father, a professional musician from Leipzig, led the choir that day.[81] Clearly, parents had been schooled in their homes when young and now were grooming their children in much the same way.

At the conclusion of the meeting, when they sang, "God Be with You Till We Meet Again," their "Auf Wiedersehen, auf Wiedersehen" brought tears to Elder Monson's eyes. To him, they were "the most wonderful Saints to be found anywhere" because they lived "after the pattern of the Savior."[82]

The singing of the German Saints always stirred his heart. At one leadership session, he heard singing from another room and he asked if that was the choir practicing. "No," he was told, "the men are just passing the time until their meeting." Elder Russell M. Nelson once reported that a priesthood leader in Germany had told him if he wanted to get the attention of anyone in his congregation, he simply had to ban that person from singing in the choir.[83]

During the 1970s, members and leaders flooded the East German authorities with repeated requests for travel passes to Switzerland to attend the temple. The answer was predictable: No. Still they continued submitting their petitions.

Gunther Schulze and his wife, Inge, both third-generation members of the Church, sat in a car with Elder Monson on one of his visits to the GDR where he proposed the Church send a letter of invitation for them to visit one of the temples of the Church. The Schulzes replied, "Our position is too sensitive here." As the visit concluded and they walked across the parking lot, Elder Monson looked at this faithful couple and called out to them in his limited German, "Bruder und Schwester Schulze, kommen Sie hier, bitte." They came back, and he said, "I feel that the Lord would like to see you endowed in His holy house. You are worthy people; you are exemplary in your conduct; you are faithful in the pursuit of your Church responsibilities. Let's trust in the Lord. Let's allow our faith to exceed our doubt." The three "knelt in the parking lot in the rain and poured out [their] hearts to God."[84] The invitation was sent, and permission was subsequently granted by the government for Brother and Sister Schulze to attend the temple.

In 1978, following conferences in the Dresden area, Elder and Sister Monson visited a small cemetery to honor a missionary who many years before had died in the service of the Lord. With a flashlight illuminating the headstone, Elder Monson read:

Joseph A. Ott
Born: 12 December 1870, Virgin, Utah
Died: 10 January 1896, Dresden, Germany

He recognized immediately something curious about the grave. Someone had polished the marble headstone to a sheen, pulled the weeds that encroached on all the surrounding markers, edged the bit of lawn, and placed flowers on the grave. He asked who had cared for the grave.

At first there was silence. Then Henry Burkhardt acknowledged that his twelve-year-old son, Tobias, was caring for the grave of the young American who had died shortly after arriving as a missionary. Tobias did not expect to have an opportunity to fulfill a proselyting mission but wanted to serve in some way, and he had felt that caring for the grave would be appropriate. He, like so many of the youth in this sequestered land, "made the decision between the world and the Church. They stayed with the Church."[85]

The small group held a brief service at the cemetery, which lay near the foot of the hill where Elder Monson had earlier dedicated the land for the preaching of the gospel.

Elder Monson's journal details many significant events relating to the buildings, dedications, and meetings. Also included are accounts of visits to hospitals to see the sick and to cemeteries to honor the dead. When the furnace failed in the Leipzig chapel and the meetings were held in the cold, he noted that the members sang the songs of Zion shoulder-to-shoulder, wearing their overcoats. "There was no lack of warmth, however, in the hearts of the members." Of the thirty-nine members of record, thirty-seven were in attendance, their scriptures open.[86]

A letter from an East German member conveyed the feelings of many: "With the Saints who have come from that part of the world and who have taken a keen interest in all the events concerning the building of the Kingdom, we want to express our most heartfelt thanks to you, President Monson, for the untiring service rendered and the special love extended to the Saints behind the curtain. You may never know the deep love they have for you and the leadership of the Church."[87]

In April 1978, Elder Monson met with the Quorum of the Twelve and the First Presidency to report formally on the progress of the Dresden Mission. When Elder Mark E. Petersen asked him if he had any reservations about crossing the border into East Germany, he assured them, "Absolutely not!" His assignment to supervise the area was then extended, though he had already been carrying the responsibility for ten years.

Later in April 1978, Elder Monson and Elder Charles Didier crossed into East Berlin, where President Burkhardt advised them that the government had monitored previous meetings at the meetinghouse. So they met in an apartment above a bakery to discuss plans and review decisions of the Brethren regarding the Dresden Mission. The homes in East Germany were cold and dreary, as well as drab and in need of repair; however, the homes of the members were warm with the Spirit, though they had little in the way of adornment or furnishings.

In that small apartment, they discussed combining the Zwickau and Karl-Marx-Stadt Districts and reviewed plans for visits from General Authorities and general auxiliary board members. At the conclusion of the meeting, Elder Monson felt impressed to bless the home and the family who lived there— father, mother, sixteen-year-old daughter, and nine-year-old son. He later wrote, "I cannot help but feel that our Heavenly Father will reward the devotions of such choice members of the Church who live and who worship under such difficult circumstances."[88]

It would not be long before the truth of those feelings would be fully manifested.

20

FAITH OF THE PEOPLE

*Germany was a tremendous assignment for him. He was the only one to go
behind the Iron Curtain. You have to give him credit for keeping the gospel
alive there during that very difficult period.*

ELDER L. TOM PERRY
Quorum of the Twelve Apostles

FOLLOWING GENERAL CONFERENCE in April 1975, Elder Monson
arranged a meeting between President Spencer W. Kimball
and Henry Burkhardt. Henry's responsibility as president of the
Dresden Mission included making direct contacts on behalf of
the Church with the East German officials. The government had
made it clear they would not work directly with representatives
from the West. The year before, in April general conference,
President Kimball had entreated the membership of the Church
to "lengthen their stride" and in the process reshape the way the
Church was viewed. No longer was it accurate to cast the Church
as a religion of the western United States. The gospel was for
everyone, everywhere, in every country and walk of life. President
Kimball's goal was to break out of the narrow geographical definition and recast the Church as a worldwide body of Saints with
faith in Jesus Christ and love for all men.

Now, in his inimitable manner, President Kimball challenged
Henry Burkhardt to change his own way of thinking: "Now,

Brother Burkhardt, if you want to see a change of things in East Germany, it must begin with you personally. It must begin with you because you are the leader of the Saints there, and you must have a change of heart, which means you must force yourself to befriend the Communists. You cannot hold any grudges against them. You must change your whole outlook and attitude."[1]

President Kimball was asking much from this tireless leader struggling with the ironhanded government system in East Germany, which had labeled Henry "an enemy of the state." But, faithful and ever obedient, Henry accepted President Kimball's charge and slowly changed his approach with the officials. President Kimball had counseled him to ask the government leaders, "What must we do to get full rights to operate as a church?"[2] It was the hardest thing Henry ever had done, and yet walls in the hearts of the Saints and the leaders began to come down long before the massive concrete symbol of oppression—the Berlin Wall—crumbled.

Henry was not the only one President Kimball charged to make things happen.

What the people behind the Iron Curtain needed was access to a temple. Later that month, April 27, 1975, Elder Monson, in his rededication of the country, petitioned the Lord, "Heavenly Father, wilt Thou open up the way that the faithful may be accorded the privilege of going to Thy holy temple, there to receive their holy endowments and to be sealed as families for time and all eternity."[3] The few who were allowed to go to Salt Lake City where they could attend the temple were just that—a few. Elder Monson understood that "worthy people feel deprived" when they cannot have the blessings of the temple. Such became "their prayer of faith, their expression of hope." As he would meet with the General Authorities every Thursday, he "would express this same hope."[4]

After one Thursday meeting in the temple in the spring of 1978, Elder Monson had returned to his office when he received a message: "President Kimball would like to see you in the temple, now." He remembers his first thought being, "What have I done wrong?" He later wrote of the meeting, "There was President Kimball with his counselors, President Nathan Eldon Tanner and President Marion G. Romney. President Kimball said to me, 'Brother Monson, you have a great love for the people of the German Democratic Republic. I have heard you lament the fact that they have not had their endowments or their sealings. I have heard you state that they are worthy to go to the temple and that with all of your heart you want them to have a temple.' He continued, 'The Lord will not deny temple blessings to those worthy members.' And then with a smile, he said, 'You find the way.'"[5]

"We explored every possibility" to provide temple blessings, Elder Monson later reported. "A trip once in a lifetime to the temple in Switzerland? Not approved by the government. Perhaps mother and father could come to Switzerland, leaving the children behind. Not right. How do you seal children to parents when they cannot kneel at an altar? It was a tragic situation."[6] Elder Monson, with the help of Elder Robert D. Hales, then a member of the First Quorum of the Seventy who had administrative responsibility for parts of Europe, explored with the First Presidency the possibility of authorizing sealings outside the temple, constructing ordinance rooms in a chapel building, or establishing an endowment house, as in the early days in the Salt Lake Valley.

Despite the challenges, which seemed insurmountable, Henry Burkhardt continued to press the government for permission for six couples at a time to visit the Swiss Temple. The theory was that the six would establish a credible record of leaving and returning to East Germany. Perhaps others would then be allowed to follow until all the worthy but unendowed members in the Dresden Mission received the blessings of the temple.

Finally, in May 1978, the East German leaders stunned Henry with a solution of their own: "Why don't you build a temple here?"

Elder Monson reported the breakthrough to the First Presidency. There were still issues, however: Would the government demand access to the temple? Would the Church own the building and the land? What guarantees would the Church have, after dedicating a house of the Lord, that the government would not confiscate the property and the temple?

Elder Monson arrived in East Berlin on Saturday, February 10, 1979, with plans for a temple in his briefcase. When Henry

Burkhardt saw the drawings, tears filled his eyes. He would "respond to his government's invitation" with plans in hand that the Church build a temple in that country rather than requesting permission for citizens of the GDR to go to Switzerland.

On March 28, 1979, Henry, who had been allowed by the East German officials to attend general conference, "indicated that the government authorities liked the building plans" and had given "the green light for us to proceed."[7] Initially the Church favored building in Karl-Marx-Stadt because of the large number of Saints living in that area, but the German government was insisting on a smaller community such as Freiberg.

The government's permitting the Church to build chapels in Dresden, Zwickau, Leipzig, Freiberg, and Plauen, as well as a temple in Freiberg, in a country hostile to all religion suggested that more was at play than just a softening of the officials' hearts regarding the spiritual welfare of the people. Elder Monson noted, "The allure of Western currency to be infused into their faltering economy was a significant incentive in allowing construction of the temple in Freiberg and other Church buildings in Karl-Marx-Stadt and Dresden."[8] The Church would be paying in Western currency—Dutch guilders and Swedish krona—which had a value much higher than the East German marks.[9]

But not to be discounted in the negotiations with the government was the role Church members played in their steadfast obedience to the laws of their land. In contrast, some other religions were far more abrasive and even confrontational. That the Saints had proven themselves industrious, reliable, long-suffering, and dutiful gave additional credibility.

The members were not aware of the negotiations and plans under consideration for a temple. Elder Monson and other General Authorities challenged the East German Saints to prepare themselves for a temple. They didn't question; rather, they organized temple preparation courses, believing that one day they would have the privilege of receiving those blessings.

Meanwhile, the Church leaders continued to work at providing temple blessings in other ways, such as inviting East German LDS leaders to Salt Lake City for general conference. At first only the leaders of the Dresden Mission were allowed to attend conference. In 1979 President Monson asked if others in district or branch leadership positions might be invited to general conference so that they might be endowed and sealed in the temple. The answer was, "Only if they go in lieu of a member of the Dresden Mission presidency." Not wishing to give up any ground with the government, Elder Monson suggested still submitting a request for additional members to attend.

As President Kimball had counseled, the mission presidency worked at establishing better relations with the government officials. Gottfried Richter, second counselor in the mission presidency, had attended a meeting in Dresden of leaders of various religions. When asked for suggestions on how to "best honor the thirteenth anniversary of the founding of their country," Brother Richter had spoken up boldly, quoting from the Doctrine and Covenants "that governments were instituted of God for the benefit" of the people.[10] The officials were impressed with the comment. When East Berlin officials denied a request for a local branch president to travel to Utah for general conference, the government officials from Dresden were asked to intercede on his behalf—and he and his wife were allowed to attend. Elder Monson recognized that "Heavenly Father brought about the opportunity."[11] During their 1979 visit to Salt Lake City, the couple attended more than twenty sessions in the temple.

Eventually, step-by-step, the Lord opened the way. Relations improved, respect for the Church increased, and requests were granted—but still at great peril that at any time, for no apparent reason, the approvals could be cancelled. Over the next few years, a mere trickle of Church leaders from behind the Iron Curtain were permitted to attend general conference. Permission was also occasionally given for some German-speaking representatives of the general boards of the Sunday School, Young Men, Young Women, Primary, and Relief Society to come into the country to teach. General Authorities visited when possible so that members would become acquainted with their faces.

During his many years on assignment in East Germany, Elder Monson was impressed that although the Saints were fewer than five thousand in number, the activity levels there exceeded those found anywhere else in the world. This, he noted, was in spite of "the absence of spacious chapels with multiple teaching stations and grounds featuring the greenery of lawns and the blossoms of flowers. The meetinghouse libraries, as well as the personal libraries of our members, consist only of the standard works, a hymnbook, and one or two other volumes. These books do not remain on bookcase shelves. Their teachings are engraved on the hearts of members. They are displayed in their daily lives. Service is a privilege. A branch president, forty-two years of age, has served in his calling for twenty-one years—half his life. Never a complaint—just gratitude."[12]

There was no question that those Saints were worthy of a temple, but the significance of the Church's receiving permission to construct that temple behind the Iron Curtain cannot be overstated. The use of all land was controlled by the government, and private construction approval from the government was very limited. Since the end of World War II, construction approval for a new church building had been unheard of in East Germany. When Henry Burkhardt informed the government officials that the building would be off-limits to all but worthy LDS members after its dedication, the officials agreed to comply. That surprised the German Saints, who were accustomed to having their lives constantly under the eyes of the government.

Quality materials and skilled craftsmen were readily available for work on the temple, although the construction process in the GDR was bewildering and unpredictable. Applications for construction were most often denied. But the ones that were not outright rejected were never actually "approved." That meant the government could halt any project at any time, hiding behind its "never having given approval" to the work. Since the Church's application was not denied, plans went ahead. Locating and acquiring property took three years. Freiberg was ultimately selected because of its location right in the heart of what Elder Monson called the triangle of Church members in Leipzig, Karl-Marx-Stadt (once Chemnitz), and Dresden. Finally, in February 1982, a site was secured—miraculously, with GDR currency—for both a temple and a stake center. As the project developed, patron housing was added. In October 1982, the First Presidency announced publicly that a temple would be built in Freiberg, the first temple of The Church of Jesus Christ of Latter-day Saints in a Communist country.

Because of their financial struggles, the members in the GDR were not initially asked to contribute money to build the temple, as was then the pattern in other countries. Knowing that the usual system was to expect member donations in the financing, they wondered when their contributions might be expected. "Are we second-class Mormons?" they asked. "Do you expect that we can't donate for the temple?" So a temple donation project was undertaken, and the members were asked to donate whatever they could. No limit or goal was set. At the same time, another temple fund-raising project began in West Germany for the announced Frankfurt Temple, with a goal of 150,000 West German marks to be raised in two years. That was the equivalent of 50,000 marks in the GDR currency. When Elder Hans B. Ringger met with President Burkhardt three months after the fund-raising began, he learned that the members in East Germany had already raised 50,000 East German marks and planned to have a total of 150,000 marks in three months—three times what was expected. Elder Ringger directed that a letter be sent thanking the members for their contributions, but the letter stirred even more donations. The East German members continued donating for two years, and at the time of the dedication, 880,000 East German marks, far more than what had been asked of the stakes in the West, was in the coffers.[13]

Purchasing construction materials within East Germany was difficult. Emil Fetzer, architect for the Church, said of the project, "In East Germany at the time, if you wanted a sack of cement, you did not go the nearest lumber yard. There were no lumber yards and no sacks of cement. All of the materials had to be allocated by the East German government."[14]

As plans for the temple progressed, Elder Monson created the first stake in the German Democratic Republic on August 29, 1982. He called it "a day of rejoicing and thanksgiving." The boundaries created a triangle of Karl-Marx-Stadt, Dresden, and Erfurt, with the official name being the Freiberg German Democratic Republic Stake of The Church of Jesus Christ of Latter-day Saints. Nearly one thousand of the 1,800 stake members attended the historic meeting. Leadership was "abundant," as were the faith and devotion of the members. These were people whose "spirit of devotion and sacrifice and desire to serve the Lord" was unequalled.[15] Brother Wilfred Möller, a professor of English from Dortmund in West Germany, served as Elder Monson's interpreter for this conference, as he had on many other occasions.

On that memorable day, Elder Monson stood at the pulpit looking at a congregation of people whom he loved for their "unwearyingness." He spoke to them of the many years the Brethren had listened to his reports of their faithfulness. He related that, when meeting with other Apostles on one occasion, Elder Harold B. Lee had said, "Tom, I hope one day we have a stake in that country." Elder Spencer W. Kimball had echoed the same sentiment. Elder Monson could not at that time imagine how that could happen, but he trusted two senior members of the Quorum of the Twelve who had expressed that faith. At the stake's creation, with joy and gratitude, Elder Monson said, "That day is today."[16]

It was certainly a day "never to be forgotten," a day when "prophecy was fulfilled." Elder Monson later recorded, "At my second visit to the Dresden Mission, I stood at the pulpit and told the people I had never seen greater faith and that surely the Lord would reward such faith by providing every blessing that other members of the Church would receive. I have seen the step-by-step unfolding of this prophecy and know it came from the Lord."[17]

Those called to direct the new stake were men whose service was counted not in years but in decades. Frank Herbert Apel was called to serve as stake president. He was an automobile electric systems supervisor, forty-two years of age, who had served eighteen years in the district presidency and had been executive secretary of the Dresden Mission. Named as counselors were Heinz Koschnicke and Reimund Dörlitz. Later the government gave clearance to President and Sister Apel to make the pilgrimage to

Salt Lake City in March 1983. Elder Monson had the privilege of sealing them in the Salt Lake Temple amid tears of gratitude.[18]

Elder Monson called Rudi Lehmann as the new stake patriarch. Brother Lehmann had been one of those present in that first Görlitz meeting with Elder Monson fifteen years before and had served as president of the district for sixteen years. In humble, broken English, Brother Lehmann testified, "I did all these things for the Lord." These were people, Elder Monson observed, who had "been strengthened here in a special way through want, sorrow, and tests."[19]

"Sometimes, in certain areas, men strive to become a stake president or a bishop and maybe almost have a campaign for the position," Elder Monson once explained. In East Germany, "there is a total absence of office seeking. You would talk to a man and ask, 'Whom do you think should be a stake president?' And he would say, 'Any one of the brethren would make a wonderful stake president.' 'Would you be willing to sustain them?' 'Absolutely.'"[20]

This was also the beginning of Elder Monson's "clothing project." He noticed that Werner Adler, the senior high councilor, a man about his same height and build, was dressed in a near-threadbare suit. What happened next was pure Thomas S. Monson. He found a little room, took off his suit, put on a pair of trousers and a casual shirt, and presented his suit of clothes to Brother Adler. As Brother Adler tried them on, his elation was evident: "It fits just fine—just fine."

Brother Adler later wrote in grateful thanks: "The beautiful suit you gave me in Dresden fits me, and I wear it with great joy. Our daily prayers to our Heavenly Father are also for you, our dear Brother Monson." He continued, "It is a great blessing to see how the promises you have expressed over this land on top of Lossnitzbergen by Dresden are systematically fulfilled. You said that the Lord will awaken in the hearts of men the desire to know and the will to listen to the gospel. Today these promises are fulfilled and we recognize from this the deep obligations we have to do everything in our power to magnify our callings and to be active with all of our strength."[21]

Elder Monson gave away his shoes and came home in his

slippers. He gave away his calculator. While addressing a large congregation of Saints, he turned to President Burkhardt and motioned for him to come forward; he then handed this longtime German leader his own set of marked scriptures, knowing that the East German members were not allowed to bring in Church materials from the West themselves. He gave away the cashmere coat that had kept him warm in Canada. Frances caught the spirit of giving and sent her clothing for the sisters to take home. Thus began the suitcases of clothes—suits, shirts, ties, belts, shoes, even socks—that Elder Monson left behind on his visits to the Dresden Mission.

When he invited a man in for an interview, that man might come out dressed in a whole new suit of clothes. Other areas in the world also received his largesse. No one has kept count, but his secretary Lynne Cannegieter estimates he has given away up to ten suits a year for forty years, not to mention the other items of clothing he has shared.

Elder Monson had developed the pattern of stuffing his pockets with packs of chewing gum—nowhere available in the GDR—to give to the youth whenever he traveled to East Germany. Beatrice Bartsch had been one of those youth. Years later, in April 2004, she sat in the choir right behind President Monson at a regional conference in Berlin. She carried in her pocket a stick of chewing gum still in the wrapper that she "had kept for a long time as a memory of shaking hands with an Apostle of God." He had given her that piece of gum at a district conference in Erfurt, East Germany, when she was fifteen years old. She had not even been a member of the Church then; her father, a Communist, would not allow her to be baptized until she was eighteen. Still, she had attended faithfully and had been baptized two weeks after her eighteenth birthday. For more than thirty years she had carried that gum with her. It was her "Apostle gum."[22] Following the conference session in Berlin, she spoke with President Monson, showed him the stick of gum, and told him how much it had meant to her through the years.

Elder Monson's ministry was a striking combination of individual, personal acts of service and guidance of what became sweeping historical events. On Saturday, April 23, 1983, the Saints in East Germany, in company with Elder Monson, Elder Robert D. Hales, Hans B. Ringger, Emil B. Fetzer of the Church Building Department, F. Enzio Busche, and Amos Wright, director of temporal affairs for the area, witnessed a "miracle of miracles" as they broke ground for the Freiberg Temple. For Elder Monson it was a very special date in his life, for he felt he had fulfilled the assignment and the promise to the faithful East German Saints. With tongue in cheek, he put Elder Hales "in charge of the weather" to ensure that they had sunshine on "this great occasion." Elder Hales was evidently successful; the weather was beautiful. Though no public announcement invited onlookers, a "nice crowd" of members and government officials gathered at the site.[23]

Elder Monson pronounced the prayer of dedication of the ground, setting it apart for its special purpose to accommodate a house of the Lord. He had invited each one in the audience to bow his head. Heinz von Selchow of the Church Educational System in Germany took a peek during the prayer to see the response of the visitors from the government. They were Communists by political persuasion, yet all but one bowed their heads.[24]

As Elder Monson took the shovel in hand to turn the first soil, a member of the Church Building Department called out, "Be careful how you lean on the shovel. When Brother Packer broke ground for a new temple in another country, the shovel broke under the weight of his foot." Elder Monson quipped back, "German-made shovels don't break."[25]

Elder Monson wrote of the experience, "I left the German Democratic Republic rejoicing in my heart and soul, now that a temple of God has been approved for construction and the dedication of the ground accomplished."[26]

Just a few days later, on Sunday, May 1, 1983, Elder Monson dedicated a newly completed chapel in Bonn, West Germany—on the other side of the wall. He counted it a great privilege to dedicate the building in the capital city of the nation. The facility was filled to overflowing with members and government guests.

Earlier he had gone to the church building in Wittenberg

where Martin Luther had nailed his famous proclamation to the door in 1517. In his journal, rather than write about the historical event, he noted his observations regarding one individual he met at the site. He referred to the guide, who "was most gracious. She would not accept any contribution for herself, simply suggesting that any contribution could go toward the maintenance of the church."[27] He made an offering in the designated box. Of significance is the fact that he singled out the guide for a comment of praise she would never even read. That is Thomas S. Monson. To him, little-known individuals are as worthy of notice as famous landmarks, events, or heads of state.

In June 1984 Elder Monson and Elder Robert D. Hales created the second stake in East Germany, the Leipzig Stake. All Saturday afternoon they conducted interviews. When the two entered the Leipzig chapel, Elder Monson was "amazed that all of the priesthood brethren who had assembled for interviews" were singing. Always the Germans were singing! "It is almost as though there has been a time warp take place in their lives. They are unpolluted by the softness and degeneracy which one sees in many countries, including our own." They were, he noted, "as pure a group of priesthood brethren" as he had ever met and were equal in every way to the priesthood brethren he had interviewed prior to the creation of the Freiberg Stake the year before.[28]

On Sunday, Elder Monson stood before the bulging congregation and spoke of establishing the Dresden Mission back in 1969. It had served as a forerunner, he said, of the stake organization put in place that day in Leipzig and previously with the creation of the Freiberg Stake.

Members in East Germany were always examples of faithful devotion to the Church and to each other. On one occasion, Elder Monson's tightly packed schedule in East Germany showed a break and he felt prompted to attend the district conference at Annaberg in the Dresden Mission. Unannounced, he and Elder Ringger arrived at the meeting as it began. Striding up the aisle, he noticed that the members were overwhelmed at his sudden appearance. One eighty-four-year-old brother, Willi Schramm, who had been a member for sixty years, began to weep. Through an interpreter, he related a dream he had had the night before in which he saw Elder Monson in attendance at the next day's meeting. He said, "Brother Monson, I believe in dreams and visions."[29]

Elder Monson remembered another occasion when "a sweet, older sister came forward and asked, 'Are you an Apostle?'

"When I answered, 'Yes,' she reached in her purse and brought forth a picture of the Quorum of the Twelve Apostles. She asked, 'Which one are you?'

"I looked at the picture. The junior member of the Quorum of the Twelve in that picture was Elder John A. Widtsoe. She had not seen a member of the Twelve for a very long time!"[30]

As Elder Monson sat down on the makeshift stand for one Church meeting, he noticed a brother in a very coveted seat on the front row looking around the room. He watched as the brother stood and walked over to an elderly man standing at the back. The man escorted the older brother to the front row, had him sit in his seat, and then walked to the back, where he stood for the rest of the meeting. When Elder Monson stood to speak, he used the example of that brother as his theme: "This is the type of silent yet meaningful courtesy," he began, "that is demonstrated by one who truly loves his brother as himself."[31]

Because of his responsibilities for Europe, Elder Robert D. Hales often accompanied Elder Monson on visits to East Germany. On one such visit, they inspected the temple and the new stake center, both located on the same large piece of property. The government architect had encouraged them to build the temple patron housing on a two-acre plot immediately adjacent to the temple property and even made the necessary arrangements with the government for the Church to purchase the land. Elder Monson continued to marvel at the Lord's hand in the work; property in the GDR was simply not made available and was not ever for sale.

The increasing visibility of the Church, as new buildings went up, spawned some envy from people of other faiths, who protested to the government. In addition, the new stake structure and the new stake leaders confused the government authorities, who were used to dealing only with Henry Burkhardt. The government was getting skittish about its commitments. In a full day of meetings in East Germany, Elder Monson and the area presidency, with the help of Church legal advisers in the GDR and in Frankfurt, Germany, prepared a "statement-of-purpose" document for government officials. The document would help to resolve growing government concerns and in turn help the officials to reassure other congregations that the Church had not grown in numbers and that the Church itself was providing the financial resources to upgrade its buildings.[32]

As he flew home from Europe on September 17, 1984, Elder Monson felt impressed to meet immediately with President Gordon B. Hinckley, then a counselor in the First Presidency, to review the statement-of-purpose document. Weary from the long plane flights, he still went straight to the Church offices and read over the document with President Hinckley, who made one change to one word and then approved it to be sent to the authorities in the GDR. The statement calmed the tensions, and the building went forward.

Four months later, on January 23, 1985, Elder Monson, in company with Elder Joseph B. Wirthlin, then supervisor of the Europe area, and Brother Hans B. Ringger, met with Minister Gysi, an impressive East German civil servant who "knew a great deal about our Church and spoke fluent English." Minister Gysi complimented the Church officials on the statement of purpose and then asked, "How is it that your church is sufficiently rich to construct buildings in our country?"[33]

Elder Monson answered that the Church was not wealthy but followed the ancient biblical principle of tithing, reemphasized in modern scripture, which made it possible to construct the buildings, including the temple then under way. When explaining tithing to the government leaders, he said, "We believe in a lay ministry, who do not receive a salary. People serve because of the love of their Heavenly Father and their fellow man. . . . The members of the Church freely live the law of tithing, an Old Testament law which asks that a tenth of one's increase should be returned to God. So in a very real way, this building was provided by the members of the Church all over the world: one family in its poverty, another in its wealth, and so on, all over the world. The tithes of the membership of the Church have provided the buildings."[34]

At the close of the meeting, Minister Gysi offered his help with the upcoming temple dedication. That was just another illustration of the great changes Elder Monson had seen in the years he had been coming to Communist Germany. The government had developed confidence in the members of the Church and in their leaders, knowing they would keep their word.

Attendance at the Freiberg Temple open house in June 1985 exceeded expectations. Nearly 90,000 people passed through the temple in sixteen days. The number was staggering, given that the entire population of the city of Freiberg was only 40,000. Most visitors were not members of the Church, yet many drove hundreds of miles to be there. Some slept in their cars. Some stood in line for as long as five hours, even in the rain, to go inside; they were people accustomed to standing in line for everything. As crowds increased, hours for the open house were extended as well, from 8:00 A.M. to 10:30 P.M., but one day the size of the crowd required that the doors remain open until 1:30 A.M. When asked, "Why do you stand in line to visit a temple of the Mormon Church?" one woman responded quickly, "Because I want to. I don't mind standing in line when it is my choice."

Elder Monson's thoughts turned to that 1975 prayer of dedication on behalf of the German Democratic Republic when he had asked Heavenly Father to instill within the citizenry a curiosity concerning the Church and a desire to learn more of its teachings.[35] The open house turnout fulfilled that supplication.

Prior to the dedication, on June 28, 1985, President Gordon B. Hinckley and Elder Monson hosted a special open house for government officials from Berlin and Dresden. In a break with tradition, they held the special meeting for the government and Church officials in the undedicated temple, with an overflow audience in the Freiberg stake center located on the property. The cornerstone ceremony followed this meeting, allowing the dignitaries to witness the unusual and significant service. A special luncheon for the honored guests followed.

Elder Monson, familiar to many of the officials because of his "file," though they had not been introduced, welcomed them. He was at home with these people. He told them: "I am confident that the things which unite us are greater than any thoughts which may separate us. We endorse wholeheartedly your emphasis on the family. We believe in honoring the country in which we live and in complying strictly with the rules and the regulations of that country, for in this way we demonstrate our allegiance. Similarly, we believe in honoring the laws of God and thus demonstrate our allegiance to our Heavenly Father." He concluded, "I believe the government of this nation will find no more loyal citizens, no more supportive electorate than will be found among the membership of our Church. I express to our Heavenly Father my gratitude. I look forward to our future meetings and future dedications of buildings."[36] The ceremonies included presenting the mayor of Freiberg with a bronze statue of a pioneer woman with her daughter.

Dr. Dieter Hantzsche from the government's "Building Academy" in Dresden, who had helped with construction issues concerning the temple, responded, "That which has been brought here today shows first that in our country a principle has been set in stone, which we could perhaps view as representing a tolerance and openness for all religious belief. I believe you can see you have been given our full support on matters such as approvals, permits, and the execution of the completed buildings."[37]

President Gordon B. Hinckley reminded the group of the remarks Elder Monson had made at the groundbreaking for the temple in April 1983, when he had noted that peace is a priceless gift that is well worth the expenditure of a great deal of effort. "These words, and, may I say, this advice, is more important than ever in view of the increasingly difficult international situation," he said.[38]

For the dedication, the visiting Church officers were staying in Dresden and traveling by coach to Freiberg, about an hour's journey. In spite of the evidence of good relations with the government at their special open house, when it was time for the visiting Church leaders to travel to their accommodations, the government provided a guide, "ostensibly to provide answers to questions, but more particularly," Elder Monson surmised from experience, "to monitor" their activities.[39]

On the morning of June 29, 1985, President Hinckley, with Elder Monson at his side, presided at the dedicatory sessions of the Freiberg Temple. The significance of that day was without equal in the lives of the East German people. The Freiberg Temple was, in the minds of the members, a physical manifestation of the power of God and His special awareness of them and their long and difficult journey. It was a highlight in the life of Thomas S. Monson as well. It had now been seventeen years since his promise to the people of Görlitz and ten years since he had dedicated the land near Dresden.

Of the experience, he wrote: "To have the opportunity to be the first speaker at the first dedicatory session of the Freiberg Temple was not only a great honor but also the fulfillment of a deep and long-held desire for the wonderful Saints in the GDR to have the blessing of a temple. It was difficult for me to control my emotions as I spoke, for racing through my mind were examples of the faith of the devoted Saints in this part of the world. Frequently people will ask, 'How was it possible for the Church to obtain permission to build a temple behind the Iron Curtain?' My feeling is simply that the faith and devotion of our Latter-day Saints in that area brought forth the help of Almighty God and provided for them the eternal blessings which they so richly deserved."[40]

The dedication continued the next day, with multiple services accommodating all those attending in the temple. The Relief Society provided refreshments between sessions. "The table was spread as an artist would paint a scene on canvas. All of the food was artistically displayed, using geometric patterns, even the placement of the glasses," Elder Monson noted. "I have never during my lifetime seen such meticulous care devoted to what some may consider a mundane assignment."[41]

Henry Burkhardt was called as the first president of the Freiberg Temple, with his wife, Inge, as matron. Beloved of the people, Henry had shepherded the flock for many years, and he and Inge were "truly persons without guile and totally dedicated to the work of the Lord."[42] During one regional conference years later, President Monson asked for a show of hands of all who at some time in their lives had received a blessing from, or been called by, or been set apart or counseled by President Burkhardt. A significant majority in the hall raised their hands.[43]

The Freiberg Temple was immediately busy. The people had waited a long time and had been actively engaged in preserving genealogical records and finding the names of their ancestors. One bishop commented to Elder Monson, "I'm having a difficult time getting my home teaching done among my ward members because the priesthood and their wives are always at the temple." Elder Monson thought: "What better place could they be?"[44]

He considered it nothing short of a miracle that the members of the Church in the GDR could enjoy the blessings they now did, including patriarchal blessings, the full Church program, and a beautiful temple dedicated and in use right in their midst. Every member of the Church in the GDR was now a member of a stake. But the magnitude of what would come from having a temple behind the Iron Curtain was yet to be realized.

Edith Krause, wife of Patriarch Walter Krause, who typed his more than 1,000 blessings, said after the temple dedication: "We tried to do what the Lord wanted us to do, so that brought us nearer to a temple. Walter always said the Lord has the might and the power and that we should never have doubt. All things will happen for us—because prophets, apostles, and other authorities had come to the country in the new day and had left their prayers and their blessings with us. And we could feel it. If you are in such a situation as we are, you can feel it. These are not only words, it is a blessing, and you feel stronger, and you feel thankful, and you feel humble to the Lord that is so great and so dear to you, that the distance from you to Him is the same as from America to Him. And you can shorten this distance by your belief. And that's what we learned at the temple. I think it was a great time. When the temple was ready we all said now let us be worthy and let us live better and better so that the temple can remain in this country. We hope it will."[45]

In his journal, Elder Monson reflected: "In the evening on the way back to Dresden [after the temple dedication], I contemplated that it had been seventeen years since I had made my first visit to Germany as a member of the Council of the Twelve. I entered the German DR at that time, being the first General Authority . . . to go to our membership there following the erection of the Berlin Wall and the tightening of security on the part of the government. Some of the milestone events were the dedicatory prayer which I offered; the organization of the Dresden Mission and the establishment of districts for training for eventual stakehood; the creation of the Freiberg Stake and later, the Leipzig Stake; groundbreaking services for the Freiberg Germany Temple and the prayer of dedication which I was privileged to offer on that occasion; and now the culmination, the completion and dedication of a house of the Lord. All honor and glory belong to our Heavenly Father, for it is only through His divine intervention that these events have taken place. I am simply gratified beyond words to have been a part of what I consider one of the historic and faith-filled chapters of Church history."[46]

21

THE WALL COMES DOWN

I watched the miracle happen when Erich Honecker said, "President Monson, we trust you." All those years they had been keeping track of him. The Communists keep really good records of people who come in and out. They had monitored his sermons, and Erich Honecker said, "We trust you. Therefore your requests are granted."

ELDER RUSSELL M. NELSON
Quorum of the Twelve Apostles

WHAT INFLUENCE DID THE Freiberg Temple have on the collapse of the Berlin Wall? A look at the string of events in this cordoned-off nation is telling: A country is cut off from the world by miles of concrete, barbed wire, land mines, and guard towers, yet it is blessed by miracles that can only be attributed to the Lord and His gospel. Stakes are created; patriarchs are called; a holy temple is completed and tens of thousands line up just to walk through it. Missionaries come in and go out, a practice unheard of in this closed-door land. Members of the Church show their devotion to their Father in Heaven by living and exemplifying the teachings of Jesus Christ, often at great peril. And then the wall—and with it, the government—comes down.

Whatever role politicians and presidents may have played, reflection at the end of this dispensation may well show that it was the diligence and faith of the German Saints, coupled with the inspiration of modern-day prophets and the prayers of the faithful in all lands, that chipped away at that wall.

President Dieter F. Uchtdorf was an eyewitness. "I remember when I first got into my hands the dedicatory prayer of this country. This was way before the wall came down and I read through those things Elder Monson promised in the name of the Lord and I thought how can that happen? Over the years, I had the prayer in my little binder where I had important things and I checked them off as they happened. It was amazing how these things came to pass. He influenced our country in a wonderful way that unification came about, much faster than anyone could have expected. I knew Germany would be reunited at one time. I knew it in my heart and in my soul. But I thought it would happen, if my kids were lucky, during their lifetime but more likely during the lifetime of my grandchildren or my great-grandchildren. A long time. Overnight it happened, largely because of the many things President Monson did after giving the blessing."[1]

Germany is indeed a story of latter-day miracles. They were as dramatic as the collapse of an oppressive government, as simple as one individual reaching out to lift another.

The Saints' challenge in East Germany was as monumental as that of a poverty-stricken people trying to place a temple on the rough frontier of America in the early days of the Church. And in both cases, the Lord opened the way for the priesthood and temple blessings to flow. Elder Monson brought faith, courage, and perseverance to the task. He sat with men of the highest political office in a nonreligious nation and, as an Apostle of the Lord, talked of things sacred and holy. And they listened. It was never about visas and permits, though they were the necessary tools. It was always the principle that mattered. He was obedient to the Lord; he asked the right questions and followed the promptings. He showed faith for years; he gave hope to those faithful living there.

The marvel is that the Saints built a temple and God brought down a wall. The Berlin Wall.

For years, German Saints visiting Salt Lake City went in and out of the office of Elder Monson at 47 East South Temple. It was for them a visit to the pool of Bethesda, and Elder Monson was poised to help them into the healing water—or to do whatever else he could to lift their burdens. Henry Burkhardt, president of the Dresden Mission for fifteen years and the first temple president in Freiberg, was one of them. On a visit in 1992, a little discouraged after having completed his assignment at the Freiberg Temple, Brother Burkhardt appealed to President Monson, "What now?"

President Monson, ever the teacher, saw an opportunity to point Henry, who had carried heavy administrative responsibilities for so many years, to the pure joy of serving the one. He listened and then gave Henry an assignment, "Perhaps one of the most unique assignments you have ever received," he said. "I am asking you to visit with Brother Walter Stover. He is in his nineties and is not in good health. I don't think he'll be with us much longer. I want you to go sit by his bed and ask him to tell you about his life. He will enjoy the opportunity, and you will treasure the memory of your visit."

President Monson knew of what he spoke. Early in his European assignment he had gone to visit with Walter Stover, the first mission president assigned to East Germany after the war. He learned much from this German convert who had later moved to Utah and built a successful business. President Monson, who so admired Brother Stover, said, "If ever there was a man who exemplified the scripture—'for everything which inviteth to do good, and to persuade to believe in Christ'—Walter Stover was that man." With his own funds, Brother Stover "constructed two chapels in Berlin—a beautiful city that had been so devastated by the conflict. He planned a gathering in Dresden for all the members of the Church from that nation and then chartered a train to bring them from all around the land so they could meet, partake of the sacrament, and bear witness of the goodness of God to them." He counseled the youth wanting to flee to West Germany "to be patient and faithful to the Lord's commandment until the Lord in His own due time would open the doors to full privileges to them."[2] He went to the Netherlands Mission seeking food and supplies for the defeated German people, who were starving.

Brother Burkhardt noted that he would have to speak to Brother Stover in German, the only language he knew. "Brother Stover will enjoy conversing with you in German," Elder Monson replied. Henry went, and his report was just as President Monson had hoped: "I left his presence a better man and more determined to serve our Heavenly Father than ever before."[3]

In 1985, when Elder Monson was called to be a counselor to President Ezra Taft Benson, he passed the baton for supervision of the countries of Eastern Europe, including the German Democratic Republic, Czechoslovakia, Yugoslavia, and Poland, to Elder Russell M. Nelson, who would oversee Europe along with Elder Joseph B. Wirthlin. Still, President Monson kept his guiding hand in the work of the Church behind the Iron Curtain.

President Monson was privileged to return to Leipzig, East Germany, to dedicate the beautiful stake center that had been built there. He gave a "valedictory address" on August 24, 1986, in a rented hall filled with "all of our members from the German Democratic Republic." On what was a "particularly touching occasion," he recounted his years of service and paid tribute to those, such as Henry Burkhardt and his counselors, who had served so faithfully for so long. At one point, the Primary children came forward from their seats with their parents to join the choir in singing the Primary songs "Called to Serve" and "I Am a Child of God." President Monson observed that some of the ever-present government officials "had tears in their eyes when they saw this evidence of love."[4]

In addition to meetinghouses in Leipzig, Freiberg, and Annaberg, in February 1987 the Church Appropriations Committee approved a new chapel building for East Berlin; in April they approved one for Dresden. With unprecedented consent from the government that had been negotiated a few years earlier to build ten chapels in the GDR, President Monson felt impressed to make sure that the buildings were put in place, relying on the members to put forth "every effort in member missionary work" so that the member base "is replenished with converts as well as by births."[5]

For nearly twenty years Elder Monson had been visiting the Saints behind the Iron Curtain. On every visit, the state had monitored his work. These officials had come to know the Latter-day Saints. They had permitted the building of chapels and a temple. Now, in October 1988, Elder Monson was approaching the next big hurdle, asking that missionaries be admitted from other countries and that Latter-day Saints from the German Democratic Republic be permitted to serve in other countries as well.

On October 24, 1988, State Secretary of Religious Affairs Kurt Löffler hosted a lunch in East Berlin for President Monson, Elder and Sister Russell M. Nelson, and others, including Günter Behncke, assistant to Herr Löffler, and Herr Zeitl from the ministry of Foreign Trade. A member of the Church, Brother Wilfred Möller, again served as President Monson's interpreter. President Monson noted that the only drinks on the table were orange juice and water, an unmistakable sign of respect for the Church leaders. At one point Kurt Löffler drew President Monson to the window and gestured from far left to far right, saying, "Following World War II, as far as you could see from this position, only seven buildings were standing." He was clearly proud of the rebuilding that had taken place in the city.[6]

The next day an entire busload of government dignitaries from East Berlin, including Herr Löffler, traveled to the Dresden stake center for a tour of the building and a special meeting. They brought beautiful bouquets of flowers, and as each one of the LDS leaders concluded his remarks, they presented him with one of the bouquets as a sign of cooperation and appreciation for one another's beliefs.

Dedication services were held with the Church members in the late afternoon at the Dresden stake center and the next day at the Zwickau chapel, where again government workers and leaders were present. One of the speakers was the oldest member of the Church in that area, who had joined in 1924. More than 6,000 people had come to the open house prior to the dedication of the chapel in Zwickau. In Dresden, 29,740 had attended the open house.[7]

At the close of the dedication services at Zwickau, a brother approached President Monson and asked that he give his greeting to President Ezra Taft Benson, adding, "He saved my life. He gave me food to eat and clothing to wear following the war. He gave me hope. God bless him!"[8] Those thoughts were taken home to President Benson.

The following day, in Potsdam, the group, hosted by Herr Wünsche, the Church's legal counsel in the GDR, toured the city and its significant sites where the Allied powers had divided Germany at the end of the war. Herr Wünsche treated them to lunch in the beautiful Cecilienhof Hotel. President Monson noted, looking out the window of the dining hall, "that the workmen, dressed as European workmen dress—in long, flowing smocks—were loading leaves on a wagon pulled by a beautiful horse." The old-fashioned scene symbolized to him "those traditions from which Europeans hate to depart."[9]

He had an experience at a sumptuous dinner in East Berlin's best hotel that evening with Herr Behncke, Herr Löffler's assistant, who confided to him, "I know you; I trust you. You and I can speak honestly as friends." He then said, "I believe some of the same principles you believe," and he commented about his wife and the many happy years of their marriage. He concluded, "If I were joining a church today, I would join your church."[10] Quite an admission from a man who, like other government officials, had authorized "watching" Elder Monson travel in and out of their country for years.

These government leaders were not used to their rules being honored by religions. The uniqueness was, as Elder Russell M. Nelson would later call it, "disarming."[11]

Friday, October 28, 1988, was an enormously significant day in the history of the Church in East Germany. President Monson, Elder Nelson, and other Church leaders were invited to make an official state visit to the halls of government of the German Democratic Republic. It was a meeting for which the Church representatives were well prepared.

They sat at a huge round table with one of the most feared leaders of the Communist world, Erich Honecker, general secretary for the entire German Democratic Republic, the head of state since 1960.[12] Besides President Monson and Elder Nelson, the Church delegation included Elder Hans B. Ringger, President Henry Burkhardt, stake president Frank Apel, Manfred Schütze, and interpreter Wilfred Möller. Herr Honecker had his deputies in his company, including Kurt Löffler. Again they showed their respect for the Church members by serving only orange juice and water.

President Monson presented Herr Honecker a statue entitled "First Steps," which depicts a mother bending over and steadying her child as the child walks to its father. Herr Honecker seemed particularly pleased with this gift and emphasized that his people also advocated the strength of the family. In his welcome, Herr Honecker explained that he had observed Elder Monson and the Church's activities for many years and had seen that the Church taught its members to obey and sustain the law of the land, that it emphasized the family, and that Church members were ideal citizens. He then gave Elder Monson the floor to present the matters previously submitted. (The early submittal of any request to the government leaders was customary so that the leaders would not be surprised.)

In a declaration at the meeting, President Monson said: "The members in many lands are observing this meeting with great joy and hope, especially all those among us who come from German stock." He continued, "We live in a time when it is imperative that men and women live together in peace and strive to protect their environment. Our Church has learned that here in your country we share common points of view in many of these basic goals, which in turn have led to trust-filled, uplifting cooperation. This is another reason that this development is being watched with great interest throughout the world." Thanking Herr Honecker for the cooperation and trust between the Church in the GDR and civic officials on every level, he continued, "From experience in many lands, we know that this is not to be taken for granted, but is rather the result of a calibrated governmental religious policy, as well as the efforts of the Church leadership, which makes every effort to notice common points and build on them.

"As a church we are not politically active, and we abstain from every attempt at political influence. Nevertheless, we encourage our members to do their utmost to assist in the development of the government under which they live and to promote a joining and mutually beneficial existence with their fellow men and women."[13]

In response, Kurt Löffler described the heartfelt meeting as one "of complete agreement on the basic ideology of life":

"We and your church are dependent upon great human ideals. These include the protection of life . . . the surety of peace . . . good and honest work . . . the strengthening of homeland . . . freedom of family . . . raising children. These will be important to society in the future."[14]

Clearly the government leaders were aware of and grateful for how the Saints had lived their lives.

President Monson explained that the Church had been established in the German Democratic Republic for many years prior to World War II. He emphasized that Germany had been one of the "most productive areas" for missionary activities in the entire world but that now the membership base was barely holding steady. He gratefully acknowledged the government's permission to build the Freiberg Temple and chapels and then described the open houses held at the buildings, indicating that large numbers of people had stood in line for lengthy periods of time to see the buildings and to inquire concerning the Church. (President Monson later learned that had the government expected such a dramatic response from the populace, they never would have allowed the Church building program to go forward.)

He then sought permission to recommence the work of full-time proselyting missionaries in the German Democratic Republic. He explained that these missionaries would come from other nations. Experience had shown that when they returned to their homes, they would become advocates of the ideals of those people with whom they had worked for two years. He illustrated his point by telling of the Argentinean ambassador who, while touring Brigham Young University, met with two hundred missionaries who had served in Argentina and who he recognized as having a great love for his country and his people.

With boldness, President Monson next asked permission for young men and women who lived in the German Democratic Republic to receive mission calls to serve elsewhere in the world, explaining that this would be a broadening benefit both for the people with whom they labored and for the young missionaries themselves.[15] Permission was being asked from a government that still severely restricted the travel of its citizens to non-Communist countries.

The issue of missionaries was resolved quickly. "Permission granted," said Herr Honecker, both for missionaries from other nations to enter the German Democratic Republic and for missionaries from the German Democratic Republic to serve outside the country.

For the next thirty minutes Herr Honecker responded, describing the brief forty-year history of the German Democratic Republic and the remarkable strides made in reconstruction following the devastation of World War II. He then agreed to the request for the youth of the Church to meet together in conferences, using state facilities if necessary, explaining that he "trusted" and "admired" them.

Elder Monson called the meeting with Erich Honecker "one of the historic days of his ministry to the Saints beyond the Iron Curtain." It was one he would "ever remember." He treasures Chairman Honecker's comment as they sat in session: "We have known you through your many visits in the past, and we trust you."[16]

On March 30, 1989, eight experienced elders chosen from the five German-speaking missions then in Europe crossed the border into East Germany; they were the first full-time missionaries coming from outside the country in fifty years. One missionary described crossing the border into the GDR to his family in a letter: "Our hearts pounded with excitement as the green-suited guards stamped our passports. The Lord was truly with us. The guards' hearts were softened. They did not open a single suitcase. No bags were checked."[17]

The president of the new Germany Dresden Mission, Wolfgang Paul, assigned the newly arrived missionaries to East Berlin, Dresden, Leipzig, and Zwickau.[18] Eventually more missionaries were added. Their success was immediate. In the next eighteen months, more than 1,100 converts were baptized members of The Church of Jesus Christ of Latter-day Saints. One missionary wrote home to his parents, "This place is door-to-door heaven. Four out of five people invite us in and want to make an appointment."[19]

Elder William Powley, one of the first missionaries in the GDR, wrote to his family, "Indeed the prophecy of Thomas S. Monson, which he gave in this land in 1975, is being fulfilled."[20]

Just two months later, May 28, 1989, ten missionaries from the German Democratic Republic arrived at the Missionary Training Center in Provo, Utah; they were the first from their country to serve abroad. Among them was Tobias Burkhardt, Henry's son. Tobias was the young deacon who had cared for the grave of missionary Joseph A. Ott.[21] His call was to the Salt Lake City Mission. The First Presidency—President Ezra Taft Benson, President Gordon B. Hinckley, and President Thomas S. Monson—met personally with the ten East German missionaries, bore their testimonies to them, and invoked "the blessings of Heavenly Father upon them in their missionary assignments."[22] The government had put no restrictions on where the missionaries might serve, commenting to President Monson, "You may send them anywhere you like." They were assigned to England, the United States, Canada, Argentina, and Chile.[23]

When the ten missionaries left their country, State Secretary for Religious Affairs Löffler sponsored a luncheon in their honor. These young men were pioneers, fitting the definition of a pioneer so oft quoted by President Monson: "One who goes before, showing others the way to follow."

That summer of 1989, East German Latter-day Saint youth were allowed by the government for the first time to attend a youth conference in West Germany. From July 27 to August 4, young men and women from both Germanys met as one; no other group of any kind had ever been allowed to bring busloads of young people across the border to join with their peers in the free West.

By early November of that year, 1989, unrest was erupting across Eastern Europe. Hungary opened its borders, and an avalanche of cooped-up Germans poured out. Large crowds took trains or automobiles or walked from East Germany to Hungary. They did not intend to come back. From Hungary they made their way to the West and freedom. Others used a route through Austria, with no protest from the governments that welcomed them. Marches in Poland and Hungary were flashed on television screens around the world as the people of many of the Eastern European nations pushed for freedom.[24]

Change came so fast that it was almost unfathomable. Herr Honecker was forced to resign from office, and many of his cabinet went with him. President Monson watched the drama with great interest. He knew the people, the places, and the hearts of those who longed for the opportunity to live where they wished without the heavy hand of Communism upon them. His journal entries at the time are telling:

Thursday, November 9, 1989. "There is a demand for the Berlin Wall separating East from West to come down. . . . Interestingly, we had received notification privately through Herr Löffler and Herr Behncke of the Ministry of Religion that Chairman Honecker would step down this week."

Sunday, November 12, 1989. "The Berlin Wall is indeed crumbling. . . . The prognosis is that the border will be opened and the repressive wall become less and less of a factor of separation. How will this affect the Church? I really believe no one knows at this point. . . . One thing is certain. The strong grip of Communism in these Eastern European countries is slipping as the people yearn for freedom and independence."[25]

The wall did come down, both physically and figuratively. No longer were the citizens of the German Democratic Republic, Poland, Hungary, and Romania sequestered from the world of nations. Months later, on March 16, 1990, KBYU interviewed President Monson about the massive changes in the Eastern Bloc countries. "The vacuum that now exists will provide for good leadership or despotic leadership," he said, concluding, "Let us hope that, step by step, democracy may come to these nations and that good leaders will emerge."[26]

Historians have credited churches in East Germany with helping bring down the government. Groups of dissatisfied citizens met in churches of many denominations, where individuals expressed their frustrations, their fears, and their hopes for the future. Many of the faithful marched on government halls; they demanded that government officials be accountable.[27] One observer of the collapse noted: "The church proved itself capable of serving as a mouthpiece for those who could not speak."[28]

At the Church's invitation, Gunther Behncke, still serving as assistant secretary of religious affairs for East Germany, attended general conference in Salt Lake City in early April 1990. Long before the collapse of the German Democratic Republic government, the Church also had invited Herr Kurt Löffler and his wife to visit Salt Lake. They were unable to come at that time, but the offer remained open. Herr Behncke had been instrumental in the Church's building program, particularly with the temple, and in assisting LDS Church leaders in opening the country and its youth to full-time missionary opportunities. President Monson reminded him that he had mentioned, "If I were going to become a member of any church, I do believe I would seriously give thought to becoming a member of your church." Herr Behncke was surprised that President Monson remembered the comment. He obviously didn't know President Monson very well.

Herr Behncke met with the First Presidency and listened attentively as President Benson told of his own service in war-torn Europe dispensing substantial amounts of welfare commodities. Herr Behncke also spoke to a group at the Monson home. In other gatherings, Herr Behncke spoke of his country's need to emerge from Communism and look to the West. Under a new regime, although freedom and access to the West might be assured, he worried that many might suffer, deprived of the basic necessities of life. President Monson commented that Herr Behncke "left us with no illusion that the pathway of the East Germans would be easy."[29]

President Monson was curious about the changes to the country he knew so well. On May 31, 1990, he and Frances flew to Berlin to "see the remnants of the Berlin Wall." To their surprise, in most parts of this once-divided city, the wall was already gone. At the famous Brandenburg Gate, near where he had queued up so many times to pass through Checkpoint Charlie, "there was not even a trace of the wall."[30] Taking a cruise along a river, he noticed an East German patrol boat making its last rounds. It was the end of an era as the two Germanys moved toward reconciliation. On October 3, 1990, the two governments merged into one.

By the time the wall came down in November 1989, the Church had a solid base in Eastern Europe. Now it moved quickly to establish its presence in the countries once closed to religious activity, approving plans for a new mission home in Hungary as well as one in East Berlin.

On October 21, 1990, President Monson returned to Berlin to help reorganize the Church units in that part of Europe. Although he had made that journey to Berlin dozens of times over the past twenty-two years, this time what awaited him was a culmination of all those visits. A robust corps of priesthood leaders from the Berlin, Leipzig, and Dresden stakes set the tone for the two days of Church meetings. "The Spirit," President Monson observed, "was absolutely of the highest inspirational quality." The Eastern brethren had not met with their friends or family from the West for thirty years, and emotions were high. President Monson noticed that the West Berliners were "better dressed and had nicer automobiles" than those from the East. But members from "Leipzig and Dresden, if anything, had greater faith."[31]

In the Saturday evening session, Sister Dantzel Nelson and Sister Frances Monson spoke, as did regional representatives Dieter Berndt and Johann Wondra. Following that meeting, a sister from East Germany handed President Monson a note of gratitude. She related how her husband had been baptized, thanks to the missionaries in her area, and how her son had been called on a full-time mission to California. She explained how the mission call was a fulfillment of Elder Monson's prophecy.

"My son was nine years old at the time you met him in Dresden," she wrote. "He and I were sitting there with grateful hearts. We were happy to have good seats. You, dear Brother Monson, gave a fine message and made our hearts feel good. You kept looking at my son, Thomas, and you smiled and said, 'Here in front of me is sitting a young man with blond hair and brown eyes named Tom. He will serve a mission one day.' . . . He was often discouraged and sad in life because he was so very short of stature, but we knew what Heavenly Father had in store for him. Now he is worthy to go on a mission—the fulfillment of his greatest wish."[32]

In the Sunday morning meeting, 2,438 members filled the International Congress Center in Berlin. In true German fashion, a "splendid choir" sang the hymns of Zion "with all their hearts." Not surprisingly, Herr Behncke, former assistant secretary of religious affairs, sat with his wife on the front row and sang with the congregation.

Elder Hans B. Ringger, whom President Monson describes as "one of the great moving forces in the expansion of the work in Europe," presented the realignment of stakes, consolidating East and West Berlin into one stake, the Berlin stake, and adjusting the boundaries of the Dresden and Leipzig stakes as well.

Reminiscent of a previous conference in East Germany, a children's chorus assembled at the front, singing "I Am a Child of God." Those from the American servicemen's units sang one verse in English, the German children sang the next in their native language, and the final verse was sung by all of them in German. President Monson appreciated that simple expression of God's children setting the tone for the whole meeting.

Speakers included each of the stake presidents, men trained under the hand of President Monson: President Schütze from Leipzig; President Apel from Dresden, who would later serve as president of the Freiberg Temple; President Grünewald from Berlin. President Burkhardt, then president of the Freiberg Temple, also gave remarks. Elder Russell M. Nelson and President Monson concluded the session.

These were sweet moments for President Monson. He reminded the congregation of his 1968 visit to Görlitz, the deprivation of the people, and their resolute conviction. "The gospel flourished through their faith and their reliance upon the Lord and upon one another," he said. "Almost without notice, and little by little," the promised blessings came.[33] The first patriarchal blessings were provided by Percy K. Fetzer, followed by Hans B. Ringger and then Walter Krause.

President Monson told of blessing the land and of having the Lord guide him throughout the years. This was a sweet and tender moment in the ministry of this Apostle whose service had spanned the world but whose heart had stayed with a ragtag band of believers behind a wall of political oppression. He could not describe the joy he had felt "over the last twenty-two years in playing a part in the Lord's plans for His Saints." And he ascribed "all honor and glory to Him" who had guided the efforts of so many.[34]

The conference marked the conclusion of President Monson's official work in the area. He acknowledged that by having stayed close to the work in Germany for this extended period—very unusual in the pattern of assignments among the Quorum of the Twelve—he "was able to establish the continuity which developed trust on the part of government officials and resulted in our having missionary work permitted in the nation." He ascribed that to be "the great breakthrough."[35] Other blessings followed.

The Spirit of the Lord filled the meetings. As the choir concluded with "Auf Wiedersehen, auf Wiedersehen," which is sung in many nations as "God Be with You Till We Meet Again," President Monson looked over the crowd, tears flowing freely. He had begun his service in Germany as the junior member of the Quorum of the Twelve Apostles. Now, as a member of the First Presidency, he counted this conference as "one of the most spiritually satisfying weekends of my life."[36]

Of his personal ministry in this part of the world, he concluded, "I am happy to have been a part of this most significant saga in the history of the Church in Germany."[37]

"I have learned from my experience," President Monson expressed in his journal, "that man's extremity is but God's opportunity. I am a living witness of how the hand of the Lord has been made manifest in watching over the members of the Church in what once were Communist-ruled countries."[38]

In 1994, President Monson again visited Leipzig, flying into the area where at one time access was possible only by automobile.

This time, there were no government troops, no one watching, no throngs of soldiers with guns. He spoke at the Leipzig stake conference in a dedicated, Church-constructed building and asked that the congregation sing the song from his first visit to the old German Democratic Republic, "If the Way Be Full of Trial, Weary Not." He asked all those who had been in attendance when he had first spoken to raise a hand. He was surprised at how many had come into the Church or had been born during the intervening years. But the stalwarts who had weathered those early years were still on hand.

In Leipzig, to the 945 in attendance in the stake center he had dedicated, he pointed out how they had been the recipients of the guiding hand of the Lord, how by putting their confidence in Heavenly Father and keeping His commandments, they had been blessed in accordance with the prayer he had offered in their behalf. Truly, step-by-step, they had received every blessing available to any member of the Church, anywhere. "All in all," he said, "the Lord opened His basket literally and bestowed upon them, beyond their finest and dearest expectations, His abundant blessings."[39]

President Monson spoke with the missionaries in both Dresden and Leipzig. In Leipzig he noticed a large young man on the front row. He had each one of the missionaries introduce himself, and he said to the one he had noticed, "You're a large man. I'd hate to guard you on the basketball court." He noted that the missionary had a fine suit, which fit him very well. He later learned that it was one of the suits he had given Brother Adler, who had in turn given it to the missionary, who did not have adequate clothing for his mission.

In subsequent meetings in Dresden and Leipzig, President Monson met others with whom he had generously shared his clothing, a stick of gum, or other possessions. Following a return visit to the grave of Joseph Ott, he asked the members to continue to care for the site. He reminisced about the evening years before when, with a flashlight in hand and rain falling furiously, he had been shown to the grave for the first time and learned that it was Henry and Inge's son Tobias who had cared for the little plot,

341

making it presentable and befitting a servant of God. He thought it appropriate that Tobias had been among the first group of missionaries called to leave the German Democratic Republic to serve in other countries.

He also took some solitary time to visit the outcropping above the Elbe River where he had dedicated the land years before. In that holy spot, he meditated and thanked God for His watchful care of the German people. "The presence of the Lord was very near. It was quiet. The surroundings were beautiful, with no one to intrude or disturb. I looked heavenward as I expressed my thanks aloud in the simple prayer and received a spiritual confirmation that the prayer had been heard and the gratitude had been accepted."[40]

In reflecting upon the German Democratic Republic, President Monson is drawn to the words of Rudyard Kipling:

> *The tumult and the shouting dies;*
> *The captains and the kings depart.*
> *Still stands thine ancient sacrifice,*
> *An humble and a contrite heart.*
> *Lord God of Hosts, be with us yet,*
> *Lest we forget, lest we forget.*[41]

President Monson added his book *Faith Rewarded: A Personal Account of the Prophetic Promises to the East German Saints* to other artifacts placed in the cornerstone time capsule of the newly constructed Church History Library in Salt Lake City on March 25, 2009. He could have chosen any one of his other books, but most precious to him was this account of his years crossing the Atlantic to minister to the members behind the Iron Curtain.

The most significant pages of the history of the German Democratic Republic were not written when the Berlin Wall came down. They were written years before—in the humble homes and hearts of a believing people, in a dilapidated warehouse in Görlitz, in a clearing above the Elbe River, in the quiet little town of Freiberg that hosted 90,000 people for an open house prior to the dedication of the Freiberg Temple. Once dedicated, the temple's influence for good upon an entire nation whose leaders tried to dismiss God, His people, and His ways was without equal. The totalitarian state was doomed; the writing of its demise was . . . on the wall.

22

THE WORK GOES FORWARD

There is no show in him. Most folks know where the photographers are in the room. He walks into a room full of cameras and he never knows they are there. Most folks in public life see themselves as powerful; he doesn't even look for the cameras in the room. It doesn't cross his mind. He is just real.

PRESIDENT HENRY B. EYRING
First Counselor in the First Presidency

ELDER MONSON WAS KNEELING IN prayer with a stake presidency in Hyrum, Utah, prior to their conference on Sunday, January 18, 1970, when the counselor petitioned the Lord to comfort Sister McKay at the death of her husband, President David O. McKay. This was the first Elder Monson had heard of it. Joseph Anderson, secretary to the First Presidency, finally reached him an hour later and confirmed that President McKay had died at six o'clock that morning.

"I was [President McKay's] last appointee to the Council," Elder Monson recalled, "and I shall ever remember and treasure the association."[1] President McKay left a remarkable legacy of leadership with those he called to the Quorum of the Twelve: Marion G. Romney, LeGrand Richards, Adam S. Bennion, Richard L. Evans, George Q. Morris, Hugh B. Brown, Howard W. Hunter, Gordon B. Hinckley, Nathan Eldon Tanner, and Thomas S. Monson. Three of them eventually were called of God as Church President; an additional three served as counselors in the First

344

Presidency. President Monson looked up to those he described as fourteen "exceptional men" senior to him in the Twelve and the First Presidency. He would see each of them return home, one by one.

President McKay was ill for the last few years of his life. Eventually he was able to attend temple meetings with the General Authorities only intermittently, and he reached a point where he watched sessions of general conference on television from his apartment in the Hotel Utah next door to the Church Administration Building. Just six months before President McKay's death, Elder Monson recorded: "All of us watch the door each Thursday at 10:00 A.M. to see if by chance President McKay may attend the meeting. We miss him so much. He has not met with us in the temple since last autumn, although we did meet with him in his apartment just prior to Christmas."[2]

President McKay, who was ninety-six years old when he passed away, "was universally loved by Church members and nonmembers alike."[3] "When one is in the presence of President McKay, he always feels uplifted and leaves the interview a better man," Elder Monson said of his mentor and friend.[4] When Elder Monson was born in 1927, President McKay had already been an Apostle for twenty-one years. Under his leadership, the Church had grown from approximately one million members to three million. When President McKay was sustained as President of the Church, there were 180 stakes; on the day he died, the landmark 500th stake was organized in Reno, Nevada.

President McKay's body lay in state for three days in the foyer of the Church Administration Building, where mourners filed past in respectful silence. Elder Monson took Tom, Clark, and Ann to pass by the casket of the prophet who had indeed changed the Monson family's lives forever.

At the funeral on Thursday, January 22, 1970, President Joseph Fielding Smith, who in just days would feel the mantle on his shoulders, spoke of the role of a prophet: "No man of himself can lead this church. It is the Church of the Lord Jesus Christ; he is at the head. The Church bears his name, has his priesthood, administers his gospel, preaches his doctrine and does his work."[5]

The next day, Friday, the Apostles gathered in the temple and took their seats in order of seniority. President Smith, the presiding authority as President of the Quorum of the Twelve, opened the meeting, calling upon the junior member of the Twelve, Elder Monson, to express his innermost feelings regarding the reorganization of the First Presidency. Elder Monson had not expected the invitation to speak, at least not first. This was his initial experience watching the guiding hand of the Lord in selecting the new President.

Elder Monson would experience such a scenario five more times before the prophetic mantle would fall on his own shoulders. "In the passing of each President," taught Elder Harold B. Lee, who had in his nearly thirty years as an Apostle seen the deaths of President Heber J. Grant, President George Albert Smith, and now President David O. McKay, "the records of their lives and their works, their words, and their ministries are fortunately lesson books, documented in the written history of the Church and in the memories of those who have followed after them."[6]

Elder Monson had worked with President Joseph Fielding Smith on manuscripts of several books to be published. President Smith had called then-Bishop Monson to serve in a stake presidency. As he looked at the august leader, Elder Monson remembered that singular moment when President Smith, acting under the direction of President McKay, had ordained him an Apostle.

At ninety-three, President Smith was the oldest man to be called as President of the Church in the 140 years since the Church's organization at Fayette, New York. The seniority system established by God and followed from the time of the Prophet Joseph was not in question. The Lord's plan is that men called as Apostles will age in office, as had President McKay. Since Brigham Young was sustained in 1847, the President of the Church has been—by divine design—the senior Apostle, schooled in the ways of the Lord through years of experience in Church administration, uniquely qualified to commune with the Lord on behalf of His children. The vibrancy, skill, and leadership of the Quorum of the Twelve, their collective wisdom and experience, would provide any needed support to the President.

After each member of the Twelve had spoken, Elder Harold B. Lee nominated Joseph Fielding Smith as the prophet, seer, and revelator, the President of the Church, and the trustee in trust for the Church. Elder Spencer W. Kimball seconded the nomination, and it was unanimously approved.

President Smith selected as his counselors Elder Harold B. Lee, who would, by seniority, be President of the Quorum of the Twelve Apostles, and Elder Nathan Eldon Tanner, who had served with President McKay as Second Counselor. Elder Hugh B. Brown, former member of the First Presidency under President McKay, returned to his position as a member of the Quorum of the Twelve. "This is as it should be," Elder Brown said. "I am happy with the decision." The reorganization could not have been easy for him. But Elder Monson noted that Elder Brown, with great dignity, "showed his sterling character and true worth."[7] Elder Spencer W. Kimball was named Acting President of the Quorum of the Twelve. Elders Alvin R. Dyer and Thorpe B. Isaacson, who had also been serving as counselors to President McKay, returned to their positions as Assistants to the Twelve.

For Elder Monson, "it was a particularly humbling experience" to place his hands along with the others upon the head of the new President of the Church as he was ordained and set apart by President Lee. Elder Monson recognized the humility of the new President: "I can truly say that, in my judgment, President Smith never coveted the position of President of the Church. He was most content to honor and sustain President David O. McKay in this position. His humility has been a lesson to all of us."[8] With both President Lee and President Tanner in supporting roles to President Smith, Elder Monson expected that "the work will go forward at an accelerated pace."[9]

At the solemn assembly in the Tabernacle on April 6, 1970, the membership of the Church sustained President Joseph Fielding Smith. When President Lee called for the patriarchs to stand and sustain Joseph Fielding Smith as prophet, seer, and revelator and President of the Church, Elder Monson surveyed the righteous leaders, their hands to the square, and observed one stump with a hook attached held high. Elder Monson knew that this was James Womack, and he knew of Brother Womack's remarkable life. Seriously injured in World War II, handicapped with the loss of both hands and a good portion of one arm, this good brother had nonetheless completed law school and was well respected in his field. He was beloved in his ward and stake congregation. But when President Spencer W. Kimball felt impressed to call him as a patriarch, the man questioned, "How can I lay hands upon someone's head and provide a blessing when I have no hands?" President Kimball sat down in a chair in front of Brother Womack and asked him to place his "stumps" on his head. "I can reach you," the man cried out with joy. "I can reach you." When Brother Womack's name was presented the next morning for sustaining as a patriarch, everyone's hands went high into the air. The new patriarch, though handicapped in the sight of men, was not handicapped in the sight of God.[10]

At this conference in April 1970, Elder Kimball, Acting President of the Quorum of the Twelve, said of President Smith what years later could be said of President Monson as well: "When he was a very young man, he was called of the Lord, through the then living prophet, to be an apostle—member of the Quorum—and was given the precious, vital keys to hold in suspension pending a time when he might become the senior apostle and the President."[11]

Elder Boyd K. Packer, an Assistant to the Twelve, was called as the new Apostle. Elder Monson had been the junior member of the Twelve for more than seven years, the second longest in history; only Elder John A. Widtsoe had sat in the last chair longer. Elder Packer was not a new face to Church administration; he had been serving as an Assistant to the Twelve since 1961. For the next fifteen years, until Elder Monson was called to the First Presidency, the two sat next to each other. President Packer describes Elder Monson as "extraordinary in an ordinary and extra special way, a spiritual way."[12]

Both of those Apostles were shaped by the Depression—Elder Monson on the west side of Salt Lake City and Elder Packer in

Brigham City to the north. Both kept pigeons; President Monson still does. "Once in a while he will bring a pair of pigeons out to my grandchildren," President Packer says with a smile. Both came to Church service young. "We worked together all those years," President Packer observes. "We've kind of grown up together, grown old together."[13] He remembers with a chuckle the Saturday morning near the end of a conference session when Elder Monson nudged him and said, with a note of longing, "In ten minutes duck hunting season opens."[14]

Elder Monson continued to supervise the Leadership Training Committee, which identified a large number of less-active members, mostly men who held no priesthood, senior members of the Aaronic Priesthood, and less-active elders. The problem would be on his mind for years, and at every opportunity he would emphasize the critical importance of bringing back those who were lost.

He didn't just teach about it; he worked at it. One example is a man who was at one time proprietor of a Husky gas station near President Monson's home. "Each time I purchased gas, I also reminded Ray of his responsibility to go to the temple of the Lord," President Monson said. Ray's brother, a bishop, told President Monson, "Please don't fail to buy gasoline from Ray, as your counsel to him on these occasions is bringing him ever closer to the temple."[15] Ray not only made it to the temple, he eventually became a temple worker.

Another of Elder Monson's assignments was to chair the Adult Correlation Committee. Now that committee was turning its attention to the various periodicals and publications the Church was producing. The auxiliaries had developed their own publications to serve their particular needs and reflect their individual focus. At general conference in 1970, Elder Monson announced in general priesthood meeting the creation of a new adult magazine, the *Ensign,* to replace three well-known publications: the *Improvement Era,* the *Relief Society Magazine,* and the *Instructor.* The *Ensign* would be written for the adults of the Church, that they "might be more adequately prepared to be examples to their children and to the world." Elder Monson encouraged, "Subscribe to it. Read its contents. Apply in your lives its lessons [that you might] be as an ensign, even the light of the world, a city of righteousness set on an hill that cannot be hid." He described its "initial press run" as over 325,000 copies.[16]

In the same message, Elder Monson also introduced the new Teacher Development Program, which had the potential "to improve the quality of teaching throughout the Church." Under the direction of the President of the Church, he, with others, had created the new program, which was not "restricted to Sunday School" but reached across all lines to Primary, MIA, Relief Society, and the quorums of the priesthood. The role of teaching weighed heavily on the minds of the First Presidency. President Smith had identified that "teaching members of the Church to keep the commandments of God" was their "greatest challenge." Elder Monson made clear the purpose of the new priesthood-sponsored, Churchwide emphasis: "The aim is to inspire the individual to think about, feel about, and then do something about living gospel principles."

Each member will "likely have an opportunity to become a teacher," he said. "There is no privilege more noble, no task so rewarding." He spoke of the meridian of time, when "in Galilee there taught a master teacher, even Jesus Christ the Lord. He left his footprints in the sands of the seashore, but left His teaching principles in the hearts and in the lives of all whom He taught."[17]

A heavy agenda greeted the Quorum of the Twelve and the First Presidency on January 13, 1971, and Elder Monson had responsibility for twelve of the twenty-six items. President Lee announced a change in Elder Monson's assignment from chairing the Adult Correlation Committee to chairing the Youth and Young Adult Correlation Committee. Elder Monson had developed a close association with members of the Adult Correlation Committee. In a letter expressing their gratitude for his superior leadership, the committee members[18] wrote:

"Among many great qualities which characterize you, may we mention three: 1) Your devotion to the Lord. We realize His picture in your office is a symbol of that devotion. 2) Your total concern for having the influence of the Holy Ghost in your life. We are deeply impressed with your spiritual sensitivity. 3) Your concern for every child of our Heavenly Father. We have noted many manifestations of this concern. . . . May we say: 'Though we will not feel the touch of your hand, we will feel the touch of your soul, eternally.'"[19]

In shifting Elder Monson's assignment, President Lee expressed confidence in his ability to do exactly as he had done in helping put the Adult Correlation Committee on track. He now had responsibility for the entire youth curriculum, including seminaries and institutes, the LDS Student Association, and the M Men and Gleaner programs.

"Prior to this meeting I didn't see how a man could be busier than was I," Elder Monson lamented, "but now I suppose with this added responsibility I will learn that it is possible to assume greater responsibility and yet work it into one's schedule."[20]

Nearly every weekend, Elder Monson was off to a stake reorganization or regular quarterly conference. If he saw a familiar face in the congregation—Charlie Renshaw, his boyhood chum, now living in California's Concord Stake, was one—he would call that person up to bear testimony. He divided stakes from Tacoma, Washington, to Leicester, England, where on one occasion he stayed in the home of the stake president and had his first home-cooked meal in more than forty days. He had been on the road that long. For a stake reorganization, he would perform as many as thirty ordinations or settings apart following the meetings—this after having interviewed up to fifty people regarding the reorganization.

When he divided the Chesapeake Stake, he came home absolutely exhausted. "I don't know when I have had a heavier day of ordinations, settings apart, and otherwise putting together a new unit of the Church," he recorded.[21] Those involved commented to him that "their reorganization went more smoothly and diplomatically than any in which they had previously participated." One couple wrote President Kimball "a note of praise for Apostle Monson. He was here this past weekend to split our stake and did so with great efficiency and inspiration." Passing the note along to Elder Monson, President Kimball penned, in a very recognizable hand, "Excellent, Tom!! SWK."[22]

At stake conferences, particularly at reorganizations, Elder Monson would pay tribute to those who had served faithfully in previous years. Francis Winters in the Star Valley Stake in Afton, Wyoming, is a good example. New officers had been named and sustained that April day in 1970, when Elder Monson asked President Winters, who had served as stake president for twenty-three years, to come to the pulpit and stand by him. He asked everyone in the congregation who had been named, confirmed, interviewed, called to a position, or blessed by President Winters to stand. "It appeared as though the entire congregation stood. I don't know when I have been more impressed with the sweet spirit of humility and service which a person could possess as I was with President Winters. The inspiration directed that he be ordained a patriarch, which proposition was presented to the congregation and enthusiastically received."[23]

When Elder Monson reorganized the Chicago South Stake in September 1970, he met for the first time Dallin H. Oaks, who had been a counselor in the stake presidency for seven years. Brother Oaks was thirty-eight years old. "I was extremely impressed at [Elder Monson's] intelligence, energy, insight, and decisiveness," Elder Oaks recalls, as he describes being interviewed by Elder Monson. "Please understand," he said to Elder Monson as he thought of his young family, the hour-long commute to the stake offices, and the separation from his home ward, "I have no aspirations to continue in this stake presidency in any capacity. I'd love to serve in a bishopric sometime." Elder Monson looked at him intently and said, "Don't count on it." Brother Oaks was called to be first counselor in the new stake presidency.[24]

The following May, when Elder Monson participated as a member of the BYU Board of Trustees in selecting a new university president, he spoke highly of academic leader Dallin H. Oaks, University of Chicago law professor. After the inaugural of President Oaks as the eighth president of BYU on November 12, 1971, Elder Monson wrote, "I am very impressed with this splendid young man and know that his appointment was made under the inspiration of the Holy Spirit."[25]

For Elder Monson, one of the responsibilities that particularly "stirred his soul" was selecting new patriarchs. His journal is filled with accounts of the inspiration that came as he sought to find a patriarch, the Spirit's promptings most often pointing to one man who would speak the words of God for those seeking a patriarchal blessing. "In no other area does one feel greater inspiration than in the naming of a patriarch," he has expressed repeatedly.[26]

Sometimes he would know that a man was to be called as a patriarch when he met him in the hall or walked past him down the aisle of the chapel. Sometimes he would look over the congregation and the patriarch would be "shown" to him, or he would glance across the room and know a certain individual was the one whom the Lord had prepared. On one occasion he was surprised to find sitting in the congregation in a San Diego, California, stake a man who he knew had been in the Church Building Department in Australia. "As I walked down the aisle after the Saturday evening session and took him by the hand, I had the definite impression that he was to be the patriarch," he later wrote.[27]

At a stake division in Hyrum, Utah, he received from the leadership the names of two men, either of whom they felt could serve as a patriarch for the newly created stake. Elder Monson felt impressed to select the younger of the two men, Woodrow Rasmussen, who was seventy-three years old, and advised him of his call. While sitting on the stand Sunday morning, he observed the other candidate, Samuel Bryson Cook, who was eighty years of age and somewhat impaired in his walking. "As I looked at him and heard him offer the invocation," Elder Monson said later, "I knew that he too should be a patriarch. I stepped to the pulpit and read the information relative to the division, had the new officers sustained, and then advised the congregation, 'There are two patriarchs for you to sustain today. One of the men is aware of his calling and in the other instance, this will be the first notification.'" The congregation raised their hands enthusiastically for both, and as Elder Monson took his seat, he saw that Samuel Cook was weeping tears of gratitude. "I feel confident," Elder Monson said, "that he was foreordained to fill the position."[28]

As the Church increased in numbers, the calling of patriarchs by the Apostles was growing unwieldy. A new procedure was

approved in February 1981 that authorized stake presidents to recommend names of prospective stake patriarchs for consideration
by the Quorum of the Twelve Apostles. Once approved, those patriarchs were ordained and set apart by stake presidents.

At a special training meeting, Elder Monson felt moved by the
Spirit, as he discussed the new procedure for calling patriarchs,
to relate personal experiences from his life. He had come to the
meeting with laryngitis, but as he spoke, his voice got stronger.
Following the meeting, Elder M. Russell Ballard sent him a note:
"We had an in-depth blessing this morning, and those of us who
were present will never be the same. You [Elder Monson] have
always been a giant of a man in my eyes, and this morning I saw in
you a future President like David O. McKay." Elder Monson noted,
"Tears came easily to the Brethren in the room, and I realized
that we had been beneficiaries of the Holy Spirit's guidance."[29]

Such guidance took him to the bedside of a young man,
Robert Williams, who "subsequently died an agonizing death
from lung cancer." A high priest in Robert's ward had rescued
him from a life of inactivity and helped him get to the temple
with his wife and small children. Elder Monson visited him right
before his passing. Robert asked, "Brother Monson, where does
my spirit go when my body dies?"

Elder Monson "groped for an answer, but then the inspiration of the Lord came." He reached for the Book of Mormon,
which literally fell open at Alma, chapter 40, where he read aloud
that "the spirits of all men, as soon as they are departed from this
mortal body, . . . are taken home to that God who gave them life.
And then it shall come to pass, that the spirits of those who are
righteous are received into a state of happiness, which is called
paradise, a state of rest, a state of peace, where they shall rest
from all their troubles and from all care, and sorrow."[30] Robert
closed his tired eyes and said, "Thank you, Brother Monson. This
is the information I've been waiting for."[31]

Elder Monson felt similarly inspired when in 1971 he put his
oldest son, Tom, on a plane for basic training as a member of the
U.S. Army Reserve. "Before he left home, I gave him a father's
blessing and felt the Spirit of the Lord present in doing so."[32]

Basic training was grueling; young Tom contracted pneumonia and was admitted to the hospital at Fort Knox. A ward member there administered to him, and his health improved, but he remained hospitalized. Elder Monson could not help but think of his own similar experience blessing his friend during his naval training. He arranged to travel to Fort Knox to see Tom and to give him a blessing as well.

That May, young Tom sent a Father's Day card; it was one his father would keep.

"At Fort Knox in training. Just turned 20. Since yesterday I am no longer a teenager. . . . The high point of my stay here, Dad, has been your visit. To receive a blessing at the hands of his father is an opportunity no one else in that hospital enjoyed. I have listened to some of the young men here talk about their families. There seems so little real love in their homes. Some of them go home on pass and stay with friends so as to avoid their parents. . . . I have thought a lot lately that I have been blessed to have been born into our family and to have you as a father to direct me in the more meaningful matters of life and to provide an example of dedication and accomplishment. . . . I love and admire you. In the next few determinant years of life, I hope I can pull out of me whatever abilities I have inherited from you."[33]

Young Tom put those abilities to good use later when he received his mission call to Italy. His brother, Clark, would later serve in New Zealand. Thus was the missionary spirit carried on in the Monson family, not only with those calls but with Elder Monson's service for more than ten years on the Missionary Executive Committee.

Speaking at mission presidents' seminars year after year, President Monson has emphasized, "Our hands are set to the plow, and there is no looking back. When the Lord appeared to His Apostles, He could have asked anything He wanted. He didn't say, 'I will be leaving you for a season. Check on home teaching.' He didn't say, 'I will be leaving you for a season. Your percentages aren't high enough.' Nor did he say, 'I will be leaving you for a season. See that you pay your tithing.' What did He say? It's from Matthew: 'Go ye therefore, and teach all nations, baptizing them in the name of the Father, and of the Son, and of the Holy Ghost: Teaching them to observe all things whatsoever I have commanded you: and, lo, I am with you alway, even unto the end of the world.' That's a wonderful instruction from the Lord to His Apostles. It's a proper instruction from His Apostles to each of you."[34]

One year at the mission presidents' seminar, President Monson invited longtime friend Sister Pearl Sudbury to stand with him at the pulpit and tell the story of her son, whose faith and prayers while serving his mission in Australia had prompted his father, a hard-core nonbeliever, to be baptized. President Monson has seen similar blessings many times. They illustrate a scripture he uses to reassure not only missionaries but also mission presidents and their wives: "Your families are well; they are in mine hands, and I will do with them as seemeth me good; for in me there is all power."[35]

At another mission presidents' seminar, he set forth a seven-step plan for productive proselyting:

1. Reports That Reveal
2. Handbooks That Help
3. Meetings That Motivate
4. Schedules That Strengthen
5. Procedures That Produce
6. Love That Lifts
7. Interviews That Inspire[36]

Elder Quentin L. Cook, who served as managing director of the Missionary Department for five years, considers President Monson to be "in a league by himself in terms of being a great missionary. I don't think there is any part of missionary work that he hasn't influenced. He has had every role in the Missionary Department during the course of his life."[37]

On a flight from San Francisco to Los Angeles one day, he observed an off-duty flight attendant reading a premiere-bound edition of *A Marvelous Work and a Wonder.* He asked her, "Are you a member of The Church of Jesus Christ of Latter-day Saints?"

She said, "No; why do you ask?" He explained that he had

printed the book she was reading and was in the same Quorum as the author.

She remarked, "I find the book most interesting. It was given to me by a friend."

Elder Monson later wrote, "She had many intelligent questions relating to the Church. She mentioned her name was Yvonne Ramirez. I recall that one of her questions was on the financing of the Church operation; another was on eternal marriage and other significant parts of the gospel. We conversed on this subject all the way to Los Angeles. As I took my leave from her to go about my activities in California, I told her that it was not simply chance that we sat next to one another on this flight, but rather the Lord's will that she might know more about His kingdom and indeed realize that He was attempting to guide and direct her. She responded willingly to my request that I have missionaries call upon her."[38] Sister Ramirez ended up joining the Church.

When Joseph Fielding Smith served as Church President, he instituted the first area conferences, large gatherings of Saints that included many stakes or mission districts. Elder Monson was part of the planning committee and participated in the first such conference, held in Manchester, England, on August 27 through 29, 1971. Elder Monson had come for this historic occasion—the first time that the President of the Church had addressed such a congregation of Saints outside general conference—from a Scout jamboree in Tokyo, with stops in Hong Kong, India, and Switzerland. He was the last of the official party to arrive and, because of the bumpy flight, felt fortunate to get there at all. Elder Packer, who had worked at his side putting the plans in place for the conference, commented, "You look like you've been through a storm." Elder Monson assured him that he had.

The speaker's stand in the Bellevue Center, a sports and entertainment arena in Manchester, had been arranged to simulate the stand in the Salt Lake Tabernacle, with red carpeting and red upholstered seats for the General Authorities. Every one of the twelve thousand seats in the arena was filled—and then some. Members came from nine stakes and seven missions to attend the general session as well as a meeting for the priesthood brethren, one for the Relief Society sisters, another for all adults, and one that Elder Monson conducted for the youth. The British Area Conference was followed by similar gatherings over the next few years in Mexico, Germany, Sweden, South America, and East Asia.

Elder Monson's message to the British Saints was one of love, a recurring theme in his talks, in his life, and in the life of the Savior. Elder Monson testified of Jesus Christ: "His was a gospel of love, not of hate; it was one of encouragement, not of finding fault or being critical. However, more than just teaching the law of love, Jesus lived that law."[39]

Drawing from one of his favorite books, *The Mansion,* by Henry Van Dyke, Elder Monson described the effects of "a life of wretched selfishness." The book tells of a wealthy man, John Weightman, who gave only "those coins which would be seen of men and honor thus accorded him." Then one night he dreamed that he visited the Celestial City, where he was given a tiny, dilapidated hut in which to live. Feeling that this was unjust, because in his own eyes he had lived a successful life, Weightman inquired of the Keeper of the Gate, "What is it that counts here?" "Only that which is truly given," the Keeper replied. "Only that good which is done for the love of doing it. Only those plans in which the welfare of others is the master thought. Only those labors in which the sacrifice is greater than the reward. Only those gifts in which the giver forgets himself."[40]

The very example calls up images of Elder Monson walking down dimly lit hallways or hospital corridors, visiting the poor, the widows, the needy, the sick. What he has learned in his many acts of mercy and love is clear: "Perhaps when we face our Maker, we will not be asked, 'How many positions did you hold,' but rather, 'How many people did you help?' One can never love the Lord until he serves Him by serving His people."[41]

On one such occasion, Elder Monson went to visit his mother in the hospital. As he got off the elevator, he was met by two women who, recognizing him, asked if he would provide their father a blessing. "My entrance on the scene," Elder Monson later wrote, "was an answer to their prayers." As he administered to their father, Abraham Godfrey, he learned that the man had known Frances's mother "for many, many years," having been an employee of the Federal Reserve Bank where she ran the cafeteria. Brother Godfrey also knew Elder Monson's father. Elder Monson counted it "a delightful experience to thus give one who knew both sides of my family a blessing for his health." As he was leaving the room, he heard someone call his name. In a bed across from Brother Godfrey lay a former member of the Sixth-Seventh Ward, Lee E. Nielsen, who had suffered a heart attack. Elder Monson "was delighted to give him a blessing."

As he went to leave, a nurse approached him in tears and asked if he had any intention of going to Primary Children's Hospital. "I told her no, but that if she had someone there whom she would like me to see, I would be happy to do so." She explained that her cousin had suffered polio many years ago and now at age eighteen was having more difficulties. Elder Monson went to Primary Children's Hospital and gave the cousin a blessing. As he was about to leave, a young man asked him if he would have time to administer to a ten-year-old girl who was suffering from what appeared to be incurable leukemia. Once again he knew that his visit at that particular moment was an answer to someone's prayer. He provided a blessing to the young girl.

"I came away from these two hospitals," he said, "realizing that our Heavenly Father is very mindful of those who suffer here in mortality and who desire, at the hands of the priesthood, a blessing."[42]

One of those suffering was Elder Richard L. Evans, a member of the Quorum of the Twelve, who in 1971 returned from foreign assignments dangerously ill. The Brethren planned a special fast and prayer for his recovery. On the designated day, Elder Monson and his son Clark were duck hunting in northern Utah. At noon Elder Monson said, "Let's kneel down right here and say a prayer. All of the members of the Quorum of the Twelve have agreed to do so right at this hour, no matter where they are in the world. We are petitioning the Lord for our dear brother Richard L. Evans." The recovery was not to be. But kneeling in the marsh with his father had a lasting impact on Clark; he cites that as one of his most cherished experiences.[43]

The Lord called Elder Evans home just a week later, on November 1, 1971. Elder Monson was in Guatemala for a mission presidents' seminar when he received the news. He left the seminar "in the capable hands of Elders Haight and Dyer"[44] and returned to Salt Lake City. En route, at the Los Angeles airport, he met Elder Marion G. Romney, who was returning from the Orient; President N. Eldon Tanner, returning from the Holy Land; and Elder Gordon B. Hinckley, returning from Germany. President Joseph Fielding Smith appointed Marvin J. Ashton to the vacancy in the Quorum of the Twelve. Elder Monson and Elder Ashton had served together on committees for years.

The Monson family were spending a few days at their Vivian Park cabin when, during the night on July 2, 1972, Elder Monson's father and brother Scott arrived unexpectedly from Salt Lake City. It was one o'clock in the morning. Because there was no phone service at the cabin, they had driven up to tell him that President Joseph Fielding Smith, tenth President of the Church, had passed away.

Within the hour, Elder Monson was on the road back to Salt Lake, knowing he would need to be in the office early to meet with the Brethren.

23

POISED FOR GROWTH

When he was in the Quorum of the Twelve, I think he was the most domi-
nant member in terms of his contributions. He was always ready for the
committees he served on; the Brethren always gave him the difficult com-
mittees, even when he was down at the bottom end of the Quorum.

ELDER L. TOM PERRY
Quorum of the Twelve Apostles

IT WAS A SPRING EVENING WHEN an attendant at a gas station in
Holladay, a suburb of Salt Lake City, glanced out his window
to see what he remembers as a green Chevy Impala pull up to a
pump. His first thought was, "He sure needs a new set of shocks."

The driver filled his car and went into the station to pay his
bill. As the young attendant counted out the change, the man
began to quiz him. The young man told the driver of the car that
he was in his senior year of high school and played ball for his
ward team. He didn't divulge that he barely qualified to play; the
requirement was attendance at just one sacrament meeting and
one priesthood meeting a month.

The man then asked the attendant what he planned after
graduation and what he wanted to do with his life. "I don't remember what I said in response until he asked if I was a Latter-day
Saint. I responded that I was. He then asked if I planned to serve a
mission, to which I answered that I didn't know." The young man
didn't explain his Word of Wisdom problem or the questioning in

his heart. The driver paused and then said, "I encourage you to do so. It will be the greatest thing you could ever do at this point in your life." He then shook the attendant's hand and left.

The young man spent the rest of the evening reflecting again and again on what the stranger had said. Twenty years later he described his experience:

"The thing that would not leave me was the memory of his friendliness and the look in his eyes. It was that night I decided to throw away the cigarettes. Two months later I received my patriarchal blessing, which confirmed that I would be called to serve a mission and I would say 'yes.' But it wasn't until the next October while watching general conference that I received a bit of a shock and a testimony that God knew who I was. I don't remember who was conducting that particular session of conference, but he announced that Thomas S. Monson would be the next speaker. As [he] came to the pulpit I recognized [him] as the man at the Metro station those many months before."[1] The young man did go on to serve a mission.

How many stories there are like that, no one will ever know. But what is known is that Thomas S. Monson has rescued many a soul with his personal interest and his Christlike countenance. President Monson has always woven such acts of personal service into his life. It cannot have been easy, given the responsibilities he has carried.

At the death of President Joseph Fielding Smith, the Quorum of the Twelve met to reorganize the First Presidency. It was a sunny morning, indicative of the light that would soon pour down upon the Apostles of the Lord Jesus Christ.

For Elder Monson, "It was a day of spiritual rejoicing." In particular he appreciated "the orderly manner which has been provided by the Lord for transition of authority within His Church as a testimony . . . to all who have a part in such significant and important matters."[2]

The Church had bidden farewell to President Smith at his funeral in the Tabernacle just the day before, July 6, 1972. Elder Monson had sat in council with President Smith, taken his guidance, listened to his prayers. "I shall ever remember him as one who prayed so beautifully that he would endure to the end and that each one of us would be true to the covenants we had made in the holy temple," Elder Monson said as he paid tribute to his friend and leader who had passed on.[3]

Three months later, at October conference, President Harold B. Lee announced that Bruce R. McConkie, an Assistant to the Twelve, would fill the vacancy in the Quorum of the Twelve. Elder McConkie, son-in-law to the recently deceased President Smith, had been serving as a General Authority since his call to the First Council of the Seventy in 1946. On October 12, 1972, the Quorum of the Twelve and First Presidency stood in a circle as President Lee ordained Bruce R. McConkie an Apostle of the Lord Jesus Christ. "It was a pleasure for me to join others of the group in placing my hands upon his head and ordaining him," Elder Monson wrote. "Likewise, most worthwhile was the solemn charge which President Lee delivered to Elder McConkie. It was as though he were speaking to each one of us, and perhaps indeed he was."[4] Also called at conference was James E. Faust, to serve as an Assistant to the Twelve. Elder Monson and Elder Faust had been friends for years; Elder Monson reached out to Elder Faust shortly after his call, "orienting him to his responsibilities as they related to the temple and other aspects of the work."[5]

Elder Monson knew President Lee as a most adept administrator in Church government, one who was thoughtful and deeply spiritual. Members of the Church expected that, at age seventy-three—the youngest man to be sustained as President of the Church in more than forty years—President Lee would lead the Church for many years.

The new President described his own soul-searching by referring to an 1853 message of Elder Orson Hyde, member of the Quorum of the Twelve: "It is invariably the case, that when an individual is ordained and appointed to lead the people, he has passed through tribulations and trials, and has proven himself before God, and before His people, that he is worthy of the situation which he holds . . . that when a person that has not been tried, that has not proved himself before God, and before His people, and before the councils of the Most High, to be worthy, he is not going to step in to lead the Church and people of God. It never has been so, but from the beginning some one that understands the Spirit and counsel of the Almighty, that knows the Church, and is known of her, is the character that will lead the Church."[6] It was an apt description, one that characterized Presidents of the Church in the past and those who would be called in the future.

Elder Monson's relationship with President Lee went far beyond that of "colleague" or even "mentor." He and President Lee were dear friends. They were of like mind, both highly organized and focused. In nearly every significant decision or juncture in Elder Monson's life, President Lee had been there. Now, he rejoiced in the opportunity to bear witness of President Lee as the prophet: "I declare that we are led by a prophet of God, even President Harold B. Lee," he told students at BYU, "a man from whom we can learn important lessons, a man who teaches all of us the beautiful lesson of humility."[7]

Throughout their service together in the Quorum of the Twelve, their association had reached beyond the walls of 47 East South Temple to the Monson home. President Lee influenced each of the Monson children for good.[8] Looking back, Elder Monson recalled, "President Lee treated everyone as though he were the father and they were a beloved son or daughter."[9]

As a teenager, Elder Monson's son Tom developed a lump on his leg that concerned family doctor Maurice J. Taylor. Often such cases were cancer; Dr. Taylor's nephew had lost his leg from the disease. Two specialists, Dr. Thomas Smart and Dr. Merrill Wilson, recommended surgery. Prior to the operation, Elder Monson asked President Lee to accompany him to the hospital to give young Tom a blessing. The two met at 5:00 P.M. outside the hospital, where President Lee spoke comforting words to an anxious father: "Elder Monson, there is no place in the world I would rather be; there's no one with whom I would rather be; there's nothing I would rather be about to do than to give a blessing to your son."

Frances joined them in the hospital room, and President Lee explained to the youth the purpose of an anointing and sealing of the anointing. He then gave young Tom a "beautiful blessing." The surgery went well; the growth was benign.[10]

President Lee visited again with young Tom when he was serving a mission in Italy. "Your boy looked wonderful," he reported to Elder Monson. "He was seated on the front row handling the recording equipment of the mission president. He introduced himself as Elder Thomas Lee Monson." Elder Monson noted with appreciation, "Parents long for this type of report."[11]

On another occasion, Elder Monson introduced daughter Ann to President Lee, and he remarked to her "that he could perceive that she was as beautiful inside as outside."[12]

When Elder Monson and son Clark—soon to be a deacon—met President Lee one day on the stairs of the Church Administration Building, the President looked into Clark's eyes and asked, "What happens when you become twelve?" Elder Monson worried that Clark might answer, "I become a Boy Scout," but he made his father proud when he declared, "I will be ordained a deacon." President Lee smiled and said simply, "God bless you, my boy."[13]

President Lee saw in Elder Monson a master orator and doctrinal teacher. He encouraged Elder Monson to publish some of his sermons in a book; he even offered to write the foreword. *Pathways to Perfection* began with President Lee's tribute to Elder Monson: "To listen to him is to be inspired. To work with him is to be uplifted; and to feel of his devotion and the strength of his conviction and powerful testimony is to know that there is no doubt but that his calling as a special witness as an apostle of the Lord, Jesus Christ, is well merited."[14]

Elder Monson was, President Lee recognized, "only in the midday of his life and service." He would continue to grow and develop from the experiences he was having in his worldwide associations. That overview would provide invaluable perspective for him as "a teacher, and a leader, and an inspirer."[15]

During his administration, President Lee faced a time of racial unrest across the United States. The Church became a target because of its position restricting those of black lineage from holding the priesthood or entering the temple. National magazines and newspapers called for change; militants demanded, "We will either integrate the Mormon Church or we will destroy it."[16]

The Church was not prepared to handle major threats and protests. For the first time in fifty years, a security guard was posted at the entrance of Church headquarters, and a modest staff of mostly night watchmen was quickly replaced with a team of more highly trained security professionals. President Lee even had a police escort when he went to the barbershop.

In a series of meetings, President Lee reflected on the damage being done to the Church's image, to national leaders who were members of the Church, and to members of the Quorum of the Twelve. "I continue to be amazed at President Lee's capacity," Elder Monson observed after one of the meetings, "and know for certain that our Heavenly Father is giving him health and strength, as well as the guidance of His Holy Spirit."[17]

During this time, what began as a study of public communications grew into a major restructuring of all Church communications. Two new departments emerged—a Department of Internal Communications and a Department of Public Communications, now known as Public Affairs.

It is surprising, given the public pressure at the time, that the Internal Communications Department was organized first. It handled the review and distribution of instructional materials, publications, and translations for the worldwide Church. Elder Hinckley was named chairman, with Elder Monson and Elder Packer as advisers.[18] Six months later, Elder Hinckley was moved to the newly created Public Communications Department, and Elder Monson became chairman of the Internal Communications Committee (ICC), with Elders Packer, Ashton, and McConkie on the committee. The age-group Correlation Committee advisers were now the ICC advisers. Under the watchful eyes of these Brethren would pass all matters of correlation, teaching, instructional materials, publications, periodicals, services for translation, and many other projects. It reminded Elder Monson of the Adult Correlation Committee. He voiced concern that this broad organization could become a mammoth bureaucracy if precautions were not observed. President Lee relied on him to make certain that didn't happen.

The Church was now poised to handle its communication needs during its steady growth across the globe, both internally and externally. In the years to come, changes would adjust the structure, the personnel, the reporting lines, and even the nomenclature of the organization laid down in that highly charged atmosphere, but the system would serve the Church well, and its oversight by the Quorum of the Twelve and the First Presidency would continue.

In June 1971, President Lee turned to Elders Monson, Hinckley, and Packer to determine what the Church could do "to maintain a unified spirit among our black members." Recommendations included creating a social unit or branch in Salt Lake City for the black members of the Church. President Lee counseled the three to "go as far as [they] could in providing opportunities for our black brethren, short of the priesthood, and then seek the inspiration of Heavenly Father for further light and knowledge."[19]

From a series of meetings with representatives of the black community—Ruffin Bridgeforth, Darius Gray, and Eugene Orr—emerged the Genesis Group.

Elder Monson had met Brother Bridgeforth only briefly, though they had a significant tie. While serving as mission president in eastern Canada, President Monson and his missionaries had faced repeated challenges to the Church's policy on priesthood and the blacks. President Monson wrote to one of his black friends in Salt Lake City, asking if he could prepare something that could help calm and reassure those caught up in the issue. His friend suggested that Ruffin Bridgeforth was the one to address the matter. Brother Bridgeforth, a convert of eighteen years, recorded his testimony so that missionaries could use it when faced with the charge that "no black members in your Church have a testimony."

The three Apostles now laid their hands on the heads of each of the three black members, setting apart Brother Bridgeforth as the group president, Brother Gray as first counselor, and Brother

Orr as second counselor. The Genesis Group, an auxiliary unit attached to the Liberty Utah Stake, would sponsor a monthly meeting, including speakers and testimony bearing. They would also hold weekly sessions for Relief Society, Primary, and the youth. Genesis members would attend sacrament meetings in their home wards. The first meeting of the Genesis Group drew a capacity audience, many of whom were white.

Some months later, after Elder Monson had watched the three leaders shape and administer the Genesis Group, he wrote: "I am very impressed with these three black brethren who comprise the presidency of this group. Certainly they have been subjected to a lot of injustice and long for the day when they may be able to hold the priesthood." He confided, "I can honestly say that I have no racial prejudice whatsoever toward such individuals and join with them in a desire that their request might one day be granted by the Lord."[20]

Other issues in the Church were surfacing in this era as well. The correlation system had helped address the need to strengthen the members' testimonies and understanding of the principles of the gospel through a standardized study of the scriptures. Still, lack of scriptural understanding was a monumental challenge. Many were not reading the scriptures or did not know how to find answers in their study.

To remedy the situation, President Lee appointed Elder Monson to head up a Bible Study Aids Committee. It would become one of the most significant efforts of the Church in the twentieth century. That Elder Monson was called was no surprise. He had shown great organizational and administrative ability in other major assignments; he had the total confidence of the senior members of the Twelve, seemingly unmatched energy, professional printing skills, and an eye for detail that would be important in the process.

Thomas Monson was—and is—known as one who looks at a book and sees much more than words on a page. He sees the typeface, with its serifs, as well as the margins—top, bottom, and sides. He handles the paper and checks its grain. He seems to have an extra sense that can spot an error in the middle of the text. This ability has earned him the designation "eagle eye." He has been known to deny proposals not for content but for spelling or grammatical errors. When working at the Deseret News, he reviewed proofs for advertising. Once he presented a prominent real-estate broker with the man's proposed advertisement for review. The man pronounced it "Fine, just fine," until Tom pointed out a mistake in the text. Instead of reading, "Our uniformed sales people will be on hand," the copy read, "Our *uninformed* sales people . . ." The grateful businessman bought Tom a milk shake.

Also called to the Bible Study Aids Committee were Elder Packer and Elder Ashton. The three, already advisers to the ICC, were aware, because of their general oversight responsibility, of the issues relating to scripture study. Later Elder McConkie was named to the group when Elder Ashton was called to another assignment.

Before the 1970s, new manuals were introduced nearly every year for the adult curriculum of the Church, both for Gospel Doctrine classes and for the Melchizedek Priesthood quorums and Relief Society. New manuals were also published each year for the deacons, teachers, and priests. The Young Women followed suit. With the correlation of all adult classes drawing from the scriptures as their "manual" came a dilemma: the Bible was not cross-referenced to the other scriptures, which handicapped a complete study of the doctrines of the kingdom. In addition, multiple printed versions of the King James Bible were in use in the Church. The Primary used one, the seminaries another, and the missionaries yet another. That meant a Primary child might learn from one edition of the Bible, switch to another while in seminary, and have a third presented for use as a missionary.

What became readily apparent was the need to expand the cross-references in the scriptures beyond the Bible to include the Book of Mormon, the Doctrine and Covenants, and the Pearl of Great Price. The First Presidency and Quorum of the Twelve wholeheartedly approved of that idea. The Bible Study Aids Committee became the Scriptures Publication Committee, and the project of creating a comprehensively referenced edition of the scriptures would reach into the 1980s for the English version; other languages would follow.

The work on the scriptures could have consumed all of Elder Monson's time, but his travel schedule during this period also increased as he took some of the more strenuous and extended assignments. He knew Canada; it was his second home and increasingly a stronghold for the Church. He had supervised and traveled extensively and often in the Pacific Islands, Europe, and Mexico. He had journeyed to South America, the Holy Land, and the Far East.

He helped plan the British area conference and subsequent conferences in Mexico City, Stockholm, and Munich, doing much of the groundwork to ensure that the arenas would appropriately house religious services.

In the summer of 1973, a young missionary from California, Elder David A. Bednar, serving at the time in the leadership of his mission in Germany, attended a meeting to review final preparations for the Munich area conference. "There was a meeting in the conference room in the mission office, and Elder Monson came in to preside and provide direction," he recalls. "I had never seen a meeting orchestrated and executed quite like that one. He wasn't commanding; he wasn't domineering, but you knew who was in control. He said, 'We are going to do this and this and this.' People were prepared and things were done and then he said, 'Thank you very much' and we had a closing prayer and we were gone. As a twenty-year-old missionary, I remember watching how it was supposed to work—not in theory but in practice. It was really amazing."[21]

On his way to the Munich conference, Elder Monson met his missionary son Tom, who had just completed his mission in Italy. "It was a day long to be remembered," he says, indicating that he can still picture Tom coming through the gate carrying his hand luggage. "It was good to see him again." The two took a cab to the train station, where young Tom, with permission, proceeded on to Birmingham, England, home of the Birmingham roller pigeons. Elder Monson flew on to Zurich, where Frances met him for a missionary conference of the Switzerland Mission.

On his forty-sixth birthday, August 21, 1973, Elder Monson and his wife joined young Tom for another "glorious reunion" and flew to Munich for the area conference there. On Friday, August 24, the members presented a floor show for an opening social, with every country in the area participating. "The shock of the evening" was when President Lee invited Elder Monson to be the speaker following the event. Speaking without notice or notes, he relied wholly on the Spirit for his remarks.

More than 15,000 attended the Munich area conference; the program included the Mormon Tabernacle Choir. "They truly rose to great heights," Elder Monson wrote in his journal; the Choir presented the famed *Music and the Spoken Word* broadcast to a worldwide audience.[22]

Elder Monson's entries in his journal concerning the Munich area conference are typical of him. To him, people matter, especially the people who are noticed less and rarely heralded. He noted "the German singing" as the highlight of the conference. He described the "superb coordination" of those who worked behind the scenes handling the details—J. Thomas Fyans, F. Enzio Busche, Jacob de Jager—and paid tribute to their service. He wrote of the "joy" he felt in watching "the expression on the face of Walter Krause, the newly ordained patriarch to the Dresden Mission, as he listened with rapt attention to the conference and particularly the music by the Tabernacle Choir." For President Monson, what really matters is always the people, their work ethic, their testimonies, their happiness, their willingness to acknowledge the Lord's hand. So it is when he is home. He noted in his journal at the end of that assignment, "We are indebted to [Aunt] Blanche for caring for the children."[23]

That summer, 1973, the Monsons' only daughter, Ann, announced her engagement to Roger A. Dibb, an accounting student at BYU. "It was rather interesting to go through the traumatic experience of having Roger petition me for the hand of my daughter," Elder Monson recalled. Roger promised "he would care for her properly and love her most sincerely." She would be the first married of the three children; she would be missed, particularly by Frances.[24]

"My father has always expected me to honor my mother," says Ann. "It wasn't hard." She and her mother had a close and devoted relationship, the two girls in a house with three strong-willed men. Ann has always seen her mother as "just so sweet and kind" and "so devoted to her family." When other teenagers were claiming independence and drawing away from parents, Ann would stay up late into the night talking to her mother about her dates or her evening activities. "She has always been quiet," Ann says. "That's what I grew up with, but she would say her opinion. 'I don't know if I feel very good about that,' she would say to my dad, and he would listen."[25] Frances shied away from activities that would draw attention to her, always careful not to complicate her husband's life by saying or doing anything that might reflect on him.

To this day, when Ann walks up the driveway and in the front door of the house where she was raised, she is "home." "My dad will say, 'Oh, look who's here. And aren't we glad, and isn't she beautiful?' My parents always give me some compliment; it doesn't matter what I look like or what I've been doing." She learned through the example set in her home the truths of the gospel described in "The Family: A Proclamation to the World": "Parents have a sacred duty to rear their children in love and righteous-ness, to provide for their physical and spiritual needs, [and] to teach them to love and serve one another."[26] "I believe when you teach the plan of salvation, it's all about being able to go home," Ann explains. "When I go and visit my parents, I know I am loved, I am complimented, I am made welcome, I am home—and that's the way it is going to be in the eternities."[27]

Elder Monson performed Ann and Roger's sealing in the Salt Lake Temple on March 5, 1974. Days before the marriage, the Monson family attended the temple with Ann and Roger. On the day of the wedding, "Ann looked absolutely stunning in her wed-ding dress, kneeling at a sacred altar in the house of the Lord," Elder Monson wrote. "I don't know when I have felt a sweeter spirit during a ceremony than prevailed on this occasion. . . . We are grateful to our Heavenly Father for such a lovely spirit as Ann."[28]

Just eight weeks later, April 26, 1974, the Monsons were in the temple again as Elder Monson had "the cherished experience" of sealing oldest son Tom and his bride, Carma Rhodehouse. He has high praise "for the steadfastness of . . . youth who have the courage to choose the right way of marriage."[29]

It would be another eight years before their last child, Clark, was married. Elder Monson considered it a "privileged opportunity" to seal each of the three children to their spouses and give them a father's blessing. Clark and Patricia Shaffer were married in the Salt Lake Temple on April 28, 1982.

Between assignments during the summer of 1973 in Zurich, Nairobi, and Athens, Elder Monson arranged to take Frances to the Holy Land, where they toured sites "sacred to Latter-day Saints." When they reached the Garden Tomb, they were disappointed to learn that it was closed for the day. They knocked, but to no avail. After visiting the Temple Mount, the Garden of Gethsemane, Via Dolorosa—the Way of the Cross—and other sites around Jerusalem, they returned a second time. And a third. At long last, someone came to the gate, whereupon Elder Monson explained that they had come all the way from America for the purpose of visiting the Garden Tomb. "Could we have just ten minutes there?" he asked. They were invited in and the door closed behind them. "Take all the time you wish," the guard said. The Monsons were overwhelmed with what they experienced. To them, the tomb became "the most beautiful and inspiring site in the Holy Land. One cannot visit here without feeling close to the Savior and His divine mission."[30]

The Monsons saw firsthand—from continent to continent— the stirrings of major growth in the Church. Elder Monson was in Europe one week, paying for a hotel room that cost $50 a night (a cost he considered exorbitant), and then was off to Nairobi, Kenya, on the African continent, and then the next week to Japan, Hong Kong, and Sydney, Australia, with a one-day stop at home. In between, he flew throughout the United States every weekend on assignments. Readjusting his time clock after each trip was difficult. Night would be day and vice versa for him for about a week, though his schedule did not provide any leisure for being tired.

Elder Monson and President Spencer W. Kimball both liked to work, and both approached their tasks with great zeal. For several summers, President Kimball had worked on writing a book titled *The Miracle of Forgiveness*. "As one reads the book," Elder Monson later observed, "particularly the first portion, one wonders if anyone will make it to the celestial kingdom." The final portion, he noted, provides the assurance that "with effort, all can qualify."[31]

One day President Kimball, then President of the Quorum of the Twelve, entered Elder Monson's office and said, "I don't know if I should have printed the book or not. I have people coming in to confess mistakes which they made long years ago. Could you help me talk to some of them?"

Elder Monson agreed to help, to which President Kimball responded, "I'll send several people in to see you."

When Elder Monson asked, "What would you like me to tell them?" President Kimball answered simply, "Forgive them, brother; forgive them."[32]

Elder Monson tried, as often as possible, to provide counsel to those who petitioned him for help. One young man, the son of a fellow pigeon fancier, who was trying to get his life in order so he could submit his mission papers, wrote after visiting with Elder Monson in his office: "I was honored to have you meet me, counsel me, and bless me. Since our time together I have felt an old strength come home, chains fall, and hope return. I didn't think I could ever have strength again that would aid my repentance. Thank you."

The young man closed his letter, "This is, for me, the largest indirect blessing from having a father who raises pigeons."[33]

Pigeons. Elder Monson, with all he was doing, still took time to visit the Utah State Fair each year to see the pigeons on exhibit, and the chickens, too. He had to go twice, since the two presentations used the same building, one taking the first half of the fair and the other the latter half. He still kept his pigeon loft full at home, though his days of showing the birds were behind him.

In the midst of all the pressures, the travel, the hours in committee meetings, and the speaking assignments, Elder Monson looked forward to spring and summer because it meant he could mow the lawn. While some might enjoy golfing or working at handyman projects around the house, Elder Monson liked to mow the lawn. For him there was—and is—something therapeutic in the ordered rows of freshly cut grass. Depending on the need, he would also paint the fence, the chicken coop, or the pigeon loft.

When he was in London or New York, he and Frances would sometimes take an evening to attend a musical. One of his favorites is *The Student Prince.* Another is *The Music Man;* he loves the line spoken by Harold Hill, the music man, to his sweetheart, Marian, the librarian: "You pile up enough tomorrows, and you'll find you've collected a lot of empty yesterdays." He also likes *Camelot, Fiddler on the Roof, Showboat, Man of La Mancha, The Phantom of the Opera, Annie,* and many others.

Elder Monson was now entering an era when his loved ones began to pass away. In 1973 Frances's mother, Hildur Augusta Booth Johnson, died of cancer. Frances's father had been gone for years. Elder Monson felt honored to speak at Hildur's funeral, describing her as "a truly marvelous woman whom we shall sorely miss."[34] Mormor, as she was affectionately called, had often stayed with the children when the Monsons traveled abroad on assignments. She was a renowned Swedish cook at the cafeteria in the Federal Reserve Bank in Salt Lake City. When she catered a large dinner, buffet, or wedding, she had the reputation of preparing delicious food, serving it efficiently, and staying out of the way. Though Frances, named for her father, Franz, has all her mother's recipes, she says they are of little use. They are all in Swedish, and Frances has not spoken or read Swedish since she was a very small child.

Later that year, Elder Monson was in Hong Kong at a mission presidents' seminar when, returning to the hotel, he received a message from Frances that his own mother had passed away. Gladys Monson hadn't been well for the last few years and at one point had been hospitalized. When the family had celebrated her husband's birthday in May 1973, Gladys had looked weak and was not her jovial self. It was still "a shock to learn of the passing of one's mother," Elder Monson noted. She had been suffering from a malignancy in the pleura of the lung area, but no one expected her "to pass so suddenly" on Thursday afternoon, September 13, 1973.

Elder Monson could have returned home immediately after receiving the news of his mother's passing but "felt the necessity to continue on." He modified his schedule so he would be home in time for the funeral. When he had a short break between meetings in the Philippines, he visited the American Memorial Cemetery, "a tranquil place where a spirit of reverence permeates the atmosphere." Acres of beautifully kept green grass are marked only by white crosses arranged in perfect symmetry, the only variation being the occasional Star of David where the deceased was of the Jewish faith. "In beautiful colonnades the history of the War in the Pacific is graphically told. Maps of ceramic tile depict every battle." Being a student of history, particularly of World Wars I and II, and being in a sober frame of mind, having just lost his mother, Elder Monson was impressed by some of the inscriptions on the colonnades and recorded them in his journal, such as this one: "O Lord, support us all the day long until the shadows lengthen and our work is done. Then, in thy mercy, grant us a safe lodging and a holy rest and peace at last."

Elder Monson concluded his journal entry for that day, "I came away from the cemetery revived spiritually and satisfied that all was well with my dear mother."[35]

He spoke to the Manila stake members that weekend and felt they responded to every inflection of his voice. He could have gone home Saturday after the session and skipped Sunday's meetings, but, "remembering the words of the Lord to keep one's eyes focused upon the kingdom of God and a hand to the plow, I remained."[36] After his address to the Saints in Manila, he confessed, "The spirit of the Lord directed my remarks, for I have never felt greater freedom in speaking to an audience nor felt that my message sank deeper into the hearts of the people assembled."[37]

He flew home through Tokyo, arriving on Monday, September 17, just before the viewing for his mother. More than 500 people "came to pay respect to Mother and Dad." Many General Authorities attended, as did members of the old Sixth-Seventh Ward and even Joe Merabelle, Elder Monson's tailor and friend for many years.[38]

The funeral service for Gladys, held on September 18 in the

Rosecrest Second Ward of the Salt Lake Canyon Rim Stake, was well attended. Many General Authorities supported Elder Monson and his family. John Burt—neighbor, friend, former bishop of the Sixth-Seventh Ward, and a longtime member of the Temple View Stake presidency—spoke, as did Gladys's former bishop, Merlin Lybbert. Gladys's cousin Richard Condie, director of the Mormon Tabernacle Choir, sang a solo. President Harold B. Lee concluded the meeting, paying tribute to Gladys's "jovial nature," her "radiant and youthful zest for living," and her "remarkable family." Speaking to the family, he said, "When there is turmoil all around you, follow the course of Gladys and Spence. Be on your guard," he counseled. "Let heaven be close. Remember the Monson name and how important it is."[39]

Elder Monson dedicated the grave. He so appreciated President Lee's kindness in speaking at the service, and recorded in his journal, "We were humbled as a family to think that the prophet of God would not only attend the service and speak, but that he and his counselors would journey to the cemetery to be with us for the graveside services incident to the burial. Let us hope that we can live worthily to merit such wonderful friendships."[40]

Indicative of the close ties forged from years of sitting in council together, his dear friend Elder Gordon B. Hinckley, on his way to an assignment overseas, wrote a note of condolence: "Our hearts reach out to you and your loved ones on this sad occasion. To lose one's mother is always a devastating experience. . . . Our prayers will be with you, and we know that the comforting Spirit of the Lord will give you peace and assurance that she has only gone hence to prepare for happy reunions."[41]

Two weeks later, Elder Monson, with sons Tom and Clark, would attend general priesthood meeting, "the first time in a considerable period that the two boys and I have been together in such a session."[42]

Not surprisingly, at October conference, Elder Monson's address was titled "Behold Thy Mother." In a tender expression, he spoke of his memory of Sunday School on Mother's Day when he was a boy. "We would hand to each mother present a small potted plant and sit in silent reverie as Melvin Watson, a blind member, would stand by the piano and sing, 'That Wonderful Mother of Mine.' This was the first time I saw a blind man cry. Even today, in memory, I can see the moist tears move from those sightless eyes, then form tiny rivulets and course down his cheeks, falling finally upon the lapel of the suit he had never seen. In boyhood puzzlement I wondered why all of the grown men were silent, why so many handkerchiefs came forth. Now I know. You see, mother was remembered. Each boy, every girl, all fathers and husbands seemed to make a silent pledge: 'I will remember that wonderful mother of mine.'"[43]

President Harold B. Lee closed the conference without prepared remarks—at his best, Elder Monson believed, when he spoke "from his heart to the people."[44] It was a singular moment—a prophet training a prophet, the two not knowing the Lord's intent but acting with complete devotion in their responsibilities.

On December 26, 1973, the day after Christmas, the Monsons were hosting a dinner for the parents of Roger Dibb, Ann's fiancé. As the group chatted, the telephone rang with a report from the Pennsylvania mission president, Hugh W. Pinnock, that two of his missionaries had been assaulted and one was currently in surgery. Elder Monson explained to the guests that members of the Missionary Executive Committee received calls at all times of the night and day with reports of perilous experiences.

No sooner had he put down the phone than it rang again. The Dibbs watched as Elder Monson's face paled. Regional representative Rex C. Reeve reported that he had just heard a news report of the sudden passing of President Harold B. Lee. It was the first that Elder Monson had heard the news. The phone rang again, with his friend John Burt on the other end, confirming what Elder Reeve had said. Then President Marion G. Romney called to tell him that he was at the hospital and President Lee was indeed gone.

The Monsons were stunned. So were their guests. That night Elder Monson soberly recorded, "Certainly we have lost a dear friend, and the Church has lost a truly dynamic and inspired leader."[45] Elder Monson had looked forward to continued service under President Lee's masterful hand; he had led the Church for only a year and a half. Now President Lee was gone, and Elder Monson would feel his absence for years to come.

The next day, the Apostles gathered, shocked and saddened as they made preparations for the funeral of their dear leader. They watched as President Kimball assumed his responsibility as the presiding officer "in an intelligent yet humble and efficient manner."[46]

On December 29, a cold, overcast day, members of the Church filled the Tabernacle on Temple Square to pay tribute to President Harold B. Lee. While some had hoped for sunshine, "Frances commented that it seemed fitting that the day would be overcast when the President of the Church was buried."[47] The Monson family had lost not only a prophet but a dear and valued personal friend.

The death came without warning, though, looking back, Elder Monson had noted that President Lee "seemed particularly weary" in a temple meeting some weeks before. President Lee had fulfilled forty-two speaking assignments in the first twenty-three days of December, a staggering load.[48]

Gone was a man Elder Monson had "loved, honored, and followed" since his youth. "Prophetic in his utterance, powerful in his leadership, devoted in his service, President Lee inspired in all of us a desire to achieve perfection," Elder Monson said of the prophet-leader whose counsel to the Saints was clear and simple: "Keep the commandments of God. Follow the pathway of the Lord."[49]

It was not the end of an era. The coming decades of tremendous international growth and missionary service would build on the foundations put painstakingly in place by President Lee and carried on by those who followed.

On Sunday, December 30, after "reflection and meditation," the Quorum of the Twelve again assembled in an upper room of the Salt Lake Temple. Being sensitive to the new experience ahead for Elder Bruce R. McConkie, the junior member of the

Quorum, Elder Monson prepared him for the process that would be followed in that meeting.

The First Presidency was dissolved with the death of President Lee, and Elder Tanner and Elder Romney took their seats back in their places of seniority in the Quorum of the Twelve.

The Lord's chosen servants joined in prayer, and then President Spencer W. Kimball asked each of the Twelve to bear testimony and to express himself in a most candid fashion. He asked Elder Ezra Taft Benson, the next senior Apostle, to speak first. After this had taken place, proper nominations were made and President Spencer W. Kimball was named to the most holy calling of prophet, seer, and revelator and President of The Church of Jesus Christ of Latter-day Saints, the twelfth man so named in this dispensation. He selected N. Eldon Tanner and Marion G. Romney as counselors. Elder Ezra Taft Benson was named President of the Quorum of the Twelve.

Elder Monson described "a sweet spirit of harmony and support. . . . It was a joy to participate in the setting apart for each of these choice Brethren. A piano stool was arranged so that Hugh B. Brown could be seated as he placed his hands upon the head of the person being set apart, the rest of us standing in a circle surrounding the person being blessed."[50]

President Kimball, "untiring in his labor, humble in his manner, inspiring in his testimony," invited those gathered in that sacred setting to "continue the chores charted by President Lee."[51] For Elder Monson, that was familiar ground.

At the time, the Church had 15 temples in operation, 630 stakes, 108 missions, and a membership exceeding 3.3 million.

President Benson met with each member of the Twelve "to let each know of his love" and to measure "the workload and assignments" each carried. Elder Monson's responsibilities were heavy—Missionary Executive Committee, Scriptures Publication Committee, Melchizedek Priesthood Committee, Church Board of Education, adviser to the Internal Communications Committee—the list was long. The new administration intended to make present programs work without constantly altering them. "In short," Elder Monson noted after an All-Church Coordinating

Council, "now that we have the house of correlation erected, let's live in it, rather than constantly remodeling the structure."[52]

The year 1973 had been an eventful year for Elder and Sister Monson, marked with the passing of both of their mothers. But the Lord had been good to them. Elder Monson acknowledged in his journal "the many blessings of our Heavenly Father to us as a family and to me in my calling"[53] and recommitted, "As for me and my house, we will serve the Lord."[54]

24

OPENING DOORS

As an Apostle of the Lord Jesus Christ, Elder Monson is filled with the pure love of Christ, and he radiates this to others. People love him because he loves them. His witness to the world is one of love and understanding.

PRESIDENT SPENCER W. KIMBALL
President of The Church of Jesus Christ
of Latter-day Saints, 1973–1985

ELDER THOMAS S. MONSON AND President Spencer W. Kimball shared a love for those who lived on the margins. The two first became acquainted in the early 1950s when Elder Monson was a young bishop. He answered the telephone one morning at his home and heard, "This is Elder Spencer W. Kimball. I have a favor to ask of you." Elder Kimball then explained, "Hidden away behind a large building on Fifth South Street is a trailer home. Living there is Margaret Bird, a Navajo widow. She feels unwanted, unneeded, and lost. Could you and the Relief Society presidency seek her out, extend to her the hand of fellowship, and provide her a special welcome."

Elder Kimball had called the right man for a rescue.

Margaret Bird blossomed as she was drawn into the loving arms of the members of the Sixth-Seventh Ward. Elder Monson wrote, "Despair disappeared. The widow in her affliction had been visited. The lost sheep had been found. Each one who participated in the simple human drama emerged a better person."[1]

President Monson has taught that lesson many times. The names, faces, and places change but his message is the same: "Let us listen for the sound of sandaled feet. Let us reach out for the Carpenter's hand. Then we shall come to know Him. He may come to us as one unknown, without a name, as, by the lakeside, He came to those men who knew Him not. He speaks to us the same words, 'Follow thou me,' and sets us to the tasks which He has to fulfill for our time. He commands. And to those who obey Him, whether they be wise or simple, He will reveal Himself in the toils, the conflicts, the sufferings that they shall pass through in His fellowship, and . . . they shall learn in their own experience who He is."[2]

President Kimball, all his years, had been in tune with the Master's voice. Following the sustaining vote at the solemn assembly on April 6, 1974, he promised in his message to the Saints: "We shall serve you, our people, and love you and do our utmost to guide you to your righteous, glorious destiny, with our hearts overflowing with love and appreciation for you."[3] This prophet, small in stature but with the gait of a giant, demonstrated the principle he taught so frequently: "Lengthen your stride." The phrase would become a hallmark of his administration, and Elder Monson would be in step right behind him. Elder Monson described the new President as one who "moves with decisiveness and carries the mantle of his solemn calling."[4]

President Kimball appointed L. Tom Perry as an Apostle to fill the vacancy in the Quorum of the Twelve. Elder Perry had been serving as an Assistant to the Twelve for two years. Later, at the death of Hugh B. Brown, President Kimball called David B. Haight to the apostleship. He too had been serving as an Assistant to the Twelve. When Elder Delbert L. Stapley passed away in August 1978, President Kimball called James E. Faust, of the First Quorum of the Seventy, as an Apostle. Elder Monson had years of experience working with these brethren; he was pleased to sustain them.

For years President Kimball had faced severe health issues that might have crippled or conquered an ordinary man. Many years earlier, doctors had operated for throat cancer, turning his melodic tenor voice into a scratchy but recognizable whisper. He underwent open-heart surgery in 1972; the Apostles were in the temple that day, fasting, and they were "filled with hopeful anxiety" as they waited for word. When the phone rang, President Harold B. Lee left the room to take the call. "President Lee was a master at masking his feelings, and he walked back into the room as somber as he could be. He said, 'That was Brother Nelson [speaking of President Kimball's heart surgeon, Dr. Russell M. Nelson]. Spencer is off the pump!'" Elder Monson's journal entry at the end of the day was tender: "We all smiled and said a prayer of thanksgiving."[5]

Much happened to shape Church policy, programs, and reporting lines during the Kimball administration: The First Quorum of the Seventy was organized; general conferences were reduced to only two days, Saturday and Sunday; the first Missionary Training Center opened; stake conferences were reduced from four to two per year; General Authority attendance at stake conferences was cut back to once a year per stake; and sacrament meetings were discontinued on the Sunday of stake conferences.

At a 1975 stake conference in Modesto, California, with the assignment to divide the stake, Elder Monson realized that more than ten years earlier he had attended a conference in that same area. He tried to remember the name of the stake president back then, and it came to him: Clifton Rooker.

He said to the current stake president, as the meeting was about to start, "Is this the same stake over which Clifton Rooker presided?"

The stake president responded, "Yes. He is our former president."

Elder Monson stepped to the pulpit and asked, "Is Clifton Rooker in the audience?" There he was—far back in the cultural hall, hardly in view of the pulpit. Elder Monson felt inspired to make the invitation, "Brother Rooker, we have a place for you on the stand. Would you please come forward?" With every eye watching him, Clifton Rooker made that long walk from the rear of the building right up to the front and took a seat at Elder Monson's side.

Later in the meeting, Elder Monson called on Brother Rooker to bear his testimony, "to give him the privilege to tell the people, whom he loved, that he was the real beneficiary of the service he had rendered his Heavenly Father and which he had provided the stake members."

When the meeting concluded, he asked Brother Rooker to join him in setting apart the two new stake presidencies. Brother Rooker responded, "That would be a highlight of my life." The two proceeded, placing hands on the head of each person and embracing one another when the work was finished.

The next morning Elder Monson received a phone call from Brother Rooker's son, who said, "Brother Monson, I'd like to tell you about my dad. He passed away this morning; but before he did so, he said that yesterday was the happiest day of his entire life." Elder Monson recorded, "I thanked my God for the inspiration which came to me in the twinkling of an eye to invite this good man to come forward and receive the plaudits of his stake members, whom he had served, while he was yet alive and able to enjoy them."[6]

Of all the blessings Elder Monson treasures in his life, he has said that one of the greatest is "that feeling which the Lord provides when you know that He, the Lord, has answered the prayer of another person through you."[7]

During the Kimball years, two particularly significant events in the history of the Church came to fruition: the publication of the new LDS editions of the scriptures and the revelation that all worthy males were invited to receive the priesthood and its fulness. Elder Monson was integrally involved in both.

For ten years Elder Monson chaired the massive project to publish editions of the printed scriptures containing LDS cross-references and study helps. His assignment began with the Bible Study Aids Committee, which was enlarged and became the Scriptures Publication Committee. The assignment suited not only his training in printing and publishing but also his skills as an administrator and one who loved the scriptures. He would count the assignment as one of the most significant of his apostolic service.

"In our dispensation," he has explained, "we would trace the important events of Church history as they relate directly to the scriptures. It was through reading the Bible that Joseph Smith went to the grove made sacred and received the First Vision. There were visitations from Moroni, an angel, who taught the young prophet Joseph about the golden plates from which the Book of Mormon was translated. We would remember the efforts to compile the revelations received by the Prophet into a book of commandments which represented the doctrines and covenants of the Church. And we would reflect on the miraculous events that brought ancient papyri into the possession of the Prophet, who valued its translated message as a pearl of great price."[8]

Elder Monson's love for the scriptures began as a youth when he would sit in sacrament meetings and listen to President Charles S. Hyde of his stake presidency explain verses of scripture. One particular meeting will always stand out in his mind. President Hyde read and explained the seventy-sixth section of the Doctrine and Covenants. Frances has related, "It impressed Tom so much that he had a great desire to read and study the scriptures for himself." To this day, he has a great love for the seventy-sixth section of the Doctrine and Covenants. He saw the aids to the scriptures—cross-references, maps, Bible dictionary, Topical Guide—as engaging the members in a similar manner.

Frances recalls that when her husband was called as a bishop, "he felt very strongly that if he were to lead the members of his ward, he would have to have a better knowledge of the scriptures." He set a goal that by the end of the year he would read all of the standard works of the Church. It was May 1950, and by December 31 of that year he had completed reading every word, including all the footnotes and ready references. "He always reads with a red pencil," Frances has said, "underlining the passages that he feels are important for him."[9]

In addition, his years of work with the General Authorities while at the Deseret Press, before being called as an Apostle, where he helped to compile, edit, and print their books, had educated him further concerning the scriptures. In particular, his work with President J. Reuben Clark, Jr., and his monumental volume, *Our Lord of the Gospels,* enhanced his understanding in an intimate, scholarly, and spiritual manner. Of his personal study he noted: "Of late I have been studying the teachings of the early Apostles, including their calls, their ministries, and their very lives. It is a fascinating experience and brings one closer to the Lord Jesus Christ."[10]

As the chair of the Scriptures Publication Committee, Elder Monson oversaw the technical aspects, including the new footnote style, which began with new superscript letters in every verse. "It was very interesting how his expertise and his training came to bear," President Boyd K. Packer has explained. Elder Packer worked with grammatical and printing revisions and historical materials; Elder Bruce R. McConkie prepared new chapter headings and introductions. The three met frequently, sometimes daily, to keep the work moving, and they met with the whole expanded committee monthly, without fail. "The three of us got along," Elder Packer remembers, "with a singleness of purpose to advance the work."[11]

A challenge was getting all the "aids" into the Bible without making it so large as to be cumbersome, awkward, and hence deemed unusable. President Packer credits Elder Monson with packaging a tight single volume. "He was an expert on such things as paper and told them, 'If you get this kind of paper you can put twice the information in the same thickness of the book as you could if you used this other kind of paper.'"[12]

"The publication of the Latter-day Saint edition of the King James Version of the Bible, with its cross-referencing to the other standard works and the mammoth endeavor of the Topical Guide, really represents an advance in the publication of the scriptures unequalled in our time," Elder Monson wrote in his journal. "The advent of the computer was absolutely necessary before the Topical Guide could have been prepared."[13]

He worked closely with scholars and professionals who had served in various correlation assignments previously and had broad experience in studying and teaching from the standard works: Daniel H. Ludlow, director of correlation; William James Mortimer, general manager of Deseret Book; and Ellis G.

Rasmussen, Robert J. Matthews, and Robert Patch, all professors at BYU with lengthy careers teaching and studying the scriptures. Others from the Church Educational System also contributed.[14]

"From the very first meeting," Brother Mortimer observed, "there continued a spirit of love and brotherhood as the staff worked under the careful supervision and direction of Elder Monson and his committee."[15] Brother Matthews said of working for nearly a decade at the side of Elders Thomas S. Monson, Boyd K. Packer, and Bruce R. McConkie in the preparation of the new editions of the standard works: "We saw them work with divine inspiration in the day-to-day activities of that committee, and often marveled at their clarity of vision and quickness of perception in deciding the course to follow. Each of the Brethren had his respective areas of responsibility, all of which were important to the success of the undertaking."[16]

Every change, down to the placement of a comma, was approved at the highest level. Elder McConkie said of the decade of effort, "There is no question that major decisions were made by the spirit of inspiration and that the conclusions reached were in accord with the mind and will of the Lord."[17]

Elder Monson's leadership style suited what needed to be done. He surrounds himself with able, faithful, dedicated individuals, who speak up and share their opinions, who work to their fullest. He believes strongly in committee efforts. He was not—and is not—a micromanager. In that ten years of meetings he listened, he counseled, he gave direction, and he let the Spirit guide.

During the summer of 1979, Elder Monson walked through the printing plant of Cambridge University Press in Great Britian as pages of the new edition of the LDS Bible were running simultaneously on a long battery of twelve presses. He was right at home.

Feeling prompted, he said to one of the press operators, "Pull me a sheet." The man did, and Elder Monson scanned it quickly. "Stop the presses," he announced. "You've got an error here."

The pressman balked. "Not possible. We've read this twelve times."

"Well, you missed it twelve times," Elder Monson responded.

Perhaps the words "for such a time as this" from the book of Esther applied that day. Elder Monson was in England at the university press that had been printing Bibles since 1611, with his finger pointing to a missing vertical rule line at the bottom of the page. No one else had caught it. The error wasn't glaring; it didn't impact the message or the study of the scriptures. But to Elder Monson, "eagle eye" printer and proofreader, it was unacceptable. A mistake is a mistake. It was fixed quickly, and the presses began humming again.[19] And he paused to thank Heavenly Father for His hand in all things.

On August 29, 1979, the Scriptures Publication Committee met with the First Presidency and the Quorum of the Twelve, where it was Elder Monson's "opportunity to introduce the new Bible edition." He explained, "We have produced what is perhaps the most significant advancement in Church scholarship in a century. The Bible, of course, is the King James Version, but includes a revolutionary system of footnoting to the other standard works, and then includes the Topical Guide, making it a reference Bible without equal." He noted, "The Brethren seemed very pleased with the result."[19]

The LDS edition of the Bible included new summary headings for every chapter in the Old and New Testaments that more clearly represented an LDS perspective; wide-ranging footnotes cross-referenced to all four standard works, 300 excerpts drawn from the Joseph Smith Translation in passages that vary considerably from the King James Version; a topical guide and concordance with more than 2,300 subjects; a 195-page Bible dictionary expanded to include revealed knowledge of the latter days; and a 24-page section of full-color maps with a gazetteer. The committee made no alteration to the text of the King James Version.

The 1981 publication of the Triple Combination followed. It included a significantly expanded and combined index for the Book of Mormon, Doctrine and Covenants, and Pearl of Great Price; new introductions to each of the three; revised headings summarizing each chapter or section; four Church history maps; and at least 265 corrections to errors made in previous printings of the Book of Mormon and Doctrine and Covenants. An all-important phrase was added to the title: "The Book of Mormon: Another Testament of Jesus Christ."

The Doctrine and Covenants contained two new sections—137 and 138—accepted by the membership of the Church and published in the 1979 edition of the Pearl of Great Price. Also added were supplementary material from President Wilford Woodruff regarding the Manifesto, in Official Declaration—1, and President Kimball's 1978 revelation on priesthood, which became Official Declaration—2.

The director of the publishing of Bibles and other religious materials at Cambridge University Press, Roger Coleman, said of the LDS edition, "Nothing is perfect in this world . . . but *this* Bible is as nearly perfect as human beings can manage."[20]

Elder Monson was pleased with the recognition and "great achievement" for the Church when the Bible was awarded national and international prizes, but he returned to the real purpose of the project with the perspective, "but what are [the awards] when compared to helping others to receive a testimony of the truth?"[21]

When he encourages the Latter-day Saints, youth in particular, to "become acquainted with the lessons the scriptures teach," he is saying much more than "take your scriptures to church" or "read your scriptures." He is saying, "Become familiar with the lessons taught." President Monson takes his own counsel; he is always teaching from the life and lessons of the Savior.[22]

He wanted his own children to feel the power of the scriptures in their lives. He remembered the impact a visit to the grave of Martin Harris at the Clarkston cemetery in northern Utah had had on him as a young man and, later, on those in his ward when he was bishop. On April 21, 1973, he and Frances took Ann and Clark to see the tombstone of Martin Harris, one of the Three Witnesses of the Book of Mormon. "As we surrounded the grave, I read to the family the personal account of Martin Harris as contained in the book *The Three Witnesses,* by Preston Nibley. We also read from the flyleaf of the Book of Mormon, which of course contains the statement of the Three Witnesses."[23]

To encourage use of the new scriptures, on Sunday, March 10, 1985, the First Presidency broadcast a Churchwide satellite program, "Using the Scriptures," followed by a succession of Church magazine articles by President Hinckley, Elder Monson, Elder Packer, and Elder McConkie.

In the broadcast, Elder Monson admonished the members: "The holy scriptures are for children, to fill their eager minds with sacred truth. They are for youth, to prepare them for the challenges of our fast-moving world. They are for the sisters . . . to be scholars of the scriptures. . . . They are for the brethren of the priesthood, that each may qualify for the description given in the Book of Mormon to the sons of Mosiah: 'They were men of a sound understanding and they had searched the scriptures diligently, that they might know the word of God.' I know these sacred books of scripture are the word of God. With all my soul, as a special witness, I testify that they are true. As we search them, as we understand them, as we live them, may we one day be privileged to meet Him who beckoned us with His words, 'Come. . . . Learn of me,' and abide His holy presence forever and ever."[24]

It was difficult and costly for some members to make the transition to the new volumes. Elder Monson understood and quipped, "Can you imagine making everyone's scriptures obsolete!"[25] However, he and the committee and other General Authorities recognized that with use, the new scriptures would produce successive generations of faithful members who would know the Lord Jesus Christ and be determined to obey the commandments.

It is little wonder that later, when the Church had taken the printing of the scriptures "in-house," Elder Monson took his children and grandchildren on an escorted tour of the Church printing facilities. "There, all of us saw the missionary edition of the Book of Mormon coming off the delivery line—printed, bound, and trimmed, ready for reading," he remembered of that singular day. "I said to a young grandson, 'The operator says that you can remove one copy of the Book of Mormon to be your very own. You select the copy, and it will then be yours.' Removing one finished copy of the book, he clutched it to his breast and said with sincerity, 'I love the Book of Mormon. This is *my* book.'"[26] The casual acceptance and use of the scriptures once plaguing the Church had been changed.

At a reunion twenty-five years later of those who worked on the "prodigious" project, President Monson said, "You have affected the world; you have affected the youth; every missionary who has gone out is [better prepared] because of the work you did."[27]

Translation of the scriptures into other languages would stretch out for decades. Not until 2009, more than a year into President Monson's tenure as President of the Church, did the Church produce the Latter-day Saint edition of the Holy Bible in Spanish. There were 800,000 copies in the first print run.

The publication of the new editions of the scriptures came just after President Kimball received the revelation on the priesthood. In 1978, at the October general conference, President N. Eldon Tanner read to the gathering of the Saints around the world that revelation. Cited as Official Declaration—2 in the Doctrine and Covenants, it stated "that the long-promised day has come when every faithful, worthy man in the Church may receive the holy priesthood, with power to exercise its divine authority, and enjoy with his loved ones every blessing that flows therefrom, including the blessings of the temple."[28] President Tanner called for a sustaining vote to include the revelation in the scriptures; it was unanimously approved.

Elder Monson considers the June 1978 revelation that provided the priesthood to all worthy males, regardless of race, a hallmark of President Kimball's presidency. Prior to that time, neither men nor women of African descent could participate in making temple covenants, though in the early days of the Church a few black men had been ordained to the priesthood. For years the First Presidency and Quorum of the Twelve had wrestled with the issue. It came with a history of discussions at every level in the Church and constant importuning of the Lord. President Kimball had always taken the position regarding the issue: "We shall stand

and defend as did Peter, 'though the whole world be against us.' . . . When the Lord is ready to relax the restriction it will come whether there is pressure or not."[29] In 1974, amidst great controversy, the First Presidency reiterated that male black members could attend elders quorum meetings the same as other prospective elders. But the time had not yet come for change.

President Kimball's announcement in 1975 of a temple in São Paulo, Brazil, and its subsequent construction brought a new pressure. Brazil was such a racially mixed country—who would be eligible to enter the Lord's house?

What followed was the model scriptural pattern for revelation—study, ask, pray, and "you shall feel that it is right."[30] President Kimball beseeched the Lord repeatedly in solitary visits to the temple, and he invited each member of the Quorum of the Twelve to express his personal opinion concerning the subject. Elder Monson was one of the few who submitted his feelings in writing, as he has long advocated "that one, when asked, should express his honest opinion, regardless of whether the viewpoint is that which the presiding officers seek or with which they would agree."[31] He favored petitioning the Lord again with the plea to extend the priesthood to all men counted worthy.

On Thursday, June 1, 1978, President Kimball asked the Apostles to stay in the room in the Salt Lake Temple at the completion of the day's business with all the General Authorities. All had come to the meeting fasting, and he asked that they extend their fast and give prayerful consideration to conferring the priesthood upon the blacks.

Elder Monson recorded: "President Kimball asked each member of the Twelve to make a specific comment on this subject. At the conclusion of the meeting with the First Presidency and Quorum of the Twelve, we had a special prayer at the altar where President Kimball was voice. He implored the Lord for light and knowledge on this issue which has such far-reaching consequences. It was a source of great comfort to the Brethren to hear his humble pleadings as he sought guidance in his lofty calling."[32] At the conclusion of the prayer, a great outpouring of the Spirit came over them. The revelation was clear. The prophet of God had received the Lord's answer, and it was confirmed by those members of the Twelve who, with him, received the same revelation at the same time.

The First Presidency later expressed gratitude that "the spirit of peace and unity which prevailed in the meeting . . . was the finest it had ever been and that it [was] evidence that the Lord was pleased with our discussion."[33] Two of the Apostles were missing from the meeting: Elder Delbert L. Stapley was in the hospital, and Elder Mark E. Petersen was on assignment in South America. Both were consulted and added their wholehearted support to the received revelation.

The temple meeting on the next Thursday, June 8, 1978, was historic. President Kimball announced to the Quorum of the Twelve that the Lord had revealed to him that they should move forward quickly in granting the priesthood blessings to all worthy male members of the Church, regardless of race or color. For Elder Monson and all those in the room, "It was a moment of exultation, for we had heard the Lord's prophet declare the Lord's revelation for this time."[34] Again, each of the Apostles present was asked to respond and express an opinion.

President Kimball led the group in prayer to receive the Lord's confirmation. They surrounded the altar in prayer and President Kimball "told the Lord at length that if extending the priesthood was not right, if the Lord did not want this change to come in the Church, he would fight the world's opposition."[35] Elder Monson would later note that had the revelation not come, President Kimball "would have defended the previous policy to his dying breath."[36]

Later that day, Elder Monson met with Bill Smart, editor of the *Deseret News,* and quietly told him, "Reserve space for an important announcement tomorrow."

Smart inquired what was coming.

"I can't say anything now; it is confidential."

"Can you tell me whether to put it on the front page or on B-1 [the front page of the local news section]?"

Elder Monson replied, "You will know when you see it."[37]

The next morning, June 9, the First Presidency, the Quorum of the Twelve, and all other General Authorities met again in a special session at 7:00 A.M. "During the meeting, President Kimball reviewed with the Brethren the decision concerning the revelation that all worthy male members might receive the priesthood. Every person in the room expressed himself individually and voluntarily as being in favor and sustaining the presentation by President Kimball as a revelation from the Lord."[38]

The announcement ran not only on the front page of the *Deseret News* but on the front pages of major newspapers across the country, including the *New York Times* and the *Washington Post*. Both *Time* and *Newsweek* magazines stopped their press runs to insert the story in their upcoming weeklies. Most commentary spoke favorably of what some called "a sudden move" by the LDS Church.

Elder Monson telephoned two of his friends in the Genesis Group, Ruffin Bridgeforth and Monroe Fleming, to congratulate them on the opportunity that was now theirs to receive the priesthood. "Both were elated," he reported.[39]

On June 21, Elder Monson, as chairman of the Missionary Executive Committee, assigned the first black missionary, Montreal member Jacques Jonassaint, to the Florida Fort Lauderdale Mission, which included Puerto Rico and Haiti, "where he would have the opportunity to preach the gospel to many of his own race."[40] Two days later, he performed the first sealing for a black family in the temple. In the Salt Lake Temple, Brother Joseph Freeman, Jr., his wife, Toe Isapela Leituala Freeman, and their two children, Zachariah and Alexander, received the ordinance sealing them together for all eternity.

The evening of June 25, Elder and Sister Monson attended the Genesis Group, "where the sacrament was served for the first time at such a gathering, being administered to and passed by black members who now held the priesthood."[41] Five men bore inspiring testimonies of the great blessing given them by God. One young man explained, "When I heard the news, I was on a cloud, but I soon came off my cloud when I realized that now that I would hold the priesthood, I would have the responsibility to do home teaching, to do genealogical work, and to go on a mission. Am I happy!"[42]

The Lord's direction that the holy priesthood should now go to all who were worthy, without exclusion of nationality or race, opened wider the door for the fulness of the gospel to be taken to every nation, kindred, tongue, and people.

The Quorum of the Twelve Apostles in 1963. Left to right, seated: Ezra Taft Benson, Mark E. Petersen, President Joseph Fielding Smith, LeGrand Richards; standing: Gordon B. Hinckley, Delbert L. Stapley, Thomas S. Monson, Spencer W. Kimball, Harold B. Lee, Marion G. Romney, Richard L. Evans, Howard W. Hunter.

The Quorum of the Twelve Apostles in 1982. Left to right, seated: President Ezra Taft Benson, Mark E. Petersen, LeGrand Richards, Howard W. Hunter; standing: Thomas S. Monson, Boyd K. Packer, Marvin J. Ashton, Bruce R. McConkie, L. Tom Perry, David B. Haight, James E. Faust, Neal A. Maxwell.

With Elder Boyd K. Packer at general conference. The two sat side by side in the Quorum of the Twelve from 1970 to 1985, when Elder Monson was called to the First Presidency.

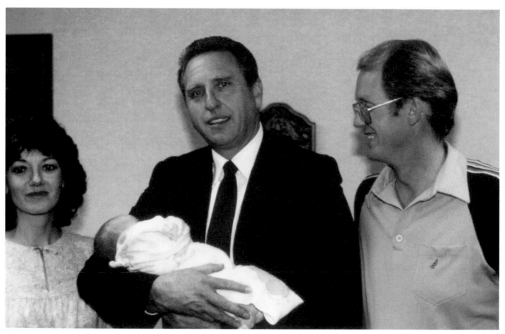

Celebrating with Lynne and Bill Cannegieter on October 2, 1981, at the arrival of Jennifer Lynne, their first daughter. Lynne has been President Monson's personal secretary for more than forty-five years.

At the Jefferson Memorial, Washington, D.C., September 17, 1987, on the two-hundredth anniversary of the signing of the U.S. Constitution.

The First Presidency in April 1986. President Monson and President Hinckley
served as counselors to President Ezra Taft Benson for nine years.

President Monson felt that President Benson treated him like a son.

With U.S. President Ronald Reagan and President Hinckley at the
Ogden Cannery on a special tour of the welfare facility.

Receiving the Bronze Wolf Award, the highest honor of the World Organization of Scouting, at general priesthood meeting in the Tabernacle on October 2, 1993. Presented by Scout officials Eugene F. "Bud" Reid and Jere B. Ratcliffe.

At the annual "Breakfast of Champions" on April 13, 2002, sponsored by Great Salt Lake Council of the Boy Scouts of America.

At the Fifteenth World Scout jamboree held at
Martin's Cove in Wyoming, June 14, 1997.

With about 3,600 Scouts on August 3, 1997, at Fort A. P. Hill, Virginia.

Called as second counselor to President Howard W. Hunter in the summer of 1994. President Gordon B. Hinckley was first counselor.

With friend and music impresario Eugene Jelesnik, recipient of BYU's Presidential Medal, at commencement exercises on Thursday, April 22, 1993.

Joining an evening of tribute, September 28, 1988, honoring former professor
Royal Garff at the establishment of the Royal L. Garff Presidential Chair at
the David Eccles School of Business, University of Utah.

Greeting members of the Quorum of the Twelve at general conference in 1994. Left to right:
Elders James E. Faust, Neal A. Maxwell, Russell M. Nelson, and Dallin H. Oaks.

Speaking with Janice and Agnes Woodbury at a reunion for members
of the Sixth-Seventh Ward on February 25, 1994.

Interacting with young adults after a Church Educational System
fireside at BYU on February 5, 1995.

At the dedication of the Deseret News Building in Salt Lake City.
Left to right: President Thomas S. Monson, President Gordon B. Hinckley,
and President James E. Faust.

Helping a youngster break ground for the
Palmyra New York Temple on May 25, 1999.

On a fishing trip with close friend Elder Jon Huntsman, Area Seventy,
near Driggs, Idaho, on June 4, 2001.

Tying a fly with items from his fishing tackle box at the
airport in Juneau, Alaska, July 17, 1996.

At a small town on Inland Passage, Alaska, on a fishing expedition, July 14, 1996, with Elder Jeffrey R. Holland.

Displaying a Mackinaw trout caught at Flaming Gorge.

Shaking hands with U.S. President George Bush in the Church
Administration Building on July 17, 1992.

The First Presidency honoring former Prime Minister Margaret Thatcher
at a luncheon on March 8, 1996.

Meeting in the First Presidency council room with President George W. Bush, along with President Henry B. Eyring, on May 29, 2008.

With the King and Queen of Sweden at the Stockholm Temple grounds on August 23, 1995.

25

NEIGHBOR HELPING NEIGHBOR

Any religious organization in the state would say Tom Monson is their friend.

ELDER M. RUSSELL BALLARD
Quorum of the Twelve Apostles

IN EARLY MAY 1977, PRESIDENT Nathan Eldon Tanner, First Counselor in the First Presidency, surprised Elder Thomas S. Monson with the request that he become president and chairman of the board of the Deseret News Publishing Company. At the time he was serving on the boards of both the Deseret News and Bonneville International Corporation, the Church's broadcast entity. He had come a long way since selling classified ads.

President Tanner expressed "full confidence" in Elder Monson's ability "to chart the destiny of the Deseret News."[1] Elder Monson, having served as vice chairman of the board while Elder Gordon B. Hinckley was chairman, was a familiar face to those who worked for the Deseret News and the Press.

President Tanner acknowledged the heavy load Elder Monson carried and asked if there were any responsibilities he could shed, allowing more time for the newspaper appointment. Elder Monson suggested that he step down from his position on the Utah State Board of Regents, although it was a post he had thoroughly enjoyed for the past seven years. He had spoken at commencements, participated on search committees for university presidents, and taken up a shovel to break ground for new campus facilities. When the Utah State Technical College wanted to start a printing course, he went to all the printers in town and lined up donated equipment to get the program started. He didn't want their old machines, he told his former associates; he wanted presses like the ones the students would use when they went to work at printing firms.

He officially became president and chairman of the board of the Deseret News Publishing Company on May 16, 1977. Elder Hinckley moved to chair the board at Bonneville International Corporation. Elder Monson selected new Deseret News board members who, for the most part, had worked with him in other capacities, including James E. Faust, who became vice president and vice chairman of the board.[2]

Elder Monson did just as President Tanner intended, leading with vigor, insight, and inspiration, and drawing upon the collective counsel of those on the board. Board member Emma Lou Thayne, a well-known poet, wrote him a note several years after he took charge: "It is apparent that you operate always out of a generosity of spirit that is as inspirational as it is rare."[3]

The senior post of publisher had long been vacant. Elder Monson recommended that Wendell J. Ashton, former managing editor of the Deseret News, be named as publisher and executive vice president, making him the chief operating officer of the corporation. "If you were going to cross the plains," he said to the Deseret News employees gathered to meet their new leader, "you would want Wendell Ashton out in front."[4]

In 1985 he was asked to form a printing advisory committee, the purpose of which was to lift the Deseret Press operation out of the Deseret News Publishing Company and merge it with the existing Church Printing Services. For years he had attempted to persuade the First Presidency, Elder Hinckley, and others who had a hand in the management of the Deseret News Publishing Company to make that change. He asserted that for the Deseret Press to attempt to act as a general line printer in the increasingly specialized world of printing was ill advised. He lobbied for the Deseret Press to withdraw from the commercial field and for the Church to funnel all printing through the Church Printing Services to maximize the use of the expensive equipment.

The Church Printing Services would operate as a division of the Materials Management Department. Elder Monson described the merger as "the culmination of a long-awaited dream for me, for I feel it is only good business to use our equipment to the maximum."[5] In its first year, the printing division of the Church operated in the black, and the Deseret News was able to funnel funds once allocated for equipment replacement to other areas.

On December 4, 1988, President Monson dedicated the Church's new 185,000-square-foot Printing Center, with a large web press now giving the Church the capability to print its own scriptures. "I have a great love for Church printing work because it produces material that bears witness of Jesus Christ, the Son of God," President Monson told those in attendance at the event. "From the work produced here go forth pages which become part of the conversion process that brings individuals to know the gospel of Jesus Christ."[6]

There were other issues to be addressed at the Deseret News. Early in 1980, as chairman of the board, Elder Monson began to negotiate a renewal of the Newspaper Agency Corporation (NAC) contract. For thirty years, the morning *Salt Lake Tribune* and the afternoon *Deseret News* had shared printing production facilities, provided joint circulation, and shared advertising staff. Elder Monson was now standing where his mentor Elder Mark E. Petersen had been decades earlier when he had helped craft the first contract. Tom, at the time, had just joined the Deseret News staff. Though the two newspaper entities split the costs fifty-fifty, the *Tribune* Sunday newspaper had grown in circulation, while interest in evening newspapers had given way to electronic news. Still, the contract, which would expire September 30, 1982, had been a blessing to both papers.

Elder Monson described the challenge ahead: "The circulation spread and the level of advertisers' acceptance are such that our competition, the *Salt Lake Tribune,* has a stronger position than does the *Deseret News* in negotiations. We will have to be at our best in order to obtain a satisfactory agreement. We will furthermore need the Lord's help."[7]

To begin negotiations, he invited John (Jack) Gallivan, longtime publisher of the *Tribune,* to meet with him, Elder James E. Faust, and *Deseret News* publisher Wendell Ashton in the office of President N. Eldon Tanner. They were competitors—but friends. For years, Elder Monson had worked tirelessly in community programs, often at Jack's side. Elder Monson left the meeting recognizing that Jack "intended to be a sharp negotiator with the profit split favoring the *Tribune.*"[8]

Initial efforts to negotiate a 50 percent interest in the Sunday paper went nowhere. Elder Monson and his associates then tried to purchase the Sunday *Tribune.* This offer was summarily rejected. Elder Monson brought in local attorney Wilford W. Kirton as chief negotiator, with Wendell J. Ashton assisting him. That allowed Elder Monson to step back, free of the rigors and rankle of the negotiations.

Wilford Kirton's role blunted confrontations between the two publishers who were, though good friends, understandably fierce rivals. Donald Holbrook, counsel for the Salt Lake Tribune, joined Mr. Gallivan on his side of the table. A year and a half later, on June 1, 1982, the two parties officially signed a contract in the office of President N. Eldon Tanner renewing the Newspaper Agency Corporation agreement between the Deseret News Publishing Company and the Kearns-Tribune Corporation. President Monson has kept as a memento the pen he used for the formal signing on behalf of the Deseret News Publishing Company. Jack Gallivan signed for the Salt Lake Tribune. The event was nothing short of historic for both papers, and it happened on the birthday of Brigham Young, who had founded the *Deseret News.* Both sides had tugged, pulled, and stormed to achieve their objectives.

In the end, the Tribune got much of what it wanted, and the Deseret News got concessions to publish its own Sunday paper and a Saturday morning edition. The two would share the national news services that had been exclusive to the Tribune; the

Newspaper Agency Corporation would increase its efforts to promote the afternoon *Deseret News* and the share of profits would divide 58 percent for the Salt Lake Tribune and 42 percent for the Deseret News, with the unilateral option on the part of the Deseret News to extend the thirty-year agreement at its conclusion in 2012. In addition, the Deseret News had the right to direct its own promotion program and invest its own funds, correlating with NAC. Mr. Gallivan would serve as president of the Newspaper Agency Corporation, with Elder Monson as vice president, Wendell Ashton as secretary, and Arthur Deck, managing editor of the Tribune, a member of the board.

Elder Monson was "very pleased," confessing, "I don't know of any assignment I have had which has been more time-consuming or demanding upon one's nervous energy than this particular assignment."[9] He considered the successful negotiation of the Newspaper Agency Corporation contract one of his major contributions as an officer of the Deseret News Publishing Company. In 1983, the arrangement provided a shareholder dividend to the Church, the first-ever cash dividend from the joint operating agreement.[10]

There was no question that Thomas S. Monson moved well in circles outside the Church environment. He knew the community; he had dealt with many different individuals when he was in the newspaper and printing business and working in civic groups. They knew him as a capable, outgoing, and respected leader. He was reasonable and forward thinking. He could grasp what was needed and knew who could make it happen. At university commencements, state inaugurals, and building dedications he was usually the one giving the opening or closing prayer; the Catholic bishop was often the other.

Elder Monson always felt privileged "to mingle with prominent men and women within our state, many of whom are not necessarily members of the Church but are community spirited and civic minded individuals."[11] And he enjoyed the challenge of associating with those in the business world and was ever mindful of the danger for Church leaders to become "ivory towered."

"He was not one to talk all the time or push his own interests," observed Duane Cardall, reporter for KSL. But he was one who could put the votes together in such a way as "to win the day."[12]

The two years of negotiations between the Tribune and Deseret News did little to stand in the way of Elder Monson's close friendship with Jack Gallivan and Don Holbrook. He and Jack would partner on a number of other community causes. They would lunch at the Alta Club, making plans to address some need in the community, from upgrading conditions in the blocks surrounding Pioneer Park—Elder Monson's old neighborhood—to revitalizing South Main Street. Jack would invite Elder Monson to services, celebrations, and functions at the Cathedral of the Madeleine, where Jack played a prominent role. And the Monsons would attend. At the funeral mass for Grace Ivers Gallivan, Jack's wife, the Monsons attended and later received a heartfelt note from Jack, "I treasure your friendship." Elder Monson referred to Jack as "Utah's best all-around-one-man ecumenical crusade,"[13] "a man of integrity and a man of honor. He is also a man of keen judgment and intellect."[14]

When Jack was named "Giant in Our City," President Monson gave the tribute. In 2001, President Monson attended the BYU commencement exercises where Jack Gallivan was awarded an honorary doctorate. President Monson had been the driving force in Jack's receiving this honor. Jack was both exuberant and grateful for the recognition. When Jack or anyone in his family was seriously ill, he or she would be remembered in Elder Monson's prayers.

In February 1993, President Monson joined with Jack Gallivan; Bishop William Weigand of the Salt Lake Catholic Diocese; Cardinal Roger Mahony, Archbishop of Los Angeles; and Agostino Cacciavillan, Apostolic Pro-Nuncio to the United States, for the dedication services of the restored Cathedral of the Madeleine. President Monson was accorded the singular honor of speaking at the luncheon held in conjunction with the dedication, the only cleric on the program who was not a Catholic. The Church had extended the hand of fellowship to the Catholic community, donating considerable funds to help in the massive restoration of the edifice, which had been dedicated originally in 1909.

Its presence on South Temple reached back to the days of the silver-mining boom in the surrounding Wasatch Mountains. Jack was pleased at his friend's attendance at the mass, as were others. Pat Shea, a prominent attorney who had helped the Church with some legal work and who was a Catholic, drew from a Robert Frost poem to express appreciation to President Monson and the Church for their involvement:

> *Men work together, I told him from the heart,*
> *Whether they work together or apart.*[15]

For President Monson, business is never just business. He makes acquaintances—even rivals—into friends. Tribune attorney Donald Holbrook was one he had served with on the State Board of Regents; Don was the chairman of that board, and they developed a close relationship.

President Monson spoke at the Catholic services in St. Ambrose Chapel for both of Don's sons, whose untimely deaths, several years apart, devastated the parents. President Monson was one of the first to the Holbrook home when he heard the news. His objective was simply "to help them."[16]

On another occasion, when one of Don's law partners was being set apart as a mission president, President Monson motioned to his friend and said, "Don, you're an elder, aren't you?" Don, who was raised a Mormon but had married a Catholic and subsequently had not been active in the LDS Church, responded, "Yes, sir."

President Monson beckoned, "Come and join us in setting apart your associate."

Don, pleased at the invitation, stepped forward. President Monson later acknowledged, "It was probably the first time he had ever participated in a blessing. It was a gratifying experience for me to have him stand in the circle."[17]

In 2005, for a third time, President Monson laid to rest another of the Holbrook family in services in the St. Ambrose Chapel. Don had died of cancer.

President Monson's attention to Don Holbrook and Jack

Gallivan is not unusual. There are countless people who have turned to him, who have been schooled in sheer goodness by his actions and words, and who have been rescued by his steady hand. Those who have observed Thomas S. Monson over the years see in him a pattern of following the Spirit promptly. He doesn't stop to check his watch or his schedule; he just responds and follows the inspiration to wherever it leads him.

"That has been Thomas S. Monson's ministry for lo these fifty-plus years," states Elder Jeffrey R. Holland. "The gospel is to get to the person in need. It might be a spiritual need, a temporal need; it might be the widow of whom he often speaks; it might be the rescued young woman or an Aaronic Priesthood young man."[18]

President Monson has spoken of the islanders in the South Pacific whose fishing efforts have been driven by a simple principle: "We pray and we go." His reaching out to others follows the same pattern. Elder Ballard, when serving as a mission president in Canada, called and asked Elder Monson "if he would mind stopping by the hospital and seeing his father if he had time." Elder Monson always had time for someone in need. He went that afternoon. On December 27, 1982, he spoke at Elder Ballard's father's funeral.[19]

It was no different with Helen Ivory, one of President Monson's widows from the old Sixth-Seventh Ward. Elder and Sister Monson went to visit her in a care center, where the attendant pointed them to the dining area, explaining that Helen sat there most days speaking to no one, clutching a card and envelope in her hands, which she would hold to her lips and kiss regularly. They pulled up chairs to Helen's side and said to her reassuringly, "We're here." They talked to her of their days in the Sixth-Seventh Ward, but they got no response. Frances finally persuaded Helen to let her see the envelope she held tightly. As she took it, she recognized it immediately; it was a Christmas card she had sent to Sister Ivory.[20]

When Elder Monson went to the Veteran's Hospital to provide a blessing for his dear friend Hyrum Adams, he spent an hour with this friend. It was a tearful discussion. Elder Monson sensed as he left that he had "accomplished more good in that visit than in a week of meetings at Church headquarters."[21]

"Often we live side by side," President Monson has taught, "but do not communicate heart to heart. There are those within the sphere of our own influence who, with outstretched hands, cry out, 'Is there no balm in Gilead?'"[22]

While he may have preferred to be blessing the sick and the infirm, he was also adept at handling the many tasks consistently piled on his desk. He served on the Ecclesiastical Studies Committee in 1978, charged with recasting the workload of the First Presidency and Quorum of the Twelve. Chairing the committee was Elder Hinckley, with Elder Monson, Elder Perry, and Elder Haight serving as members. The four men "discussed the duties of the Twelve, the Seventy, the Presidency of the Seventy, the regional representatives, and the entire matter of supervision of the work throughout the world." Elder Monson recognized that this was a "very significant task committee" and one that would have far-reaching impact on the work.[23]

After months of meetings, the committee presented a plan to move a substantial portion of the duties then held by the Twelve to the Presidents of the First Quorum of the Seventy, which would free the Apostles "to act more wisely in their calling as Apostles and in general Church management and place the Presidency of the First Quorum in a true position of presidency over their quorum members and indeed over the work."[24]

In 1984, under Elder Monson's chairmanship, the restructured committee, then called the Organizational Studies Committee, looked at the growth of the Church and attendant leadership needs. Elder Monson was masterful in his role, providing balance and institutional memory as the committee considered many options. At a June meeting in 1984, the committee proposed what Elder Monson viewed as one of the most significant changes presented during his twenty years as a member of the Quorum of the Twelve—to create Area Presidencies to regulate Church affairs in thirteen geographical areas, seven in the United States and six in other parts of the world. They replaced executive administrators in various nations. In the next several years, the number of areas would increase as the Church grew. Area Presidencies were later discontinued in the United States and Canada, where Church leadership is deep and experienced, but they have continued to operate in all other areas.

Following that June meeting, with the recommendation having been heartily accepted by all of the First Presidency and the Twelve, Elder Bruce R. McConkie expressed "special commendation" on behalf of the committee and other members of the Twelve "for the efficient and able leadership provided by Elder Thomas S. Monson in recent deliberations which culminated in the announcement by the First Presidency of administrative changes to be effective in the near future."[25]

Elder Monson was "humbled as well as honored" by Elder McConkie's gesture. He confided in his journal, "To my knowledge, this is the first time that any motion has ever been formally moved, seconded and acted upon expressing commendation to any member of the Twelve."[26]

The First Presidency had created a Welfare Services Department in April 1973, bringing together health services, social services, and welfare services into one correlated body. The General Welfare Services Committee had been charged to address the major issues of each of the services. Five years later, a Welfare Executive Committee was announced, with President Marion G. Romney, long a "welfare man," as chairman; Elder Monson, another "welfare man," as first vice chairman; and Presiding Bishop Victor L. Brown as second vice chairman to lead an effort to heighten the visibility of welfare principles and programs within the Church.

Welfare had long been a focus of Elder Monson, who as a young bishop had been schooled in the blessings of the Church welfare program. In the last half of 1979, Church officers were training stake leaders on welfare principles at stake conferences, showing a newly produced film, "Welfare Services: Another Perspective." Elder Monson in a general conference address called for "personal and family preparedness efforts, including food storage." He emphasized the "continuing need to insure that gainful employment is had by heads of families. Beyond this effort is the desirability to upgrade employment for those who may be underemployed."

In his message, he also called for increased participation in welfare projects, giving as an example his experience topping beets. "I am grateful I learned to top sugar beets on our stake welfare farm," he said. "I am also grateful that we do not have to top beets in the same way today. That farm was not situated in a fertile belt of land, but rather in the area of today's industrial section of Salt Lake City. I testify, however, that when put to this sacred service, the soil was sanctified, the harvest blessed, and faith rewarded."[27]

President Monson can see God's hand in a field of beets, just as he does in a home where righteousness overcomes the difficulties of the day by sheer faith in Jesus Christ. As an example of such a home, he has used the personal experience of Randy Spaulding from northern Utah, who as a young man wrote President Monson a letter describing the gradual onset of an illness that took his father from a healthy, strong individual to a "weak and crippled, middle-aged man." His father was confined to a wheelchair and was nearly helpless, but never did he or his wife ask, "Why us?" Wrote Randy, "Oh, how I long to take him back in time to the Pool of Bethesda and to ask our Master if He would please have mercy on us, so that my father, also, could take up his bed and walk."[28]

Letters telling of such hardship pour into President Monson's office. "Let us remember," he counsels, "that it was not the waters of Bethesda's pool which healed the impotent man. Rather, his blessing came through the touch of the Master's hand."[29]

Welfare to President Monson is that tender touch offered to anyone who needs it. It is also farms and storehouses, bishops' orders, employment centers, and skill training. The Church's once labor-intensive Church farms and properties are now part of an aggressive agribusiness providing commodities for the welfare system. Said Elder Monson, "The changes are inspired and long overdue." Yet, he contends, "The best storehouse is the individual storehouse of each family."[30]

In 1981, United States President Ronald Reagan appointed

Elder Monson to his "Task Force on Private Sector Initiatives." For more than a year, Elder Monson made repeated trips to Washington, D.C., to meet with thirty-four other business, religious, minority, nonprofit, and government leaders to address the notion of "neighbor helping neighbor."

At their first meeting, President Reagan outlined his desire to engage the private sector in a more vigorous manner to solve community needs. He then pointed to Elder Monson and said, "Seated at the table is Elder Monson, who represents The Church of Jesus Christ of Latter-day Saints, an organization which truly knows how to care for its own."[31] He then described how the Church had instituted its own welfare program during the Depression. Being singled out surprised Elder Monson, but he was gratified "for the high compliment" paid to the Church.[32]

President Reagan, who had during his tenure as governor of California visited some of the Church welfare canneries and was much impressed "with the independent spirit of the Mormon people," asked for advice and counsel from Elder Monson and others to solve a particularly vexing problem that, he said, "has weighed heavily upon me." What he hoped for was a "resurgence of the American spirit of generosity," an unprecedented outpouring of good deeds. He hoped the task force could help realize that vision.[33]

As part of his task force assignment, Elder Monson was invited to meet with all of the major religious leaders of America to explain the welfare program of the Church. Three other religious leaders also participated—one from the Catholic church, one from the Evangelical church, and one from the Jewish faith. The meeting represented "a true outpouring of brotherly love and kindness." Elder Monson used the Teton Dam disaster as his case study, prepared a brochure giving a brief explanation of the welfare plan, and showed the welfare film. He explained that the collapse of the Teton Dam in southeastern Idaho on June 5, 1976, had devastated communities along the Upper Snake River Valley. A wall of water, an estimated 80 billion gallons at a height from 12 to 20 feet, narrowly missed the communities of Teton and Newdale, but slammed with full force into Sugar City, Salem, and

Hibbard, destroying more than 50 percent of the homes and damaging all structures in those rural towns. St. Anthony, Roberts, and other communities were also flooded. Forty thousand people, more than 90 percent of them Church members, were driven from their homes. To the rescue, for months to come, came more than 35,000 Church members from surrounding states and truckloads of goods from the storehouses of the Church—on hand for immediate response to such a disaster.[34]

William Verity, the chairman of President Reagan's task force and chief executive officer of one of the nation's largest steel companies, wrote to Elder Monson, telling him how impressed he was with "the good works and the spirit of the Mormon Church." He called the film "a knockout" and concluded his note by saying, "If all of us could do as well as the Mormon Church, our problems would be over."[35]

In December 1982, the work of President Reagan's task force was completed. Elder Monson had felt honored to serve his country in this capacity and to make a contribution toward preserving proper welfare principles.

Humanitarian Aid, which would become a hallmark of the Church welfare system in years to come and a favorite focus of President Monson, got its start in 1985 when the members of the Church in the United States and Canada were asked to observe a special fast day and to be generous in donating fast offerings, which would be utilized in aiding the starving people in Ethiopia. Elder Monson said, "I am happy to see such a humanitarian program where the recipient who is in need can receive help regardless of whether or not the individual is a member of the Church. I think we need to do more of this type of endeavor."[36] The Church collected $6.8 million in donations. A new era in welfare had begun.

26

There Are No Coincidences

Some of the most superb moments I can remember about President Monson have been at mission presidents' seminars as he has talked about missions, mission experiences, and his tenderness for missionaries. I suspect not many people have equated those two things: love of missionaries and President Monson. He has a deep, abiding respect and love, interest, and consciousness of what happens to those in the mission field.

BISHOP H. DAVID BURTON
Presiding Bishop

THE LORD DECIDES WHERE YOU go on your mission, Elder Monson has told missionaries for many years. He has testified that "divine inspiration attends such sacred assignments" and "the faith and hopes and dreams of many people [are] involved."[1]

While attending a stake conference in Paris, France, Elder Monson indicated, as he often does, that he would like to hear from one of the missionaries. As he looked toward the back of the hall, he saw a tall young elder whom he recognized as a son of some friends of the Monsons. He called him forward. As the missionary spoke, Elder Monson seemed to see in his mind a picture of Heber J. Grant in a Japanese garden, the same painting that was produced as a cover for a pamphlet about this famed Church President. He didn't tell anyone about the experience and even wondered what it meant, assuming that it may have been triggered by his knowledge that President Grant was this elder's great-grandfather. When Elder Monson returned to Salt Lake City, he looked up the missionary's parents to give them a report on their son. He learned that another son had just turned in his missionary papers. As Elder Monson later reviewed that missionary's application, he knew why he had received the strong impression concerning President Grant. He changed the young missionary's assignment to Tokyo—the city and land where his great-grandfather, Heber J. Grant, had opened the work. Not only did the missionary serve in the land so significant to the family, he was present for the dedication of the Japan Tokyo Temple, an occasion, Elder Monson knew, that would have pleased his great-grandfather immensely.[2]

On another occasion, Elder Monson designated a mission assignment for a young man, only to return back to it several times. Still not feeling right, he asked Elder Carlos Asay, a member of the Seventy who was assisting him in the assignment meeting, to read him the whole file. In the initial review they had somehow missed the information that the young man had learned Spanish "at his mother's knee." Elder Monson assigned him to a Spanish-speaking mission, and the Spirit said, "Yes."

"It never ceases to amaze me how the Lord can motivate and direct the length and breadth of His kingdom," Elder Monson has said, "and yet have time to provide the inspiration on the call of a single missionary."[3]

Elder Monson became chairman of the Missionary Executive Committee in 1976 after having served for more than a decade on that committee. As chairman, he sat with Elders David B. Haight and Bruce R. McConkie at his side and was involved in the processes of selecting mission presidents, assigning missionaries, recommending the creation of new missions, approving the acquisition of mission homes, recommending training programs, caring for missionaries assigned to foreign- and English-speaking countries, and providing oversight of visitors' centers and the Language Training Mission.

Through his hands passed tens of thousands of missionary applications. Elder Monson has said, "Many are the faith-promoting experiences which have occurred in the assignment of missionaries. I so testify. Hardly an assignment day goes by when we don't have it evidenced that our Heavenly Father has, in an unusual way, prompted us to send particular missionaries to serve in locations, only to learn that this has fulfilled their earnest prayers and, in many instances, the wishes and hopes of their families."[4]

When the Monsons' son Clark received his mission call, he was hesitant to open it. Frances asked, "Aren't you anxious to find out where you are going?" Clark shrugged, "I know where I'm going. Dad wants me to go to Canada, so no doubt that's where I'll go." Elder Monson spoke up, "Clark, you'd better open the call because I didn't make your assignment. I think a father should not assign his own son to his mission." Clark then opened the call and expressed delight, with some surprise, that his call was to New Zealand.[5]

President Monson feels strongly the importance of preparing missionaries for service while they are young. His counsel to youth has been clear: "Preparation for a mission is not a spur-of-the-moment matter. It began before you can remember. Every class in Primary, Sunday School, seminary—each priesthood assignment—had a larger application. Silently, almost imperceptibly, a life was molded, a career commenced, a man made. . . . You who hold the Aaronic Priesthood and honor it have been reserved for this special period in history. The harvest truly is great. Let there be no mistake about it; the opportunity of a lifetime is yours. The blessings of eternity await you."[6]

A young man serving in the South Dakota Rapid City Mission wrote Elder Monson, describing the time when the Apostle had started him thinking about serving a mission:

"You spoke at a stake conference at the San Diego South Stake. There you taught the principle of tithing by using a demonstration. You called two girls up and a boy—I was the boy. You gave the one girl a penny, the other a dime and me a dollar. I remember the words you used to call me up, 'You, the one in the middle with the messy hair.' I knew you were talking about me. Then you taught the law of tithing in a simple and nice form. Afterwards you gave the penny to the one girl and sent her back to her seat, and went through the same process with the girl with the dime. Then you put your arm around me and told me that I could keep the whole dollar to start my missionary fund. Well, I'm 20 now instead of 11 and I am out on a mission."[7]

The responsibility of missionaries to be faithful representatives of the Lord was always on Elder Monson's mind, and he reminded them of that responsibility at every opportunity, explaining, "[You] are building a foundation upon which many hundreds shall indeed build further. . . . Remember [your] sacred calling and . . . be good examples to all the members and to the population at large."[8]

With his responsibility for the Missionary Committee, Elder Monson had to be available night and day for questions and issues about missionary work. He dealt with kidnappings, missionary disappearances, illnesses, deaths, natural disasters, and even military coups.

He and the other committee members also dealt with any errant activity in the field. He attended a mission conference in an area that had posted a suspiciously high number of baptisms, in which there was some evidence that the converts were being baptized without having been taught sufficiently the doctrines of the Church. He had been assigned by the First Presidency to visit and get the mission back to the "approved" missionary program. He could not have known he was also on a mission to rescue one single elder who was floundering.

He recognized among the zone leaders an elder from St. Thomas, Ontario, Canada. Elder Monson had attended a district conference in London, Ontario, when the missionary was six months old. At that time, the boy's mother and father had recently been involved in a terrible auto accident that had seriously injured his mother and had eventually led to her death. "I was able to recite to the young man how I administered to his mother and held her hand when she knew that she was dying. I explained to him that her great concern was for her son. She hoped that our Heavenly Father would bless him and guide him throughout his stay in mortality."

The young missionary wept as he learned of the caring feelings of a mother he had never known. Elder Monson later learned that the young Canadian's adjustment had been particularly difficult. "It was providential that I was the General Authority assigned to this particular task in this mission, that I might, being the only one among the General Authorities who knew his parents, convey to him this special plan and prayer from his mother."[9]

He is quick to say, "There are no coincidences."

Elder Monson conducted mission presidents' seminars in all areas of the world. On October 20, 1982, at a mission presidents' seminar in Great Britain, a fire broke out in the kitchen of the Caledonia Hotel in Edinburgh, where the mission presidents and their wives were staying. All guests were evacuated. He remembers the night well. When the wife of the England Manchester Mission president saw him, she put her hands over her hair, exclaiming, "My hair is in curlers!" He responded, "That's all right; I don't have a tie on."[10]

At a mission presidents' seminar in the midwestern United States in 1978, in a more relaxed social setting one evening, Elder Monson looked at Sister Jan Callister, eight months pregnant, whose husband, Douglas, presided over the Minnesota Minneapolis Mission, and asked each person present, "Do you think Sister Callister is going to have a boy or a girl?" Because Sister Callister earlier had disclosed that the physicians thought her baby was likely a boy because of the heartbeat, every individual in the room said it was going to be a boy. Except Elder Monson. He said, "You are all wrong. It will be a girl." It was.

Twenty years later, Elder Callister, then a regional representative, was attending a regional conference in Palm Springs, California, at which President Monson was presiding. "He walked in," Elder Callister describes, "with no . . . recognition that he knew me or had ever met me. When he stood to speak he said, 'I have been thinking about Elder Callister sitting behind me on the second row on the stand. Twenty years ago I met him in Chicago; his wife was expecting. Everyone else thought she would have a boy, but I said, "Not true, it will be a girl."' And he turned around and said to my wife sitting next to me, 'Sister Callister, it was a girl, wasn't it?' She said, 'It was.' He said, 'I thought so.'" The Callisters were amazed by Elder Monson's memory, "having not seen him, having not had one word with him for twenty years."

Said Elder Callister, "He makes every person he greets feel like one of the special people in his life, and he remembers some incident concerning that person that he'll tell. That is one of the things that causes him to be loved."[11]

Elder Monson took President Spencer W. Kimball's clarion call to members of the Church, "Lengthen your stride," as a personal challenge to look for more opportunities to share the gospel. When he was attending the installation of a new university president at a local college, the man who helped him in and out of the cap and gown was an old friend. As he was leaving, the two "exchanged a few pleasantries," and Elder Monson hurried on his way. But, he explains, "I felt impressed to go back and bear to him my testimony." The man was not a member of the Church, though his wife and daughter were.

He remembers saying, "Gene, I feel impressed to mention one or two things to you. First, may I say that it is not my desire or my disposition to impose my religious persuasions upon another person who may not wish to receive them. However, I have known you for a long time. You have a lovely wife and a choice daughter who are members of the Church and who, more than anything in this world, would like you to be a member so that you could go to the temple as an eternal family." Elder Monson then expressed his testimony that the gospel of Jesus Christ was true and could be of inestimable worth in the man's life, noting later, "He thanked me and was somewhat emotional in doing so."

A few weeks later, Elder Monson received word that Gene had suddenly decided to be baptized. When Gene's daughter was married a few years later, her father was sitting in the witness chair in the temple as Elder Monson performed the ceremony.[12]

In connection with his "Lengthen your stride" counsel, President Kimball encouraged Latter-day Saints to petition the Lord for the doors of then-closed countries to be opened for the preaching of the gospel. As a result of the prayers of the members, he said, "We may get all of the missionaries that are needed to cover the world as with a blanket," and he indicated that "when we are prepared, the Lord will open the gates."[13] President Monson would renew that call as a priority in his first general conference address as President of the Church in April 2008.

Portugal was one such land just opening its doors. Elder and

Sister Monson arrived for a visit there in 1975, at a time when national elections were filling the streets with calls for change. The Communist government had a clear advantage. The Church had learned much from working with the Communist governments behind the Iron Curtain and did not want to see missionary work limited in this recently opened mission in Portugal.

As they drove from the airport to the mission home, they saw crude signs scrawled on beautiful statues and fences: "Vote Communista." Elder Monson readily recognized that the political situation could well mark the end of a brief beginning of missionary work in Portugal. The next morning, the Monsons, missionaries, and a handful of members stood on a hilltop where Elder Monson dedicated Portugal for the preaching of the gospel. Mission President Grant Bangerter leaned over before Elder Monson began to pray and said, "Ask our Heavenly Father to intervene in the election."

As Elder Monson offered the prayer, he asked for divine guidance as the Church struggled to get established. "We recognize that from this land went navigators and seafaring men in days of yore and that the Portuguese people had an adventuresome spirit as they trusted in Thee when they looked for lands unknown. Grant that they may trust in Thee as they now search for those truths which will lead them to life eternal." He concluded the prayer by asking that the election might come out in such a way that missionary work would not be impaired.[14]

Two days later, as he and Frances prepared to leave, the European edition of the *Herald Tribune* announced, "Moderates Sweep Portugal Election—Communists a Poor Third." Elder Monson gratefully thanked Heavenly Father "for His intervention" in the election.[15] There are no coincidences.

Fifteen years later, when President Monson was again on assignment in Portugal, a missionary serving there handed him a letter. The young man had written, "When a sophomore in high school, my life was a very difficult one to live. I had problems with school, friends, low self-esteem, and even with my family at times. But one thing I always loved was to listen to the conference talks given by Thomas S. Monson. They made me forget my troubles.

416

. . . One day when my mother got mad at me and chewed me out, I asked, 'Why can't the Lord send me someone to carry this load?'"

The elder, then a young teenager, had written Elder Monson describing his plight. He had received a package with "Thomas S. Monson" on the return address, containing a letter and a book by Elder Monson, *Be Your Best Self.* In the letter, Elder Monson had written, "You asked, 'Why can't the Lord send someone to help me carry this load?' Well, maybe He has, for I wish to help you carry it by uniting my prayers with yours." Elder Monson had also written, "I can relate to that which you write, because I remember the time when I was the last boy to be chosen on a softball team."

The young missionary now concluded, "I don't know if a great man like you could ever know how much that meant to me, and looking back, I can say that that experience saved me spiritually."[16]

As the work proceeded in various lands, Elder Monson had the privilege of dedicating other places. A prayer of dedication had been offered for all the Scandinavian nations in the early days of the Church, before individual missions were created for the different countries, but no prayer had ever been given specifically for Sweden. On July 7, 1977, at the Stockholm Third Ward chapel, Elder Monson importuned the Lord: "We place this land, Father, and all who live herein in Thy care and under Thy watchful supervision. We plead with Thee to bring to the people a desire to know the truth, we plead with Thee to bring to them the ability to recognize the truth when they hear it and when they see it, and we plead with Thee to cause that their hearts may rejoice and that they may embrace the gospel wholeheartedly and become converted to the truth."[17]

Bo Wennerlund, regional representative, translated for Elder Monson, who called him "Brother Bo." He recalls, "I stood by [Elder Monson's] side. I prayed, may the same spirit that guides him, guide me. I was the instrument to put his words into Swedish. The words just flew from him and from me. Always to me, it was a spiritual experience to translate for him."[18]

Elder Monson would be back in Sweden on March 17, 1984, to break ground for a temple. The ground was frozen solid. Braving 16-degree-Fahrenheit weather, with about 400 people in attendance,

Elder Monson said, "The temple is the pinnacle of happiness. Today we shall call upon our Heavenly Father to . . . sanctify our sacrifices and to let this be a dwelling place for Him."[19] He spoke tenderly of his Swedish heritage and mentioned how pleased his Grandfather Monson and his grandfather's brothers and sisters must have felt "to think that a descendant of theirs would play a historic role in the beautiful city of Stockholm in dedicating a plot of ground for a temple of God."[20] Sister Monson addressed the gathering as well.

Many members of Elder Monson's family—mother, aunts, and uncles—had died. His father's health had been deteriorating for many months, until on Sunday, May 13, 1979, he too passed away. Elder Monson had dreamed the night before that his father had died. "Strangely enough," he said, "Marilyn, Bob, and Barbara [his siblings] had similarly had such a dream."[21] At about 9:30 P.M., his father slipped away from mortality. Elder Monson considered the passage of scripture that was most reflective of his father's life to be: "For where your treasure is, there will your heart be also."[22] His father's treasure had been his family. Elder Monson spoke at the funeral, as did President Kimball.

In March 1982 Elder Monson was released from the Missionary Committee and received a new assignment at headquarters as chairman of the Priesthood Executive Council. He had served in missionary work since President McKay was the prophet, more than sixteen years. The Priesthood Executive Council included "just about everything in the Church, with the exception of Family History and Missionary Service," the other two major councils. After one of the first meetings, he said, "Already I can see that this Council will handle 90 percent of the detail work of the Church." He indicated that he had the "finest" committee, which included Elder David B. Haight, Elder Neal A. Maxwell, Bishop Victor L. Brown, Elder M. Russell Ballard, and Elder Dean L. Larsen.[23]

While most members of the Church had seen him at the pulpit and loved his messages and his spirit, they hadn't seen his influence and impact on the Church's structure, its programs and administration. He worked long hours and was often the last to leave the Church Administration Building. He came in on

Saturdays and Mondays when he was not out of town. He kept his secretary busy with enough work for three people. His remarkable memory made him invaluable in looking back at precedents, and his forward thinking was always insightful. He brought back astute observations from the field and worked effectively to implement needed change. He supervised revisions of the General Handbook of Instructions all the way through to the printing. From that close attention to how things were to be done, he became very knowledgeable about Church policy and procedures. That knowledge, coupled with his remarkable memory, made him a formidable force in committee work. Those who served with him in those years concur that if they wanted to get something through the system, they gave it to Tom Monson.

Elder Monson oversaw the completion of the 1985 hymnbook, the first new edition in 37 years, after Elder Mark E. Petersen died. Elder Monson had served on the hymnbook committee throughout its twelve years and had left his personal touch on the completed volume: Several older hymns were replaced by new ones, including "Hark, All Ye Nations," one of President Monson's favorites. The book was larger than the previous edition, as was the type. Elder Monson credited Michael Moody, who had served all twelve years as managing director of the Church Music Committee, as the moving force deserving of "a mountain of praise for his persistent and capable efforts."[24] For Elder Monson, his involvement with the hymnbook was a treasured experience.

Elder Monson conceived the idea of multistake conferences to replace area conferences; these were instituted in 1984. He pondered what the Lord would have him say on such assignments. "Resolve to make room in your life for Jesus Christ. We have time for jogging, time for working, time for playing. Let us make time for Christ," he told one gathering.[25] To another, at the beginning of a new year, he said, "Contemplate the next twelve months. First we should resolve to be good listeners. And to whom should we listen? To the prophets of God, to the whisperings of our conscience, to the whisperings of the still small voice."[26]

Temple worship accelerated with the dedication of a number of new temples. The Jordan River Temple dedication used as "overflow" the Salt Lake Tabernacle. Elder Monson admitted, "While I had originally some doubts concerning whether or not this would be a suitable accommodation for a temple dedication overflow, located so far from the temple, all doubt ceased when I saw the Tabernacle filled to overflowing. During the Hosanna Shout, to see 8,000 to 9,000 handkerchiefs waving simultaneously overhead was a thrill ever to be remembered."[27]

It was an era of "taking the temples to the people." Elder Monson spoke at the rededications of the Logan and Manti temples. At the Atlanta Temple dedication on June 1, 1983, for the first time in his apostolic ministry, he led the Hosanna Shout. He spoke again at the Dallas Temple dedication on October 19, 1984. Temple dedications would never become casual to him, though he would attend and speak at dozens in the years to come. They were a clear indicator that the Church indeed was on course "in so great a cause,"[28] and he felt privileged to be a part of that holy work.

In April 1981 BYU honored Elder Monson with a Doctor of Laws Degree, the first presented under the hand of the newly named president, Jeffrey R. Holland. The tribute described his loyalty, a quality "universally admired." "A friend of Thomas Monson's is a friend forever—through good times, through bad times, and through years of separation," it read. "Furthermore, business associations, civic causes, political beliefs and above all, principles of the gospel of Jesus Christ are also defended with a conviction and loyalty that surely must be considered uncommon to a world in which values are increasingly relative and ideals are increasingly rare."[29] He would receive similar honors from the Salt Lake Community College (1996), University of Utah (2007), Utah Valley University (2009), Southern Utah University (2009) and Weber State University (2010).

His daughter, Ann, so proud of her father, wrote to him in 1983: "On this, your twentieth anniversary of your calling to the Twelve, I want you to know how proud I am of you and how proud I am to be your daughter. Having been only nine when you received your call, I only understood that it was important. Now I understand what a sacred responsibility was entrusted to you twenty years ago. Through the years I've seen the great effort you have continually expended in order to magnify your calling. I also know, through your shared experiences, how the Lord has truly worked miracles through you in order to bring to pass His desires and bless His children. I am sure that even though there must be times of discouragement, the knowledge that you have assisted the Lord in accomplishing His purposes must be a great source of comfort and assurance that He is pleased with your efforts. . . . I love you, I admire you, and I shall be eternally grateful that I was born under the covenant into yours and Mother's home."[30]

The pace of the work took its toll on the senior leaders, President Kimball included. Elder Monson wrote in his journal after the President had improved from a long siege of illness, "What a delight to hear from President Kimball. His spirit inspires a greater devotion to duty on the part of each one of us."[31] President Tanner and President Romney were failing as well. At one point early in 1982, the presiding officer of each quorum of the Church was in the hospital: President Spencer W. Kimball, First Presidency; President Ezra Taft Benson, Quorum of the Twelve; Elder Franklin D. Richards, First Quorum of the Seventy; and Bishop Victor L. Brown, Presiding Bishop.[32]

Elder Monson had been close to all three members of the First Presidency, but his bond with President N. Eldon Tanner went back to his days in Canada. "It is a sad thing to see a giant oak commence to lean," Elder Monson wrote. "President Tanner, in my judgment, will go down in Church history as one of the greatest counselors who has ever served a Church President. I think his contribution is equal to that of President J. Reuben Clark."[33]

President Tanner died November 28, 1982. Elder Monson had lost a real friend, and the Church had lost an exceptional administrator. President Marion G. Romney was named as First Counselor in the First Presidency and President Gordon B. Hinckley as Second Counselor. (President Hinckley had been serving as a third counselor to President Kimball since July 1981.)

A year later, January 11, 1983, Elder LeGrand Richards died, just three days short of his ninety-seventh birthday. Then, on January 16, 1984, Elder Monson spoke at the funeral of one of his mentors, Elder Mark E. Petersen. In a later tribute to Elder Petersen in the Church magazines, he wrote:

"Few men are given the opportunity to influence the Church in the manner Elder Mark E. Petersen influenced it for nearly forty years as one of the Lord's special witnesses. His was a pen of spiritual power. Mark Petersen combined an insightful mind with a faith-filled heart to work wonders with his words. His style was distinctively his own."[34]

Added to the Quorum of the Twelve to fill the two vacancies were Russell M. Nelson, a heart surgeon and former general president of the Sunday School, and Dallin H. Oaks, Supreme Court justice in the state of Utah and former president of BYU.

Elder Bruce R. McConkie died April 19, 1985. Another dear friend was gone. Elder Monson had visited Elder McConkie the previous Monday and had given him a blessing. "He was bedfast but could communicate with me. He expressed his friendship for me as I did for him," Elder Monson recalled. "His philosophy always was: do the very best you can in the assignments you fulfill. It is a good philosophy."[35]

Elder Monson was assigned to the committee to handle Elder McConkie's funeral, "quite an undertaking, with many aspects, all the way from security to flowers to speakers to funeral processions."[36] One of those attending a planning meeting was Ronald D. John, new manager of Temple Square. At the close of the meeting, Elder Monson called on one of the security men to say the prayer and asked if anyone in the room had heard what the weather forecast might be on Tuesday, the day of the funeral. It was the consensus opinion that the weather would be bad. He said to the man giving the prayer, "It can't rain on Bruce's funeral; please take care of that in your prayer, will you?'"

Brother John later described his feelings in a letter: "Elder Monson, I have been a first counselor to two bishops; I've been a bishop two times; I've served on two high councils, and I'm currently serving as first counselor in a stake presidency. I've had some special experiences, but never have I felt what I felt in that room at that time. I never understood childlike faith until that moment. I had come to me an absolute knowledge that the elements would obey." He raced home and called his best friend, local television weatherman Mark Eubank, and asked: "What will the weather be on Tuesday?" Mark answered that the pattern of bad weather would stay for at least four or five more days. "I then told him of my experience in your office. . . . On Monday evening, Mark alone forecast clear and warm weather until at least 3:00 P.M. on Tuesday. You and Elder Packer were the last two to leave the cemetery. As you drove away, the large awning we had set up for the family almost blew down. . . . As I looked toward the west, the black clouds were coming across the lake. Elder Monson, it wasn't the sign that was the teacher but your example of absolute faith that I shall never forget."[37]

M. Russell Ballard, member of the Presidency of the Seventy and former president of the Canada Toronto Mission, was called to fill the vacancy in the Twelve.

Church leadership was entering a unique period. Both President Kimball and President Romney were ill. "President Hinckley found himself in a most challenging situation, because President Kimball was still the prophet," Elder Monson has described, looking back. "Even though a man may be impaired physically, he might not be impaired mentally or spiritually. President Hinckley had the unenviable task of not going too far too fast, but of going far enough. . . . He was the only member of the First Presidency in attendance many times in our meetings of the Presidency and the Twelve. We made certain we were in total agreement on any issue before we moved forward. We had worked many years with President Kimball, and we knew how President Kimball felt about many matters and what his decisions would most likely be. . . . Short of assuming that prophetic mantle, he [President Hinckley] moved as far as he could."[38]

On November 5, 1985, President Hinckley called the members of the Quorum of the Twelve together and told them that President Kimball was in a precarious state of health. It appeared that the end could be imminent. Elder Monson looked around the room and realized that every member of the Quorum was in attendance. Just twenty-four hours earlier, fully a third of them had been elsewhere in the world, some oceans away.

President Spencer W. Kimball died that evening at 11:00 P.M. at age ninety. He had served as Church President for twelve years.

27

ORDAINED IN HEAVEN

He has this energy, this liveliness and bounce. He goes through the halls like a whirlwind; sometimes the paintings have to be straightened after he has gone by.

ELDER JEFFREY R. HOLLAND
Quorum of the Twelve Apostles

IT WAS SUNDAY, NOVEMBER 10, 1985, and Elder Monson was making one of his frequent visits to a care center near his home to participate in the church services with the elderly residents. When he walked in, he was greeted with smiles. These were people who knew him and loved him. Being with such pure hearts prepared him for the rest of his day.

At 3:00 that afternoon, he and thirteen of the living Apostles met in one of the most sacred meetings that is ever held on earth.[1] A new President of The Church of Jesus Christ of Latter-day Saints was to be chosen. President Ezra Taft Benson, as President of the Quorum of the Twelve, conducted the session. Seven of the Twelve had never before participated in a reorganization of the First Presidency. Elder Ballard had been an Apostle only one month.

After each one present expressed his feelings, Elder Howard W. Hunter nominated Ezra Taft Benson as the thirteenth President of the Church. Elder Gordon B. Hinckley seconded the motion, and it carried unanimously. The words of Joseph Smith rang true: "Every man who has a calling to minister to the inhabitants of the world was ordained to that very purpose in the Grand Council of heaven before this world was."[2] Like those before him, President Benson had not been elected "through committees and conventions with all their conflicts, criticisms, and by the vote of men," but was "called of God and then sustained by the people." The divine pattern "allows for no errors, no conflicts, no ambitions, no ulterior motives. The Lord has reserved for himself the calling of his leaders over his Church."[3]

President Benson responded humbly to the call and indicated that he had prayerfully and with much fasting considered the matter of his counselors. He indicated he had been to the temple earlier in the day and petitioned for divine guidance and then announced that his first counselor would be Gordon B. Hinckley and his second counselor would be Thomas S. Monson. Again, the Apostles approved—unanimously.

Elder Monson was completely surprised but certainly able, worthy, qualified, and willing to so serve. He was fifty-eight years old, the youngest counselor called in more than 100 years. President Benson was eighty-six; President Hinckley was seventy-five.

President Benson, in a circle of Apostles laying hands on Elder Monson's head, set him apart "in the authority of the holy priesthood of God and in the power of the holy apostleship." The Prophet blessed his new counselor with "strength to carry forward" as he had in the past and thanked the Lord for Elder Monson's "glorious memory, which is almost unequaled among men."[4]

At a press conference held the following day, President Benson said, "The Lord, through President Kimball, has sharply focused on the threefold mission of the Church: to preach the gospel, to perfect the Saints, and to redeem the dead. We shall continue every effort to carry out this mission."[5]

What would distinguish the Benson presidency was the renewed emphasis on the Book of Mormon. "When President Ezra Taft Benson warned that we had neglected the Book of Mormon and urged every member to read and study this sacred volume, new printing presses were required to produce more and more copies of the book,"[6] noted President Monson.

Elder Monson approached the calling to the First Presidency with "deep humility." That the First Presidency would be "upheld by the confidence, faith, and prayer of the Church" was comforting.[7] The knowledge that Jesus Christ stands at the head of His Church and directs it through His chosen servants eased immediately the burden President Monson felt.

He understood the hierarchical nature of the Church and the fact that, as described in scripture, "three Presiding High Priests . . . form a quorum of the Presidency of the Church,"[8] the highest governing body. He was grateful for every experience he had had in Church administration and for his mentors J. Reuben Clark, Jr., Harold B. Lee, Mark E. Petersen, N. Eldon Tanner, and others.

He perhaps did not fully realize the impact he himself was having in the lives of others. As Rex E. Lee, then president of BYU, wrote to him: "I know of literally no one who has your combination of leadership talent together with personal sensitivity and ability to touch the human, spiritual chords within each of us. You are a great man, President Monson, and I always feel better about myself when I am in your presence."[9]

His years in the Quorum of the Twelve had been a remarkable training period for President Monson. "As you pass through the chairs of seniority in the Quorum of the Twelve, you have a lot of assignments so you can learn how the Church works: Missionary Department, Priesthood Department, Correlation, Temples, and the business aspects or corporations, like the Deseret News," explains Elder Russell M. Nelson.[10] Elder Monson had worked in them all. Elder Monson had also supervised the work in the South Pacific, Mexico, Northwest United States, and Europe, with sole responsibility for East Germany for nearly twenty years.

President Monson brought his love, loyalty, and stability to President Benson's side. He moved his office downstairs to the southwest corner on the main floor of the Church Administration Building. His secretary, Lynne Cannegieter, went with him. Elder Gordon B. Hinckley's office was directly across the hall.

The work and the workload at the office changed dramatically. President Spencer W. Kimball, after a few months in the highest quorum, had commented to his Brethren, "I never dreamed of the detail the First Presidency has to deal with. It has been like night and day."[11] Like President Kimball, President Monson enjoyed detail, had a prodigious work ethic, and also knew how to work with people.

President Monson soon learned that the work was not only different from his Quorum assignments but also worldwide in perspective. In 1985, the Church had on record almost 5,920,000 members, 12,939 wards and branches, and 1,582 stakes. Thirty-seven temples were blessing the people around the world, and 29,265 missionaries were serving in 188 missions.[12]

The First Presidency met every Tuesday, Wednesday, Thursday, and Friday at 8:00 A.M. and then were together many times during the day as they attended additional meetings. President Monson soon found his appointments, consultations, and presentations taking on a different cast, as the First Presidency originated fewer programs but passed final judgment on everything of significance. "The work of the Twelve is somewhat different than that of the Presidency," he recognized quickly. "The Presidency finds it most difficult to be away from the office even for a week at a time, for the avalanche of mail never ceases, and the problems from the field do not take a holiday."[13]

By revelation, the First Presidency directs the day-to-day operations of the Church as well as temple work, those ecclesiastical affairs supervised by the Quorum of the Twelve, and the temporal affairs administered by the Presiding Bishop.

One of the dynamics that did not change with his call to the First Presidency was the need for unity among the First Presidency and Quorum of the Twelve. "That scriptural mandate requires everyone to pay attention to everyone else," notes Elder D. Todd Christoffersen, a member of the Quorum of the Twelve who was called by President Monson. "Everybody has to be heard, everyone has to contribute, everyone has to be on board before we take any action. No one can be waved off."[14] That attention to one another's viewpoints is by divine design: "And every decision made by either of these quorums must be by the unanimous voice of the same; that is, every member in each quorum must be agreed to its decisions."[15]

The deliberative process fits President Monson's style. "There will come a moment, usually after a lot of hard work, lots of thinking, he does charts, he reads minutes, he really does his homework, asks for lots of opinion, prays a long time, and when he's there, you know he's there," his first counselor, President Henry B. Eyring, describes. "He will never say, 'I had an impression from the Lord.' He will just say, after a lot of prayer, 'I think this is what we ought to do.' He waits until he receives revelation and then he acts."[16]

The First Presidency and Quorum of the Twelve met occasionally with no structured agenda, usually on a Sunday, where they discussed the issues pressing on the Church. President Monson said of such a meeting held on December 13, 1992, "I feel that a uniform commitment resulted from the discussions."[17]

Elder Francis M. Gibbons, former secretary to the First Presidency before being called to the Quorum of the Seventy, wrote to President Monson, "The mantle of the First Presidency fits very well indeed. Your openness, your enthusiasm, and your spirituality are sources of inspiration to us all."[18]

Again, many "firsts" began to unfold in President Monson's life. It had been a first that November day in 1985 to sit under the hands of a prophet and to be set apart to the Quorum of the First Presidency and as his Second Counselor; a first in the next temple meeting to be seated next to President Benson and, although only ten feet from the Quorum of the Twelve, to realize "what an altered assignment" he had.[19] It was a first to sit in council with the First Presidency and make assignments to the Quorum of the Twelve. "Those men did a lot of work in a very short period of time," Elder Russell M. Nelson recalls. "They started with the senior Brethren and went down the line and gave them their assignments. They said to me, 'Elder Nelson, you are responsible for the affairs of the Church in Africa and in Europe, with the specific assignment to open the doors in Europe that are now under the yoke of Communism.'" Elder Nelson admits to thinking,

"Who, me?"[20] Without question, President Monson knew he was committing his precious countries of Eastern Europe to able hands, and he kept close to developments, joining Elder Nelson and others in several momentous meetings in East Germany and Poland, in particular.

Bishop Richard Sager of President Monson's home ward, Valley View Ninth, invited him to speak in the ward on November 17, his first public address as a member of the First Presidency. In addition, he made his first calls to new mission presidents. He attended his first Investment Policy Committee meeting and, at the New Year, wrote in his journal, "Today began my first new year as a member of the First Presidency of The Church of Jesus Christ of Latter-day Saints. My new assignments bring a spirit of humility to my soul, coupled with a desire to do my very best."[21] His first meetings to consider restoration of temple blessings prompted him to grieve, "This is a particularly arduous assignment when one realizes the enormity of the decisions to be made. Some few of our members certainly have a variety of problems."[22]

He prepared a dedicatory prayer, his first, for the Buenos Aires Argentina Temple and barely arrived on January 5 in time to read it. Airline delays en route placed him on the ground with just enough time to take a cold shower, put on his white suit, and dash to the cornerstone-laying ceremony, where, with an umbrella blocking the pouring rain, he placed mortar around the stone. The words of the dedicatory prayer resonated with the 10,000 in attendance in the eleven sessions. In part, the prayer stated:

"Bless with health and wisdom Thy servant, President Ezra Taft Benson, whom Thou hast called to lead Thy Church in this day. Reveal to him Thy mind and will concerning the growth and advancement of Thy work among the children of men. . . .

"As we dedicate this temple, we dedicate our very lives. We desire to lay aside anything petty or sordid, and reach to thee in daily prayer and supplication, that our thoughts may be pure, our hearts and hands clean, and our lives in conformity with Thy teachings. . . .

"May all who enter this, Thy house, be privileged to say, as did the Psalmist of old, 'We took sweet counsel together, and walked unto the house of God in company.' (Psalm 55:14.)"[23]

His work in Communist countries was not finished. President Monson and Elder Nelson met with Poland's minister of religion, Adam Wopatka, and his deputy for non-Catholic churches on May 31, 1986. The Brethren had prayed fervently that they would be received in a proper spirit and that their two objectives would be realized—that the Church would be permitted to have more than one missionary couple in Poland and that it would find a way to properly accommodate the members there in appropriate meetinghouses. President Monson reported, "When I asked the question regarding an additional missionary couple so that we would have an overlap, the minister suggested that we be granted three or four additional couples. When I talked about buildings, he indicated we would have his full approval in remodeling an existing building or in acquiring properties and building chapels designed for our specific purpose. I could not have wished for a more positive reception."[24] The next day, June 1, President Monson offered a prayer, "bringing a current dimension to the previous prayer of dedication." In it, he indicated that "a new emphasis and thrust of members are soon to take place, and this land, together with the people whom Thou hast prepared to receive the gospel, will blossom as the rose and will take its place among the nations where Thy Spirit has directed the on-rolling of the work."[25]

He dedicated a meetinghouse in Budapest, Hungary, on October 17, 1989; 128 Saints attended. He noted later that as he drove past the Parliament Building, "little did we realize that within the building that very day the parliament was sitting to discuss the overthrow of Communist rule in Hungary and the declaration of Hungary as a free republic. This represented perhaps one of the most historic days in the history of Hungary."[26]

His first release of a general auxiliary officer was that of Patricia Holland, wife of BYU president Jeffrey R. Holland, who had been serving as a counselor in the Young Women general presidency. Afterward, President Holland expressed his gratitude in a letter, saying, "I felt I was in the presence of angels, as well as in the presence of one who knows how angels work. I said to you in parting that perhaps somewhere, someday someone will ask my advice on how a release should be extended to one who has faithfully served. Wherever and whenever that day comes, I will remember yesterday's moment with you."[27]

President Monson's first experience ordaining an Apostle and setting him apart as a member of the Quorum of the Twelve came that fall, October 9, 1986, when Elder Joseph B. Wirthlin was called to fill the empty chair. President Benson had not called an Apostle in the spring, though he had added three new members to the Quorum of the Seventy. Just a month before, in September 1986, President Monson had set Elder Wirthlin apart as one of the Presidents of the Seventy. The two had worked closely in Europe; they shared a love for Germany.

In 1988 President Benson would again turn to President Monson to ordain the new Apostle, Richard G. Scott, who was called at the death of Elder Marion G. Romney. The Scotts had first met the Monsons at a mission presidents' seminar in Argentina. Elder Scott remembers of that meeting, "Elder Monson just seemed like he was a current Joseph Smith, powerful, articulate, loving; he was just an inspiration. So you can imagine what it meant to have President Benson ask that he be the one, the voice, in setting me apart for the Twelve."[28]

Elder Scott will always remember the big hug that President Monson gave him, welcoming him into that very select circle. Elder Scott has watched him for years working with people in committees, in conferences, in interviews, and just passing in the hall. He notes: "Whatever way it starts, it ends up with the under-standing that he truly loves you. Not just a glitzy smile and a pat on the back. He truly loves you, and that makes all the difference in the world."[29]

What President Monson hadn't contemplated with his new calling was the increased speaking assignments and conducting of meetings. At general conference in April 1986 he had to give three talks rather than one, which necessitated his using a tele-prompter rather than memorizing his addresses. His daughter, Ann, remembers him down in the basement of their home all those years, memorizing his talks. He was good at it. After a particularly stirring talk, Ann had sent him a note, "Congratulations on doing a wonderful job on your address. It is difficult to memorize a talk. The miracle is that you can memorize a talk, attend endless meetings, answer ever-ringing phones and cut lawns all in the same day."[30] He had long held off reading his talks on the screen, but now he had no choice. He had too many talks to give and certainly not enough time to memorize them as he had for so many years.

Although much had changed for President Monson, much remained the same, as evidenced by his journal entry on December 23, 1986: "Spent a considerable amount of time delivering a nice roasting chicken and a copy of my new book to each of the widows whom I have traditionally visited at Christmastime. I enjoyed each visit, as I trust each one of them did."

"He has this incredible capacity to communicate love," says Elder Scott. "Whether it's a tiny child waiting in the doorway or an adult suffering the last stages of an illness, he has this incredible ability to make that person feel like he is a personal friend. He can be joyous, and he can be very serious; he can be jovial when that's the proper spirit. And he can be profoundly spiritual. He is just a remarkable individual."[31]

That winter he visited his friend Stan Cockrell many times. Stan was confined to a wheelchair, and President Monson had once found him discouraged, sitting in his wheelchair at the edge of a swimming pool, trying to decide whether to end his life. President Monson was able to counsel him and convince him that life was worth living. Now Stan was in the hospital once again— and this time, he would not go home. President Monson gave him a blessing and then gave one to Stan's bishop, who was visiting at the time. Both men had cancer. Months later, President Monson spoke at Stan's funeral with such "a greater fluidity of thought and expression" that he, with gratitude, acknowledged the hand of the Lord with him that day.[32]

If you are President Monson, "you rescue the one," Elder Holland emphasizes. "If you are swimming at the Deseret Gym as he once was, and have the impression to get out and go to the hospital, you get out, dress, and go to the hospital and save some-one's life."[33]

President Monson thoroughly enjoyed serving with President Benson. "While he leaves most of the administrative detail to President Hinckley and to me," he wrote, "he truly enjoys meeting the people and attending regional conferences and such activities where he can meet with large numbers of the members of the Church."[34]

Every year President Monson called new mission presidents, dividing the 100-plus interviews with President Hinckley. In 1988, Neil L. Andersen was busy at work at his business in Florida when his secretary informed him, "Thomas Monson from Salt Lake is on the phone." Elder Andersen remembers standing up out of respect, right there at his desk, to take the call. President Monson chatted with the startled Brother Andersen and then extended a call for him to serve as a mission president with his wife, Kathy. They would later learn of their assignment to Bordeaux, France, which was a return "home" for Brother Andersen, as he had served in France as a young missionary.

Brother Andersen was thirty-seven years old. "You're a young man," President Monson said, and then advised, "Don't ever let your youth be an excuse. Joseph Smith was young; the Savior was young."

When President Monson said that, Elder Andersen remembers thinking, "and Thomas Monson was young."[35]

President Monson also began extending calls to full-time service in the Quorums of the Seventy. Elder Monte J. Brough told President Monson about the sweet experience he and his wife had had when meeting with President Monson and being called to the First Quorum of the Seventy:

"When I sold my computer business some years ago, one of the conditions of sale was for me to sign a five-year employment agreement. The new owners wanted to assure themselves of my service until their acquisition of our technology was complete. The employment agreement required several pages with much effort from attorneys on both sides to complete. It is interesting to me, after worldly experience, that you and I entered a lifelong agreement without signing a contract, entering into an extended negotiation, or even having a discussion of the mutual benefits which each would expect from a lengthy relationship. Only in the Church could we find such a high level of personal and organizational commitment from one to another."[36]

Elder Russell M. Nelson has watched President Monson's personal, attentive style, saying, "I have learned from him that there are things more important than the clock. I've tried to be more like him when I am meeting with people. Even with my family. Don't be so overridingly concerned with what time it is; just make sure that you are blessing the people while you are there, that they go away from that interchange better than they would have been."[37]

President Monson created the 1,600th stake in the Church on June 22, 1986, in Kitchener, Ontario, Canada. Elder M. Russell Ballard and regional representative Alexander B. Morrison were at his side. As if being "home" in Canada weren't enough, President Monson announced to the members that a new temple had been approved for the Toronto area in the township of Brampton. The next year, on October 10, 1987, he returned to break ground for that temple. Some 3,000 members filled the temple site under threatening clouds that had poured rain for three days. As the service began, the clouds dissipated, and the first shovelfuls of dirt were turned under a clear sky. At the last minute, President Monson called upon Frances to speak. Her expression was heartfelt as tears filled her eyes. She said, "I am so grateful we had the mission experience in Canada, one of the greatest of my life."[38]

The temple would serve members in the Canadian provinces of Ontario, Nova Scotia, and Quebec, as well as parts of Ohio, Michigan, New York, and Vermont. But its construction faced delays. At one point President Hinckley turned to President Monson and said, "I don't know if we can justify some of the added elements proposed for the Toronto Temple." He then asked President Monson, "Can you guarantee that we will have 35,000 members in Ontario?" President Monson did not hesitate. "Brother Hinckley," he said, "we will have 35,000 members in the city of Toronto, without considering all of Ontario."

"Will you guarantee it?" President Hinckley asked.

"I will guarantee it," President Monson stated firmly, "and Brother Ballard will second the motion."[39] The temple construction began.

One of the highlights of the August 25, 1990, Toronto Temple dedication for President Monson was conducting the cornerstone-laying ceremony. With trowel in hand, he and each of the Brethren in attendance placed a little mortar to lay the cornerstone, and then President Monson noticed a small, red-haired boy. President Monson called on the boy to come forward and have the opportunity of placing some of the mortar. "It marked a beautiful example of a young boy participating in a ceremony which affected eternity," he noted.[40]

He presided at the concluding sessions of the dedication and then stood on the grounds looking up at the angel Moroni and reflecting on the words of his former mission counselor, Everett Pallin: "On a clear day, one standing where the angel Moroni is affixed could see clear to Cumorah." President Monson thought it a comforting thought that the Moroni statue was facing a place "very dear to Moroni himself."[41]

The First Presidency focused extensively on locating temple sites, breaking ground, reviewing construction progress, and participating in dedications. President Monson looked at sites in many locations, among them Missouri, the Dominican Republic, and England. In November 1991, President Monson and Elder Jeffrey R. Holland walked the ground where the Preston Temple now stands. President Monson "felt well" about recommending the purchase of the site, but his most significant memory of the property was the twenty-six acres of bluebells that carpeted the ground. "It was a beautiful day," Elder Holland remembers. "We walked the full length of the property. He was very impressed. In his mind's eye he could see much that is there now—a stake center, an MTC, patron housing, and a beautiful temple."[42]

President Monson celebrated his sixty-second birthday in the Portland Oregon Temple conducting four dedicatory sessions. During his closing remarks, he noticed a beautiful little girl about eleven years of age sitting to the side of the pulpit in the celestial room. Two bouquets of white roses sat on either side of the podium.

"I felt impressed to take one of the white roses and hand it to this little girl, whom I had invited to stand by my side at the pulpit. I told her that these roses could not have been grown for a more glorious purpose than to adorn either side of the pulpit in the celestial room at the dedication of a holy temple, and this white rose symbolized purity, and that she symbolized purity as a sweet young girl. I handed her the rose as a reminder that she should plan one day to return to the temple of God, there to be married for time and all eternity."[43]

The building of temples is fraught with challenges. Few neighbors, planning commissions, zoning boards, or other entities are able to understand the pastoral setting being proposed or the spiritual peace that will settle on the neighborhood when the temple is dedicated.

In 1989, when the cost estimates for the San Diego Temple came in far in excess of projections, President Monson, President Hinckley, Elder Packer, and Elder Gene R. Cook flew to California to meet with the stake presidents in the proposed temple district. They identified three options: go forward and pay the higher bill, scale down the specifications, or scrap the footings and plans and start over with a Toronto Temple design. They all agreed that scaling back was the best choice. The temple, dedicated April 25, 1993, was honored by the San Diego Press Club as Headliner of the Year for 1993 in the landmark category.

When President Monson, President Hinckley, and Bishop H. David Burton visited Vernal in eastern Utah to assess the possibility of converting its pioneer tabernacle to a temple, they found the building in such bad shape that the cost of restoration would be astronomical. But, President Monson conceded, he couldn't see how they could tear down such a pioneer structure. When President Benson said "Yes" to the recommendation that the tabernacle be renovated as a small temple, plans went forward and the stake presidents in the area "were ecstatic." As President Monson presented the plans to preserve the structure, he described the great faith and courage of the people in such valleys during times of severe winters and extreme privation and hardship, when harsh weather, lack of food, and other difficulties, including problems with the Indians, made settlement so difficult. "I touched a tender vein," he realized, "for many of the stake presidents descend from the early pioneer families." He could see the tears in their eyes when they realized that the work of their forebears would be preserved in the beautification and remodeling of the tabernacle into a house of the Lord.[44]

The First Presidency did not know at the time that an earlier President of the Church, Joseph F. Smith, in the August 1907 dedicatory service of the Uintah Stake Tabernacle in Vernal, had told those assembled that he would not be surprised if a temple were in their midst someday. That someday was November 2, 1997, when the Vernal Utah Temple was dedicated, the fifty-first temple of the Church.[45]

In those years as a counselor in the First Presidency, President Monson would participate in other dedications, including rededications of temples in Cardston, Alberta, Canada; London, England; and Bern, Switzerland. Brother Wilfred Möller, his translator for twenty years in East Germany, was his interpreter in the temple in Switzerland. At the conclusion of the last session, President Monson gathered "the General Authorities and their wives in together where we had a kneeling prayer in which we expressed our gratitude to our Heavenly Father."[46] Gratitude to a loving Father in Heaven is a consistent theme in his life.

At the groundbreaking for the Bountiful Temple, the full First Presidency attended. President Hinckley called on a couple of boys to help him turn the sod; President Monson "was impressed to call upon three little girls to help." He expressed to those gathered, "I think it is so fitting that President Ezra Taft Benson, who loves the Book of Mormon as much as any Latter-day Saint who has ever lived, is here today in Bountiful. I am sure he is contemplating the meaning of the name and the loveliness of the land."[47]

Because stake conferences were no longer part of his assignments as a member of the First Presidency, President Monson rarely attended one, except in special circumstances when prompted by the Spirit. Being in the presence of a General

Authority or a member of the First Presidency is always a blessing to the people. One man, Grant Johnson, later described waiting with anticipation for President Monson to enter the chapel and begin the meeting.

"It was a couple of minutes past the hour and you and our stake president had not yet come into the hall. I suddenly felt a great increase in the Holy Ghost. I looked around, but saw nothing unusual. The Spirit seemed to fill the room, and within a few seconds you walked in through the front doors. This was a witness to me that the holy angels precede your arrival. For I felt the presence of holy ones even though I could not see them. I said within myself, I know that this is one of God's prophets."[48]

The regional conference format was instituted to make it possible for a member of the First Presidency and members of the Twelve to speak to more priesthood leaders as well as the general membership of an entire area. "The large number of stakes and the limited opportunity of members of the Presidency to visit them precludes our being in attendance in such areas other than through the regional meeting arrangement," President Monson commented.[49] With the growth of the Church, regional meetings were broadcast to several stake centers at once, and though the broadcasts meant less face-to-face contact, the televised meetings allowed for members to receive direction from General Authorities, including members of the First Presidency, specifically for their area.

President Monson presided at regional conferences in many countries. He made a difference not only for those in the congregation but also for those who sat with him on the stand. Elder Alexander B. Morrison, Area President for Europe in 1988, wrote to President Monson after joining him for meetings, "Your comment in Scotland that you were proud of me humbled me nearly to tears. There is no man on earth whose approval means more to me than does yours; my prayer is that I do nothing to betray or fail to be true to that trust."[50]

At a regional conference in Mexico City on April 28, 1990, President Monson marveled at "the miracle which has taken place." When he had become a member of the Quorum of the Twelve, there had been only one stake in the colonies of Mexico; a stake was soon thereafter created in Mexico City. "To think that I would meet with fifty-nine stake presidents," he said as he looked over the group of men, "and that Richard Scott met with perhaps forty-five more in a similar gathering the week before gives one an idea of the explosive growth that has occurred." He left the regional conference "feeling that the Lord loves these children of Father Lehi and has performed a work and a wonder in their lives."[51]

He dedicated the Kirtland stake center in what he called "the shadow of the Kirtland Temple," which is owned by the Community of Christ church. His thoughts were on more than bricks and mortar as he remarked that the Church has beautiful buildings because of the faith of the tithe-paying members. Everyone from the widow to the workman has a part in every chapel built throughout the world.

President Monson has always endeared himself to congregations through his messages filled with true accounts from his own life and the lives of others. Some of those who are touched write to tell him of experiences they had when they heard his words.

A woman from Edmonton, Alberta, Canada, wrote of her experience years earlier as a single woman, a music graduate from Queensland University. "Friends started to take me to various churches. One even offered me a paid position as an organist," she said. But she didn't feel right in any of the congregations, and she determined that she had been to enough churches. The next Sunday, she stayed home. She explained, "I turned on the TV; a magnificent choir was singing, so I sat there and listened. After the choir a speaker started to talk about a family and what one could do to obtain an eternal family. The speaker inspired me and touched me so much that I started to cry. The Spirit was so strong I couldn't stop." She said that after the speaker concluded, he was referred to as "Elder Monson."

Elder Monson's message on that occasion was one of God's love. "Love is the guide to mortal happiness and a requisite for eternal life," he said. "God so loved the world that He gave His Son. The Redeemer so loved mankind that He gave His life. To you and to me He declared, 'A new commandment I give unto you, that ye love one another as I have loved you. . . . By this shall all men know that ye are my disciples.' With all my heart I pray that we will be obedient to such a heavenly vision, for I testify it came from the Son of God, who is our Redeemer, our mediator with the Father, even Jesus Christ, the Lord."[52]

The woman acknowledged that as he "gave the powerful testimony" and then the choir sang "O My Father," she "was completely converted." She turned on the TV each Sunday after that, looking for the program. After a few Sundays of disappointment, she looked up the Church's number, called, and reached an institute of religion. A few days later, two missionaries delivered a Book of Mormon to her door. She was baptized and has "not missed a conference broadcast since." She assured him he was still her "favorite speaker."[53]

From speaking assignments to business issues, President Monson always sought ways to bless people's lives. When the institute building at Snow College needed to be replaced and the school hoped to purchase it for additional classroom space, President Monson convinced the Church Appropriations Committee to give it to them at no cost as a gesture of goodwill, "given the declining population in the area."[54]

He spearheaded donating the Twenty-fifth Ward meetinghouse to the Salvation Army and then reroofing it, painting the interior, and furnishing it with an organ, piano, pews, and chairs. He even had it stocked with supplies from the recently closed Hotel Utah, including silverware, dishes, tables, and chairs. Bill R. Lane, major in the Salvation Army, responded, "You carry a great responsibility in the leadership position of your church, yet you always open your heart to meet the needs and requests of the Salvation Army. Certainly you and your associates have overwhelmed us with your warmth and gracious spirits."[55]

He sponsored the donation of a 1.8-acre parcel of property valued at $100,000 adjacent to Neighborhood House, a United Way participant.

At the sesquicentennial of the Relief Society, he encouraged the sisters to renew the spirit of their beginnings in this work. "We see the stirrings of strength," he said as he paid tribute to the women, whose charge, "Charity Never Faileth" was close to his heart. Characteristically, he renewed that charge with a verse of poetry:

> *Go gladden the lonely, the dreary;*
> *Go comfort the weeping, the weary,*
> *Go scatter kind deeds on your way.*
> *Oh, make the world brighter today.*[56]

He has taken his own counsel to heart. At the BYU commencement in April 1992, he watched as President Rex Lee led the congregation in applause for the graduates and similarly led the graduates in applause for the parents. President Monson then stood and said, "All who would like to join me in giving a round of applause for our university president, please do so." Instantly every person in the Marriott Center stood and gave a prolonged and sincere applause for Rex Lee, a dedicated president of BYU who faced daunting health issues. President Monson noted in his journal, "They tell me that the camera showed Rex during this emotional period and that his chin was quivering and his heart full through this expression of gratitude."[57]

"The bottom line is that when he leaves a meeting, conference, or gathering, everybody feels edified. They feel loved and validated," observes Elder Spencer J. Condie of the Seventy. "They do not feel like unprofitable servants of the Lord. They believe President Monson feels they are okay, so maybe Heavenly Father thinks they are okay. They know they have got to do a lot better than they are doing, but they are going to do better because he has shown them such love and respect."[58]

There is no show in President Monson, unless it is showing how much people matter to him. He doesn't walk away from the multitude; he is always looking to lift. At the conclusion of a recent temple cornerstone ceremony, as Church leaders prepared to go back inside, President Monson paused and looked around. He saw a little girl, about age seven, standing by the front rope, her head down, obviously disappointed she had not been picked to participate. He went right over to her and brought her up to the cornerstone, got out the trowel and mortar, and guided her hand. That's President Monson.

28

——————

"LOYAL, HELPFUL, FRIENDLY . . ."

For me, President Monson is like the Savior would be if He were here. His ministry, his sensitivity to the one is incredible, but so, I think, are his perceptions. I know he knows what I am thinking and feeling. It is tender to see the "seer" part of him.

ELAINE S. DALTON
Young Women General President

PRESIDENT EZRA TAFT BENSON came to the calling of Church President late in life. He was eighty-six. Others, too, have carried the mantle in their advanced years, and the Church members have sustained and supported them with devotion. When President Benson had a series of slight strokes and surgery for a subdural hematoma, his counselors recognized that their role was to carry on for him.

At general conference, President Monson and President Hinckley read President Benson's talks for him at the pulpit and spoke on his behalf, relating incidents in the President's life that taught gospel truths, using some of his favorite scriptures. President Monson saw it as "a good solution to a situation where the Church is more and more realizing that President Benson is just not physically able to speak or deliver a message due to his advanced age."[1]

When President Benson attended general conference, he "seemed pleased" with what was said. "His spirit is bright,"

443

President Monson related. "He would put his hand on mine and turn to me and extend a warm, loving smile. When I told him that there were many children in the audience and that they love him so, tears would come to his eyes."[2]

When President Benson was absent, his chair seemed "so empty." One of President Monson's journal entries about the aging president is poignant: "He is not so well as he was a year ago."[3]

There were several scares as President Benson was rushed to the hospital and then, rallying, would be returned home. The Benson family gathered at the hospital on October 15, 1990, fearing that their father, who had recently undergone surgery, might not recover. President Hinckley and President Monson went to give their prophet-leader a priesthood blessing. President Hinckley asked President Monson to seal the anointing. As he spoke, he "felt impressed to promise President Benson that he would not leave mortality one day sooner than the Lord wanted him to and that he would be given the gift of healing, that he might enjoy life until his time for departure was at hand. A sweet feeling of peace filled the room."[4]

President Monson had been scheduled to attend an area conference in Germany, the first such meeting bringing together Saints from the east and the west now that the two governments had reunited. He wanted to be there, but he did not feel comfortable leaving with President Benson in his fragile condition. Frances listened as he weighed the options and then agreed that he couldn't go.

Following the blessing at the hospital, however, President Benson began to improve. He left intensive care and returned home, and President Monson caught the first flight he could find to Germany, arriving in time to participate in what would be one of the most "significant gatherings in the history of the Church in Germany." In attendance at the Saturday meeting on October 20, 1990, were priesthood leaders from the Berlin, Leipzig, and Dresden stakes. He wrote with great thanksgiving, "The Spirit was absolutely of the highest inspirational quality. Just to think that brethren from the East who have not had the opportunity to meet with their friends and family from the West are now being permitted to do so after a thirty-year period gives some idea concerning the emotional height which was reached."[5]

President Benson treated his Second Counselor like a son. Some of that connection came from their shared love for Scouting. When President Benson had retired from the National Executive Board of the Boy Scouts of America in 1969, Elder Monson had been asked by the First Presidency to take his place. President Benson had replaced President George Albert Smith on the board. All three shared a love for the organization and a commitment to its place in the youth program of the Church. For more than forty years, President Monson has attended regular meetings of the board, national and international jamborees, annual conventions, and Eagle Scout courts of honor, and he has been a merit badge counselor. His enthusiasm for Scouting has never been about tying knots; it has been about touching lives. To him, Scouting is "the building of boys,"[6] and he has enunciated that duty to Scouters in many nations.

On Tuesday, June 8, 1982, Elder and Sister Monson toured Westminster Abbey in London, England, viewing the monuments and tombs of the great and famous and finally pausing in Poet's Corner before the marker they had come to see:

ROBERT BADEN-POWELL, 1857–1941
FOUNDER OF BOY SCOUTS
FRIEND OF ALL THE WORLD

President Monson recognized in Baden-Powell a kindred soul. "Unlike others memorialized within the walls of Westminster Abbey, Baden-Powell had neither sailed the stormy seas of glory, conquered in conflict the armies of men, nor founded empires of worldly wealth. Rather, he was a builder of boys, one who taught them well how to run and win the race of life."[7] The description begs the question, How many boys have had their lives blessed—even saved—by the Scout movement begun by Baden-Powell? Certainly Thomas Monson would count himself in such company.

The Church adopted the Boy Scout program in America in

1913, embracing the concepts of "Do a good turn daily" and "Be prepared." Certainly both describe Tommy Monson in his youth and President Monson as an adult. He quotes often, "The greatest gift a man can give a boy is his willingness to share a part of his life with him."[8] He believes it; he teaches it; he practices it.

He can look back in his life and see the John Burts and the Paul Childs, and even the burly Scoutmaster who took Troop 60 up to Brighton canyon, just east of Salt Lake City, for a summer campout, dropped them off, asked Tommy—the most responsible of the lot—if he had brought his fishing pole, and then ordered, "Catch trout for breakfast for each of the boys for the two days you are here. I'll see you Saturday and take you home." He drove off; Tommy did his "Scout duty"; no one went hungry.[9]

President Monson has worked closely with general Young Men leaders Jack H Goaslind Jr., Marion D. Hanks, Robert L. Backman, Vaughn J. Featherstone, Robert K. Dellenbach, Charles Dahlquist, and David L. Beck, each of whom also labored tirelessly in Scouting at both the Church and national levels. These were men who saw what President Monson saw "in the great cause of Scouting." He has served with some of the nation's most successful businessmen, men of the highest caliber. They have come to know him and The Church of Jesus Christ of Latter-day Saints, which he represents.

"You can't get him away from Boy Scouts," attests Elder L. Tom Perry, who has participated in his share of jamborees. "He *is* Boy Scouting. He goes to every camporee he can. If you want to excite him, go to one of these Boy Scout affairs and report it in the temple."[10]

President Monson has attended jamborees all around the world. When prompted, he leaves an apostolic blessing upon the Scouts, such as the one he pronounced in Las Vegas in 2006: "that you may find joy in your lives [and] that you may have peace within your homes."[11]

He has been a voice of reason and determination to hold fast to the traditions of Scouting. Challenges have come to Scouting over the years that would change the very nature of the young men's experience. He has taken a firm posture when efforts have been made to dismiss such basics as the Scout Oath and the "Duty to God" award, when a push came to admit girls to troops, when homosexuals demanded the opportunity to be Scoutmasters. He was not shaken by the confrontations, nor did he step back when the arguments were taken to the press and bitter public attacks ensued. His steady position has kept the discussions focused on principles and preserved the purpose of Scouting. If he has seen the slightest wavering or possible shifts in Scouting's administrators, he has been quick to respond, stating decisively his position and that of the Church. President Monson acknowledges that Scouting is "more expensive than other endeavors" but "well worth the money."[12]

President Monson received the Silver Buffalo Award, the highest honor bestowed by the Boy Scouts of America, in 1971. He was in good company. That year, Jimmy Carter, thirty-ninth president of the United States, received the award as well. President Monson feels honored to be included with other recipients, which include aviator Charles A. Lindbergh, artist Norman Rockwell, film producer Walt Disney, and baseball Hall of Famer Hank Aaron.

In 1993, in a general priesthood meeting, Present Monson received the Bronze Wolf, the highest award given by the World Organization of Scouting Movement. "President Monson is one of the Boy Scouts of America's most distinguished friends," stated Jere B. Ratcliffe, Chief Scout Executive, at the presentation. "He has very much dedicated his life to upholding and to placing into practice the teachings of the Church and the mission of the Boy Scouts of America, a mission of teaching values to last a lifetime."[13]

A wooden walking stick four feet high, with the symbol for every Boy Scout merit badge carefully carved into it by Jacob J. Dietz, sits in one corner of his office. Scouting has provided common ground for him as he has met with leaders around the world. When he met with the king of Sweden on the Church temple grounds in Stockholm, the two talked of their experiences in Scouting; both were recipients of the Bronze Wolf award.

For decades President Monson has faithfully taken his seat at Scout meetings in New Orleans, Chicago, Washington, New York,

Dallas—even in Tehran. As the keynote speaker at BSA national meetings in May 1992, he spoke with concern about the plight of society: "Throughout our country, we have been screaming ever louder for more and more of the things we cannot take with us, and paying less and less attention to the real sources of the very happiness we seek. We have been measuring our fellowmen more by balance sheets and less by moral standards. . . . We have become so concerned over the growth of our earning capacity that we have neglected the growth of our character. Perhaps this is indicative of the days in which we are living—days of compromise and diluting of principles, days when sin is labeled as error, when morality is relative and when materialism emphasizes the value of expediency and the shirking of responsibility. Well might a confused boy cry out using the words of Philip of old, 'How can I [find my way], except some man should guide me?'"[14]

As a young Scout himself, Tommy's first time away from home was when his Scout troop went to Tracy Wigwam in Millcreek Canyon near Salt Lake City. It was winter, and it was cold. Looking back, he has said it was "a terrible time to go."[15] The old lodge had one dilapidated stove to heat the whole drafty place. The boys were shivering and wet, having spent the first thirty minutes after their arrival launching snowballs at each other. Though they wouldn't admit it, they were homesick, too. The next day, up the canyon came Tommy's mother and father with a treat for the whole troop—a freezer full of ice cream. "We were freezing to death," he recalls. "They should have brought chili. But their intentions were good."[16]

As the Scouts bedded down for the night in their cabin, Tommy and the others watched as their ward Scout leader, Carl, removed his artificial leg and set it next to his sleeping bag. During the night, one of the boys wiggled from his sleeping bag and "swiped Carl's artificial leg and hid it in his own bunk."

When Carl awoke and discovered his leg missing, he did not raise his voice or even demand that the boys bring it back. Saying he needed to step outside the cabin for a moment, he hopped on his one leg out the door. "Every boy felt ashamed," remembers President Monson. When Carl returned, his artificial leg rested where he had left it the night before. "I don't know how I overlooked this the first time," he said, "but I'm sure glad it's here." His mild response to the boys' prank taught them much more than an angry accusation would have.[17]

On one occasion, a Scouting skill saved a life in President Monson's own family. He relates, "My nephew's son, eleven-year-old Craig Dearden, successfully completed his requirements for Scouting's swimming award. His father beamed his approval, while mother tenderly placed an affectionate kiss. Little did those attending the court of honor realize the life-or-death impact of that award. Later that very afternoon, it was Craig who spotted a dark object at the deep end of the swimming pool. It was Craig who, without fear, plunged into the pool to investigate and brought to the surface his own little brother. Tiny Scott was so still, so blue, so lifeless. Recalling the life-saving procedures he had learned and practiced, Craig and others responded in the true tradition of Scouting. Suddenly there was a cry, breathing, movement, life. Is Scouting relevant? Ask a mother, a father, a family who know a Scouting skill saved a son and brother."[18]

"Of vital importance to our success," President Monson has emphasized to Scout leaders, "is learning to win the confidence and respect of the very boys we seek to build. To do this, love is required. You who love and guide our precious youth may never open gates of cities or doors to palaces, but your success will come as you gain entrance to the heart of a boy."[19]

President Monson sees Scouting as "a spiritual program, a builder of men." He has said, "If ever there were a time when the principles of Scouting were vitally needed—that time is now. If ever there were a generation who would benefit by keeping physically strong, mentally awake, and morally straight—that generation is the present generation."[20]

Between Scouting and all the other tasks demanding his attention, President Monson scarcely had time to notice when, in late November 1993, he began suffering from a sore toe. He has generally enjoyed good health, although he has diabetes, so he thought perhaps the problem was his shoes, and he changed to another pair. He tried elevating his foot in meetings and walking as little as possible; given his frenetic schedule, that was difficult. The pain continued, but he just kept going. He went to Vernal to view the tabernacle there as a possible site for a temple, to the Cathedral of the Madeleine to give a Thanksgiving message, to the St. Vincent de Paul Center to honor Father Terence Moore, to San Bernardino, California, for a conference, to meetings in the temple, to funerals, and to the hospital to visit the sick.

As he prepared to leave town on an assignment on December 3, 1993, Frances looked at his foot and insisted he visit the doctor instead. Late that morning he was able to see his physician, who immediately had him admitted to the hospital for a "raging infection" in his left foot. The doctors weren't sure they could save it.

It was the first time he'd been in a hospital gown since he was four years old and had his tonsils removed. This time he was not on "short stay."

Two days later, on Sunday, he was excused from the First Presidency Christmas Devotional, although he briefly considered putting on his suit and heading for the Tabernacle to do his duty. His frustration was clear: "This is the first time, for a very long time, if ever, that I have been absent from a meeting at which I had been assigned to speak."[21]

On December 20, 1993, he recorded: "Still in hospital. Missed the Council on the Disposition of Tithes meeting, Manti Temple workers speaking assignment, First Presidency staff luncheon, Beneficial Life Christmas party, open house for Key Bank of Utah."[22] Fortunately, the holidays had interrupted much of the work he normally would have been doing.

Those with diabetes are at great risk for foot infections because of inhibited blood circulation and even nerve damage. President Monson's infection was severe, but when he left the hospital three weeks later, his toe had greatly improved.

Doctors released him from the hospital on December 22 with orders to return every other day for whirlpool treatments on his foot and rebandaging. Frances was his nurse; she was a good one.

On Christmas Eve, he gratefully acknowledged "the love and prayers extended in my behalf by many whom I know."[23] Two of his physicians had administered to him when he first entered the hospital. President Hinckley had also done so on his visit a few days later. President Hinckley and Elder Wirthlin administered to him on yet another occasion. President Monson had unquestioning faith that he would get well.

"We are glad to learn that you are on the mend," Elder Hugh W. Pinnock wrote. "It is good that so many thousands have been praying for you because of the unnumbered times you have focused your prayers on others."[24]

He went back to his office on January 5, 1994, sitting in a wheelchair, with his foot elevated. He conducted mission presidents' interviews—that year he had fifty-two—and attended meetings, including the ones in the temple, though navigating the doorways, corridors, elevators, and rooms was a bit tricky.

On January 23, six weeks from his initial hospitalization, he participated in the general Primary satellite broadcast, "Behold Your Little Ones." Until the week prior to the broadcast, he wasn't sure if he would be able to stand for twenty minutes to deliver his message. He had rehearsed once, putting all his weight on his right foot and using his left simply for balance. With the aid of a special "athletic" shoe provided by the physical therapy department at the LDS Hospital, he was able to present his message, the first since his illness was treated on December 3.

At the end of six months, the doctors reported that all was progressing nicely and that the healing had been miraculous. He was informed that only one in fifty patients who suffered such an extensive infection was able to avoid having a toe or foot removed. "I think you never once doubted that your foot would heal and you would not suffer any amputation," one doctor said when the ordeal was mostly behind them. "You are a man of great faith." President Monson responded, "I am grateful to our Heavenly Father and to skilled surgeons."[25]

Dr. Gary Hunter and Dr. Greg Anderson have become his dear friends. President Monson's regular visits with them "are social get-togethers as well as examinations" of his feet. But nonetheless, the two are "very meticulous and careful," making certain that all is well.[26]

At one point during President Monson's hospital stay, one

of his doctors asked, "If I am able to save this foot, would you be willing to confer upon my son his Eagle Scout award?" When President Monson later mentioned that "invitation" at the Eagle Scout's court of honor, he grinned, saying, "Both of us are happy with the outcome."

With his foot in a cast, he spent New Year's Day at home watching football. "I can start out neutral watching two football teams," he explains, "but within minutes I have selected the team which I think ought to win, and I pull for that particular team."[27]

If Michigan is playing, there is no question which team he favors. He has long been a Michigan fan. That reaches back to the days of Bo Schembechler, who coached at Michigan from 1969 to 1989 and made some favorable comments to BYU coach LaVell Edwards about the LDS Church. When he watches Michigan play, President Monson dons the maize and blue as a true fan. His journal records the football wins and losses on New Year's Day, especially when Michigan is playing.

It is a rite of passage to be invited to join Grandpa in the basement on game day. He presents each grandchild a Michigan cap in a special ceremony with the Michigan fight song playing in the background. If the team falters in the first half, he switches the maize and blue hats to blue and maize ones to spur the team on. For years, when his team was ahead, he would call his friend John Burt and play the Michigan fight song over the phone. John was not a Michigan supporter. When the Wolverines won, he called John yet again, enjoying his success.

But President Monson's legendary loyalty is extended not so much to teams as to people. The list of funerals at which he has spoken reads like a phone book: Lucy Gertsch Thompson, whom he called "the finest teacher I have ever known"; Donald Dean Balmforth, lifelong friend and counselor in the Sixth-Seventh Ward bishopric; Isabel Moon, a widow whose funeral fell on a Thursday, but "miraculously" the temple meeting adjourned early and President Monson made it to the funeral and spoke; Elder Franklin D. Richards, "one of the great missionaries of our time"; Alton "Moose" Carman, his uncle; another uncle, Myron Bangerter; Elder Jeffrey Brent Ball, a missionary who was killed in La Paz, Bolivia; Marian Clark Sharp, daughter of J. Reuben Clark, Jr.; Phillip Jacobsen, bindery foreman at Deseret Press; Elder Theodore M. Burton; Arthur J. Kirk, who bought night crawlers from enterprising Tommy at Vivian Park in the 1930s; O. Preston Robinson, mentor at the University of Utah and at the Deseret News Publishing Company; Elder Joseph Anderson, emeritus General Authority; D. Arthur Haycock, secretary to five Presidents of the Church; John Fife, fancier of Birmingham roller pigeons; Huston Johnson, a handicapped man who lived in the Sixth-Seventh Ward and worked his entire life as a busboy at a downtown coffee shop. President Monson represented the Church at the funeral of former U.S. President Richard M. Nixon; he spoke at the Catholic funeral of civic leader Frank Granato, at a pulpit with a candle on each side. Those are only a few of the hundreds of funerals he has attended, and at most of them he also spoke.[28]

His participation on the national scene included attending the inauguration of U.S. President George H. W. Bush on January 20, 1989, with President Ezra Taft Benson. It was like going home for President Benson, who had served in the Eisenhower cabinet as secretary of agriculture. The Mormon Tabernacle Choir participated in the parade on the final float, singing "The Battle Hymn of the Republic" as they passed the reviewing stand. President Monson received a "thank you" from President Bush for attending, with a personally signed note at the bottom, "With respect."

At a national Boy Scouts of America prayer breakfast at the White House that spring, May 4, 1989, he sat at a table with President Bush, and the two quickly learned that they shared a common interest in family values and a love for English springer spaniels. After the meeting, President Bush invited President Monson to his kennel to view his dog Millie's new litter of pups. "Which one would you choose if you were to keep just one?" the president asked. The two men discussed the merits of the breed. President Monson picked out a pup with strong legs, a well-proportioned body, and a square head with substantial room for an active brain, and added, "If you can get good markings in addition to these attributes, so much the better." President Bush named the puppy Ranger, and when he traveled to Salt Lake City and visited the two counselors in the First Presidency on July 17, 1992, he brought President Monson up to date on "their" dog.[29]

The First Presidency and other Church leaders faced a host of problems in the 1980s and 1990s that reflected society's increasingly "self-absorbed" style. They issued a statement about the growing problem of AIDS: "We, with others, hope that discoveries will make possible both prevention and healing from the dread affliction. But regardless of such discoveries, the observance of one clearly understandable and divinely given rule would do more than all else to check this epidemic. That is chastity before marriage and total fidelity in marriage."[30]

The Church's position that the institution of marriage is reserved for a man and a woman was under fire. Protestors attacked the Church, demanding that marriage be redefined to include those in same-sex relationships. The issue did not go away but gained momentum.

On May 30, 1994, President Ezra Taft Benson passed away at the age of ninety-four. On June 3, an estimated 20,000 people filed by his casket. "Most said no words," noted President Monson, "but many tears could be seen and a sweet, reverential gratitude prevailed."[31] At the funeral, President Monson described President Benson as "a giant among men." Services were carried on three television stations.[32]

As the Apostles left the stand, they formed an honor guard for the casket leaving the hall. The Monsons drove in the funeral procession to Whitney, Idaho, where President Benson was to be buried next to his wife, Flora, who had died two years earlier. President Benson had said to his counselor some time before, "Regardless of what anyone may say, Brother Monson, I want to be buried in Whitney, Idaho."[33]

On June 4, 1994, Howard W. Hunter, senior Apostle of The Church of Jesus Christ of Latter-day Saints, was unanimously approved by the members of the Quorum of the Twelve to become President of the Church.

29

AN INDOMITABLE SPIRIT

Sometimes people are different personalities at the pulpit than they are personally. With President Monson, what you see at the pulpit is what you get personally.

ELDER DALLIN H. OAKS
Quorum of the Twelve Apostles

AT FOUR O'CLOCK ON THE AFTERNOON of May 16, 1989, President Monson, Second Counselor in the First Presidency and vice chairman of the BYU board of trustees, welcomed fifty invited guests to the dedication services of the BYU Jerusalem Center for Near Eastern Studies, located on Mount Scopus overlooking the Mount of Olives. The multimillion-dollar building would house the Jerusalem branches of the Church and serve as a home for BYU Semester Abroad students. Speakers at the dedication included President Howard W. Hunter, Elder Boyd K. Packer, Elder Jeffrey R. Holland, and others. President Monson called on President Hunter, who had shepherded the building through ten stormy years of approvals and construction, to pronounce the dedicatory prayer: "The building wherein we are seated has been constructed for the housing of those who love Thee and seek to learn of Thee and follow in the footsteps of Thy Son, our Savior and Redeemer. . . . May all who enter herein to teach, to learn, or for whatever purpose be blessed of Thee and feel Thy Spirit."[1]

"President Monson was conducting," Elder Holland recalls. "He was junior to President Hunter in the Quorum but senior to him as far as the presiding council. He had the wonderful, wonderful courtesy to call on President Hunter to give the dedicatory prayer, a nice touch, a very nice touch. That is a Monson characteristic. He will defer; he will reach out; he will reach down repeatedly. His antenna is out all the time about what is the nice thing to do."[2]

President Monson had sat next to President Hunter during the years when President Hinckley had served as a counselor to President Kimball; he had served with President Hunter on committees, and the two had attended so many conferences together that neither was counting. He had been in the congregation in the Tabernacle when Howard W. Hunter was sustained as a new member of the Quorum of the Twelve. President Hunter was a man with a reputation of being Christlike, humble, and kind.

Howard W. Hunter and Thomas S. Monson had first worked together in 1956, when Brother Hunter was regional chairman for the Los Angeles Temple dedication and Brother Monson printed the tickets. "His assignment was mammoth," Tom said at the time. "I saw only that portion which pertained to the tickets, which were color coded, intricately labeled, and numbered in the most orderly fashion I had ever seen."[3]

The two had also shared a moment on October 3, 1963, as they met in the outer office of President David O. McKay. Elder Hunter was just concluding some business, and Tom was there to visit with the President, not knowing why he had been summoned. Elder Hunter knew. "I noted the tears in his eyes, yet the smile on his lips, the catch in his voice," President Monson would later relate. "I did not understand why he was so emotional. After visiting with President McKay, where he extended to me my call to the Twelve, I understood. Howard W. Hunter had known why I was there that afternoon. He had been where I was now going. He had felt the feelings I was soon to experience."[4]

One year, during a highly contested campaign for the post of governor of the state of Utah, President Monson, a serious-minded citizen, had asked Frances which candidate she had chosen at the polls. She replied, "I didn't vote for either candidate. They promised too much for any man to deliver." He looked at her and said, "What did you do? Leave it blank?" She said, "Why no, of course not. I wrote in the name of Howard W. Hunter. He is so modest, so humble; surely he is the type of man Heavenly Father would guide to success." He shared that story with President Hunter, who smiled and said, "Tell her thank you."[5]

President Hunter was a prodigious journal keeper, not unlike Thomas Monson, and a scholar of ancient ruins. Before Elder Monson went to Peru in 1978 to create the Trujillo stake, Elder Hunter encouraged him to "be certain to visit the ruins at Chan Chan." The largest pre-Columbian city in South America, Chan Chan was once home to 30,000 people. "There is nothing like [these ruins] in all the world," Elder Hunter said excitedly as he shared a copy of his three-page journal entry detailing his visit to the archaeological site. When Elder Monson got to Chan Chan, his journal entry was much briefer: "All I saw was sand. Took me fifteen minutes. Brother Hunter saw ruins of a culture, a people, even a civilization long gone but preserved in memory."[6]

The meeting of the Twelve following the death of President Benson was the fifth time President Monson would participate in the naming of the man the Lord had chosen as His prophet. President Hunter retained President Hinckley and President Monson as his counselors. At a press conference two days later, President Monson pledged his support, saying, "I would like one and all to know that you [President Hunter] are a man of talent, you are a man of great compassion, and you are a leader whose heart goes out to the hungry, to the homeless. And in the spirit of the Master, your great desire has ever been to lift others upward toward Him. God bless you in your ministry."[7]

The new First Presidency of the Church got down to business. President Hunter called Jeffrey R. Holland to fill the vacancy in the Quorum of the Twelve, and on June 23, 1994, the new Apostle was ordained in the regular temple meeting of the First Presidency and Quorum of the Twelve. He had served as president of BYU from 1980 to 1989, when he was called as a member of the First Quorum of the Seventy. He and President Monson had long shared a sweet association. "You interviewed me when I was hired by the Church Educational System in 1965 and have, at every major turning point of my life since that time, been standing at the crossroads cheering me on and marking the way," Elder Holland wrote in a touching note of appreciation to President Monson just days after his call to the Twelve. "I feel I have no better friend, no greater defender, no more vocal advocate, no more loving example."[8]

President Monson expressed similar feelings to his friend and frequent fishing companion. "In the fifth grade at age eleven, I won a marble championship," he explained in a note to Elder Holland. "I was very proud of a special flint marble which permitted me to win, and many asked if I would loan to them this special marble for their rounds of competition. I would only loan it to my own younger brother. To you I would give the marble."[9]

The letters in the "Special Book" in President Monson's office—which is a bit of a misnomer, given there are numerous volumes—are filled with expressions from "just a few" of those whose hearts he has touched and lives he has changed. Neal A. Maxwell was another in the Quorum who had great affection for Tom Monson. For years President Monson has kept a note from this close friend. "I love you," it says simply, and is signed, "Neal."

After President Hunter was set apart, and meetings resumed, President Monson commented in his journal, "This is the first time in a long while that we have had the President of the Church in his customary chair."[10] He was not as excited about the First Presidency being "subjected to"—in President Monson's words—a photo session in the First Presidency board room. For someone who balks at having his photograph taken, it might be considered ironic that there are dozens of scrapbooks full of such photographs, chronicling his nearly fifty years in front of the cameras.

President Monson conducted the solemn assembly on October 1, 1994, noting in his journal, "Today is an important day in Church history. Howard W. Hunter was sustained as President of the Church . . . and as prophet, seer and revelator."[11]

President Hunter came to the office having had his share of health challenges. President Monson noted, "It is a joy to serve as counselor to President Howard W. Hunter, who carries an indomitable spirit. Even though his body is frail, his desire is to serve with all his heart and soul in the sacred position to which the Lord has called him."[12]

Seven years earlier, President Hunter's diabetes had impaired the nerves and muscles in his right leg, and the doctors had projected that he would "spend the balance of his life in a wheelchair." At that time, he had asked President Monson to give him a blessing. Words of reassurance had flowed from President Monson "that the Lord did not call him to the Council of the Twelve because of his legs and that all of the portions of his body and mind which warranted his call can still function effectively."[13] At the time, President Hunter was serving as Acting President of the Quorum of the Twelve. One year later, on June 22, 1988, with the death of President Romney, Elder Hunter was set apart as the President of the Quorum of the Twelve.

On Sunday morning, April 1, 1988, conference viewers watched as Howard W. Hunter slowly rose from his chair and, with the aid of a walker, made his way to the pulpit. "As he came toward the end of his message, he lost his balance and tumbled backwards," Elder Monson recorded in his journal. "I was able to put my hand under his shoulder and help break his fall. Elder Packer and I immediately helped him to his feet, and he carried on without missing a syllable in delivering his message from the teleprompter."

President Monson felt "that we had witnessed a miracle in Howard W. Hunter being able to come to the pulpit, and even a second miracle, as he came to the pulpit for a second time."[14]

Two years later, in April 1990, at the conclusion of the Thursday meeting of the First Presidency and the Twelve in the temple, President Hunter had asked if anyone had anything to bring up that had not been covered on the agenda. The room was still, since the Apostles had been made aware that their President did have a matter he wished to mention. He said simply, "I thought I'd just let you know that I'm going to be married this afternoon." He then spoke of Inis Stanton, an acquaintance from California with whom he had been visiting for some time. President Hinckley was going to perform their marriage in the Salt Lake Temple, he explained. "I've invited President Monson to be one of the witnesses and Inis's bishop will be the other one." President Monson had spoken at the funeral of President Hunter's wife, Clair Hunter, on October 9, 1983.[15]

During his presidency, Howard W. Hunter dedicated the Orlando and Bountiful temples and announced that three new temples would be built, in Nashville, Tennessee; Cochabamba, Bolivia; and Recife, Brazil. He created the Church's 2,000th stake, in Mexico City, and participated in commemorative services for the 150th anniversary of the martyrdom of the Prophet Joseph Smith.

In his address to the members following the solemn assembly in October, President Hunter had invited them "to look to the temple of the Lord as the great symbol of your membership. It is the deepest desire of my heart to have every member of the Church worthy to enter the temple. . . . Let us be a temple-attending people."[16] That call brought increased attention to temple worship.

When President Hunter dedicated the Church's forty-sixth temple, in Orlando, Florida, on October 9, 1994, it had been five years since a President of the Church had been able to attend a temple dedication. President Hunter, with the dignity and mantle of the Lord's chosen prophet, presided at seven dedicatory sessions and delivered four addresses. President Monson spoke in one of the sessions on courtesy, a quality he was taught in his youth and has valued in associations with others. "Whenever the word *courtesy* flows through my mind, I think of those who seem to exemplify courtesy in all that they do," he said, citing the temple as "a place of courtesy. There will be those coming to the temple who will not know which way to go, and you wonderful workers, who shall work here in the temple and labor diligently, always be kind, always go out of your way to let every person know that he or she is welcome in the house of the Lord."[17]

On January 8, 1995, President Hunter dedicated the Bountiful Utah Temple. He asked President Monson to conduct the cornerstone ceremony and the actual placement of the cornerstone on that cold and windy Sunday morning. Dressed in overcoats, each member of the First Presidency wielded the trowel, and then

Sister Hunter was called forward to do the same on behalf of the women of the Church.

At President Hunter's request, President Monson had prepared the dedicatory prayer. President Hunter, frail but determined, read the prayer in the first two sessions, which included the great hope: "We seek to be like Thee; we seek to pattern our lives after the life of Thy Son; we desire righteousness of ourselves and our children and our children's children."[18]

President Hinckley presided at the Monday dedicatory sessions at the Bountiful Temple. President Monson had responsibility for Tuesday's sessions. On Monday evening he realized he did not have a pair of special white elastic stockings for the next day. He telephoned the LDS Hospital pharmacy to see if they had a pair, and the young woman who answered the phone promised she could find what he needed. But the conversation did not end with the socks. The attendant, with some hesitation, asked if he possibly would give a blessing to a young man, Joshua Holdaway, who had been lost in subzero weather in the mountains near Salt Lake City and was in serious condition in the hospital. He told her he would be happy to do so.

That evening he went to Joshua's hospital room, where he found "a splendid young man" about eighteen years of age. His feet were bandaged much like the President's foot had been when he lay in the hospital just over a year before. Each of his fingers was individually bandaged as well. The worry was that the severity of frostbite might require amputation of his fingers, his toes, and possibly his feet. President Monson noted, "I was able to talk to him about the whirlpool bath for the afflicted feet . . . and asked him if Corky, the physical therapist who took care of me, was still there, and he said he was. We exchanged views concerning the hyperbaric chamber, which both of us endured. It was nice that I had been through some of these things from the standpoint of being able to empathize with him."[19] After they talked for a time, Josh's father joined President Monson in giving Josh a priesthood blessing.

The attendant at the pharmacy was Joshua Holdaway's cousin. The next day, a letter from her arrived at President Monson's office. She indicated that she was rarely at the pharmacy on Monday evening; in this case she was substituting for another pharmacist. She rarely answered the phone but felt "it was inspiration from on high" that President Monson would telephone that night, when he was so needed.[20]

Joshua's mother wrote a letter of appreciation as well, commenting that Josh had said to her that day, "Mother, I want you to wash my hair, for I have the feeling that President Monson will come to my hospital room while I am here."[21]

On Tuesday and Thursday of that week, President Monson presided at the Bountiful Temple dedication sessions in his white suit—and special socks. He mentioned his visit to Joshua Holdaway and asked all there to unite their faith in Josh's behalf.

President Monson was back at the hospital on Friday, this time to see President Hunter, who had left the temple after the Tuesday morning session, saying, "Tom, I'm not feeling well. I think I'd better go home." He had struggled in that session to turn the pages of his talk and had finally allowed his secretary to assist him. President Monson recorded in his journal, "I held his hand and kissed it gently. I told him I was so pleased he had been able to dedicate the [Bountiful Temple] and likewise the Orlando Temple." President Hunter smiled, nodded, and said, "Thank you. I am too."[22] The next day, Saturday, President Monson presided at the final four dedicatory sessions and conveyed President Hunter's love to the people in the temple. During the six days of dedication, 201,655 people had attended sessions in the Bountiful Temple, the Salt Lake Tabernacle, the Bountiful Regional Center, and the tabernacles in Ogden, Brigham City, and Logan.

In his work with humanitarian and community projects, President Monson had developed a good relationship with many of the local church leaders of other denominations. Two weeks after the dedication of the Bountiful Temple, President and Sister Monson attended a prayer service and blessing of the Episcopal Insignia for Bishop George H. Niederauer, who had been named by the Pope to succeed Bishop William Weigand as the Catholic bishop in Salt Lake City. Bishop Weigand had been transferred to the diocese at Sacramento, California. It was an evening of pageantry in the Cathedral of the Madeleine. President Monson had been asked to speak, along with the governor of the state of Utah and a Lutheran minister who had responsibility for the Salt Lake Ministerial Association. The Monsons felt welcome as Bishop Niederauer mentioned them in his opening remarks and "expressed his pleasure in being able to visit the Bountiful Temple open house, which he then indicated he had enjoyed very much."[23]

The next day, the Monsons and Elder and Sister Faust were invited to the cathedral for the official ordination and installation of Bishop Neiderauer, presided over by Roger Cardinal Mahony from California. Also in attendance was the Papal Nuncio to the United States, Agostino Cacciavillan. The ordination took three hours and fifteen minutes. One of the priests filing by nodded to the Monsons and said, "Aren't you glad we were not honoring the Pope? That would have been much longer."[24]

President Monson was asked to address those present in the cathedral. Elder Gene R. Cook later wrote to him: "What you did at the Cathedral of the Madeleine Tuesday night was absolutely masterful, speaking with no notes but with the Spirit and a gracefulness that was evident to all present." In his judgment, he continued, President Monson "had an impact on the nonmember world and especially the Catholic church in really telling them that we are Christians and want to cooperate with them and yet still firmly hold to what we believe and know to be true."[25]

LDS Church leaders honored the new Catholic bishop at a luncheon on February 7, 1995, with President Monson acting as master of ceremonies. The event brought together the First Presidency and the Quorum of the Twelve with Bishop Niederauer and his associates from the Catholic diocese in Salt Lake, including Monsignor Terrence Fitzgerald, Reverend Monsignor M. Francis Mannion, Reverend Monsignor John J. Hedderman, Father Joseph M. Mayo, and Deacon Silvio Mayo.

President Monson has made friends with scores of strangers he has met flying from one assignment to another. He was taking his seat on a plane for a cross-country flight and asked the man next to him if he would mind trading places with President

Monson's traveling partner from Church headquarters. The man, Ron Gunnell, willingly agreed. But as he stood, he mentioned to President Monson that a mutual friend in northern Utah had given him a few of President Monson's chickens. President Monson smiled and said to him, "Sit down," and the two chatted about chickens for the entire flight.[26]

President Monson addressed students at a CES broadcast the first Sunday in February, the largest such gathering ever held in the Marriott Center at BYU, and shared some of his tender experiences with President Hunter. Earlier that day he had gone to see the President and found him warm, responsive, and articulate. "I am going to tell the students some of the lessons I've learned from you," he explained, but added that he wasn't sure if he would tell about the shoes. President Hunter looked at him quizzically.

"In our temple meetings," President Monson explained, "I have sat next to you all these years, and my shoelaces kept coming untied. And your shoelaces never did. One day I had the courage to say to you, 'Howard, how come my shoelaces always come untied and yours never do?'"

"Because I tie them in a square knot," Elder Hunter had responded. "You're tying a granny knot, and here's how you tie a square knot." He reached down and tied President Monson's shoes. President Monson has followed that procedure ever since.

When President Monson took his shoes into a local repair shop to be shined, the manager—who was quite an unusual character, always wearing cowboy boots and a black hat and sporting a beard—surprised him as he attempted to pay for the newly shined shoes. "I'll catch you next year," he said. "Happy New Year." It was a simple thing, but it touched President Monson. "I think there are good people everywhere," he noted in his journal, "and if you treat them with respect, regardless of their occupation or their position or status, they will respond affirmatively."[27]

He continued visiting nursing homes and care centers, finding that his visits were longer because he was greeting almost all of the patients, even those he didn't know, and posing for pictures with the staff. One Christmas, as he visited with Louie McDonald, a friend from his childhood, one of the other patients caught his arm as he left the room and asked if President Monson would bring him some M&M's candies the next time he came. "I will try to do that," President Monson responded. A week later, he was back with chocolates for Louie and the bag of M&M's for his new friend. He remembers that, as he plunked down the large bag, the man seemed shocked—and delighted. For the busy Apostle, who was never too busy for those in need, it "made" his Christmas.[28]

President Hunter took a turn for the worse in February 1995, and his inspired words from the past October general conference came to mind for many: "When a President of the Church is ill or not able to function fully in all of the duties of his office, his two counselors, who, with him, comprise a Quorum of the First Presidency, carry on the work of the Presidency. Any major questions, policies, programs, or doctrines are prayerfully considered in council by the counselors in the First Presidency and the Quorum of the Twelve Apostles. No decision emanates from the First Presidency and the Quorum of the Twelve without total unanimity among all concerned. Following this inspired pattern, the Church will move forward without interruption."[29]

On March 3, 1995, at 8:30 A.M., President Hinckley and President Monson were meeting with the Presiding Bishopric when they received the news of President Hunter's passing. The two immediately went to the Hunter residence in a high-rise near the Church offices. President Hunter had been failing since the Bountiful Temple dedication, when President Monson had observed, "The outlook does not appear optimistic."[30] Inis Hunter shared with the two Brethren her husband's final words. They "were not a sermon of length nor a detailed code for our conduct, but rather, a divine message from his heart to our hearts. It is powerful. It is penetrating. It is memorable. To those who were attending him, he said simply, 'Thank you,' and then was gone."[31] In his journal President Monson recorded: "A great and gentle giant of the Lord has passed away. He served well as President, although for just a brief period of nine months. A new era of leadership will now begin."[32]

The funeral committee, comprised of Elder Thomas S. Monson; Elder Boyd K. Packer; F. Michael Watson, secretary to the First Presidency; Elaine Jack, general Relief Society president; Ray Bryant from the Tabernacle staff; and Richard Bretzing, head of security, met to make the necessary plans. They scheduled a private viewing for family members as well as General Authorities and their families on March 6 at Larkin Mortuary, and a public viewing on March 7. The crowds were so large that the closing time was extended from 7:00 P.M. to 9:00 P.M. At the funeral in the Tabernacle on Temple Square, President Hunter's two counselors took their seats on either side of his empty red chair.

In a final tribute to President Hunter on behalf of the Church, nine million strong, President Monson said: "Like the Master, Howard W. Hunter grew from a humble beginning to a magnificent mission to the entire world. He, too, 'increased in wisdom and stature and in favour with God and man.' He, too, lifted up the hands which hung down. He, too, remembered the fatherless and the widows in their affliction. He, too, gave of himself for the blessing of others."[33] President Monson knew—from personal experience—of what he spoke. He, too, lives such a life.

30

___

THE CONSUMMATE COUNSELOR

There was never a time when we knew of any view he had that was sepa-rate from President Hinckley. He clearly had opinions on issues; he clearly had vast experience. In those years, to not find even the slightest gap or dif-ference of view between the President of the Church and his counselor was really quite remarkable; it was a completely united presidency.

ELDER QUENTIN L. COOK
Quorum of the Twelve Apostles

IT WAS AUGUST 21, 2006. "We're here for Tom's birthday," President Gordon B. Hinckley announced to the group of General Authorities and Church employees gathered in the west board room of the Church Administration Building for the traditional celebration. As the congratulations came to a close, President Hinckley handed President Monson a plate and mo-tioned for him to step forward and start the buffet lunch. "Tom," he said, "you lead out; you're the birthday boy."

Without a pause, President Monson smiled and said, "No, President, you go first. I always follow you."

The example is simple but so illustrative. From 1985 to 2008, President Monson served as a counselor to three Church Presidents: second counselor to Presidents Benson and Hunter and first counselor to President Hinckley. "He's very high energy in the best sense, intellectually vibrant," states Elder Dallin H. Oaks, "and yet, depending on the position he's in, that is subdued or put to work in the need of the moment."[1]

467

At the solemn assembly on April 1, 1995, when President Monson proposed the name of Gordon Bitner Hinckley for a sustaining vote of the membership of the Church, he asked priesthood holders, as had been the pattern at general conference since John Taylor became the third President of the Church, to stand and raise their arms in support. Then, for the first time in Church history, the Relief Society (all women over the age of eighteen) and the Young Women (ages twelve to eighteen) were invited to participate in sustaining the prophet of God. A new tradition was established, one that President Monson would continue when he was sustained as President of the Church thirteen years later.

"Wherever you are," President Monson announced, "you are invited to stand when requested and express by your uplifted hand whether you choose to sustain those whose names will be presented."[2] That sustaining of President Hinckley was hardly a perfunctory experience for the members. President Monson received a tender letter that described one man's reaction to the "extraordinary occasion":

> On that particular morning, I needed to haul hay for my livestock. I was enjoying conference on my truck radio. I had picked up the hay, backed into the barn, and was throwing down hay bales from the back of the truck. When you called for the brethren of the priesthood, "wherever you are," to prepare to sustain the prophet, I wondered if you meant me. I wondered if the Lord would be offended because I was sweaty and covered with dust. But I took you at your word and climbed down from the truck.
>
> I shall never forget standing alone in the barn, hat in hand, with sweat running down my face, with arm to the square to sustain President Hinckley. Tears mixed with sweat as I sat for several minutes contemplating this sacred occasion. . . .
>
> In our lives, we place ourselves at particular places when events of large consequence occur.

That has happened to me, but none more spiritual
or tender or memorable than that morning in the
barn with only cows and a roan horse looking on.
Sincerely,
Clark Cederlof[3]

President Monson read for sustaining vote: "Thomas Spencer
Monson as President of the Quorum of the Twelve, and Boyd K.
Packer as Acting President of the Quorum of the Twelve." He also
presented the members of the Quorum of the Twelve to be sustained, with the newest member, Henry B. Eyring, called to fill
the vacancy created by the death of President Howard W. Hunter.
He then invited Elder Eyring to take his place with the Apostles
on the stand. Every time he sees a new member join the Quorum,
President Monson remembers as if it were yesterday that long
walk he took decades before. (It would be October 2004, another
nine years, before he again would read the names of two new
Apostles, Dieter Friedrich Uchtdorf and David Allan Bednar, and
give a nod of welcome to them. They filled vacancies created at
the deaths of Elders Neal A. Maxwell and David B. Haight.
Quentin L. Cook would follow in October 2007, when Elder
Eyring was called to the First Presidency at the death of President
James E. Faust.)

That evening, at the general priesthood session, President
Monson bore a powerful witness of the fifteenth President of the
Church, President Hinckley:

"With moist eyes and tender hearts, we have said fare-
well to that gentle giant of a man, even a prophet of God,
President Howard W. Hunter. We have sustained this day
President Gordon B. Hinckley as the President of the Church and
the prophet, seer, and revelator of God. I know that President
Hinckley has been called of our Heavenly Father as the prophet
and that he will lead us along those pathways the Savior has out-
lined. The work will go forward and the people will be blessed.
It is an honor and distinct privilege to serve with President
Gordon B. Hinckley and with President James E. Faust in the First
Presidency of the Church."[4]

President Hinckley had extended the call to President Monson to serve as First Counselor in the First Presidency, and the two would again sit side by side for the next thirteen years.

Upon hearing of the new First Presidency, a former member of the Sixth-Seventh Ward, Jack Fairclough, wrote to President Monson: "I am honored to call you a dear friend for these many years. Your marvelous work in the Church of the Lord does you enormous credit. The Sunday your calling to the Quorum of the Twelve was announced, I was in the old South Visitors' Center as a guide preparing to take tourists on a tour of Temple Square. I was very gratified then that a former Sixth-Seventh Ward bishop and very caring home teacher to my mother and sister had been so honored. The feeling is much magnified today at your calling as First Counselor in the First Presidency."[5]

President Monson fits the description in Doctrine and Covenants Section 81, the only revelation given—originally—to a counselor in the First Presidency. That revelation, received for Frederick G. Williams, perfectly defines President Monson's many years of service to Presidents of the Church, whether he was on their right hand or on their left.

The passage of scripture identifies three important duties: "[Be] faithful in counsel . . . [proclaim] the gospel . . . succor the weak, lift up the hands which hang down, and strengthen the feeble knees."[6] Elder Quentin L. Cook suggests that President Monson has been such a counselor. "Because of the strength of his personality, there can be no question that he would have given his very best advice and counsel. He values unity, he values loyalty, he will let his voice be heard when it is appropriate to do so in that counsel. But as a decision is reached, he fully and wholeheartedly supports it. The unity of the First Presidency in their important decisions is a great example to the whole Church."[7]

President Monson was the consummate counselor to President Hinckley, as he had been to President Hunter and President Benson. President Monson has been remarkably able, yet deferential; bold, yet humble; resolute and innovative, yet a voice for precedent.

Elder David A. Bednar agrees that one of the "marvelous

lessons in the life of President Monson is that he was the perfect counselor. He didn't presume to take upon himself initiatives or responsibilities that were the purview of the President of the Church." Elder Bednar noted that in board of education meetings he attended as president of Ricks College, which became BYU–Idaho, President Monson "would express his views very appropriately and even emphatically. But whenever a decision was made, he would always sustain and support."[8]

What the members of the Church haven't seen is how, from his chair next to President Hinckley, he helped move the work forward with the faith and capacity of a world leader. "He is a man of *great* faith, *great* faith," Bishop H. David Burton testifies. "When I talk to the First Presidency about issues that are very difficult, very complex, or have some implications that are very dramatic, he, more often than not, will be the first to say, 'We'll leave it in the Lord's hands. Don't worry, Bishop. We'll leave it in the Lord's hands.'"[9]

President Gordon B. Hinckley became the most traveled President of the Church in its history. In June 1997, at President Hinckley's eighty-seventh birthday celebration, President Monson said of his friend, "President Hinckley is gradually circumventing the world, meeting with our members who have rarely, if ever, seen a living President of the Church."[10] While President Hinckley was gone, President Monson as First Counselor in the First Presidency carried much of the administrative burden at headquarters. The two had worked together for so many years that President Monson knew basically how President Hinckley thought and what his response would be to most matters put before him. They consulted on the phone, President Hinckley in Africa or some such place, President Monson at his office in Salt Lake City.

Much of President Hinckley's travel was to dedicate temples. Each recent Church President has helped expand temple work. President Spencer W. Kimball prophesied, "We look to the day when the sacred ordinances of the Church, performed in the temples, will be available to all members of the Church in convenient locations around the globe."[11] President Brigham Young had foreseen such a day, proclaiming in 1856, "To accomplish this work there will have to be not only one temple but thousands of them, and thousands and tens of thousands of men and women will go into those temples and officiate for people who have lived as far back as the Lord shall reveal."[12]

That day came closer when, in the October 1997 general conference, President Hinckley announced plans to construct smaller temples, built to "temple standards" in areas of the Church "that are remote."[13] The first of these was constructed and dedicated in 1998 in Monticello, Utah.

Since his call to the holy apostleship in 1963, President Monson has participated in dedications and rededications of more than fifty temples. At the cornerstone ceremony for the temple in Stockholm, Sweden, he said, "Each of us has a cornerstone, or two, or three, in his life, even points of reference to guide us." As with all his messages, he shaped this message to those in the congregation. "A cornerstone in my life," he said, "is my association with my grandfather's sisters who came from Sweden. As a little boy, I would sit upon their knees and they would tell me stories of Sweden, stories which I have never forgotten. Then they would show me some slide pictures of the country. During the presentation of most of the pictures placed in the viewer they would speak with reverential respect. It was as though the picture portrayed holy ground. Inevitably my aunts would pause before exclaiming, 'Here is a picture of Stockholm.' Then there was a moment of silence and I was supposed to have the same reverence that they had." He has never forgotten that experience, which became a cornerstone to him—a cornerstone of heritage, a cornerstone to remind him of his duties, and a cornerstone to remind him of those who went before.[14]

The Tampico Mexico Temple dedication in 2000 was for President Monson a glorious return to that part of Mexico; he had created the Tampico stake twenty-eight years earlier. That dedication was also a part of temple history: three temples were dedicated in two days. President Monson dedicated the Tampico Mexico Temple on May 20 in four sessions; that same day, President James E. Faust dedicated the Nashville Tennessee Temple. The next day, President Monson dedicated the Villahermosa Mexico Temple. Total attendance at Tampico was 5,066; at Villahermosa the next day it was 3,850. President Monson shared with the congregations his limited Spanish language ability, learned mostly in high school, commenting, "It isn't up to par by far but at least I can understand more than I once could."[15]

At the Veracruz Mexico Temple dedication six weeks later, he spoke of the temple helping the members there. "We all have certain talents, and the Lord knows what they are," he said. "We all have limitations and the Lord knows what they are. Whatever our limitations may be, the Lord said this: 'Be ye therefore perfect, even as your Father which is in heaven is perfect.' [Matthew 5:48.] He would not give us commandments we could not fulfill. We can become perfect in our love of God. We can become perfect in our love of our fellow men. We can become perfect in the payment of our tithing. We can become perfect in living the Word of Wisdom. We can become perfect in our home teaching. In other words, all of those degrees of perfection are within our reach. . . . We know what we must do."[16]

He makes it simple: "Seek the Spirit of the Lord in your families. Kneel down with your children. Counsel them from your heart and be kind. Don't take life too seriously and remember that disappointments will come and we have to recognize that and live within those parameters."[17]

President Monson felt prompted to call young Carlos de Jesus Contreras Madrigal, who was sitting on the front row in the celestial room at the Veracruz Mexico Temple dedication, to come forward and stand by his side, that "he might represent all the boys and girls at the temple that day." President Monson asked him how old he was and he replied that he would be thirteen the next day. With a smile, President Monson then suggested that his experience in the temple would be his birthday present and that he should make a note of it in his journal. Later, President Monson learned that the boy's mother, Elvira Madrigal Gonzalez de Contreras, was one of the most faithful sisters in a branch in the Villahermosa stake, and that his father was not a member of the Church.[18]

"My, but the temples have blessed the people of the Church," President Monson states. His family members have gathered in sealing rooms of the Salt Lake Temple to participate in ordinances for deceased ancestors. "There was an overwhelming feeling of binding together," he wrote one evening when the family participated in sixty-nine sealings. The work had been for Frances's family, which had been one of Frances's mother's last wishes before she passed away.[19]

"Surely this will be known as an era of temple building as we move forward under the direction of our inspired President, Gordon B. Hinckley," President Monson wrote in his journal after the First Presidency review of an actual model of a proposed sealing room for small temples.[20]

"I have never seen a more supportive counselor as it relates to temple work than President Monson," Bishop Burton says as he recalls the many discussions in the Temple Sites Committee meetings regarding temple construction. The Presiding Bishop's office oversees temple construction as part of its charge. Bishop Burton notes, "The first person to make a motion about spending the resources of the Church for temple work was Brother Monson. While he has not been quite as vocal in public about that, his influence on temple construction, temple work, and family history work is pretty extensive." When we think of temples, Bishop Burton continues, "we immediately think of President Hinckley; I think that is appropriate. But not many steps behind, if any, is our current President. He has a great testimony of why we build temples and all the work that goes on in temples."[21]

Every Thursday, President Monson and President Hinckley rode in a little open cart along the underground tunnel leading from the Church Administration Building to the temple. "As it went under Main Street in the tunnel, and as soon as we were in the part where the temple began, Brother Hinckley took his hat off for the rest of the trip," President Monson observed. "No one said anything, but I noticed. He's a very spiritual President."[22] Every time President Monson sees Church members, youth in particular, coming and going to the temple, he reflects on how "they have done something of eternal value for someone else. And this is what life is all about."[23] To him, temple work is rescue work.

President Monson still remembers when he was a bishop counseling a couple whose disagreements were escalating. He felt inspired to ask them, "How long has it been since you have been to the temple and witnessed a temple sealing?"

"A long time," they replied. These were worthy people who went to the temple and did ordinance work for other people, but they had not witnessed a sealing in many years.

"Will you come with me to the temple on Wednesday morning at eight o'clock?" he asked.

The next Wednesday the three were in one of the beautiful sealing rooms. Bishop Monson's couple started out far apart on a little bench against the wall. As the ceremony proceeded, they drew closer and closer together; by the end, they were reunited, holding hands, their differences put aside. They had remembered their covenants made in the house of God. "When we remember our covenants, we will keep them," states President Monson. "Covenant keepers are happy people."[24]

"I think there is a lot to be said about his influence on where we have gone as a Church over the last forty years," states Bishop Burton. "During that period of time Thomas Monson has certainly been a strong advocate and voice."[25]

Another area of the Church in which President Monson's influence has been powerful is missionary work. Elder M. Russell Ballard views President Monson as "one of the great missionaries of all dispensations. He understands missionary work, he understands the role of tying the members to the missionary effort."[26]

As chairman of the Missionary Executive Committee, Elder Ballard took a rough draft of *Preach My Gospel,* then a proposed missionary guide, to the three members of the First Presidency one Sunday afternoon. At President Monson's home, the two chatted and even took a stroll in the backyard to see the pigeons in President Monson's lofts. Then Elder Ballard asked him to read the manuscript of several hundred pages. "I know you will read every word of it," Elder Ballard said and encouraged his longtime friend and colleague to make any changes.

And then Elder Ballard added, "I need it back in two days."

"You've got to be kidding," President Monson replied as he felt the weight of the manuscript. To his credit, President Monson stayed up most of the night reviewing that manuscript, and two days later Elder Ballard had his corrections and suggestions.

One thing that was missing in that early draft of *Preach My Gospel* was the personal touch of real-life accounts. Elder Quentin L. Cook, who at the time was executive director of the Missionary Department, explains, "President Monson never calls them stories because he wants them always to be true accounts. He has always recognized that a vast majority of people can see and understand such accounts, whereas if you are talking in terms of concepts, people might not grasp the message."[27]

President Monson made it clear that any such account has to teach a principle. He could have used the experience of Shelley, a member of the Sixth-Seventh Ward, to illustrate effective missionary work. Shelley had not embraced the gospel, though his wife and children were active in the Church. When Tom left for Canada to serve as mission president, he had almost given up on Shelley. "Had I been asked to name anyone I knew not likely to become a member of the Church," he says, "I believe I would have thought of Shelley."

After he was called to the Twelve, Elder Monson had a telephone call from Shelley. "Bishop, will you seal my wife, my family, and me in the Salt Lake Temple?" Shelley asked.

Elder Monson hesitated. "Shelley, you first must be a baptized member of the Church."

Shelley laughed. "Oh, I took care of that while you were in Canada. My home teacher was the school crossing guard, and every weekday as he and I would visit at the crossing, we would discuss the gospel."[28]

President Monson's life is full of such examples. Another came to his attention when George Watson, who was serving in a stake presidency in 1999 in Naperville, Illinois, decided to write to President Monson to let him know what had happened to him.

In 1957, at age twenty-one, George Watson emigrated from Ireland to Canada, took a job in Niagara Falls, and found a room at the "ridiculously inexpensive cost of $6 per week." The only drawback was that he had to drive his landlady, age seventy-three, to church each Sunday in St. Catherines, Ontario. She used the twenty-five-minute drive to encourage George to "see the missionaries from her church." He resisted for more than a year, until one day she invited him to join her and "two young ladies coming to supper." He found it very difficult to be rude to lady missionaries.

He "did a great deal of thinking" during the next several months, but kept dismissing the Church. By now eleven missionary companionships had taught him the gospel. It felt right but required giving up too much. The landlady persisted in inviting him to church, and finally he determined to accompany her—in "an open neck shirt, sneakers, and sports slacks," intending to embarrass her so she would not ask him again. They were late; he sat in the hall, refusing to attend Sunday School, and talked with "a very fine man who was crippled" and who, George felt, understood him. When George told the member he was returning to Ireland in eight days, the man pressed him to be baptized before he left. He agreed. All week long George ignored the man's phone calls to confirm the Saturday baptismal service. On Sunday, however, "after a very sleepless night," George phoned him, apologized, and arranged for his baptism to take place on the way to the airport.

"I have no idea where you or the missionaries found my address in Ireland," he wrote to President Monson thirty years later, but "I had a letter from you welcoming me into the Church." It read, "We are thrilled to welcome you as a newly baptized member of our Father's kingdom. Your Father in Heaven loves you deeply and desires to bless you richly with His spirit." One Sunday in Ireland, at 9:00 A.M., there was a knock on George's door, and "a President Lynn was on the doorstep," saying he had had a letter from the president of the Canadian Mission, Thomas S. Monson, asking him to watch over George.[29] A small act by a loving leader had helped keep a brother safely in the fold.

The true accounts in *Preach My Gospel* were included largely as a result of President Monson's prodding, and many of them were his suggestions. *Preach My Gospel* came together in a short fourteen months, guided by the hand of the Lord through His servants, President Monson among them. "He was chairman of the Missionary Executive Council forever," explains Elder Ballard. "He knows missionary work, and the fact that the manual spoke to the missionary and taught him, instead of just laying out a lesson, was one of the magical parts of it."[30] It has proven to be a divinely inspired and successful approach to missionary work.

Every fall, stretching into the winter, President Monson and President Faust extended calls to men whose names had been recommended by Church leaders and approved by the First Presidency and Quorum of the Twelve to serve as mission presidents. Some years there were as many as 135, and the two counselors each took approximately half. President Monson would prepare before each meeting, reviewing the file and checking with the Missionary Department for further detail if there were any concerns or questions. In the interviews, he rarely spent less than an hour with each couple and sometimes took longer. He personalized the interview so that when the couple left his office, they would feel as though they had received his undivided attention, as indeed they had.

As the missionary work went forward, and the Church continued to grow, the need for new physical facilities increased as well. April general conference in 2000 was held in the newly completed Conference Center. President Monson described the transition from the Tabernacle to the Conference Center as nothing short of miraculous. "I don't think that many people have been moved on and off of Temple Square in the history of the Square," he said.[31] Some 6,500 usually squeezed into the Tabernacle for general conference; the Conference Center seated approximately 21,000.

"We have needed a much larger building to accommodate those who attend conference and other activities throughout the year," said President Monson at the Sunday conference session in the new facility. "Workmen with finely honed skills have labored with their hearts and hands to provide a structure worthy of [the Lord's] divine approbation."[32]

With the construction of the Conference Center, along with technological innovations in satellite broadcasting and computer streaming, more people than ever could participate more personally in general conference. And many of them particularly loved hearing from Thomas S. Monson. One family required their children to listen to two speakers in each general conference session; the rest of the time the children were allowed to play. The mother wrote in a letter to President Monson that her son had said to his father, "Call me when the last speaker is up—or when President Monson is speaking. I'll come in for that."[33] Another mother wrote of watching her youngest sit captivated before the television as President Monson spoke; when he was nearly finished, the child rushed forward and planted a kiss on President Monson's smiling face on the screen.[34]

President Monson's love for people shines through. He loves to be out among the Saints. Elder David B. Haight once commented, after the two of them attended a stake conference in President Monson's home stake, "The 1,500 people that filled the stake center would gladly have stayed another hour listening to your wisdom and feeling of your love."[35] President Monson's great capacity to engage the membership of the Church with his personal experiences and warm delivery prompted President Hinckley to remark, when he stood to speak after President Monson, "How would you like to follow him!"[36]

Bishop H. David Burton said: "I was on a speaking assignment [out of town], and my mom was in assisted living. My wife, Barbara, had called and said Mom had a little bit of a setback, but not to worry. Then I got a call from President Hinckley, who said, 'I think it is important for you to come home.' I hadn't hung the phone up a minute when President Monson called. He'd been to see Mom a couple of days before. I don't know if he and President Hinckley had been speaking with each other or not, but he said, 'I think it's time for you to come home.' I did. I arrived about an hour before she passed away. President Monson has those kinds of tender feelings about people and their circumstances, almost like an antenna."[37]

In May 1997, President Monson presided at a regional conference in Lyon, France. He hadn't been to France in nearly a decade. As President and Sister Monson and Elder and Sister

Neil L. Andersen made their way to the car through the throngs of members hoping to get a glimpse up close or even a handshake, Elder Andersen pointed out a couple standing in the crowd and told President Monson their touching story. Their son, Elder Richard Charrut, had died in a tragic accident after serving with the Andersens in the France Bordeaux Mission.

Elder Andersen had spoken at the funeral service in the little branch in Chambéry, France. This was the first time he had seen the parents since that service five years earlier. As Elder Andersen concluded the account, the couples had reached the car. Rather than climbing in, President Monson said, "Let's go back and see them." Nothing was more important to President Monson at that moment than expressing his love to these faithful parents whose son had perished while in the Lord's service.

Worried, Elder Andersen checked his watch and looked at the members pressing in around them. But President Monson would not be dissuaded. "President Monson insisted we go back and find the Charruts," Elder Andersen remembers. President Monson put his arms around Gerard and Astrid Charrut and said, through Elder Andersen, who was translating, "Brother and Sister Charrut, as you remain faithful, I promise you, you will have your son forever."

The Charruts melted into tears. "It wasn't so much his words as the feeling that came over all of us," remembers Elder Andersen. Twelve years later, the Charruts' stake president contacted Elder Andersen to report that Brother Charrut had just passed away. He added, "The love and attention President Monson showed to this couple strengthened and lifted them in a marvelous way during the years, and they have remained true and faithful."[38]

Following a regional conference in Hamburg, Germany, President Monson insisted on visiting a former president of the Hamburg Stake, Michael Panitsch, who was seriously ill. He had been a faithful leader in the Church when times were hard. Born in the Ukraine, fluent in Russian and Ukrainian, Brother Panitsch had fought in the Second World War with the German army; he had served long and ably as president of the Hamburg Stake, with his wife at his side.

Elder Uchtdorf, president of the Europe area at the time, tried to dissuade President Monson from making the visit, explaining that Brother Panitsch lived on the fifth floor of his building. There was no elevator. President Uchtdorf was also aware that, only months before, President Monson had been hospitalized because of a serious problem with his left foot. But Brother Panitsch and President Monson had been friends for years; he was going. He and President Uchtdorf climbed the stairs, stopping every second or third step to rest. They found Brother Panitsch in his bed, gravely ill. He lived alone now, his wife having died years before. His family lived close by, his daughter a floor above him and his son a floor below. The longtime friends reminisced and shared testimony, and then President Monson promised Brother Panitsch that he would be remembered on the prayer roll of the First Presidency and the Quorum of the Twelve. Brother Panitsch began to weep. "Danke, danke, mein Bruder," he said to President Monson. It would be the last time the two would be together.[39]

To President Monson, the climb up and down the stairs had nothing to do with his feet and everything to do with his hands. He has taught from personal experience: "'God's sweetest blessings always go by hands that serve Him here below.' Let us have ready hands, clean hands, and willing hands, that we may participate in providing what our Heavenly Father would have others receive from Him."[40]

Dan and Mabel Taylor were another couple blessed by the loving hands of President Monson. They had lived in Canada when President Monson was mission president there and they knew the Monsons very well. Mabel, in fact, had served as a counselor to Frances in the mission Relief Society presidency. The Taylors had moved to California, and then-Elder Monson visited with them when he was on assignment there to divide their stake. He suggested that the Taylors might consider serving a mission. The next week the two of them showed up at his office at Church headquarters, saying, "You said we ought to serve a mission, and here we are."

"Have you visited with your bishop or stake president?" Elder Monson asked.

"No," the two responded.

He suggested they return home and let their bishop know they would like to serve. They were called to the Washington D.C. Mission, and then on a second mission to the visitors' center in Laie, Hawaii. They subsequently moved to Salt Lake City.

In the fall of 2003, President Monson was notified that Dan Taylor was in a Salt Lake City hospital, having suffered a heart attack. He went to see Dan and, when they arrived at the hospital, had his driver confirm the room number. President Monson walked into the room, "looked around, and didn't know a single soul." Surprised, he said, "I understand this is the room of Dan Taylor."

The patient responded that he was Dan Taylor.

Wrong Dan Taylor.

But before President Monson could excuse himself, the man's wife spoke up, "We've been praying that someone who held the priesthood would come and give a blessing to my husband. We just concluded our prayer and here, Brother Monson, you've come."

President Monson gave the man a blessing and expressed how happy he was to meet him. Then, explaining that he had another Dan Taylor to visit, he slipped out of the room, but not before the patient and his wife and family expressed their great appreciation for the blessing.

Checking with the desk, he found there was indeed another Dan Taylor in the hospital. It was *his* Dan Taylor, and President Monson gave him a blessing as well.[41]

When President Monson has such experiences, he knows that the hand of the Lord has guided him. He feels the mix-up with the two Dan Taylors was no mistake. So many times he has borne witness "that the sweetest spirit and feeling in all of mortality is when we have an opportunity to be on the Lord's errand and to know that He has guided our footsteps."[42]

As willing as he was to reach out, President Monson realized that "the desire to help another, the quest for the lost sheep, may not always yield success at once. On occasion, progress is slow— even indiscernible."[43] Fritz Hoerold, a boyhood friend of President

Monson's, was a good example. Fritz was "short in stature but tall on courage." He enlisted in the United States Navy at age seventeen and was off to war on a large battleship in the Pacific, where the crew faced a number of bloody engagements. His ship was repeatedly damaged; many sailors were killed or wounded. Thomas Monson and Fritz Hoerold lost track of each other—for fifty years. Then one day, when President Monson was reading a magazine article featuring battles in the Pacific, he thought of his friend. Was he still alive? Did he live in Salt Lake City? With a little investigation, this years-ago president of Fritz's teachers quorum got him on the phone and sent him the magazine. Fritz had long since stopped attending church altogether. Twice in only a few months, the two ran into each other. Both times, President Monson encouraged Fritz to qualify for the blessings of the temple. Fritz's wife, Joyce, urged, "Keep working with this man of mine."

Joyce passed away, and President Monson lamented, "How I wish that I had been more successful with my private project to get Fritz to the temple." He went to Joyce's funeral service. Fritz, seeing him, "made a beeline to his side." President Monson described what happened: "We both shed a few tears. He asked me to be the final speaker. When I arose to speak, I looked at Fritz and his family and said, 'Fritz, I am here today as the president of the teachers quorum of which you and I were once members.' I proffered how he and his family could become a 'forever family' through temple ordinances—ordinances at which I pledged to officiate when that time came.

"Then I said, 'Now, Fritz, to use naval terms, since we were both in the navy, our ship is about to weigh anchor, and Joyce is on it. And it is destined for the port of the celestial kingdom of God, and I don't want you to miss that ship. The boatswain's mate's whistle has sounded, and now is the time.' As I said that, Fritz jumped to his feet and saluted me, saying, 'Yes, sir.' I returned his salute. It was a very touching moment for all of us."

Not long afterward, at the October 2001 general priesthood meeting, President Monson spoke of Fritz in his talk. The following Monday morning, Fritz called to say thank you, explaining that his home teacher had taken him to the priesthood meeting. He was shocked when President Monson told his story. His home teacher turned to him and asked, "Did you get the message?" Fritz's son-in-law, who also accompanied him, jumped to his feet and introduced Fritz to the men gathered as the man about whom President Monson had just spoken. "President," Fritz said, "I began to shed tears." On August 31, 2002, President Monson sealed Fritz's wife and children to him in the temple. Less than a year later, on March 4, 2003, President Monson ordained Fritz a high priest, with Fritz's stake president, bishop, and home teacher standing in the circle.[44]

Reaching the one is important, but it is also important to reach everyone. To that end, on January 4, 2003, the First Presidency taped the first in an ongoing series of worldwide leadership training meetings. The program was broadcast one week later, and the training meetings have continued each year. President Monson recognizes that "there is really no substitute for being present in person, where you can provide open discussion and answer questions,"[45] but the introduction of satellite sessions for priesthood leaders has great advantages. Topics are discussed, refined, correlated, and translated, which means that everyone can receive the same message at the same time throughout the world in his or her own language.

The worldwide expansion of the Church also made it necessary to eliminate some programs that had been in place for many years. It was President Spencer W. Kimball who announced the discontinuance of the MIA's June Conference, with its dance and music festivals, drama presentations, and all-Church basketball and softball competitions. He stated that they were being eliminated because the Church had grown too large to bring youth to one central location for such grand activities. In their place, he recommended such activities be held on a regional basis. Unfortunately, such events were extremely scarce.

Years later, seeing a need for events to strengthen the youth, President Monson gave each member of the First Presidency and the Quorum of the Twelve a copy of President Kimball's statement concerning such festivals. "That was the genesis that sparked a rethinking of the desirability of something like a youth celebration held in multiple cities," President Monson has explained.[46]

The Day of Celebration at Rice-Eccles Stadium in Salt Lake City on July 16, 2005, a gigantic youth program commemorating the 200th birthday of the Prophet Joseph Smith and the 175th anniversary of the organization of the Church, was the largest presentation in decades. President Monson was thrilled with the program, calling it "magnificent." Some 42,000 youth from across the Salt Lake Valley and Wyoming performed, including 16,000 singers, 5,200 dancers, and 2,400 flag bearers. Other such extravaganzas, though on a smaller scale, have celebrated temple dedications or milestones in Church history, with great success.

President Monson's love for the youth has been apparent in his addresses at many Scout gatherings. In the summer of 1996 he spoke at a jamboree at Valley Forge, Pennsylvania. Chris Rasband was a twelve-year-old Scout at the event. Earlier that summer, he had moved with his parents to New York, where his father presided as mission president. It was a hard move. There he sat in the mass of 5,000 eager Scouts as President Monson took the podium at a devotional.

Chris knew President Monson from the years he and his father had sat right in front of President Monson at Utah Jazz basketball games. Chris remembered cheering and exchanging "high fives" with the President when a shot would go in, so having him speak at the Jamboree was a touch of home for the lonesome Scout. As President Monson prepared to leave the jamboree, he began shaking hands with the Scouts, who all pressed forward. The President looked out over the crowd and saw Chris in his Scout uniform. He called out, "Chris Rasband, come up here and say hello!" The Scouts parted like the Red Sea, and Chris walked up as President Monson reached out to take his hand and pull him up on the podium.

Chris needed that attention. He needed his friend, who found him. "He is never too busy," Elder Ronald Rasband, Chris's father, says with emotion, "never too busy for people."[47]

He is never too busy to pick up the phone to call a friend from high school who just lost her husband, never too busy to sit by the side of a friend as he passes on, never too busy to write a letter of encouragement to one of his friends with a note at the bottom, "It's time to come back." President Monson is never too busy to reach out to rescue.

Elder Neil L. Andersen has watched President Monson and has learned: "He doesn't act as if he is an administrator who has to get through all of the issues. He acts more like a shepherd. That's who he is, someone whose impact on people is more important than are his calculations or strategies for the Church."[48]

Still, his travel schedule has always been rigorous and his Church assignments heavy. He and Sister Monson would rarely take a break—unless they were in Germany. Scenic Southern Germany has always been their favorite getaway if they were in Europe. Part of the lure is the countryside, another part is the relative anonymity afforded them so far from home. On one European trip, in August 1995, they started out in Stockholm, Sweden, where President Monson was dividing the stake he had created in 1975. It was a historic occasion, for Sweden's royalty, His Royal Majesty King Carl XVI and Her Royal Majesty Queen Silvia, visited the LDS temple as part of their revival of a tradition dating back to the thirteenth century when the king traveled throughout the country to meet the citizens. President Monson presented the queen with a two-volume history of her family and gave His Royal Majesty a bronze statue of the "First Steps" figurine.

The Monsons had arranged to take two days off before they were expected in Görlitz to dedicate the new chapel that had been completed there. Gerry Avant of the *Church News* had been dispatched to cover the events at the last minute with a packet of airline tickets based, she was told, on President and Sister Monson's itinerary. She didn't take time to look through them.

When the ceremonies in Sweden ended, a new adventure began. Gerry explains: "I made my way to the ticket counter, and a smiling agent said, 'I see you're going to Munich today.' I said, 'No, I'm going to Dresden.' The agent riffled through my packet of tickets and said, 'You go to Dresden in three days; today you are going to Munich.' I figured President Monson was going to speak at an area meeting or a fireside, or meet with missionaries. Whatever he did, I would cover it for the *Church News.*

"As we got out of the car at the hotel in Munich, I asked, 'What time are the meetings tomorrow?'

"President Monson said, 'We don't have any meetings in Munich.'

"I was somewhat at a loss for words, but asked, 'Then, why did we come to Munich?'

"President Monson said, 'I don't know why you're here, Gerry, but Frances and I thought we would take a couple of days to sightsee.'

"I said, 'That's great! This will give me some time to meet a few members and take some photos.'

"President Monson said, 'You've been working hard. You ought to take some time off, too. Go sightseeing.'

"The next morning I went to breakfast, expecting to hear that they would drop me off at some tourist site and would then be on their way. However, after breakfast, President Monson said, 'I told Frances last night, I know Gerry; as soon as we're gone she'll call a bishop or a Primary president or someone and go to work. Then everyone will know we are here. We'd better take her with us.'

"So off I went on the most memorable 'vacation' of my life. We visited Berchtesgaden on a very foggy day, and went to Salzburg for lunch. The next day, we went out on Lake Königsee. It was raining, but it was a most beautiful experience. Because of the weather, few other tourists were on the boat, and no one else was in the little round chapel by the lake when we got there. We sat for a few minutes in that chapel, and I soaked up every word President Monson said. That evening, we went back to Salzburg for dinner."[49]

They later met Elder Dieter F. Uchtdorf of the Seventy and his wife, Harriet, in Dresden, and the group visited Elder Joseph A. Ott's grave and then went to the hill east of the Elbe River where President Monson had dedicated the land twenty years earlier. "It was the same kind of day, misty and rainy," President Monson noted, "as we walked down the lane toward the mountain out-look. As I reminisced with those present concerning the events of that earlier period, the sun burst forth with all its splendor, as it had done on that dedication day. The Elbe River far below in the valley flowed ever onward as it has done through the years, in both good times and bad."[50]

Elder Uchtdorf later wrote to President Monson, sharing his observations upon visiting such a sacred spot:

"I recognized two most significant names given to a street and a building. The street leading to the spot has the name *Sonnleit,* which translates into 'guided by the sun.' The closest building to the spot is called *Friedensburg,* which translates into 'fortress' or 'castle of peace.' I know that the fulfillment of your blessing has brought healing rays of sunlight and peace to our people. Harriet and I received in these two extraordinary days another testimony that, 'Surely the Lord God will do nothing, but he revealeth his secret unto his servants the prophets.' Thank you for being a prophet of the Lord Jesus Christ."[51]

Of his visit to Görlitz in 1968, President Monson said: "Under the inspiration of the Lord, I promised those worthy Saints who had nothing—nothing—that if they were faithful to the Lord, He, in His kindness and fairness, would provide them with all the blessings any other member of the Church in a free country received."[52] In the intervening years, the Freiberg Temple had been built and the members in Görlitz had received all the blessings of worthy members in free nations. But they didn't have a meetinghouse—until President Monson arrived on August 25, 1995, to dedicate the structure that, twenty-seven years earlier, he had promised would be built.

When the Monsons arrived in Görlitz, they were met by members thrilled with their new chapel and with the visit of President Monson, as well as a visit from Lord Mayor Matthias Lechner, a young man who had helped plan the day's proceedings. The day stood in sharp contrast to what a young Elder Monson had encountered twenty-seven years earlier when "there were informers in the audience, fear in the hearts of all citizens, and the presence of Russian troops in full military regalia and East German police with their machine guns at their side and their Doberman dogs straining at leashes. . . . Gratitude filled my heart and soul," said

President Monson, "for the privilege of seeing the hand of the Lord in the blessing of this choice people."[53]

Over the years, President Monson has taken every opportunity to return to Germany. In December 2003 he completed a regional conference in England on a Sunday afternoon and flew immediately to Dresden to give a fireside for "his friends." He invited Elder Marlin K. Jensen, Area President, to join him. "As we walked into this Dresden building packed with about 1,100 people," Elder Jensen recalls, "it was just electrifying. They all stood as he came in. He didn't just walk to the stand like most would. He went out and circulated among the people for about ten or fifteen minutes on his way to the pulpit, embracing them and shaking hands. It was what he had done for so many years and was amazing to see."[54]

When President Monson has tried to "lift up the hands that hang down," as he did in Germany for so many years, he has seen the blessings of the Lord pour down into other people's lives. Yet it often takes years for "the rest of the story" to reveal itself.

For example, it was a full five years after the death of prominent Church educator Rex E. Lee, who had suffered with cancer, when President Monson received a touching letter from his widow, Janet, describing "a sweet experience" she had had in the temple. She explained that she and her son had been talking about the last days of her husband's life. Her son mentioned that one of his regrets had been that when he left the hospital for lunch one day, President Monson had come and given his father a blessing. He was so disappointed to have missed it, and mentioned that the experience was probably not as meaningful to the respiratory therapist who had been asked to assist in giving the blessing. "It would have meant a great deal to my son," she wrote, "and as he spoke, his emotions were very close to the surface."

Sister Lee continued:

"During a temple session last March, a lovely young woman in her thirties caught my eye. We seemed to exchange glances each time we changed rooms. When the session was over, she came to me and asked if we could talk a minute. She told me that she and her husband were heartbroken over the recent death of their seven-year-old daughter, but said that what had helped them the most was an experience her husband had had five years ago at the hospital, when he was a respiratory therapist and had assisted you [President Monson] in giving my husband a blessing. She said that the day of the blessing, her husband had shared some very spiritual insights into the passing from this world to the next of which you had spoken in the blessing. She said they had often talked about the comfort that blessing would bring them someday if they had to lose someone close to them. Little did they know it would be their young daughter! She wept when she told me how the understanding they had been given helped and sustained them in their days of sorrow. When I told my son, he wept as well, finally understanding why it was more important for the therapist to be there at that time than for him—as much as he would have liked to have been. We don't always understand why things happen the way they do, but my heart rejoiced in the new insight I had been given."[55]

President Monson had his own brush with potentially losing a loved one in January 2000. His daughter, Ann, had stopped by the Monsons' home on the afternoon of January 5 to drop off some Swedish flatbread fresh from her oven for her parents. She walked into the kitchen unprepared for what she saw. Her mother lay unconscious on the floor in a pool of blood. Ann called 911 and then her father; then she started to pray. President Monson said he would meet her at St. Mark's, the nearest hospital. He arrived before the ambulance did and watched as they brought Frances in. She had a severe laceration on the back of her head and a large lump on her forehead. When he told her, "We're here," she said, "I hurt."

A later look at the kitchen made it clear she had gashed the back of her head on an open drawer—it was covered with blood—and then had fallen facedown on the floor.

The doctors quickly decided to life-flight Frances to the LDS Hospital, a larger trauma facility. Her physicians and Dr. Rich, who had cared for her nearly eighteen years before when she had suffered a serious fall, were there to meet them. The doctors worked into the night to stabilize her condition, inserting a breathing tube and a feeding tube and making her as comfortable as possible. She was heavily sedated. President Monson stayed at the hospital all night, as did his security officer, Tracy Monson (who is not related, though he has the same last name).

Although Frances had spoken those two words, "I hurt," while on the stretcher at St. Mark's Hospital, she did not utter another word for two and a half weeks. President Monson stayed close to her side. His journal entry for January 7 notes: "We were hoping that she would wake up soon, but the doctors caution that with head injuries it takes longer, particularly with one who is diabetic. . . . It is very painful to see your eternal companion suffer and feel so helpless in not being able to be of assistance to her. . . .

"Gordon B. Hinckley, James E. Faust, and Russell M. Nelson joined me in giving her a blessing. I asked President Faust to anoint, and President Hinckley sealed the anointing." It was a beautiful blessing. Among other things, President Hinckley said, without equivocation, "You will rise from this affliction, you will awaken and you will be healed under the Spirit of the Lord."

The hospital gave President Monson a room where he could do some paperwork, and for the next few weeks he spent most of each day with Frances, slipping out only for the temple meetings on Thursdays and to a viewing or two. The children and grandchildren were attentive but worried.

Son Clark recalls, "Dad demonstrated faith like I have never seen any other time from anybody. Dad was praying, and he would not admit to the possibility that she might die. I don't think he had very often prayed for anything for himself. He was always willing to let the Lord decide what was best for him. In this case, he was determined not to lose her."[56]

On Monday, January 10, President Monson wrote in his journal: "There is still no glimmer of recognition, and she still has not gained an awareness of where she is or what has happened, which is very disconcerting. Eyes remain closed, pain persists, and faith comes forth to bless her. The doctors say to be patient."

On Friday, January 14: "Not yet regained consciousness. Ann and Carma have been attentive, as have the grandchildren."

On Thursday, January 20: "We have been praying for a break-through in the next few days, that the coma she is in may not hold her captive."

On Friday, January 21: "Frances was opening her eyes and tracking very clearly my conversation, then Tommy's conversation. My, but it was good to see this happen. I went home a happier man than I have been for more than two weeks."

On Saturday, January 22: "Frances was just wonderful today. She was alert. She smiled several times. She followed me with her eyes and held my hand. Dr. Fowles said, 'She has turned the corner.'"

Her first words to her husband were, "I forgot to mail the quarterly tax payment." He assured her he would take care of it.

In the midst of the crisis, President Monson prepared and presented a message for a satellite missionary broadcast, speaking on "Hallmarks of a Happy Home." "We are responsible for the home we build," he counseled. "We must build wisely, for eternity is not a short voyage. There will be calm and wind, sunlight and shadows, joy and sorrow. But if we really try, our home can be a bit of heaven here on earth."[57] He looked forward to that bit of heaven—Frances was coming home.

It was fortunate that Frances could stay in mortality longer, because her support would be particularly needed in the years ahead. On January 10, 2008, President Hinckley attended the temple meeting but asked President Monson to conduct. He did not attend the Temple Sites Committee Meeting. He was not well, but in the weeks ahead, he pushed on as he always had done. He gave a dedicatory prayer at the restored state capitol and rededicated the Garden Park Ward chapel on Sunday, January 20. He attended the First Presidency meeting on Tuesday, January 22, and seemed to be a little better. He came into the office on Wednesday, January 23.

On Saturday, January 26, President Monson, President Eyring, and F. Michael Watson, secretary to the First Presidency, went to the bedside of the much beloved leader. Wrote President Monson of the visit: "The doctors indicated he might not survive this illness. . . . Family members had gathered and he was sedated. I had

Congratulating longtime friend Thelma Fetzer on her
one-hundredth birthday, April 8, 2010.

With Elder L. Tom Perry, bidding a final farewell at the
cemetery to President Gordon B. Hinckley.

Photo by Keith Johnson, Deseret News

"It is proposed that Thomas Spencer Monson be sustained as prophet, seer, and revelator and President of The Church of Jesus Christ of Latter-day Saints."

"Let us relish life as we live it," President Monson counsels Saints
at general conference, "and find joy in the journey."

Entering the Conference Center for general conference
with that familiar spring in his step.

The First Presidency. Left to right: President Henry B. Eyring, President Thomas S. Monson,
and President Dieter F. Uchtdorf. The tenor of President Monson's administration
is one of unity, cooperation, and love.

Sharing post-conference moments with (right to left) Elders Jeffrey R. Holland, Robert D. Hales, and Richard G. Scott, along with President Henry B. Eyring, in April 2010.

Embracing Elder Joseph B. Wirthlin following the solemn assembly on April 5, 2008.

Photo by John Luke, © IRI

A smile and handshake for (left to right) Elders D. Todd Christofferson, Quentin L. Cook, and David A. Bednar of the Quorum of the Twelve, April 2009.

Joining Elder Glen L. Rudd for his ninetieth birthday celebration at Welfare Square. The two had been bishops in neighboring wards more than fifty years earlier.

Paying tribute to business leader Larry H. Miller on February 28, 2009, for the little things he did every day that weren't in the newspapers.

Joining in annual Pioneer Day festivities at the Days of '47 Parade.

Pulling the "devil's tail" on a replica of the Gutenberg printing press at the opening of the Crandall Historical Printing Museum in Provo, Utah, April 21, 2009.

Honored with the game ball as the "distinguished University of Utah fan of the game" when Utah played Air Force at Rice-Eccles Stadium on October 24, 2009. Left to right: U of U athletic director Chris Hill, U of U president Michael Young, and Deseret News publisher Jim Wall.

Visiting with Bishop George H. Niederauer of the Catholic Diocese of
Salt Lake City after a ceremony at the Cathedral of the Madeleine.

Joining Rabbi Benny Zippel at the January 5, 2009,
inaugural of Governor Jon Huntsman, Jr.

Speaking in the Cathedral of the Madeleine for the centennial celebration
"A Civic Service of Thanksgiving," Sunday, August 9, 2009.

Draped in Mexican serapes to stay warm, President Thomas S. Monson and President Henry B. Eyring salute the crowd of 87,000 inside Mexico City's Azteca Stadium during the LDS cultural event prior to the Mexico City Temple rededication. Ann Monson Dibb (seated, right) looks on.

Photo by Jason N. Swensen, Deseret News

Helping a young girl apply mortar to the cornerstone of the
Twin Falls Idaho Temple on August 24, 2008.

Taking a moment with brothers Jacob Jonathan and Nicholas James Lowry
at the Cebu City Philippines Temple dedication.

Catching the eye of a member of the congregation at general conference in October 2008.

Enjoying time with the members at the cultural celebration
prior to the Twin Falls Idaho Temple dedication.

The Monson family in 2008.

President and Sister Monson at the Oquirrh Mountain Utah Temple after the first dedicatory session on August 21, 2009, which was also President Monson's eighty-second birthday.

Photo by Gerry Avant, LDS Church News

the feeling I would probably never see President Hinckley again with his eyes open."[58]

Returning to the office, the three were uneasy. President Monson made plans to give President Hinckley a blessing the following day—the Lord's day—Sunday, January 27.

President Packer was invited to join them, and the next day at 3:00 P.M. they were again at President Hinckley's bedside. The entire family had assembled. "After some conversation, in which his doctor mentioned the gravity of President Hinckley's health, we joined in giving him a priesthood blessing. I invited President Packer to anoint, and I was voice in the sealing of the anointing. We were joined by all the priesthood holders in the Hinckley family and by Don Staheli [President Hinckley's personal secretary], Michael Watson, and others present who held the priesthood."

President Monson recorded, "I have known Gordon B. Hinckley for many, many years, beginning before either of us was a General Authority. Long ago I did the printing for the missionary literature and he handled the buying of the printing. Today I found him about like he was the day before. However, his breathing seemed a little deeper. I held him by the wrist and had a distinct feeling this was the last time I would see my beloved President and friend alive in mortality."[59]

Three and a half hours later, at 7:20 P.M., Michael Watson called. President Hinckley had passed away.

31

REACHING OUT TO THE ONE

President Monson is warm and attentive, with a wonderful sense of humor and a spontaneous love for people. I think as a prophet he is irresistible. He goes out in the kitchen to thank the people who prepared a meal; he gives a thumbs-up acknowledging your efforts; he shakes hands with everyone he can reach and high-fives the youth. When he interacts with children, he almost always bends down so that he is at eye level. If everybody were like President Monson, we'd have heaven on earth.

ELDER WILLIAM R. WALKER
First Quorum of the Seventy

PRESIDENT MONSON PRESIDED, conducted, and spoke at the funeral service of his "cherished friend and colleague," President Gordon B. Hinckley, on February 2, 2008. "I cannot adequately express how much I miss him," he said to the worldwide audience, which included more than 16,000 people in the Conference Center and many more watching via satellite, the Internet, and BYU Television. "It's difficult to recall a time when he and I did not know each other," President Monson continued. "We have served side by side for over forty-four years in the Quorum of the Twelve Apostles and in the First Presidency. We have shared much over the years—heartache and happiness, sorrow and laughter. . . . Wherever I go in this beautiful world, a part of this cherished friend will always go with me."[1]

With the passing of President Hinckley, the First Presidency had been dissolved. President Monson and President Eyring, who had served as his counselors, returned to their places in the Quorum of the Twelve Apostles, and that quorum became the presiding authority of the Church. On Sunday, February 3, 2008, all fourteen ordained Apostles living on the earth assembled in an upper room of the Salt Lake Temple. They met in a spirit of fasting and prayer. President Monson described, "During that solemn and sacred gathering, the Presidency of the Church was reorganized in accordance with well-established precedent, after the pattern which the Lord Himself put in place."[2]

President Boyd K. Packer was voice in formally ordaining and setting apart Thomas S. Monson as the sixteenth President of The Church of Jesus Christ of Latter-day Saints. President Monson was eighty years old.

Many times he had borne his testimony of Jesus Christ to this august body of the Lord's servants, as he had to members of the Church everywhere and would as the President of the Church in years to come: "With all my heart and the fervency of my soul, I lift my voice in testimony . . . as a special witness and declare that God does live. Jesus is His Son, the Only Begotten of the Father in the flesh. He is our Redeemer; He is our Mediator with the Father. He loves us with a love we cannot fully comprehend, and because He loves us, He gave His life for us. My gratitude to Him is beyond expression."[3]

Those in the room remember the Spirit confirming immediately the sacred calling of President Monson. Elder Russell M. Nelson describes the moment as being "unlike any ascension to high office in any other part of life—political, academic, governmental—where there is always some striving, competition, vying for favor, but not so at that time. It is a sweet and sacred experience, one that is just such a sacred privilege."[4]

Elder Quentin L. Cook recalls receiving "the marvelous spiritual confirmation that President Monson was to be the prophet" as he sat, the most junior member of the Twelve, in his first meeting in the temple to select—by revelation—the President to lead the Church. He noted that President Monson seemed "a very pure receptacle for divine inspiration."[5]

In the days before the temple meeting, President Monson prayed earnestly for guidance in selecting his counselors. He studied the matter "very carefully, considering seniority, precedent, and the talents which [he] felt were needed at the time and those who would make a nice, compatible presidency."[6] And then he humbly took his selections to the Lord for confirmation.

President Monson named Elder Henry B. Eyring, age seventy-four, as First Counselor in the First Presidency. The calling was not a surprise. Elder Eyring had served as Second Counselor in the First Presidency since the October 2007 general conference. The two had worked together for many years, as Elder Eyring had served as Church Commissioner of Education, as a counselor in the Presiding Bishopric, and as a member of the Quorum of the Seventy before being called by President Hinckley in 1995 as an Apostle.

President Monson selected Elder Dieter Friedrich Uchtdorf, age sixty-seven, to serve as Second Counselor in the First Presidency. A convert to the Church and former stake president in Germany, a member of the Quorum of the Seventy since 1994 and of the Presidency of the Seventy since 2002, Elder Uchtdorf had been called to the Quorum of the Twelve in October 2004. He brought international, business, and Church experience to the new responsibility.

President Monson wanted to reach out into the world, Elder L. Tom Perry suggests, "and the most logical one to reach out with was Elder Uchtdorf. President Monson was showing, 'We are a worldwide church.'"[7]

Neither counselor had much seniority in the Quorum of the Twelve, but President Monson knew he had "enough senior years to balance his counselors." The three have vastly different experiences but, he notes, they are united, and "in unity there is great strength. We come together, united, on every major issue."[8]

That Sunday evening, as had been tradition at the Monsons' for decades, the family came over to the house. President Monson did not speak of what had happened in the temple that day. Not until his daughter, Ann, pressed him for the timing of the public announcement did he share the plan for a press conference the next morning.

On Monday, February 4, 2008, President Thomas S. Monson, sixteenth President of The Church of Jesus Christ of Latter-day

Saints, with his counselors on either side of him and the members of the Quorum of the Twelve seated in full support, met with the press in the Church Office Building lobby directly in front of the mural depicting the beckoning Savior.

President Monson read a prepared statement, first addressing the passing of President Gordon B. Hinckley. "We shall miss him," he said, "yet we know that he has left us with a wonderful legacy of love and goodness." The President then promised to "continue the commitment of those who have gone before us in teaching the gospel, in promoting cooperation with people throughout the world, and in bearing witness of the life and mission of our Lord and Savior, Jesus Christ."

True to what would become a central theme of his presidency, he spoke of reaching out "in the spirit of brotherhood which comes from the Lord Jesus Christ" and emphasized the importance of rescuing the one.

Someone from the press asked, "What will you do differently?"

Given that he and President Hinckley had met together in various meetings nearly every day for twenty-three years in three different First Presidencies, making decisions and setting future objectives, he responded, "It is inevitable that our thinking would be similar." He identified "no abrupt change," emphasizing a continuation of temple building around the world, further development of the Perpetual Education Fund, and emphasis on personal prayer and on helping others.[9]

Both counselors acknowledged their new leader's commitment to people. "I've come to know of his goodness," said President Eyring.[10] "I know of his heart, his soul, his commitment, his wonderful love for the people," added President Uchtdorf.[11]

As Thomas S. Monson began his presidency, there were 13.1 million members of the Church in 178 nations and territories, 2,740 stakes, 27,827 wards and branches, 348 missions, 52,686 missionaries, and 124 temples throughout the world.[12]

When the General Authorities met the next Thursday in the temple with the new First Presidency, President Monson instinctively went to his chair of thirteen years and sat down—until he realized the chair in the middle was empty. "This is going to be hard to get used to," he quipped. For years he had stood back in support of the three Presidents of the Church he served as a counselor.

"We never talked at home about my dad someday becoming President of the Church," his son Tom explains.[13] "Any task he takes on, he finds a way to magnify it and to put more into it."[14]

Words of support and congratulations poured into his office. Elaine S. Dalton, who would become the Young Women general president, viewed the new First Presidency as "a mighty force" for the Lord. "Combined, they have such a grasp of the whole; they see a bigger picture than anyone in the room can see."[15]

One treasured note came from the Reverend Monsignor Terence Moore of the Saint John the Baptist Catholic Church in Draper: "You are such a prayerful, thorough spiritual leader. I feel so blessed by our friendship and your graciousness towards me." This was not a form letter but a communication friend to friend. The two had worked on several of the same community causes and attended a host of formal dinners and celebrations, and President Monson would be a comfort to the Reverend Monsignor Moore in his battle with cancer.[16]

Without question, President Monson's committee assignments over the years and his supervisory responsibilities had helped prepare him to lead every aspect of the Church organization. Over the years, he has been closely associated with correlation, printing, missionary work, temples, priesthood service, auxiliaries, youth, and welfare; he has traveled to every continent; he has addressed so many gatherings that he long ago quit counting. But his service is most often manifest in reaching out, in caring for the one in need, in being prompted by the Spirit and then acting on the prompting.

His first opportunity to speak to members of the Church came quickly. He recorded a message for the worldwide leadership training broadcast to be aired on February 9. The theme of the meeting, "Building up a Righteous Posterity," was one of his favorite topics, something about which he had preached for years. He spoke with fervor and conviction, saying, "More and more the world is filled with chaos and confusion. Messages surround us which contradict all that we hold dear—enticing us to turn from that which is 'virtuous, lovely, or of good report or praiseworthy' and embrace the thinking which often prevails outside the gospel of Jesus Christ. However, when our families are united in purpose, and an atmosphere of peace and love prevails, home becomes a sanctuary from the world."[17]

On February 10, 2008, he was in Rexburg, Idaho, to dedicate the Church's 125th operating temple, an event he described as his first official act as Church President. He told news media he was "filling in" for President Hinckley, who had intended to dedicate the temple that February. The words of that dedicatory prayer were particularly poignant:

"We thank Thee that since the restoration Thou hast never left Thy Church alone. From the days of the Prophet Joseph Smith, Thou hast chosen and appointed a prophet to this people who has held and exercised all the keys of the everlasting priesthood for Thy children in the earth."[18]

Many of those attending the proceedings described receiving a personal witness of President Monson as the prophet of God.

Members of the Church stood to sustain President Thomas S. Monson at the 178th Annual General Conference of The Church of Jesus Christ of Latter-day Saints on April 5, 2008. He later acknowledged, "I have felt your prayers in my behalf and have been sustained and blessed during the two months since our beloved President Hinckley left us. Once again, I appreciate your sustaining vote."[19]

In the general priesthood meeting that evening, he issued a charge to priesthood leaders: "We who have been ordained to the priesthood of God can make a difference. When we qualify for the help of the Lord, we can guide boys, we can mend men, we can accomplish miracles in His holy service."[20]

To the membership of the Church in his Sunday morning address, he referred to the fifteen men who had preceded him as President of the Church. Many of them he had known personally; he had served in the Quorum of the Twelve with six of them and as a counselor to three. "My earnest prayer," he said, "is that I might continue to be a worthy instrument in His hands to carry on this great work and to fulfill the tremendous responsibilities which come with the office of President."[21]

In the following session, on Sunday afternoon, Elder Jeffrey R. Holland said on behalf of the General Authorities and the Church as a whole:

"Of the many privileges we have had in this historic conference, including participation in a solemn assembly in which we were able to stand and sustain you as prophet, seer, and revelator, I cannot help but feel that the most important privilege we have all had has been to witness personally the settling of the sacred, prophetic mantle upon your shoulders, almost as it were by the very hands of angels themselves. Those in attendance at last night's general priesthood meeting and all who were present in the worldwide broadcast of this morning's session have been eyewitness to this event. For all the participants, I express our gratitude for such a moment. I say that with love to President Monson and especially love to our Father in Heaven for the wonderful opportunity it has been to be 'eyewitnesses of his majesty.'"[22]

President Monson concluded the final session of that general conference saying, "My dear brothers and sisters, I love you, and I pray for you. Please pray for me. And together we will reap the blessings our Heavenly Father has in store for each one of us."[23]

"I simply want to serve in such a way that the Lord would be pleased with whatever I do," President Monson has said.[24] His messages at general conference are a high priority in his life. "I look every day of my life for topics that might help someone," he says. "I am thinking of general conference every day."[25]

Six months later, at the conclusion of one session of the October 2008 general conference, as he passed along the line of the Quorum of the Twelve shaking hands, as is the custom, President Monson suddenly turned and made his way into the congregation. It was not something he had ever done before, nor had any Church President in recent times.

He had caught sight of his longtime friend Elder Royden G. Derrick, an emeritus General Authority, seated near the front in a wheelchair. Making his way up the aisle, the President embraced Elder Derrick and quickly spoke of their treasured past experiences, including duck hunting when they "never shot a single one!" Then he strode back to the stand, shaking a hand here and there, giving a thumbs-up to the missionaries, smiling broadly and encouragingly at everyone. It was Thomas S. Monson doing what he does best—reaching out. Elder David A. Bednar calls it "his inherent, instinctive goodness focused on 'the one.'"[26]

Allie Derrick, sitting next to her husband, described the day when "President Monson put into action that which he has taught: 'Never assume; we should always let them know we love them.'" Just over a year later, Elder Derrick passed away, but that special encounter and expression of love by President Monson "was cherished to the end of his mortal life."[27] President Monson spoke at his funeral.

"This warm, engaging giant of a man fills the room," his sister Marilyn suggests. "It doesn't matter how large the room is."[28]

Elder Dallin H. Oaks suggests that "what is emerging is Thomas Monson the bishop, not Thomas Monson the manager. He is very good in both roles. His concerns are with the individual. I have seen enough Presidents of the Church to see differences. Some are very conscious of policy and procedures and so on; President Monson, of all the leaders that I have observed, is concerned for the individual. It comes out in his talks; it comes out in his meetings. He is sensitive to policy, he participated fully in making it and he often reminds us we need to follow it, but his personal creative energies are focused on the one."[29]

General Authorities see a concerted effort on the part of the President to increase members' awareness not only of others' needs but also of the privilege and duty to respond. "When we go to the temple on Thursdays, and we, each member of the Twelve, give our reports as called upon by President Monson, we describe what we did with the callings and assignments we have been given," Elder Robert D. Hales explains. "But when it comes to him, he speaks of his sweetheart and how he's been caring for her. He speaks with appreciation of his family, his children, grandchildren, and great-grandchildren. He speaks of going to care centers and homes or to hospitals or neighbors to give blessings. As we leave, we remind ourselves as Apostles what he has taught us that day about what we should be and how we should conduct our lives."[30]

Says Elder Holland: "He will show up, probably unannounced, at the funeral of a rank-and-file employee. I can't think of anything that exemplifies more the ministry of President Monson than that kind of individualized attention. That's what the Savior taught, and President Monson does it and reflects it and embodies it more than anybody I have ever seen."[31]

"Some people, if they are really prominent," Elder Bruce D. Porter of the Seventy explains, "he will treat very kindly but he probably won't visit their homes. But if you are the lowly of the earth, he is likely to drop in any time." Elder Porter saw that in President Monson's attention to a resident, Paul Tingey, living in a local care center. Paul and Elder Porter had been mission companions in Germany. Paul had married, had a family, even been a bishop. Now, severely impaired by multiple sclerosis, he was younger by decades than most of the care center's residents.

President Monson was visiting the center one evening, and as he spoke to Paul, he realized that Paul was the son of his good friend Burton "Buzz" Tingey. The two struck up a friendship. They shared a natural optimism and enthusiasm for life. From then on, every time President Monson went to that facility, he talked to Paul.

Two or three years later, Paul passed away. Elder Porter, who attended the funeral, recalls, "I had this feeling as I sat down that President Monson would come." Five minutes before the service was to begin, President Monson walked in. Elder Porter knew of President Monson's busy schedule; he also knew that President Monson cares about people. The President was the concluding speaker at the funeral, and at the next general conference priesthood session, President Monson spoke about Paul.

"Held captive by this malady, Paul Tingey struggled valiantly but then was confined to a care facility," President Monson explained. "There he cheered up the sad and made everyone feel glad. Whenever I attended Church meetings there, Paul lifted my spirits, as he did all others. When the World Olympics came to Salt Lake City in 2002, Paul was selected to carry the Olympic torch for a specified distance. When this was announced at the care facility, a cheer erupted from those patients assembled, and a hearty round of applause echoed through the halls. As I congratulated Paul, he said with his limited diction, 'I hope I don't drop the torch!'

"Paul Tingey didn't drop the Olympic torch. What's more, he carried bravely the torch he was handed in life and did so to the day of his passing. Spirituality, faith, determination, courage—Paul Tingey had them all."[32]

"At our monthly General Authority testimony meetings in the temple," Elder Porter explains, "President Monson shares many personal experiences with us, like his association with Paul. The more I've listened, the more I have thought, 'He is teaching us how to be Christlike. He is not teaching how to be great administrators, though he is that, but how to be Christlike.'"[33]

President Monson has reiterated, "There are feet to steady, hands to grasp, minds to encourage, hearts to inspire, and souls to save."[34] He considers such actions as going "to the rescue." He issued a challenge to the General Authorities to carry that theme to the membership of the Church. "I am pleased that the Brethren, especially the Seventy, have caught hold of that message and are teaching it everywhere they go," Elder D. Todd Christoffersen notes. "President Monson has said it enough that there is no doubt how strongly he feels about it."[35] Quoting Jesus' words that "whosoever will save his life shall lose it: but whosoever will lose his life for my sake, the same shall save it,"[36] President Monson has concluded, "I believe the Savior is telling us that unless we lose ourselves in service to others, there is little purpose to our own lives."[37]

At general conference in October 2009, President Monson made reference to a large, clear jar he had received, filled with little multicolored puff balls called "warm fuzzies," each one representing a kind deed done by a Primary child. He described sitting with his wife and reading the hundreds of notes and cards sent to him on his eighty-second birthday describing acts of service performed by Church members, young and old, the world over. A year earlier, on his eighty-first birthday, he had been interviewed by the *Church News* and asked what he would most like for his birthday. "Do something for someone else on that day to make his or her life better," he had responded.[38] The cards, the notes, the warm fuzzies, and other creative items had been sent in response to that wish.

His daughter, Ann, has observed his natural interest in others for many years. "He has no inhibitions in taking the first step to strike up a conversation. And he always sees the best in people. No matter what their situation may be, he lifts them where they are and inspires them so they can lift themselves."[39]

President Monson has always reached out to those estranged from the Church, saying, "In the private sanctuary of one's own conscience lies that spirit, that determination to cast off the old person and to measure up to the stature of true potential. In this spirit, we again issue that heartfelt invitation: Come back. We reach out to you in the pure love of Christ and express our desire to assist you and to welcome you into full fellowship."[40]

Many have been shepherded back to the fold by his warmth and gentle urging. One General Authority tells of an older man who, after nearly twenty years of being out of the Church, came to him and asked how to "come back." The two talked, and the Church leader asked him, "What made you decide after all this time to want to be rebaptized?" The man pulled a letter from his pocket, unfolded it, and held it out. It read, "You have been long enough away, and it is time to come back. Tom."[41]

President Monson's approach is consistent and simple. "I am a people person," he explains. "If I see someone who will be happy that I stopped or took time to talk, I do it. I find there is a little bit of sainthood in everybody, and I look for it."[42] He expects members to do no less than "befriend the new converts, to reach out to them, to surround them with love, and to help them feel at home."[43]

No man was better prepared to engage the Church in such a concerted effort to reach out to those facing the loneliness of the self-absorbed, self-centered cultures of today. President Monson lives by the creed he teaches, says Bishop H. David Burton. He has said many times: the five most important words in the English language are *"I am proud of you."* The four most important are *"What is your opinion?"* The three most important are *"If you please."* The two most important are *"Thank you."* The least important is *"I."*[44]

That focus has been emphasized in materials being distributed. In 2009, with the global economy in a slump, the Church produced a DVD and pamphlet reemphasizing "Basic Principles of Welfare and Self-Reliance," featuring messages by President Monson, Elder Hales, Bishop Burton, and Sister Julie B. Beck, Relief Society general president. "We have to teach our people thrift, frugality and industry. We have to teach them to put away for a rainy day," asserts President Monson.[45]

The welfare system of the Church in early 2009 included 138 warehouses in the western hemisphere, with 108 of those being in the United States and Canada. It operated fourteen Church canneries, which produced 12.6 million cans of food. Its Deseret Bakery produced 453,594 loaves of bread, Deseret Pasta produced 938,505 pounds of pasta, and Deseret Soap produced 2.6 million pounds of soap; Deseret Dairy produced 9.87 million pounds of milk, 1.5 million pounds of powdered milk, and 727,251 pounds of cheese.[46]

The new Church handbook prepared for release in the fall of 2010 lists caring for the poor and the needy as one of the purposes of the Church, along with tenets from its well-recognized threefold mission: to proclaim Christ's gospel worldwide, to perfect the Saints through their receiving ordinances and instruction en route to gaining exaltation, and to redeem the dead by performing vicarious ordinances for them.

"Anyone who knows President Monson," explains Bishop Richard C. Edgley, counselor in the Presiding Bishopric, "knows his wonderful experiences and the wonderful example that he's set for the rest of us. He has, by example, taught us in how we can reach out and help with those who are suffering."[47]

"Our Heavenly Father has placed an upward reach in every one of us," President Monson has said. "No problem is too small for His attention nor so large that He cannot answer the prayer of faith."[48] "There are those throughout the world who are hungry;

there are those who are destitute," he has reminded the Saints. "Working together, we can alleviate suffering and provide for those in need. In addition to the service you give as you care for one another, your contributions to the funds of the Church enable us to respond almost immediately when disasters occur anywhere in the world. We are nearly always among the first on the scene to provide whatever assistance we can."[49]

For years, he has witnessed staggering humanitarian needs in the aftermath of earthquakes and other natural disasters that have crippled communities and even countries. On September 29, 2009, the islands of Samoa and part of Tonga experienced an 8.3 magnitude earthquake; four tsunamis roared to land. There were nearly two hundred deaths, with many more people injured and still others unaccounted for. The Associated Press reported that nearly 90 percent of residents in American Samoa were left homeless and without resources. Within a week, seventy-eight pallets containing sixty tons of food, hygiene kits, clothing, wheelchairs, and water containers were gathered from the Church's Salt Lake City warehouses and placed on a twelve-hour charter flight to the Pacific islands of Samoa. The Church also has contributed humanitarian aid to ongoing efforts in the Philippines, Vietnam, Indonesia, Turkey, and numerous other spots around the world.

On January 10, 2010, an earthquake rocked the small Caribbean nation of Haiti. More than 230,000 people, twenty of them Latter-day Saints, lost their lives in the quake, which measured 7.0 and had thirty-three aftershocks. President Monson knew the nation and its people. In 1983, he had dedicated the land of Haiti for the preaching of the gospel.

Immediately the Church opened the doors and grounds of its half-dozen meetinghouses in the capital of Port-au-Prince, which were remarkably still standing, to anyone needing assistance. Available were food, blankets, tents and tarps, medical supplies, and teams of LDS doctors, nurses, and other health specialists who had come to the island to provide assistance.

President Monson became Church President at almost the exact time that a major national and international economic crisis hit. It wasn't a tsunami, a flood, or a hurricane, but it was a wholesale global concern about employment, potential poverty, and whether people had food to eat and a roof over their heads. "We could not have a prophet better prepared and more skilled than President Monson during this period of serious welfare and humanitarian need," explains Elder Hales, who as Presiding Bishop from 1985 to 1994 saw firsthand President Monson's passion for helping the poor and administering relief. There is no question that President Monson finds himself on familiar ground when he encourages Church members to be involved in their communities, to don the trademark yellow T-shirts of the Mormon Helping Hands program.[50]

President Monson's vision of the Church, Elder Marlin K. Jensen suggests, is that "we are to become not only hearers of the word but doers. He still speaks at a funeral or two a week, and still makes his visits to the individual person. He is trying through that and through his teachings to get us to be galvanized into becoming real Christians at the very personal level, one person at a time, one soul at a time."[51]

When he called Elder D. Todd Christofferson to be the ninety-sixth Apostle in this dispensation after President Hinckley's death, it was not a quick meeting. President Monson had issued the call to Elder Christofferson to serve in the First Quorum of the Seventy fifteen years earlier. Elder Christofferson's account of being called as an Apostle is poignant:

"It was not remarkable in the sense of there being a lot of fanfare or activity surrounding the call. I think in the simplicity of it is the power and beauty. It was like a sealing in the temple, not complicated, not a lot of ceremony, but great power in the purity of it. There was nothing to distract from what was happening, what the focus ought to be."[52]

When President Monson extended the call to Elder Neil L. Andersen, then Senior President of the Seventy, to fill the vacancy in the Quorum of the Twelve at the death of President Monson's dear friend Elder Joseph B. Wirthlin, those close to the process saw his interest for others in action.

"President Monson commented about the burden, the weight of that responsibility, a few times in our Thursday meetings in the temple," remembers Elder Christofferson, who was observing the process for the first time. "Some of the senior Brethren commented early on, 'We don't have to worry—President Monson knows how to get revelation.'"[53]

President Uchtdorf described watching the selection of a new Apostle from his position in the First Presidency. "As a counselor," he said, "I want to let you know what I am learning about our prophet. I have watched him closely during the process of selecting the next Apostle. At one time he said, 'I haven't got an answer from the Lord yet, but I don't worry, because when the time comes that I absolutely need it, He will let me know.'"[54]

Elder Andersen will never forget the day he was invited to President Monson's office. First the President described his experiences being called as a mission president and later as an Apostle. "He has such a personal touch," says Elder Andersen. "At one point he got his Kleenex for me. He said, 'Don't worry. This is a good time to be tearful and emotional. I am not in a hurry.' This was Wednesday afternoon. Starting the next morning he was speaking to all the General Authorities and all the Area Seventies of the world. He had many messages in front of him in coming days, including talks for all the sessions of general conference. But he would not be rushed. This is President Monson."[55]

After President Monson extended a call to Elaine Dalton to serve as Young Women general president, he walked her and her husband to the door. Reaching over to his table, which had on it a bouquet of white roses, and pulling out one of the blossoms, he said, "This is for the Young Women general president."

"The minute he handed me the rose," Sister Dalton recalls, "my thoughts went back to my own experience as a young woman when we had the bandelos and we had to choose a symbol of something to sew on as our own emblem. I chose a white rose. He had handed me a white rose. The Spirit said, 'This is how we want every young woman to be, clean and growing and blossoming and prepared to come back home to her Father in Heaven.'"[56]

President Monson has seen many men called of God as apostles and prophets. He has watched them and their wives as they have gone about doing the Lord's work. In meetings with

General Authorities, he will speak lovingly about experiences he had with President David O. McKay, President J. Reuben Clark, Jr., President Spencer W. Kimball, and President Hugh B. Brown, among others. One of his favorite experiences with President Brown, who was called as an Apostle in 1958 and served in the First Presidency from 1963 to 1970, happened one day when the two were attending a commencement at BYU; President Brown was to conduct the exercises and Elder Monson was to speak. Elder Monson stopped at the home of President Brown to pick him up. President Monson tells that as he was pulling out of the driveway, President Brown stopped him and said, "Wait a minute." He looked toward the large bay window of his home as the curtains parted. Sister Brown, his beloved companion of more than fifty years, was at the window, propped up in a wheelchair, waving a small white handkerchief. President Brown reached inside his coat pocket for his handkerchief and returned her wave. Then he turned to Elder Monson with a smile and said, "Let's go."

Elder Monson assumed there was more to the interaction than just a friendly good-bye. He inquired of President Brown, who explained, "The first day after Sister Brown and I were married, as I went to my daily work, I heard a tap at the window, and there she was, waving a handkerchief. I found mine and waved in reply. From that day until this I have never left my home without that little exchange. It is a symbol of our love for one another, an indication to one another that all will be well until we are joined together at eventide."[57]

A similar incident fairly characteristic of President Monson occurred at a weekday General Authority training meeting in April 2008 before general conference. All of the Brethren were seated twenty minutes before the hour the meeting was scheduled to begin, as had been the practice for years, and then they waited. President Monson arrived late—ten minutes past the hour—and explained that he had been doing something for Sister Monson. Interestingly, many of the General Authorities remember that meeting not for what was said but for what was demonstrated by a prophet of God. Commented Elder David A. Bednar, "If he focused on efficiency and timeliness, he would have said, 'I have to be there.' But he was taking care of his wife."[58] There was a lesson to be learned that has stayed with those who waited patiently. That morning Frances was the one on whom he needed to focus.

The whole Church shared in his obvious pleasure at Frances's attendance at general conference in April 2010. So pleased was he in her recovery from a recent illness that he departed from his prepared text to welcome her with tender words that would long be remembered by those in attendance.

Elder Neil L. Andersen says, "He has never asked Sister Monson to be anyone different than she is. One time when we were at a regional conference in Lyon, France, I didn't know him that well. I was a General Authority serving in Europe and had not had much exposure to the senior Brethren. 'Is Sister Monson going to speak?' I asked. President Monson replied, 'I don't know yet.' A little more time went by, and I asked again, 'Do you know yet if Sister Monson is going to speak?' And finally he said, 'We won't know until we are in the meeting. I will pass you a note.' I thought, 'How thoughtful that he would not require her to speak.' She ended up speaking and did a wonderful job."[59]

What does it feel like to be President of the Lord's Church on the earth? "Humbling," President Monson says. "You immediately search your style, you search your thinking, you search your heart, and you realize you have an obligation to tell the people how you feel about things and to bear testimony. It isn't the time for oratory. You realize you are going to need God's help and then you live so you can earn it. He knows me. He has come to my aid before, and He will come again and again."[60] He has admonished the members to "acquire the language of the Spirit. It is not learned from textbooks written by men of letters, nor is it acquired through reading and memorization. The language of the Spirit comes to him who seeks with all his heart to know God and keep His divine commandments. Proficiency in this 'language' permits one to breach barriers, overcome obstacles, and touch the human heart."[61]

Like prophets of old and others of this dispensation, President Monson has repeatedly issued a clarion call to live the gospel, to avoid sin, and to live righteously. His direction has been clear:

"The philosophies of men surround us. The face of sin today often wears the mask of tolerance. Do not be deceived; behind that facade is heartache, unhappiness, and pain. You know what is right and what is wrong, and no disguise, however appealing, can change that." With passion borne of years of experience, he said, "Be the one to make a stand for right, even if you stand alone. Have the moral courage to be a light for others to follow."[62]

He has cautioned in particular about the degradation of pornography, "one of Satan's enticements." With great concern for the growing problem, he looked into the camera at general conference in May 2009 and stated, "If you have allowed yourself to become involved in this behavior, cease now."[63] Many commented that they felt powerfully the mandate of the prophet in those words, "Cease now."

After addressing a combined sacrament meeting of three young single adult wards one Sunday early in 2010, he recorded: "I felt the Spirit of the Lord as I counseled this special group of young men and women, . . . showing how the Lord blesses young people in the selection of a mate and in determining what they might study or what they might become in their vocation."[64]

The Lord's Spirit and message were received. One sister, a returned missionary who had served in Belgium, had gone to sacrament meeting not intending to stay for the whole meeting. She was struggling with her place in life and missed desperately the spiritual environment of the mission field. That day the Lord had a message just for her. "This prophet is the one well-known for touching the one," she later described. "I was sitting in a sea of people thinking, he has no idea that I am here and that I am struggling. Yet, the Spirit was an amazing tool, and President Monson was, literally, the conduit for the Lord. That's how the prophet does it, that's how he touches the one, through his ability to work with the Spirit. I felt it."[65]

President Monson's ability to affect individual lives is remarkable, especially considering the schedule he keeps. His typical day begins with a First Presidency meeting, and his regular schedule generally includes Thursday meetings with the Quorum of the Twelve and General Authorities, the General Welfare Committee, and the Priesthood Leadership Council. Other meetings range from the Board of Education to Budget and Appropriations, Temple Sites, Presiding Bishopric, Deseret Management Corporation, Printing Advisory, Human Resources, and many more. He also meets with many people. Some are dignitaries from around the world; others are friends he has known over the years.

President Monson has had vast experience in executive roles—he delegates, communicates, and organizes—but he also listens to the promptings of the Spirit. He knows that in the end, everything will work out. He has that kind of faith.

As an administrator, he is relaxed and inclusive. "He starts right on the dot but he'll come in and visit before the meeting begins," Elder L. Tom Perry explains. "He'll talk about the BYU game or the Jazz; he's a great sports fan. And then he'll get down to business." Elder Perry has appreciated President Monson's open manner in discussing Church finances, making certain he hears what those at the table have to say. "In the Budget and Appropriations Committee I can ask questions and he'll accept them, and we will work together in council."[66]

"He can hear from God and does hear from God," President Henry B. Eyring has observed. "He makes decisions in the most interesting way. He does his homework. He ponders and prays a long time. In other words, he doesn't shoot off quickly. He is not predisposed to a particular direction or decision until he decides it is right. But I'll tell you there will come a moment, usually after a lot of hard work—he does charts, he reads minutes, he asks for lots of opinions, he ponders and prays a long time—and then, very interesting, he's all settled."[67]

As Elder D. Todd Christofferson has observed, "There is always the underlying sense this is the Lord's work and His Church and therefore He will see it through. Whatever obstacles you face, whatever unsettledness about which way to turn in a given moment, the direction is there. He exhibits this underlying confidence that things will sort out; they always have and always will because the Lord's hand is in it."[68]

Whatever the focus of the meeting may be, he is always open to counsel. No one is waved off. If he is choosing artwork for a temple, he takes counsel from members of the Temple Sites Committee and others who work closely with him. He sincerely wants to hear other views and perspectives and have meaningful discussions, usually before divulging his own opinion. President Eyring has seen the pattern often. "He wants your opinion, but he is very, very good at telling what your motives are. So if you shade anything for him at all, he sees it. If you hedge, he will say nicely but with a smile, 'But you don't help me. You don't help me.' He wants it absolutely straight. Most people like to win arguments. He likes to get to the truth. He is very interesting that way, very rare."[69]

"He is not nearly as concerned about the agenda as he is about hearing people's opinions concerning the issue at hand," explains Elder William R. Walker, who participates in meetings with the President as executive director of the Temple Department. "He honestly wants to know what people think, and he won't voice his own opinion until he has gone around the table. He trusts people who have assignments to do their best."[70]

Often, in order to answer a question, to shift the direction the meeting is going, or to break growing tensions, President Monson will share a personal account from his life or from his vast experience with others. That informality invites participation. The experiences he shares are never random but rather address the very issue on the table.

Elder Christofferson was touched by a pre-conference leadership meeting when President Monson addressed General Authorities on the subject of audits and following the financial stipulations in the handbook. "He took what could have been a fairly dry presentation," Elder Christofferson recalled, "and, typical of him, said, 'We're talking about people's souls here.'" He described a man who was a clerk who embezzled some funds in his stake or ward and was excommunicated. It was a great hardship for the family and a trial to the man, and he committed suicide. President Monson's words have stayed with Elder Christofferson. "The President said, 'We cannot let that happen to a man or his family. We must follow procedures and do the audits, and we'll prevent it. This is much more than clerical procedures; this is the worth of a soul.'" Elder Christofferson continued, "The worth of each individual always comes through, no matter what President Monson talks about. And he has lived his life that way."[71]

Though his focus is on individuals, President Monson's skills extend to more general concerns as well. The businessman in him has kept an eye on the City Creek project begun in downtown Salt Lake City in President Hinckley's era and scheduled for completion in 2012. The Church undertook the City Creek project to protect the environment around Temple Square. The new urban community in the heart of downtown will cover approximately 20 acres and will create an altered cityscape and skyline with residences, offices, and retail stores. One of the first occupants of the center in 2010 was—fittingly—the flagship location of the Church-owned Deseret Book store.

His business acumen was again put to the test with the reorganization of Beneficial Financial Group, a company the Church had sponsored since 1905. When the economy went into a severe downturn in 2008, losses were so substantial that the company closed its doors to new business and maintained only a small force to manage its existing accounts. "Our corporations take the same bumps others do," President Monson explains. "We are in the same competitive business, and some years are better than others."[72] Also in that difficult economic climate, Deseret Management Corporation (the Church's holding company for business enterprises) shifted its focus to becoming predominantly a media company with its remaining businesses: Deseret Book, the Deseret News, KSL TV and radio, and a new Internet division called Deseret Digital Media.

In dividing up responsibilities among members of the First Presidency, President Monson chose to supervise personally the 360-voice Mormon Tabernacle Choir. He gave the choir a special send-off on June 14, 2009, in preparation for their summer tour of seven cities, during which they would travel from Ohio to Colorado in thirteen days. "You are going on a mission for the Church," he said. "For every applause you hear, there will be applause in their hearts for the memory they will have of having heard the Mormon Tabernacle Choir sing."[73]

If he is asked about the Choir, his eyes light up. He considers that "members of the Mormon Tabernacle Choir are the Lord's emissaries in their singing and music."[74] He often attends *Music and the Spoken Word* broadcasts on Sunday mornings, and when Choir members retire, he enjoys handing out plaques to them with Choir president Mac Christensen and music director Mack Wilberg. After the April 2009 retirement ceremony, he was invited to sit down at the organ and play. He stared at the five keyboards of sixty-one keys each and the thirty-two organ pedals at his feet. When the Choir urged him to play something, he obliged with one of the "renowned" piano selections he learned as a child, "To a Birthday Party," from the John Thompson book *Teaching Little Fingers to Play*. Organist Linda Margetts showed him how to use the many organ stops, but when she asked if he wanted to play the sound of the harp as one of the stops, he quipped, "I'm not ready to play the harp. Someone up there might get ideas."[75]

In 2009, online current affairs publication Slate.com ranked President Monson number one on its list of the eighty most powerful octogenarians in America. He was ranked ahead of former U.S. Presidents Jimmy Carter and George H. W. Bush, former secretary of state Henry Kissinger, and news personality Barbara Walters, among others. Slate.com reported, "The top spot this year goes to 82-year-old Thomas S. Monson, president of The Church of Jesus Christ of Latter-day Saints, and the only person on the list to rule over millions of people as a prophet of God."[76]

There is no question that he has a high profile, but, as Elder Kenneth Johnson of the First Quorum of the Seventy has observed, "President Monson will not be influenced by popularity or press. He will know or seek to know the Lord's will and then act on it. Courage and character stand out as two of his greatest strengths."[77]

Courage and character have been called for as, in recent years in the United States and other countries, a movement promoting same-sex marriage has divided voters. In some cases legislation has been passed to secure that shift. This radical change, Church leaders contend, is one of the great moral issues of our time because it strikes at the very heart of the family. As traditional marriage and family—defined as a husband and wife with children in an intact marriage—have come increasingly under assault, President Monson has said, "We owe it to our people to let them know the moral issue. We stand firm for true principles in a changing society."[78]

In letters to Church members, the First Presidency has reaffirmed the principle of marriage being between a man and a woman and has encouraged families to review the Church document "The Family: A Proclamation to the World" to more fully understand the LDS doctrine on marriage: "We, the First Presidency and the Council of the Twelve Apostles of The Church of Jesus Christ of Latter-day Saints, solemnly proclaim that marriage between a man and a woman is ordained of God and that the family is central to the Creator's plan for the eternal destiny of His children."[79]

The Church joined a coalition of other religious organizations, including evangelical and Catholic leaders in California, in support of Proposition 8, the "California Marriage Protection Act," which provided that "only marriage between a man and a woman is valid or recognized in California." The ballot proposal was accepted by the voters but faced court challenges. In similar election contests in other communities and nations, the Church has reiterated its support of traditional marriage but has not involved itself institutionally. The Church has supported local initiatives that are "fair and reasonable" and do "not do violence to the institution of marriage," such as protection from discrimination in hospitalization and medical care, fair housing and employment rights, and probate rights.[80]

The Church's position has always been one of "mutual respect and civility" towards others. President Monson is "a man of remarkably good will, someone who is not interested in being divisive, who wants to further good things for the benefit of mankind," explains Elder M. Russell Ballard.[81]

His attention to family is nowhere more apparent than in temples. President Monson has said, "Millions of ordinances are performed in the temples each year in behalf of our deceased loved ones. May we continue to be faithful in performing such ordinances for those who are unable to do so for themselves."[82] In 2008 he dedicated temples in Rexburg, Idaho; Curitiba, Brazil; Panama City, Panama; and Twin Falls, Idaho, and he rededicated the Mexico City Mexico Temple after it was refurbished. In 2009 he dedicated the Draper Utah and Oquirrh Mountain Utah Temples. In 2010 he dedicated temples in Vancouver, British Columbia; Gila Valley, Arizona; and Cebu City, Philippines, and he has continued to push forward with new temples, including structures in Kyiv, Ukraine (announced by President Hinckley); Calgary, Alberta, Canada; Córdoba, Argentina; Kansas City, Missouri; Philadelphia, Pennsylvania; Rome, Italy; Brigham City, Utah; Concepción, Chile; Fortaleza, Brazil; Fort Lauderdale, Florida; Sapporo, Japan; and Payson, Utah. In 2009, 83 percent of Church members lived within 200 miles of a temple. "That percentage will continue to increase," he has assured the Saints, "as we construct new temples around the world."[83]

What he witnesses at temple dedications, President Monson explains, is "a renewed dedication to the gospel by those who participate." He admonishes the children assembled, "Boys and girls, remember this day."[84] He notes, "It is a time of renewal. It is a time to consider how our lives could be improved with regard to our family unity and our service to the Lord and our fellow men. At the end of the day, one feels the strain of multiple dedication sessions but also the wonderful exhilaration that a house of the Lord will now be open for the glorious work to be performed there."[85]

In the planning of the Oquirrh Mountain Utah Temple dedication, he did "not feel settled" with the schedule of three sessions on Saturday and three on Sunday, August 22 through 23, 2009. Meeting with the Temple Department, he directed that three sessions be added on Friday, August 21. "The Lord has not let me feel at ease about the earlier decision," he said. "We need to have more sessions. I want more young people to be in the temple to have this experience."[86]

As he left a session of that temple dedication, he saw at the back of the celestial room a man in a wheelchair. He realized the man couldn't get up to greet him, so he went to the man and gave him an embrace. He then stopped at the doors of each room along the hall to greet the children gathered to see him.

For years, the Church has sponsored open houses prior to temple dedications. President Monson stressed the importance of well-crafted open houses at the newest temples in the Salt Lake Valley, Draper and Oquirrh Mountain. He invited countless individuals who were not members of the Church, including representatives from the national news media, to tour the temples. "What it does for them," he explains, "is to provide them an opportunity to understand the purpose of the temple, and to help them understand that the work we do in temples is not secret, but sacred. The temple itself is a missionary."[87] Total attendance at the Draper Utah Temple open house was a staggering 684,721.

The tenth session of the Draper Utah Temple dedication, on Sunday at 11:30 A.M., was broadcast to all stakes in the temple district, and the twelfth and final session that afternoon was broadcast to all the stakes in Utah.

Dedicating a temple brings with it a "feeling of gratitude," he explains, for the blessings made possible by the tithes and offerings of the people throughout the world. Temples are representative of great sacrifices of time, effort, and funds. "I am humbled by the fact that the worker's mite in some countries has helped to build that house of the Lord," he explains, "that the people might have the ultimate ordinances of the gospel now. That's why we have temples."[88]

"There is nothing like the dedication of a temple to bring out the best in people," he says. "When a building is dedicated for its holy purposes, it reflects a welcome sign to all who are worthy: 'Come, here you shall find peace, here you shall find a formula for happy families.'"[89]

As he came to the close of his first year as President of the Church, President Monson reflected on his experiences. "I have always needed the help of the Lord, and I have always asked for it. I simply put my faith and trust in Him and move along day by day and week by week."[90] He has admonished the members to do the same. "Reflect gratitude for our Lord and Savior, Jesus Christ," he has said. "He is our Master. He is our Savior. He is the Son of

God. He is the Author of our Salvation. He beckons, 'Follow me.' [Mark 2:14.] He instructs, 'Go, and do thou likewise.'[Luke 10:37.] He pleads, 'Keep my commandments.'[D&C 11:6.] Let us follow Him. Let us emulate His example. Let us obey His word. By so doing, we give to Him the divine gift of gratitude."[91]

When asked if his assignment as President were lonely, he replied, "You are never alone when you are on the Lord's errand. The Lord is always there. I rely on Him. I know what it is like to have Him lead me."[92]

32

JOY IN THE JOURNEY

I have known President Monson for many years. As the Presiding Bishop, I worked by his side for over a decade. I have traveled with him throughout the world. I have been with him and watched him and felt of his spirit. I know that his caring and love is who he is as a prophet. That's how he conducts his life. He loves the Lord, he loves us, and he loves and cares for those over whom he has been called to serve in this part of the dispensation of time before the Second Coming of our Savior.

ELDER ROBERT D. HALES
Quorum of the Twelve Apostles

PRESIDENT MONSON LOOKED OVER THE many members gathered outside the temple in Curitiba, Brazil, on June 1, 2008, for the historic of the cornerstone prior to the dedication of the temple. It was the second temple to be dedicated by President Monson since he became President of the Church.

He put a little mortar in the crack between the granite slabs and then looked around. He said, pointing to a young man in a cap not far from him, "There is a little boy there. He looks cold. Let's have him come up."

A photographer snapping images of the scene suggested that someone take the boy's hat off so she could get a good picture of his face. He was bald.

Elder Russell M. Nelson, standing at the side of President Monson, knew immediately who the young lad was. Before going to Curitiba, Elder Nelson had been contacted by leaders in Brazil about a six-year-old boy, Lincoln Vieira Cordeiro, who suffered from a very high-grade malignancy and was undergoing chemotherapy. He had a poor prognosis. The local leaders had asked if Elder Nelson could give the child a blessing while he was in Brazil for the dedication.

Elder Nelson was right at the President's side as the youngster pulled the hat back on, came up to put a little mortar on the wall, and then went back to sit with the other children. "It was my job to make sure that President Monson got back in the temple to finish the ceremony on schedule," Elder Nelson explained, "so I suggested it was time for us to return."

The President shook his head. "No, I want to call up one more," he said. He scanned the crowd, looked and looked, and finally spotted a woman at the back and said, motioning to her as their eyes made contact, "Will you come up? I want you to put a little mud in the crack."

Not until the next day did Elder Nelson learn that the woman, Odilene Cordeiro, was Lincoln's mother.

"That's President Monson," Elder Nelson states with conviction. "He knows how to draw revelation from God Almighty to bless the life of one person." The little boy died a short time later, "but you can imagine what it meant to the mother of that family. That was the Lord's way of saying, 'I know you, I am concerned for you, and I want to help you.' That's the kind of man we've got in this prophet of God."

On the airplane on the way to Brasilia to meet with the nation's vice president, Elder Nelson told President Monson about the mother and son he had called up to participate in the cornerstone ceremony. "President, how did you know they were related?" Elder Nelson asked. President Monson responded, "I didn't know, but the Lord knew. I've learned how to respond to His promptings."[1]

Such is a hallmark of President Monson's service. He has taught, "The worth of souls is indeed great in the sight of God. Ours is the precious privilege, armed with this knowledge, to make a difference in the lives of others."[2] That day outside the Curitiba Brazil Temple, that loving service was provided for a woman who would soon lose her son.

Elder Alexander B. Morrison, emeritus member of the Quorum of the Seventy and "fellow Canadian," has said to

President Monson, "You have a rare talent to translate celestial principles into practical application and to see the true grandeur in the lives of humble people."[3]

Those who have worked with him, fished at his side, or joined him for an evening of relaxation at the theater or rodeo see greatness. Elder Jon M. Huntsman, Area Seventy and business icon, has noted, "I have the privilege of meeting some most unusual leaders around the world, but Thomas Monson stands the tallest and exemplifies the best of the human spirit."[4]

People notice and appreciate his attention not just to themselves but to others. A woman attending a BYU Women's Conference watched as President Monson left the stand and then stopped in the flurry of getting to his next appointment to shake hands with a woman in a wheelchair. "It wasn't just what he said that day," the woman concluded, "it was what he did."[5] Often, after delivering a message, he will pick someone out in the congregation and give that person the paper copy of the outline of his talk—and he generally signs it. A grateful father wrote to him of the impact of that simple act at a devotional: "You reached out to my daughter in the crowd and handed her the copy of your talk. She's winning her struggle to grow up and be committed to the Lord. In this, you have been a special help to her."[6]

President Monson has been at the Lord's work for a very long time. Elder Bruce D. Porter recalls, "My first real exposure to the charm and powerful spirit of Thomas S. Monson was when I was a young new missionary at the Center in Provo and he came down to speak. He must have been in his early fifties, very young, very vibrant, very vigorous. He talked to us for probably well over an hour, and he reminded me of accounts I've read about what Joseph Smith was like. We were laughing one moment and crying the next. He was just mesmerizing; the force of his spirit was so great. At the end of that talk about missionary work, he put his arms out and pronounced upon us an apostolic blessing. He promised us we would remember that night and the feelings we had. When he left, everyone was in tears—nobody moved. All those missionaries just sat there. Then they gathered together in small groups and made pledges to each other about what kind of missionaries they would be. It was an amazing experience."[7]

President Monson also reaches those who are of different religions. "I have never doubted God's infinite wisdom," wrote Don Flanders, one of his national Scouting friends, "but I want you to know that my faith is strengthened in watching God's hand on your shoulder as he has called you to successive important missions in his work. You must know what your example has meant to your admirable LDS followers, but I thought you might be pleased to know how much your life has brightened our paths, even as Methodists."[8]

To those attending a general priesthood meeting, he said, "Yours is the privilege to be not spectators but participants on the stage of priesthood service."[9] Certainly he has been on that stage. When the *Deseret News* published its "Top 10 LDS stories of the century,"[10] President Monson, as a member of the Quorum of the Twelve or the First Presidency, had been a participant in one way or another in every one of them:

1. The revelation extending priesthood to all worthy males
2. A great increase in temple building worldwide
3. The First Presidency's statements on God; the origin of man; proclamations to the world, including on the family
4. Scriptures published, new editions; new sections added to the Doctrine and Covenants
5. Missionary work: more missionaries called, new training centers, standard discussions
6. Growth of the Church to 10 million members, internationalization of the Church
7. Expansion of family history activity, worldwide microfilming of records
8. Impact and use of technology, including radio, television, video, and satellites, to expand the reach of the Church
9. Creation of the Quorums of the Seventy and decentralization of many Church administrative functions
10. Priesthood correlation and development of the Correlation Committee, formalization of home teaching and family home evening

Since his call to the holy apostleship in 1963, President Monson has sat in nearly every chair in succession in the Quorum of the Twelve and in the First Presidency. He told a general conference congregation, "The changes . . . that were incremental now seem monumental."[11]

"He has respect for his predecessors," explains President Henry B. Eyring, who acknowledges President Monson's reverence for the continuing revelation in the Church. "He will always measure new directions against what the Lord has revealed before. But if the Lord wants to move in some new direction, he will move."[12] President Eyring admits to gaining an even greater respect for the Lord's prophets who have gone before. Still, President Monson is open to innovation, which has marked his presidency in many ways.

He counsels those just starting out in their families and careers to seek "the abundant life." Wishing will not make it so, he says. "The Lord expects our thinking. He expects our action. He expects our labors. He expects our testimonies. He expects our devotion."[13] He cautions: "To measure the goodness of life by its delights and pleasures and safety is to apply a false standard. The abundant life does not consist of a glut of luxury. It does not make itself content with commercially produced pleasure, the nightclub idea of what is a good time, mistaking it for joy and happiness." He measures the abundant life by the capacity "to face trouble with courage, disappointment with cheerfulness, and triumph with humility."[14]

President Monson's responsibilities have brought before him the cases of many who have violated sacred covenants and subsequently desired to make things right with the Lord. As a young bishop, he sat as a "judge in Israel." As a counselor in the First Presidency and then as President of the Church, he has addressed those issues that require the highest mortal judgment. Elder Douglas Callister, who as a General Authority worked with the First Presidency in determining cancellations of sealings and restoration of blessings, has described President Monson as one "most anxious to close ugly chapters in people's lives and to help them move forward with a newness of life."[15]

"Marriages start out happy," President Monson explains. "And then people don't get along, and the pattern for the Church is that the President will be the ultimate determiner of whether the cancellation of sealing should be approved or not. Some circumstances are tragic. These are hard decisions."[16]

Elder Callister states, "I would rather have Thomas S. Monson judge me than any man I have known in this dispensation because, when in doubt, he leans into the winds of mercy."[17]

President Monson often turns to the picture of Jesus that has hung on his office wall since he was a bishop. "I will say, 'Lord, this is a tough one. On this hand there's mercy, on this hand there is justice. Where is the weight heaviest?'" And then he ponders, "What would the Savior do?" Generally, when he comes to that point, mercy wins.[18]

A letter from a husband who had strayed "far from the priesthood path of service and duty" is typical:

> Dear President Monson:
>
> I had so much and now have so little. I am unhappy and feel as though I am failing in everything. The gospel has never left my heart, even though it has left my life. I ask for your prayers.
>
> Please don't forget those of us who are out here—the lost Latter-day Saints. I know where the Church is, but sometimes I think I need someone else to show me the way, encourage me, take away my fear and bear testimony to me.[19]

President Monson has responded to such tragedy drawing upon a painting he has seen by Joseph Mallord William Turner showing heavy-laden black clouds, the fury of a turbulent sea, and a vessel stranded far off. He has said, "Amidst the storms of life, danger lurks; and men, like boats, find themselves stranded and facing destruction. Who will man the lifeboats, leaving behind the comforts of home and family, and go to the rescue?"[20]

In his penchant for quoting poetry, he has shared verses that have made this same point. In his office is a bronze statue of a bridge with an inscription attached bearing one of his favorites:

An old man, going a lone highway,
Came at evening, cold and gray,
To a chasm, vast and deep and wide
Through which was flowing a sullen tide.
The old man crossed in the twilight dim;
The sullen stream had no fears for him;
But he turned when safe on the other side
And built a bridge to span the tide.

"Old man," said a fellow pilgrim near,
"You are wasting strength with building here;
Your journey will end with the ending day;
You never again must pass this way;
You have crossed the chasm, deep and wide—
Why build you the bridge at eventide?"

The builder lifted his old gray head:
"Good friend, in the path I have come," he said,
"There followeth after me today
A youth whose feet must pass this way.
This chasm that has been naught to me
To that fair-haired youth may a pitfall be;
He, too, must cross in the twilight dim.
Good friend, I am building the bridge for him."[21]

"I believe that among the greatest lessons we are to learn in this short sojourn upon the earth are lessons that help us distinguish between what is important and what is not," he has taught. "Let us relish life as we live it, find joy in the journey, and share our love with friends and family."[22]

One of those treasured "joys" in his life was standing with Sister Monson as the two received honorary degrees from Utah Valley University in May 2009. She was new to the rostrum but not new to the humanitarian service for which she was being honored. Reflecting on that experience, he says with great tenderness in his voice, "If there ever was a heroine in my life, it would have to be Frances."[23] He explains, "As I look back to our beginnings, I realize just how much our lives have changed since then. Our beloved parents, who stood beside us as we commenced our journey together, have passed on. Our three children, who filled our lives so completely for many years, are grown and have families of their own. Most of our grandchildren are grown, and we now have great-grandchildren."[24]

This is a man who loves Birmingham roller pigeons, Vivian Park and the Provo River, fishing, duck hunting, and cream soups for lunch—especially tomato, which he orders at the Little America Hotel coffee shop owned by his friend Earl Holding. If he starts a book, he will finish it. He likes to eat Wheaties in the morning, a habit stemming clear back to his childhood. He favors orange juice and lime-flavored yogurt, and he likes to drink milk with his meals. He loves elderly people, dogs, chickens, and mentors such as J. Reuben Clark, Jr., and Mark E. Petersen. He likes lines from Broadway musicals, like King Arthur's statement in *Camelot*: "Violence is not strength, and compassion is not weakness." He is simple in his faith, firm in his resolve to do things "right," and possessed of a half-century-long work ethic difficult to match. He rarely changes the lightbulbs in his home—his wife did that for years—but he is a light to everyone who encounters him, hears him tell of personal experiences, or sees in him boundless hope, love of life, and joy in the journey.

He is a missionary of the gospel message, a testifier of principles he has seen change lives and hearts, a pure vessel speaking truths that connect heaven and earth:

- "When God speaks and a man obeys, that man will always be right."[25]
- "Whom the Lord calls, the Lord qualifies."[26]
- "Decisions determine destiny."[27]
- "When you are on the Lord's errand, you are entitled to the Lord's help."[28]
- "Your decision to think right, choose right, and do right will rarely if ever be the easiest course to follow."[29]
- "You do not find the happy life—you make it."[30]

- "The power to lead is the power to mislead, and the power to mislead is the power to destroy."[31]
- "Good habits . . . are the soul's muscles; the more you use them, the stronger they grow."[32]
- "Life is like a candid camera; it does not wait for you to pose."[33]
- "The door of history turns on small hinges, and so do people's lives."[34]
- "As we look heavenward, we inevitably learn of our responsibility to reach outward."[35]

What will the legacy of President Thomas S. Monson be? Observers have a tendency to set the starting point at the beginning of a man's presidency of the Church. But his legacy goes all the way back to when he began following the Spirit and heeding promptings, when he began reaching out with the power of the Spirit, one-on-one, to anyone and everyone, especially the forgotten. His legacy will be Christlike living.

As the sixteenth President of The Church of Jesus Christ of Latter-day Saints, Thomas S. Monson has testified far and wide. His message has been clear from the beginning: "Our Savior Jesus Christ is at the head of this Church, which bears His name. I know that the sweetest experience in all this life is to feel His promptings as He directs us in the furtherance of His work. I felt those promptings as a young bishop, guided to the homes where there was spiritual—or perhaps temporal—want. I felt them again as a mission president in Toronto, Canada, working with wonderful missionaries who were a living witness and testimony to the world that this work is divine and that we are led by a prophet. I have felt them throughout my service in the Twelve and in the First Presidency and now as President of the Church. I testify that each one of us can feel the Lord's inspiration as we live worthily and strive to serve Him."[36]

TIMELINE

21 August 1927	Born to G. Spencer and Gladys Condie Monson in Salt Lake City, Utah.
2 October 1927	Given a name and a blessing by Peter S. Condie, his mother's uncle.
27 October 1927	Frances Beverly Johnson born to Franz and Hildur Johnson.
21 September 1935	Baptized in the font at the Salt Lake Tabernacle. Confirmed 29 September 1935.
5 November 1939	Ordained a deacon by Frank B. Woodbury, patriarch.
15 March 1944	Received patriarchal blessing from Frank B. Woodbury.
21 August 1944	Ordained a priest by John R. Burt.
Fall 1944	Enrolled at University of Utah at age 17; met Frances.
1945–46	Completed naval training course and continued service in San Diego.
August 1948	Graduated with honors from University of Utah with a bachelor of science in marketing; became part-time instructor.
Fall 1948	Accepted position at Deseret News. Became assistant classified manager, later classified advertising manager.
7 October 1948	Married Frances Beverly Johnson in the Salt Lake Temple.
12 March 1950	Sustained as second counselor to Bishop John R. Burt.
May 1950–July 1955	Bishop of Sixth-Seventh Ward, Temple View Stake. Sustained at age 22.
28 May 1951	Son Thomas Lee Monson born.
1 September 1952	Appointed assistant classified advertising manager of newly formed Newspaper Agency Corporation.
1953–1959	Deseret News Press assistant sales manager, later sales manager, and then assistant general manager.
30 June 1954	Daughter Ann Frances Monson born.

June 1955–June 1957	Served as second counselor in the Temple View Stake presidency.
April 1959– January 1962	Served as Canadian Mission president. Frances became president of mission Relief Society, assisted in Primary and Young Women.
1 October 1959	Son Clark Spencer Monson born in Toronto, Canada.
1962	Named General Manager of Deseret News Press.
1962–1963	Named to Church's Priesthood Missionary Committee, Priesthood Genealogy Committee, Adult Correlation Committee, and Priesthood Home Teaching Committee.
4 October 1963	Sustained as a member of the Quorum of the Twelve.
10 October 1963	Ordained an Apostle by Quorum President Joseph Fielding Smith.
November 1964	Participated in Oakland Temple dedicatory services, first temple dedication he would be assigned to as a member of the Quorum of the Twelve.
1965–1968	Supervised South Pacific, including New Zealand, Polynesian islands, and Australia.
1965–1996	Served on Deseret News Publishing Company Board of Directors; 1971, vice president and vice chairman; 1977, president and chairman of the Board.
March 1965	Became chairman of Adult Correlation Committee, which included everything not assigned to missionary or temple work.
14 June 1965	Hired Lynne Fawson (Cannegieter).
6 July 1965	Assigned to Missionary Executive Committee with Spencer W. Kimball, chairman, and Gordon B. Hinckley.
1967	Became chairman of Leadership Training Committee, responsible for regional representatives' seminar, priesthood leadership training, teacher development, and other programs.
1968–1985	Supervised work in Europe, including Austria, Switzerland, Italy, West and East Germany, and other Eastern Bloc countries.
1968–1985	Chairman of the Bible Aids Study Committee, which became the Scriptures Publication Committee.
2 May 1968	Dedicated New Caledonia for preaching of the gospel.
9–10 November 1968	First visit to Görlitz, East Germany, where he "promised the faithful Saints that if they continued to live worthily and to obey the commandments of God, every blessing . . . would in time be theirs."

1969–1988	Served on Mountain Bell board of advisors and board of directors.
1969–1993	Served on board of directors of Commercial Security Bank (later Key Bank).
14 June 1969	Organized Dresden Mission, calling Henry Burkhardt as president with Walter Krause and Gottfried Richter as counselors.
November 1969	Named member of National Executive Board of Boy Scouts of America, taking Ezra Taft Benson's place.
18 January 1970	Death of President David O. McKay, age 96.
23 January 1970	Participated in reorganization of the First Presidency: Joseph Fielding Smith became President, with counselors Harold B. Lee and N. Eldon Tanner.
3 October 1970	Announcement made that *Ensign, New Era,* and *Friend* would replace previous Church publications.
23 February 1971	Received Scouting's Silver Beaver Award.
27–29 August 1971	Helped organize and participated in first area conference, held in Manchester, England.
1971–1977	Served on State Board of Higher Education and State Board of Regents.
2 July 1972	Death of President Joseph Fielding Smith, age 95.
7 July 1972	President Harold B. Lee named eleventh president of Church, with N. Eldon Tanner and Marion G. Romney as counselors.
30 June 1973	Death of Hildur Booth Johnson, Frances's mother.
13 September 1973	Death of Gladys Condie Monson, mother.
26 December 1973	Death of President Harold B. Lee, age 74.
30 December 1973	Participated in ordination of Spencer W. Kimball, twelfth President of the Church, who called N. Eldon Tanner and Marion G. Romney as counselors.
5 March 1974	Performed marriage ceremony for daughter Ann Monson and Roger Dibb in Salt Lake Temple.
April 1974	Received master's degree in business administration from BYU.
26 April 1974	Performed marriage ceremony for son Tom Monson and Carma Rhodehouse in Salt Lake Temple.
22 April 1975	Dedicated Portugal for the preaching of the gospel.
27 April 1975	Rededicated East Germany (GDR), marking the "dawning of a new beginning" for that Communist country.
1976–1982	Served as chairman of Missionary Committee, with David B. Haight and Bruce R. McConkie as members.

7 July 1977	Rededicated Sweden for preaching of the gospel.
19 May 1978	Received Silver Buffalo award of Boy Scouts of America.
9 June 1978	First Presidency announced revelation that "all worthy males" would receive the priesthood.
13 May 1979	Death of G. Spencer Monson, father.
September 1979	Church published new 2,400-page edition of the King James Version of the Bible with special features, including Topical Guide, Bible Dictionary, and revolutionary footnote system.
1980	Church Printing Services created, merging Deseret Press with Church Printing Department.
September 1981	New edition of the Triple Combination (Book of Mormon, Doctrine and Covenants, and Pearl of Great Price) published, including extensive scripture helps.
1981–1982	Member of President Ronald Reagan's Task Force on Private Sector Initiatives.
1982–1985	Chaired Priesthood Executive Council.
28 April 1982	Performed marriage ceremony for Clark S. Monson and Patricia Shaffer in Salt Lake Temple.
1 June 1982	Signed renegotiated Newspaper Agency Agreement between the Deseret News Publishing Company and the Kearns-Tribune Corporation.
29 August 1982	Created first stake in communist East Germany in Freiberg. On 3 June 1984 the second stake was created, in Leipzig. All Church members living in East Germany then resided in stakes.
17 April 1983	Dedicated Haiti for preaching of the gospel.
23 April 1983	Presided at groundbreaking for Freiberg Germany temple.
1985	Supervised preparation of new hymnbook, first revision in 37 years.
29 June 1985	Participated in Freiberg Temple dedication, "one of the highlights" of his life.
October 1985	Dedicated chapel in Zagreb, Yugoslavia. Pronounced dedicatory prayer for that nation.
5 November 1985	Death of President Spencer W. Kimball, age 90.
10 November 1985	Ezra Taft Benson ordained and set apart as thirteenth President of the Church, with Gordon B. Hinckley and Thomas S. Monson as counselors. At age 58, TSM was youngest counselor in First Presidency in the twentieth century.
28 October 1988	Erich Honecker, head of state in East Germany, granted permission for full-time proselyting missionaries to enter the country and for East

	Germans to receive mission calls to serve elsewhere in the world.
30 March 1989	First missionaries in fifty years arrive in East Germany.
28 May 1989	First ten missionaries called from East Germany arrive at the Provo Missionary Training Center.
17 October 1989	Dedicated first meetinghouse in Budapest, Hungary.
November 1989	Germans began tearing down the Berlin Wall erected in 1961.
3 October 1990	East and West Germany formally reunited as one nation.
20–21 October 1990	Conference held to reunite East and West Church units within Germany.
2 October 1993	Received International Scouting's highest award, the Bronze Wolf.
30 May 1994	Death of President Ezra Taft Benson, age 94.
5 June 1994	Quorum of the Twelve met to reorganize First Presidency, with Howard W. Hunter as President, Gordon B. Hinckley as first counselor, Thomas S. Monson as second counselor.
3 March 1995	Death of President Howard W. Hunter, age 87.
12 March 1995	Ordained Gordon B. Hinckley as fifteenth President of the Church. Thomas S. Monson became first counselor, James E. Faust second counselor.
1 January 2000	The First Presidency and Quorum of the Twelve—fifteen special witnesses—issued their testimony of Christ's divinity before all the world in a document titled "The Living Christ."
27 June 2002	President Hinckley dedicated rebuilt Nauvoo Temple. Thomas S. Monson had "the privilege of being the first speaker."
10 August 2007	James E. Faust died. Henry B. Eyring sustained as new second counselor in the First Presidency at October general conference.
27 January 2008	Death of President Gordon B. Hinckley, age 97.
3 February 2008	Ordained and set apart as sixteenth President of The Church of Jesus Christ of Latter-day Saints by Boyd K. Packer, President of the Quorum of the Twelve. Henry B. Eyring became first counselor, Dieter F. Uchtdorf second counselor.
4 February 2008	Addressed press conference with counselors and members of the Quorum of the Twelve in attendance.
9 February 2008	First message as President of the Church for worldwide leadership training broadcast.

10 February 2008	Dedicated the Rexburg Idaho Temple.
5 April 2008	Solemn Assembly. Church members sustained sixteenth President of the Church and counselors. D. Todd Christofferson sustained as member of the Quorum of the Twelve.
1 June 2008	Dedicated temple in Curitiba, Brazil.
10 August 2008	Dedicated temple in Panama City, Panama.
24 August 2008	Dedicated Twin Falls Idaho Temple.
15 November 2008	Rededicated Mexico City Mexico Temple.
20 March 2009	Dedicated Draper Utah Temple.
2 April 2009	Delivered training message to General Authorities, "To the Rescue."
4 April 2009	Neil L. Andersen sustained as member of the Quorum of the Twelve.
20 June 2009	Dedicated Church History Library, using pulpit from old Sixth-Seventh Ward chapel.
21 August 2009	Dedicated Oquirrh Mountain Utah Temple.
2 May 2010	Dedicated Vancouver British Columbia Temple.
23 May 2010	Dedicated The Gila Valley Arizona Temple.
13 June 2010	Dedicated Cebu City Philippines Temple.

NOTES

INTRODUCTION: TO THE RESCUE

Epigraph. Interview with Boyd K. Packer, 19 August 2009.

1. Thomas S. Monson (hereinafter referred to as TSM in interviews, letters, and journal entries) Journal, 2 December 1979.
2. As quoted by Thomas S. Monson in "The Upward Reach," *Ensign,* November 1993, 50.
3. TSM Journal, 2 December 1979.
4. Acts 10:38.
5. John 5:3–4.
6. Thomas S. Monson, "Christ at Bethesda's Pool," *Ensign,* November 1996, 18.
7. See John 5:2–10.
8. Interview with TSM, 8 December 2008.
9. Thomas S. Monson, Salt Lake City South Stake Conference Broadcast, 18 October 2009.
10. Interview with TSM, 15 April 2009.
11. Thomas S. Monson, "Looking Back and Moving Forward," *Ensign,* May 2008, 89–90.
12. Monson, "Looking Back and Moving Forward," 90.
13. Interview with Dieter F. Uchtdorf, 2 September 2009.
14. Doctrine and Covenants 84:88.
15. Thomas S. Monson, "The Long Line of the Lonely," *Ensign,* February 1992, 2.
16. Ann Monson Dibb, "My Father Is a Prophet," BYU–Idaho Devotional, 19 February 2008, 10.
17. "I'll Go Where You Want Me to Go," *Hymns* (Salt Lake City: The Church of Jesus Christ of Latter-day Saints, 1985), no. 270.
18. Interview with TSM, 18 June 2009.
19. Thomas S. Monson, "'Behold Thy Mother,'" *Ensign,* April 1998, 6.
20. Joseph B. Wirthlin, "Concern for the One," *Ensign,* May 2008, 17.
21. TSM Journal, 13 February 1981.
22. TSM Journal, 25 March 1983.
23. Interview with Jeffrey R. Holland, 22 September 2009.
24. Interview with Robert D. Hales, 8 April 2009.
25. Interview with Ronald Rasband, 12 November 2008.
26. Thomas S. Monson, "Sugar Beets and the Worth of a Soul," *Ensign,* July 2009, 7.

27. Interview with Bruce D. Porter, 16 December 2009; Interview with TSM, 17 December 2009.
28. Gerry Avant, "On Lord's errand since his boyhood," *Church News,* 9 February 2008.
29. Interview with L. Tom Perry, 22 August 2008.
30. James 1:27.
31. Interview with TSM, 15 April 2009.
32. Monson, "Long Line of the Lonely," 4–5.
33. Interview with Henry B. Eyring, 26 August 2009.
34. Thomas S. Monson, "'Be Thou an Example,'" *Ensign,* November 1996, 45.
35. Monson, "Looking Back and Moving Forward," 88.

CHAPTER 1: A HERITAGE OF FAITHFUL SOULS

Epigraph. Thomas S. Monson, "Looking Back and Moving Forward," *Ensign,* May 2008, 88.
1. James R. Clark, comp., *Messages of the First Presidency of The Church of Jesus Christ of Latter-day Saints,* 6 vols. (Salt Lake City: Bookcraft, 1965–75), 2:33.
2. Jeremiah 3:14.
3. See Thomas S. Monson, "Come Follow Me," *Liahona,* November 1988, 2.
4. Richard L. Evans, *A Century of Mormonism in Great Britain* (Salt Lake City: Publishers Press, 1984), 83.
5. See *Coming to Zion,* edited by James B. Allen and John W. Welch (Provo, Utah: BYU Studies, 1997), 269.
6. Conway B. Sonne, *Saints on the Seas, A Maritime History of the Mormon Migration 1830–1896* (Salt Lake City: University of Utah Press, 1983), 1.
7. "President Monson Visits Sweden and Germany," *Ensign,* November 1995, 112.
8. Thomas S. Monson, remarks at Stockholm Sweden Temple dedication, 1985.
9. Interview with TSM, 10 December 2008.
10. James P. Condie, "Life of the Early Condies," unpublished manuscript.
11. Thomas S. Monson, *On the Lord's Errand* (hereinafter referred to as *Errand*), autobiography (Salt Lake City: privately published, 1985), 16.
12. Thomas S. Monson, "Pioneers All," *Ensign,* May 1997, 93.
13. Monson, *Errand,* 16–17.
14. See Sonne, *Saints on the Seas,* 73.
15. Gibson Condie, *Reminiscences and Diary, 1865–1910,* 33–35. (Privately published; grammar and spelling corrected.)
16. Thomas A. Condie, *History of Gibson and Cecelia Sharp Condie,* 1937. Privately published.
17. Gerry Avant, "Travelers Encouraged on Journey," *Church News,* June 21, 1997, 4; see also article in quarterly newsletter of family organization of Condies and Sharps, January–March 2005.
18. Avant, "Travelers Encouraged on Journey," 4.
19. Condie, *History of Gibson and Cecelia Sharp Condie.*
20. John L. Hart, "Ground Is Broken on Cold Day for Temple in St. Louis," *Church News,* 30 October 1993.
21. Thomas S. Monson, remarks at Bern Switzerland Temple rededication, 1992.
22. Sonne, *Saints on the Seas,* 126, 130, 133.
23. Family records show both *Nils* and *Nels* as a first name and *Akeson* and *Akesson* as a last name. His certificate of citizenship in the United States

is in the name of Nels Monson, as is his 1898 missionary call to Sweden. The Swedish tradition of patronymics—a component of a personal name based on the name of the father—creates a curious pattern. The father of Nels Monson was not named Monson at all, but rather Mons Akesson; his father's name was Oke Pederson; his father's name was Peter Monson; and his father's name was Mons Lustig. When Mons Akesson came to America, he changed his last name to Monson so that it would be the same as his children's, as was the pattern in his new home.

24. See "Missionary Journal of Nels Monson," in Monson family history records.
25. Thomas S. Monson, remarks at Stockholm Sweden Temple dedication, 1985.
26. Thomas S. Monson, "Abundantly Blessed," *Ensign,* May 2008, 111. See also "Missionary Journal of Nels Monson."
27. Interview with TSM, 9 September 2008.
28. See "Missionary Journal of Nels Monson."
29. Monson, "Abundantly Blessed," 111.
30. Thomas S. Monson, "Truth, Service, Love," Copenhagen area conference, 5 August 1976.
31. Monson family tape recording, 1950s, in the family's possession.
32. Thomas S. Monson, "Treasure of Eternal Value," *Ensign,* April 2008, 4.
33. Thomas S. Monson, "Traditions," Dixie College homecoming address, 2 November 1986.

Chapter 2: Between the Railroad Tracks

Epigraph. As quoted in Gerry Avant, "Serving Others Is His Way of Life," *Church News,* 25 August 2007, 6.

1. Thomas S. Monson, "The Race for Eternal Life," Seminary Day address, 3 February 1968.
2. G. Spencer Monson, "Compilation of Poetry."
3. Audiotape of Scott Monson's mission farewell prior to his leaving for Sweden, 1962.
4. Thomas S. Monson, "Great Expectations," BYU Devotional, 11 May 1965.
5. *Through Our Eyes: 150 Years of History as Seen through the Eyes of the Writers and Editors of the Deseret News,* ed. Don C. Woodward (Salt Lake City: Deseret News, 1999), 103.
6. As quoted in Ezra Taft Benson, "A Marvelous Work and a Wonder," *Ensign,* May 1980, 32.
7. Thomas S. Monson, "From Here to Eternity," BYU Commencement Exercises, 24 April 1997.
8. *Through the Years: A Brief History of the Sixth-Seventh Ward, 1849–1955* (Salt Lake City: privately published), 8.
9. "History of George Spencer Monson."
10. Copy of invitation in TSM Scrapbook.
11. Audiotape of Gladys Condie Monson's funeral, 18 September 1973, in LDS Church Archives.
12. Interview with TSM, 15 April 2009.
13. Interview with TSM, 9 September 2008.
14. Thomas S. Monson, "An Attitude of Gratitude," *Ensign,* May 1992, 54.
15. Interview with TSM, 9 September 2008.

16. Thomas S. Monson, "Heavenly Homes, Forever Families," Worldwide Leadership Training Broadcast, February 2006, 18.
17. Monson, "Attitude of Gratitude," 59.
18. Interview with TSM, 9 September 2008.
19. "Pioneer Son," *Deseret Evening News,* 20 June 1947.
20. Thomas S. Monson, "Only a Teacher," Provo Utah Oak Hills Stake Fireside, 21 November 2005.
21. Monson, "Only a Teacher."
22. Dell Van Orden, "Pres. Monson Launches Stake Jubilee," *Church News,* 18 January 1997, 4.
23. Van Orden, "Pres. Monson Launches Stake Jubilee," 4.
24. Marjorie Monson Dearden, "Remembrances of Uncle John."
25. Monson, *Errand,* 65.
26. Interview with TSM, 15 October 2008.
27. Audiotape of Gladys Condie Monson's funeral, 18 September 1973, in LDS Church Archives.
28. Thomas S. Monson, "A Sanctuary from the World," Worldwide Leadership Training Broadcast, February 2008, 29. Thomas S. Monson, "Dedication Days," *Ensign,* November 2000, 64–66.
30. Thomas S. Monson, "Hallmarks of a Happy Home," *Ensign,* October 2001, 2.

Chapter 3: "I Want to Be a Cowboy!"

Epigraph. Interview with M. Russell Ballard, 9 September 2009.
1. Monson, *Errand,* 42.
2. Interview with Marilyn Monson Martin, 10 January 2009.
3. Interview with Clark Spencer Monson, 4 November 2008.
4. Thomas S. Monson, "Peace, Be Still," *Ensign,* November 2002, 54.
5. Monson, *Errand,* 44.
6. Interview with TSM, 15 April 2009.
7. Monson, *Errand,* 178.
8. Thomas S. Monson, "Primary Days," *Ensign,* April 1994, 65.
9. Monson, *Errand,* 19.
10. Monson, *Errand,* 19.
11. Thomas S. Monson, "A Sanctuary from the World," Worldwide Leadership Training Broadcast, February 2008, 30.
12. Monson, *Errand,* 31.
13. Interview with TSM, 12 November 2008.
14. Interview with Thomas Lee Monson, 6 November 2009.
15. Interview with TSM, 9 September 2008.
16. Monson, *Errand,* 42.
17. Mosiah 2:17.
18. Thomas S. Monson, "Boyhood Revisited," unpublished essay.
19. Interview with Thomas S. Monson, 10 December 2008.
20. Thomas S. Monson, "Primary Days," *Ensign,* April 1994, 66.
21. Quoted in Monson, "Primary Days," 66.
22. Monson, *Errand,* 28.
23. Interview with TSM, 11 November 2009.
24. TSM Journal, 19 December 1981; 23 January 1994.
25. Interview with TSM, 10 December 2008.

26. Interview with TSM, 9 September 2008.
27. Thomas S. Monson, "Compassion," *Ensign*, May 2001, 17, 18.
28. G. Spencer Monson, "Compilation of Poetry."
29. Matthew 2:2.
30. Monson, "Primary Days," 66.
31. Thomas S. Monson, "Models to Follow," *Ensign*, November 2002, 62.
32. Thomas S. Monson, "Let Us Keep Christmas," First Presidency Christmas Devotional, 1 December 2002.
33. Thomas S. Monson, quoting President David O. McKay, in "What Is Christmas?" *Ensign*, December 1988, 2.
34. "The Real Meaning of Christmas," *Church News*, 8 December 2007.
35. Thomas S. Monson, "Your Jericho Road," *Ensign*, February 1989, 5.
36. Monson, *Errand*, 33.
37. Thomas S. Monson, "If Ye Are Prepared Ye Shall Not Fear," *Ensign*, November 2004, 115.
38. Alma 56:47.
39. Interview with Thomas S. Monson, 9 September 2008.
40. Matthew 25:35, 40.

CHAPTER 4: LIKE HUCK FINN ON THE RIVER

Epigraph. Interview with D. Todd Christofferson, 24 September 2009.
1. Sinclair Lewis, "Nobel Lecture," 12 December 1930.
2. Luke 5:10.
3. TSM Journal, 8 February 1974.
4. TSM Journal, 26 July 1986.
5. Monson, *Errand*, 37.
6. Interview with TSM, 15 October 2008.
7. Monson, *Errand*, 37.
8. Interview with TSM, 9 February 2009.
9. Monson, *Errand*, 78.
10. See John 9:7.
11. Monson, *Errand*, 34–35.
12. Interview with TSM, 19 February 2009.
13. Thomas S. Monson, "Happiness—The Universal Quest," Ensign, October 1993, 4.
14. Thomas S. Monson, "Who Honors God, God Honors," *Ensign*, November 1995, 49.
15. Monson, *Errand*, 62.
16. Thomas S. Monson, "An Invitation to Exaltation," *Ensign*, May 1988, 53.
17. Interview with TSM, 19 February 2009.
18. See Thomas S. Monson, "The Way to Eternal Glory," BYU Devotional, 15 October 1991.

CHAPTER 5: BECOMING A GENTLEMAN

Epigraph. Interview with Marlin K. Jensen, 28 October 2009.
1. Interview with Robert C. Monson, 28 January 2009.
2. Letter from Lucy Gertsch Thomson to TSM, 30 March 1968.

3. Thomas S. Monson, "Examples of Great Teachers," Worldwide Leadership Training Meeting, February 2007.
4. Thomas S. Monson, "The Faith of a Child," *Ensign*, August 1998, 2.
5. Luke 24:32.
6. Acts 20:35.
7. Thomas S. Monson, "Your Personal Influence," *Ensign*, April 1992, 22.
8. Monson, *Errand*, 26–27.
9. Letter from Lucy Gertsch Thomson to Thomas S. Monson, 30 March 1968.
10. Thomas S. Monson, "The Bridge Builder," *Ensign*, November 2003, 68–69.
11. Thomas S. Monson, "Priesthood Profiles," Priesthood Commemoration Satellite Broadcast, 17 May 1987.
12. Thomas S. Monson, remarks at rededication of the Carl F. Eyring Science Center, Brigham Young University, 10 March 1998.
13. "Master, the Tempest Is Raging," *Hymns* (Salt Lake City: The Church of Jesus Christ of Latter-day Saints, 1985), no. 105.
14. Thomas S. Monson, "Peace, Be Still," *Ensign*, November 2002, 53.
15. "Come, All Ye Sons of God," *Hymns*, no. 322.
16. Thomas S. Monson, "Your Eternal Voyage," *Ensign*, May 2000, 46.
17. Thomas S. Monson, "The Priesthood—A Sacred Trust," *Ensign*, May 1994, 50.
18. Thomas S. Monson, "'Be Thou an Example,'" *Ensign*, November 2001, 99–100.
19. Thomas S. Monson, "'Be Thou an Example,'" *Ensign*, November 1996, 46.
20. Monson, *Errand*, 57.
21. Interview with TSM, 15 April 2009.
22. See Monson, *Errand*, 47–49.
23. Thomas S. Monson, "That All May Hear," *Ensign*, May 1995, 49.
24. Thomas S. Monson, "Who Honors God, God Honors," *Ensign*, November 1995, 48.
25. Thomas S. Monson, "The Priesthood—Mighty Army of the Lord," *Ensign*, May 1999, 49.
26. Thomas S. Monson, "Welcome to Conference," *Ensign*, November 2008, 6.
27. See "Returning to where his 'roots run deep,'" *Church News*, 25 May 1996, 4.
28. Monson, *Errand*, 63–64.
29. H. David Burton, "What Manner of Men and Women Ought Ye to Be?" Church Educational System Fireside, 2 November 2008.
30. Thomas S. Monson, *Be Your Best Self* (Salt Lake City: Deseret Book, 1979), 53.
31. Thomas S. Monson, *Be Your Best Self* (Salt Lake City: Deseret Book, 1979), 53–54.
32. See Thomas S. Monson, "To Learn, to Do, to Be," *Ensign*, November 2008, 62.
33. Thomas S. Monson, "The Army of the Lord," *Ensign*, May 1979, 35; see also Thomas S. Monson, "Anxiously Engaged," *Ensign*, November 2004, 56–57.
34. Monson, "Priesthood—Mighty Army," 49.
35. Monson, *Errand*, 55–56.

Chapter 6: School Days

Epigraph. Interview with Ronald Rasband, 12 November 2008.
1. Thomas S. Monson, Boy Scout National Jamboree, Ft. A.P. Hill, Virginia, 31 July 2005.
2. See Thomas S. Monson, "Your Eternal Voyage," *Ensign*, May 2000, 47–48.

3. Thomas S. Monson, address at General Authority training meeting, 28 September 1999.
4. Interview with TSM, 12 November 2008.
5. Interview with G. Ray Hale, West High School Alumni President, 23 March 2009.
6. See Thomas S. Monson, "The Call for Courage," *Ensign*, May 2004, 57.
7. Monson, *Errand*, 80–81.
8. Richard O. Cowan, The Latter-day Saint Century (Salt Lake City: Bookcraft, 1999), 126.
9. Letter from Terese Patton to TSM, 29 April 1969. See also Thomas S. Monson, "Mrs. Patton—the Story Continues," *Ensign*, November 2007, 23–24.
10. Letter from Blanche Carter to TSM, 1944.
11. Gerry Avant, "Among Friends," *Church News*, 13 September 2008, 5.

Chapter 7: The Greatest Lessons

Epigraph. Interview with Lynn Cannegieter, 26 August 2008.
1. Thomas S. Monson, "Honorary Doctorate Remarks," University of Utah, 3 May 2007.
2. Thomas S. Monson, "Three Gates to Open," Church Educational System Satellite Broadcast Fireside, Ricks College, 14 January 2001.
3. Thomas S. Monson, "An Attitude of Gratitude," *Ensign*, February 2000, 5.
4. Thomas S. Monson, "Constant Truths in Changing Times," address at Utah State University Stake, 12 January 1969.
5. Interview with TSM, 15 April 2009.
6. Thomas S. Monson, "Guideposts for Life's Journey," University of Utah Commencement address, 4 May 2007.
7. Monson, *Errand*, 89.
8. Gerry Avant, "Pres. and Sister Monson note their Swedish roots," *Church News*, 26 August 1995, 12.
9. Avant, "Pres. and Sister Monson note their Swedish roots," 12.
10. Thomas S. Monson, "The Mission of Life," address at Copenhagen Area Conference, Mothers-Daughters Session, 4 August 1976.
11. Interview with TSM, 15 October 2008.
12. Frances J. Monson, unpublished essay on "Establishment of values and a personal morality."
13. Monson, "Three Gates to Open."
14. Monson, *Errand*, 94.
15. See Thomas S. Monson, "The Three R's of Choice," address at Brigham Young University, 5 November 1963; *Errand*, 97–98.
16. Monson, *Errand*, 98.
17. Doctrine and Covenants 4:1–2.
18. See Thomas S. Monson, "Priesthood Profiles," Priesthood Commemoration Satellite Broadcast, 17 May 1987.
19. Monson, *Errand*, 10; see also Thomas S. Monson, "The Master's Blueprint," *Ensign*, January 2006, 4.
20. Letter from Edward (Eddie) Foreman to TSM, 22 September 1989.
21. TSM Journal, 1 November 1992.
22. Monson, *Errand*, 99.

23. Interview with TSM, 12 November 2008.
24. Interview with TSM, 12 November 2008.
25. Thomas S. Monson, "In Remembrance," Freedom Festival, Provo, Utah, 28 June 1998.
26. Monson, *Errand*, 101.
27. See Monson, "Priesthood Profiles."
28. Monson, *Errand*, 108.
29. TSM Journal, 15–16 May 1971.
30. Interview with TSM, 12 November 2008.
31. Letter from TSM to G. Spencer Monson, 21 April 1946.
32. Thomas S. Monson, "A Royal Priesthood," *Ensign*, November 2007, 61.
33. Interview with TSM, 12 November 2008.
34. Thomas S. Monson, "In Remembrance," Freedom Festival, Provo, Utah, 28 June 1998. Poem "In Flanders Fields" by Lieutenant Colonel John McCrae, MD, Canadian Army, 1872–1918.
35. Gerry Avant, "War divides but the gospel unites," *Church News*, 19 August 1995, 5.
36. Letter from Ralph A. Curtis to G. Spencer and Gladys Monson.
37. Monson, *Errand*, 111.
38. Monson, "Honorary Doctorate Remarks."

Chapter 8: Starting a Family

Epigraph. Ann Monson Dibb, as quoted in Monson, *Errand*.
1. M. Russell Ballard Oral History, in the James Moyle Oral History Program, LDS Church Archives, 31.
2. Thomas S. Monson, "In Search of Treasure," BYU Devotional, 11 March 1997.
3. Thomas S. Monson, "Honor Thy Father and Thy Mother," BYU Fourteen-Stake Fireside, 3 December 1978.
4. Thomas S. Monson, "Constant Truths in Changing Times," address at Utah State University Stake, 12 January 1969.
5. Interview with TSM, 12 November 2008.
6. Thomas S. Monson, "Honorary Doctorate Remarks," University of Utah, 3 May 2007.
7. Thomas S. Monson, "An Attitude of Gratitude," *Ensign*, May 1992, 59.
8. Thomas S. Monson, address at BYU College of Business, 14 March 1973.
9. Monson, BYU College of Business.
10. Thomas S. Monson, "Building a House for Eternity," address to Jordan River Temple workers, 28 October 2007.
11. TSM Interview, 15 October 2008.
12. Thomas S. Monson, address at Stockholm Sweden Temple dedication, 1985.
13. Monson, *Errand*, 128.
14. Monson, *Errand*, 128.
15. MIA at that time included both youth and adult programs, so the number was particularly discouraging.
16. Thomas S. Monson, "Life's Greatest Decisions," Church Educational System Fireside, Conference Center, 7 September 2003.
17. Monson, "Life's Greatest Decisions."
18. Gerry Avant, "60th Anniversary," *Church News*, 4 October 2008, 10.
19. Monson, address at Stockholm Sweden Temple dedication, 1985.

20. Monson, *Errand,* 145.
21. Monson, *Errand,* 178.
22. Monson, *Errand,* 178.
23. Interview with Boyd K. Packer, 19 August 2009.
24. Interview with Richard G. Scott, 28 August 2009.
25. Doctrine and Covenants 88:119.
26. Thomas S. Monson, "Heavenly Homes—Forever Families," Family Satellite Broadcast, 12 January 1986.
27. Thomas S. Monson, "Becoming Our Best Selves," *Ensign,* April 2006, 4.

Chapter 9: "Decisions Determine Destiny"

Epigraph. Interview with Robert C. Oaks, 8 November 2008.
1. Thomas S. Monson, address at BYU College of Business, 14 March 1973.
2. Hal Knight, "We Were There," in *Through Our Eyes: 150 Years of History as Seen through the Eyes of the Writers and Editors of the Deseret News,* ed. Don C. Woodward (Salt Lake City: Deseret News, 1999), 195.
3. Thomas S. Monson, "Honorary Doctorate Remarks," University of Utah, 3 May 2007.
4. Interview with TSM, 12 November 2008.
5. Monson, BYU College of Business.
6. Monson, "Honorary Doctorate Remarks."
7. Interview with M. Russell Ballard, 20 October 2009.
8. TSM Journal, 25 February 1977.
9. Interview with TSM, 19 February 2009.
10. *Sheldon James Weight and Florence Beatrice Brailsford: Their Lives, Their Ancestry and Their Posterity,* edited by Dale and Melvin Weight (Privately published, 2006), 9.
11. Interview with TSM, 19 February 2009.
12. Eleanor Knowles, *Deseret Book Company: 125 Years of Inspiration, Information, and Ideas* (Salt Lake City: Deseret Book, 1991), 92.
13. Thomas S. Monson, "The Call of Duty," *Ensign,* May 1986, 37.
14. See John A. Widtsoe, "President J. Reuben Clark: A Defender of the Gospel," *Improvement Era,* August 1951, 560.
15. Thomas S. Monson, "Miracles of Faith," *Ensign,* July 2004, 3–4.
16. Monson, *Errand,* 176.
17. Gerry Avant, "Missionary Training Center Expands," *Church News,* 19 March 1994, 11.
18. Monson, BYU College of Business.
19. Monson, *Errand,* 155–56.
20. Interview with TSM, 17 June 2009.
21. Jason Swenson, "Printing Industry Lauds LDS Leader," *Church News,* 25 April 2009, 3.
22. Interview with TSM, 17 June 2009.
23. 1 Peter 3:15.
24. Doctrine and Covenants 38:30.
25. Thomas S. Monson, "Dedicatory Address and Prayer: David O. McKay Building," BYU, 25 April 2003.
26. Interview with TSM, 13 May 2009.
27. Matthew 25:21.

28. Thomas S. Monson, "Traditions," Dixie College homecoming address, 2 November 1986.
29. Interview with TSM, 12 November 2008.
30. Interview with TSM, 17 June 2009.
31. Interview with TSM, 13 May 2009.
32. Swenson, "Printing Industry Lauds LDS Leader," 3.

CHAPTER 10: ALWAYS A BISHOP

Epigraph. Harold B. Lee, Foreword to Thomas S. Monson, *Pathways to Perfection* (Salt Lake City: Deseret Book, 1973), vii.
1. Monson, *Errand,* 11.
2. *Deseret News 2006 Church Almanac,* 654–55.
3. Thomas S. Monson, "A New Spirit Will I Put within You," Satellite Priesthood Leadership Training Broadcast, 21 June 2003, 18–19.
4. "An Old Chapel Carries On," *Deseret News Church Section,* 16 February 1935, microfilm page 223, LDS Church Archives.
5. 1 Timothy 3:1–6.
6. Thomas S. Monson, "The Bishop—Center Stage in Welfare," *Ensign,* November 1980, 89.
7. Thomas S. Monson, "Yellow Canaries with Gray on Their Wings," *Ensign,* July 1973, 41.
8. Thomas S. Monson, "My Brother's Keeper," address at Salt Lake Rotary International meeting, 20 January 2007.
9. Interview with TSM, 12 July 2010.
10. Thomas S. Monson, "Looking Back and Moving Forward," *Ensign,* May 2008, 90.
11. Interview with TSM, 9 September 2008.
12. "Carry On," *Hymns* (Salt Lake City: The Church of Jesus Christ of Latter-day Saints, 1985), no. 255.
13. Thomas S. Monson, *Inspiring Experiences That Build Faith: From the Life and Ministry of Thomas S. Monson* (Salt Lake City: Deseret Book, 1994), 256.
14. "Friendships are strong in ward Pres. Monson once served as bishop," *Church News,* 5 March 1994, 11.
15. See Monson, *Errand,* 133.
16. Thomas S. Monson, remarks at rededication of the Carl F. Eyring Science Center, Brigham Young University, 10 March 1998.
17. Monson, *Errand,* 144.
18. See Monson, *Errand,* 129.
19. Interview with TSM, 9 September 2008.
20. Letter from Harold B. Lee to TSM, 5 July 1951.
21. Ecclesiastes 12:13.
22. As quoted in Thomas S. Monson, "The Call of Duty," *Ensign,* May 1986, 38.
23. David O. McKay, in Conference Report, 9 April 1951, 151.
24. J. Reuben Clark, Jr., in Conference Report, 9 April 1951, 154.
25. Thomas S. Monson, "A New Spirit Will I Put within You," Satellite Priesthood Leadership Training Broadcast, 21 June 2003.
26. *A Guide to Happiness through Gospel Service, Sixth-Seventh Ward* (Salt Lake City: privately published), 3–6; see also Monson, "A New Spirit."
27. *A Guide to Happiness,* 3–6; see also Monson, "A New Spirit."
28. *A Guide to Happiness,* 3–6; see also Monson, "A New Spirit."

29. Monson, "Duty Calls."

30. Thomas S. Monson, address at General Authority training meeting, 27 March 1990.

31. Monson, "A New Spirit."

32. Monson, *Errand*, 130.

33. Monson, *Errand*, 162.

34. Interview with H. David Burton, 27 August 2009.

35. Thomas S. Monson, "The Long Line of the Lonely," *Ensign*, February 1992, 2.

36. TSM Journal, 15 December 1974; 8 February 1981.

37. Thomas S. Monson, "Called to Serve," *Ensign*, November 1991, 47.

38. Monson, "Called to Serve," 48.

39. See Thomas S. Monson, "Becoming Our Best Selves," *Ensign*, April 2006, 6.

40. Poem by Meade McGuire, as quoted in Thomas S. Monson, "Yellow Canaries with Gray on their Wings," *Ensign*, July 1973, 44.

41. Doctrine and Covenants 76:5–6.

42. Thomas S. Monson, "Your Personal Influence," *Ensign*, May 2004, 23.

43. Thomas S. Monson, "I Know That My Redeemer Lives," *Ensign*, May 2007, 24.

44. Richard O. Cowan, *The Latter-day Saint Century* (Salt Lake City: Bookcraft, 1999), 165.

45. Monson, *Errand*, 150.

46. Monson, *Errand*, 168.

47. See TSM Journal, 7 May 1950.

48. "Bishop Monson, Tops in the World of Men," lyrics written in tribute to Bishop Thomas S. Monson.

Chapter 11: "He Went About Doing Good"

Epigraph. Interview with David A. Bednar, 20 October 2009.

1. Thomas S. Monson, *Inspiring Experiences That Build Faith: From the Life and Ministry of Thomas S. Monson* (Salt Lake City: Deseret Book, 1994), 188.

2. Thomas S. Monson, *Be Your Best Self* (Salt Lake City: Deseret Book, 1979), 179.

3. Glen L. Rudd, *Pure Religion: The Story of Church Welfare Since 1930* (Salt Lake City: The Church of Jesus Christ of Latter-day Saints, 1995), 20.

4. Doctrine and Covenants 64:33–34.

5. Interview with TSM, 19 February 2009.

6. Thomas S. Monson, "Guiding Principles of Personal and Family Welfare," *Ensign*, September 1986, 5.

7. *Through the Years: A Brief History of the Sixth-Seventh Ward, 1849–1955* (Salt Lake City: privately published), 30.

8. Glen L. Rudd, "The First Presidency and Welfare," Lectures, July 1999.

9. Interview with Henry B. Eyring, 26 August 2009.

10. Thomas S. Monson, "Back to Basics," address at regional representatives' seminar, 3 April 1981.

11. See Thomas S. Monson, "Christ at Bethesda's Pool," *Ensign*, November 1996, 18–19; see also Monson, *Errand*, 131–32.

12. Monson, *Errand*, 132; Thomas S. Monson, "Yellow Canaries with Gray on Their Wings," *Ensign*, July 1973, 41–42.

13. See Thomas S. Monson, "Do Your Duty—That Is Best," *Ensign*, November 2005, 59.

14. Monson, *Errand*, 134–36.

15. Letter to TSM, 29 June 1955.
16. Interview with TSM, 9 September 2008.
17. George Albert Smith, in Conference Report, April 1950, 169, as quoted in Thomas S. Monson, "Tabernacle Memories," *Ensign*, May 2007, 41.
18. Thomas S. Monson, "A New Spirit Will I Put within You," Satellite Priesthood Leadership Training Broadcast, 21 June 2003.
19. Thomas S. Monson, "The Call of Duty," *Ensign*, May 1986, 39.
20. See Monson, *Errand*, 143–44; TSM Journal, 26 June 1996.
21. Monson, "A New Spirit."
22. Thomas S. Monson, "The Lord's Way," *Ensign*, May 1990, 93.
23. See Thomas S. Monson, "Preparing the Way," *Ensign*, May 1980, 9; see also TSM Journal, 3 January 2003.
24. Monson, "Do Your Duty—That Is Best," 58.
25. TSM Journal, 3 January 2003.
26. Letter from Richard Casto to TSM, 29 January 1994.
27. Letter to TSM, 6 November 1980.
28. Thomas S. Monson, "The Lord's Way," New Budget Program Satellite Broadcast, 18 February 1990.
29. *Deseret News Semi-Weekly*, 6 August 1878, 1; as quoted in Monson, "A New Spirit," 20.
30. Thomas S. Monson, "Heavenly Homes—Forever Families," Worldwide Leadership Training Broadcast, February 2006.
31. Thomas S. Monson, "True to Our Priesthood Trust," *Ensign*, November 2006, 58.
32. Thomas S. Monson, address at general conference leadership session, 4 April 1986.
33. Thomas S. Monson, "Looking Back and Moving Forward," *Ensign*, May 2008, 87–90.

Chapter 12: "Have Courage, My Boy"

Epigraph. Interview with Richard G. Scott, 28 August 2009.
1. Interview with TSM, 15 April 2009; see also Thomas S. Monson, "The Priesthood—a Sacred Gift," *Ensign*, May 2007, 57.
2. "The Priesthood—a Sacred Gift," 57.
3. Letter from Presiding Bishopric to TSM, 28 July 1955.
4. Monson, *Errand*, 182.
5. See Thomas S. Monson, "The Perfection of the Saints," regional representatives' seminar, 1 April 1988; see also Monson, *Errand*, 169–71.
6. Doctrine and Covenants 107:99.
7. TSM Journal, 1 March 1981.
8. TSM Journal, 1 March 1981.
9. Doctrine and Covenants 59:21.
10. Monson, *Errand*, 184.
11. Monson, *Errand*, 185.
12. Monson, *Errand*, 185.
13. Luke 15:4–5.
14. Thomas S. Monson, "Dedication Day," *Ensign*, November 2000, 64; see also Thomas S. Monson, "Hallmarks of a Happy Home," *Ensign*, November 1988, 69.

15. Thomas S. Monson, "The Best Christmas Ever," *Ensign,* December 2008, 5.
16. Charles Dickens, *A Christmas Carol,* in *A Christmas Treasury* (Orem, Utah: Granite Publishing, 2007), 16.
17. Monson, "Best Christmas Ever," 7.

CHAPTER 13: "O CANADA"

Epigraph. Interview with Quentin L. Cook, 18 September 2009.
1. Thomas S. Monson, address at mission presidents' seminar, 23 June 2005.
2. Interview with TSM, 9 September 2008.
3. Interview with Quentin L. Cook, 18 September 2009.
4. Thomas S. Monson, address at Harold B. Lee Library Dedication, 15 November 2000.
5. Doctrine and Covenants 112:10.
6. Thomas S. Monson, "To Learn, to Do, to Be," *Ensign,* November 2008, 67.
7. Monson, *Errand,* 192–93.
8. Monson, *Errand,* 191.
9. Letter from J. Reuben Clark, Jr., to Clark Spencer Monson, 1 October 1959.
10. See "Autobiography of Bathsheba Smith," 14–15, LDS Church Archives.
11. TSM Journal, 21 February 1959.
12. As quoted in John Hart, "Mission presidents told to prepare for 'greatest experience,'" *Church News,* 3 July 1993, 6.
13. The same geographical area of the Canadian Mission now is sectioned into three missions: Canada Montreal, Canada Toronto East, and Canada Toronto West.
14. Interview with Stephen Hadley, 14 October 2009.
15. Interview with Everett Pallin, 15 October 2009.
16. "The Canadian Missionary," Canadian Mission Newsletter, Toronto, Canada, 1959.
17. Thomas S. Monson, address at General Authority training meeting, 29 September 1998.
18. Interview with Everett Pallin, 15 October 2009.
19. Thomas S. Monson, address at mission presidents' seminar, 25 June 2007.
20. Monson, *Errand,* 239–41.
21. Interview with M. Russell Ballard, 9 September 2009.
22. Letter from Bruce R. McConkie to TSM, 3 September 1959.
23. "Church Officer Reports on Canadian Tour," *Church News,* 3 September 1960, 10.
24. *A History of the Mormon Church in Canada, 1830–1846* (Alberta, Canada: Lethbridge Stake, 1968), 5.
25. Doctrine and Covenants 100:3.
26. Thomas S. Monson, address at mission presidents' seminar, 27 June 2006.
27. Thomas S. Monson, "Principles from Prophets," address given at BYU, 13 September 2009.
28. Thomas S. Monson, "Motivating Missionaries," mission presidents' seminar, 22 June 2008; Doctrine and Covenants 108:7.
29. Thomas S. Monson, address at mission presidents' seminar, 28 June 2008.
30. Thomas S. Monson, in Conference Report, April 1964, 132.
31. Interview with TSM, 17 June 2009.
32. Monson, address at mission presidents' seminar, 23 June 2005.

33. Interview with Ann Monson Dibb, 6 June 2009.

34. Monson, address at mission presidents' seminar, 23 June 2005.

35. John Farrington, "Return to Canada," *Church News,* 8 May 2004, 3.

36. Interview with Everett Pallin, 15 October 2009.

37. Interview with Stephen Hadley, 14 October 2009.

38. Monson, address at mission presidents' seminar, 23 June 2005.

39. See Interviews with Stephen Hadley, 14 October 2009; Michael Murdock, 29 October 2008.

40. Interview with Michael Murdock, 29 October 2008.

41. Interview with Everett Pallin, 15 October 2009.

42. Interview with Everett Pallin, 15 October 2009.

43. Interview with Stephen Hadley, 14 October 2009.

44. Interview with Stephen Hadley, 14 October 2009.

45. Thomas S. Monson, "The Prophet Joseph Smith—Teacher by Example," Twenty-first Annual Joseph Smith Memorial Sermon, 11 December 1963.

46. Monson, "The Prophet Joseph Smith."

47. Monson, *Errand,* 222–23.

48. Thomas S. Monson, address at General Authority training meeting, 23 June 2005.

49. Thomas S. Monson, address at General Authority training meeting, 2 April 2003.

50. Ossington Chapel Reunion, July 2002, videotape, LDS Church Archives.

51. Gerry Avant, "Church in Upper Canada: rich history is celebrated," *Church News,* 16 August 1997, 8.

52. Canada Mission handbook, 1959.

53. Canada Mission handbook, 1959.

54. Thomas S. Monson, address at General Authority training meeting, 28 September 1999.

55. *A History of the Mormon Church in Canada,* 32.

56. Monson, *Errand,* 197–98.

57. See Thomas S. Monson, address at BYU College of Business, 14 March 1973; address at regional representatives' seminar, 30 March 1990.

58. Thomas S. Monson, "Your Choice," BYU Devotional, 10 March 1998.

59. Monson, *Errand,* 226.

60. Monson, address at mission presidents' seminar, 23 June 2005.

61. Thomas S. Monson, "Timeless Truths for a Changing World," address at BYU Women's Conference, 4 May 2001.

62. TSM Journal, 23 February 1964.

63. Monson, *Errand,* 227.

64. Monson, address at mission presidents' seminar, 25 June 2007.

65. Wayne Chamberlain, address at South Salt Lake Regional Meeting, Conference Center, 2009.

CHAPTER 14: CALLED TO GENERAL CHURCH COMMITTEES

Epigraph. Interview with Neil L. Andersen, 7 October 2009.

1. Monson, *Errand,* 231.

2. Thomas S. Monson, "Missionary Report," 3 February 1962.

3. Monson, *Errand,* 241.

4. Letter from Franklin D. Richards to TSM, 9 January 1963.

5. Letter from Wilford Wood to TSM, 16 May 1962.

6. Letter from Max Zimmer to TSM, 28 March 1983.

7. See "The Beehive Coinage of Deseret," *The Utah Genealogical and Historical Magazine,* Volume 2, 35.

8. See Thomas S. Monson, address at Primary annual conference, 4 April 1973; *Errand,* 230.

9. Thomas S. Monson, "Examples of Great Teachers," Worldwide Leadership Training Broadcast, 10 February 2007.

10. Romans 1:16.

11. Monson, "Examples of Great Teachers."

12. TSM Journal, 1 July 1967.

13. Interview with Clark Spencer Monson, 4 November 2008.

14. Interview with Thomas Lee Monson, 6 November 2009.

15. Letter from Vaughn Featherstone to TSM, 2 September 1999.

16. Letter from Vaughn Featherstone to TSM, 15 July 2001.

17. Monson, *Errand,* 233.

18. Monson, *Errand,* 234.

19. Letter from Spencer W. Kimball to TSM, 20 February 1962.

20. Letter from Spencer W. Kimball, Ezra Taft Benson, Mark E. Petersen, and Delbert L. Stapley to Mission Area Supervisors, 9 April 1962.

21. Letter from Spencer W. Kimball to TSM, 20 February 1962.

22. Thomas S. Monson, "Teach Ye Diligently," regional representatives' seminar, 3 April 1987.

23. Missionary Department Circular, 26 October 1962, LDS Church Archives.

24. Missionary Department Circular.

25. Other committee members included Gordon Owen, Paul Royall, Lorin Pace, Zelph Erekson, Quinton Cannon, Vernon Sharp, Henry Chace, Earl E. Olson, Henry Christiansen, George H. Fudge, Leslie Derbyshire, Frank Smith, David Romney, and John E. Carr.

26. General Church Office Building, Memorandum of Suggestions, 29 March 1940.

27. Richard O. Cowan, *The Church in the Twentieth Century* (Salt Lake City: Bookcraft, 1985), 307.

28. Harold B. Lee, in Conference Report, October 1961, 79–80.

29. David O. McKay, in Conference Report, October 1961, 77.

30. See Monson, *Errand,* 234.

31. Joseph F. Smith, in Conference Report, October 1916, 6.

32. Thomas S. Monson, "A Man For All Seasons," Church Educational System Satellite Broadcast Fireside, BYU, 5 February 1995.

33. Thomas S. Monson, "How Firm a Foundation," *Ensign,* November 2006, 62.

34. Thomas S. Monson, "The Key of Faith," Third Annual Priesthood Genealogical Seminar, BYU, 13 August 1968.

35. Interdepartmental Meeting with First Presidency, General Authorities, Department and Organization Heads, 7 May 1981.

36. "Temple work is mandate from the Lord," *Church News,* 19 November 1994, 4–5.

37. The Adult Correlation Committee included Wendell Ashton, Christine Robinson, Keith Oakes, Irene Woodford, Ruth Funk, Augustus Faust, Norman Bowen, Alden Anderson, Hortense Child, and Thomas Monson.

38. Interview with TSM, 17 June 2009.
39. Thomas S. Monson, "The Perfection of the Saints," regional representatives' seminar, 1 April 1988.
40. Monson, "Perfection of the Saints."
41. Monson, "Perfection of the Saints."
42. As quoted in Monson, "Perfection of the Saints."
43. *Initial Training for Priesthood Home Teachers* (Salt Lake City: Deseret Press).
44. Home Teaching Committee members in 1964 included L. Brent Goates, Hugh C. Smith, Henry G. Tempest, Richard Summerhayes, A. Lewis Elggren, Franck C. Berg, Heber J. Heiner, Jr., Harold R. Boyer, Cecil E. Hart, Donald Elsworth, Owen G. Reichman, George Z. Aposhian, and M. Elmer Christensen.
45. Monson, *Errand,* 236.
46. Interdepartmental Meeting, 7 May 1981.
47. "Hold High the Correlation Torch," All-Church Coordinating Council, 18 May 1993. See TSM Journal, 31 December 2005.
48. TSM Journal, 11 March 1999.
49. Monson, *Errand,* 242.

CHAPTER 15: A SPECIAL WITNESS

Epigraph. Interview with Jeffrey R. Holland, 22 September 2009.
1. See Monson, *Errand,* 246.
2. TSM Journal, 3 October 1963.
3. *Church News,* 26 April 1975.
4. TSM Journal, 3 October 1963.
5. Letter from Max Zimmer to TSM, 28 March 1983.
6. See Conference Report, October 1963, 3.
7. David O. McKay, in Conference Report, October 1963, 3.
8. David O. McKay, in Conference Report, October 1963, 7.
9. Hugh B. Brown, in Conference Report, October 1963, 9.
10. Monson, *Errand,* 248.
11. Thomas S. Monson, in Conference Report, October 1963, 14.
12. Interview with Russell M. Nelson, 3 September 2009.
13. Interview with TSM, 15 October 2008.
14. TSM Journal, 4 October 1963.
15. Interview with Michael Murdock, 29 October 2008.
16. TSM Journal, 5 October 1963.
17. "I Know That My Redeemer Lives," *Hymns* (Salt Lake City: The Church of Jesus Christ of Latter-day Saints, 1985), no. 136.
18. TSM Journal, 6 October 1963.
19. Interview with David A. Bednar, 20 October 2009.
20. TSM Journal, 25 February 1989; *Deseret News 2006 Church Almanac.*
21. Edward L. Kimball and Andrew E. Kimball, Jr., *Spencer W. Kimball* (Salt Lake City: Bookcraft, 1977), 338.
22. TSM Journal, 7 October 1963.
23. TSM Journal, 7 October 1963.
24. TSM Journal, 7 October 1963.
25. TSM Journal, 25 November 1963.
26. Letter from William James Mortimer to TSM, 8 October 1963.

27. "The Church's Eternal Progress," *Deseret News* editorial, 5 October 1963, 14A.
28. Harold B. Lee, address at regional representatives' seminar, 13 December 1969.
29. TSM Journal, 10 October 1963.
30. TSM Journal, 10 October 1963.
31. David O. McKay, as quoted in Kimball and Kimball, *Spencer W. Kimball,* 344.
32. Monson, *Errand,* 253.
33. Harold B. Lee, in Conference Report, April 1970, 123.
34. TSM Journal, 14 October 1963.
35. Interview with Glen L. Rudd, 17 January 2009.
36. TSM Journal, 13 October 1963.
37. Monson, *Errand,* p. 252.
38. TSM Journal, 17 October 1963.
39. Thomas S. Monson, "Dear to Our Hearts, Always," BYU Devotional, 12 September 2000.
40. Monson, "Dear to Our Hearts, Always."
41. David O. McKay, in Conference Report, October 1963, 9.
42. Poem by Edwin Markham, as quoted by David O. McKay in Conference Report, October 1962, 119.
43. TSM Journal, 10 December 1964.
44. Marba C. Josephson, "Thomas S. Monson," *Improvement Era,* November 1963.
45. Thomas S. Monson, "Finding Joy in the Journey," *Ensign,* November 2008, 84.

CHAPTER 16: SERVING IN THE TWELVE

Epigraph. Letter from Neal A. Maxwell to TSM, 9 September 1987.
1. Matthew 20:28.
2. Thomas S. Monson, "Mark E. Petersen: A Giant among Men," *Ensign,* March 1984, 11.
3. TSM Journal, 24 October 1963.
4. TSM Journal, 7 November 1963.
5. TSM Journal, 31 October 1963.
6. TSM Journal, 4 April 1964.
7. TSM Journal, 2 March 1967.
8. TSM Journal, 5 March 1964.
9. TSM Journal, 5 November 1963.
10. TSM Journal, 4 November 1966.
11. Jack E. Jarrard, "Walk in the Lord's Way for a Really Happy Life," *Church News,* 26 April 1975, 13.
12. TSM Journal, 15 February 1964.
13. Isaiah 54:2.
14. See TSM Journal, 18–19 September 1965.
15. Matthew 17:4.
16. TSM Journal, 19 November 1964.
17. Interview with Marlin K. Jensen, 28 October 2009.
18. TSM Journal, 7 February 1964.
19. TSM Journal, 17 August 1964.
20. Interview with Thomas Lee Monson, 6 November 2009.
21. TSM Journal, 9 July 1965.

22. Interview with Thomas Lee Monson, 6 November 2009.

23. TSM Journal, 27 October 1967.

24. TSM Journal, 14 July 1967.

25. TSM Journal, 19 August 1979.

26. TSM Journal, 12 November 1963.

27. TSM Journal, 31 January 1964.

28. Certificate in Thomas S. Monson collection, 12 March 1965.

29. TSM Journal, 24 October 1963.

30. TSM Journal, 3 February 1964.

31. TSM Journal, 4 February 1964.

32. TSM Journal, 7 September 1971.

33. Monson, *Errand,* 272.

34. TSM Journal, 2 October 1981.

35. TSM Journal, 3 April 1984.

36. Thomas S. Monson, "Welcome to Conference," *Ensign,* November 2008, 4–6.

37. Thomas S. Monson, address at MIA June Conference, 28 June 1969.

38. Monson, address at MIA June Conference.

39. See Thomas S. Monson, "A Royal Priesthood," *Ensign,* November 2007, 60.

40. TSM Journal, 1 June 1965.

41. Interview with Ronald A. Rasband, 12 November 2008.

42. See Edward L. Kimball and Andrew E. Kimball, Jr., *Spencer W. Kimball* (Salt Lake City: Bookcraft, 1977), 364.

43. Letter from John R. W. Purdell to TSM, 3 January 1968.

44. Thomas S. Monson, "A Man for All Seasons," Church Educational System Satellite Broadcast Fireside, 5 February 1995.

45. Acts 3:6–7.

46. Thomas S. Monson, "Is There a Doctor in the House?" *Collegium Aesculapium,* Vol. 21, no. 1, 11.

47. Interview with TSM, 8 September 2008.

48. Sarah Jane Weaver, "A worker's gift: Children, missionaries benefit," *Church News,* 24 December 2005, 6.

49. Thomas S. Monson, "May You Have Courage," *Ensign,* May 2009, 124.

Chapter 17: "He Was Everywhere"

Epigraph. Interview with Jeffrey R. Holland, 22 September 2009.

1. TSM Journal, 5 October 1966 .

2. TSM Journal, 6 October 1966.

3. TSM Journal, 6 October 1966 .

4. TSM Journal, 3 November 1966.

5. Thomas S. Monson, in Conference Report, April 1965, 46.

6. Interview with TSM, 13 May 2009.

7. Interview with M. Russell Ballard, 9 September 2009.

8. Interview with TSM, 12 November 2008.

9. See Richard L. Evans, in Conference Report, October 1962, 74.

10. See Ruth Funk, "Ruth, Come Walk with Me," in *He Changed My Life* (Salt Lake City: Bookcraft, 1988), 119.

11. TSM Journal, 25 March 1965.

12. Interview with TSM, 12 November 2008.

13. "Outline of General Procedures for Developing the Curriculum for

Organizations of the Church with Membership on the Adult Level," 1965, LDS Church Archives.

14. "Guidelines for developing a correlated program for adults," Adult Correlation Committee minutes, 1965, 4.

15. Thomas S. Monson, "Duty Calls," regional representatives' seminar, 30 March 1990.

16. Thomas S. Monson, "The Bishop and the Spiritual and Temporal Well-Being of the Saints," Worldwide Leadership Training Broadcast, June 2004, 5.

17. Hugh B. Brown, in Conference Report, October 1967, 25–26.

18. Francis M. Gibbons, *Harold B. Lee: Man of Vision, Prophet of God* (Salt Lake City: Deseret Book, 1993), 414.

19. Thomas S. Monson, "Hold High the Correlation Torch," All-Church Coordinating Council, 18 May 1993.

20. See Donald Q. Cannon, Richard O. Cowan, and Arnold K. Garr, eds., *Encyclopedia of Latter-day Saint History* (Salt Lake City: Deseret Book, 2000), s.v. "Regional Representatives."

21. Thomas S. Monson, "The Search for Jesus," address at Lethbridge, Alberta, Canada, Centennial Service, 11 June 1967.

22. Thomas S. Monson was elected to the alumni board with Graham W. Doxey, June Wilkins Nebeker, Hugh W. Pinnock, and Rex W. Williams. Other members included George L. Nelson, Mark B. Garff, Ernest L. Wilkinson, Frank M. Browning, Henry R. Pearson, and Arch L. Madsen. Truman B. Clawson was the association executive director, E. Earl Hawkes was executive vice president, and D. Arthur Haycock was secretary.

23. TSM Journal, 11 February 1975.

24. Letter from Maurice P. (Pat) Shea to TSM, 26 March 1993.

25. TSM Journal, 11 December 2003.

26. TSM Journal, 30 May 2001.

27. TSM Journal, 4 March 1964.

28. G. Homer Durham, *N. Eldon Tanner: His Life and Service* (Salt Lake City: Deseret Book, 1982), 236.

29. TSM Journal, 24 September 1965.

30. Thomas S. Monson, "A Time to Choose," address at Brigham Young University, 16 January 1973.

31. TSM Journal, 20 January 1975.

CHAPTER 18: NEAR AND FAR

Epigraph. Joseph Smith, *History of The Church of Jesus Christ of Latter-day Saints,* 7 vols. (Salt Lake City: The Church of Jesus Christ of Latter-day Saints, 1932–1952), 4:227.

1. Letter from Mark Mendenhall to Heidi S. Swinton, 2 February 2009.

2. Letter from Mark Mendenhall to Heidi S. Swinton, 2 February 2009.

3. TSM Journal, 24 April 1964.

4. Monson, *Errand,* 281; TSM Journal, 15 February 1965.

5. Interview with TSM, 15 October 2008.

6. TSM Journal, 9 November 1965.

7. Thomas S. Monson, "Building Your Eternal Home," *Ensign,* May 1984, 16.

8. TSM Journal, 17 October 1965; Monson, *Errand,* 283–84.

9. Thomas S. Monson, "We Should Love as Jesus Loves," address to Deseret Sunday School Union, 4 April 1965.

10. Thomas S. Monson, "Hallmarks of a Happy Home," Missionary Open House Satellite Broadcast, 20 February 2000.

11. Monson, "We Should Love as Jesus Loves," 4 April 1965.

12. TSM Journal, 8 March 1965.

13. Thomas S. Monson, in Conference Report, October 1966, 10.

14. Thomas S. Monson, "For I Was Blind, but Now I See," *Ensign,* May 1999, 56; John 8:12.

15. Monson, "We Should Love as Jesus Loves," 4 April 1965.

16. TSM Journal, 20 November 1965.

17. TSM Journal, 20 November 1965.

18. At the time, all missionaries leaving from the Salt Lake mission home were assigned to a General Authority to be set apart. That responsibility was later given to stake presidents.

19. Letter from John Telford to TSM, 18 January 1988.

20. John H. Groberg, *The Fire of Faith* (Salt Lake City: Bookcraft, 1996), 174; Monson, *Errand,* 289–92.

21. Groberg, *Fire of Faith,* 174–75.

22. TSM Journal, 6 September 1968.

23. TSM Journal, 7 September 1968; Monson, *Errand,* 291–92.

24. Thomas S. Monson, address at MIA June Conference, 28 June 1969.

25. TSM Journal, 13 May 1967.

26. Thomas S. Monson, "The Race for Eternal Life," address at Ricks College, 10 May 1967.

27. Oral History, Karl M. Richards, August 1973, 50, LDS Church Archives.

28. TSM Journal, May 2, 1968.

29. See Thomas S. Monson, "Building Bridges," Beneficial Life Convention, 14 July 1988.

30. TSM Journal, 25 June 1968.

31. See TSM Journal, 29 July 1968.

32. TSM Journal, 24 April 1969.

33. TSM Journal, 11 August 1968.

34. Interview with Ann Monson Dibb, 29 July 2010.

35. TSM Journal, 21 October 1968.

Chapter 19: "Weary Not"

Epigraph. Interview with Dieter F. Uchtdorf, 2 September 2009.

1. Though the official name of the socialist state established in 1949 was German Democratic Republic (GDR), it was informally called East Germany by those in the West. Geographically it bordered West Germany (officially Federal Republic of Germany) to the south and west, the Baltic Sea to the north, Poland to the east, and Czechoslovakia to the south.

2. Interview with TSM, 9 September 2008.

3. KBYU Interview with TSM for documentary *A Fortress of Faith,* October 1988.

4. Thomas S. Monson, *Faith Rewarded: A Personal Account of Prophetic Promises to the East German Saints* (Salt Lake City: Deseret Book, 1996), 1.

5. Winston Churchill, "The Sinews of Peace," address at Westminster College,

Fulton, Missouri, 5 March 1946. Churchill served as Prime Minister of Great Britain from 1940 to 1945 and again from 1951 to 1955.

6. Justus Ernst, comp., *Highlights from the German-Speaking Latter-day Saints Mission Histories, 1836–1960,* LDS Church Archives, 97.

7. Ernst, *Highlights,* 115.

8. Ernst, *Highlights,* 117.

9. "Ever since its founding in 1959, East Germany lost a steady stream of citizens who emigrated to the Federal Republic [West Germany] in order to claim citizenship as guaranteed by the [West German] Basic Law. Before 1961, such emigration proved fairly easy in that one needed only to cross from the eastern to the western zones of Berlin. The building of the Berlin Wall put a halt to such direct emigration, but not before the Federal Republic received the staggering total of 3,419,042 emigrants from the East." Richard A. Leiby, *The Unification of Germany, 1989–1990* (Westport, CT: Greenwood Press, 1999), 25–26.

10. Bruce W. Hall, "And the Last Shall Be First: The Church of Jesus Christ of Latter-day Saints in the Former East Germany," *Journal of Church and State,* vol. 42 (Summer 2000):485–89.

11. Hall, "And the Last Shall Be First," 487–88.

12. Roger P. Minert, *In Harm's Way, East German Latter-day Saints in World War II* (Provo, UT: Religious Studies Center, Brigham Young University, 2009), 23; see also Presiding Bishopric, "Financial, Statistical, and Historical Reports of Wards, Stakes, and Missions, 1884–1955," *Der Stern,* final no. for 1939–41.

13. Gilbert W. Scharffs, *Mormonism in Germany: A History of The Church of Jesus Christ of Latter-day Saints in Germany* (Salt Lake City: Deseret Book, 1970), xiv.

14. Garold and Norma Davis, "Behind the Wall: The Church in Eastern Germany," *Tambuli,* February 1992, 12.

15. Rodney Taylor, "Karl G. Maeser memorialized in native Germany," *Church News,* 21 July 2001.

16. David F. Boone, *The Worldwide Evacuation of Latter-day Missionaries at the Beginning of World War II,* master's thesis (Provo, UT: Brigham Young University, 1981), 1–2.

17. Minert, *In Harm's Way,* quoting East German Mission Quarterly Reports, 1938, no. 40.

18. Boone, *Worldwide Evacuation,* 4.

19. Robert C. Freeman, "When the Wicked Rule the People Mourn: The Experiences of the German Saints during World War II," in Donald Q. Cannon and Brent L. Top, eds., *Regional Studies in Latter-day Saint Church History—Europe* (Provo, UT: Brigham Young University, 2003), 90; see also Ernst, *Highlights,* 47–48.

20. See Scharffs, *Mormonism in Germany,* 107.

21. See Freeman, "When the Wicked Rule," 91.

22. Scharffs, *Mormonism in Germany,* 109.

23. Minert, *In Harm's Way,* 181.

24. The sacrament was passed in Sunday School worship service (opening exercises) until 1980, when the Church implemented the "Church Consolidated Meeting Schedule." See "News of the Church, Church Consolidates Meeting Schedule," *Ensign,* March 1980, 73.

25. Doctrine and Covenants 84:117.

26. Letter from Lt. Col. John Richard Barnes to President Thomas McKay; Thomas McKay Correspondence 1939–1946, European Mission, LDS Church Archives.

27. Sheri Dew, *Ezra Taft Benson: A Biography* (Salt Lake City: Deseret Book, 1987), 219.

28. KBYU Interview with TSM for *Fortress,* October 1988.

29. Ezra Taft Benson, in Conference Report, April 1947, 154; see also *Improvement Era,* vol. 5 (May 1947): 293.

30. KBYU Interview with TSM for *Fortress,* October 1988.

31. Dew, *Ezra Taft Benson,* 226.

32. Monson, *Faith Rewarded,* vii.

33. KBYU Interview with TSM for *Fortress,* October 1988.

34. Monson, *Faith Rewarded,* 12.

35. Monson, *Faith Rewarded,* 13.

36. Monson, *Faith Rewarded,* 3.

37. The earliest published accounts of the February 13–14, 1945, bombing of Dresden used information gathered from the Nazi and Soviet governments. During the next forty years, death estimates for the Dresden bombing varied greatly, ranging from 18,000 to 450,000, but most frequently cited in excess of 100,000. Since the reunification of Germany and the review of newly available government files, historians now place the estimated death count between 25,000 and 40,000. See Frederick Taylor, *Dresden, Tuesday, February 13, 1945* (New York: HarperCollins Publishers, 2005), 441–48.

38. Monson, *Faith Rewarded,* 3–4.

39. Doctrine and Covenants 112:21.

40. KBYU Interview with TSM for *Fortress,* October 1988.

41. KBYU Interview with TSM for *Fortress,* October 1988.

42. Monson, *Faith Rewarded,* 6.

43. Monson, *Faith Rewarded,* 6.

44. KBYU Interview with TSM for *Fortress,* October 1988.

45. "Weary Not," *Deseret Sunday School Songs* (Salt Lake City: Deseret Sunday School Union, 1909), no. 158; see Monson, *Faith Rewarded,* 4.

46. KBYU Interview with TSM for *Fortress,* October 1988.

47. See Monson, *Faith Rewarded,* 4–5; TSM Journal, 22 October 1978.

48. KBYU Interview with TSM for *Fortress,* October 1988.

49. Monson, *Faith Rewarded,* 5.

50. KBYU Interview with TSM for *Fortress,* October 1988.

51. Monson, *Faith Rewarded,* 7.

52. Psalm 46:10.

53. Minert, *In Harm's Way,* 176.

54. KBYU Interview with TSM for *Fortress,* October 1988.

55. TSM Journal, 8 May 1969.

56. Monson, *Faith Rewarded,* 11.

57. Monson, *Faith Rewarded,* 11.

58. Monson, *Faith Rewarded,* 11–12.

59. Karin Sommer, "An Account About Great Events in My Life," unpublished manuscript in possession of TSM.

60. KBYU Interview with TSM for *Fortress,* October 1988.

61. KBYU Interview with TSM for *Fortress,* October 1988.

62. Monson, *Faith Rewarded*, 66–67.

63. Monson, *Faith Rewarded*, 66–67.

64. KBYU Interview with Hans B. Ringger for documentary, *A Fortress of Faith*, October 1988.

65. Monson, *Faith Rewarded*, 18–19.

66. Monson, *Faith Rewarded*, 109–11; Interview with Dieter Berndt, 3 July 2009.

67. Monson, *Faith Rewarded*, 15–16.

68. See Hall, "And the Last Shall Be First,"488–89. In the late 1980s the "uncharacteristically favorable treatment of the LDS Church" by the GDR was a benefit of the information the government gathered over many years. They concluded the members were "responsible citizens and people of high moral character" and could be trusted.

69. Monson, *Faith Rewarded*, 16.

70. TSM Journal, 23 October 1970.

71. See Monson, *Faith Rewarded*, 16.

72. KBYU Interview with TSM for *Fortress*, October 1988.

73. Monson, *Faith Rewarded*, 107–8.

74. Monson, *Faith Rewarded*, 26–27.

75. KBYU Interview with Russell M. Nelson for documentary *A Fortress of Faith*, 1988.

76. See Monson, *Faith Rewarded*, 84.

77. KBYU Interview with TSM for *Fortress*, October 1988.

78. See Monson, *Faith Rewarded*, 37.

79. KBYU Interview with TSM for *Fortress*, October 1988.

80. Monson, *Faith Rewarded*, 38; TSM Journal, 27 April 1975.

81. Monson, *Faith Rewarded*, 38.

82. See Monson, *Faith Rewarded*, 153; Thomas S. Monson, "Examples of Great Teachers," *Ensign,* June 2007, 112.

83. KBYU Interview with Russell M. Nelson for *Fortress*, 1988.

84. Monson, *Faith Rewarded*, 48–49.

85. KBYU Interview with Hans B. Ringger for *Fortress*, October 1988.

86. Monson, *Faith Rewarded*, 62.

87. Letter from Harold W. Schreiber to TSM, 12 April 1989.

88. Monson, *Faith Rewarded*, 46.

CHAPTER 20: FAITH OF THE PEOPLE

Epigraph. Interview with L. Tom Perry, 22 August 2008.

1. Edward L. Kimball, *Lengthen Your Stride: The Presidency of Spencer W. Kimball* (Salt Lake City: Deseret Book, 2005), 367.

2. Kimball, *Lengthen Your Stride*, 367.

3. Thomas S. Monson, *Faith Rewarded: A Personal Account of Prophetic Promises to the East German Saints* (Salt Lake City: Deseret Book, 1996), 36.

4. KBYU Interview with TSM for documentary *A Fortress of Faith*, October 1988.

5. KBYU Interview with TSM for *Fortress*, October 1988.

6. Thomas S. Monson, "Thanks Be to God," *Ensign,* May 1989, 50.

7. Monson, *Faith Rewarded*, 58–59.

8. TSM Journal, 29 March 1979.

9. See Bruce W. Hall, *Gemeinde Geschichte als Vergleichende Geschichte, The Church*

of Jesus Christ of Latter-day Saints in East Germany 1945–1989, master of arts thesis (Provo, UT: Brigham Young University, June 1998), 92.

10. Doctrine & Covenants 134:1.
11. Monson, *Faith Rewarded,* 60–61.
12. Thomas S. Monson, "Those Who Love Jesus," *Ensign,* November 1985, 34–35.
13. See KBYU Interview with Hans B. Ringger for documentary *A Fortress of Faith,* October 1988.
14. Hall, *Gemeinde Geschichte,* 90.
15. Monson, *Errand,* 402.
16. Monson, *Faith Rewarded,* 81.
17. Monson, *Faith Rewarded,* 78.
18. Monson, *Faith Rewarded,* 87.
19. KBYU Interview with TSM for *Fortress,* October 1988.
20. KBYU Interview with TSM for *Fortress,* October 1988.
21. Letter from Werner Adler to TSM, 22 November 1982.
22. Letter from Beatrice Bartsch to TSM, 21 June 2004.
23. Monson, *Faith Rewarded,* 88–89.
24. See Monson, *Faith Rewarded,* 90.
25. Monson, *Faith Rewarded,* 89.
26. Monson, *Faith Rewarded,* 91.
27. Monson, *Faith Rewarded,* 88.
28. Monson, *Faith Rewarded,* 92–93 .
29. TSM Journal, 28 February 1982.
30. Monson, "Thanks Be to God," 51.
31. KBYU Interview with TSM for *Fortress,* October 1988.
32. KBYU Interview with TSM for *Fortress,* October 1988.
33. Monson, *Faith Rewarded,* 99–100.
34. KBYU Interview with TSM for *Fortress,* October 1988.
35. See Monson, *Faith Rewarded,* 36.
36. Thomas S. Monson, remarks at Freiberg Germany Temple cornerstone meeting held prior to first dedicatory Session, 28 June 1985.
37. Dieter Hantzsche, remarks at Freiberg Germany Temple cornerstone meeting.
38. Gordon B. Hinckley, remarks at Freiberg Germany Temple cornerstone meeting.
39. TSM Journal, 29 June 1985.
40. TSM Journal, 29 June 1985.
41. Monson, *Faith Rewarded,* 108.
42. TSM Journal, 8 October 1984.
43. Interview with TSM, 17 June 2009.
44. KBYU Interview with TSM for *Fortress,* October 1988.
45. KBYU Interview with Edith Krause for documentary *A Fortress of Faith,* 1989.
46. TSM Journal, 29 June 1985. For a brief overview of Thomas S. Monson's service in East Germany, see Monson, "Thanks Be to God," 50–53.

CHAPTER 21: THE WALL COMES DOWN

Epigraph. Interview with Russell M. Nelson, 3 September 2009.
1. Interview with Dieter F. Uchtdorf.
2. Letter from Henry A. Matis to TSM, 5 April 1989.

3. Thomas S. Monson, *Faith Rewarded: A Personal Account of Prophetic Promises to the East German Saints* (Salt Lake City: Deseret Book, 1996), 161.

4. Monson, *Faith Rewarded,* 123.

5. Monson, *Faith Rewarded,* 125.

6. Monson, *Faith Rewarded,* 127.

7. Monson, *Faith Rewarded,* 128.

8. Monson, *Faith Rewarded,* 130.

9. Monson, *Faith Rewarded,* 131.

10. Monson, *Faith Rewarded,* 131.

11. Russell M. Nelson, "Drama on the European Stage," *Ensign,* December 1991, 10.

12. Erich Honecker was the General Secretary of the Central Committee of the socialist unity party of Germany 1971–1989; Chairman of the State Council for the German Democratic Republic 1976–1989 and Chairman of the National Defense Council of the German Democratic Republic 1971–1989.

13. Declaration on the occasion of the meeting with the Chairman of the State Council for the German Democratic Republic, Erich Honecker, October 24, 1988.

14. "Response on the occasion of the meeting with the Chairman of the State Council for the German Democratic Republic," Kurt Löffler, 24 October 1988, document in Monson collection.

15. Monson, *Faith Rewarded,* 133–34.

16. TSM Journal, 29 May 1994.

17. Letter from Will Powley to his family, 30 March 1989, shared in letter from Harrison Powley to TSM, 17 April 1989.

18. Wolfgang Paul was sustained to the Second Quorum of Seventy on 2 April 2005.

19. Letter from Will Powley to his family, 30 March 1989, shared in letter from Harrison Powley to TSM, 17 April 1989.

20. Letter from Will Powley to his family, 30 March 1989, shared in letter from Harrison Powley to TSM, 17 April 1989.

21. Monson, *Faith Rewarded,* 139–40.

22. Monson, *Faith Rewarded,* 140.

23. Nelson, "Drama on the European Stage," 10.

24. Richard A. Leiby, *The Unification of Germany, 1989–1990* (Westport, CT: Greenwood Press, 1999), 10–11.

25. Monson, *Faith Rewarded,* 142–43.

26. Monson, *Faith Rewarded,* 143.

27. Leiby, *Unification of Germany,* 12–15.

28. KBYU Interview with Dr. Horst Dohle of Humboldt-Universität zu Berlin, historian and former representative of the State Secretariat for Church Affairs of the GDR, for *A Fortress of Faith,* 1991.

29. Monson, *Faith Rewarded,* 143–46.

30. TSM Journal, 31 May 1990.

31. TSM Journal, 21 October 1990.

32. Monson, *Faith Rewarded,* 154.

33. TSM Journal, 21 October 1990.

34. Monson, *Faith Rewarded,* 152–53.

35. Monson, *Faith Rewarded,* 153.

36. Monson, *Faith Rewarded*, 153.
37. Monson, *Faith Rewarded*, 147.
38. Monson, *Faith Rewarded*, 165.
39. Monson, *Faith Rewarded*, 166–68.
40. Monson, *Faith Rewarded*, 168–71.
41. Rudyard Kipling, "Recessional" (1897), text for "God of Our Fathers, Known of Old," *Hymns* (Salt Lake City: The Church of Jesus Christ of Latter-day Saints, 1985), no. 80.

CHAPTER 22: THE WORK GOES FORWARD

Epigraph. Interview with Henry B. Eyring, 26 August 2009.
1. Thomas S. Monson, *Be Your Best Self* (Salt Lake City: Deseret Book, 1979), 125.
2. TSM Journal, 15 May 1969.
3. TSM Journal, 18 January 1970.
4. TSM Journal, 9 November 1965.
5. Dell Van Orden, *Joseph Fielding Smith: A Prophet Among the People* (Salt Lake City: Deseret Book, 1971), 2.
6. Harold B. Lee, in Conference Report, April 1970, 122.
7. TSM Journal, 23 January 1970
8. TSM Journal, 23 January 1970.
9. TSM Journal, 29 January 1970.
10. See Thomas S. Monson, "Each Must Choose," Manchester Area Conference, 29 August 1971.
11. Spencer W. Kimball, in Conference Report, April 1970, 118.
12. Interview with Boyd K. Packer, 19 August 2009.
13. Interview with Boyd K. Packer, 19 August 2009.
14. Interview with Boyd K. Packer, 19 August 2009.
15. TSM Journal, 7 April 1971.
16. Thomas S. Monson, in Conference Report, October 1970, 105–6.
17. Thomas S. Monson, in Conference Report, October 1970, 106–8.
18. Serving on the committee were Reed H. Bradford, Jim Barton, Ardeth G. Kapp, Ruth Funk, Leon Hartshorn, and Ethelyn Graham.
19. Letter from Adult Correlation Committee to TSM, 1 March 1971.
20. TSM Journal, 6 October 1970.
21. TSM Journal, 13 September 1970.
22. Letter from Dale and Karen Harris to President Spencer W. Kimball, 13 September 1970, copy in TSM collection.
23. TSM Journal, 12 April 1970.
24. Interview with Dallin H. Oaks, 3 September 2009.
25. TSM Journal, 12 November 1971.
26. TSM Journal, 29 April 1973.
27. TSM Journal, 10 December 1971.
28. TSM Journal, 4–5 August 1979.
29. Letter from M. Russell Ballard to TSM, 13 March 1981; TSM Journal, 13 March 1981.
30. Alma 40:11–12.
31. TSM Journal, 6 February 1970
32. TSM Journal, 26 March 1971.
33. Letter from Tom L. Monson to TSM, 29 May 1971.

34. Thomas S. Monson, address at new mission presidents' seminar, 25 June 1997.
35. Doctrine and Covenants 100:1.
36. Thomas S. Monson, address at mission presidents' seminar, 24 June 1976.
37. Interview with Quentin L. Cook, 28 September 2009.
38. TSM Journal, 15 September 1972.
39. Thomas S. Monson, address at stake conference broadcast, 25 May 2008.
40. See Thomas S. Monson, "Anonymous," *Ensign,* May 1983, 55; quoting Henry Van Dyke, *The Mansion,* 364–68.
41. Monson, "Each Must Choose," 29 August 1971.
42. TSM Journal, 27 April 1972.
43. Interview with Clark Spencer Monson, 4 November 2008.
44. Interview with TSM, 12 December 2009.

Chapter 23: Poised for Growth

Epigraph. Interview with L. Tom Perry, 22 August 2008.
1. Letter from Jerrald M. Jensen, president of Jordan Oaks Stake, to TSM, 26 April 2003.
2. TSM Journal, 7 July 1972.
3. TSM Journal, 6 July 1972.
4. TSM Journal, 12 Oct 1972.
5. TSM Journal, 13 October 1972.
6. *Journal of Discourses,* 26 vols. (London: Latter-day Saints' Book Depot, 1854–1886), 1:123.
7. Thomas S. Monson, "A Time to Choose," BYU Devotional, 16 January 1973.
8. Monson, *Errand,* 325.
9. Thomas S. Monson, address at Harold B. Lee Library Dedication, 15 November 2000.
10. Monson, *Errand,* 326.
11. TSM Journal, 29 September 1972.
12. TSM Journal, 27 June 1970.
13. Monson, *Errand,* 326.
14. Harold B. Lee, Foreword, *Pathways to Perfection* (Salt Lake City: Deseret Book, 1973), viii.
15. Lee, Foreword, *Pathways,* viii.
16. Francis M. Gibbons, *Harold B. Lee: Man of Vision, Prophet of God* (Salt Lake City: Deseret Book, 1993), 423.
17. TSM Journal, 11 January 1972.
18. J. Thomas Fyans, later called as a General Authority in April 1974, was named managing director of the four divisions: James M. Paramore, who became a General Authority in 1977, administrative services; Daniel H. Ludlow, instructional materials; Doyle Green, editorial; and John Carr, translation.
19. Monson, *Errand,* 360.
20. TSM Journal, 29 March 1972.
21. Interview with David A. Bednar, 20 October 2009.
22. TSM Journal, 25–26 August 1973.
23. TSM Journal, 26–27 August 1973.
24. TSM Journal, 28 August 1973.

25. Interview with Ann Monson Dibb, 19 July 2008.
26. "The Family: A Proclamation to the World," *Ensign,* November 1995, 102.
27. Interview with Ann Monson Dibb, 19 July 2008.
28. TSM Journal, 5 March 1974.
29. TSM Journal, 10 August 1973.
30. TSM Journal, 22 July 1973.
31. Monson, *Errand,* 342.
32. Monson, *Errand,* 342.
33. Letter from Steven (Arvil) Stone to TSM, 10 February 1984.
34. TSM Journal, 3 July 1973.
35. TSM Journal, 14 September 1973.
36. TSM Journal, 16 September 1973.
37. TSM Journal, 16 September 1973.
38. TSM Journal, 17 September 1973.
39. Harold B. Lee, address at funeral service for Gladys Condie Monson, 18 September 1973.
40. TSM Journal, 18 September 1973.
41. Letter from Gordon B. Hinckley to TSM, 15 September 1973.
42. TSM Journal, 6 October 1973.
43. Thomas S. Monson, in Conference Report, October 1973, 28.
44. TSM Journal, 7 October 1973.
45. TSM Journal, 26 December 1973.
46. TSM Journal, 27 December 1973.
47. TSM Journal, 29 December 1973.
48. TSM Journal, 29 December 1973.
49. Thomas S. Monson, *Be Your Best Self* (Salt Lake City: Deseret Book, 1979), 107.
50. TSM Journal, 30 December 1973.
51. TSM Journal, 30 December 1973.
52. TSM Journal, 30 January 1974.
53. TSM Journal, 30 December 1973.
54. Joshua 24:15.

CHAPTER 24: OPENING DOORS

Epigraph. Spencer W. Kimball, Foreword to Thomas S. Monson, *Be Your Best Self* (Salt Lake City: Deseret Book, 1979), ix.
1. Monson, *Be Your Best Self,* 111.
2. Monson, *Be Your Best Self,* 111, quoting Albert Schweitzer, *The Quest of the Historical Jesus* (New York: MacMillan, 1948), 104.
3. Spencer W. Kimball, "What Do We Hear?" *Ensign,* May 1974, 47.
4. TSM Journal, 14 March 1974.
5. TSM Journal, 12 April 1972 .
6. Thomas S. Monson, address at BYU Fourteen-Stake Fireside, 11 October 1981.
7. Monson, BYU Fourteen-Stake Fireside, 11 October 1981.
8. Thomas S. Monson, "'Come, Learn of Me,'" *Ensign,* December 1985, 46.
9. Talk by Frances J. Monson to Relief Society.
10. TSM Journal, 5 October 1996.
11. Interview with Boyd K. Packer, Oral History project, LDS Church Archives.
12. Interview with Boyd K. Packer, Oral History project, LDS Church Archives.

13. TSM Journal, 12 February 1980.
14. Many specialists brought particular expertise to the process: Eldin Ricks, computer expert at BYU, had placed every verse of all four standard works into a computer database. To fast-track the scriptures project, the committee asked for access, and he gave it. Stephen Howes provided invaluable printouts of scriptural texts and cross-references in a sophisticated program he designed for the task. The major work on the Topical Guide came from a committee of Alma Gardiner, retired seminary administrator; Edward Brandt from the University of Utah Institute of Religion; George Horton, director of curriculum for seminaries and institutes; Bruce Harper of Church editing; and Eleanor Knowles, accomplished editor at Deseret Book. More than one hundred scholars, computer specialists, and students of ancient scripture worked days, nights, and weekends to complete the complicated task.
15. William James Mortimer, "The Coming Forth of the LDS Editions of Scripture," *Ensign*, August 1983, 36.
16. In Joseph Fielding McConkie, *The Bruce R. McConkie Story: Reflections of a Son* (Salt Lake City: Deseret Book, 2003), 383–84.
17. Bruce R. McConkie, address at General Authority training meeting, 2 October 1981.
18. TSM Journal, 13 May 2009.
19. TSM Journal, 29 August 1979.
20. Lavina Fielding Anderson, "Church Publishes First LDS Edition of the Bible," *Ensign*, October 1979, 15.
21. "Prodigious project," *Church News*, 5 March 2005.
22. Thomas S. Monson, "A Time to Choose," *Ensign*, May 1995, 97.
23. TSM Journal, 21 April 1973.
24. Monson, "'Come, Learn of Me,'" 46.
25. Church Audiovisual Department Interview with TSM, 26 January 1994; Interview with TSM, 10 December 2008.
26. Thomas S. Monson, "Hallmarks of a Happy Home," *Ensign*, November 1988, 70.
27. "Prodigious project," *Church News*, 5 March 2005.
28. Doctrine and Covenants, Official Declaration—2.
29. Edward L. Kimball, *Lengthen Your Stride: The Presidency of Spencer W. Kimball* (Salt Lake City: Deseret Book, 2005), 204.
30. D&C 9:8.
31. TSM Journal, 30 June 1983.
32. TSM Journal, 1 June 1978.
33. TSM Journal, 9 June 1978.
34. Monson, *Errand*, 360.
35. See "President Kimball says revelation was clear," *Church News*, 6 January 1979.
36. Monson, *Errand*, 361.
37. Edward L. Kimball, *Lengthen Your Stride*, 226.
38. TSM Journal, 9 June 1978.
39. TSM Journal, 10 June 1978.
40. TSM Journal, 21 June 1978.
41. TSM Journal, 25 June 1978.
42. TSM Journal, 25 June 1978.

Chapter 25: Neighbor Helping Neighbor

Epigraph. Interview with M. Russell Ballard, 9 September 2009.
1. See TSM Journal, 16 May 1977.
2. Named to the board were Victor L. Brown, Robert H. Bischoff, Dallin H. Oaks, Emma Lou Thayne, L. Glenn Snarr, and Neal A. Maxwell. Jeffrey R. Holland joined the board later, taking the seat of Elder Oaks. William James Mortimer served as a board member until he was named general manager of Deseret Press.
3. Letter from Emma Lou Thayne to TSM, 15 February 1981.
4. Interview with TSM, 9 September 2008.
5. TSM Journal, 27 March 1980.
6. TSM Journal, 4 December 1988.
7. TSM Journal, 4 January 1980.
8. Monson, *Errand*, 399.
9. TSM Journal, 1 June 1982.
10. Monson, *Errand*, 400–401.
11. TSM Journal, 24 October 1972.
12. Interview with Duane Cardall, KSL, 13 November 2009.
13. Letter from TSM to Jack Gallivan, 4 April 1990.
14. TSM Journal, 26 April 2001.
15. Letter from Patrick Shea to TSM, 22 February 1993.
16. TSM Journal, 28 May 1993.
17. TSM Journal, 5 March 2005.
18. Interview with Jeffrey R. Holland, 8 October 2009.
19. TSM Journal, 27 December 1982.
20. TSM Journal, 18 July 1980.
21. TSM Journal, 22 July 1979.
22. Thomas S. Monson, "What Have I Done for Someone Today?" *Ensign,* November 2009, 85.
23. TSM Journal, 29 June 1978.
24. TSM Journal, 19 December 1978.
25. TSM Journal, 7 June 1984.
26. TSM Journal, 20 June 1984.
27. Thomas S. Monson, "The Bishop—Center Stage in Welfare," *Ensign,* November 1980, 89–91.
28. Letter from Randy Spaulding to TSM, as quoted in Thomas S. Monson, "Christ at Bethesda's Pool," *Ensign,* November 1996, 16.
29. Thomas S. Monson, "Christ at Bethesda's Pool," *Ensign,* November 1996, 18.
30. TSM Journal, 7 January 1983.
31. Monson, *Errand*, 407.
32. Monson, *Errand*, 407; TSM Journal, 21 September 1981.
33. Monson, *Errand*, 407.
34. Thomas S. Monson, "Mormon Church Welfare Services: An Account of the Teton Dam Disaster," prepared for the President's Task Force on Private Sector Initiatives, Washington, D.C., 14 April 1982, 2.
35. Letter from William Verity to TSM, 6 November 1982.
36. TSM Journal, 27 January 1985.

Chapter 26: There Are No Coincidences

Epigraph. Interview with H. David Burton, 27 August 2009.

1. TSM Journal, 27 March 1979.
2. See TSM Journal, 15 June 1981.
3. TSM Journal, 30 November 1981.
4. TSM Journal, 22 March 1982.
5. TSM Journal, 13 May 1979.
6. Thomas S. Monson, "The Army of the Lord," *Ensign,* May 1979, 36, 35.
7. Letter from Elder Pickett to TSM, 14 January 1982.
8. TSM Journal, 17 April 1983.
9. TSM Journal, 25 July 1979.
10. TSM Journal, 20 October 1982.
11. Interview with Douglas L. Callister, 26 October 2009.
12. TSM Journal, 28 December 1981.
13. Spencer W. Kimball, "Insights from June Conference," *Ensign,* October 1975, 70.
14. Prayer of dedication in Portugal, 22 April 1975.
15. TSM Journal, 28 April 1975.
16. Letter to TSM, 31 May 1991.
17. Prayer of dedication in Sweden, 7 July 1977.
18. Interview with Bo Wennerlund, 7 October 2008.
19. *Church News,* March 25, 1984, 7.
20. Thomas S. Monson, remarks at Stockholm Sweden Temple groundbreaking, 17 March 1984.
21. TSM Journal, 13 May 1979.
22. Matthew 6:21.
23. TSM Journal, 5 May 1982.
24. TSM Journal, 31 July 1985.
25. Thomas S. Monson, address at multistake conference, 15 January 1984.
26. Monson, multistake conference, 15 January 1984.
27. TSM Journal, 16 November 1981.
28. Doctrine and Covenants 128:22.
29. Monson, *Errand,* 388.
30. Letter from Ann Monson Dibb to TSM, 1 October 1983.
31. TSM Journal, 21 January 1982.
32. TSM Journal, 4 February 1982.
33. TSM Journal, 5 April 1980.
34. Thomas S. Monson, "Mark E. Petersen—A Giant among Men," *Ensign,* March 1984, 6.
35. TSM Journal, 19 April 1985.
36. TSM Journal, 22 April 1985.
37. Letter from Ronald D. John to TSM, 1 July 1985.
38. In Sheri Dew, *Go Forward with Faith: The Biography of Gordon B. Hinckley* (Salt Lake City: Deseret Book, 1997), 401.

Chapter 27: Ordained in Heaven

Epigraph. Interview with Jeffrey R. Holland, 22 September 2009.

1. Marion G. Romney, the only member of the Twelve absent, was confined to his home due to a lengthy illness.

NOTES

2. Joseph Fielding Smith, comp., *Teachings of the Prophet Joseph Smith* (Salt Lake City: Deseret Book, 1976), 365.

3. Spencer W. Kimball, "'We Thank Thee, O God, for a Prophet,'" *Ensign,* January 1973, 33.

4. TSM Journal, 10 November 1985.

5. Richard O. Cowan, *The Latter-day Saint Century* (Salt Lake City: Bookcraft, 1999), 252.

6. Thomas S. Monson, "You Make a Difference," *Ensign,* May 1988, 42.

7. D&C 107:22.

8. D&C 107:22.

9. Letter from Rex E. Lee to TSM, 5 February 1992.

10. Interview with Russell M. Nelson, 3 September 2009.

11. James E. Faust and James P. Bell, *In the Strength of the Lord: The Life and Teachings of James E. Faust* (Salt Lake City: Deseret Book, 1999), 219.

12. Church Statistical Report from 1985, in *Deseret News 2002 Church Almanac,* 583.

13. TSM Journal, 29 July 1994.

14. Interview with D. Todd Christoffersen, 24 September 2009.

15. Doctrine and Covenants 107:27.

16. Interview with Henry B. Eyring, 26 August 2009.

17. TSM Journal, 13 December 1992.

18. Letter from Francis M. Gibbons to TSM, 12 June 1990.

19. TSM Journal, 14 November 1985.

20. Interview with Russell M. Nelson, 3 September 2009.

21. TSM Journal, 1 January 1986.

22. TSM Journal, 3 January 1986.

23. Dedicatory prayer, Buenos Aires Argentina Temple, 17 January 1986.

24. TSM Journal, 31 May 1986.

25. Prayer of dedication in Poland, 1 June 1986.

26. TSM Journal, 18 October 1989.

27. Letter from Jeffrey R. Holland to TSM, 12 March 1986.

28. Interview with Richard G. Scott, 28 August 2009.

29. Interview with Richard G. Scott, 28 August 2009.

30. Letter from Ann Monson Dibb to TSM, 1 October 1983.

31. Interview with Richard G. Scott, 28 August 2009.

32. TSM Journal, 10 March 1986.

33. Interview with Jeffrey R. Holland, 8 October 2009.

34. TSM Journal, 16 December 1986.

35. Interview with Neil L. Andersen, 7 October 2009.

36. Letter from Monte J. Brough to TSM, 16 April 1991.

37. Interview with Russell M. Nelson, 3 September 2009.

38. See TSM Journal, 10 October 1987.

39. TSM Journal, 10 October 1987.

40. TSM Journal, 25 August 1990.

41. Interview with Everett Pallin, 6 October 2009.

42. Interview with Jeffrey R. Holland, 22 September 2009.

43. TSM Journal, 19 August 1989.

44. TSM Journal, 16 January 1994.

45. See *Teachings of Presidents of the Church: Joseph F. Smith* (Salt Lake City: The Church of Jesus Christ of Latter-day Saints, 1998), 305.
46. TSM Journal, 25 October 1992.
47. Thomas S. Monson, address at Bountiful Temple groundbreaking, 2 May 1992.
48. Letter from Grant Johnson to TSM, 27 February 1994.
49. TSM Journal, 26 May 1991.
50. Letter from Alexander B. Morrison to TSM, 1 November 1988.
51. TSM Journal, 28 April 1990.
52. Thomas S. Monson, in Conference Report, October 1968, 82.
53. Letter from Emily Ong to TSM, 10 May 1995.
54. TSM Journal, 16 December 1986.
55. Letter from Bill R. Lane to TSM, 20 August 1988.
56. See Thomas S. Monson, "The Spirit of Relief Society," *Ensign*, May 1992, 100–104.
57. TSM Journal, 26 April 1995.
58. Interview with Spencer J. Condie, 30 September 2009.

CHAPTER 28: "LOYAL, HELPFUL, FRIENDLY . . ."

Epigraph. Interview with Elaine S. Dalton, 2 December 2009.
1. TSM Journal, 1 April 1990.
2. TSM Journal, 5 October 1991.
3. TSM Journal, 4 August 1990.
4. TSM Journal, 15 October 1990.
5. TSM Journal, 20 October 1990.
6. Thomas S. Monson, *Live the Good Life* (Salt Lake City, Deseret Book, 1988), 19.
7. Thomas S. Monson, "'Run, Boy, Run!'" *Ensign*, November 1982, 19–20.
8. Monson, "'Run, Boy, Run!'" 19.
9. Interview with TSM, 9 September 2008.
10. Interview with L. Tom Perry, 22 August 2008.
11. Jason Swenson, "Scouting offers young men 'welcome rain,'" *Church News*, 21 October 2006, 4.
12. TSM Journal, 23 January 1993.
13. "Scouting Award presented to President Thomas S. Monson," *Ensign*, November 1993, 46.
14. Thomas S. Monson, "The Family's Treasured Friend," Boy Scouts of America National Meeting, Cincinnati, Ohio, 15 May 1992.
15. Interview with TSM, 9 September 2008.
16. TSM Journal, 12 November 2008.
17. Jason Swenson, "Face-to-face with President Monson about young men," MormonTimes.com, 24 May 2008.
18. Thomas S. Monson, "'Called to Serve,'" *Ensign*, November 1991, 47.
19. Thomas S. Monson, "Builders of Boys," WW Clyde Boy Scouts of America Lodge Dedication, 29 June 1991.
20. Monson, "'Called to Serve,'" 47.
21. TSM Journal, 5 December 1993.
22. TSM Journal, 20 December 1993.
23. TSM Journal, 24 December 1993.
24. Letter from Hugh Pinnock to TSM, 31 December 1993.

25. TSM Journal, 14 June 1994.
26. TSM Journal, 27 July 1999.
27. TSM Journal, 1 January 1994.
28. TSM Journal, 9 May 2006; 17 November 1987.
29. TSM Journal, 17 July 1992.
30. "First Presidency Statement," *Church News*, 26 September 1987, 5.
31. TSM Journal, 3 June 1994.
32. Thomas S. Monson, "President Ezra Taft Benson—A Giant among Men," *Ensign*, July 1994, 35.
33. TSM Journal, 4 June 1994.

CHAPTER 29: AN INDOMITABLE SPIRIT

Epigraph. Interview with Dallin H. Oaks, 3 September 2009.
1. Eleanor Knowles, *Howard W. Hunter* (Salt Lake City: Deseret Book, 1994), 225.
2. Interview with Jeffrey R. Holland, 22 September 2009.
3. Thomas S. Monson, "A Man for All Seasons," Church Educational System Satellite Broadcast, BYU, 5 February 1995.
4. Monson, "Man for All Seasons."
5. Monson, "Man for All Seasons."
6. Interview with TSM, 19 February 2009.
7. "Pres. Hunter is ordained prophet," *Church News*, 11 June 1994, 14.
8. Letter from Jeffrey R. Holland to TSM, 28 June 1994.
9. Letter from TSM to Jeffrey R. Holland, 1986.
10. TSM Journal, 7 June 1994.
11. TSM Journal, 1 October 1994.
12. TSM Journal, 31 December 1994.
13. TSM Journal, 27 July 1987.
14. TSM Journal, 1 April 1989.
15. Interview with TSM, 17 June 2009.
16. Howard W. Hunter, "'Exceeding Great and Precious Promises,'" *Ensign*, November 1994, 8.
17. Thomas S. Monson, address at Orlando Florida Temple dedication.
18. TSM Journal, 8 January 1995.
19. TSM Journal, 9 January 1995. A hyperbaric chamber is used for medical purposes to provide oxygen at a level higher than atmospheric pressure. It enhances healing in certain types of wounds.
20. TSM Journal, 9 January 1995.
21. TSM Journal, 9 January 1995.
22. TSM Journal, 13 January 1995.
23. TSM Journal, 24 January 1995.
24. TSM Journal, 25 January 1995.
25. TSM Journal, 26 January 1995.
26. Interview with Ron Gunnell, 28 February 2010.
27. TSM Journal, 31 December 1994.
28. TSM Journal, 10 December 1994.
29. Hunter, "'Exceeding Great and Precious Promises,'" 7.
30. TSM Journal, 13 January 1995.
31. Thomas S. Monson, "President Howard W. Hunter: A Man For All Seasons," *Ensign*, April 1995, 31.

32. TSM Journal, 3 March 1995.
33. Monson, "President Howard W. Hunter," 32.

<h2>CHAPTER 30: THE CONSUMMATE COUNSELOR</h2>

Epigraph. Interview with Quentin L. Cook, 18 September 2009.
1. Interview with Dallin H. Oaks, 3 September 2009.
2. "The Solemn Assembly Sustaining of Church Officers," *Ensign,* May 1995, 4.
3. President Thomas S. Monson, "The Call to Serve," *Ensign,* November 2000, 49.
4. Thomas S. Monson, "That All May Hear," *Ensign,* May 1995, 48.
5. Letter from Jack Fairclough to TSM, 2 February 2004.
6. Doctrine and Covenants 81:3, 5.
7. Interview with Quentin L. Cook, 18 September 2009.
8. Interview with David A. Bednar, 20 October 2009.
9. Interview with H. David Burton, 27 August 2009.
10. TSM Journal, 23 June 97.
11. Spencer W. Kimball, "'We Feel an Urgency,'" *Ensign,* August 1980, 2.
12. See Richard O. Cowan, *The Latter-day Saint Century* (Salt Lake City: Bookcraft, 1999), 288.
13. Gordon B. Hinckley, "Some Thoughts on Temples, Retention of Converts, and Missionary Service," *Ensign,* November 1997, 49.
14. Thomas S. Monson, remarks at Stockholm Sweden Temple cornerstone ceremony, 2 July 1985.
15. TSM Journal, 21 May 2000.
16. Thomas S. Monson, address at Veracruz Mexico Temple dedication, 9 July 2000.
17. Thomas S. Monson, address at Reno Nevada Temple dedication, 23 April 2000.
18. TSM Journal, 21 May 2000.
19. TSM Journal, 2 August 2007.
20. TSM Journal 15 June 1999.
21. Interview with H. David Burton, 27 August 2009.
22. Monson, Reno Nevada Temple dedication.
23. Thomas S. Monson, address at Buenos Aires Argentina Temple dedication, 17 January 1986.
24. Monson, Buenos Aires Temple dedication.
25. Interview with H. David Burton, 27 August 2009.
26. Interview with M. Russell Ballard, 9 September 2009.
27. Interview with Quentin L. Cook, 18 September 2009.
28. Thomas S. Monson, "Home Teaching—a Divine Service," *Ensign,* November 1997, 46.
29. TSM Journal, 20 October 2000.
30. Interview with M. Russell Ballard, 9 September 2009.
31. Interview with TSM, 15 April 2009.
32. Thomas S. Monson, "Your Eternal Home," *Ensign,* May 2000, 52.
33. Letter from William R. Walker to TSM, 2 May 2006.
34. Letter from Joan Ellen Fox to TSM, 3 October 1975.
35. Letter from David B. Haight to TSM, 7 February 2003.
36. TSM Journal, 1 April 2006.
37. Interview with H. David Burton, 27 August 2009.

38. Interview with Elder Neil L. Andersen, 7 Oct 2009.
39. TSM Journal, 9 May 1999; Interview with Dieter F. Uchtdorf, 2 September 2009.
40. Thomas S. Monson, "Priesthood Power," Salt Lake City Utah South Stake Conference Broadcast, 17 October 2009; poem, "Living What We Pray for," by Whitney Montgomery.
41. TSM Journal, 9 November 2003.
42. See "Guideposts for Life's Journey," *BYU Magazine*, Spring 2008.
43. Thomas S. Monson, "My Brother's Keeper," *Ensign*, May 1990, 48.
44. See Thomas S. Monson, "Duty Calls," *Ensign*, November 2001, 51; TSM Journal, 8 October 2001.
45. TSM Journal, 5 March 2006.
46. TSM Journal, 16 July 2005.
47. Interview with Ronald A. Rasband, 12 November 2008.
48. Interview with Neil L. Andersen, 7 October 2009.
49. Letter from Gerry Avant to Heidi S. Swinton, 30 March 2010.
50. TSM Journal, 27 August 1995.
51. Letter from Dieter F. Uchtdorf to TSM, 21 August 1995.
52. Gerry Avant, "Dedication of meetinghouse fulfills 27-year-old promise," *Church News*, 2 September 1995.
53. TSM Journal, August 1995.
54. Interview with Marlin K. Jensen, 28 October 2009.
55. Letter from Janet Lee to TSM, 12 July 2001.
56. Interview with Clark Spencer Monson, 4 November 2008.
57. Thomas S. Monson, "Hallmarks of a Happy Home," Missionary Satellite Broadcast, 20 February 2000.
58. TSM Journal, 28 January 2008.
59. TSM Journal, 27 January 2008.

CHAPTER 31: REACHING OUT TO THE ONE

Epigraph. Interview with William R. Walker, 14 January 2010.
1. Julie Dockstader Heaps, "He was a 'giant' of faith, love, vision," *Church News*, 9 February 2008.
2. Thomas S. Monson, "Looking Back and Moving Forward," *Ensign*, May 2008, 88.
3. Monson, "Looking Back and Moving Forward," 90.
4. Interview with Russell M. Nelson, 3 September 2009.
5. Interview with Quentin L. Cook, 18 September 2009.
6. TSM Journal, 3 February 2008.
7. Interview with L. Tom Perry, 22 August 2008.
8. Interview with TSM, 19 February 2009.
9. Adam C. Olson, "Maintaining the Course," *Ensign*, April 2008, 10–14.
10. Interview with Henry B. Eyring, 21 July 2010.
11. Interview with Dieter F. Uchtdorf, 2 September 2009.
12. "Statistical Report, 2008," *Ensign*, May 2009, 30.
13. Interview with Thomas Lee Monson, 6 November 2009.
14. Interview with Thomas Lee Monson on "Legacy of Life," DVD shown at Legacy of Life Awards Ceremony, 14 April 2005.
15. Interview with Elaine S. Dalton, 2 December 2009.

16. Letter from Terry Moore to TSM, 6 April 2008.
17. Thomas S. Monson, "A Sanctuary from the World," Worldwide Leadership Training Meeting, 9 February 2008.
18. "Rexburg Idaho: 'We come humbly,'" *Church News,* 16 February 2008.
19. Thomas S. Monson, "Abundantly Blessed," *Ensign,* May 2008, 112.
20. Thomas S. Monson, "Examples of Righteousness," *Ensign,* May 2008, 65.
21. Monson, "Looking Back and Moving Forward," 88.
22. Jeffrey R. Holland, "'My Words . . . Never Cease,'" *Ensign,* May 2008, 91.
23. Monson, "Abundantly Blessed," 112.
24. Interview with TSM, 15 October 2008.
25. Interview with TSM, 15 April 2009.
26. Interview with David A. Bednar, 20 October 2009.
27. Letter from Allie Derrick to Heidi S. Swinton, 20 April 2010.
28. Interview with Marilyn Martin, 10 January 2008.
29. Interview with Dallin H. Oaks, 3 September 2009.
30. Interview with Robert D. Hales, 8 April 2009.
31. Interview with Jeffrey R. Holland, 8 October 2009.
32. Thomas S. Monson, "The Call for Courage," *Ensign,* May 2004, 56.
33. Interview with Bruce D. Porter, 16 December 2009.
34. Thomas S. Monson, "How Firm a Foundation," *Ensign,* November 2006, 62, 68.
35. Interview with D. Todd Christofferson, 24 September 2009.
36. Luke 9:24.
37. Thomas S. Monson, "What Have I Done for Someone Today?" *Ensign,* November 2009, 85.
38. Gerry Avant, "Ideal birthday gift for Pres. Monson," *Church News,* 15 August 2009.
39. Interview with Ann Monson Dibb, 19 July 2008.
40. Monson, "Looking Back and Moving Forward," 90.
41. Interview with Erich Kopischke, 20 September 2008.
42. Interview with TSM, 15 April 2009.
43. Thomas S. Monson, "Welcome to Conference," *Ensign,* November 2009, 6.
44. H. David Burton, "What Manner of Men and Women Ought Ye to Be?" Church Educational System fireside, 2 November 2008.
45. Interview with TSM, 29 March 2010.
46. "The Journey of a Peach," Mormons Giving Aid Globally, 17 June 2009, http://mormonchurch.org/174/the-journey-of-a-peach.
47. Scott Taylor, "Care for needy has been longtime emphasis for Mormons," *Deseret News,* 12 December 2009.
48. Thomas S. Monson, "Your Celestial Journey," *Ensign,* May 1999, 96.
49. Thomas S. Monson, "Until We Meet Again," *Ensign,* November 2008, 106–7.
50. Interview with Robert D. Hales, 8 April 2009.
51. Interview with Marlin K. Jensen, 28 October 2009.
52. Interview with D. Todd Christofferson, 24 September 2009.
53. Interview with Dieter F. Uchtdorf, 2 September 2009.
54. Interview with Dieter F. Uchtdorf, 2 September 2009.
55. Interview with Neil L. Andersen, 7 October 2009.
56. Interview with Elaine S. Dalton, 2 December 2009.
57. Thomas S. Monson, address at BYU 102nd Commencement Exercises, 22 April 1977.

58. Interview with David A. Bednar, 9 September 2009.
59. Interview with Neil L. Andersen, 7 October 2009.
60. Interview with TSM, 15 October 2008.
61. Thomas S. Monson, "To the Rescue," *Ensign*, May 2001, 50.
62. Thomas S. Monson, "Examples of Righteousness," *Ensign*, May 2008, 65, 68.
63. Thomas S. Monson, "Until We Meet Again," *Ensign*, May 2009, 113.
64. TSM Journal, 10 January 2010.
65. Interview, name withheld, December 2009.
66. Interview with L. Tom Perry, 22 August 2008.
67. Interview with Henry B. Eyring, 26 August 2009.
68. Interview with D. Todd Christofferson, 24 September 2009.
69. Interview with Henry B. Eyring, 26 August 2009.
70. Interview with William R. Walker, 14 January 2010.
71. Interview with D. Todd Christofferson, 24 September 2009.
72. Interview with TSM, 19 February 2009.
73. TSM Journal, 14 June 2009.
74. Interview with Mac Christensen, 6 October 2009.
75. Interview with Mac Christensen, 6 October 2009
76. "80 Over 80," Slate.com, posted 20 October 2009.
77. Interview with Kenneth Johnson, 24 July 2008.
78. Interview with TSM, 15 April 2009.
79. "The Family: A Proclamation to the World," *Ensign*, November 1995, 102.
80. Aaron Falk and Scott Taylor, "Mormon church supports Salt Lake City's protections for gay rights," *Deseret News*, 11 November 2009.
81. Interview with M. Russell Ballard, 9 September 2009.
82. Thomas S. Monson, "Welcome to Conference," *Ensign*, November 2009, 4–5.
83. Monson, "Welcome to Conference," 4.
84. Sarah Jane Weaver, "President Monson dedicates edifice, thousands celebrate," *Church News*, 30 August 2008.
85. TSM Journal, 21 March 2009.
86. Interview with William R. Walker, 14 January 2010.
87. Interview with TSM, 19 February 2009.
88. Interview with TSM, 19 February 2009.
89. Gerry Avant, *Church News*, 28 March 2009.
90. Interview with TSM, 15 April 2009.
91. Thomas S. Monson, "Finding Joy in the Journey," *Ensign*, November 2008, 87, 88.
92. Interview with TSM, 19 February 2009.

CHAPTER 32: JOY IN THE JOURNEY

Epigraph. Interview with Robert D. Hales, 8 April 2009.
1. Interview with Russell M. Nelson, 3 September 2009.
2. Thomas S. Monson, "To Learn, to Do, to Be," *Ensign*, November 2008, 61.
3. Letter from Alexander B. Morrison to TSM, 14 January 1991.
4. Interview with Jon M. Huntsman, 14 December 2009.
5. Interview with Ann Monson Dibb, 13 May 2009.
6. Letter to TSM, name withheld.
7. Interview with Bruce D. Porter, 16 December 2009.

8. Letter from Don Flanders to TSM, 24 July 1992.

9. Thomas S. Monson, "To the Rescue," *Ensign*, May 2001, 48.

10. *Through Our Eyes: 150 Years of History as Seen through the Eyes of the Writers and Editors of the Deseret News,* ed. Don C. Woodward (Salt Lake City: Deseret News, 1999), 203.

11. Thomas S. Monson, "Finding Joy in the Journey," *Ensign*, November 2008, 84.

12. Interview with Henry B. Eyring, 21 July 2010.

13. Monson, "To the Rescue," 49.

14. Thomas S. Monson, "In Quest of the Abundant Life," *Ensign*, March 1988, 2.

15. Interview with Douglas L. Callister, 26 October 2009.

16. KBYU Interview with TSM for *A Fortress of Faith,* 1988.

17. Interview with Douglas L. Callister, 26 October 2009.

18. Interview with Douglas L. Callister, 26 October 2009.

19. Letter to TSM, name withheld.

20. Monson, "To the Rescue," 48.

21. Thomas S. Monson, "The Upward Reach," *Ensign*, November 1993, 47.

22. Monson, "Finding Joy in the Journey," 84, 86.

23. Interview with TSM, 13 May 2009.

24. Monson, "Finding Joy in the Journey," 84.

25. Thomas S. Monson, *Be Your Best Self* (Salt Lake City: Deseret Book, 1979), 136.

26. Thomas S. Monson, "Duty Calls," *Ensign*, May 1996, 44.

27. Monson, "Upward Reach," 48.

28. Monson, "Duty Calls," 44.

29. Thomas S. Monson, "Learning the ABC's," address given at BYU, 8 February 1966.

30. Thomas S. Monson, "Faces and Attitudes," *New Era*, September 1977, 49.

31. Thomas S. Monson, address given at ASU Institute of Religion, 2 February 1973.

32. Monson, *Be Your Best Self,* 93.

33. Wendy Leonard, "UVU grads told to reach out, press forward," *Deseret News,* 2 May 2009.

34. Thomas S. Monson, "The Priesthood in Action," *Ensign*, November 1992, 48.

35. Thomas S. Monson, "Guideposts for Life's Journey," *BYU Magazine,* Spring 2008.

36. Thomas S. Monson, "Looking Back and Moving Forward," *Ensign*, May 2008, 88.

INDEX